A Philosophy for Communism

Historical Materialism Book Series

Editorial Board

Loren Balhorn (*Berlin*)
David Broder (*Rome*)
Sébastien Budgen (*Paris*)
Steve Edwards (*London*)
Juan Grigera (*London*)
Marcel van der Linden (*Amsterdam*)
Peter Thomas (*London*)

VOLUME 211

The titles published in this series are listed at *brill.com/hm*

A Philosophy for Communism

Rethinking Althusser

By

Panagiotis Sotiris

BRILL

LEIDEN | BOSTON

Library of Congress Cataloging-in-Publication Data

Names: Sotiris, Panagiotis, author.
Title: A philosophy for communism : rethinking Althusser / by Panagiotis Sotiris.
Description: Leiden ; Boston : Brill, 2020. | Series: Historical materialism book
   series, 1570-1522 ; volume 211 | Includes bibliographical references and index.
Identifiers: LCCN 2020007393 (print) | LCCN 2020007394 (ebook) |
   ISBN 9789004291355 (hardback) | ISBN 9789004291362 (ebook)
Subjects: LCSH: Althusser, Louis, 1918–1990. | Communism–Philosophy.
Classification: LCC B2430.A474 S68 2020 (print) | LCC B2430.A474 (ebook) |
   DDC 194–dc23
LC record available at https://lccn.loc.gov/2020007393
LC ebook record available at https://lccn.loc.gov/2020007394

Typeface for the Latin, Greek, and Cyrillic scripts: "Brill". See and download: brill.com/brill-typeface.

ISSN 1570-1522
ISBN 978-90-04-29135-5 (hardback)
ISBN 978-90-04-29136-2 (e-book)

Copyright 2020 by Koninklijke Brill NV, Leiden, The Netherlands.
Koninklijke Brill NV incorporates the imprints Brill, Brill Hes & De Graaf, Brill Nijhoff, Brill Rodopi,
Brill Sense, Hotei Publishing, mentis Verlag, Verlag Ferdinand Schöningh and Wilhelm Fink Verlag.
All rights reserved. No part of this publication may be reproduced, translated, stored in a retrieval system,
or transmitted in any form or by any means, electronic, mechanical, photocopying, recording or otherwise,
without prior written permission from the publisher.
Authorization to photocopy items for internal or personal use is granted by Koninklijke Brill NV provided
that the appropriate fees are paid directly to The Copyright Clearance Center, 222 Rosewood Drive,
Suite 910, Danvers, MA 01923, USA. Fees are subject to change.

This book is printed on acid-free paper and produced in a sustainable manner.

To Despina and Eleni-Ernestina

The most beautiful sea hasn't been crossed yet
NAZIM HIKMET

∴

Contents

Introduction 1

PART 1
Structure, Conjuncture, Encounter

1 The Many Readings and Misreadings of Althusser 9

2 The Never-Ending Confrontation with Hegel 25

3 'This Man is Indeed Alone in Facing His Task': Althusser on Montesquieu 36

4 Structure Revisited 50

5 Materialism as Philosophy of the Encounter 84

6 From the Critique of Natural Law to the Void of the Forest and the Inexistence of the Origin: Althusser on Rousseau 98

7 From the 'Hidden God' to the Materialism of the Encounter: Althusser on Pascal 126

8 The Difficulties of being a Materialist in Philosophy: Assessing Aleatory Materialism 142

9 Spinoza in Althusser-as-Laboratory 169

10 Structure and/as Conjuncture 200

PART 2
A New Practice of Philosophy

11 Althusser's Struggle with the Definition of Philosophy 215

12 Philosophy as Laboratory 246

13   A Philosopher Always Catches a Moving Train   302

14   Althusser and Gramsci on Philosophy   312

PART 3
Is There an Althusserian Politics?

15   Althusser 1960–65: Attempting a Theoretical Correction of a Political Strategy in Crisis   339

16   The Politics of Theoretical Anti-humanism   353

17   Althusser's Self-Criticism   378

18   Althusser in the 1970s: Break and Open Critique of Communist Reformism   396

19   The Politics of the Encounter: Machiavelli and Beyond   460

20   Ideology and Political Subjectivity   504

21   The Limits of Althusserian Politics   523

   Conclusion   529

   References   535
   Index   553

Introduction

This book is the result of many years of confrontation with the work of Louis Althusser, ever since the preparation of my PhD dissertation in the second half of the 1990s.[1] Yet, the book is also the result of a second encounter with Althusser in the past years. In both encounters, the motivating question was the same: what philosophy, what practice of philosophy, can be useful for a politics of social change and emancipation? In a certain way, this is the guiding thread of the book: it marks an attempt to rethink the political effectivity of materialist philosophy as part of any attempt to rethink communism as historical movement and potentiality. Consequently, it is important to return to the work of Althusser, the work of a philosopher who attempted in a self-critical and, in certain respects, tragic manner to remain a communist in philosophy. The results of these constant returns and new departures from Althusser are presented in this book.

The book is divided into three parts. Part 1 is organised around three concepts that define the contours of Althusser's confrontation with the (im)possibility of a Marxist dialectic: structure, conjuncture, encounter. I begin with an overview of the criticisms regarding Althusser's supposed structuralism, anti-humanism or lack of connection between epistemological or philosophical demarcations and political exigencies, in order to suggest the possibility of another reading of Althusser. We begin by revisiting Althusser's confrontation with Hegel, in order to demonstrate both Althusser's knowledge of Hegel but also his attempt to distinguish Marxism from Hegelianism, before moving on to his reading of Montesquieu in which we can see the first elements of his own highly original version of historical materialism. Then, I attempt to examine whether we can read the evolution of Althusser's work as an opposition between structure and conjuncture or as a transition or shift from structures to conjunctures. I try to bring out the fact that the emphasis on the singularity of conjunctures and on the contradictory and contingent character of structures was a defining feature of the entire Althusserian endeavour. In light of this, the notion of the encounter, in its entire trajectory in the work of Althusser from its emergence in 1966 until the 1980s texts on aleatory materialism, becomes the central pillar not of a metaphysics of contingence and freedom but rather of a highly original attempt to break with any form of metaphysical historicism. It is here that we also deal with two important philosophical 'detours' by Althusser:

---

1 Sotiris 1999.

Rousseau and the way that each return to the reading of his work also marked an important shift in Althusser's own conception of historical materialism; and Pascal and how, in many instances, beginning with the years of his captivity at a German POW camp during WWII, Althusser returned to his work. At the same time, I stress the limits and shortcomings of some of Althusser's formulations as evidence of the necessarily contradictory process of constantly 'bending the stick to the other side'. It is here that I also deal with Althusser's constant references to Spinoza, exemplified in his well known phrase *'we were Spinozists'*. Finally, I attempt to rethink the possibility of thinking structure and/as conjuncture.

Part 2 returns to the question of philosophy. Althusser was above all a philosopher who not only intervened politically into theory, but also attempted to see the role of philosophy in politics. Consequently, his work also confronts the questions around the theoretical status as well as the social effectivity of philosophy. I begin with Althusser's initial conception of the Theory of theoretical practice as part of his strategy for a theoretical correction of a political deviation, what one could define as 'the politics of the epistemological break', and I attempt to retrace the trajectory of corrections and self-criticism of the second half of the 1960s and Althusser's attempt to rethink the very role of philosophy that led to the second definition of philosophy as, in the last instance, class struggle in theory. I then turn to two important manuscripts from the 1970s, *How to be a Marxist in Philosophy* and *Philosophy for Non-Philosophers*, which have recently been published, since they not only offer us Althusser's attempt to see philosophy as a conceptual and ideological laboratory for dominant ideologies, but also enable us, along with other texts from the same period that had remained unpublished during Althusser's lifetime, to realise that the philosophy of the encounter was not a product of Althusser's period of isolation after 1980 but a problematic upon which he had already worked to a significant degree. It is from this reading that the conception for a new liberating practice of philosophy emerges in the same period as Althusser's intensification of his left-critique of communist reformism. I then turn towards the particular imagery of philosophy we can find in the post-1980 texts. This part of the book closes with an attempt towards a comparative reading of Gramsci's conception of the philosophy of praxis and Althusser's conception of a new practice of philosophy in order to show that despite Althusser's many critical references to Gramsci, there are in fact many important common elements that can help us to redefine a philosophy for communism.

Part 3 attempts to answer an important question: *is there an Althusserian politics?* I begin by examining the aporias of Althusser's initial attempt to think of political intervention against the crisis of the communist movement in the

1960s in terms of a theoretical correction that would supposedly also lead to changes in the political line. I suggest that the limits of this initial conception of political intervention are at the beginnings of Althusser's long period of self-criticism after the second half of the 1960s. I point to the increased apprehension of the depth of the political and theoretical crisis of the communist movement and also of Marxist theory, the confrontation with mass movements, such as May 68, and the realisation that what is needed is a new practice of politics. I also point to the increased emphasis on the importance of social movements, popular initiatives, forms of organisations from below, 'traces of communism' or 'virtual forms of communism' emerging as part of these movements. In light of this, I revisit both Althusser's texts on the crisis of Marxism but also his interventions regarding the crisis of Western communist parties, and the big debate on state theory with Balibar and Poulantzas, but also Althusser's confrontation with the work of Gramsci. What becomes evident through this reading is Althusser's attempt to actually offer a left-wing critique of Stalinism and communist reformism. Moreover, I also revisit the notion of the encounter, in order to see its particular political significance and Althusser's oscillations and shifts regarding the very possibility of 'organizing good encounters'. It is here that I return to Althusser's reading of Machiavelli and how it is exactly in this reading that we can see the possibility and at the same time the difficulty of a politics of the encounter, of an attempt to intervene politically in the radically contingent terrain of social antagonism. I then turn to the question of political subjectivity in order to see if we can think of new forms of non-subjectivist forms of collective subjectivity. Finally, I discuss the importance and the limits of Althusser's conception(s) of politics.

The book ends with conclusions which are rather more open in character and consciously unstable in the sense that they offer points and open questions for future research, rather than definite answers, in an attempt to think what it means to be a communist in philosophy or what a philosophy for communism might be like.

Earlier versions of some of the arguments presented here have appeared in the form of articles in theoretical journals or edited volumes. These are:
1. 'The Difficult Encounter with Materialism' (Review article of Louis Althusser, *Philosophy of the Encounter: Later Writings, 1978–1987*, London: Verso, 1987), *Historical Materialism*, 16, no. 3: 147–78, 2008.
2. 'Rethinking Aleatory Materialism', in *Encountering Althusser: Politics and Materialism in Contemporary Radical Thought*, edited by K. Diefenbach, S. Farris, G. Kirn and P. Thomas, London: Bloomsbury, 2013.

3. 'How to Make Lasting Encounters: Althusser and Political Subjectivity', *Rethinking Marxism*, 26, no. 3: 398–413, 2014.
4. 'Rethinking Structure and Conjuncture in Althusser', *Historical Materialism*, 22, no. 3–4: 5–51, 2014.
5. 'The Laboratory of Philosophy: Gramsci and Althusser on Philosophy', *Décalages*, 2, no. 1, 2016.
6. 'From the "Hidden God" to the Materialism of the Encounter: Althusser and Pascal', in *Althusser and Theology: Religion, Politics and Philosophy*, edited by A. Hamza, Leiden: Brill, 2016.

The comments and suggestions by the referees and editors have been crucial in improving my understanding of important questions.

This book would not have been written without the help of many people. Sebastian Budgen and Peter Thomas were the ones who suggested this project and have been always more than supportive, offering friendship, intellectual dialogue, and support. Tassos Betzelos has always been there to discuss questions, offer suggestions coming from his own deep knowledge of Althusser and his own highly original reading, and bibliographical help. Many of the questions of this book have been discussed with Giorgos Kalampokas, whose comments and suggestions are always important. A seminar with Giorgos and Tassos back in 2013 formed the background of large segments of the book and my discussions with both of them have had a definite influence on this book. Spyros Sakellaropoulos has always reminded me of the need to actually finish the book, patiently waiting in order to reactivate our project for a book on Imperialism. G.M. Goshgarian was always available to answer queries about details of the Althusserian oeuvre and the Althusserian archive. Discussing Althusser with Stathis Kouvelakis has always been a critical process that I hope has been transmitted into the book's final content. Jason Read, Ted Stolze, William Lewis, Agon Hamza, Alberto Toscano, Thomas Carmichael, Sara Farris, Bruno Bosteels, Dhruv Jain, Giorgos Fourtounis, John Milios, Fabio Frosini, Sevasti Trubeta, Constantine Boundas, and many who I have probably forgotten have contributed to my understanding of Althusser, philosophy, and social theory, and I am more than grateful for my discussions with them. Moreover, since many of the ideas in this book were first presented at Historical Materialism Conferences in London and Toronto, one might say that this book is also a product of the comradely yet rigorous discussion during such conferences. Félix Boggio Éwanjé-Épée and Stella Magliani-Belkacem have offered inspiration, friendship, and passionate discussion on politics and theory. Finally, my family, Despina Koutsoumba and our daughter Eleni-Ernestina have had to put up with all of the chaos that usually accompanies the writing of a book, at the same time contributing both of them – Despina with her ruthless criticism of abstract theorising and Eleni-Ernestina in her almost Socratic tendency to question everything – to important aspects of it.

The writing of the book coincided with a period of social and political crisis, but a time that has also seen an impressive return of mass movements and mass political mobilisation in Greece. I hope that the anger, hope, and passion of this period are reflected in these pages ...

    August 2019
    Athens

PART 1

Structure, Conjuncture, Encounter

CHAPTER 1

The Many Readings and Misreadings of Althusser

Jürgen Habermas is well known to have insisted that he had hardly read Althusser.[1] In a similar manner, G.A. Cohen described *Reading Capital* as 'critically vogue'[2] and warned against Althusserianism endangering the lucidity of Marxism. Leszek Kołakowski practically accused Althusser of offering an empty verbosity without substantial content.

> These two books of Althusser provide a disagreeable example of empty verbosity which, as noted earlier, can be reduced either to common sense trivialities in new verbal disguise, or to traditional Marxist tenets repeated with no additional explanation, or to wrong historical judgments. In understanding Marx, or Hegel, or political economy, or the methods of social science, they give us nothing except pretentious language.[3]

Yet, in contrast to such outright rejections, there have been many readings of Althusser, many of them – at least depending upon where you stand – *mis*readings. We are familiar with the *leitmotif* of the accusations: that Althusser's structuralism leads him to overlook human agency and subjectivity, and that his rigid conception of theory, science, and philosophy lead him to an underestimation of the importance of the role of revolutionary practice. For many Marxists, this remains the dominant image of Althusser. In what follows we will try to go through some of these readings and the challenges that they pose for any critical reading of the dynamics of the Althusserian text.

1 The Polemic against Theoreticist Structuralism

In E.P. Thompson's polemic against Althusser, we find the epitome of the attack on theoreticism and structuralism. Early on, Thompson sets out to define the enemy: Althusser's rejection of the category of experience and consequently of historical evidence and his adoption of a structuralism of '*stasis*, departing from Marx's historical method' that made Althusser and his followers 'unable to

---

[1] Habermas 1985, p. 77.
[2] Cohen 2000, p. x.
[3] Kołakowski 1971, p. 127.

handle, except in the most abstract and theoretic way, questions of value, culture – and political theory'.[4] It is the result of a particularly French conception of philosophical theorising, of Cartesian origins, that leaves aside the defining role of experience in the emergence of social consciousness. The outcome is an idealism that expresses a deeply problematic relation between Marxist intellectuals and revolutionary politics in a period of crisis in the socialist movement.

> In the West a bourgeois soul yearns for a 'Marxism' to heal its own alienation; in the 'Communist' world a proclaimed 'socialist basis' gives rise to a 'superstructure' of orthodox Christian faith, corrupt materialism, Slav nationalism and Solzhenitsyn. In that world 'Marxism' performs the function of an 'Ideological State Apparatus', and Marxists are alienated, not in their self-identity, but in the contempt of the people. An old and arduous rational tradition breaks down into two parts: an arid academic scholasticism and a brutal pragmatism of power.[5]

Thompson is extremely suspicious of Althusser's anti-empiricism, devoting many pages to a polemic against what he sees as an underestimation of the importance of historical facts in their complex interrelation with ideologies, political dynamics, and social conflicts, and insists that our notions are not the simple products of theoretical speculation but actually say something about what exists 'out there':

> Insofar as a notion finds endorsement from the evidence, then one has every right to say that it does exist, 'out there', in the real history. It does not of course actually exist, like some plasma adhering to the facts, or as some invisible kernel within the shell of appearances. What we are saying is that the notion (concept, hypothesis as to causation) has been brought into a disciplined dialogue with the evidence, and it has been shown to 'work'; that is, it has not been disproved by contrary evidence, and that it successfully organises or 'explains' hitherto inexplicable evidence; hence it is an adequate (although approximate) representation of the causative sequence, or rationality, of these events, and it conforms (within the logic of the historical discipline) with a process which did in fact eventuate in the past. Hence it exists simultaneously both as a 'true' knowledge and as an adequate representation of an actual property of those events.[6]

---

4 Thompson 1995, p. 6.
5 Thompson 1995, p. 33.
6 Thompson 1995, p. 59.

For Thompson, this leads to a *static* conception of history, a structuralism of stasis and closure and an 'eviction of dialectics'.[7] In Thompson's view, Althusser 'evicts process from history'.[8] For Thompson, who had indeed written on socialist humanism in the *New Reasoner*, theoretical humanism was exactly a reaction to Stalinism and not a theoretical apology for it: 'socialist humanism was, above all, the voice of a Communist opposition, of a total critique of Stalinist practice and theory'.[9] Consequently, Althusser was accused of proposing a version of theoretical Stalinism. 'Thus we can see the emergence of Althusserianism as a manifestation of a general police action within ideology, as the attempt to reconstruct Stalinism at the level of theory'.[10] Thompson accuses Althusser of underestimating the importance of agency, 'of men and women as subjects of their own history',[11] expressed also in the underestimation of 'human experience',[12] and of crucial aspects of social interaction such as morality and values, exactly the aspects that Thompson had tried to explore in his historical work.

> Historical and cultural materialism cannot explain 'morality' away as class interests in fancy dress, since the notion that all 'interests' can be subsumed in scientifically-determinable material objectives is nothing more than utilitarianism's bad breath. Interests are what interest people, including what interests them nearest to the heart. A materialist examination of values must situate itself, not by idealist propositions, but in the face of culture's material abode: the people's way of life, and, above all, their product and familial relationships. And this is what 'we' have been doing, and over many decades.[13]

Thompson creates a certain image of Althusser as at the same time a theoreticist refusing the effectivity of human praxis and an apologist for Stalinism by means of the rejection of socialist humanism. In political terms, this helps Thompson present this polemic against Althusser as a defence of libertarian Communism and the need for it to be an independent current, demarcating itself from the developments within a broad Left which, to Thompson, still

---

7   Thompson 1995, p. 153.
8   Thompson 1995, p. 120.
9   Thompson 1995, p. 178.
10 Thompson 1995, p. 176.
11 Thompson 1995, p. 217.
12 Thompson 1995, p. 221.
13 Thompson 1995, p. 237.

seemed like varieties of Stalinism. In this sense, his polemic against Althusser is also related to his own political perception of the developments within the British Left.

> What I mean is, rather, this. First, libertarian Communism, or a Socialism which is both democratic and revolutionary in its means, its strategy and objectives, must stand firmly, on an independent base, on its own feet, developing its own theoretical critique and, increasingly, its own political forms and practices. Only on these presuppositions can any 'alliance' be negotiated; and if emergencies demand such an alliance, then it cannot be on orthodox Communism's usual imperative terms: that ulterior theoretical and strategic differences be obscured or silenced, in the interests of a 'Broad Left' (whose interests, are, in turn, ultimately those of the Party).[14]

It is obvious that in the case of Thompson, we are dealing with a polemic that is aggressive in its attack on Althusser's supposed structuralism and theoreticism but also against Althusser's anti-humanism, conceived as an attack on the possibility of left communism-humanism and consequently as a justification for Stalinism. It is exactly this combination of a rejection of structuralism, a defence of humanism, an emphasis on subjectivity and praxis, and an accusation of Stalinism that makes Thompson's critique read like a summary of a certain line of criticism against Althusser that in many respects has been repeated many times since the 1960s.

Norman Geras, in his defence of a theoretical humanism, encapsulates this view in his insistence that

> the texts of Althusserianism are strewn with such assertions, 'structuralist', sociologically reductionist, in truth historicist, in character, as that the agents of production are 'never anything more than the occupants' of places determined by the structure of the relations of production, that 'individuals are merely the effects' of the structure, that 'they are only *class representatives*', '*are nothing more than masks*', and so forth.[15]

Yet it is interesting that echoes of such polemics can also be found in critics of Althusser coming from different traditions. André Glucksmann in his tra-

---

14   Thompson 1995, pp. 256–7.
15   Geras 1983, p. 52.

jectory from Maoism to the virulent anti-communism of the '*nouveaux philosophes*' offered a polemic against Althusser that, while emerging from within certain aspects of the Althusserian paradigm, nevertheless accuses Althusser of a metaphysical attempt to present Marx's theory as a closed system.

> Althusser is right to refer us to *Capital* for the principles of a critical reading of them. But his metaphysical passion for a system threatens to obliterate this new body of knowledge, over which the Marxist critique of political economy must exercise its permanent power.[16]

Even Paul Ricœur, in his discussion of Althusser's theory of ideology, makes the specific claim that Althusser, by means of his conception of the epistemological break, misses the necessary emphasis on real people and the necessity for non-idealistic anthropology:

> For my part, Althusser's representation of the epistemological break does great damage not only to the theory of ideology but to the reading of Marx. [...] The great damage done to Marx by Althusser is that he forces us to put under one heading – anthropological ideology – two different notions. The first is an ideology of consciousness, which Marx and Freud have rightly broken. The second, though, is the ideology of real, concrete human being [...] The latter notion can be expressed in non-idealist terms.[17]

The same emphasis on Althusser's supposed structuralism and its inability to think actual political praxis and the emergence of social groups that orient themselves towards social emancipation by means of their social and communicative collective interaction, forms the basis of Axel Honneth's critique of Althusser:

> Because Althusser's historical materialism conceives the capitalist process of history only as a reproduction of the social-structural formation not as the experiential process of social groups and classes, it cannot even forge a political link with the self-interpretation of social revolutionary movements. This is why Althusser is politically tied to Lenin's conception of the party. In place of a theoretical relation to the consciousness and

---

16   Glucksmann 1972, p. 92.
17   Ricœur 1986, pp. 152–3.

interests of the class movement steps the party, as a surrogate for class consciousness. The political acts of the party with respect to social movements are instrumental, just like Althusser's representation, of systematic practice in general.[18]

Althusser's emphasis on the autonomy of theoretical disciplines and elements of his theoreticism can also be found in discussions of his work that are in general sympathetic to important elements of the Althusserian endeavour such as Ted Benton's *The Rise and Fall of Structural Marxism*, itself a comprehensive presentation of Althusser's work. There the problem is located in the 'absolute conceptual autonomy and mutual incommensurability of theoretical disciplines'.[19] Even critics who have actually attempted to enter into a dialogue with Althusser's work, such as Pierre Vilar, insist upon the rather abstract and schematic character of Althusser's conceptualisation of the mode of production and of historical time.[20]

2   Althusser as the Repetition of Communist Orthodoxy

The accusations that Althusser in a certain manner reproduced aspects of the Stalinist orthodoxy have been repeated in various forms. However, it is interesting that one of the most aggressive attacks against Althusser, insisting upon the continuity of his work with the communist orthodoxy, came from one of Althusser's own students and collaborators in the collective project of *Reading Capital*, namely Jacques Rancière. *Althusser's Lesson* is a singular text, both in its polemical tone but also in the degree of Rancière's actual confrontation with the work of Althusser. Rancière's attacks are mainly targeted against Althusser's more political interventions in the 1970s and especially the *Reply to John Lewis*, insisting that they mark Althusser's attempt to maintain both his authority and the authority of the Party.

> From the beginning, though, something more important has been at work behind the fight Althusser the philosopher wages against a declining existentialism and the one Althusser the 'communist' wages against those of his 'comrades' who have been corrupted by bourgeois humanism. All along, this has been the fight of a 'communist philosopher' against that

---

18   Honneth 1994, p. 101.
19   Benton 1984, p. 230.
20   Vilar 1973.

which threatens both the authority of his Party and of his philosophy: Cultural Revolution on a global scale, and students who contest the authority of knowledge on a local scale.[21]

Rancière is particularly critical of Althusser's strategy in the 1960s. He thinks that Althusser's emphasis on the autonomy of theory in fact was an attempt to safeguard rather than subvert the role of the Communist Party.

> This new orthodoxy was not based on Stalin's words, but on Marx's texts. Althusser's *detour* foreclosed the possibility of providing the politics of the Party with a theoretical foundation. But giving its politics a theoretical foundation was decidedly not the point; others had already tried, much too assiduously, to do so. The real task was to keep its politics from being contested. If Althusserianism could serve the Party, it was because it warned against the dangers of hasty theorizations – insisting instead on the need to learn to raise the problems before arriving at conclusions – and against the risk that by attempting to 'modernize' Marxism, one might actually restore the tendencies of bourgeois humanism.[22]

For Rancière, the problem with Althusser's conception of the role of theory in *Reading Capital* was that it reproduced the classical position that theory was the responsibility of intellectuals and scientists, in a form reminiscent of Kautsky's position that socialist consciousness must be conveyed to the working class from the outside. In Althusser's case this takes the form of an underestimation of the importance of social practices, since social practices represent the terrain of ideology and 'false ideas'.

> *Reading Capital* grounds this autonomy [of theory] on the thesis that agents of production are necessarily deluded. By agents of production, we are to understand proletarians and capitalists, since both are simply the agents of capitalist relations of production and both are mystified by the illusions produced by their practices. Put bluntly, the thesis that grounds the autonomy of theory is this: *false ideas originate in social practices*. Science, conversely, must be founded on a point extrinsic to the illusions of practice.[23]

---

21   Rancière 2011, p. 21.
22   Rancière 2011, p. 35.
23   Rancière 2011, p. 47.

In light of this criticism, Rancière insists that Althusser's greater emphasis on class struggle in *Lenin and Philosophy* does not alter the basic conception of the autonomy of science and philosophy. 'The class struggle does not touch the different forms of scientific activity or the power relations that inform them: the functioning of scientific institutions is not one of the stakes of the class struggle'.[24] In a similar manner, Rancière is also critical of Althusser's critique of economism because it does not go all the way in order to challenge the hierarchy of production and in general the hierarchical social relations reproduced inside communist politics:

> The professor's 'Maoism' says the same thing as the cadre's economism or the manager's humanism: it defends the privilege of competent people, of the people who know which demands, which forms of action and which words are proletarian, and which bourgeois. It is a discourse in which specialists of the class struggle defend their power.[25]

In fact, Rancière accuses Althusser of using references to class struggle in order to reinstate a new form of revisionism. 'Only the language of class struggle can serve the double function of normalization and recuperation that defines the relationship of revisionism to revolt'.[26] To this Rancière contrasts not another reading of Marx but the actual practices of the masses in their struggles: 'only mass struggles can shake up the theoretical and political apparatus of representation that blocks the autonomous expression of revolt'.[27]

For Rancière, the danger is that a theory that claims to be revolutionary will become the opposite: 'cut off from revolutionary practice, there is no revolutionary theory that is not transformed into its opposite'.[28] In this sense, Rancière's verdict is that Althusser's turn to the masses and their practices was not enough since it was still based upon a classical conception of the division of labour between theory and mass politics and also upon a classical conception of political organisation and did not pay sufficient attention to the initiatives of the masses themselves.

---

24   Rancière 2011, pp. 63–4.
25   Rancière 2011, p. 109.
26   Rancière 2011, p. 117.
27   Rancière 2011, p. 123.
28   Rancière 2011, p. 154.

3 Althusser's Work as Rupture of the Dialectic of Theory and Practice

Leaving aside those more polemical readings of Althusser, other writers have chosen a different approach. These writers have attempted a more sincere dialogue with the work of Althusser, stressing its many theoretical, philosophical and epistemological virtues, yet at the same time they have remained, to varying degrees, critical of the interrelation between Althusser's theory and his politics or, more generally, the political exigencies of a Marxist-inspired politics.

Alex Callinicos's *Althusser's Marxism*[29] from 1976 is one of the most sympathetic approaches to Althusser of that period. Callinicos stresses both the many merits but also the idealist elements of Althusser's initial epistemological endeavour and acknowledges the force of Althusser's self-critical redefinition of philosophy as in the last instance class struggle in theory, seeing it as a way out of the impasse of his original conception of Marxist philosophy as a Theory of theoretical practice and as a way to rethink the emergence of historical materialism out of the development of class struggles.

> I think we can see that Althusser has been able to rescue his system from an internal critique by abandoning the whole notion of epistemology. In the process, he has succeeded in producing the elements of a theory of the relation between the sciences and the class struggle, which captures both the autonomy of theoretical practice and the necessity for certain class conditions to be established in theory before a particular science can be constituted. He does so by means of a theory of philosophy, not as the Science of Sciences, but as the instance which, mediating between the sciences and politics, establishes these conditions. He thereby also provides us with a much clearer idea of the process whereby historical materialism emerged.[30]

However, it is upon the question of politics that Callinicos is much more critical of Althusser. On the one hand, he criticises Althusser for not being able to offer a complete account of the rise of Stalinism, which for Callinicos is the crucial question that has to be answered, and he also attacks Althusser's dismissal of the importance of Trotskyism as an alternative. Moreover, Callinicos is very critical of Althusser's position towards Mao and the Cultural

---

29   Callinicos 1976.
30   Callinicos 1976, p. 88.

Revolution as a resource for a potential left critique of the Stalinist deviation in the Communist Movement: 'Althusser's Maoism, on the other hand, serves merely as a certificate of revolutionary militancy that enables him to evade the real questions that are Stalin's heritage'.[31] Callinicos extends this criticism to Althusser's theory of ideology. For Callinicos, the entire conception of ideology in general runs the risk of underestimating the determining role of class struggle and the historical specificity of capitalism and seems like a regression to an epistemological and not class-oriented conception of ideology.

> There remains, therefore, a contradiction in Althusser's work. It derives from the juxtaposition of his altered theory of ideology, which sees ideologies as the site of class struggles and the reflections of class interest, rather than as the illusions that precede the Truth of Science, and his rejection of any form of epistemology, on the one hand, and the assertion that ideology is necessary to any society, on the other. This results from a survival from his previous position, an epistemological conception of ideology.[32]

For Callinicos, the problem lies exactly in Althusser's inability to actually think of a deeper break with the Stalinist tradition in the Communist Movement, 'criticising, understanding and rejecting the reformism of the western Communist Parties and the state capitalist bureaucracies of the eastern Communist Parties'.[33] This is the result of Althusser's 'failure to discuss the unity of theory and practice',[34] which leads to a 'practical, political evasion of the problem of revolutionary practice'.[35] Moreover, his conception of ideology and of the Ideological State Apparatuses underestimates the need to smash the state and establish forms of workers' power. Instead Althusser's position runs the risk of falling back into a reformist position of simply taking over and using the state. Consequently, Callinicos's critique is that 'on the questions that divide revolutionaries from reformists, the questions of the revolutionary party and the struggle against the capitalist state, Althusser is silent or misleading'.[36]

---

31   Callinicos 1976, p. 94.
32   Callinicos 1976, pp. 100–1.
33   Callinicos 1976, pp. 103–4.
34   Callinicos 1976, p. 103.
35   Callinicos 1976, p. 104.
36   Callinicos 1976, p. 106.

This line of critique, which is based upon the rupture of the dialectic between theory and practice in Western Marxism, is the theoretical and analytical guiding thread of Perry Anderson's *Considerations on Western Marxism*, which is aimed at not only Althusser, but also a great part of the Marxism of the twentieth century.

> Thus, from 1924 to 1968, Marxism did not 'stop', as Sartre was later to claim; but it advanced via an unending detour from any revolutionary political practice. The divorce between the two was determined by the whole historical epoch. At its deepest level, the fate of Marxism in Europe was rooted in the absence of any big revolutionary upsurge after 1920, except in the cultural periphery of Spain, Yugoslavia and Greece. It was also, and inseparably, a result of the Stalinization of the Communist Parties, the formal heirs of the October Revolution, which rendered impossible genuine theoretical work within politics even in the absence of any revolutionary upheavals – which it in turn contributed to prevent. The hidden hallmark of Western Marxism as a whole is thus that it is a product of defeat.[37]

Moreover, it was on the basis of this rupture in the dialectic of theory and practice that could, according to Anderson, account for the tendency of major figures in Western Marxism to turn to philosophical references before Marx, such as Hegel in the case of Lukács, Kant in the case of Della Volpe, and Spinoza in the case of Althusser. 'Nearly all the novel concepts and accents of Althusser's Marxism, apart from those imported from contemporary disciplines, were in fact directly drawn from Spinoza'.[38] This was also the result of the fact that postwar Marxism mainly flourished in academic environments. Consequently, the 'loss of any dynamic contact with working-class practice in turn displaced Marxist theory towards contemporary non-Marxist and idealist systems of thought, with which it now typically developed in close if contradictory symbiosis'.[39] This led to a 'predominance of epistemological work', an emphasis on 'cultural superstructures' and a 'consistent pessimism'.[40] Anderson's conclusion, echoing the post-1968 optimism of the revolutionary Left, was for the masses to speak instead of intellectuals detached from the actuality of working-class struggle.

---

37   Anderson 1979, p. 42.
38   Anderson 1979, p. 64.
39   Anderson 1979, p. 93.
40   Ibid.

> When a truly revolutionary movement is born in a mature working class, the 'final shape' of theory will have no exact precedent. All that can be said is that when the masses themselves speak, theoreticians – of the sort the West has produced for fifty years – will necessarily be silent.[41]

In *Arguments within English Marxism*,[42] his reply to Thompson's polemic against Althusser, Anderson offers a more balanced account that highlights some of the injustices done by Thompson in his critique. He defends Althusser against the accusation of Stalinism, stressing instead the problematic character of Althusser's turn towards the Cultural Revolution: 'he must be criticized for his ingenuous misjudgment of Mao's regime in China, rather than suppositious hankerings for Stalin's in Russia'.[43]

However, it is interesting that this line of Althusser as an interesting thinker in terms of epistemology and a rethinking of historical materialism who remained trapped within the limits of communist politics and could not actually articulate elements of a revolutionary strategy, falling into various forms of problematic positions in his attempt at self-criticism, is also the guiding thread in Gregory Elliott's *Althusser: The Detour of Theory*.[44] A seminal study and one of the most comprehensive monographs on Althusser in the English-speaking world, written by someone who also provided important translations of Althusser's texts.[45] At the same time, Elliott's work followed, in certain respects, the line offered by Callinicos and Anderson. Althusser was to be considered as an important and highly original thinker, yet the problem lay precisely in the politics and in the relation between theory and political practice. According to Elliott, the aim of Althusser's initial programme was 'twofold':

> to construct an authentically – non-empiricist – Marxist philosophy (in accordance with tradition, 'dialectical materialism') and to reconstruct Marxist science ('historical materialism') in non-economistic, non-humanist and non-historicist form. The provision of a philosophy was the prime desideratum, because it could prevent a repetition of the Zhdanovist delirium; it would act as a bulwark against other kinds of theoretical pragmatism; and it would provide an epistemological foun-

---

41 Anderson 1979, p. 106.
42 Anderson 1980.
43 Anderson 1980, p. 110.
44 Elliott 2006. The first edition appeared in 1987.
45 E.g. Althusser 1990; Althusser 1999a.

dation and guarantee for historical materialism, thus defending it against the enemy within and without the gates.[46]

Althusser tried to answer this mainly by turning towards epistemology as a way to redefine Marxist philosophy, 'a transformed, *marxisant* Bachelardian epistemology combined with certain Spinozist and structuralist theses, and with elements of Marx's own reflections'.[47] However, this led to an unresolved tension in Althusser's work:

> [T]here was a contradiction between Althusser's epistemological project – the provision of a philosophy *for* science, one 'genuinely adequate to constantly developing scientific thought' – and the means by which he attempted to realise it. The effect of his particular assimilation of Spinoza and Bachelard was an unresolved tension between the realism to which he was committed as a Marxist and the relativism or rationalism to which their philosophies led. Oversimplifying, we might say that, having turned to conventionalism to escape the verities of diamat, Althusser depended upon rationalism to conjure away relativism, therewith partially returning to diamat.[48]

Elliott thinks that, in the end, 'Althusser's co-option of Bachelardian epistemology misfired' and that his 'epistemology was not an adequate approach to the commencement and development of scientific research programmes in general'.[49]

Elliott offers a relatively positive account of Althusser's reformulation of the dialectic by means of the centrality of the notion of overdetermination, and regarding the relationship between modes of production and social formations he stresses how

> [r]ather than 'return[ing] us to the conceptual prison (mode of production = social formation)', as Thompson has it, Althusser and Balibar helped release us from it (to put it no higher) by emphasising the structural complexity of the social formation per se and the combination and articulation of at least two modes of production in any social formation.[50]

---

46   Elliott 2006, p. 42.
47   Elliott 2006, p. 49.
48   Elliott 2006, p. 95.
49   Elliott 2006, p. 122.
50   Elliott 2006, p. 152.

Elliott's general assessment of the importance of the first phase of Althusser's interventions is positive. He insists that

> whatever the flaws in Althusser's reconstruction of historical materialism, and however tenuous its title to orthodoxy, it represented – and was widely experienced as – a liberation. If Althusser's constructions were problematic, the majority of his criticisms were pertinent and powerful. They released Marxists from more than one conceptual prison, re-establishing historical materialism as a research programme – one whose potential had been negated rather than exhausted in the enumeration of iron stages and laws, the incantation of derisory formulae, the reiteration of 'famous quotations'.[51]

However, his stance towards Althusser's more self-critical approach in the second half of the 1960s, and the new definition of philosophy as in the last instance class struggle in theory, is much more negative and Althusser is accused of falling back into a *gauchisant* variation of Marxist-Leninist orthodoxy.

> Here, the 'class struggle in theory' – a motley of Bachelard and Mao – assumes a shape, and takes on accents of the Communist *langue de bois*, which the earlier Althusser might have recognised as foes. Pursued to its conclusion, the road taken in *Reply to John Lewis* terminates in the quasi-Zhdanovite tutelage over the intellectuals – in the name of Marxism-Leninism – against which Althusser had once so eloquently intervened.[52]

Part of the motivation behind this criticism is political, mainly relating to Elliott's disbelief as to the political significance of the Chinese Cultural Revolutions, but it also has to do with his critical approach towards the renewed emphasis on the class struggle as the driving force of history. According to Elliott, 'Althusser opted for the worst of both worlds in retaining strict anti-humanist theoretical protocols while relaxing structural causality to accord an exorbitant role to class struggle'.[53] For Elliott, Althusser's turn towards the Cultural Experience was a grave error that 'produced an evasive account of Stalinism' and 'condemned himself to an incongruous position in the PCF'.[54] Elliott is also critical of Althusser's interventions in the second half of the 1970s,

---

51 Elliott 2006, pp. 164–5.
52 Elliott 2006, p. 188.
53 Elliott 2006, p. 203.
54 Elliott 2006, p. 232.

basically accusing him of initially seeking a 'third way' between revolutionary socialism and Eurocommunism, by means of his conception of a renewed form of a popular front combined with de-Stalinisation of the Party. Yet he acknowledges that *What Must Change in the Party*[55] is 'Althusser's single most powerful text',[56] a position also shared with Anderson.[57]

Elliott's overall conclusion is that while Althusser attempted a highly original renewal of historical materialism as a theory, this was undermined 'by a "theoreticism" that toppled over into idealism and conventionalism; by an astringent theoretical anti-humanism which occluded human agency in its prioritisation of structural necessity; by an ultimately anti-histori*cal* anti-histori*cism*'.[58] He rejects Althusser's renewed emphasis on class struggle as an attempt to substitute a 'schematic Marxism-Leninism'[59] for his theoretical system, and stresses that his later turn towards 'centrism or left Eurocommunism' was combined with 'increased scepticism as to the explanatory merits of historical materialism'.[60] In a certain way Althusser is accused on both sides of his tension, the theoretical and the political, and for his apparent inability to actually combine the theory and the politics of a new revolutionary socialist strategy. It is interesting to note that Elliott also maintains and stresses this position in his 2006 postscript to the second edition of *Althusser: The Detour of Theory*, which also takes account of Althusser's texts that were not available in the 1980s.

> To conclude: thus to fix Althusser in his limits is to recognise the limitations of the 'imaginary Marxism' with which he sought to supplant the 'Hegelo-Stalinism' he had subscribed to at the beginning of his career; to register its essentially destructive charge, in spirit and substance alike; to record the self-evident failure of its ambition, which subjectively and objectively governed everything else, to renew communist politics; and thereby, just this once giving him the last word, stifle any inclination to tell (ourselves) stories – even (or especially) about Louis Althusser.[61]

---

55   Althusser 1978c.
56   Elliott 2006, p. 287.
57   'Althusser's manifesto of April 1978 is the most violent oppositional charter ever published within a party in the post-war history of Western Communism' (Anderson 1980, p. 113).
58   Elliott 2006, p. 302.
59   Elliott 2006, p. 303.
60   Elliott 2006, pp. 303–4.
61   Elliott 2006, p. 371.

4   The Possibility of Another Reading

There is no innocent reading and Althusser was the one who actually set the protocols to realise the inexistence of any innocent reading. To this we can add that there is no reading that is completely devoid of sense or that is completely off the mark. Every reading, even when motivated by a desire for complete refutation, in a certain way brings forward some of the modalities of the text under consideration. In this sense, the readings I have chosen to highlight here indeed manage to capture the many contradictions of a work that set out from the beginning to be contradictory and – to use Lenin's metaphor that Althusser appreciated – always bending the stick to the other side. And Althusser himself was aware of the contradictions of his own work. The importance he accorded to the constant practice of self-criticism, the very fact that he treated self-criticism as an indispensable philosophical strategy and political practice, attest to this consideration. Consequently, in respect of the readings discussed above, we have to admit that, indeed, in Althusser's work we find at the same time the originality and the limits of an epistemological conception of theory, the problems caused by taking the existing Communist movement as a starting point, the difficulty in thinking the relation between theory, strategy, and the practices of the masses, and the oscillation between an emphasis on the reproduction of structures and the constant effectivity of class struggle in the singularity of concrete movements and experiences. Yet, the work of Althusser over the whole course of his theoretical and political trajectory cannot be reduced to a series of impasses or the constant reaching of political and theoretical limits.

At the same time, Althusser's work is an attempt to confront these questions and offer crucial starting points. That is why, in contrast to the readings discussed above, I will attempt to show that Althusser's theory of structures and conjunctures cannot be reduced to a variation of structuralism, but instead can be shown to initiate a novel way of thinking social relations and practices along with the singularity of conjunctures; that his reading of other philosophers is highly original and cannot be limited to anti-Hegelianism or Spinozism; that the materialism of the encounter represents an attempt to rethink exactly these questions along with the possibility of a left critique of the existing Communist movement; that Althusser's constant redefinition of a new materialist practice of philosophy is an effort to rethink that collective intellectual practice that could actually help the liberation of the social practices and collective creativity and ingenuity of the subaltern classes; that his work remains deeply political from the beginning, representing, despite its many contradictions and shortcomings, an attempt towards a renewal of revolutionary strategy for the Communist movement, an attempt that is more relevant than ever.

CHAPTER 2

The Never-Ending Confrontation with Hegel

Althusser's entrance into the philosophical scene in the early 1960s, first by his articles and then by the appearance of *For Marx* and *Reading Capital*, was a defining moment of the evolution of Marxist debates on philosophy, theory, and to a certain extent politics. Despite not offering a systematic exposure (*For Marx* was a collection of essays and *Reading Capital* a collection of presentations at a seminar), Althusser's insistence on the possibility of a novel way to rethink structures, contradictions, decentred totalities and singular conjunctures, along with his insistence upon theoretical anti-humanism, indeed seemed not only a philosophical position but also an attempt to redefine the entire terrain of Marxist philosophy, re-posing all the strategic philosophical questions regarding the role of materialist philosophy, the content, place, form and function of the dialectic, and the conceptualisation of social totalities.

This position had a polemical and confrontational tone against other readings and conceptualisations of Marxism. In particular it was turned against the possibility of a Hegelian Marxism. Defining the '*structural differences*'[1] between Marx's and Hegel's conceptions of the dialectic was one of the declared aims of *For Marx*. More generally we can say that the rupture with Hegel and the attempt to redefine Marxist philosophy in opposition to the tendency to think of it as an inverted materialist form of Hegelianism was one of the most important traits of this philosophical endeavour. However, Althusser's relation with Hegel was not just one of simple rejection, despite the fact that the better known part of his work is an attempt to draw a very strict line of demarcation between Marxist philosophy and the philosophy of Hegel. In fact we are dealing with a more complex relation between Althusser and Hegel, which we need to retrace before moving on to Althusser's attempt to think of the possibility of a historical materialism beyond Hegel.

1   The 1947 Thesis

First of all, we have Althusser's confrontation with Hegel in his 1947 Master's thesis *On Content in the Philosophy of Hegel*.[2] This is an important text, despite

---

[1] Althusser 1969, p. 94.
[2] In Althusser 1997c. The text remained unpublished until 1994, even though, according to

being disavowed by Althusser himself. Its importance lies in the fact that at the moment of Althusser's turn from Christianity towards Marxism and communist politics, this reading of Hegel was crucial. It demonstrates an extensive knowledge of Hegel's texts and of the relevant literature. It also shows that from the beginning of this process of political and philosophical conversion, Althusser was interested in separating his own philosophical orientation from any personalistic or moralistic 'philosophy of consciousness'; rather, he was much more interested in a philosophy of history and transformation and the role that collective ideological and theoretical practices play in this. 'The problem of the content in Hegel's philosophy is, first of all, an historical problem'.[3] For the young Althusser, Hegel is a thinker who attempts to present thought as a process that 'discloses' a void 'in the very act of filling it',[4] this void being 'the Enlightenment',[5] of which he offers an extraordinary description in the *Phenomenology of Spirit*. Althusser discerns a positive side to the void, as 'promise of fulfilment', thus a '*necessity of the void*' which can explain Hegel's famous reference to 'tarrying with the negative'.[6]

Althusser is particularly interested in Hegel's criticism and supersession of Kant and his conception of consciousness and subjectivity which are presented as 'an empty unity abstracted from its content'.[7] Regarding the importance of the void in the Hegelian *Logic*, Althusser insists that it is not a question of an abstract logic, but of the necessary condition in order to arrive at the totality in the end of the process instead of taking it as a pure given. Althusser approaches the dialectic of form and content in Hegel and in particular the conception of content as *reflection* and traces the contradictions associated with this attempt. The 'impossibility of reducing reflection to substance'[8] leads to the alternative of a conception of totality as a beyond leading to 'reality without totality; on the other hand totality without reality'.[9]

Regarding Hegel's conception of the content as Self, Althusser turns to the centrality of the concept in Hegel's endeavour. According to Althusser, the 'Hegelian concept can be reduced neither to one absolute term (intuition), nor

---

Althusser, Merleau-Ponty had suggested to Althusser, Jacques Maritain and Jean Deprun to publish their theses, something they all refused (Althusser 1993b, p. 161). Instead Althusser decided to subject it to the 'gnawing criticism of the mice' (Althusser 1993b, p. 327).

3   Althusser 1997c, p. 36.
4   Althusser 1997c, p. 41.
5   Althusser 1997c, p. 44.
6   Althusser 1997c, p. 49.
7   Althusser 1997c, p. 55.
8   Althusser 1997c, p. 83.
9   Ibid.

to two contradictory terms (general, formal ideas / concrete content). Rather it is accomplished in the third term [...] There are not three terms, for Hegel, but one, the concept'.[10] In light of these we can understand the importance of the 'transformation of the substance into subject'[11] as the foundation of Hegelian freedom: 'Viewed from this angle, then (substance becoming subject), history is the progressive development of the forms of self-consciousness'.[12]

For Althusser it is important to stress that Hegel included 'the philosopher in its field of reflection',[13] as a 'concrete, historical man, who dwells in eternity in his own time and his own time in eternity',[14] in a process mediated by language. Althusser acknowledges that at first sight Hegel's presentation of dialectical necessity 'creates the impression that Hegel has reverted to a philosophy of laws, to formalism'.[15] Althusser suggests that we must turn to Hartmann's reading of Hegel and his insistence on the 'purity of the object',[16] even though he admits that even Hartmann did not manage to think the full complexity of the Hegelian dialectic, and the contradictory ways in which it can be viewed from the viewpoint of substance and subject, respectively.

Althusser turns to what he defines as the 'sins of the content',[17] confronting Marx's critique of Hegel's *Philosophy of Right*. Marx is credited with linking content to revolutionary transformation: 'Marx was to work out the truth of this basic, mutually compensatory interaction characteristic of economic relations by showing that the concept, i.e., the appropriation of this relation, could only consist in the revolutionary transformation of the social order'.[18] Althusser also points to the importance of Marx's critique as realisation of the 'necessity of error' in Hegel's philosophy: 'The perversion of the content is not happenstance or inconsistency, but rather the most consistent of phenomena: the false content emerges, in that case, as the truth of a falsified Idea. Thus it would be possible to speak of the necessity of error in Hegel'.[19]

However, it is interesting that Althusser does not simply endorse the criticism of Hegel by the young Marx. Instead he points to certain questions where Hegel's thinking still has an advantage over that of the young Marx.

---

10   Althusser 1997c, p. 86.
11   Althusser 1997c, p. 90.
12   Althusser 1997c, p. 97.
13   Althusser 1997c, p. 101.
14   Althusser 1997c, p. 103.
15   Althusser 1997c, p. 112.
16   Althusser 1997c, p. 113.
17   Althusser 1997c, p. 116.
18   Althusser 1997c, p. 120.
19   Althusser 1997c, p. 127.

> If thought could really reappropriate the alienation that spawned it, and repossess in reality what it endeavours to apprehend in a figure, it would abolish the real alienation of the world and reconcile the world with itself through the power of its discourse. This childish aspiration lies at the heart of every philosophy; Marx denounced it as a kind of magic. Hegel's grandeur lies in the fact that he consciously renounced this aspiration (at least in the *Phenomenology*) and demonstrated the necessity of that renunciation; he showed, in other words, that alienation cannot either be eliminated in a figure, nor even simply thought as the essence of thought, before being concretely overcome in history.[20]

Althusser insists that 'Marx is thoroughly informed by Hegelian truth'.[21] For the young Althusser it is important to return to the question of how to separate the good form from the bad content, as suggested by Marx and Engels. For Althusser, 'Marx's critique helped us grasp the perversity of the Hegelian state, but we saw that, far from succeeding in its attempt to extend the perversion of the content to the form, this critique was itself, down to its deepest levels, drawn back into the embrace of Hegelian necessity'.[22] Althusser reminds us that especially in the *Phenomenology* '[i]t was not the world he lived in that reflected Hegel's audacity back to him; it was Hegel who held up the mirror to the world's audacity, that is, to the truth of the world'.[23] He denies that the Hegel of the *Philosophy of Right* does not fully abandon this position. Instead, he points to a situation where necessity becomes a *ruse*.[24] This circularity of thinking justifies depicting Hegel as the last philosopher, opening up the way towards the Marxist conception of emancipation.

> Marx is right when he says that Hegel is the last philosopher – but he does not mean this in the way Hegel did. Hegel is the last philosopher because, in the form of the circularity of the concept, he wrests philosophy's own kingdom from philosophy. All that remains is to translate Hegelian circularity into reality, to transform philosophy into a world, and, to that end, to seek in the actually existing historical worlds the dialectical element that will enable man to overcome alienation and render history circular. This is

---

20   Althusser 1997c, p. 132.
21   Althusser 1997c, p. 140.
22   Althusser 1997c, p. 141.
23   Althusser 1997c, p. 145.
24   Althusser 1997c, p. 148.

the Marxist transition from contemplation to action and the transformation of history into universal history, i.e. the elevation of the content to the level of freedom.[25]

It is interesting that for Althusser, the emergence of phenomenological thinking is a result of the decay of Hegel and its transformation into ideology. This is one of the first indications of Althusser's rejection of phenomenology and phenomenological readings, a critical position that would also be a defining aspect of his 'mature' work.[26]

> Whether or not it realizes its dependence, contemporary thought has been created out of Hegel's decay, and draws sustenance from it. Ideologically speaking, then, we are dominated by Hegel, who comes back into his own in modern philosophical endeavour; and this dependence is genuine, since it does not break free of the decay of Hegel, i.e., the transformation of Hegelian truth into ideology. Modern *ideologies* are reappropriated by Hegelian *ideology* – right down to their deliberate ingratitude – as if by their mother – truth.[27]

For Althusser, Hegel's thought retains its importance. The decomposition of the Hegelian system did not just lead to the emergence of various ideologies. 'Hegel had become our world' also in the sense of the '*real world* in the form of the workers' movements and revolutionary action'.[28] And this brings out the importance of Marx's intervention:

> Marx understood that the transcendental was history but he did not consider it possible to think history in general, apart from the *concrete content* of the dominant historical reality. He therefore determined the socioeconomic structure of capitalist society, positing this world as a contradictory totality [...] He conceived this totality as dialectical.[29]

Even more importantly, all these relate to a revolutionary effort. The 'Marxist movement is a materialism [...] but also a humanism'.[30] Althusser's final con-

---

25   Althusser 1997c, p. 150.
26   Cf. Montag 2013.
27   Althusser 1997c, p. 151.
28   Ibid.
29   Althusser 1997c, p. 155.
30   Althusser 1997c, p. 156.

clusion concerns the need to confront the disintegration of the Hegelian system and the emergence of the Marxist outlook not in the sense of – what are presented as Marxist – definite answers but rather as a challenge to be answered.

> We do not find ourselves in the transparent circularity of the Hegelian truth but in a concrete world whose significations are enveloped by concrete totalities. The Marxist movement *is* its own signification; it is not necessarily the one it gives out as its own. The disintegration of Hegelianism is tangible even in the difficulty reality has in conceiving its own truth. If we attempt to determine the intellectual structure of this post-Hegelian world, our objective cannot be to re-establish a definitive schema. For us, the future is in the secret movements of the present content; we are caught up in a still obscure totality which we must bring into the light.[31]

2   The Polemics against French Hegelianism

We also have two more texts by Althusser from the period of his Master's thesis. One is called 'Man that night'. The title comes from a phrase of Hegel. For Althusser, 'Hegel saw in man a sick animal who neither dies nor recovers, but stubbornly insists on living on in a nature terrified of him. The animal kingdom reabsorbs its monsters, economy its crises: man alone is a triumphant error who makes its aberration the law of the world'.[32] However, the main target is the work of Alexandre Kojève. For Althusser, Kojève's interpretation is 'brilliant' yet as an 'anthropology' it 'develops the subjective aspect of Hegelian negativity'. Consequently, 'the partiality of this approach leads him to a dualistic perspective'.[33] To this subjectivism – dualism – Althusser opposes the dialectic of substance and subject in Hegel as a dialectic of freedom.

> Hegel himself clearly felt this obscure imperative; that is why he showed that the totality was the Kingdom, not merely of nothingness (of the Subject), but also of being (of Substance). That is why nature is neither a shadow, nor the conjunction of human projects (as in Sartre for example), nor the opposite of man, another world governed by laws of its own (as

---

31   Ibid.
32   Althusser 1997c, p. 170.
33   Althusser 1997c, p. 171.

in Kojève). The Hegelian totality is the totality Substance – Subject. [...] But this is only one aspect of the Hegelian totality. The other is the becoming-Subject of Substance, the production of Spirit by a concrete nature, that is the production of man by nature, and the objective working out of human freedom in the course of an exacting history.[34]

Althusser accuses Kojève of coming close to existentialist positions: 'Kojève's existentialist Marx is a travesty in which Marxists will not recognize their own'.[35] Even more aggressive is another text by Althusser from 1950 that offers a polemical account of the rediscovery of Hegel by French philosophy, and in particular of the work of Jean Hippolyte and Kojève, the philosophers and the readings upon which he had, at least partially, relied in his own Master's thesis.

Althusser begins with a historical detour, tracing the fate of Hegelianism after the death of Hegel. For Althusser, Hegelian philosophy was viewed in the nineteenth century as an attempt to legitimise monarchy. At the same time, Marx and Engels 'acknowledged the important role Hegel had played in their development, and, though they subjected him to a thorough-going critique, revealed the extent to which his thought stripped of its mystifications, had contributed to the creation of scientific socialism'.[36] In contrast, liberalism and especially neo-Kantian liberalism 'constituted a fallback position for the ideological legitimization of the bourgeoisie, and, at the same time, was the natural philosophy of petit-bourgeois intellectuals in their blindness'.[37] However, the broader evolution and crisis of 'monopoly capitalism' led to a retreat from liberalism and the emergence of 'experience', 'action', 'intuition', 'existence', 'life', the 'hero' and, soon, 'blood'.[38] In this intellectual climate, the readings he criticised 'zeroed in on the reactionary aspects of Hegel's philosophy'.[39] All these show that '[w]ith the generalized imperialist crisis, the bourgeoisie has entered the world of tragedy, in the *actual exigency of self-seeking*, whose expression is war'.[40] These readings target Marxism and the way it was inspiring millions of human beings. Therefore the current 'return' to Hegel was openly reactionary:

---

34 Ibid.
35 Althusser 1997c, p. 172.
36 Althusser 1997c, p. 175.
37 Althusser 1997c, p. 177.
38 Althusser 1997c, p. 178.
39 Althusser 1997c, p. 179.
40 Althusser 1997c, p. 181.

> Today we see that the question of Hegel is, for the bourgeoisie, merely a matter of impugning Marx. This Great Return to Hegel is simply a desperate attempt to combat Marx, cast in the specific form that revisionism takes in imperialism's final crisis: *a revisionism of a fascist type*.[41]

It is interesting that in this condemnation of the current return to Hegel, Althusser accused even Hyppolite, whose interpretation of Hegel was one of the guiding lines of his work in the Master's thesis.[42] This polemic is interesting not only because of his attempt, from an early stage, to present analyses of politico-intellectual conjunctures, but also because of his drawing a line of demarcation of any subjectivist and personalistic readings of Hegel. This critique should not be viewed as simply a 'cold war era' polemic against 'bourgeois' philosophers. Althusser, who was indeed a very attentive reader of Hegel, attempts to actually think of a non-subjectivist, 'objective', 'anti-humanist' Hegel that could be combined with a Marxist outlook. Althusser is historicist, in terms of his own terminology, but his historicism is not that of a messianic Subject; rather it is the historicism of a historical contradictory dialectical process, that has as an integral aspect the emergence of a form of a collective conscience that is itself part of the historical process. When almost 20 years later Althusser praised Hegel for bringing forward a conception of the process that is in reality 'without a subject', in a certain way he returns to elements of his early confrontation with Hegel: 'While remorselessly abandoning all Hegel's influence, Marx continued to recognize an important debt to him: the fact that he was the first to conceive of history as a "process without a subject"'.[43]

3   The Critique of Hegel

A reading of Althusser's early texts on Hegel also enables us to fully realise that his critique comes out of knowledge of Hegel; it is not a set of arbitrary accusations. It can also account for Althusser's continuous return to the question of the necessary line of demarcation with any form of historicism and theoretical humanism. Althusser's critique of any possibility of separating Hegel's dialectical method from its idealist content, a critique that is one of the main motifs of *For Marx* and *Reading Capital*, is based upon his own attempt, especially

---

41   Althusser 1997c, p. 183.
42   Cf. Montag 2013, p. 30.
43   Althusser 1971, p. 84.

in his Master's thesis, to think the dialectic of form and content in Hegel. One can see this relation between Althusser's earlier confrontation with Hegel and his later critique of Hegelian Idealism in passages such as the following from 'Contradiction and Overdetermination':

> Indeed, a Hegelian contradiction is never *really overdetermined*, even though it frequently has all the appearances of being so. For example, in the *Phenomenology of Mind*, which describes the 'experiences' of consciousness and their dialectic, culminating in Absolute Knowledge, contradiction does not *appear* to be *simple*, but on the contrary very complex. Strictly speaking, only the first contradiction – between sensuous consciousness and its knowledge – can be called simple. The further we progress in the dialectic of its production, the richer consciousness becomes, the more complex is its contradiction. However, it can be shown that this complexity is not the complexity of an *effective overdetermination*, but the complexity of a cumulative *internalization* which is only apparently an overdetermination.[44]

In a similar manner, Althusser's famous rejection of Hegelian totality in favour of his own attempt towards a materialist notion of a decentred and overdetermined totality is an attempt to answer, in a different and even opposite way, questions that had haunted him from the time of his Master's thesis. In 1947 he was confronting the question of Hegelian totality in terms of the dialectic between substance/content and subject:

> We have here the two aspects of the Hegelian totality before us. *In the substance*, the solid, homogeneous aspect of the content and the obscurity of its soul are paramount – and in this sense there is no dialectic. *In the subject*, in contrast, it is the soul that triumphs, in other words, the conscious process, though still in the form of externality – and in this sense there is a dialectic, though it is a formal one. The totality is constituted through the development, accomplishment and mutual recognition of these two aspects: in the totality, dialectic and non-dialectic profoundly coincide. At this stage, dialecticity is the depth of non-dialecticity, the 'soul of the content', i.e., its own concept. [...] Moreover, we know that negativity is the soul of the concept. It can therefore be said that the Hegelian dialectic is the concept of negativity, that is, negativity's own cognition of itself.[45]

---

44   Althusser 1969, p. 101.
45   Althusser 1997c, p. 115.

In contrast, in 1965 the Hegelian totality is criticised and rejected, in terms of its inability to include complex, uneven and overdetermined relations and also its inability to think the contradictory co-existence of different temporalities. Here, the main point of critique is exactly the possibility of an 'essential section' offered by the Hegelian conception of totality.

> The contemporaneity of time, or the category of the historical *present*. This second category is the condition of possibility of the first one, and in it we find Hegel's central thought. If historical time is the existence of the social totality we must be precise about the structure of this existence. The fact that the relation between the social totality and its historical existence is a relation with an *immediate* existence implies that this relation is itself *immediate*. In other words: the structure of historical existence is such that all the elements of the whole always co-exist in one and the same time, one and the same present, and are therefore contemporaneous with one another in one and the same present. This means that the structure of the historical existence of the Hegelian social totality allows what I propose to call an *'essential section'* (*coupe d'essence*), i.e., an intellectual operation in which a *vertical break* is made at any moment in historical time, a break in the present such that all the elements of the whole revealed by this section are in an immediate relationship with one another, a relationship that immediately expresses their internal essence.[46]

It is interesting that although especially in *Reading Capital* he attempted to present an image of an absolute and total break with Hegel, in the late 1970s he returns to the theme of the persevering Hegelian influences to Marx. Thus, in 1978 he admitted the Hegelian and in general idealist elements in the thought of the mature Marx. In *Marx in his Limits* Althusser acknowledges that we can find 'in Marx – increasingly subject to criticism, yet always present just beneath the surface – the idea of a philosophy of history, of an Origin and an End'.[47] In 'Marxism Today', again from 1978, he admits that:

> The latent or manifest idealism of these themes haunts not only *The German Ideology* (a veritable 'materialist' philosophy of history) but also the evolutionism of the 1859 Preface (the 'progressive' succession of modes of

---

46 Althusser et al. 2016, pp. 240–1.
47 Althusser 2006a, p. 36.

production) and the tautological finalism of the famous sentences that delighted Gramsci: 'No social order is ever destroyed before all the productive forces for which it is sufficient have been developed. [...] Mankind thus inevitably sets itself only such tasks as it is able to solve'. In an infinitely more subtle form, the same idealism haunts *Capital* itself. We have learned to recognize in *Capital*'s 'mode of exposition', however impressive, the fictive unity imposed upon it from the outset by the requirement of beginning with the abstraction of value – i.e. with the homogeneity presupposed by the field of commensurability – without having previously posited capitalist relations of exploitation as the condition of its process.[48]

This does not mean that Althusser abandoned any conception of the break between Hegel and Marx. He feels obliged to problematise it, rather than simply assert it: Marx 'remained sufficiently attached to this Idea to consider himself obliged to begin with value, to regard the "inverted" Hegelian dialectic as his own, and to think what he had discovered within the impressive but fictitious unity of the (in principle) one and only order of exposition in Capital'.[49]

If Hegel was in a certain way, in the history of philosophy, the alternative to any attempt to create a philosophy of transcendental consciousness, whether Kantian or phenomenological, an alternative towards a philosophy of historical process and practice, then for Althusser it was a constant challenge of how to elaborate such an alternative without falling back into some sort of metaphysical idealism. The critique of Hegel – and at the same time the acknowledgement of the influence of Hegel on Marx – was a way to deal with this challenge. Hegel was never a philosophical ally for Althusser in the sense that Spinoza or Machiavelli were, that is, philosophers who actually dealt with the same open questions and offered conceptual breakthroughs. Nevertheless he remained a critical reference in the sense that the contradictory conceptual dynamics emerging from Hegelian philosophy and the questions they posed were indispensable elements in Althusser's thought laboratory.

---

48 Althusser 1990, p. 272.
49 Althusser 2006a, p. 42.

CHAPTER 3

'This Man is Indeed Alone in Facing His Task': Althusser on Montesquieu

Although Althusser's book on Montesquieu belongs to the period of 'Althusser before Althusser', namely the long period during which he had developed his distinctive philosophical intervention, it is an important first expression of many aspects of his entire philosophical endeavour. If we want to retrace Althusser's philosophical interventions and his redefinition of the conceptual terrain of Marxist philosophy, it is important to revisit his reading of Montesquieu exactly as one of his first attempts towards a rethinking of historical materialism as a highly original materialist social theory.

Although Althusser became known mainly for his reading of key texts of the Marxist tradition, such as Marx's *Capital* or Lenin's texts on the revolutionary conjuncture in Russia or on philosophy, his initial project of a *grande thèse* on political philosophy of the eighteenth century led to a series of readings of political philosophers such as Machiavelli, Rousseau, and of course Montesquieu. One can find in Althusser's confrontation with the work of Montesquieu some of the theoretical preoccupations that also marked Althusser's mature work, such as how to conceive of societies as totalities or the need to avoid the teleology or finalism of any conception of an origin of societies. His reading of Montesquieu can also be considered the first example of a *symptomatic* reading of a text, in the sense of going beyond the intentions of the writer: 'Let us do him the duty, which is the duty of every historian, of taking him not at his word, but at his work'.[1]

1   Montesquieu's Revolution in Method

For Althusser, Montesquieu represents a revolution in method compared to other philosophers and theorists of the eighteenth century. Although he shares the same quest for a political physics with other theorists from the sixteenth century onwards, he is different insofar as he does not opt for theorising an

---

1 Althusser 1972a, p. 15.

abstract conception of society in general, but instead wants to 'set out not from essences but from facts'.[2]

> Hence it is clear both what unites Montesquieu with the theoreticians who preceded him and what distinguishes him from them. He has in common with them *the same project*: to erect a political science. But *he does not have the same object*, proposing to produce the science not of society in general but of all the concrete societies in history. And for this reason *he does not have the same method*, aiming not to grasp essences, but to discover laws. This unity in project and difference in object and method make Montesquieu both the man who gave his predecessors' *scientific exigencies* the most rigorous form – and the most determined opponent of their *abstraction*.[3]

The basic novelty of Montesquieu is the absence in his work of a theory of the origin of society, in a line similar to Althusser's later insistence that teleology and finalism are the main forms of idealism. He insists that philosophers of natural law and of the social contract 'pose the same problem: *what is the origin of society?*',[4] with the social contract ensuring the transition from the state of nature as originary 'negation of society to the existing society'.[5] For Althusser, although this 'idea is both a protest against the old order and the programme for a new order', at the same time it is a theoretical conception marked by '*abstraction and idealism*'.[6] In contrast, Montesquieu goes beyond the question of origin, since he insists that society is always already given, offering a 'condemnation of the problem of origins as absurd'.[7] This can account for the radical novelty of the endeavour of Montesquieu and his radical break with the teleology and idealism of the theorists of natural law:

> Rejecting the theory of natural law and the contract, Montesquieu at the same time rejects *the philosophical implications of its problematic*: above all the *idealism* of its procedures. [...] He only knows *facts*. If he refuses to judge *what is* by *what ought to be*, it is because he does not draw his principles from his 'prejudices, but from the nature of things'.[8]

---

2 Althusser 1972a, p. 20.
3 Ibid.
4 Althusser 1972a, p. 25.
5 Althusser 1972a, p. 26.
6 Althusser 1972a, p. 27.
7 Althusser 1972a, p. 29.
8 Ibid.

In order to accomplish this task Montesquieu attempts to actually apply the new conception of the laws derived from natural sciences and especially Newtonian physics to history and society, a conception of law not as 'an order and an end pronounced by a master', but 'as a relation'.[9] All these suggest that Montesquieu was in fact attempting to think in terms of historical laws and in sharp contrast to other theorists of that period:

> The Montesquieu who refuses precisely to judge what is by what ought to be, who only wants to give the real necessity of history the form of its law, by drawing this law from the diversity of the facts and their variations, this man is indeed alone in facing his task.[10]

For Althusser, this represents a theoretical revolution:

> We must face up to the implications of this theoretical revolution. It presupposes that it is possible to apply a Newtonian category of law to matters of politics and history. It presupposes that it is possible to draw from human institutions themselves the wherewithal to think their diversity in a uniformity and their changes in a constancy: the law of their diversification and the law of their development. This law will no longer be an ideal order but instead a relation immanent to the phenomena.[11]

Althusser then turns to what he defines as the 'dialectic of history'[12] in Montesquieu. He stresses the importance of Montesquieu's distinction between the *nature* and the *principle* of a government. The *nature* refers to how government is constituted, in the sense of the holder of power and the way power is organised, while the principle refers to how a government is made to act, its specific disposition to a 'certain way of acting and reacting', what he designates the 'specific *passion*' which 'each government necessarily desires'.[13] For Althusser, this relation between nature and principle prevents Montesquieu's schema from turning into formalism.

> Montesquieu has been accused of formalism because of his way of defining a government by its *nature*, which does indeed consist of a few words

---

9   Althusser 1972a, p. 33.
10   Althusser 1972a, p. 30.
11   Althusser 1972a, p. 34.
12   Althusser 1972a, p. 43.
13   Althusser 1972a, p. 45.

of pure constitutional law. [...] The *principle* is thus the intersection of the *nature* of the government (its political form) with the real life of men. It is thus *the point and aspect in which the real life of men has to be resumed in order to be inserted into the form of a government*. The principle is the concrete of that abstract, the nature. It is their unity, it is their totality, that is real. Where is the formalism?[14]

More importantly, Althusser seeks in Montesquieu a new theoretical conception of *totality*, attempting to explain both the multiplicity and diversity and their inner logic. Montesquieu was not the first to think in terms of totality, but he was the first to think of it as a scientific hypothesis.

> I do not claim that Montesquieu was the first to think that the State should of itself constitute a *totality*. This idea is already lurking in Plato's reflection and we find it again at work in the thought of the theoreticians of natural law, at any rate in Hobbes. But before Montesquieu this idea only entered into the constitution of an *ideal* State, without lowering itself to the point of making *concrete* history intelligible. With Montesquieu, the totality, which was an *idea*, becomes a scientific *hypothesis*, intended to *explain the facts*.[15]

However, Althusser is careful to stress that the danger of formalism is not completely avoided, especially if '*an idea which is only valid for pure models and perfect political forms* has been taken for a category applicable to all existing categories'.[16] What prevents Montesquieu from falling and makes evident that there is a sense of history in his work is his distancing from any form of teleology, of any sense of end in history, attempting instead to think of societies in their real history, to think of them as concrete totalities in their history.

> *Montesquieu was probably the first person before Marx who undertook to think history without attributing to it an end*, i.e. without projecting the consciousness of men and their hopes onto the time of history.[17]

Althusser disagrees with Ernst Cassirer's assertion that in Montesquieu's conception of totality no element is considered more important than another and

---

14 Althusser 1972a, p. 46.
15 Althusser 1972a, p. 47.
16 Althusser 1972a, p. 48.
17 Althusser 1972a, p. 50.

that no element can be considered the 'motor of history'.[18] Such a conception, which may be in accordance with the letter of some of Montesquieu's formulations, runs the risk of leading to a conception wherein every form will be producing its own principles, expressed in their turn in this form.

> We would seem here to be in a real *circular expressive totality* in which each part is like the whole: *pars totalis*. And the movement of this sphere which we think is moved by a cause is no more than its displacement onto itself.[19]

It is obvious that we are dealing here with a first version of Althusser's distancing from what he later designated and criticised as the expressive conception of totality, which he attributed mainly to Hegel, a critique that is one of the main points in Althusser's texts from 1960–65. Here what guarantees this distancing is exactly the emphasis on a potential motor of history, or of a determining 'in the last instance' element (or a structure in dominance). Montesquieu avoids this danger by insisting that there is 'in the last instance *a determinant form: the principle*',[20] and for Althusser there are obvious analogies with the importance attributed by Marx to the determining in the last instance role of the economy, which at the same time also left a space for the efficacy of politics.

> However hazardous a comparison it may be, and one that I put forward with all possible precautions, the type of this *determination in the last instance by the principle*, determination which nevertheless farms out a whole zone of subordinate effectivity to the *nature* of the government, can be compared with the type of determination which Marx attributes *in the last instance to the economy*, a determination which nevertheless farms out a zone of subordinate effectivity to *politics*.[21]

It is interesting to note that although Althusser here presents a version of the insistence on the determining in the last instance role of the economy, while attempting to think of the distinctive yet subordinate effectivity of other instances and in particular politics, he still lacks a concept of overdetermination.

---

18   Althusser 1972a, p. 51.
19   Althusser 1972a, p. 52.
20   Ibid.
21   Althusser 1972a, p. 53.

Althusser knows very well that in the traditional reading of Montesquieu, external factors such as the climate play an important role in determining human societies, especially since they are determining manners and morals. How can the primacy of the principle and the political exigencies it expresses be combined with these external factors? For Althusser, in the end Montesquieu attempts to think within the limits of this contradiction.

> All Montesquieu's ambiguity is linked to this tension. He did feel that the necessity of history could only be thought in the unity of its forms and their conditions of existence, and in the dialectic of that unity. But he grouped all these conditions, *on the one hand in the manners and morals*, which are indeed produced by real conditions, but whose concept remains vague (the synthesis of all these conditions in the manners and morals is no more than cumulative); and *on the other hand in the principle*, which, divided between its real origins and the exigencies of the political form it has to animate, *leans too often towards these exigencies alone*.[22]

2   Montesquieu's Politics

Althusser stresses that for Montesquieu '*the age of republics is over*',[23] although he admits that in democracy the 'category of the citizen realizes the *synthesis of the State* in man himself'.[24] Apart from this 'retrospective apologia'[25] for democracy, Montesquieu, in contrast to Rousseau, brings forward the problem of political representation, since for Montesquieu power 'cannot fall into the hands of the common people'.[26] In contrast Montesquieu thinks that 'feudal monarchy belongs to modern times'.[27] Consequently, Althusser thinks that Montesquieu's endorsement of monarchy is the result of a certain realist conception of social and political contradictions.

Althusser then proceeds to Montesquieu's insistence that '*in despotism all politics can always be reduced to passion*',[28] without any social structure, lowering 'all subjects to the same *uniformity*'.[29] However, this is a passion that is

---

22   Althusser 1972a, p. 59.
23   Althusser 1972a, p. 61.
24   Althusser 1972a, p. 62.
25   Althusser 1972a, p. 63.
26   Althusser 1972a, p. 65.
27   Ibid.
28   Althusser 1972a, p. 76.
29   Althusser 1972a, p. 77.

not educated or social. In contrast Montesquieu defends 'against the politics of absolutism [not] so much *liberty in general* as the *particular liberties* of the feudal class'.[30] That is why Montesquieu's fear is that despotism can lead to '*the regime of popular revolution*'.[31]

Althusser insists on the 'myth of the separation of powers'.[32] He follows Charles Eisenmann's thesis that the famous theory of the separation of powers '*simply does not exist in Montesquieu*'.[33] Montesquieu is concerned not with the separation of powers, but with the combination of *puissances* and the attempt to identify which combinations must be excluded in order to avoid monarchy collapsing into despotism, such as the investment of the judiciary into the executive. The aim is exactly the '*protection of the nobility* against the political and legal arbitration of the prince' and in general to guarantee the privileges of the nobility '*against the undertakings of either the king or the people*'.[34] This might explain why his preference for the English constitution should not be understood as evidence of republicanism.

For Althusser, all these attest to the theoretical difficulties regarding 'the nature of *absolute monarchy* on the one hand, of the *bourgeoisie* on the other, in the historical period in which Montesquieu lived'.[35] It was a period marked on the one hand by nostalgia for '*primitive* monarchy'[36] that would be based upon nobility, and on the other hand, by a bourgeois support for enlightened despotism based upon the bourgeoisie. Althusser generalises this in terms of a certain historicisation of thinking, insisting that a degree of distance is necessary if we want to actually understand historical reality.

> Thinking a history whose deeper springs escaped them, it was easy for them to limit their thought *to the immediate categories* of their historical life, most often taking political intentions for reality itself, and superficial conflicts for the basis of things.[37]

Moreover, it is necessary to avoid projecting onto the seventeenth or eighteenth centuries the image of the advanced bourgeoisie of the nineteenth century

---

30 Althusser 1972a, p. 83.
31 Althusser 1972a, p. 85.
32 Althusser 1972a, p. 87.
33 Althusser 1972a, p. 89.
34 Althusser 1972a, p. 93.
35 Althusser 1972a, p. 97.
36 Ibid.
37 Althusser 1972a, p. 98.

and the industrial revolution. Such a projection risks asserting a contradiction between feudal social forms and mercantile capitalism which in fact did not exist.

> [T]he gravest danger confronting the historian of the seventeenth and even of the eighteenth century, at least of its first half, is to project onto the 'bourgeoisie' of this period the image of the later bourgeoisie which made the Revolution, and of the bourgeoisie which emerged from the Revolution. The true modern bourgeoisie, which transformed the previous economic and social order from top to bottom, is the *industrial* bourgeoisie, with its mass-production economy, concentrating entirely on profit subsequently reinvested in production. But in its generality this bourgeoisie was unknown to the eighteenth century; the bourgeoisie of that period was quite different: in its most advanced elements it was essentially dependent on the *mercantile economy*.[38]

This brings forward the broader question of how to theorise absolute monarchy and the relation of the bourgeoisie to it, and in particular whether there was a conflict between the feudal lords and the bourgeoisie. In contrast to the received images of class conflicts within absolute monarchy, Althusser insists that

> *the fundamental antagonism at that time did not counterpose the absolute monarchy to the feudal lords, nor the nobility to a bourgeoisie which was for the most part integrated into the regime of feudal exploitation and profited by it, but the feudal regime itself to the masses subject to its exploitation.*[39]

Althusser contends that the mercantile bourgeoisie were not in fact against the nobility and the political arrangements of absolute monarchy; rather, they were aiming at being incorporated into it and therefore were not in opposition to absolute monarchy:

> The aim of the 'bourgeois' enriched by trade thus consists of *directly entering the society of the nobility,* by the purchase of lands or the refurbishing of a family whose daughter he marries, or of *directly entering the State*

---

[38] Althusser 1972a, p. 99.
[39] Althusser 1972a, p. 103.

apparatus by the gown and offices, or of *sharing in the profits of the State apparatus* via rents. This is what gives this upstart 'bourgeoisie' such a peculiar situation in the feudal State.[40]

Consequently, Althusser opposes the traditional view that the 'confrontation and involuntary equilibrium of two antagonistic classes, each powerless to triumph over the other'.[41] He even criticises Marx for taking a similar position in *The German Ideology*.[42] For Althusser, we have to reject the 'anachronism ... to lend the *bourgeoisie* of absolute monarchy the traits of the later bourgeoisie, *in order to think it even in this epoch as a class radically antagonistic to the feudal class*'.[43] Avoiding this anachronism also implies avoiding the danger of treating the state as an arbiter between classes, a position that would imply in fact a negation of the class character of state power. And even if some members of the feudal class regarded the absolute monarchy as a hostile force, in reality the latter guaranteed the class interests of the feudal class.

> It is hardly surprising that the advent of absolute monarchy, centralization and its epiphenomena (and even that gilded political internment camp, Versailles) had the appearances of a usurpation, an injustice and a violence directed at their class in the eyes of the individual feudal lords, stripped, even by force, of their ancient personal political prerogatives. But it is impossible not to reckon this precisely *a fixed idea of theirs which masked the real from them, and a true historical misunderstanding which made them confuse these ancient personal political prerogatives with the general interests of their class*.[44]

There was also another form of social antagonism. For Althusser, a gap separates the political and ideological conflict between the king, the nobility and the bourgeoisie, and another fundamental class antagonism between the pop-

---

40   Althusser 1972a, p. 100.
41   Althusser 1972a, p. 101.
42   Here is Althusser's footnote: 'See even in Marx [...] a passage on Montesquieu which still (in 1845) inclines towards this interpretation: "For instance in an age and in a country where royal power, aristocracy and bourgeoisie are contending for mastery and where, therefore, mastery is shared, the doctrine of the separation of powers proves to be the dominant idea and is expressed as an 'eternal law'."' (Althusser 1972a, p. 101). Cf. Goshgarian 2006 for bringing attention to the importance of these points and of the book on Montesquieu.
43   Althusser 1972a, p. 102.
44   Althusser 1972, p. 103.

ular masses and the social and political configuration of absolute monarchy, a dynamic that found outlets in various forms of riots but also in the revolutionary dynamic of the French Revolution.

> Between the masses of the exploited, peasants subject to feudal rights, small craftsmen, shopkeepers, minor professions in the towns, on the one hand, and the feudal order and its political power on the other, it was hardly a question of theoretical disputes but rather a matter of silence or violence. It was a struggle between power and poverty, most often settled by submission and for brief periods by riots and arms. Now these starvation rebellions were very frequent in town and country throughout the seventeenth century in France, which had not only the peasants' wars and jacqueries of sixteenth-century Germany, but also urban riots; these risings were ruthlessly suppressed. Now we can see what the king, the absolute *power*, and the *State apparatus* were for, and what side the famous '*puissances*' which occupied the forestage were on; until certain '*journées révolutionnaires*' of the Revolution, the first that achieved a victory – and brought a certain disorder both to theories and powers.[45]

Consequently, for Althusser, there is a certain historical illusion in treating Montesquieu as '*the herald, even the disguised herald, of the cause of the bourgeoisie which was to triumph under the Revolution*'.[46] However, the anachronism of Montesquieu's political project does not imply that in the end his theoretical endeavour was not highly original and did not open up new paths for theoretical inquiry, paths that in fact, in theoretical terms, rendered impossible the return to the past that Montesquieu politically envisaged.

> And if I should close by returning to my first words, let me say of this man who set out alone and truly discovered the new lands of history, that nevertheless his own notion was always to return home. The conquered land he salutes on his last page, as I pretended to forget, was the land of return.[47]

---

45   Althusser 1972a, p. 104.
46   Althusser 1972a, p. 105.
47   Althusser 1972a, p. 107.

3   Montesquieu as Anti-teleology

As G.M. Goshgarian has stressed, in Althusser's book on Montesquieu there is a double attempt at drawing a line of demarcation with teleology and finalism. On the one hand, there is the appreciation of Montesquieu as a thinker who refuses to think in terms of teleology and finalism; on the other, in the end Althusser 'applies Montesquieu's anti-teleological principles to Montesquieu'.[48] Moreover, Goshgarian refers to a 1959 letter in which Althusser referred to a 'singular encounter' in *Politics and History* of 'two ideas about the late feudal French bourgeoisie: that the "primary conflict" of the day pitted it against the nobles; and that in this conflict, the king "sided with" it, or "should have or could have"'.[49] For Goshgarian, Althusser attempts to think not in the classical sense of a teleological evolution between the feudal mode of production and capitalism, according to which the feudal bourgeoisie was the expression of the decay of the feudal mode of production. In contrast, Goshgarian insists that:

> One sees, then, once the mirage of retrospective history is dispelled, why the encounter of the two received ideas about the late feudal period is dangerous. The idea that the conflict at its heart pitted bourgeoisie against nobility, and that, in this conflict, the king 'sided with' the former, breeds the illusion that the king played one off against the other in order 'to raise himself above' these 'two antagonistic classes' – or 'should have or could have'. That is, it encourages a 'notion of [...] the State' according to which 'a political power can be established outside classes and over them'. Marx, too, once entertained this illusion, writing in *The German Ideology* that in eighteenth-century France, where 'aristocracy and bourgeoisie [were] contending for domination', 'domination [was] shared'. But that, in Althusser's view, was the tribute he advanced to the un-Marxist myth of the state. Class domination, he saw soon thereafter, cannot be shared.[50]

Goshgarian also links Althusser's break with any form of teleology in *Montesquieu, Politics and History*, to his insistence in the 1970s, and especially in *Marx in his Limits*, that the 'state results from the transformation of an *excess*

---

48   Goshgarian 2006, p. xxxi.
49   Ibid.
50   Goshgarian 2006, p. xxxiii.

of class force'.⁵¹ In sum, then, for Goshgarian, the importance of the book on Montesquieu is that it offers the first emergence of a profoundly anti-teleological, anti-metaphysical and relational conception of social reality:

> An aleatory-materialist axiom affirms 'the primacy of the structure over its elements' 'once the encounter has been effected'. Montesquieu illustrates it. It asserts, against the teleological Marx or his stand-ins, that the feudal bourgeoisie is thoroughly feudal, not an embryo of bourgeois society gestating in a late feudal womb, because it is a subordinate element of a structure constituted by a feudal class dictatorship.⁵²

Montesquieu also plays an important role in Althusser's 1962–63 seminar on structuralism, and Warren Montag has offered a very interesting reading of this seminar. In it, in order to trace the historical path to structuralism, Althusser sets out from Montesquieu to Dilthey. According to Montag,

> Althusser's identification in 1962 of Montesquieu as the founding moment of structuralism's prehistory makes visible the way in which his analysis of some of Montesquieu's key concepts, notable those of law, spirit, nature, and principle, is simultaneously a meditation on what he will later explicitly identify as the central problems of structuralism.⁵³

Althusser in 1962 attempts to link Montesquieu's conception of law – his application of a Newtonian version of law to human societies – to Lévi-Stauss's conception of 'unconscious laws'.⁵⁴ However, he does not fully consider Montesquieu as a precursor of structuralism; rather 'he draws a line of demarcation through Montesquieu's text, making visible the antagonism proper to the latter's philosophical endeavour'.⁵⁵ Montag suggests that this is exactly an operation performed in Althusser's attempt to defend Montesquieu against the accusation of 'formalism'. At the same time, Althusser, according to Montag, brings forward the ambiguity that traverses Montesquieu's work in relation to the question of the relationship between essence and its expression.

---

51 Goshgarian 2006, p. xxxiv.
52 Goshgarian 2006, p. xxxv.
53 Montag 2013, p. 26.
54 Montag 2013, p. 27.
55 Ibid.

> Thus we arrive at the fatal ambiguity that sets the *Spirit of Law* against itself: either we divorce the principles from their real causes, which are not only plural (customs, religion, climate, population, etc.) but which, to the extent that they are rooted in an infinite nature that exhibits its own history, prove utterly indifferent to that of humankind, and thus arrive at static models whose transformation remains unintelligible, or the historical explanation fades in the face of an infinity of causes.[56]

In Montag's view, Althusser in the seminar on structuralism suggested that it was Hegel who attempted to resolve the contradictions of Montesquieu's endeavour. However, the price was high, since Hegel thought in terms of all the elements reduced to a simple internal principle, the position that was Althusser's main target of criticism in his 1962–63 interventions on the question of the dialectic.

Althusser's confrontation with Montesquieu was not just an aspect of his theoretical preparation before the main thrust of his work. The book on Montesquieu, curiously enough the only monograph that Althusser actually published (all the other books that Althusser chose to publish during his lifetime were collections of texts), is in fact his first attempt to deal with some of the questions that would continue to preoccupy him until the end of his life. Questions such as the possibility of theorising social reality with its multitude of determinations and contingencies, the relation between determining principles and overdetermining factors, the need to break with any teleological conception, the explicit refusal of every philosophy (and theory) of origins, the emphasis on the effectivity of class relations and determinations, delineate the terrain of Althusser's trajectory. The fact that Althusser treats Montesquieu both as a precursor of some aspects of structuralism and as a thinker that cannot be considered 'formalist', reflects the tension that runs through Althusser's own work of that period, that is, the tension about the direction that an anti-metaphysical (anti-teleological and anti-humanist) conception of history should take. It is the tension between an emphasis on 'latent' structures expressed only in their results, and an emphasis on the singularity and the contingency of the conjuncture.

In this sense, treating the book on Montesquieu as just an expression of Althusser before Althusser misses the point, and underestimates the importance of this book. Moreover, reading this book alongside his texts and courses on Rousseau and Machiavelli (and also other political philosophers) one real-

---

56   Montag 2013, p. 28.

ises that even if Althusser never fulfilled the initial project of a *grande thèse* on political philosophy, he nevertheless embarked on a major theoretical confrontation with classical political philosophy of modernity as an attempt towards rethinking a materialist conception of history and politics alongside his confrontation with the work of Marx, a 'theoretical detour' of impressive theoretical and political depth and insight.

CHAPTER 4

Structure Revisited

Although Marxism has been associated with thinking history in the *longue durée*, exemplified in texts such as the third chapter of Engels's *Socialism: Utopian and Scientific*,[1] thinking about the conjuncture has always been a major preoccupation for Marxists. Lenin's reference to the 'concrete analysis of the concrete situation' as the 'living soul of Marxism'[2] and his emphasis on the analysis of specific moments and situations exemplify this preoccupation.[3]

In the traditional Marxist treatment of the conjuncture, more general historical tendencies are considered to be more important than the particular dynamics of the conjuncture. Is it possible to suggest such a hierarchy of historical determination? Is it possible to think social reality in terms of a distinction between 'deeper' or 'structural' tendencies and 'surface' conjunctural dynamics, with the latter treated as mere epiphenomena, or does this lead to some form of historical teleology? If what actually exist are singular conjunctures, can we also think of structural tendencies as having their proper material effectivity or can we only conceive of them as theoretical constructions that generalise singular sequences of events after the fact?

It is obvious that the relation between structure and conjuncture remains a theoretical challenge for Marxism and for social theory in general. Louis Althusser's work can be a starting point in order to rethink these questions. Althusser has offered a novel reading of the notion of structure, the most thorough treatment of the conjuncture as the proper object for political practice and at the same time a most intense and even painful confrontation with all the open questions the relation between structural and conjunctural determinations raises.

1 'Althusser of the Structure' vs. 'Althusser of the Conjuncture'?

In 1991 Étienne Balibar suggested that a tension can be discerned in Althusser's conception of the dialectic. On the one hand, Althusser criticises finalism and

---

1 Engels 2003.
2 Lenin 1920.
3 See for example the recurring theme of the 'current situation' in many texts and speeches by Lenin.

determinism in the name of the 'singularity of the conjunctures, in the name of "the concrete analysis of concrete situations": the Leninist, and even more, the Machiavellian side of Althusser's analysis'.[4] On the other hand, we have the criticism of a simple and expressive totality 'in the name of the complexity of the structure, of its unequal development'.[5] Balibar calls this second conception of the dialectic the 'truly structuralist side to Althusser'. He stresses that each of these conceptions dominates each of Althusser's texts on the dialectic in *For Marx*: 'Contradiction and Overdetermination' and 'On the materialist dialectic'. It is on the basis of this analysis that Balibar suggests that there are 'Althusserians of the Conjuncture' and 'Althusserians of the Structure'.[6]

I think that this distinction can also, if read in a schematic way, lead to a misapprehension of Althusser's attempt to theorise a possible materialist dialectic.[7] Instead, I want to suggest three basic points. The first is that drawing such a sharp opposition between these two essays from *For Marx*[8] misreads the theoretical (and political) modalities of these texts, especially since both texts actually criticise the expressive conception of totality. The second is that Althusser's actual structuralism lies elsewhere, in his temptation to think of 'latent structures' and in his flirting with the idea of production as substance. The third is that instead of remaining within the contours of supposed structure/conjuncture dichotomy, it is better to try to rethink new ways to theorise the differential effectivity of both 'structural' and 'conjunctural' determinations, within a conception of social forms that combines relationality, singularity, and reproduction.

2   High Althusserianism Revisited

'Contradiction and Overdetermination' offers a novel conception of social causality. It is the first and perhaps most exemplary case of Althusser's con-

---

4   Balibar 1994a, p. 166.
5   Ibid.
6   Ibid.
7   To be fair to Balibar, we must note that in his 1996 preface to the French re-edition of *Pour Marx*, he offers a more balanced account of this tension. 'When we read and re-read closely these great essays on "Contradiction and Overdetermination" and "On the Materialist Dialectic", which present themselves as a continuation of one by the other, I think that it might be possible to actually suggest that the first takes overdetermination from the side of a thinking of the event, whereas the second does this from the side of the tendency and periodisation. Surely the solution is not to choose one point of view against the other' (Balibar 1996, p. ix).
8   Althusser 1969.

ception of an immanent social causality and his total rejection of any form of teleology. Although Althusser seems to suggest that an analysis of the conjuncture is the object of political practice, he is offering a more general position concerning the object of historical materialism. Althusser insists that the object of a possible science of history (and also of political practice) concerns concrete historical social formations, their relation of forces and the articulation and condensation of their contradictions into a unique 'historical moment'.

> If it is true, as Leninist practice and reflection prove, that the revolutionary situation on Russia was precisely a result of the *intense overdetermination* of the basic class contradiction, we should perhaps ask what is *exceptional* about this 'exceptional *situation*', and whether, like all exceptions, this one does not clarify its rule – is not, unbeknown to the rule, *the rule itself*. For, after all, *are we not always in exceptional situation*.[9]

As G.M. Goshgarian has suggested,[10] Althusser was, from the beginning, preoccupied with a conception of history where 'general historical' tendencies exist only in concrete historical situations. In his 1959 book on Montesquieu, Althusser produces an image of Montesquieu 'proposing to produce the science not of society in general but of all the concrete societies in history',[11] in sharp contrast to thinking of human societies in terms of philosophical abstractions, an image close to Althusser's own attempt to think in terms of concrete conjunctures. As we already discussed in the previous chapter, this is even more evident in Althusser's discussion of the supposed 'formalism' of Montesquieu.

It is not that Althusser denies the importance of general trends, historical tendencies, regularities, and law-like phenomena. Rather, he insists that they exist only as aspects of concrete conjunctures and relations of forces. In this sense, Althusser from the beginning, despite the terminological affinities to classical Marxism, offers a different and openly political conception of history as a contradictory terrain and of political practice as intervention. As Andrea Cavazzini recently noted:

> In this passage from one Marxism to another, namely from a Marxism as *instrumentum regni* to a Marxism that is a guide for a determinate action,

---

9   Althusser 1969, p. 104.
10 Goshgarian 2006.
11 Althusser 1972a, p. 20.

politics ceases to be able to think of itself as the art of managing [*gestion*] of people founded upon the undifferentiated unity of the march of history and finds itself confronting the finitude of the constraints and the possibilities that determined conditions specify in a conjuncture. The gesture of Althusser thus consists in 'founding' politics on the *actuality* of a historical situation that is always determined, and vis-a-vis which it is no longer possible to find refuge in totality equally undifferentiated as the ideological notion of history as manifestation of praxis: the objective knowledge of the conjuncture is related to the idea of political practice centred on the urgency of a taking of position that we can no longer differ in regards to a situation that calls for an intervention, but which no total knowledge can come and regulate [*regler*].[12]

This is made explicit in the way Althusser treats in 'Contradiction and Overdetermination' any possible 'general' or 'abstract' notion of the contradiction between Capital and Labour: 'The real contradiction was so much one with its "circumstances" that it was only discernible *through them and in them*'.[13] For Althusser the general contradiction 'between the forces and relations of production, essentially embodied in the contradiction between two antagonistic classes [...] cannot of its own simple, direct power induce a "revolutionary situation"'.[14] Different contradictions and relations, operating at different levels, necessarily co-exist *on the same plane* in terms of social ontology.

> [A] vast accumulation of 'contradictions' comes into play *in the same court*, some of which are radically heterogeneous – of different origins, different sense, different *levels* and *points* of application – but which nevertheless 'merge' into a ruptural unity.[15]

This is a rejection of the classical distinction between empirical and/or 'surface' phenomena and 'deeper' social tendencies. What emerges is the uneven contradictory co-existence of different contradictions, structures and practices in a highly original conception which transcends the essence/phenomenon distinction, at the same time acknowledging actual differences in effectivity. 'Structural' contradictions are not 'deep' structures coming to the surface as

---

12   Cavazzini 2011, p. 253.
13   Althusser 1969, p. 98.
14   Althusser 1969, p. 99.
15   Althusser 1969, p. 100.

simple phenomena and conjunctural tendencies are neither simple expressions nor random events; they have their own properly material existence and effectivity.

> But strictly speaking, it cannot be claimed that these contradictions and their fusion are merely the *pure phenomena* of the general contradiction. The 'circumstances' and 'currents' which achieve it are more than its phenomena pure and simple. They derive from the relations of production, which are, of course, one of the *terms* of the contradiction, but at the same time its *conditions of existence*.[16]

Overdetermination does not simply refer to an articulation of structural and conjunctural tendencies nor does it simply imply contingent and historically specific changes in the relative weight of each instance of the social whole. Overdetermination emerges as a more general position on the immanent complexity and unevenness of social reality. 'Simple' contradictions do not exist in isolation from the total structure of the social whole, structure used here in the more general sense of the articulation of different practices, relations and contradictions. Overdetermination is not the simple acceptance of the increased effectivity of ideology or of the political in particular conjunctures but a novel theoretical approach stressing the co-existence and articulation of various relations, contradictions and practices and their varying degrees of effectivity, within social wholes that are necessarily decentred.

> [T]he 'contradiction' is inseparable from the total structure of the social body in which it is found, inseparable from the formal *conditions* of existence, and even from the *instances* it governs; it is radically *affected by them*, determining, but also determined in one and the same movement, and determined by the various *levels* and *instances* of the social formation it animates; it might be called *overdetermined in its principle*.[17]

It is exactly here that Althusser's criticism of the Hegelian conception of totality comes into play. According to Althusser we cannot accept any conception of a deeper social essence that is 'expressed' in concrete social reality and functions as its causal mechanism. The social whole cannot be conceived as having a centre, in contrast to what Althusser defines as the Hegelian totality. On the

---

16 Ibid.
17 Althusser 1969, p. 101.

contrary, it is inherently decentred, uneven and complex. Instead of a possible 'centre' Althusser suggests the notion of *structure in dominance* that guarantees the unity of the social whole, but makes clear that this does not mean that 'secondary' contradictions or 'structures' are simple phenomena. This is one of the main points of 'On the Materialist Dialectic': 'secondary contradictions are essential even to the existence of the principal contradiction, that they really constitute its condition of existence, just as the principal contradiction constitutes their condition of existence'.[18]

Contradictions cannot be considered in the sense of the self-movement (self-alienation and consequent sublation) of the essence. Contradictions refer to the inherently antagonistic character of social reality and the ways in which class struggle always creates a decisive tension within processes of social reproduction. This is the main point of 'On the Materialist Dialectic', leaving aside its more theoreticist aspects that deal with the 'Theory of theoretical practice', particularly its tendency towards a philosophy guaranteeing of the scientificity of sciences. I do not think that there is a gap dividing the problematic of both Althusser's articles. They both target the expressive totality and any conception of a possible deeper essence expressed in surface forms.

What emerges in 'On the Materialist Dialectic' is less a definite theorisation of 'social structures' as opposed to conjunctures, and more an attempt to combine the emphasis on the concrete and conjunctural character of social reality (in the strict sense, only conjunctures exist and, as Saül Karsz has noted, Althusser's structures are 'structures *of* events'[19]) with more 'structural' determinations. 'On the Materialist Dialectic' poses the question of how to theorise the specific contradictory unity of any particular conjuncture and consequently both its intelligibility and its ability to be the object of political practice and intervention:

> Lenin knew perfectly well that he was acting on a social present which was the product of the development of imperialism [...] but in 1917 he was not acting on Imperialism in general; he was acting on the concrete of the Russian situation, of the Russian conjuncture, on what he gave the remarkable name, 'the current situation', the situation whose currency defined his political practice as such. [...] Lenin analyzed what constituted the characteristics of its structure: the essential articulations, the interconnections, the strategic nodes on which the possibility and the fate

---

18 Althusser 1969, p. 205.
19 Karsz 1974, p. 171.

of any revolutionary practice depended [...] This is what is irreplaceable in Lenin's texts: the analysis of the structure of a *conjuncture*, the displacements and condensations of its contradictions and their paradoxical unity, all of which are the very existence of that 'current situation' which political action was to transform.[20]

The introduction of the notion of *structure in dominance* is presented as a way to better theorise the complexity of conjunctures, without falling into some kind of randomised conception of social reality. That is why it is coupled with the emphasis on the determination 'in the last instance' by the economic. This should not be read as a residual economism – it is Althusser who insisted that 'the lonely hour of the "last instance" never comes'[21] – nor as some form of ontological grounding, but as an attempt to grasp the conjunctural unity of a social formation. The following passage from *Reading Capital* encapsulates this point:

[T]his dominance of a structure [...] cannot be reduced to the primacy of a *centre*, any more than the relation between the elements and the structure can be reduced to the expressive unity of the essence within its phenomena. This hierarchy only represents the hierarchy of effectivity that exists between the different 'levels' or instances of the social whole. [...] [I]n order to conceive this 'dominance' of a structure over the other structures in the unity of a conjuncture it is necessary to refer to the principle of the determination 'in the last instance' of the non-economic structures by the economic structure [...] only this 'determination in the last instance' makes it possible to escape the arbitrary relativism of observable displacements by giving these displacements the necessity of a function.[22]

---

20   Althusser 1969, pp. 178–9. Bruno Bosteels has stressed the importance of Althusser's conception of overdetermination: 'Methodologically speaking, the whole point of Althusser's reading is not simply to reiterate Lenin's well-known analysis but rather to ask how a structure actually seizes upon and becomes history or, to put it the other way around, how history eventalizes and periodizes the structure of a given situation at the site of a subjective intervention. Technically foreign to Lenin no less than to Marx yet supposedly already at work and implied in their analyses, Freud's concept of overdetermination is thus imported into Marxism by Althusser in order to articulate history and structure without separating them, for example, in terms of concrete empirical fact and abstract transcendental or ontological principle' (Bosteels 2011, p. 58).
21   Althusser 1999, p. 113.
22   Althusser et al. 2016, p. 246.

3   Structures without Structuralism?

Does all of this suggest that Althusser's relation to 'structuralism' was unproblematic? The very fact that he self-critically referred to 'flirting' with structuralism[23] suggests that we are indeed facing a theoretical contradiction running through his work. This requires coming to terms with the ambiguity of the notion of 'structuralism'. Warren Montag has recently shown how difficult it is to adapt the dominant narrative about 'structuralism' that goes from Saussure to Althusser to the actual theoretical modalities of the writers and thinkers involved in this narrative.[24]

If we consider structuralism to be a more general trend in social theory that stresses theoretical anti-humanism, the priority of relations over the agents that occupy the places in the social structure that these relations determine and the decentring or destitution of the subject in the sense of presenting it as the result of processes of subjectification, then obviously Althusser can be considered a 'structuralist' in most of his theoretical trajectory. Étienne Balibar has stressed the ambiguity of the distinction between terms such as 'structuralism' and 'post-structuralism':

> [M]y hypothesis is precisely that there is, in fact, no such thing as post-structuralism, or rather that poststructuralism [...] is always still structuralism, and structuralism in its strongest sense is already post-structuralism. [...] *I am calling 'structure,' in the sense of structuralism, a mechanism of reversal of the constituting subject into constituted subjectivity*, based on a deconstruction of the 'humanist' equation of the subject. And I am calling 'post-structuralism,' or *structuralism beyond its own explanatory constitution, a moment of reinscription of the limit on the basis of its own unpresentability*.[25]

Gilles Deleuze's well-known text 'How Do We Recognize Structuralism' exemplifies the ambivalence and the difficulty of trying to present a unifying image of 'structuralism'. Deleuze's list of criteria for structuralism includes the centrality of the symbolic – the trace *par excellence* of 'structuralism' – the topological, multi-serial and relational conception of structures, metonymic causality, differential relations, displacement and practice,[26] thus bringing for-

---

23   Althusser 1976a, p. 126.
24   Montag 2013.
25   Balibar 2003, p. 11.
26   'For structuralism is not only inseparable from the works that it creates, but also from

ward the conflicting theoretical dynamics associated with what we tend to define as structuralism.

Ted Stolze has offered a very illuminating reading of Deleuze's text that also highlights the possible influence of Althusser's comments on Deleuze's first draft of the text, comments that coincide with Althusser's own self-criticism regarding his 'structuralist deviation'.[27] More recently Warren Montag has also stressed the importance of this exchange between Althusser and Deleuze as evidence of Althusser's critical position towards 'structuralism'.[28]

However, I think that we can still discern in this broad and contradictory theoretical movement the crucial points that tendentially deviate from a materialist conception: the conception of the structure as a symbolic order presenting the deeper meaning of social reality, the treatment of the structure as a latent causal mechanism and the image of the structure as a combinatory of elements. As Montag has shown in his detailed exposition of Althusser's relation to 'structuralism', Althusser's interest in structuralism was part of an attempt to theorise social reality in a relational but non-reductionist manner as knowledge of concrete historical conjunctures in opposition to formalism, hermeneutics and historicism.[29] Therefore, it was an interest or a 'flirting' that already contained elements of a critique of the theoretical basis of structuralism.

Coming back to Althusser's texts from 1960–65, I think that the crucial question is how to treat Althusser's insistence on the '*existence of a structure in its effects*'.[30] In my opinion there are two possible readings. On the one hand, we can read it as a highly original conception of structural determinations and/or law-like tendencies that do not have any existence of their own other than that in concrete social formations. In this sense, structure is not ontologically prioritised, nor is it considered to be beneath the surface. Moreover, structural causality should not be opposed to dynamics of transformation and the possibility of historical change.[31] Therefore the structured whole is proposed by Althusser as a radically novel way to think historical existence, causality and transformation.

---

a practice in relation to the products that it interprets. Whether this practice is therapeutic or political, it designates a point of permanent revolution, or of permanent transfer' (Deleuze 2004b, p. 192).

27 Stolze 1998.
28 Montag 2013, pp. 97–100.
29 Montag 2013, especially part 1.
30 Althusser et al. 2016, p. 344.
31 Bruno Bosteels stresses this point in his reading of Badiou's relation to Althusser: 'The theory of structural causality, in this sense, is already an attempt to think through the problem of how the structure of a given situation, in the effective process of becoming historical, will have been transformed as the result of an unforeseeable event' (Bosteels 2011, p. 60).

> If the whole is posed as *structured*, i.e., as possessing a type of unity quite different from the type of unity of the spiritual whole, this is no longer the case: not only does it become impossible to think the determination of the elements by the structure in the categories of analytical and transitive causality, *it also becomes impossible to think it in the category of the global expressive causality of a universal inner essence immanent in its phenomenon*. The proposal to think the determination of the elements of a whole by the structure of the whole posed an absolutely new problem in the most theoretically embarrassing circumstances, for there were no philosophical concepts available for its resolution.[32]

The structure exists at the same ontic level with concrete historical events, providing the mechanism of their necessarily contradictory unity and articulations, in a line similar to Deleuze's concept of the plane of immanence.[33] In this sense the absence of a visible mechanical cause is exactly the manifestation of its structural effectivity.

> The structure is not an essence *outside* the economic phenomena which comes and alters their aspect, forms and relations and which is effective on them as an absent cause, *absent because it is outside them. The absence of the cause in the structure's 'metonymic causality' on its effects is not the fault of the exteriority of the structure with respect to the economic phenomena; on the contrary, it is the very form of the interiority of the structure, as a structure, in its effects*. This implies therefore that the effects are not outside the structure, are not a pre-existing object, element or space in which the structure arrives to *imprint its mark*: on the contrary, it implies that the structure is immanent in its effects, a cause immanent in its effects in the Spinozist sense of the term, that *the whole existence of the structure consists of its effects*, in short that the structure, which is merely a specific combination of its peculiar elements, is nothing outside its effects.[34]

---

32 Althusser et al. 2016, pp. 342–3.
33 'Everyone knows the first principle of Spinoza: one substance for all the attributes. But we also know the third, fourth, or fifth principle: one Nature for all bodies, one Nature for all individuals, a Nature that is itself an individual varying in an infinite number of ways. What is involved is no longer the affirmation of a single substance, but rather the laying out of a common plane of immanence on which all bodies, all minds, and all individuals are situated. This plane of immanence or consistency is a plan, but not in the sense of a mental design, a project, a program; it is a plan in the geometric sense: a section, an intersection, a diagram' (Deleuze 1988, p. 122).
34 Althusser et al. 2016, p. 344.

In passages such as this one, Althusser attempts to distance his conception of structural causality from any dualism, insisting on immanence and a conception of the structure as a combination of elements that does not exist outside its effects, hence the insistence that 'metonymic causality' does not refer to any kind of externality. However, the very reference to 'metonymic causality', a concept originally proposed by Jacques-Alain Miller, makes manifest the theoretical tension at the very centre of structural causality. Miller originally used the term to describe the particular effectivity of the unconscious as a structure upon the subject's discourse and the particular miscognition effect induced by this structure.

> The discourse that the subject emits, he also receives, and the determination inverts itself through being made in the first person [*la determination s'inverse de se faire en première personne*]. We will thus explore the space of the determination's displacement. At once univocal, repressed and interior, withdrawn and declared, only *metonymic* causality might qualify it. The cause is metaphorized in a discourse, and in general in any structure – for the necessary condition of the functioning of structural causality is that the subject takes the effect *for the cause*. Fundamental law of the action of the structure.[35]

Miller's conception, in its particular psychoanalytical context, can indeed be read as pointing to a conception of structure that exists beneath the surface, that only finds its way in a reverted and metaphorised way in appearances as an expression of a deeper reality whose effectivity is beyond the immediate understanding of social actors.

Therefore, the notion of the existence of a structure in its effects can indeed lead back to a rewriting of the essence/phenomena distinction, especially if *existence* is treated as *expression*. And indeed Althusser seems to suggest in some places that the break between science and ideology means bringing forward what exists beneath the veil of ideological mystification, a deeper or latent social reality. It is here that the actual danger of 'structuralism' lies, in the treatment of structure not as a relational conception of social reality, but as the hidden secret, the inner grammar of social reality. Indeed, Althusser's own references to a *latent* structure can point in such direction. We begin with the references that can be found in Althusser's text 'The "Piccolo Teatro": Bertolazzi and Brecht' which was included in *For Marx*. This 1962 text, one of the

---

35 Miller 2012 [1964], p. 79.

few Althusser wrote on questions of art, is an important intervention. Written as a response to the negative stance of Parisian critics to the Piccolo Teatro's presentation of Bertolazzi's *El Nost Milan*, it is not simply a text on theatre or aesthetics.[36] Althusser refers to different times and temporalities co-existing within the play. On the one hand, there is the time of the 'chronicle', the time of people presented in their ordinary lives. On the other hand, the time of *tragedy*, a dramatic time, a time of dialectical conflict. However, Althusser notes that this dialectic 'is acted marginally, so to speak, in the wings',[37] and is a dialectic of consciousness and therefore characterised by 'non dialecticity'.[38] To this non-dialectic of consciousness Althusser opposes the other world, the real experience of social reality. For Althusser, Bertolazzi's play under Giorgio Strehler's direction becomes a manifestation of the limits of the dialectic of consciousness as opposed to the real dialectic of social antagonism. The text, as Sibertin-Blanc notes, offers 'a *double critique*: a critique of the dialectic of conscience and a critique of the dramatic form as it was fixed by Hegel in his *Aesthetic*'.[39] This can also be seen as a broader philosophical statement about the complexity and unevenness of any potential Marxist knowledge, 'a knowledge that is not the place of a truth finally reflected, finally seen "in the face", but on the contrary has no other consistency than that of an act of scission that is always reactivated, always put in question, by class antagonisms and the ideological effects of cohesion and belonging they determine'.[40] Until now we can say that the text is an attempt by Althusser to put in practice his new conception of the dialectic based upon coexisting temporalities, the absence of a centre, the effectivity of relations, and the importance of ideological misrecognition. It is here that the notion of a 'latent structure' enters the theoretical stage: 'at issue here is the play's latent structure [...] what counts, beyond the words, the characters and the actions of the play, is the internal relation of the basic elements of its structure'.[41] But what is this latency of the relations? Is it some form of 'deeper' social causation or meaning? Here is Althusser's attempt to answer this:

> It should now be clear why we have to speak of the dynamic of the play's latent structure. It is the structure that we must discuss in so far as the play cannot be reduced to its actors, nor to their explicit relations – only

---

36 On the importance of this text see Montag 2005 and Sibertin-Blanc 2011.
37 Althusser 1969, p. 138.
38 Althusser 1969, p. 140.
39 Sibertin-Blanc 2011, p. 261.
40 Sibertin Blanc 2011, p. 271.
41 Althusser 1969, p. 141.

> to the dynamic relation existing between consciousnesses of self alienated in spontaneous ideology [...] This relation, abstract in itself [...] can only be acted and represented as characters, their gestures and their acts, and their 'history' only as a relation which goes beyond them while implying them; that is, as a relation setting to work abstract structural elements [...] their imbalance and hence their dynamic. This relation is necessarily latent in so far as it cannot be exhaustively thematized by any 'character' without ruining the whole critical project: that is why, even if it is implied by the action as a whole, by the existence and movements of all the characters, it is their deep meaning, beyond their consciousness – and thus hidden from them; visible to the spectator in so far as it is invisible to the actors – and therefore visible to the spectator in the mode of a perception which is not given, but has to be discerned, conquered and drawn from the shadow which initially envelops it, and yet produced it.[42]

This text is really revealing of the questions facing Althusser. On the one hand, it seems like a presentation of the concept of a structure existing in its effects and of the inability of social actors to have an immediate understanding of social reality and how it is determined by social relations. The reference to a meaning that is at the same time visible and hidden, exemplifies the fact that actual social determination is never given, despite the fact that all the elements and the relations exist on the same ontological level. On the other hand, these references to latency and depth can also be read as implying some sort of dualism between surface phenomena and deeper causal mechanisms. It is Althusser himself who signalled in that direction in the second edition of *Reading Capital* by choosing to omit certain passages and by replacing the passage on metonymic causality discussed above.[43] The following omitted fragment exemplifies this tension:

> That is why, *according to the level on which we place ourselves*, we can say that the *'Darstellung'* is the concept *of a presence of the structure in its effects*, of the modification of the effects by the efficacy of the structure that is present in its effects. – or in contrast that the *'Darstellung'* is the concept of *the efficacy of an absence*. It is in this second sense that Rancière has used the decisive concept of *'metonymic causality'*, which was profoundly elaborated by Miller last year at our seminar on Lacan. I

---

42   Althusser 1969, pp. 142–3.
43   Warren Montag has offered a close and careful reading of these omissions and their significance. See Montag 2013, pp. 82–91.

believe that understood as the concept of the *efficacy of an absent cause*, this concept is admirably convenient to designate the absence in person of the structure in its effects considered in the mundane perspective of their existence. But it is necessary to insist on the other aspect of this phenomenon, which is that of the *presence*, of the immanence of the cause in its effects in other words, *the existence of the structure* in its effects.[44]

As Montag has stressed,[45] the tension lies exactly in the different notions of a presence and an existence of structure in its effects, with the second definition pointing to the direction of an immanent conception of causality whereas presence can lead to a form of ontological dualism between underlying causes and surface expressions. As part of his self-criticism Althusser decided to omit these references to a latent structure. That is why he also omitted from the second edition of *Reading Capital* an explicit reference to the 1962 text on Bertolazzi and Brecht.[46] These omissions make manifest Althusser's decision to go beyond any references to latent structures as forms of a potential 'deeper' social grammar generating surface phenomena. It is not that Althusser had actually moved in that direction – the omitted passages offer evidence to the contrary – but that he sensed that this was a tension or a theoretical danger that needed to be corrected in order to avoid any form of essence/phenomena dualism. And this can account for why in the second edition the emphasis is on the *existence* of the structure in its effects, therefore a more immanentist conception of causality.

Following G.M. Goshgarian, we can say that the same deviation (to borrow Althusser's own terms) is evident in Althusser's treatment of production (especially in the sense of a general theory of production) as a substance. According to Goshgarian, this was the price paid for Althusser's insistence on the materiality of both ideological and theoretical practice.

> Against the conception of knowledge as a shadowy reflection of a real living outside it, *For Marx* and *Reading Capital* silently invoke the Spinozist principle that 'substance thinking and substance extended are one and the same substance', insisting that ideas, no less than their real objects,

---

44 Althusser et al. 1996, p. 646.
45 Montag 2013, p. 90.
46 Here is the omitted passage: 'In an article on Bertolazzi, Brecht, in relation exactly to the theatre, I believed that I could advance the expression "a dialectic *in the wings*" in order to take account of the *effects* of a "latent structure" that acted in its presence as an "absence"' (Althusser et al. 1996, p. 647).

are also the *real*, albeit in the form of thought. But this materialist defence of the materiality of both ideological and theoretical practice came at a price, set by the equivalent of substance that runs through Althusser's work of the 1960s.[47]

Althusser also used this reference to the Spinozist conception of substance in a 1966 text, the 'Three notes on the theory of discourse'.[48] In that text, which marks Althusser's gradual distancing from the schema of the 'Theory of theoretical practice', Althusser referred to the possibility of thinking of the combination of general theories (such as historical materialism or the general theory of the signifier) and regional theories such as the theory of the unconscious, and used Spinoza's conception of the parallelism of different attributes of one and the same substance as a way to think the relation between general and regional theories and particularly the articulation of more than one general theory in the determination of a regional theory.[49]

Although the 'flirting' with a theory or notion of production in general is indeed a 'structuralist' aspect of the original Althusserian project, this does not mean that it was the dominant aspect. Althusser himself at many points distances himself from such a conception, something made evident by the following passage from *Reading Capital*: 'It needs to be said that, just as there is no production in general, there is no history in general, but only specific structures of historicity'.[50]

---

47 Goshgarian 2003, p. xv.
48 In Althusser 2003.
49 Althusser's provisional suggestion is that the regional theory of psychoanalysis is determined by the articulation of the general theory of historical materialism and the general theory of the signifier. 'In other words, if we do not think the possibility of an articulation between GTs, we will remain at the level of the *parallelism of tile attributes* and of the temptation that constantly accompanies it, the *conflation* of the attributes. The parallelism of the attributes is tempered and corrected in Spinoza by the concept of substance: the different attributes are attributes *of one and the same substance*. It is the concept of *substance* which plays the role of the concept of the articulation of the attributes (it plays other roles, too, but that is one of them). The *distinction* between attributes is possible only on condition that they are articulated. Let us revert to our own terminology: the distinction between the GTs (which are our attributes) is possible only on condition that they are *differentially* articulated. We observe one instance of the existence of this differential articulation between the signifier-attribute and the history-attribute (that is, between the GT of the signifier and the GT of historical materialism) in the fact that the RT of the psychoanalytic object has as its GT a specified articulation of the GT of historical materialism with the GT of the Signifier' (Althusser 2003, p. 65).
50 Althusser et al. 2016, p. 257.

It was mainly Balibar, in his contribution to *Reading Capital*, who insisted that a possible periodisation of modes of production requires a notion of production in general, suggesting that this was also Marx's own position, and proposing a conception of the modes of production as a combinatory of basic historical elements.

> Periodization, thought of as the periodization of the modes of production themselves, in their purity, first gives form to the theory of history. Thus the majority of the indications in which Marx assembles the elements of his definition are comparative indications. But behind this descriptive terminology (men do not produce in the same way in the different historical modes of production, capitalism does not contain the universal nature of economic relations), there is the indication of what makes the comparisons possible at the level of the structures, the search for the invariant determinations (for the 'common features') of 'production in general', which does not exist historically, but whose variants are represented by all the historical modes of production.[51]

According to Balibar, the same elements or forms (labourer, means of production, object of labour, etc.) in different combinations form different modes of production. As a result 'we can draw up a table of the elements of any mode of production, a table of the invariants in the analysis of forms'.[52] What is particularly 'structuralist' about this conception is its abstract character, since it does not account for the priority of the relation over the elements of the relation and how they are actually conditioned by the relation itself. Moreover, it can suggest some form of transhistorical essences that are combined in different ways in different historical modes of production. Balibar himself admitted this danger associated with any general theory of production in his 1973 self-criticism regarding *Reading Capital*, where he insisted that there can be no 'general theory' of historical transition, insisting instead 'that *every historical "transition" is different*, materially and consequently conceptually'[53] and that

---

51 Althusser et al. 2016, p. 369.
52 Althusser et al. 2016, p. 376.
53 Balibar 1973, p. 45. It is interesting to note how Althusser refers to this point in his *Essays in Self-Criticism*: 'Now no-one can claim that we ever gave way to the crazy formalist idealism of the idea of producing the real by a combinatory of elements. Marx does speak of the "combination" of elements in the structure of a mode of production. But this combination (*Verbindung*) is not a formal "combinatory": we expressly pointed that out. Purposely. In fact this is where the most important demarcation line is drawn' (Althusser 1976a, p. 129).

special attention must be paid to the specific histories of modes of productions and social formations.[54]

Regarding Althusser's conception of structural causality, another important question arises. The Marxist tradition – and Althusser has insisted upon this – is one of anti-empiricism and this implies that we should oppose the 'givenness' of social phenomena to the underlying causal mechanisms that condition them, at the same time insisting that this 'givenness' is in reality a misrecognition of reality as the result of the effectiveness of ideological practices. At the same time Althusser, again in sharp contrast to any empiricism, has insisted that knowledge does not consist of registering singular facts; rather, knowledge of the concrete is the *result* of a process, based upon the transformative intervention of concepts and theoretical abstractions, that attempt to theorise the very complexity of the relations and contradictions that define a social reality, including ideological relations of misrecognition. Therefore Althusser's actual distancing from 'structuralism', before and after 1965, should not be read as a rejection of all forms of abstraction and as a relapse into some form of empiricism.[55] However, such an anti-empiricist position implies that knowledge begins with a distinction between what is directly perceived and what is not, between what is visible and what is not visible, that runs the risk of being translated into a difference between visible phenomena and invisible essences that can bring us back to traditional metaphysics. The importance of the inter-

---

54   It is worth noting here Poulantzas's criticism of any abstract conception of production: 'It follows that neither the concept of the economy nor that of the State can have the same extension, field or meaning in the various modes of production. Even at an abstract level, these modes cannot be grasped as purely economic forms deriving from an ever-changing combination of inherently constant economic elements that moves in a closed and self-limited space. But nor do they constitute combinations of these elements with unchanging elements of other instances (the State) conceived as immutable substances. In short a mode of production does not arise out of the combination of various instances, all of which posses an inalterable structure before they come in relation to each other' (Poulantzas 2000, p. 17).

55   This is how Althusser referred to this question in his period of self-criticism: 'We should note that at no time does this detour *via* relations estrange Marx from living men, because at each moment of the process of knowledge, that is, at each moment in his analysis, Marx shows how each relation – from the capitalist production relation, determinant in the last instance, to the legal-political and ideological relations – brands men in their concrete life, which is governed by the forms and effects of the class struggle. Each of Marx's abstractions corresponds to the "abstraction" imposed on men by these relations, and this terribly concrete "abstraction" is what makes men into exploited workers or exploiting capitalists. We should also note that the final term of this process of thought, the "thought-concrete", to which it leads, is that synthesis of many determinations which defines concrete reality' (Althusser 1976a, p. 206).

vention by Althusser is that it is based on the assumption that the difference or the gap between 'essence' and 'phenomena' is not some form of ontological dualism; on the contrary, it is a dichotomy at the same level of social ontology, mainly as the result of processes of ideological mystification and misrecognition. What makes something visible or invisible is not its position in a layered reality; it is determined by whether we remain within an ideological conception or not. It is not a question of seeing the invisible beneath the visible, but of realising how the structure of the visible creates the conditions of its invisibility, what Althusser describes as the 'necessity of the obscure field of the invisible, as a necessary effect of the structure of the visible field'.[56]

4 Althusser's Self-Criticism: From Structures to Enduring Relations

Althusser's own effort to distance his position from structuralism took many forms, especially in the long process of theoretical self-criticism. We begin with his 1966 criticism of Lévi-Strauss, which shows Althusser distancing himself from a conception of the structure as some kind of formal and deeper essence that conditions social reality. This is evident in Althusser's criticism of Lévi-Strauss's functionalist and reductionist conception of kinship structures that cannot actually think the complexity of social reality:

> In short, because Lévi-Strauss does not know that kinship structures *play the role of relations of production* in primitive social formations (for he does not know what a social formation or a mode of production is, and so on) he is compelled to think them either in relation to the 'human spirit' or the 'brain' and their common (binary) formal principle, or else in relation to a social unconscious that accomplished the *functions* necessary to the survival of a society.[57]

Lévi-Strauss opts for a conception of social reality as a combinatory matrix. But for Althusser this formalisation of possibilities cannot help the theorisation of social formations.[58] For Althusser, '[t]o understand a real phenomenon is not

---

56 Althusser et al. 2016, p. 18.
57 Althusser 2003, p. 26.
58 This is how Althusser repeated this line of criticism in his *Essays in Self-Criticism*: 'Ultimately (and this can be seen in certain of the texts of Lévi-Strauss, and among linguists or other philosophizing logicians) structuralism (or rather: certain structuralists) tends towards the ideal of *the production of the real as an effect of a combinatory of elements*.

[...] a matter for producing the *concept of its possibility* [...] it is, rather, a matter of producing the concept of its *necessity*.[59] The cost paid for Lévi-Strauss's formalism, according to Althusser, is an emphasis on *isomorphism*, as if the same 'human spirit' is in action everywhere. And it is here that a discussion on *singularity emerges*. Lévi-Strauss's assertion that both the 'savage mind' and modern science stress the singular and the concrete, for Althusser says very little because the crucial question is what kind of theoretical concepts can help us think the singular.

> [M]odern scientific thought sets out to think *singularity* ... [I]t is possible to think the singular and concrete only in concepts which are, consequently, abstract and 'general'. Philosophers such as Spinoza (the 'singular essences') and Leibniz did not wait until our day to assign the non-savage mind the task of thinking singularity.[60]

We have here Althusser's insistence that what marks non-ideological thinking is exactly the emphasis on *singularity*, the attempt to theorise, through theoretical concepts, the singular. This emphasis on *singular essences* can be seen as a move away from his former tendency to think production as substance. It is here, in the conditions that enable '*thinking* the singular',[61] that Althusser finds the 'precise point that distinguishes us from Lévi-Strauss himself and, *a fortiori*, from all the "structuralists"'.[62]

It is also here that we find the importance and the originality of Macherey's criticism of the structuralist effort to bring forward the inner meaning of literary texts. Warren Montag has been more than right to emphasise the importance of Macherey's writings and the extent of his influence on Althusser's distancing from structuralism.[63] Montag's research has shown how Macherey was

---

But of course since "it" uses a whole lot of concepts drawn from existing disciplines, we could not honestly accuse structuralism of being the first to use the concept of structure!' (Althusser 1976a, p. 129).

59   Althusser 2003, p. 27.
60   Althusser 2003, p. 32.
61   Althusser 2003, p. 30.
62   Althusser 2003, p. 31. The same reference to the importance of thinking in terms of Spinoza's singular essences can be seen in a 1966 letter to Franca Madonia: 'What exist, in the strong sense of existing, are real objects (that I now call, retaking this concept from Spinoza, "singular essences"), knowledge of this real objects presupposes the intervention of the concepts of the general theory and the concepts of the related regional theories, plus the knowledge (empirical) of the determinate forms of existence that make the singularity of these essences' (Althusser 1997b, p. 712).
63   Montag 1998; Montag 1998a; Montag 2003; Montag 2013.

from the beginning critical towards a conception of the 'structured whole', proposing instead a more Spinozist conception of the infinity of attributes,[64] and how Althusser formed part of his self-criticism regarding the notion of 'latent structure' on the basis of Macherey's criticism.[65]

Macherey's published texts from that period offer at the same time a proof of the gap separating 'High Althusserianism' and structuralism and of the actual structuralist tension running through some of Althusser's original formulations. Macherey criticises the use of the concept of structure in literary studies and its quest for an intrinsic meaning or a hidden structure beneath the surface of the text, thus bringing forward the affinities between a certain version of structuralism (Macherey's main target is Roland Barthes) and an idealist or even hermeneutic reading.

> The idea of structure [...] goes back to the entirely unscientific hypothesis that the work has an intrinsic meaning [...] [T]o extricate a structure is to decipher an enigma, to dig up a buried meaning: the critical reading performs the same operation on the work that the writing had to perform on the signs (or on the themes) that it combined. Criticism produces merely a pre-established truth; but that might be called an innovation because ideally it precedes the work.[66]

In *A Theory of Literary Production* Macherey offers a devastating criticism of structuralism. This criticism helps Macherey redefine the very goal of knowledge. Knowledge is no more the search for some underlying reason or deeper meaning, but that otherness that conditions the production of an object. It has nothing to do with either a presence or an interiority of meaning or reason but with a constitutive absence, that determines the production of reality, the absence of an underlying grammar or rationality:

---

64   According to Montag, Macherey counterposed Spinoza's reference to the infinity of attributes to Althusser's notion of the structured whole (Montag 1998a, p. 7). Macherey referred explicitly to Spinoza's November 1665 letter to Oldenburg: 'Hence it follows that every body, insofar as it exists as modified in a definite way, must be considered as a part of the whole universe, and as agreeing with the whole and cohering with the other parts. Now since the nature of the universe, unlike the nature of the blood, is not limited, but is absolutely infinite, its parts are controlled by the nature of this infinite potency in infinite ways, and are compelled to undergo infinite variations' (Spinoza 2002, p. 849).
65   Montag 2013, pp. 73–6.
66   Macherey 2006, p. 158.

> The goal of knowledge is not the discovery of a reason or a secret: through an indispensable sequence knowledge alludes to that radical otherness from which the object acquires an identity, that initial difference which limits and produces all reality, that constitutive absence which is behind the work. If the notion of structure has any meaning it is in so far as it designates this absence, this difference, this determinate otherness.[67]

Consequently, Macherey rejects any notion of 'organic' totality. In a move reminiscent of later aspects of 'deconstructionist' readings, he insists that 'the work exists above all by its determinate absences, by what it does not say, in its relation to what it is not. [...] [Meaning] is not buried in its depths [...] It is not in the work, but by its side'.[68] Similar positions are also evident in Macherey's contribution to *Lire le Capital* where he rejects any notion of ordered totality in favour of a conception of knowledge that struggles not to order reality but to link a possible disorder of thought to the actual disorder in social reality. For Macherey whatever order is expressed in science is the result of the production of knowledge and does not suggest an initial order: 'Knowledge does not consist in substituting order for disorder, in the arrangement an initial disorder [...] it is knowledge [of an immediate object] that constructs its content, i.e. its order'.[69] That is why he insists on this logic of diversity and unevenness. It is obvious that with this position we are as far as possible from both high structuralism and functionalism. 'Structures' are the sites of absences, conflicts and radical differences.

> True rationality and true logic are those of diversity and inequality. Producing scientific knowledge means acting with disorder as if it were an order, using it as an order: this is why the structure of science is never transparent but opaque, divided, incomplete, material.[70]

The dialogue between Althusser and Macherey can help us locate the theoretical tension inherent in the Althusserian endeavour. We can say that structuralism emerged in Althusser's work not wherever he refers to structures but to all these points where the dialectic of visible and invisible as an aspect of social reality in its immanence is treated as the dialectic between the obvious and the hidden, between the ephemeron and the eternal and between the random and

---

67 Macherey 2006, p. 168.
68 Macherey 2006, p. 172.
69 Athusser et al. 2016, p. 213.
70 Ibid.

the law-like. On the contrary, the emphasis on the singularity of modes of production and social formations, on the immanent character of social causality, on the conception of knowledge as production (and not 'extraction' of a hidden kernel of truth), on conflict, unevenness and radical difference mark the distance between 'Althusserianism' and structuralism.

Consequently, we can see Althusser's increasing emphasis on the primacy of the class struggle upon the existence of classes[71] as part of this broader process of self-criticism, as a renewed emphasis on the singularity of conjunctures and their determination by the balance of forces in class struggle. This is not to be taken simply as an example of Althusser's leftist turn[72] towards a militant 'movementism'. It is mainly a position upon social ontology and a clear break from 'structuralism'. Instead of pre-existing elements that are recombined into different forms, here it is exactly the relation itself (the antagonistic class relation) that conditions the very elements that enter into the relation. It is obvious that in light of this the very notion of structure changes since conflict, rupture and antagonism are inscribed at the centre of it. A much more *relational* conception of social reality emerges: a relation takes precedence over the elements of it.

However welcome this turn towards the class struggle as the 'motor force of history' might have been, there was still the danger of treating social reality as simply a multitude of struggles. How are we to theorise the relative stability of social forms and structures? One of the major ways Althusser tried to come to terms with these problems was his increasing emphasis on *reproduction* in his late 1960s texts, exemplified in the 1969 manuscript on Reproduction (*Sur la reproduction*).[73] The question of reproduction is essential in order to tackle the problem of how social relations and forms tend to be stable without resorting to latent structures as unconscious constraints or historical invariants. Althusser's extended writings on ideology and ideological apparatuses, whose materiality guarantees the reproduction of not only ideological (mis)recognitions but also relations of production, are an effort to think the reproduction of 'structural' forms in a non-teleological way. It is here that the existence of a mode of production is linked to its *duration* (durée) or durability and its *reproduction*. Instead of the synchronic eternity of a mode of production as latent struc-

---

71 'Revolutionaries, on the other hand, consider that it is impossible to separate the classes from class struggle. The class struggle and the existence of classes are one and the same thing' (Althusser 1976a, p. 50).
72 For criticisms of Althusser's supposed *gauchisme* see Elliott 2006.
73 Althusser 1995b; Althusser 2014b.

ture or social grammar, we have the durability of social relations as reproduced social practices, always open to transformation.[74] Social forms can last and we can have lasting forms and relations because social practices can be reproduced through apparatuses that guarantee their reproduction, mainly through the reproduction of ideological interpellations that make human subjects accept certain practices as being in the 'nature of things', these interpellations themselves being the result of practices. Instead of a previous emphasis on structural determination, here the emphasis is on reproduction and repetition through practices. This is evident in the definition of State Apparatus as a 'system of institutions, organizations and the corresponding practices'.[75] This conception of the reproduction of ideological misrecognition through the endless repetition of singular practices, within material apparatuses, is not just an attempt at a highly original theory of ideology and of the role of the state in this process. It is a theory of social practice that attempts to explain the reproduction of social relations and forms without resorting to some form of latent structure. *On Reproduction* emerges as a much broader attempt on the part of Althusser towards a reformulation of his conception of social structures. In this new conception, 'structure' is a relation that exists because it *lasts*, and lasts because it is reproduced through the material effectivity of a system of material apparatuses that guarantees this reproduction, a system that is itself conditioned by social practices and antagonistic social relations and strategies.

> It is easy to see that, if a mode of production lasts only as long as the system of state apparatuses that guarantees the conditions of reproduction (reproduction = duration) of its base, that is, its relations of production, one has to attack the system of the state apparatuses and seize state power to disrupt the conditions of the reproduction (= duration = existence) of a mode of production and establish new relations of production. They are established under the protection of a new state and new state apparatuses which ensure the reproduction (= duration = existence) of the new relations of production, in other words, the new mode of production.[76]

---

74   It is interesting to note the analogies between Althusser's preoccupation with material practices and apparatuses ensuring – in the case of ideological formation through the repetition of social rituals – the reproduction of social relations and Deleuze's preoccupation at that time with repetition and singularity. See especially Deleuze 2004c.
75   Althusser 2014b, p. 77.
76   Althusser 2014b, p. 151.

Facing the potential theoretical problems of any conception of modes of production as 'latent structures', Althusser opts for a different vocabulary of relations and material practices and apparatuses that reproduce them. The reference to practices, struggles and apparatuses serves as a way to avoid any danger of dualism and to make more evident the possibility of an immanent causality. Althusser, both in the early 1960s and the 1970s, tends to insist that what exists are only singular historical social formations. The reproduction of social relations (and primarily *relations of production*), within particular social formations, represents exactly the 'structural' aspect of social reality. The conjunctural aspect is represented by the relation of forces which can be understood as the balance of force between reproduction and rupture. The class struggle is the decisive aspect at both levels. These preoccupations are evident in Althusser's emphasis on difference and unevenness as aspects of a materialist conception of the contradiction, but also on his emphasis on not only overdetermination, but also underdetermination.

> [I]f you take seriously the nature of the Marxist whole and its unevenness, you must come to the conclusion that this unevenness is necessarily reflected in the form of the *overdetermination* or of the *underdetermination* of contradiction [...] [C]ontradiction, as you find it in *Capital*, presents the surprising characteristic of being *uneven*, of bringing contrary terms into operation which you cannot obtain just by giving the second a sign obtained by negating that of the first. This is because they are caught up in a *relation of unevenness* which continuously reproduces its conditions of existence just on account of this contradiction [...] Because the working class is not the opposite of the capitalist class, it is not the capitalist class negated, deprived of its capital and its powers – and the capitalist class is not the working class plus something else, namely riches and power. They do not share the same history, they do not share the same world, they do not lead the same class struggle, and yet they do come into confrontation, and this certainly is a contradiction since the *relation of confrontation reproduces the conditions of confrontation* instead of transcending them in a beautiful Hegelian exaltation and reconciliation.[77]

Althusser's concept of underdetermination generally does not receive the attention it deserves. For Balibar this 'enigmatic' reference in the 1975 *Souten-*

---

77   Althusser 1976a, pp. 184–5.

ance d'Amiens must be read as suggesting a philosophical programme to think besides the 'necessity of contingency', also *'the contingent of this contingence*, the "under-determined" multiplicity of possibles or tendencies that coexist within the same event'.[78] Mikko Lahtinen has offered a comprehensive examination of the importance in Althusser's thinking of the complexity and unevenness of contradictions.[79] According to Lahtinen the articulation and overdetermination of contradictions implies that at the same time other contradictions or elements of social reality or the conjuncture are underdetermined and this, along with the necessarily displaced and condensed character of contradictions, forms the basis of their very complexity. I think that both Balibar and Lahtinen offer us useful reminders of the force of the notion of underdetermination, bringing forward the fact that elements of social reality, although present and actually existing, cannot – within a historically specific conjuncture – pass a certain threshold of effectivity or 'threshold of determination'[80] and therefore cannot influence social reality.

Alain Badiou has attempted to tackle the same problem with the introduction of the concept of the *inexistent*, that which in a given situation has a minimal degree of existence until there is radical change and it obtains a maximum degree leading to the event as radical novelty and rupture.[81] As an attempt to theorise material tendencies that do not manage to cross a certain threshold of effectivity and consequently existence, it is a welcome addition to Badiou's ontological schema and an equally welcome correction to Badiou's initial quasi-miraculous eruption of the event.[82] However, I think that Althusser's notion of underdetermination has a theoretical advantage in relation to Badiou's inexistent. According to Althusser's conception, underdetermination is not an intrinsic quality of a contradiction or more generally of any given element of a contradiction, but is the outcome of a specific relation of forces between contradictions and within contradictions. The over- and underdetermination of a contradiction refers exactly to the dynamics of determination in historically specific conjunctures. The change in the degree of effectivity can be explained by the change in this relation of forces. In contrast, Badiou's reference to the inexistent in a situation does not include any explanation of

---

78   Balibar 1996, p. xiii.
79   Lahtinen 2009, pp. 33–43.
80   Althusser 1976a, p. 187.
81   '[G]iven an object in a world, there exists a single element of this object which inexists in that world. It is this element that we call the proper inexistent of the object. It testifies, in the sphere of appearance, for the contingency of being-there. In this sense, its (ontological) being has (logical) non-being as its being-there' (Badiou 2009a, p. 324).
82   For such a criticism of Badiou, see Bensaïd 2004.

how a possible change in its degree or intensity of existence can occur, even in the sense of the contingency of its necessity.

I think that this conception of the underdetermination of a contradiction or of an element can also be helpful in trying to think the relation between the visible and the invisible with the visible itself, to which I referred earlier as an important aspect of an attempt to avoid thinking latent tendencies as 'hidden structures'. Something can be invisible not only because of ideological mystification and misrecognition, but also because of its being underdetermined and therefore unable to reach the level of historical existence necessary for its direct perception or visibility. The fact that this underdetermination and subsequent invisibility is the outcome of overdetermination, displacement and condensation of contradictions allows us to avoid any dualism and to retain visibility and invisibility, existence and inexistence at the same ontological level. Visible and invisible within the very terrain of the visible do not simply co-exist, they are tied in a dialectical and necessarily contradictory relation of mutual determination and represent, in the last instance, stakes of the class struggle, as the principal motor force of the overdetermination, displacement and condensation of contradictions.

5 The Critique of Feuerbach as Critique of Phenomenology and Structuralism

In 1967 Louis Althusser prepared a course for the *aggregation* on Marx and Engels's *The German Ideology*. This offered him the possibility to return to his criticism of Feuerbach. Along with *The Humanist Controversy*, again from 1967, it represents Althusser's attempt to rethink in a more profound way the questions regarding theoretical humanism.

For Althusser, Feuerbach was the philosopher who, in the most explicit way, attempted to 'invert' Hegel, in the sense of an 'inversion of the relation between subject and attribute, Thought and Being, Idea and sensuous nature'. It is a critique that 'remains the prisoner of Hegel's system' and, at the same time, '*adds nothing* to Hegel'; moreover, it has

> the interesting effect of *deleting* something from him [...] something that constitutes an essential object of Hegelian thought – *history* or culture, and that which Hegel situates at the origins of culture: *labour*.[83]

---

83 Althusser 2003, p. 88.

The result of this attempt at an *inversion* of the Hegelian system led Feuerbach to retreat into an anthropology or a humanist materialism that is in fact a 'theoretical retreat with respect to Hegel'.[84]

Althusser begins with an examination of Feuerbach's equation of religion with the essence of man, in the sense of the objectification of what is proper to man, in contrast to Hegel where there is no conception of the essence of man and where religion is one of the moments of Absolute Spirit. Consequently, for Althusser, this means that Feuerbach's philosophy with its conception of religion as alienation just gives 'this "self-consciousness" that religion lacks'.[85] This is based exactly upon this conception of the object as objectified essence of the subject, in the form of a theory of the '*absolute horizon*'.[86] By taking Feuerbach's conception of the object as the mirror in which the essence of the subject is reflected, Althusser stresses this '*speculary* relation',[87] which is based upon a centred structure in which the subject occupies the central position. This relation is also an example of the 'structure of all ideological discourse'.[88] It is this special relation of man to his inner essence that gives a particular centrality to consciousness. Moreover, alienation explains why in Feuerbach consciousness as self-consciousness does not necessary imply transparency: 'This misrecognition, this non correspondence of the individual consciousness to generic objects and activities is the effect of alienation'.[89]

Althusser criticises Feuerbach for relapsing into a pre-Hegelian position. While Hegel had insisted on the identity of consciousness and self-consciousness in Absolute Knowledge, Feuerbach insists on the primacy of self-consciousness. Moreover, Feuerbach 'has no need for any theory of history of alienation', since consciousness is reduced to '*the disclosure of an originary self-consciousness*'.[90] The result is a 'transcendental pseudo-biology'[91] that is essentially anachronistic in nature. What is more important for Althusser is exactly the centrality of the speculary reflection of the human essence in the object, exemplified in religion. In this sense, 'the faculty of theoretical "seeing"' becomes the attribute that transcends the 'subjectivity of the species' and 'sustain the thesis of the universality of the human species'.[92] It is in light of this

---

84   Althusser 2003, p. 89.
85   Althusser 2003, p. 93.
86   Althusser 2003, p. 95.
87   Althusser 2003, p. 96.
88   Althusser 2003, p. 99.
89   Althusser 2003, p. 102.
90   Althusser 2003, p. 103.
91   Althusser 2003, pp. 104–5.
92   Althusser 2003, p. 111.

theoretical strategy that we can understand the centrality of religion. Moreover, this is not just a theory of perception, it is above all a theory of the *'intentionality of an intentional consciousness'*.[93]

Althusser here does not intend simply to offer a critique of Feuerbach. In his reading of Feuerbach he lays the ground for a full confrontation with all philosophies of consciousness and in particular phenomenology, which had been one of Althusser's main targets in the French discussion. The target in this respect is not only Feuerbach but also Merleau-Ponty's conception of a philosophy of consciousness.[94] Here is how Althusser summarises this:

> If we draw up a balance sheet of these principles we obtain the following system:
> 1. a suspension of the thesis of existence;
> 2. the method of reduction, which makes it possible to home in on signification;
> 3. the beginning of an eiditic variation carried out through an analysis of *examples*;
> 4. the original nature of the signification.
>
> Thus we have a set of theoretical principles strikingly reminiscent of the principles informing the method of the Husserlian reduction.[95]

In a certain sense, we can say that this reading of Feuerbach offers Althusser the possibility to stress the anthropology that we can find at the bottom of such a philosophy of consciousness. This anthropological conception of the essence of man, exemplified in religion where '[i]n the infinite faculties of God, it is this infinity of his faculties that man worships',[96] in fact means that in the speculary relation between object and subject the essence of the subject is on both sides of the relation. Moreover, it leads to a theory of ideology, that Althusser considers dominant in Marxism, which is based upon a relation between an essence and a phenomenon:

> (a) At one end, as *essence, an originary fact*, or a practice or empirical conditions (which can even be class relations of relations of class struggle).
> (b) *At the other end*, the corresponding ideological formation or one of its segments, the *phenomenon* of this essence.

---

93 Althusser 2003, p. 113.
94 Merleau-Ponty 2002.
95 Althusser 2003, p. 117.
96 Althusser 2003, p. 120.

(c) Between the two, the necessity of producing the *genesis* of the phenomenon, in other words, the necessity of demonstrating the persistence of the originary essence down through the long line [*filiation*] *of mediations* that ultimately culminate in the phenomenon of this essence: ideology.[97]

This has, for Althusser, an important theoretical and political consequence. For Althusser, there is a limit to the whole image of 'inversion' because it can remain within the terrain of the ideological. Althusser pays particular attention to the 'speculary relation with reduplication'[98] regarding the subject-object relation, exemplified in the relation between man and God, which can lead to 'a relation of the *absolute subordination of the first subject to the Second Subject*', thus leading to complex relations of not only reduplication but also 'submission/guarantee'.[99] Since the 'first Subject is *accountable* to the Second Subject', the specular relation 'becomes a relation of moral accountability'.[100] This means a certain *inequality* in this specular relation, '*the specular relation is asymmetrical and unequal, and that its true foundations is this specular inequality*'.[101] This is for Althusser an expression of the more general structure of the ideological:

> We must therefore reverse the apparent order of the effects of the structure, and say that *the specular relation is not the cause of the effects of reduplication and of submission/guarantee; quite the contrary, the speculary structure is the effect of a specific absence which makes itself felt, in the field of the ideological itself, in the symptom of the reduplication of the subject and the couple submission guarantee*. This absence is an absence *in propria persona* in the field of the ideological but a presence in *propria persona* outside it. This presence is that of the ideological *function* of recognition-misrecognition, a function that has to do with *what is misrecognized* in the form of the specular relation of recognition: that is, in the last instance, the *complex structure of the social whole*, and its *class structure*.[102]

---

97 Althusser 2003, p. 126. Althusser explicitly refers to Lucien Goldmann as an example of this conception of ideology.
98 Althusser 2003, p. 129.
99 Althusser 2003, p. 130.
100 Ibid. According to Montag, this affects how the 'freedom of the subject' is conceived: 'The much vaunted freedom or agency of the subject is simultaneously constituted as responsibility before a power ready to hold the subject accountable and with the means to punish if the subject should be found guilty' (Montag 2013, p. 135).
101 Ibid.
102 Althusser 2003, p. 132.

For Althusser, the danger is to embark on a '*structural analysis of an ideology*' while remaining within the ideological. For Althusser, this is the case even when one attempts to analyse 'its *unsaid*, its latent discourse, which will then be called its *unconscious*'.[103] The problem is that

> One never gets beyond the structure of the ideological when one proceeds in this fashion: bringing the structure of the ideological into relation with other *isomorphic structures* does not undermine this structure, but has the opposite effect, inasmuch as this generalized isomorphism merely reinforces, merely *repeats*, the structure of the ideological.[104]

According to Althusser, this 'repetition of isomorphism is merely the symptom of structuralism's ideological nature'.[105] He insists that is evident in Lévi-Strauss's conception of the primitive society which is presented as an 'expressive society', 'a society one can recognize in its total essence by analysing one or another of these total parts'.[106] Thus structuralism is accused of being in the end a variety of 'expressive causality' and, 'in the last instance', a 'hermeneutics'.[107] Consequently, '[t]here can be no Marxist theory of ideology in the absence of a radical break with all hermeneutics, existential or structuralist'.[108] It is also interesting that Althusser explicitly refers to Lucien Sébag's *Marxisme et structuralisme*,[109] the most ambitious attempt to insist that an historicist Marxism is the best philosophy for structuralism, which for Althusser exemplifies the relation between structuralism and a certain form of hermeneutics.

Althusser then proceeds to a critique of Feuerbach's conception of Man as a species-being in order to offer a critique of Feuerbach's ideological theory of history. According to Feuerbach every individual carries the essence of man albeit within the limits of *individuality*,[110] both real and imaginary. However, Althusser insists that Feuerbach avoids any nominalism, since this would have paved 'the way for a critique of the human essence as a *name*, as an arbitrary, contingent formulation'.[111] Instead, Althusser insists that in Feuerbach human essence exists in the human species as a whole, and here emerges the import-

---

103 Ibid.
104 Ibid.
105 Althusser 2003, p. 133.
106 Ibid.
107 Althusser 2003, p. 134.
108 Althusser 2003, p. 135.
109 Sébag 1964. On the importance of Sébag's book see Montag 2013.
110 Althusser 2003, p. 138.
111 Althusser 2003, p. 141.

ance of the relation of intersubjectivity and in particular in Feuerbach's theory of sexuality, in the form of a thesis 'that the infinity of the human essence exists *in actu* in the finitude of intersexuality, the foundation of intersubjectivity'.[112] The communism of Feuerbach is 'the communism of love, that is, the communism of the Christian religion "taken at its word"'.[113] In the end there is no history in Feuerbach except in the sense of a history of processes of alienation and disalienation. The only privileged historical locus is the 'period in which the human essence will be realized and the originary essence will exist in the very form of authenticity'.[114] But this will in fact be 'the negation of all history'.[115] Consequently, history in Feuerbach, and in general within such a humanist anthropological perspective, can exist only as an *ideological fantasy, an ideology of history*.

> History is the concept of the realization of a desire, or, rather, the phantasmagoric concept of the realization of a fantasy, the reduplication of a fantasy. If reduplication is typical of the structure of the ideological, then we are dealing, in the proper sense, with an ideology of history.[116]

It is obvious that Althusser's manuscript on Feuerbach is not just a critique of theoretical humanism. Rather it is a critique of the ideological anthropology and ideology of history that can be the philosophical supplement of structuralism, or the combination of structuralism and phenomenology, thus forming an important aspect of Althusser's polemics against a certain version of structuralism in the 1960s.

6   From Structure to the Conjuncture

Althusser's attempt towards a rethinking of the structure/conjuncture relation took various forms. The attempt to rethink a theory of politics as a materialist intervention in the conjuncture is most obvious in his enduring interest in Machiavelli, as the thinker who more than anyone attempted to theorise what it means to 'think *in* the conjuncture'.[117] For Althusser, Machiavelli is 'the greatest

---

112   Althusser 2003, p. 145.
113   Althusser 2003, p. 148.
114   Althusser 2003, p. 150.
115   Ibid.
116   Ibid.
117   'I believe it is not hazardous to venture that Machiavelli is the first theorist of the con-

materialist philosophy in history'.[118] In *Machiavelli and Us* we can find a much more balanced and dialectical conception of this relation, stressing especially the political stimulus necessary for any materialist theorisation of historical and social reality.

> We are no longer dealing with the mythical pure objectivity of the laws of history and politics. Not that they have disappeared from Machiavelli's discourse. Quite the reverse: he does not cease to invoke them, and track them in their infinite variations, so as to make them declare themselves ... But the theoretical truths thus produced are produced under the stimulus of the conjuncture; and no sooner are they produced than they are affected in their modality by their intervention in a conjuncture fully dominated by the political problem it poses, and the political practice required to achieve the objective it proposes.[119]

It is obvious that in this formulation structural determinations and/or laws (as historical tendencies) are not abandoned. What is implied is that their only form of existence is in singular historical conjunctures, something that has to be distinguished from any classical conception of materialisation or actualisation of 'latent tendencies'. The only possible way at arriving at any possible theorisation of structural determinations is through the exigencies and open questions that these singular conjunctures pose. For Althusser, the conjuncture offers at the same time an object of theory and a political task:

> The conjuncture is thus no mere summary of its elements, or enumeration of diverse circumstances, *but their contradictory system,* which poses the political problem and indicates its historical solution, *ipso facto* rendering it a political objective, a practical task.[120]

This turn towards more singular, concrete, tangible historical determinations can account for Althusser's much more critical approach towards what he took to be the idealist elements in Marx's theory of value. To an abstract conception

---

juncture or the first thinker consciously, if not to think the concept of conjuncture, if not to make it the object of an abstract and systematic reflection, then at least consistently – in an insistent, extremely profound way – to think *in* the conjuncture: that is to say, in its concept of an aleatory, singular case' (Althusser 1999a, p. 18).

118 Althusser 1999a, p. 103. On the importance of Machiavelli for Althusser, see Terray 1996 and Matheron 2012.
119 Althusser 1999a, pp. 19–20.
120 Althusser 1999a, p. 19.

of value that can easily lead to a strictly quantitative and arithmetic conception of exploitation, Althusser opposes a theoretical perspective that stresses the importance of concrete material conflicts and antagonisms.

> The whole set of these concrete forms does indeed include the extraction of value, but it also includes the implacable constraints of the labour process embedded in the process of production and, therefore, exploitation: the socio-technical division and organization of labour; the length of the 'working day' [...] speed-up; compartmentalization; the material conditions of the centralization of labour [...] work related accidents and illnesses; the practice of forcing people to take jobs below or above their level of competence; and so on.[121]

This effort by Althusser to think in new terms the relation between the more structural and the more 'historical'/'conjunctural' aspects and a new synthesis is also evident in his reading of the relation between the more 'abstract' and the more 'concrete' chapters of *Capital*, vol. 1, in his preface to Gerard Duménil's book *Le concept de loi économique dans 'Le Capital'* (*The Concept of Economic Law in* Capital). In this text Althusser insists that the more 'concrete' and 'historical' chapters of *Capital*, the ones referring to the length of the working day or primitive accumulation, are not 'external' to theory, but are indeed theoretically indispensable, even though they seem to exceed Marx's abstract order of presentation. History and class struggles in their singularity and their conjunctural dynamics are not outside the theorisation of value; they form an integral part of it.

> That the unity of *Capital* is remarkably unequal would enable us to take seriously the reason for which Marx, as they say, 'injected' inside *Capital* these analyses on the 'working day', this chapter for which he spat blood (il sua 'sang et eau') in order to treat manufacturing and machinism, the astonishing section VIII on primitive accumulation etc. in short all the chapters and pages where what we call 'concrete history' irrupt in the analysis: we have to believe that this 'exterior' singularly communicates with the 'interior', and if this communication was not clearly thought by Marx, how not to see there an exteriority effect produced by the order of exposition that was imposed to it? [...] We must not be astonished if the 'exterior' is present in *Capital*. In the chapters that transverse and exceed the order

---

121   Althusser 2006a, p. 43.

of exposition, the 'exterior' intervenes like a theoretical element indispensable for the project of the 'critique of political economy': to testify for the sense of the 'reduction' operated by the order of exposition, whose theoretical constraints Marx had accepted, to attest the real extent of the analysis that was conducted in the real space of his 'reduction' and therefore to go beyond its necessary 'limits'.[122]

---

[122] Althusser 1998, p. 262.

CHAPTER 5

Materialism as Philosophy of the Encounter

Ever since the posthumous publication of Althusser's texts from the 1980s, his conception of a potential *materialism of the encounter* or an *aleatory materialism* has been the subject of lively debate. Of particular importance has been the attempt especially in the 1990s to present these texts as marking a turning point in the evolution of his work or of bringing forward 'another' Althusser. In contrast, we are now in a position to have a much more complex and problematised conception of this relation. In fact, we can now retrace the trajectory of the emergence of the encounter as a central notion in Althusser's work since the second half of the 1960s. One might also say that the emphasis on the encounter and the parallel attempt to intervene more politically in the debates regarding the line and politics of the Communist movement are aspects of the same process, the same effort, beginning with the self-criticism of 1966.

1   An Althusserian *Kehre*?

Antonio Negri has suggested that Althusser's later writings represent a major theoretical turn, an Althusserian *Kehre*, describing these texts as indications of Althusser's endorsement of a postmodern and post-communist perspective.[1] According to Negri, Althusser moved away from his previous structuralism and embarked upon the quest for a new philosophical and political subjectivity, refusing all forms of dialectical thinking. The postmodern totalisation of power leaves no room for dialectical contradictions in social reality, only the possibility of new social and productive forms emerging at the margins and interstices of the existing social order. Negri insists that these new social forms necessarily take the form of aleatory ruptures, and instead of a negative philosophy of structures and 'processes without subjects', we need a positive philosophy of the resistance and creativity of singular social bodies, with Negri projecting onto Althusser his own ontology of the creative potentiality of the multitude.

Similarly, Yann Moulier Boutang has insisted that Althusser, faced with the crisis of Marxism in the 1970s, chose to abandon the theoretical apparatus of historical materialism and any conception of a science of history dealing with

---

1   Negri 1996.

modes of production and their succession and forms of transition in favour of a logic of the singular case and of a notion of the political practice as aleatory encounter.[2] Ichida and Matheron[3] think that the notion of the *aleatory* which Althusser introduced in his later writings has to be interpreted as the non-dialectic, in the sense of the abandonment of a conception of politics based on the relation between a dialectical order of exposition and the order of things.

Callari and Ruccio link aleatory materialism and the possibility of a postmodern Marxism and postmodern politics of the multiple and heterogeneous subjects and identities,[4] presenting Althusser's work as a clear break with classical Marxism and modernism. Modernist Marxism is presented as plagued by essentialism and teleology, with production being the causal centre of social reality and the proletariat as the historical subject of social change. For Callari and Ruccio there is the possibility of an 'other' Marxism, exemplified in the work of Althusser, that counters these essentialist, systemicist and teleological tendencies and offers the possibility to think the heterogeneity, complexity and multiplicity of social struggles and to reject classical Marxism's premises such as the primacy of the struggles in production or the determination in the last instance by the economic. This postmodern Althusser is also a post-communist one, refusing the basic tenets of communist politics, such as the political centrality of the labour movement. But this reading also has epistemological consequences: Althusser's insistence on the possibility of treating Marxism as a science and as an attempt towards scientific explanation is discarded.[5]

In contrast, G.M. Goshgarian has offered the most detailed accounts of Althusser's early confrontation with the notion of the encounter. In his 'Introduction' to the *Philosophy of the Encounter*,[6] Goshgarian stresses the element of continuity in Althusser's work, tracing the notion of the encounter in all of his mature work, beginning with the book on Montesquieu,[7] which is represented as a first clear break with historicism and teleology, and later in the

---

[2] Moulier-Boutang 1997, pp. 100–1.
[3] Ichida and Matheron 2005.
[4] Callari and Ruccio 1996.
[5] 'Of course, Althusser himself did not help matters by invoking such terms as science, society effect, structural causality, reproduction and so on – terms that a allude to a sense of closure for the objects and methods of Marxist discourse' (Callari and Ruccio 1996, p. 35).
[6] Goshgarian 2006.
[7] Althusser 1959. For Goshgarian's reading of the book on Montesquieu as the emergence of the philosophy of the encounter see especially Goshgarian 2006, pp. xxx–xxxv. See also Goshgarian 2013.

reformulation of the materialist dialectic in the 1960s, until its emergence as part of the new practice of philosophy, envisaged as an integral part of a political and theoretical strategy to counter right-wing tendencies and the crisis in the communist movement. According to Goshgarian, Althusser's rethinking in the 1970s of the crisis of communist politics and the non-accomplishment of socialism in the USSR already included the basic premise of aleatory materialism that an encounter might not take place, or that it might not last. Similarly he treats Althusser's insistence on the primacy of class struggle over the contending classes, a basic premise of his works in the 1970s, as analogous to his later insistence on the primacy of the encounter over the forms to which it gives birth.[8] Consequently, Goshgarian insists that only by reading the texts on aleatory materialism can we understand the philosophical perspective of Althusser's political battles in the 1970s.

Wal Suchting also provided, shortly before his death, a very interesting reading of Althusser's later writings,[9] in which he suggested that one possible way to understand these texts is through the conceptual strategy introduced by Wittgenstein, and especially the distinction between facts and things. He also insisted on the usefulness of aleatory materialism as a way to dissolve philosophical problems, especially those having to do with the relation of materialism to the development of modern science.

André Tosel chooses a more balanced position, at the same time trying to stress an element of continuity in Althusser, basically in his effort to think communism in a non-ideological mode 'remaining until his death a communist philosopher',[10] also stressing the open questions that mark the formulations of aleatory materialism. Mikko Lahtinen has also offered a very interesting reading of the later writings and especially Althusser's preoccupation with Machiavelli,[11] insisting that aleatory materialism is basically a way to theorise the exigencies of political practice and action in the unpredictable terrain of singular historical conjunctures.

Vittorio Morfino's writings on aleatory materialism[12] represent an original attempt at a materialist reading of the later writings and they draw clear lines of demarcation with more idealist readings, since Morfino insists on Althusser's radically anti-teleological and anti-historicist position. Especially interesting is Morfino's careful reading of Althusser's theoretical sources and his insistence

---

8   Goshgarian 2006, p. xlv.
9   Suchting 2004.
10 Tosel 2006, p. 195.
11 Lahtinen 2009.
12 Morfino 2005; Morfino 2007; Morfino and Pinzolo 2005; Morfino 2010; Morfino 2015.

that certain references by Althusser (for example the imagery of the rain or the void) must be treated more like rhetorical strategies and not like proper philosophical concepts or ontological positions.

But the question remains: While one can be in agreement with readings such as the ones proposed by Goshgarian or Morfino, that offer the possibility to treat Althusser's materialism of the encounter as something opposed to an idealism of the aleatory and as a set of theoretical positions that are continuous with Althusser's earlier formulations, the problem is that there has been a great number of interpretations that insist on a possible idealist reading. Is this a problem of the interpretations proposed, or is it an actual theoretical contradiction in Althusser's writings themselves? In my opinion it is not enough to limit ourselves to an effort to salvage the later texts from post-Marxist and postmodernist readings and to insist on an unbreakable continuity in Althusser's work. Such a reading would be in sharp violation of the protocols Althusser himself introduced for the reading of any theoretical problematic. Instead the contradictions in Althusser's conception of aleatory materialism must be brought forward.

2 Rethinking the Genealogy of the Encounter

We have now a much more complete view of the evolution of Althusser's confrontation with the notion of the encounter. In fact, a rather different image emerges, one in which the notion of the encounter is a crucial element, explored with theoretical intensity in Althusser's work ever since the book on Montesquieu. Moreover, the broader access to Althusser's unpublished texts from the second half of the 1960s and the 1970s offers ample evidence that Althusser already had a developed version of the materialism of the encounter, or at least its basic theoretical structure.

G.M. Goshgarian has meticulously traced the early emergence of references to the encounter, in the book on Montesquieu, especially through his confrontation with the Marxian concept of *Verbindung* (combination). He stresses the fact that Althusser, in his defence of Montesquieu against accusations of pluralism, refers to the *encounter* [*rencontre*] between the multiple factors and elements that determine any given society. It is 'a "chain"' that 'binds Montesquieu's apparently "different" truths':[13]

---

13   Goshgarian 2013, p. 92.

> How is this chain designated? In Ben Brewster's English translation it is a 'conjunction': 'all these causes, apparently so radically disparate, converge' in a determinate instance 'from [whose] conjunction arises what Montesquieu calls the *spirit of a nation*'. The French word is *rencontre*, now usually rendered as 'encounter'. If the sentence just quoted were retranslated today (Brewer's translation appeared in 1972), it might read: 'What Montesquieu calls the spirit of a nation derives from an encounter of causes that seem radically disparate'.[14]

The notion of the encounter resurfaces in Étienne Balibar's contribution to *Reading Capital*. Balibar here refers to the *encounter*[15] between the man with capital and the man with labour power. Here the emphasis is not on *chance* or contingency but on the conditions that make possible the reproduction of this encounter.

> Further, the analysis of reproduction destroys the appearance involved in the 'beginning' of the production process, the appearance of a 'free' contract between the worker and the capitalist, which is renewed on each occasion, the appearance which makes variable capital an 'advance' from the capitalist to the labourer (on account of the product, i.e., of the 'end' of the production process). In a word, all the appearances which seem to reduce to *chance* the face to face meeting [*rencontre*] of the capitalist and the worker as buyer and seller of labour power. Reproduction reveals the 'invisible threads' which chain the wage-earner to the capitalist class.[16]

More significant is another surfacing of the notion of the encounter, which refers to a radically anti-teleological conception of the articulation or combination of various elements in a new structure. In this conception it is exactly the encounter, the combination of the different elements or social forms that is determinant and not their effectivity in previous articulations and previous modes of productions. The different encounters therefore constitute the essence of a conception of historical discontinuity.

> Thus the unity possessed by the capitalist structure once it has been constituted is not found in its rear. Even when the study of the pre-history of the mode of production takes the form of a genealogy, i.e., when it aims

---

14   Ibid.
15   Ben Brewster translated *rencontre* as meeting, but *encounter* is also a possible translation.
16   Althusser et al. 2016, p. 434.

to be explicitly and strictly dependent, *in the question that it poses*, on the elements of the constituted structure, and on their identification, which requires that the structure is known as such in its complex unity – even then the pre-history can never be the mere retrospective projection of the structure. All it requires is that the *encounter* should have been produced and rigorously thought, between those elements, which are identified on the basis of the result of their conjunction, and the historical field within which their peculiar histories are to be thought. *In their concepts*, the latter have nothing to do with that result, since they are defined by the structure of a *different* mode of production. In this historical field (constituted by the previous mode of production), the elements whose genealogy is being traced have precisely only a 'marginal' situation, i.e., a *non-determinant* one. To say that the modes of production are constituted as combination variants is also to say that they transpose the order of dependence, that they make certain elements move in the structure (which is the object of the theory) from a place of historical domination to a place of historical subjection.[17]

It is interesting that two of the first thinkers to stress the radically anti-teleological theory of the encounter in this passage were Deleuze and Guattari in *Anti-Oedipus*. For Deleuze and Guattari,

> At the heart of *Capital*, Marx points to the encounter of two 'principal' elements: on one side, the deterritorialized worker who has become free and naked, having to sell his labour capacity; and on the other, decoded money that has become capital and is capable of buying it. The fact that these two elements result from the segmentation of the despotic State in feudalism, and from the decomposition of the feudal system itself and that of its State, still does not give us the extrinsic conjunction of these two flows: flows of producers and flows of money. The encounter might not have taken place, with the free workers and the money-capital existing 'virtually' side by side. One of the elements depends on a transformation of the agrarian structures that constitute the old social body, while the other depends on a completely different series going by way of the merchant and the usurer, as they exist marginally in the pores of this old social body.[18]

---

17 Althusser et al. 2016, p. 450.
18 Deleuze and Guattari 2004, p. 245. Deleuze and Guattari in the note attached to this passage quote Balibar from the passage we have just commented upon.

It is obvious that Deleuze and Guattari manage to grasp the importance of this conception of the encounter between different elements within the process of emergence of a new social form and a new mode of production. They note, in a way very similar to Althusser's own emphasis in later texts, that the encounter might not have taken place, in the sense that there is no prior determination, no linear historical causality, no predetermined direction in historical evolution, only the constant interplay of different elements and the (non)possibilities of their encounter. There are different histories and historicities involved in this encounter, different origins, and different forms of co-existence of these different elements prior to their encounter.

Althusser himself moves toward this direction as part of his self-critical turn after 1966. Here the notion of the encounter takes the form of a break with any form of teleology and is part of a broader process of theoretical correction that also includes rejecting any conception of 'latent structures' and confrontation with singularity in history. In 1966, Althusser notes:

> 1. Theory of the encounter or conjunction (= genesis ...) (d. Epicurus, clinamen, Cournot), chance etc., precipitation, coagulation. 2. Theory of the conjuncture (= structure) ... philosophy as a general theory of the conjuncture (= conjunction).[19]

Again in 1966 in his correspondence with René Diatkine, Althusser insists on the encounter of the various social forms that were combined in the emergence of the capitalist mode of production. Here encounter is presented as the opposite of any conception of historical genesis. Encounter thus becomes an essential aspect of determining discontinuity between different modes of production, along with the notion of combination that Marx uses.

> When one reads *Capital* rather closely, it appears that contrary to the genetic ideology currently applied to Marx [...] [t]here is no *filiation* properly (precisely) speaking between the feudal mode of production and the capitalist mode of production. The capitalist mode of production irrupts from the *encounter* (another one of your concepts to which I subscribe entirely) of a certain number of very precise elements and from the specific *combination* of those *elements* ('combination' translates the Marxist concept of *Verbindung*: your concept of *organization* would fit quite well,

---

19   Quoted in Matheron 1997a, p. 10. Althusser wrote on the margins of Macherey's book: 'Theory of the clinamen. First theory of the *encounter*' (Ibid.).

or the concept of *arrangement*). [...] The feudal mode of production in no way *engenders* either the *encounter* of those elements or the fact that they can *combine and organize themselves* in an actual unit that *functions*, an actual functioning unit that is precisely *what irrupts*. The fact that those elements are elements apt to combine (not all things eager to combine can!), the fact that they begin to function as a mode of production, and the fact that their functioning represents a real mode of production: *all that is absolutely without any genetic relation with the feudal mode of production* but obeys instead laws entirely different from those of engendering by the feudal mode of production.[20]

In a similar line, in a small note from September 1966, Althusser returns to this 'theory of the encounter' or 'theory of the conjunction'.[21] And in 1967 in his manuscript on *The Humanist Controversy*, Althusser again returns to this opposition between genesis and encounter as a clear break with any form of teleology and as an attempt to confront the open question of the emergence of capitalism as a mode of production.

[C]apitalism is the result *of a process that does not take the form of a genesis*. The result of what? Marx tells us several times: of the process of an *encounter* of several distinct, definite, indispensable elements, engendered in the previous historical process by different *genealogies* that are independent of each other and can, moreover, be traced back to several possible 'origins': accumulation of money capital, 'free' labour-power, technical inventions and so forth. To put it plainly, capitalism is not the result of a *genesis* that can be traced back to the feudal mode of production and if to its origin, its 'in-itself', its 'embryonic form', and so on; it is the result of a complex process that produces, at a given moment, the encounter of a number of elements susceptible of [*propre à*] constituting it in their very encounter.[22]

It is also interesting that on March 1969 in one of his letters to Maria-Antoinetta Macciocchi, Althusser takes up the question of May 1968 and he uses the notion of the encounter, in an opposition to 'fusion', to describe the relation between the students and intellectuals on the one side and the working class movement on the other:

---

20   Althusser 1999b, p. 61.
21   Althusser 2013b.
22   Althusser 2003, p. 296.

> What happened was an historic *encounter*, and not a fusion. An encounter may occur or not occur. It can be a 'brief encounter', *relatively* accidental, in which case it will not lead to any *fusion* of forces. This was the case in May, where the meeting between the workers/employees on the one hand and students and young intellectuals on the other was a brief encounter which did not lead, for a whole series of reasons [...] to any kind of fusion.[23]

Althusser returned on various occasions in the 1970s to the notion of the encounter. Of particular importance is the emergence of this notion in his 1972 course on Rousseau, to which we shall return in the next chapter. It is an attempt to ground in the reading of Rousseau Althusser's thesis that one of the main forms that idealism takes is a thinking of *Origins*. The main theoretical enemy is any philosophy *of origin*, a philosophy that for Althusser is always linked to varieties of philosophical idealism.

> The origin belongs to a completely different mode [*mode*] of philosophical reference, a completely different world [*monde*] of philosophical reference [...] It is *the manifestation of titles of legitimacy in the self-evidence of nature.*[24]

It is interesting that, as we have already seen, the notion of the encounter plays a rather central role also in Althusser's reading of Rousseau, especially in his 1972 course. For Althusser, in Rousseau the state of pure nature is like the pre-Cosmos situation, the situation of the rain of atoms and the chance encounters that do not last, as part of a broader anti-teleological and anti-metaphysical conception of reality: 'The encounter is the punctual event that has the property of effacing itself, leaving no trace behind, surging up out of nothingness to return to nothingness, with neither origin nor result'.[25]

The notion of the encounter also plays a central role in Althusser's reading of Machiavelli especially in the 1970s manuscript *Machiavelli and Us*.[26] For Althusser, the relation between *fortuna* and *virtù* can only be described in terms of an encounter:

> As we can see, everything revolves around the encounter and non-encounter, the correspondence and non-correspondence, of *fortuna* and

---

[23] Macciocchi 1973, p. 306.
[24] Althusser 2019, pp. 33–34.
[25] Althusser 2019, p. 130.
[26] Althusser 1999a.

virtù. If this correspondence, whether immediate or deferred, is not ensured – in other words, in the absence of this encounter – there is no New Prince and no New Principality.[27]

Moreover, for Althusser, the notion of the encounter in his reading of Machiavelli appears as the necessary condition for both political practice and political thinking, in fact for a political thinking that enables a genuine form of political practice. Althusser's starting point is that although in Machiavelli we have all the specific conditions for the encounter between *fortuna* and *virtù*, there is 'no specification of the site and subject of political practice'. For Althusser, this apparent contradiction

> can be removed only by the sudden appearance – necessary, but unforeseeable and inascribable as regards place, time and person – of the concrete forms of the political encounter whose general conditions alone are defined. In this theory that ponders and preserves the disjuncture, room is thereby made for political practice. Room is made for it through this organization of disjoined theoretical notions, by the discrepancy between the definite and indefinite, the necessary and the unforeseeable. This discrepancy, thought and unresolved by thought, is the presence of history and political practice in theory itself.[28]

The importance of the encounter as a central philosophical concept is evident in Althusser's manuscript from the 1970s entitled *Être marxiste en philosophie*, translated in English as *How to be a Marxist in Philosophy*.[29] It is interesting that we also find here references to Epicurus as a philosopher who insisted on radical contingency, rejected any sense of origin and end, and had an atomistic conception, and also to the imagery of the rain, as described by Lucretius in *De rerum natura*, and to the reference to the *clinamen* as the beginning, in the sense of an infinitesimal deviation at the beginning of world, references that we tend to associate with Althusser's texts of the 1980s.[30] Texts like *How to be a Marxist in Philosophy* suggest that not only was the elaboration of the materialism of the encounter a much broader theoretical project for Althusser, one that had begun long before the 1980s, but also that this project coincided with his attempt to offer a left-wing critique of communist reformism in the 1970s.

---

27 Althusser 1999a, p. 74.
28 Althusser 1999a, p. 80.
29 Althusser 2015a; Althusser 2017b.
30 See Althusser 2006a.

The encounter is a central concept in *How to be a Marxist in Philosophy*. For Althusser, it offers a new way to think of a singular subject, in a rather Spinozist conception of singularity: 'the different atoms, encountering each other and aggregating, produce the singular entities that [...] constitute our world'.[31] Moreover, the encounter is a 'developed concept of contingency',[32] in the sense that no encounter is predetermined, something that brings us to the notion of the conjuncture. The fact that 'everything is an encounter', and that 'every encounter is [...] necessarily contingent',[33] opens the possibility of events, of time, and of history. An encounter can happen, or not happen; it can also be undone, and Althusser cites the case of the Italian bourgeoisie of the fourteenth century as an example. What is important is how an encounter 'takes', which means that we can define its conditions only after the fact, since before it rests a 'relatively aleatory possibility'.[34] This also offers a conception of the emergence of a subject.

> What I wish to say, however, is that, with his thesis about *deviation*, *encounter*, and the *take*, Epicurus has provided us with the means of understanding precisely what the idealists had aimed at and missed: namely the irruption of a subject, *this* particular subject and no other.[35]

We also see the notion of the encounter play an important role in Althusser's manuscript *Initiation à la philosophie pour des non-philosophes*, translated in English as *Philosophy for Non-Philosophers*. Here Althusser again reiterates his anti-finalist conception of the encounter between the capitalist mode of production, the bourgeoisie and the members of the feudal aristocracy:

> it was born at the 'encounter' of these independent processes, which affected, conjointly and simultaneously, *feudal lords* who had enriched themselves or landed proprietors eager to consolidate and exploit their holdings; *bourgeois* whose wealth stemmed from international trade (thus 'owners of money' all); and, finally, *workers* who had been '*freed*' by being dispossessed.[36]

---

31 Althusser 2017b, p. 101.
32 Ibid.
33 Ibid.
34 Althusser 2017b, pp. 101–2.
35 Althusser 2017b, p. 102.
36 Althusser 2017a, pp. 134–5.

What is important is the absence of any finality or teleology in this process. Capitalism was the result of different autonomous processes, and '*was born and died several times in history*',[37] using, as in other texts, the example of the non-birth of capitalism in Italy towards the end of the fourteenth century.

For Althusser one of the main achievements of materialist philosophy is to prove that questioning why there is something rather than nothing is exactly the kind of '*meaningless questions*'.[38] In contrast, for Althusser, a materialist philosophy like that of Epicurus does not pose the question of origins but the question of the beginning.[39] The materialist thesis is that '[*t*]*here is* [...] *always already something, always already matter*',[40] and he describes the Epicurian theme of the rain of atoms falling that encounter each other after a deviation, a theme that would later be a cornerstone of the imagery of aleatory materialism in the post-1980 works:

> The *slightest* [*un rien de*] *deviation, the slightest 'deviance'*, is enough for the atoms to *encounter each other* and agglomerate: there we have the beginning of the world, and the world. Neither God nor Nothingness at the Origin: no Origin, but the beginning and, to account for the beginning, pre-existent matter, which becomes a world thanks to the (contingent, arbitrary) *encounter* of its elements.[41]

3   The Encounter as Anti-teleology and as New Practice of Politics

The encounter is an important concept, both as a break with any teleology in relation to the emergence of new social forms and modes of production and also as a way to think of new political forms and projects. It can indeed be really useful as an attempt to theorise the transition from one mode of production to the other in non-essentialist and non-teleological terms. Transition remains an open question and there have been many efforts to theorise it, from Soviet Marxism's insistence on the productive forces as the principal aspect of historical development, to more recent attempts to present the emergence of specifically capitalist social property relations in England as the essential

---

37   Althusser 2017a, p. 135.
38   Althusser 2017a, p. 28.
39   Althusser 2017a, p. 29.
40   Ibid.
41   Althusser 2017a, pp. 29–30. Cf Althusser 2006a.

aspect of the transition to capitalism,[42] all tending to view a certain aspect or element as playing the part of the self-development of an essence that marks the emergence of capitalism as the solution of the historical contradictions of feudalism. The problem is that it is very difficult to bring all the elements which are present in the expanded reproduction of the capitalist mode of production in the same essentialist historical narrative and treat them as aspects of the relation between an essence and its expressions. The emergence of English 'agrarian capitalism',[43] the first truly capitalist form of production, the development of Italian banking and credit practices (themselves having to do more with risk taking and handling of foreign trade costs than with a demand to obtain some part of the total capitalistically extracted surplus value), the emergence of the absolutist state and the unified, centralised territorial state (as opposed to the feudal fragmentation of territory and political authority), the emergence of 'bourgeois' culture and mentality as a result of the development of cities as administrative centres, were not predestined to be part of the reproduction of the capitalist mode of production, even though this is what effectively took place. The notion of the encounter can help us see the crucial theoretical difference between the transition to a mode of production and its reproduction.

In this reading the notion of the encounter marks the break with any form of historical metaphysics and does not preclude the structured character of the social whole. There is nothing contingent in the articulation of these elements as aspects of the reproduction of the capitalist mode of production. On the contrary the only way to account for this reproduction is the emergence of capitalist relations of production as a *structure in dominance*.[44] This causal primacy of the relations of production holds also for the transition itself: only under the dynamics of the emerging capitalist forms of exploitation and the social forces that came along could this combination have taken place. To Althusser's warning against any form of historical teleology that the encounter might not have taken place, we must add the materialist insistence on the possibility of historical explanation: the encounter could not have taken place without the emergence of capitalist social forms.

However, there is also another, more political overtone in the notion of the encounter. The encounter here emerges also as a strategic concept offering a much overdetermined and always at stake conception of the relations

---

42   See for example Wood 1991; 1995; 2002; 2003.
43   Brenner 1987a; Brenner 1987b.
44   Althusser 1969, pp. 200–16.

between the communist or revolutionary movement and the working and popular masses. It is obvious that what Althusser attempted was a left-wing critique of communist reformism. We can even say that from the beginning Althusser's work had a political orientation and was a critique of the communist movement's crisis. However, now it is no longer a question of a theoretical correction that would lead to a change in political direction. Now it is more a question of whether there can be an encounter between the dynamics arising from popular movements and the forms of political organisation. In all this period we have an increased reference to the potential, dynamics, and ingenuity of the popular masses. So the political and theoretical challenge is the following: How are we going to have an encounter between these dynamics and initiatives coming from the popular masses and whatever forms of communist and political organisations and theory are in place?

CHAPTER 6

From the Critique of Natural Law to the Void of the Forest and the Inexistence of the Origin: Althusser on Rousseau

One of the ways to retrace Althusser's transition towards the materialism of the encounter can be documented by retracing the different readings of Rousseau that Althusser offered in his theoretical trajectory. For Althusser, Rousseau was a constant reference point for most of his career. In 1975, on the occasion of his defence of his doctoral thesis '*sur traveux*' at the University of Picardy, he explained his relation to the study of political philosophy in the eighteenth century:

> It is however true that 26 years ago, in 1949–50, I did place before Mr Hyppolite and Mr Jankélévitch a project for a *grande thèse* (as it used to be called) on politics and philosophy in the eighteenth century in France with a *petite thèse* on Jean-Jacques Rousseau's *Second Discourse*. And I never really abandoned this project, as my essay on Montesquieu shows.[1]

Part of his duties as *caïman* at the École Normale Superieure de la Rue d'Ulm, i.e. someone whose duty was to prepare students for the *aggregation* exam, Althusser's courses on political philosophy were also a research project. Althusser only partially published his 1965–66 course in the *Cahiers pour l'Analyse*.[2] However, we now have access to four versions of his courses on Rousseau: from the following academic years: 1955–56, 1958–59, 1965–66 and 1972.[3]

1   The 1955–56 Course

In the 1955–56 course, Althusser deals with Rousseau in the context of a course on philosophy of history, admitting that this means 'confronting a paradox',[4]

---

1   Althusser 1976a, p. 165.
2   Althusser 1967. English translation in Althusser 1972a.
3   For the 1955–56 and 1965–66 courses see Althusser 2006b. For the 1958–59 course see Jalley 2014. For the 1972 course see Althusser 2013a and Althusser 2019.
4   Althusser 2006b, p. 107.

since Rousseau never wrote on history although, for Althusser, Rousseau's *Discourse on the Origin and Foundation of Inequality Among Men*[5] is a text that dominates how the eighteenth century viewed its own history. It offers a 'conceptual history' of the progress of civilisation and of the decadence of the human species, with 'abstract concepts, in appearance so far from real history and in truth so close to it', with 'revolutionary concepts' that can produce a 'new and infinitely more profound understanding [*intelligence*] of history'.[6]

For Althusser, in the eighteenth century there were two main antagonistic propertied classes with their philosophical representatives: the 'feudal-liberal party' represented by Montesquieu, and the 'bourgeois' party represented by the Encyclopedists. However, this led to petty-bourgeois masses of peasants and artisans being subjected to a combination of two kinds of exploitation, feudal and capitalist. This petty-bourgeois mass found its philosophical representative in Rousseau, who occupies a very particular position as being on the one hand a representative of the Enlightenment and at the same time an '*interior enemy*'[7] because of the 'plebeian accent' of his conception.[8] Consequently, Althusser treats Rousseau as a precursor of historical materialism:

> Rousseau conceives history as the effect, the manifestation of an immanent necessity [...] For the philosophers [of the Enlightenment] there is progress in civilization and progress in happiness; for Rousseau this development is *antinomic in itself*.[9]

For Althusser, Rousseau rejects a vision of history as the development of human nature; rather he was the first philosopher who 'systematically conceived the development of history, the development of society, as a development dialectically linked to its material conditions'.[10] Moreover, Rousseau considered human reason as 'the product of historical development',[11] thus refusing the fundamental position of Enlightenment that 'reason is the motor of history'.[12]

Regarding the state of nature, Althusser insists that Rousseau opposes the tradition that nature is a hostile environment, the forest 'gives at the same

---

5   In Rousseau 1997.
6   Althusser 2006b, p. 108.
7   Althusser 2006b, p. 110.
8   Althusser 2006b, p. 111.
9   Ibid.
10 Althusser 2006b, pp. 112–13.
11 Althusser 2006b, p. 112.
12 Althusser 2006b, p. 113.

time fruits and refuge'[13] and prefigures the social contract: 'demand of a general accord of man with his surroundings: nature already the role of general will'.[14] What initiates the transition from state of nature to state of society is the institution of property. This is the 'product of an historical development' that is 'a *necessary* development [...] produced by a series of *accidents* [*hazards*]'.[15] First, there is a man-nature scission as a 'distance between the materiality and the ideality of human nature'.[16] This leads to the development of reason and reflection and to the emergence of self-conscience. At this stage, forms of association are temporary and common interest equals 'the encounter of particular interests' since there is always the forest as refuge.[17] This development leads to the first forms of property, the 'huts', to the emergence of families and of language – an island as 'symbol of social life and not of solitude (≠ Romanticism)'[18] – of nations and of values. This is the ideal state of human sociality: An 'economic independence' superimposed by an 'abstract universality of mutual recognition', leading to Rousseau's ideal of an artisan economy, 'before the division of labour', with human relations that do not depend upon the economy.[19] In contrast, the 'accident' of the discovery of agriculture and metallurgy[20] led to the division of labour creating in the first instance a state of relative independence:

> Thus the dialectic: the forest becomes insufficient to assure the independence of man → arts: metallurgy → because of the invention of the plough nature becomes again the terrain of a relative independence.[21]

However, there is a limit to this relative independence because there is the '*end of earth*, the end of the forest' leading to new human relations: 'A new possession cannot be established at the expense of the forest but at the expense of another possession'.[22] This leads to a state of war, to servitude and domination, to struggles between poor and rich, and consequently to the social contract.[23]

---

13 Althusser 2006b, p. 116.
14 Althusser 2006b, p. 117.
15 Althusser 2006b, p. 119.
16 Althusser 2006b, p. 120.
17 Althusser 2006b, p. 121.
18 Althusser 2006b, p. 122.
19 Ibid.
20 Cf. Rousseau 1997, pp. 168–9.
21 Althusser 2006b, p. 124.
22 Althusser 2006a, p. 125.
23 Cf. Rousseau pp. 171–4.

In contrast to Hobbes, in Rousseau human beings are forced to enter a state of war; it is the effect of specific human relations. The social contract is a solution to this problem. However, the content of the contract depends upon 'existing determinate relations',[24] thus leading to recognition of possession, 'possession becomes property'.[25] Althusser's conclusion is that Rousseau is at the crossroads of a materialist and an idealist conception.

- a) If the accent is put upon the material process, upon the historical dialectic that shows the role played by economic conditions.
- b) If the accent is put upon the ideal character of human nature, and upon the character of decadence of history in relation to this ideal nature
  → we can interpret Rousseau in two ways:
  – History as alienation (Hegel).
  – Materialist and dialectical conception of history (Marx).

Thus, Rousseau is at a crossroads.[26]

2   The 1958–59 Course

Thanks to a recent book by Émile Jalley,[27] we also have access to notes from the 1958–59 course on Rousseau at the École Normale Superieure. For Althusser, Rousseau is distinct from his predecessors on social contract theory mainly in the sense that in Rousseau there are 'radical discontinuities' and a 'new structure of genesis',[28] leading to a 'double denaturalization of man'.[29] In contrast, Rousseau's predecessors 'project the structures and values of [their] contemporary state to the state of nature'.[30] In the case of Rousseau, the solution to the impossibility of going back to the state of nature was the emphasis on the heart. Althusser stresses that in Rousseau's state of pure nature, 'men are animals',[31] distinguished from other animals only in their perfectability, living in the empty space of the forest where encounters are avoided. This state of pure nature could go on perpetually were it not for natural disasters, leading to the

---

24   Althusser 2006b, p. 126.
25   Althusser 2006b, p. 127.
26   Ibid.
27   Jalley 2014.
28   Jalley 2014, p. 82.
29   Ibid.
30   Jalley 2014, p. 83.
31   Jalley 2014, p. 84.

emergence of reason, arts, and language ('because of encounters').[32] However, all these end up in the state of war that goes along with 'the progress of human faculties'.[33] This makes contingency and precariousness central to human history and to political bodies, thus marking Althusser's objection, even from the 1950s, to any teleological or finalist conception of human history.

> The development of humanity is a precarious, contingent development. This precariousness manifests itself in the contingence of accidents [...] and in the precariousness of the contract. Human history is precarious, contingent, provoked by accidents. It has no end. The social contract himself is precarious. It can be put again into question. Necessity of the death of political bodies.[34]

Althusser in 1958–59 continues to present Rousseau as, in a certain way, a precursor of historical materialism, referring to the 'real development of human faculties, a dialectical development in vaults'.[35] All these have to be related to the politics of Rousseau and his critique of the established political order.

> Hobbes and Locke had as an object to justify the existence of absolute power, or of the liberal English regime, in brief, the established fact, the established order. Rousseau is an adversary of the established order and a critic of existing things. That is why he does not project to the origin the existing social order. That is why he imagines an originary state of nature that does not bear any of the traits of the actual state.[36]

3   The 1965–66 Course

The course of the 1965–66 academic year was entitled 'Political Philosophy in the seventeenth century before Rousseau',[37] but a large part of it was dedicated to Rousseau. Althusser refers again to Rousseau as an 'opponent from the interior' of the ideology of the Enlightenment.[38] The main difference with

---

32   Jalley 2014, p. 85.
33   Jalley 2014, p. 87.
34   Ibid.
35   Ibid.
36   Jalley 2014, p. 88.
37   Althusser 2006b, p. 255.
38   Althusser 2006b, p. 301.

traditional accounts of the origins of society lies in his reference to 'radical discontinuities'. The first discontinuity 'separating the state of pure nature from that of the youth of the world and the second separating the state of the youth of the world from the state of the contract' because of accidents, first natural accidents and then the accidental discovery of metallurgy.[39] For Althusser, this marks a sharp contrast to any philosophical teleology.

> The structure of genesis is transformed: instead of bringing a formal redistribution (as is the case with Hobbes and Locke) already given at the origin, instead of a single essence that is given, in Rousseau the discontinuities are leaps: the result is radically different than the origin, it is not the same essence at the beginning and at the end, and this in multiple times.[40]

For Rousseau, the state of pure nature is a 'state of radical solitude', thus making it impossible for Natural Law to 'reign in the state of nature'. Moreover, the 'state of war becomes problematic, in the sense that it does not exist in the origin but at the end of the state of nature [...] the state of war is a product'.[41] We are dealing with a real genesis in the sense of a 'real history of the development of human society'.[42] Consequently, 'Rousseau gives *the concept of his concept and the concept of the non-concept, namely the theory of the error of his predecessors*'.[43] This implies a radical critique of the attitude of philosophers to project onto the state of nature their own preoccupations, exemplified in Rousseau's famous assertion that '[philosophers] continuously speaking of need, greed, oppression, desires and pride transferred to the state of Nature ideas they had taken from society. They spoke of Savage Man and depicted Civil Man'.[44] For Althusser, the importance of Rousseau's critique lies in the following position: 'philosophers have always commented upon the present, that is, they have definitively *justified* it. They are nothing but the valets of existing power, of present society'.[45]

Rousseau's conception of human society as denaturalisation of human essence leads to the circle of alienation. Rousseau remains within this circle: 'he

---

39 Ibid.
40 Althusser 2006b, pp. 301–2.
41 Althusser 2006b, p. 302.
42 Althusser 2006b, pp. 302–3.
43 Althusser 2006b, p. 303.
44 Rousseau 1997, p. 132.
45 Althusser 2006b, p. 303.

affirms the necessity to go to the state of nature and the impossibility of arriving there by pure reflection'.[46] His solution is to resort to the 'heart', and at the same time to a 'conjectural reasoning [...] of conjectural hypotheses'.[47] Moreover, Althusser draws our attention to the importance of the imagery of circles in Rousseau. Questions of language and how it could be invented and at the same time presupposed, or of how man could have invented things in the state of pure nature, end in circularities that Rousseau attempts to solve by exterior accidents, by the infinity of time and by a constituent initiative.[48] For Althusser, this leads to a different conception of genesis, since it is a *'constituent, productive genesis'*, a *'dialectical genesis'*, and a *'genesis of differences'*; consequently for Rousseau 'every genesis is a transformation of a contingency into necessity', that 'every order of necessity is specific', and that 'every dialectic is irreversible'. Regarding the state of nature, Rousseau refers at the same time to the animality and non-animality of man. 'Pity, perfectibility and liberty' are aspects of the heart, which are already there but will serve man later, in the establishment of the contract, technical progress and natural law.[49] For Rousseau there is a fundamental 'human solitude of man',[50] since physical needs disperse people in contrast to social needs. This means that we are dealing with *encounters*. Again, the imagery of the encounter re-emerges exactly during the period when, as we know, Althusser started rethinking his very conception of social practices and 'structures' in terms of encounters.

> It is under the form of an accidental encounter that man encounters man, an instantaneous encounter, itself and without memory: immediacy of being reverses itself into nothing (cf. Hegel). Man has no need of the other man. All these figure the theoretical exigencies of Rousseau that resume in the refusal of natural sociability.[51]

---

46 Althusser 2006b, p. 304.
47 Althusser 2006b, p. 305. Here is how Rousseau refers to conjectures: 'I admit that since the events I have to describe could have occurred in several ways, I can choose between them only on the basis of conjectures, but not only do such conjectures become reasons when they are the most probable, that can be derived of the nature of things and the only means available to discover the truth, it also does not follow that the consequences I want to deduce from mine will therefore be conjectural, since, on the principles I have just established, no other system could be formed that would not give me the same results, and from which I could not draw the same conclusions' (Rousseau 1997, p. 159).
48 Althusser 2006b, p. 306.
49 Althusser 2006b, p. 310.
50 Ibid.
51 Althusser 2006b, p. 311.

For Althusser, the '*forest is a plain space*'[52] that offers the necessary empty space for people not to be constrained to encounter each other; it offers the necessary non-possibility of the 'human non-relation of the encounter', and therefore it offers the necessary non-teleology of the encounter:

> *The forest is an empty space.* It is the infinity of the void. It is what responds to the condition of nothing of society: in order for men not to be constrained to encounter each other, the forest has to be an infinite space. Condition of possibility of the human non-relation of the encounter. It is a space without a place, a Cartesian space.[53]

Althusser insists that in Rousseau there is a refusal of natural sociability,[54] and that human needs do not necessarily bring human beings together, in contrast to utilitarianism, and that his conception of the perfectibility of man is in contrast to the infinity of needs in Hobbes, since for Rousseau

> [m]an is not a *fuite en avant* of infinite desire as in Hobbes; it is a *flight by means of accidents*, despite him. Society, produced by exterior events, becomes the real infinite. The objective of Rousseau is to regulate this infinite, the false infinite of society.[55]

That leads to the importance of pity as a foundation of morality, marking, along with the theory of needs, Rousseau's critique of the thesis of natural sociability of man and of the utilitarian conception of society. The passage from the state of nature to the youth of the world is the result of accidents and catastrophes.[56] A change in space leads to the emergence of the huts and then of villages and the gradual disappearance of the forest. The disappearance of the forest means that human beings have to settle their problems between themselves and this leads to a state of war. Although it is the rich who start to think of the contract in terms of their interest, in the end the contract opens up a space well beyond its initial conception, the space of 'juridicity'.[57] The contract entails two moments: one of civil laws, conventions, and the right of property, and one of the establishment of government. Regarding the question of the theoretical

---

52 Ibid.
53 Ibid.
54 Althusser 2006b, pp. 311–12.
55 Althusser 2006b, p. 315.
56 On the state of youth of the world see Rousseau 1997, pp. 166–7.
57 Althusser 2006b, p. 320.

status of history in Rousseau, Althusser thinks that we are dealing with a 'problematization of fundamental concepts',[58] not only in the second discourse, but also in the *Social Contract*: 'the essence of the contract would not be in its purity but in its very impurity. The Social Contract would be the purity of a concept containing in itself its impurity, to think the death, the downfall that awaits it and that contemporary society realizes'.[59]

Of all the courses on Rousseau, Althusser chose to publish only the part of the 1965–66 course that dealt specifically with Rousseau's social contract. As the French editors of the full version of the course indicate,[60] it was somewhat separate from the rest of the course which mainly dealt with the *Second Discourse*. Althusser focuses on Book 1, Chapter 6 of the *Social Contract*,[61] treating the social contract as a philosophical object that can only be articulated through a 'chain of theoretical discrepancies [*décalages*]'.[62]

For Althusser, in Rousseau the contract emerges as a result of the obstacles posed by the 'generalized state of war'.[63] The obstacles are human and internal and not external, which leads Althusser to describe the state of war as a 'universal state of *alienation*'.[64]

> So long as there 'was still some forest left', men could partially escape the tyranny of social relations and the alienating effects of their constraint. When the 'end of the forest' came and the whole of the earth came under cultivation and was seized by its first occupiers or the strong men that supplanted them, then there was no longer any refuge for human liberty. Men were forced into the state of war, i.e. into alienation. That is how they were trapped in the very relations that their activity had produced.[65]

For Althusser, 'total alienation' is a nodal point.[66] This leads to the first discrepancy: there is a difference between the two recipient parties of the social

---

58   Althusser 2006b, p. 326.
59   Althusser 2006b, p. 329.
60   Althusser 2006b, p. 330.
61   Cf. Rousseau 1999, pp. 54–6.
62   Althusser 1972a, p. 114.
63   Althusser 1972a, p. 118.
64   Althusser 1972a, p. 121.
65   Althusser 1972a, p. 122.
66   Althusser 1972a, p. 127. '[Within the social contract] we shall find that it may be reduced to the following terms. *Each of us puts his person and all his power in common under the supreme direction of the general will; and we as a body receive each member as an indivisible part of the whole*' (Rousseau 1999, p. 55).

contract, the individual in a state of total alienation and the individual as part of the community, of the people. It is a discrepancy 'between the content of the juridical content of the contract, which Rousseau imports into his problematic to give a cover, and the actual content of the contract'.[67] For Althusser, this seemingly contradictory insertion of total alienation into the social contract is his way of dealing with the legacy of Hobbes:

> Rousseau's theoretical greatness is to have taken up the most frightening aspects of Hobbes: the state of war as a universal and perpetual state, the rejection of any transcendental solution and the 'contract' of total alienation, generator of absolute power as essence of any power. But Rousseau's defence against Hobbes is to transform total alienation in externality into total alienation in internality: the Third Recipient Party then becomes the Second, the Prince becomes the Sovereign, which is the community itself, to which free individuals totally alienate themselves without losing their liberty, since the Sovereign is simply the community of these same individuals.[68]

The second discrepancy refers to the difference between total alienation and an advantageous exchange. For Althusser, the answer is the insertion of interest into the whole schema of total alienation. Interest acts as the self-regulation and self-limitation of total alienation.

> This contact which is not an exchange thus paradoxically has an exchange as its effect. We now see why this total alienation can be both 'incompatible with man's nature' [...] and not contrary to it. In the Social Contract, man does not give himself for nothing. He gets back what he gives and more besides, for the reason that he only gives himself to himself. This must be understood in the strongest sense: he only gives himself to his own liberty.[69]

The third discrepancy has to do with the relation between particular interest and general interest, particular will and general will. These notions are for Althusser interrelated in the conceptual architecture of the *Social Contract*. Althusser stresses that Rousseau assigns primacy to general interest and the general will in the sense that '[e]ach particular interest contains in itself the

---

67 Althusser 1972a, p. 131.
68 Althusser 1972a, p. 136.
69 Althusser 1972a, p. 144.

general interest, each particular will the general will'.[70] However, a contradiction emerges because particular interest is both the essence of general interest and the main obstacle to it.[71] For Althusser there is a play of words here because particular interest as obstacle to the general will refers to the particular interest of social groups, not individuals. In reality, although Rousseau refers to the general interest as real, it appears as a myth in relation to its real 'double' the 'general' interests of social groups. This is a discrepancy 'introduced into Rousseau's conceptual system by the emergence of the following irreducible phenomenon: the existence of the interests of social groups'.[72] In this sense, it is a 'Discrepancy of the theory with respect to the real'.[73] However, this confrontation with the reality of social inequality, at the heart of the attempt of the social contract to resolve it, means that Rousseau in the end reaches again what was the result of the *Discourse on Inequality*:

> It is that in the object involved in the denegation of Discrepancy III (social groups, orders, classes, etc.), Rousseau has finally reached what he began with as a problem: the result of the *Discourse on Inequality*. [...] The true Social Contract, now a 'legitimate' one, thus finds at the end of the displacement of its concepts the very same realities whose existence and implacable logic had been described in the *Discourse on Inequality*.[74]

According to Althusser, Rousseau's answer to these theoretical difficulties was a resort to ideology in order to counter the effects of social inequality by means of education, social manners and morals. Although Rousseau realised the importance of economic inequality, for Althusser Rousseau's solution seems to remain with the circle of an insufficient regression to the economy:

> Rousseau invokes as a practical solution to his problem (how to suppress the existence of social classes) an *economic regression* towards one of the phenomena of the dissolution of the feudal mode of production: the independent petty producer, the urban or rural artisanate [...]. But to what

---

70   Althusser 1972a, p. 151.
71   This view of partial interests and groups as obstacle is evident in the *Social Contract*: 'It is therefore important, if the general will is to be properly ascertained, that there should be no partial society within the state' (Rousseau 1999, p. 67).
72   Althusser 1972a, p. 153.
73   Ibid.
74   Althusser 1972a, p. 154.

saint should one entrust oneself for the realization of this impossible regressive economic reform? There is nothing left but moral preaching, i.e. ideological action. We are in a circle.[75]

For Althusser, this discrepancy can explain Rousseau's turn to literature, in the form of a *transfer*, 'the transfer of the impossible theoretical solution into the alternative to theory, literature'.[76]

4 The 1972 Course

The 1972 course comes after a course on Machiavelli, so it begins by trying to show the differences between the worlds of Machiavelli and Rousseau. Althusser thinks, in a phrasing similar to that of *Machiavelli and Us*,[77] that Machiavelli had 'the task of *thinking radical beginning* [...] the conditions of possibility of this absolute beginning'.[78] Machiavelli had to think within the fact to accomplish; the 'natural law theorists think in the accomplished fact'.[79]

> Natural philosophy's object will be political power not as a task to be accomplished, not as a contingent relationship of being to nothingness, nor as event or beginning; rather, its object will be political power as existing, as existent [*étant*], and this object will be thought in the categories of the existent and the essence of the existent.[80]

This means that instead of a philosophy of beginnings (associated with a materialist practice and outlook) we have a philosophy *of origin*, which for Althusser is always linked to philosophical idealism.

> The origin belongs to a completely different mode [*mode*] of philosophical reference, a completely different world [*monde*] of philosophical reference. [...] It is *the manifestation of titles of legitimacy in the self-evidence of nature*.[81]

---

75   Althusser 1972a, p. 159.
76   Althusser 1972a, p. 160.
77   Althusser 1999a.
78   Althusser 2019, p. 31.
79   Althusser 2019, p. 32.
80   Althusser 2019, p. 33.
81   Althusser 2019, pp. 33–4.

Althusser embarks upon a certain symptomatic reading of Rousseau, which would bring forward repressed or forgotten aspects of Rousseau's conceptual framework.

> To put it differently, there exist words in Rousseau, and perhaps concepts and arguments as well, which were not registered by philosophy in its history when philosophy drew up the accounts of its history or settled its accounts with its own history. The philosophy that has inscribed Rousseau in its history for one or another merit has drawn up its accounts, and its tallies are accurate – but with the figures it has registered. The drawback, or the boon, is that a few figures, a few words, a few concepts have been left out of account, have been neglected.[82]

For Althusser, Rousseau's resemblance to philosophers like Hobbes and Locke hides 'a difference [...] that goes much deeper: *a difference in problematic and object*'.[83] Rousseau was the first to '*think the concept of the origin in its own right*'.[84] Althusser pays particular attention to the fact that Rousseau at the same time speaks about the need to go back to the state of nature and about the fact that no previous philosopher has achieved it, since they all remained subject to their errors. This error was the fact that they all projected onto the state of nature the social reality of their respective era, 'a retrospective projection of the civil state (the present state of civil man, man as formed by society and history) onto the state of nature and natural man, both supposed to exist before history'.[85] For Althusser this is a critique both of the attempt to justify contemporary societies, but also of 'a critique of the utopianism that hopes to justify the future of the society it desires by projecting it onto the origins, by grounding it in the origins'.[86]

Althusser tends to treat Rousseau as a critic of the ideology of the Enlightenment. Moreover, in his attempt to offer a critique of the '*false origin*', Rousseau in fact offers a 'critique of the concept of the origin'.[87] Althusser reads Rousseau's critique of the previous philosophers as a critique that brings forward the limit of their thinking, that is, the fact that they reproduced in their projections the conditions of the societies of their time; this is the circle within which they remain.

---

82   Althusser 2019, p. 35.
83   Althusser 2019, p. 38.
84   Althusser 2019, p. 39.
85   Althusser 2019, p. 43.
86   Althusser 2019, p. 44.
87   Althusser 2019, p. 45.

> The theorists' circle is not in their political will; rather, it is at the very basis of their political consciousness and in their theoretical consciousness, merely the realization and repetition of a completely different circle, which simultaneously dominates politics as well as its theoretical justification: the circle of man's and present-day society's social denaturation and social alienation.[88]

It is in light of this reading that Althusser treats Rousseau's references to the disappearance of nature and the state of nature. It is a forgetting of nature as the result of a process of alienation: '*nature is alienated,* [...] *it no longer exists except in the other-than-itself*, in its contrary, the social passions, and even in reason subject to the social passions'.[89] Rousseau, in contrast to the other philosophers, does not project reason in the state of nature: 'reason is a product of human history'.[90] The human sciences are part of this loss of the state of nature exactly because they are a product of reason: 'Science [...] has been caught up, from its birth, in the forgetting that constituted it'.[91] Consequently, sciences are part of the process of denaturation and alienation, and for Althusser this offers a 'general theory of the human sciences' political determination',[92] and a theory of philosophy as mystification.

> [P]hilosophy intervenes as a socially necessary mystification of thought by way of the origin, [...] in order to provide the established order or projects of social reform with illusory, yet socially necessary, credentials.[93]

In contrast, the challenge for Rousseau is to think of origin in a radically different way:

> It is, then, necessary to think a completely different origin and gain access to it by completely different means. A completely different origin: that is, a state of nature, since it is necessary to go back to the state of nature, but one which cannot have, as its contents, a projection of the present social state, and which will not instate the result of the origin as the origin of the origin.[94]

---

88   Althusser 2019, p. 46.
89   Althusser 2019, p. 48.
90   Althusser 2019, p. 49.
91   Althusser 2019, p. 50.
92   Althusser 2019, p. 52.
93   Ibid.
94   Althusser 2019, p. 54.

For Althusser, Rousseau introduces a highly original concept that separates him from the other theorists of natural law: the 'concept *of the pure state of nature*'.[95] Moreover, he introduces another concept in order to think this access to the state of pure nature, and this is the *heart*, as opposed to reason which is linked to the processes of denaturation and alienation. However, since in Rousseau's conception 'the heart thinks', we are not dealing with a radical change of philosophising since we are still within a particular conception of subjectivity according to which 'nature is transparency in its self-evidence'.[96] For Althusser, these conceptual displacements 'from reason to the heart and from light to the voice'[97] are determined by concepts and do not correspond to external realities: 'they take their philosophical meaning not from philosophical objects, but from their philosophical intervention. [...] The heart and the voice [...] are the philosophical mark of a philosophical demarcation [...] from every existing construction of reason, from the idealism of reason'.[98] This presence of the heart and the voice attempts to exit the circle of denaturation '*by way of the inside*'[99] and at the same time it 'has the effect of constituting a new philosophical object [...] the true origin, [...] the pure state of nature'.[100]

The singularity of the pure state of nature is that without the intervention of cosmic accidents it would have remained unchanged. The heart represents the 'purity of the concept' of origin.[101] This has also to do with the fact that the pure state has completely disappeared and even the various forms of savagery that the eighteenth century used as traces of the state of nature are in fact already a 'form of denaturation'.[102] In this sense, the non-observability of the state of nature implies that only the heart can pose its existence:

> This loss [of the state of nature] would in that case be not an empirical loss, but a de jure loss: since the state of nature can only be lost, can exist only in the form of loss, of present non-existence, its existence could be posited only in the form of a de jure non-observability; it could,

---

95 Althusser 2019, p. 55. For an example of the use of the pure state of nature in Rousseau see the following phrase: 'Let us for a moment cross the immense distance that must have separated the pure state of Nature from the need of languages' (Rousseau 1997, p. 147).
96 Althusser 2019, p. 57.
97 Althusser 2019, p. 58.
98 Althusser 2019, pp. 58–9.
99 Althusser 2019, p. 59.
100 Althusser 2019, p. 60.
101 Althusser 2019, p. 66.
102 Ibid.

that is, be posited only by the heart. We might add that the heart ultimately proves the attributes of the state of pure nature, the contents of this state.[103]

In contrast, the history of denaturation can be based upon observable facts and conjectures, the use of reason. That is why the heart in Rousseau is not just a faculty. Rather it 'is a philosophical power, the power that resolves the antinomies of reason and of society, the power of the true origin'.[104] For Althusser, this brings forward a radically different conception of origin:

> To the circle of an originary specularity – which is simply a justification of accomplished fact and the form par excellence of the philosophy of the accomplished fact, of the philosophy that thinks in the accomplished fact – Rousseau thus opposes another, pure form of origin, one not compromised in its result, one so absolutely separate from its own result that we may even wonder whether it has a result that we can call *its* result. Rousseau opposes an origin as a different world, separated from our world by something like a distance or an *abyss* [*abîme*], an insurmountable distance: an origin whose purity and separation are reflected, or would be reflected, precisely, in this abyss.[105]

For Althusser, Rousseau at the same times insists on the importance of origin in order to understand what follows, namely its loss, and on the fact that we cannot understand contemporary society, government, inequality by reference to the origin. This brings forward the importance of the void created by this 'radical separation of the pure and the impure'.[106] Althusser recapitulates the difference between the notion of the origin in Rousseau and his predecessors. In them 'it is not a real genesis, […] it is not an historical genesis […] [it is] a philosophical – juridical justification of the established order'.[107] In contrast, Rousseau begins with the state of pure nature, which could be prolonged perpetually, were it not for cosmic accidents. Men were dispersed into the vast forest, but were subsequently forced to come together. This leads to a second stage of the state of nature, which includes the development of human faculties as a process of denaturation, the emergence of social relations, the invention

---

103   Althusser 2019, p. 67.
104   Althusser 2019, p. 69.
105   Althusser 2019, p. 70.
106   Althusser 2019, p. 71.
107   Althusser 2019, p. 74.

of language, what is designated as the 'youth of the world'. The second big accident – 'something which is not precipitated by previous developments, and which changes everything'[108] – was the invention of metallurgy that leads to the state of war, making necessary the intervention of the social contract. What is important for Althusser is the absence of any teleology, the absence of any essential continuity between the pure state of nature and the developments that lead to the social contract; rather it is a process based upon discontinuity.

> This genesis, however, will be a discontinuous genesis, and this genesis will be a genesis whose cause is not contained in the state of pure nature. More exactly, it will be a genesis of which the state of pure nature, that is, the state of origin, is not the beginning. In other words, things begin [*ça commence*] after the origin.[109]

In the same anti-teleological perspective, the effect of the social contract is not 'to redistribute forces deriving from natural law', but a 'constitution of a radically new reality'.[110] Consequently, the 'constituent discontinuity of the social contract in Rousseau is intelligible as denaturation only if it is a denaturation of the existing denaturation [...] alienation of the existing alienation, [...] negation of the existing negation'.[111] If the state of pure nature represents the 'radical absence [*néant*] of society, the radical absence of social relations, the radical absence of sociability',[112] if it means that no encounter can last, no encounter can repeat itself, then the forest in the *Second Discourse* is not a object, or an image of man's solitude in the state of pure nature; it is a concept:

> *The forest is the truth of the state of nature*, the concept of the state of pure nature, the condition for realizing the solitude and the condition for realizing the non-society that define man. It is a nourishing, protective forest, full because it offers men all they need, instantaneously, immediately, without labour; yet it is simultaneously empty – above all empty, because it is a space without places. It is the infinite, empty space of dispersion and the simple encounter with no morrow. The forest is a space without place, a space without *topos*. This space of the forest is at once

---

108 Althusser 2019, p. 77.
109 Althusser 2019, p. 80.
110 Ibid.
111 Althusser 2019, p. 81.
112 Althusser 2019, p. 84.

always present, in the form of nourishment and refuge, and always absent. It is the realization of the existence of the state of pure nature.[113]

Here the forest emerges as the void *par excellence*, as the 'zero-degree' of social relations, as the absence of any teleology, and forms part of an imagery of the void that for Althusser increasingly becomes the necessary space for encounters conceived in the sense of a non prefigured *clinamen*, a chance deviation that may lead to the emergence of forms and social relations.

However, this conception of the good origin that leads to no result requires solving the problem regarding in which sense it is an origin of something. Althusser again returns to Rousseau's conception of the qualities that man possesses even in the state of nature: self-love, freedom, pity and perfectibility.[114] These qualities in the state of nature cannot be practiced. This is the result of the fact that the 'inner essence of the state of pure nature is the inability to develop on its own' / it is 'incapable of producing any result'.[115] The state of pure nature lacks 'an internal logic of self-movement or self-development'.[116] This leads to the appearance of new concepts, 'the concept of the accident, the concept of contingency, the concept of event'.[117] Above all, the importance of physical nature as a constraint re-emerges, in the form of a 'catastrophic nature'[118] that leads to the first accidents. The changes involve a transformation of the nature of space, with the emergence of fixed places for men to live. For some time, there is still the forest, but when the forest no longer exists, this marks the passage to the state of war.

For Althusser, this process of denaturation means that the initial human qualities are in the end also transformed, and again we have the drawing of a line of demarcation from any teleological reading: Denaturation 'is the separation of the origin from itself; it is the non-identity of identity; it is the developed contradiction from the origin as the other of its result in the result, as the other of the origin'.[119] This conception of the process of denaturation means for Althusser that Rousseau can be considered 'the first theorist to have thought history in the category of the negation of the negation, the first to have thought the historical process as a process of antagonistic development in which nature

---

113 Althusser 2019, p. 85.
114 Cf. Althusser 2019, p. 87.
115 Althusser 2019, p. 89.
116 Althusser 2019, p. 90.
117 Althusser 2019, p. 91.
118 Althusser 2019, p. 92.
119 Althusser 2019, pp. 94–5.

is negated, the negation is negated and originary nature is re-established upon new foundations'.[120] However, we are not dealing simply with a process of internal dialectical development:

> The radical interiority presupposed by the process of the negation of the negation, or denaturation of denaturation, is contested in Rousseau himself by the following idea: one must posit an exteriority in order to think the process of interiority. An idea of exteriority is required to make the process of pure interiority possible.[121]

What form does this non-dialectic of exteriority take in the work of Rousseau? According to Althusser, it takes three forms of 'beginnings without origin'.[122] First, we have the accidents that mark the 'absence of an internal dialectic of development'.[123] Then we have the emergences that occur within what Rousseau describes as circles, such as languages or inventions. Finally, there is the 'creative nature of time'.[124] Moreover, there is a certain relation between contingency and necessity; more precisely, contingency is what necessity is based upon: 'Contingency is transformed into necessity, but the necessity created by a new contingency is not the same as the old one. There are differences in degree and level between the necessities'.[125] In the same sense, there are different laws of development in every phase of historical development. In light of these, the social contract, as an answer to historical contradictions, is not just a contract; it is 'a veritable change of regime, a veritable constitution'.[126] Since the contract is itself the outcome of a '*human* contingency',[127] it is a risk and a 'leap in the void [...] so much so that we can say that the whole edifice of the social contract is suspended over an abyss'.[128]

This is how Althusser attempts to read the conception of the state of pure nature in Rousseau in the third course. He notes that the liberty and equality of human beings in the state of nature is conditioned upon the immediate relation of human beings to nature and the absence of any relations between human beings. Only after the cosmic accidents do human beings exit the circle

---

120   Althusser 2019, p. 96.
121   Althusser 2019, p. 97.
122   Ibid.
123   Ibid.
124   Althusser 2019, p. 98.
125   Althusser 2019, p. 99.
126   Althusser 2019, p. 100.
127   Althusser 2019, p. 101.
128   Ibid.

of the state of nature. During the state of nature, a certain animality of human beings prevails.[129] Human beings are animals in the sense that they are also machines, whose material needs have to be satisfied. However, human beings, according to this reading of Rousseau by Althusser, are special animals in the sense of having multiple instincts, which means that they also have multiple ways to answer their needs. These create the condition of the 'physical independence' of man in the state of nature. Within this context the concept of the forest becomes crucial for man,

> as a form of existence of nature necessitated by Rousseau's theoretical requirements in order to satisfy – a form of existence, a way nature has to be made – in order to satisfy, everywhere and at the same time, man's two basic physical needs, hunger and sleep.[130]

Althusser insists that in Rousseau there is a 'rejection of the theory of man's natural sociability'.[131] This is a refusal of any theory of natural sociability, both in the sense of a sociability aiming at the satisfaction of need or a sociability based upon the need for friendship. For Rousseau, 'man does not naturally need man'.[132] Rather, for Rousseau, needs tend to 'disperse rather than assembling them'.[133] The only relation possible between human beings in the state of nature is *pity*, a 'negative relation of compassion'.[134] This absence of natural sociability means that in the state of nature, human beings have 'no moral relationships'.[135] The solitude of man in the state of nature 'is not founded on a negative de jure condition alone; it is also founded on a positive de facto condition'.[136] Althusser then moves to the status of sexual relation in Rousseau, which takes the form of an encounter between a man and a woman, who 'they do not know what has happened, for one thing and, for another, are incapable of recognizing each other. Neither knows who the other is and they cannot find each other again'.[137] For Althusser this concept of the encounter has a broader significance in Rousseau, it the category under which Rousseau thinks the state of nature.

---

129   'I see an animal' – this is how Rousseau refers to man in the pure state of nature (Rousseau 1997, p. 134).
130   Althusser 2019, pp. 116–17.
131   Althusser 2019, p. 118.
132   Althusser 2019, p. 120.
133   Althusser 2019, p. 121.
134   Althusser 2019, p. 122.
135   Althusser 2019, p. 123.
136   Althusser 2019, p. 124.
137   Althusser 2019, p. 127.

> This category of the *encounter*, which we have just seen emerging in connection with sexuality – the encounter as chance event without duration or sequel, as instantaneous chance event – is the category in which Rousseau thinks, in general, everything that can transpire between men in the pure state of nature. Men live dispersed, they live in solitude, but it sometimes happens that they encounter each other by chance, and it is by chance by definition, it is by definition that it does not last, it is by definition that it never has consequences, that it has no sequel.[138]

This is one of the most impressive emergences of the concept of the encounter in the work of Althusser, and one of the clearest indications that Rousseau's conception of the pure state of nature and of the chance encounters between men is one of Althusser's references in the entire imagery of the materialism of the encounter. In a way, the state of pure nature is like the pre-Cosmos situation, the situation of the rain of atoms and the chance encounters that do not last, are not lasting encounters. This conception of non-lasting, chance encounters becomes the basis for a broader anti-teleological and anti-metaphysical conception of reality:

> The encounter is the punctual event that possesses this property of effacing itself, of leaving no trace, of leaving no trace behind, surging up out of nothingness to return to nothingness, with neither origin nor result.[139]

However, this requires certain conditions: First, man must 'be an animal who realizes the concept of generic animality'; second, 'nature must stand in immediate proximity to man'.[140] Herein lies the importance of the forest. However, for Althusser, the space of the forest in Rousseau has a broader significance; it is the space of non-socialisation, of encounters that do not last, because they do not become relations. The forest

> is the space of men's dispersion, an infinite space, a space such that it prevents all encounters from producing the least tie. The forest is the space of non-recognition, of non-identification, of non-identity.
>
> Positively, therefore, the forest is defined as the immediate object of man's physical need; negatively, it is defined as the form of space that allows men to avoid being forced into society. It is a space without place

---

138 Althusser 2019, p. 128.
139 Althusser 2019, p. 130.
140 Ibid.

> in which men are subject to divagation, in which they do not run the risk of binding themselves to other men because they cannot bind themselves to space. The universality of the fullness of the object and of the void of the encounter and place: that is what the forest is.[141]

However, all these have consequences for the very notion of origin, since there is a radical separation between origin and what follows. For Rousseau it is an origin because something followed, even though it did not emanate directly from this origin. In light of the above, we can think about the faculties of man in the state of pure nature: animality, pity, freedom, perfectibility. Especially, pity 'is the relation of non-relation; it is the community of abstention in suffering. Hence it is inactive or even non-existent in the state of nature'.[142]

Moreover, freedom 'as intellectual power or intellectual awareness [...] is inactive and non-existent in the state of nature'. At the same time, 'perfectibility, the general principle of the possibility, of the virtuality, of the development of all the human faculties [...] is by definition inactive in the state of nature'.[143] Consequently, only animality is actually active in the state of nature. The other faculties 'attributes of the origin that are present by their attribution and absent by their existence'.[144] This is how the origin is separated by what follows and for Althusser this means that Rousseau can be spared the accusation that he projected in the state of nature social qualities from a later phase. In fact, pity and liberty only intervene in the social contract: 'It is in the contract – hence at the end of the risky process constituted by the process of socialization – that freedom and pity intervene as origin'.[145] This intervention of the origin in reality comes for Althusser under the form of a *'reprise*, that is, the form of a new beginning of a beginning; but, nota bene, of a beginning that has never taken place'.[146] Consequently, for Althusser there are three forms of origin in Rousseau: origin as separation; origin as virtuality; and origin as reprise.

> The repetition of an event that has never taken place, the new beginning of a beginning that has never taken place, since all that was non-existent in the origin. This is the third meaning of the origin: reprise.[147]

---

141 Althusser 2019, pp. 130–1.
142 Althusser 2019, p. 135.
143 Ibid.
144 Ibid.
145 Althusser 2019, p. 136.
146 Althusser 2019, p. 137.
147 Ibid.

For Althusser, there is also another way of describing origin as separation, virtuality and reprise: the notion of *loss*.

> If the origin has never taken place, it is because it is lost. If it is reprised, if it is the repetition of something definite that has never taken place, it is because it is lost. If it repeats that which has not taken place, it is because it repeats what is.[148]

For Althusser we can say that there are two contracts in Rousseau: one that is the closure of the *Discourse on Inequality* and another which is the subject of the *Social Contract*. In the *Second Discourse* it is the cunning of the rich that leads to the instauration of laws and political power leading to despotism and the state of war. This is 'how the reprise of the origin is lost, to be reprised again and lost again, without end'.[149] In the *Social Contract*, Althusser argues that behind the dialectic of alienation there is 'another dialectic [...] the dialectic of the death that stalks every political body and precipitates it in despotism – hence the same loss'.[150]

---

148 Althusser 2019, pp. 137–8.
149 Althusser 2019, p. 138. For Rousseau, in the *Discourse on Inequality* the rich first realise the need to put an end to the state of war: 'The rich, above all, must soon have sensed how disadvantageous to them was a perpetual war of which they alone bore the full cost, and in which everyone risked his life while only some also risked goods' (Rousseau 1997, p. 172). Consequently they devised the social contract as a means to defend cunningly their interests. 'Lacking valid reasons to justify and sufficient strength to defend himself; easily crushing an individual but easily crushed by troops of bandits; alone against all, and unable, because of their mutual jealousies, to unite with his equals against enemies united by the common hope of plunder, the rich under the pressure of necessity, at last conceived the most well considered project ever to enter the human mind, to use even his attacker's forces in his favour, to make his adversaries his defenders, to instil in them other maxims, and to give them different institutions, as favourable to himself, as Natural Right was contrary to him' (Rousseau 1997, pp. 172–3). However, the continuous existence of inequality leads to 'Despotism, gradually rearing his hideous head' (Rousseau 1997, p. 185).
150 Ibid. Cf. the following passage from the *Social Contract*, referring to the death of the body politic: 'The political body, like the human, begins to die as soon as it is born, and carries within it the causes of its own destruction. But the one and the other can be more or less robustly constituted, so as to be preserved for a longer or shorter time. Man's constitution is a product of nature; the state's is the result of artifice. It is not within men's power to extend their lives, but they are able to extend the life of the state for the longest time possible by endowing it with the best constitution that it can have. The best constituted state will come to its end, but later than others, provided that no unforeseen accident destroys it prematurely' (Rousseau 1999, p. 121).

For Althusser, this means a particular relation to politics that is different from all other philosophers of natural law. Making a comparison to Machiavelli, whom he had discussed earlier that academic year, as a thinker of the *fact to accomplish*, he suggests that Rousseau is also a thinker of the fact to accomplish:

> That is, he does not think this fact to be accomplished as a practical act to be accomplished, with certain essential political premises. Rather, he thinks it as a moralist and a philosopher who tries to adjust theoretical notions in an attempt to take the measure of a possible essence.[151]

For Althusser, all these attest to a certain utopianism in the politics of Rousseau, albeit a critical utopianism regarding the fact to accomplish, based upon 'an extraordinarily acute awareness of its necessity and its impossibility, that is, of its precariousness'.[152] What distinguishes Rousseau from other utopian thinkers is this critique of utopia within the very thinking of utopia, a constant critical self-conscience: 'It is the criticism brought to bear on the thought of utopia itself at the very moment in which the thought of utopia is thought'.[153]

It is obvious that in the 1972 course we are not just dealing with a close yet idiosyncratic reading of Rousseau's *Second Discourse*. In fact, we see Althusser in one of his most important attempts to think the importance of the notion of the encounter and its implications for the materialism of the encounter. The analysis of the state of pure nature as an open terrain of non-lasting encounters, the very conception of human relations as encounters that may or may not last, the imagery of the forest – and here it is important to keep in mind Yves Varga's observation that the forest is presented here as being much more important in comparison to the 1966 course[154] – as the open space, the necessary void, for these encounters. Moreover, we have to stress the importance of his attempt towards a non-teleological reading of the notion of the origin. This is important, because for Althusser, the notion of the origin increasingly becomes the defining feature of metaphysical thinking, attested also in other manuscripts, such as *Philosophy for Non-Philosophers*.[155] The very notion of origin is presented as epitomising the teleological and idealist conception of history, the very conception of history as having an orientation and consequently a *telos*. Moreover,

---

[151] Althusser 2019, p. 139.
[152] Althusser 2019, p. 140.
[153] Ibid.
[154] Vargas 2013.
[155] Althusser 2017a.

Althusser's reading of Rousseau's state of pure nature as an origin that is separated by whatever follows offers an opportunity to think the new emphasis on the encounter and more generally a more aleatory conception of social reality. For this conception it is important not only to view social relations as encounters – and not as essential connections – but also to present the very possibility of non-lasting encounters, of encounters that do not create social relations and social forms. In this sense, the forest, as the space that is not place, the space that represents the void that is necessary for this interplay of encounters, is one of the most forceful images that Althusser finds in order to think this empty space of – in the last instance – political practice. It does not matter that the forest is in reality full, of trees, of animals, of human beings. It is empty and void in the same sense that the Italian conjuncture for Machiavelli was empty, namely it was lacking the constitutive political intervention (or the constitutive accident) that would initiate a sequence of new encounters, of the encounters that could last and consequently of new social and political configurations.

This reading, which we can see in its fullest form in the 1972 course, leads to the inclusion of Rousseau in the genealogy of the materialism of the encounter in the post-1982 texts. This is most evident in the way he presents the imagery of the forest as void in the *Underground Current of the Materialism of the Encounter*:

> The forest is the equivalent of the Epicurean void in which the parallel rain of the atoms falls: it is a pseudo-Brownian void in which individuals cross each other's paths, that is to say, do not meet, except in brief conjunctions that do not last. In this way, Rousseau seeks to represent, at a very high price (the absence of children), a radical absence [*néant*] of society prior to all society; and – condition of possibility for all society – the radical absence of society that constitutes the essence of any possible society.[156]

That is why in this void space of non-encounters or of brief encounters, the possibility of lasting encounters has to be forced upon us by cosmic accidents and in general by constrains.

> The state of encounter has to be imposed on people; the infinity of the forest, as a condition of possibility for the non-encounter, has to be reduced to the finite by external causes; natural catastrophes have to

---

156   Althusser 2006a, p. 184.

divide it up into confined spaces, for example islands, where men are forced to have encounters, and forced to have encounters that last: forced by a force superior to them.[157]

Moreover, for Althusser this can account for the importance of the constant threat of the abyss in the theory of the Social Contract, the threat of an encounter that fails and there is a relapse into the state of pure of nature, namely a relapse into social and political death.

> This determines the true meaning of the Social Contract, which is concluded and persists only under the constant threat of the abyss (Rousseau himself uses this word [abîme] in the *Confessions*) represented by a relapse [re-chute] into the state of nature, an organism haunted by the inner death that it must exorcize: in sum, an encounter that has taken form and become necessary, but against the background of the aleatory of the non-encounter and its forms, into which the contract can fall back at any moment.[158]

It is this reading of Rousseau as a theorist of the encounter and the non-encounter that leads Althusser to insist that it is in this conception of the social contract that we can find a conception not only of the contingency of necessity but also of the necessity of the contingency, of the constitutive role of the absence of any teleology in the historical process, as the only means to think of concrete conjunctures in their singularity.

> The most profound thing in Rousseau is doubtless disclosed and covered back up [decouvert et recouvert] here, in this vision of any possible theory of history, which thinks the contingency of necessity as an effect of the necessity of contingency, an unsettling pair of concepts that must nevertheless be taken into account.[159]

The 1972 course marked a very important turning point in the evolution of the thinking of a potential materialism of the encounter. That is why, as we have shown, its main premises and conclusions are practically repeated in the post-1982 manuscripts. Along with *Machiavelli and Us*, *Philosophy for Non-Philosophers*, and *How to be a Marxist in Philosophy*, it is one of the most import-

---

157 Althusser 2006a, p. 185.
158 Althusser 2006a, p. 186.
159 Althusser 2006a, p. 187.

ant texts unpublished during his lifetime that attest to the elaboration of most elements of the whole conception of a materialism of the encounter. We are now in a much better position to assess the fact that in reality the materialism of the encounter or the whole imagery of an aleatory materialism does not constitute a philosophical *Kehre* as Antonio Negri famously suggested, but is in fact part of a broader theoretical research programme that covers the whole period of his post-1966 work, especially in the 1970s, and is contemporaneous with his whole attempt in the second half of the 1970s to provide a left-wing critique of the crisis of the communist movement.

5   A Comparison between the Courses

The courses on Rousseau offer a way to see the evolution of Louis Althusser's thinking and some of his turning points. In the 1955–56 and 1958–59 courses, Althusser reads Rousseau as a critic of the tradition of Natural Law – a position he repeats in all courses – and as a precursor of a rather classical historical materialist position, in the sense of history as a material process, based upon material constraints that lead to historical change and development. Teleology or 'materialist' metaphysics are absent but, at the same time, there are obvious references to the possibility of historical causality and in general social and economic determination of the historical process in sharp contrast to any idealised conception of human nature. In this conception, Rousseau is presented as a thinker of history as a dialectical development of material conditions and constraints, of 'history as a process', based upon an internal material logic or dialectic, 'immanent necessity'.[160] In this sense, it is a reading in a long Marxist tradition that sought to 'find Marx in Rousseau'.[161]

In the 1965–66 course we can see two complementary tendencies at work that mark that transitory phase in Althusser's work. On the one hand, the whole reading of the *Social Contract* seems like an application of a variation of symptomatic reading of Rousseau's text in the sense of bringing forward the discrepancies that traverse the text in order to find its underlying tensions and dynamics in order again to find elements of a historical materialist conception and a critique of the idealism of the Natural Law tradition. On the other hand, we have the emergence of Althusser's preoccupation with the notion of the encounter and the imagery of the void, which is also part of his broader theor-

---

160   Althusser 2006a, p. 111.
161   Vargas 2013, p. 34.

etical self-criticism, after the moment of 'High Althusserianism' of the 1960–65 texts, an evolution that led to the full emergence of the materialism of the encounter by 1972 and a series of important manuscripts such as *Machiavelli and Us* and the 1972 course on Rousseau.[162]

In contrast, in the 1972 course we have the full employment of the conceptual framework of the materialism of the encounter, along with all the imagery of the void, the space of encounter and non-encounter, exemplified in the forest, and the radical absence of any teleology. This is why the 1972 course is also an attempt to ground in the reading of Rousseau Althusser's thesis that one of the main forms that idealism takes is a thinking of the origins. In contrast, Althusser attempts, by means of his reading of Rousseau's references to the state of pure nature, a theory of the inexistence of the origin, of a radical anti-teleology. That is why now the emphasis is not simply upon accidents and encounters but also upon non-encounters and in general what he later defined as the necessity of contingency.

Althusser's confrontation with the work of Rousseau was always an important aspect of his theoretical endeavour. In a way, not only was Rousseau, along with Montesquieu, Spinoza, and Machiavelli, a constant theoretical interlocutor, but he was also a terrain upon which Althusser experimented with his evolving conceptions of historical materialism until the full emergence of the materialism of the encounter. The fact that we now have full access to his major courses on Rousseau, along with the already known passages on Rousseau in the post-1982 texts, offers us an important insight into the work of Althusser and his confrontation with the question of a non-teleological and non-metaphysical materialism. At the same time, these texts are important contributions to the literature on Rousseau offering an idiosyncratic yet not arbitrary reading of an important moment and at the same time exception in the history of philosophy.

---

162 On the period of 1966–72 as one of elaboration upon the new theme of the materialism of the encounter, see Goshgarian 2013.

CHAPTER 7

From the 'Hidden God' to the Materialism of the Encounter: Althusser on Pascal

Blaise Pascal seems to be an important reference for Althusser, beginning from his days of captivity during WWII. A highly original figure in the evolution of French Philosophy, especially in his combination of an idiosyncratic rationalism with a theological turn based upon the absence of any guarantees or certainties regarding the grounds for belief, Pascal was to be a constant interlocutor of Althusser. Any attempt to retrace the emergence of Althusser's anti-teleological stance and his philosophical transition towards what was to be termed the materialism of the encounter must necessarily include a reading of his confrontation with Pascal.

1   Althusser in Captivity and Pascal

In October 1943, a few days after resuming writing his diary of captivity in a German war camp, following a period of silence seemingly caused by a personal crisis and a bout of depression, Louis Althusser quotes a phrase by Pascal, from the fragment of the *Pensées* entitled 'The Mystery of Jesus'. The phrase quoted, supposedly spoken or thought by Jesus himself during his agony at Gethsemane, is the following: 'My concern is for your conversion; do not be afraid, and pray with confidence as though for me'.[1]

The entire passage offers an image of Jesus ready to be 'in agony until the end of the world',[2] sleepless and in uncertainty in order to redeem us. We can only add our wounds to his: 'There is no link between me and God or Jesus Christ the righteous. But he was made sin for me. [...] I must add my wounds to his and join myself to him and he will save me in saving himself'.[3] Yann Moulier-Boutang has suggested that Althusser's resuming of writing in his journal followed a period during which he came close to losing his faith, hence the period

---

1 Pascal 1966, p. 314 (L919/B553). In quoting from the *Pensées*, I indicate the passages in both the Lafuma (L) and Brunschvicg (B) numbering.
2 Pascal 1966, p. 313 (L919/B553).
3 Pascal 1966, p. 315 (L919/B553).

of silence in the journal.[4] Moreover, Althusser's new interest in Pascal, in 1943, coincides with a period with many references to solitude and silence, a desire to be 'free of words',[5] an interest in Proust, and a confrontation with subjectivity:

> 'Something' that comes out as the support of silence, that is silence itself; something that could be the support of nothing, could be this nothing itself. I will call it, because it is necessary, speaking with words, that one more word takes place at the end of the phrase, I will call it: subject.[6]

For young Althusser, Pascal was a constant reference in his confrontation with the agony of trying to believe. On Christmas 1943, he writes: 'The wait, the wait ... this is how I go, repeating in order to believe in it this phrase from Pascal "My concern is for your conversion ..." How much more time'.[7]

In April 1944, Althusser writes about an 'echo of Pascal's wager'.[8] Pascal's fragment on the wager[9] is not simply an exercise in probabilities theory, and how a potential wager on the existence of God can secure a greater return. For Pascal, in the end, there is no certainty, no sure bet; the only way to deal with uncertainty is to engage in the very rituals of religious belief, in the collective practice of belief, even if this makes someone closer to an animal, something that has to be accepted.

> You want to find faith and you do not know the road. You want to be cured of unbelief and you ask for the remedy: learn from those who were once bound like you and who now wager all they have. These are people who know the road you wish to follow, who have been cured of the affliction of which you wish to be cured: follow the way by which they began. They behaved just as if they did believe, taking holy water, having masses said, and so on. That will make you believe quite naturally, and will make you more docile [*cela vous fera croire et vous abêtira*].[10]

---

4   Moulier-Boutang 1992, Volume 1, pp. 337–41.
5   Althusser 1992b, p. 135.
6   Althusser 1992b, pp. 139–40.
7   Althusser 1992b, p. 140.
8   Althusser 1992b, p. 159.
9   Pascal 1966, pp. 149–53 (L418/B233).
10 Pascal 1966, p. 152 (L418/B233). *Abêtira* means, literally, turn you into a beast [*bête*]. According to Pierre Macherey, 'to turn into animal [*s'abêtir*] means to adopt, in his own plain consent and with awareness of the cause, pure mechanical behaviors, in which the spirit does not have to engage itself, namely what animals who act instinctively do naturally [...] This is the manner of behavior of those that act as if they believe, and who, unable

Considering Althusser's own crisis of faith during his captivity, the interest in Pascal's apologetics is revealing. Pascal did not start as a believer, and turned to religion and Jansenist theology at a later stage. Pascal's apologetics of religion reflect Althusser's own confrontation with the uncertainties of belief. To the young Althusser's eyes, the Pascalian wager seemed like a call to follow the true Life of the Church, in the sense of a conviction that faith-as-test is the only proof of faith.[11] It is interesting to see some of the passages he quotes. One is from L960/B921, where Pascal, in answering accusations of heresy, chooses a position of both humility and defiance: 'I do not deserve to defend religion, but you do not deserve to defend error'.[12] The second (L743/B859) refers to the pleasure of being 'on a boat battered by storms when one is certain of not perishing' since '[t]he persecutions buffeting the Church are like this';[13] accompanied by the insistence that the Church is in a 'fine state', 'when it has no support but God',[14] an obvious reference to faith, and Grace, being its true power. These are followed by Pascal's reference to the truth co-existing, unnoticed, among simple opinion: 'Just as Jesus remained unknown among men, so the truth remains among popular opinions with no outward differences'.[15] Althusser also quotes Pascal's insistence that 'I only believe histories whose witnesses are ready to be put to death'.[16] He refers to Pascal's position that 'Jesus wants his witness to be nothing',[17] and adds Pascal's juxtaposition between Mahomet and Jesus.[18] He quotes from L449/B556, where Pascal refuses the validity of rational knowledge as a step towards salvation.[19] He also seems attracted by Pascal's references to the elect, who can understand the obscure parts of the Scriptures.[20]

On 21 August 1944, we have another large collection of Pascal quotes. Althusser chooses quotes that refer to the need to go beyond conventional forms of expression and beyond conformity. He copies phrases on the fact that 'we are

---

        to submit their spirit, resort to first bend their body, in order to bend their spirit into good sense, by breaking little by little its resistances, whose principle cause reside in passions' (Macherey 2005a).

11   Althusser 1992b, p. 160.
12   Pascal 1966, p. 339 (L960/B921). It is interesting that in copying the phrase in his notebook, Althusser adds '[...] and injustice' (Althusser 1992b, p. 169).
13   Pascal 1966, p. 256 (L743/B859), Althusser 1992b, p. 170.
14   Pascal 1966, p. 291 (L845/B861), Althusser 1992b, p. 170.
15   Pascal 1966, p. 100 (L225/B789), Althusser 1992b, pp. 170–1.
16   Pascal 1966, p. 276 (L822/B593). Althusser 1992b, p. 174.
17   Pascal 1966, p. 33 (L1/B596), Althusser 1992b, p. 174.
18   Pascal 1966, p. 97 (L209/B599).
19   Pascal 1966, p. 169 (L449/B556), Althusser 1992b, p. 174.
20   Pascal 1966, p. 222 (L566/B575), Althusser 1992b, p. 174.

convinced more easily by reasons that we have found ourselves';[21] on 'rivers [being] ... moving roads that take us where we want to go';[22] on the fact that the 'last thing one discovers in composing a work is what to put first';[23] and on the arrangement of the material as a way to achieve novelty.[24] There is a reference to pleasure as 'the coin for which we will give people all they want',[25] but also to the need for the pleasure in eloquence to be derived from truth.[26] Althusser seems impressed by Pascal's insistence that 'one consults the ear because one is lacking in heart',[27] his appreciation of honesty and excellence,[28] and his insistence that a book is usually not the work of a sole author.[29] He also refers to Pascal's well-known phrase that 'it is not in Montaigne but in myself that I find everything I see there',[30] and to his insistence on self-knowledge.[31]

Althusser quotes from L199/B72, which deals with the limits of the human mind, and comprehension, on account of humans sharing both a corporeal and a spiritual nature, stamping their 'own composite being on all the simple things we contemplate'.[32] Althusser chooses a quote, from the beginning of the text, where Pascal refers to man contemplating the wonders of nature: 'let our imagination proceed further; it will grow weary of conceiving things before nature tires of producing them'.[33] He also quotes from another fragment, referring to the tendency of the mind to believe, and of the will to love false objects – part of the broader problematic of imagination within the *Pensées*.[34] He then

---

21 Pascal 1966, p. 255 (L737/B10), Althusser 1992b, p. 182.
22 Pascal 1966, p. 250 (L717/B17), Althusser 1992b, p. 182.
23 Pascal 1966, p. 347 (L976/B19), Althusser 1992b, p. 182.
24 'Let no one say that I have said nothing new; the arrangement of the material is new. In playing tennis both players use the same ball, but one plays it better' (Pascal 1966, p. 182 (L696/B22), Althusser 1992b, p. 182).
25 Pascal 1966, p. 248 (L710/B24), Althusser 1992b, p. 182.
26 '*Eloquence*. There must be elements both pleasing and real, but what is pleasing must itself be drawn by what is true' (Pascal 1966, p. 241 (L667/B25); Althusser 1992b, p. 182).
27 Pascal 1966, p. 233 (L610/B30), Althusser 1992b, p. 182.
28 'If, on seeing someone, we remember his book, it is a bad sign' (Pascal 1966, p. 239 (L647/B35), Althusser 1992b, p. 183).
29 Pascal 1966, p. 357 (L1000/B43).
30 Pascal 1966, p. 245 (L689/B64), Althusser 1992b, p. 183.
31 'One must know oneself. Even if that does not help in finding truth, at least it helps in running one's life and nothing is more proper' (Pascal 1966, p. 49 (L72/B66); Althusser 1992b, p. 183).
32 Pascal 1966, p. 94 (L199/B72).
33 Pascal 1966, p. 89 (L199/B72), Althusser 1992b, p. 183.
34 'The mind naturally believes and the will naturally loves, so that when there are no true objects for them they naturally become attached to false ones' (Pascal 1966, p. 241 (L661/B81), Althusser 1992b, p. 241).

chooses a phrase that perhaps signified, for him, the importance of his own temperament: 'There is little connection between the weather and my mood. I have my fog and fine weather inside me'.[35] He seems impressed by Pascal's reference to painting as vanity,[36] and by his insistence that 'only the contest appeals to us, not the victory'.[37] From L136/B139, on *Diversion*, where Pascal exposes his opinions on why human beings search for ways to divert themselves, Althusser chooses the phrase 'the sole cause of man's unhappiness is that he does not know how to stay quietly in his room'.[38] Perhaps this is an allusion to – and justification for – his forced inactivity during captivity.[39] Althusser also seems interested in Pascal's thoughts about death: 'Being unable to cure death, wretchedness and ignorance, men have decided, in order to be happy, not to think about such things'.[40] 'The last act is bloody, however fine the rest of the play. They throw earth over your head and it is finished for ever'.[41] Althusser quotes L816/B240, referring to the practice of abandoning pleasure as evidence of faith.[42] He quotes Pascal's phrase: 'Faith is a gift of God. Do not imagine that we describe it as a gift of reason',[43] and his insistence on the distance 'between knowing God and loving him'.[44] Finally, he quotes a metaphorical phrase, about how everything matters concerning grace, 'the slightest movement affects the whole of nature ... one stone can alter the whole sea',[45] and on the need to comfort ourselves, by thinking that 'it is not from yourself that you must expect it, but on the contrary you must expect it by expecting nothing from yourself'.[46]

Although we are far from the Althusser of the 1960s and his quest for a redefinition of materialism and even further from the Althusser of the materialism of the encounter, it is interesting to see the young Althusser choosing Pascal as a crucial theoretical interlocutor exactly in a period of crisis and uncertainty.

---

35   Pascal 1966, p. 220 (L552/B107), Althusser 1992b, p. 184.
36   Pascal 1966, p. 38 (L40/B134).
37   Pascal 1966, p. 240 (L773/B135).
38   Pascal 1966, p. 67 (L136/B139), Althusser 1992b, p. 184.
39   Pascal 1966, p. 69 (L136/B139), Althusser 1992b, p. 184.
40   Pascal 1966, p. 66 (L133/B169), Althusser 1992b, p. 184.
41   Pascal 1966, p. 82 (L165/B210), Althusser 1992b, p. 185.
42   Pascal 1966, p. 273 (L816/B240).
43   Pascal 1966, p. 227 (L588/B279), Althusser 1992b, p. 185.
44   Pascal 1966, p. 137 (L377/B280), Althusser 1992b, p. 185.
45   Pascal 1966, p. 319 (L927/B505), Althusser 1992b, p. 185.
46   Pascal 1966, p. 95 (L20/B517), Althusser 1992b, p. 185.

2 Lucien Goldmann and the 'Hidden God'

Some years later, Lucien Goldmann wrote one of the most important Marxist philosophical confrontations with Pascal, *Le Dieu caché*.[47] For Goldmann, who is interested in the relation between social structures, social groups and particular intellectual and literary currents, Jansenism, the philosophy expressed in the *Pensées* and the theatre of Racine, express the same tragic vision of the world, exemplified in the thematic of the *hidden God*: the God that makes Himself hidden. For Goldmann, this is an expression of a particular social group, the *noblesse de robe*, during the transition towards absolute monarchy. The rise of the *tiers état*, with its particular rationalism, and empiricism, suppressed the social foundation of this particular current.[48]

> The nature of the tragic mind in seventeenth-century France can be characterized by two factors: the complete and exact understanding of the new world created by rationalistic individualism, together with all the invaluable and scientifically valid acquisitions which this offered to the human intellect; and, at the same time, the complete refusal to accept this world as the only one in which man could live, move and have his being.[49]

The hidden God (*Deus absconditus*) means that 'God's voice no longer speaks directly to man'.[50] The tragic vision is based upon a combination of 'extreme realism' and a demand of absolute values in the confrontation with the 'fundamental ambiguity of the world'.[51] Pascal's thinking represents the 'truth of the opposites' and is essentially *static*, because it denies any possibility of realising a potential synthesis, *paradox*, because it conceives of reality as a unity of opposites, and *tragic*, since 'he sees man as unable either to avoid or to accept this paradox'.[52] The tragic vision is the result of Pascal's conception of man being in the middle of corporeality and spirituality, as opposing extremes. At the same time, Pascal represents an appreciation of individuality missing from the work of Descartes: 'individuality exists in the Cartesian system only by virtue of the union between the soul and the body [...] by distinguishing

---

47 Goldmann 1959; Goldmann 2013.
48 Goldmann 2013, pp. 26–7.
49 Goldmann 2013, p. 33.
50 Goldmann 2013, p. 36.
51 Goldmann 2013, p. 58.
52 Goldmann 2013, p. 195.

matter from empty space, Pascal maintained the individuality even of physical bodies'.[53] Although Pascal 'certainly does not use Hegelian and Marxist vocabulary', there is a dialectical sense in Pascal's fragments on the relation between the heart and reason,[54] such as his well-known phrase that 'the heart has its reasons of which reason knows nothing',[55] and his assertion that 'to have no time for philosophy is to be a true philosopher'.[56] Goldmann insists that the 'wager' puts emphasis on human practice and on human beings as active actors in social reality, since the 'wager' proposes that one must act and change one's conditions in order 'genuinely to assimilate the truth'.[57] For Goldmann, Pascal offers both a conception of the problematic of the hidden God, and a dialectical conception of natural, and social, reality:

> man can no longer find a sure and certain refuge by simply withdrawing from the world. It is in the world, or at least in the presence of the world, that man must now express both his rejection of any relative values and his quest for values that shall be authentic and transcendent.[58]

For Goldmann, the Pascalian wager is close to a conception of human *praxis*. It is not simply the affirmation of the rationality of gambling on the non-importance of certain mundane goods, in order to win infinite happiness. The central idea is that

> man can never achieve any authentic values by his own efforts, and that he always needs some supra-individual help on whose existence he must wager [...] Risk, possibility of failure, hope of success and the synthesis of these three in the form of a faith which is a wager are the essential constituent elements in the human condition.[59]

---

53 Goldmann 2013, p. 234.
54 Goldmann 2013, p. 251.
55 Pascal 1966, p. 154 (L423/B277).
56 Pascal 1966, p. 212 (L513/B4).
57 Goldmann 2013, p. 259.
58 Goldmann 2013, p. 284.
59 Goldmann 2013, p. 302.

3 From the Materiality of Ideological Practices to Aleatory Materialism

Although Althusser's texts in the 1940s and early 1950s do not contain many references to Pascal, Althusser never abandoned his constant dialogue with Pascal. In his book on Montesquieu, in a passage referring to Montesquieu's attempt to constitute a science of politics, he insists that this kind of 'rational necessity rejects, along with scepticism which is its pretext, all the temptations of Pascal's apologetics, espying in human unreason the admission of a divine reason'.[60] In *Philosophy and the Spontaneous Philosophy of the Sciences*, Pascal is used as a reference to the fact that 'behind assigned science by philosophy there lurks religion',[61] and is characterised as an 'authentic scientist' who 'used his science to justify his philosophy'.[62] There is also a passage on the contradiction between Pascal's materialist philosophical conception of scientific practice and his religiosity.

> All the scientific genius of Pascal did not prevent him from deriving beautifully eloquent flourishes of rhetoric, dedicated to the (slightly heretical) Christianity he professed, from the contradictions of the mathematical infinite itself, and from the religious 'terror' inspired in him by the new (Galilean) 'infinite spaces' of a world of which man was no longer the centre and from which God was 'absent' – which made it necessary, in order to save the very idea of God, to say that He was in essence a '*hidden* God' [...] But he was too alone in his time, and like everyone else was subject to such contradictions, such stakes and such a balance of power (think of the violence of his struggle against the Jesuits) that he could not avoid the obligatory 'solution', which was also no doubt a consolation to him, of resolving *in religion* (his own) the most general and conflict-ridden contradictions of a science in which he laboured as a genuine materialist practitioner.[63]

The Pascalian references in Althusser's *On the Reproduction of Capitalism*, the 1969 manuscript from which the famous 1971 article on 'Ideology and the Ideological Apparatuses of the State' was taken, are well known:

---

60 Althusser 2007, p. 21.
61 Althusser 1990, p. 111.
62 Althusser 1990, p. 112.
63 Althusser 1990, p. 121.

> Pascal says, more or less, 'Kneel down, move your lips in prayer *and you will believe*'. He thus scandalously inverts the order of things, bringing, like Christ, not peace, but strife, and, what is more, in a way that is hardly Christian (for woe to him who brings scandal into the world!) – scandal itself. A fortunate scandal which makes him speak, with Jansenist defiance, a language designating reality as it is, with nothing imaginary about it.
>
> We may perhaps be allowed to leave Pascal to the arguments of his ideological struggle with the religious Ideological State Apparatuses of his day, in which he waged a little class struggle in his Jansenist Party, constantly on the brink of being banned, that is of excommunication.[64]

Indeed, we can find in Pascal's *Pensées* elements of a theory of ideology through material rituals, associated with his conception of faith in a condition of fundamental uncertainty about the very existence of the 'hidden god'. This is evident in the importance Pascal attributes to *custom* as a road towards faith, but also political subjection and apprehension of the world.

> Custom is our nature. Anyone who grows accustomed to faith believes it, and can no longer help fearing hell, and believes nothing else.
> Anyone accustomed to believe that the king is to be feared ...
> Who then can doubt that our soul, being accustomed to see number, space, movement believes in this and nothing else?[65]

The relation between power and ideology is also expressed in the following passage on how power can exploit opinion:

> Power rules the world, not opinion, but it is opinion that exploits power.
> It is power that makes opinion. To be easygoing can be a fine thing according to our opinion. Why? Because anyone who wants to dance the tightrope will be alone and I can get together a stronger body of people to say there is nothing fine about it.[66]

---

64   Althusser 2014b, p. 186. This is the fuller version, since in the article on the ISAs the reference to the 'class struggle' within the Jansenist movement is omitted (for the article version see Althusser 2014b, p. 260). For Pascal's intervention in religious debates and in particular the struggle against the Jesuits, see Krailsheiner 1966, pp. 11–18.
65   Pascal 1966, p. 153 (L419/B419).
66   Pascal 1966, p. 220 (L554/B303).

Pascal had an apprehension of the politics of ideology, and of the power of ideological manipulation. Imagination is 'the dominant faculty in man',[67] and it is impossible to avoid its efficacy: 'Reason never wholly overcomes imagination, while the contrary is quite common'.[68] From the 'red robes' of magistrates, 'gowns and mules' of physicians, to 'drums and trumpets' of armies,[69] all these attest to the use of imagination, in order to impose a certain image of things or an opinion, especially since man 'has no exact principle of truth, and several excellent ones of falsehood'.[70] This is linked to Pascal's conception of the animality of human nature, exemplified in his suggestions that 'Man's nature is entirely natural, *wholly animal*',[71] and that 'Man is properly speaking *wholly animal*'.[72] This must be linked to his conception of human beings as *automata*. Pascal was not only one of the first thinkers to work on the possibility of a thinking machine, exemplified in work on a potential calculating machine, but he also used the analogy of the machine as a way to refer to the human body, and the corporeal nature of human beings. As Pierre Macherey has shown,[73] Pascal was not simply concerned with reproducing a Cartesian dualism of body and soul; he was more concerned with the question of how the body influences the mind, in a reversal of classical philosophical dualisms that open up the way for a highly original materialist conception. Macherey directs our attention to those passages in which Pascal sketches 'his project of a "discourse of the machine"'.[74]

> *Order*. A letter of exhortation to a friend, to induce him to seek. He will reply: 'But what good will seeking do me? Nothing comes of it.' Answer: 'Do not despair.' Then he in turn would say that he would be happy to find some light, but according to religion itself it would do him no good even if he did thus believe, and so would just as soon not look. The answer to that is 'the Machine'.[75]
>
> *Letter showing the usefulness of proofs, by the Machine*. Faith is different from proof. One is human and the other a gift of God. *The just live by faith.*

---

67   Pascal 1966, p. 38 (L44/B82).
68   Pascal 1966, p. 40 (L44/B82).
69   Pascal 1966, pp. 40–1 (L44/B82).
70   Pascal 1966, p. 42 (L44/B82).
71   Pascal 1966, p. 236 (L630/B94).
72   Pascal 1966, p. 241 (L664/B94b).
73   Macherey 2005a.
74   Ibid.
75   Pascal 1966, p. 33 (L5/B247).

> This is the faith that God himself puts into our hearts, often using proof as the instrument. *Faith commeth by hearing*. But this faith is in our hearts, and makes us say not 'I know' but 'I believe'.[76]
>
> *Order*. After the letter urging men to seek God, write the letter about removing obstacles, that is the argument about the Machine, how to prepare it and how to use reason for the search.[77]

The potential influence of Pascal on Althusser's conception of ideology goes beyond the simple use of a metaphor regarding the importance of material practices and rituals in the reproduction of ideological representations. There is, in Pascal, a potentially materialist conception of beliefs and customs being reproduced through material practices, themselves grounded in the animal and machine-like aspects of human nature. Beliefs, attitudes, and ideological representations are not acts of consciousness; rather, consciousness is nothing but the aggregate of the results of repetitive material social practices and interactions, especially since the very nature of human being is much more bodily and material than spiritual and ethereal. This conception of repetitive social practices and rituals is a crucial part of Althusser's attempt to rethink the reproduction of social relations without resorting to 'latent structures'. In his autobiography, Althusser encapsulated the influence of Spinoza and Pascal on his conception of the materiality of ideology:

> Following his [Spinoza's] example on this point, as well as that of Pascal whom I greatly admired, I was later to insist strongly on the material existence of ideology, not only the material *conditions* of its existence (an idea which is found in Marx as well as in a number of earlier and later writers) but also on the *materiality* of its very existence.[78]

Althusser also uses one of the most famous passages from the *Pensées* ('The Mystery of Jesus' L919/B553), where Pascal discusses the redemptive role of the agony of Christ. He turns to the phrase 'I shed these drops of blood for you',[79] in order to theorise the relation between subject and Subject in the mechanism of ideological interpellation, in a passage that links interpellation and the reproduction of material rituals and practices, with the assumption that individuals are always already interpellated as subjects. Althusser links two of his

---

76 Pascal 1966, p. 33 (L7/B248).
77 Pascal 1966, p. 34 (L11/B246).
78 Althusser 1993b, p. 217.
79 Pascal 1966, p. 314 (L919/B553).

more important influences regarding the theory of ideology, namely, the Pascalian insistence on repetitive material rituals, and the Lacanian emphasis on the nodal role of a Subject in the process of ideological interpellation.

> if it calls these individuals by their names, thus recognizing that they are always-already interpellated as subjects with a personal identity (to the extent that Pascal's Christ says: 'It is for you that I have shed this drop of my blood!'); [...] if everything does happen in this way (in the practices of the well-known rituals of baptism, confirmation, communion, confession and extreme unction, etc. ...), we should note that all this 'procedure' to set up Christian religious subjects is dominated by a strange phenomenon: the fact that there can only be such a multitude of possible religious subjects on the absolute condition that there is a Unique, Absolute, *Other Subject*, i.e. God.[80]

The other sets of Althusser's references to Pascal can be found in his post-1982 writings. In his 1984 interview with Fernanda Navarro, he stated that:

> Pascal is an interesting, because paradoxical, instance. By way of the religious problems that he raises, epistemological problems also appear, problems of the theory of the history of the sciences and a theory of social relations, so that we may affirm that he exhibits profoundly materialist features. [...] [W]ithout realizing it, I had already borrowed a few philosophical ideas from him: the whole theory of ideology, of misrecognition and recognition, is to be found in Pascal.[81]

In a passage from his autobiography, which was not included in the first edition, Althusser refers to the importance of Pascal's 'theory of the apparatus of the body' as the basis of a theory of the materiality of ideology.

> I had duly read Pascal in captivity [...] I was still a believer, but that was not the reason. What fascinated me was certainly Pascal's theory of justice and force, his theory of relations among men, but especially his theory of the apparatus of the body: 'Kneel and pray', which was later to inspire my 'theory' of the materiality of ideology (see what Michel Foucault appropriately calls the disciplines of the body in the seventeenth century; they

---

80 Althusser 2014b, pp. 266–7.
81 Althusser 2006a, p. 269.

have obviously not disappeared since), of the *semblance* I was to rediscover later, that is further on, in Machiavelli.[82]

Althusser also suggests that we can find in Pascal an actual theory of the history of sciences, a theory of the historicity of scientific theories and discoveries, in a non-teleological and non-metaphysical way.

> What do I not owe to Pascal! and in particular to that astonishing sentence on the history of science, in which the moderns are said to be greater than the ancients only because they stand on the latter's shoulders [...] I found in this sentence a theory of scientific experimentation related not to its conditions of possibility (as later in Kant) but to its material conditions of historical existence, thus the essence of a genuine theory of history; when Pascal speaking of new experiments that contradict those of the ancients, utters this extraordinary sentence: *'Thus it is that without contradicting [the ancients] we can advance the contrary of what they said'*! Without contradicting them: because the conditions of our scientific experiments have changed and are no longer the same as those of the ancients [...] I did not stop reflecting on this sentence, infinitely more profound than all that the philosophers of the Enlightenment were able to say (which was ultimately very simple-minded, because teleological) about history.[83]

Althusser finds in Pascal a conception of the actual historicity of science, in sharp contrast to any rationalist and/or teleological conception of some scientific theories being more 'rational' or 'correct' than others. Rather, the emphasis is on the changing conditions of experimentation and theorisation that can account for theories being different but not 'contradictory', in the sense that there is no point in treating them as being in a simple dialogue, since they refer to different conditions of production and experimentation. The new knowledge changes our view through the very historicity of our experimentation and exploration. The passages Althusser refers to are both from the *Preface to a Treatise on the Void*. There, referring to the evolution of our knowledge, Pascal insists that it is not a question of authority, but rather of expanding knowledge through experimentation and discovery.

---

82   Althusser 1997a, p. 3.
83   Althusser 1997a, pp. 3–4.

> It is in this manner that we may today adopt different sentiments and new opinions, without despising *the ancients* [...] *and* without ingratitude, since the first knowledge which they have given us has served as a stepping-stone to our own, and since in these advantages we are indebted to them for our ascendency over them; because being raised by their aid to a certain degree, the slightest effort causes us to mount still higher, and with less pain and less glory we find ourselves above them. Thus we are enabled to discover things which it was impossible for them to perceive. Our view is more extended, and although they knew as well as we all that they could observe in nature, they did not, nevertheless, know it so well, and we see more than they.[84]
>
> Thus it is that, without contradicting them [*the ancients*], we can affirm the contrary of what they say.[85]

In the 'Underground Current of the Materialism of the Encounter', Althusser relates Pascal to the problematic of the *philosophical void* as a crucial aspect of an aleatory materialist tradition, which is

> not only the philosophy which says that the void pre-exists the atoms that fall in it, but a philosophy which creates the philosophical void [*fait le vide philosophique*] in order to endow itself with existence: a philosophy which [...] *by evacuating all philosophical problems, hence by refusing to assign itself any 'object' whatever* [...] in order to set out from nothing, and from the infinitesimal, aleatory variation of nothing constituted by the swerve of the fall. Is there a more radical critique of all philosophy, with its pretension to utter the truth about things?[86]

Althusser praises Pascal for attempting to introduce the void as a philosophical concept, although he deplores the fact that Pascal related this to religious apologetics; a curious observation, taking into account the fact that Pascal treated the void in terms of scientific observation and experimentation.[87]

> Is there a more radical critique of all philosophy, with its pretension to utter the truth about things? Is there a more striking way of saying that philosophy's 'object' par excellence is nothingness, nothing, or the void?

---

84   Pascal 2001, p. 7.
85   Pascal 2001, p. 10.
86   Althusser 2006a, pp. 174–5.
87   Cf. Macherey 2005b, p. 60.

In the seventeenth century, Pascal repeatedly approached this idea, and the possibility of introducing the void as a philosophical object. He did so, however, in the deplorable context of an apologetics.[88]

Althusser attempts to combine the conception of philosophy not having an object in the proper sense (his famous reference to the *'emptiness of a distance taken'*),[89] with the rain of atoms in Lucretius moving in empty space, as an imagery for an open, non-teleological conception of reality. In this non-ontology, the notion of the *void* acquires a more general philosophical significance as the necessary ground or space for aleatory encounters and new social forms.

Moreover, in any conception of an *aleatory* materialism, in the very notion of the *alea*, one can also find echoes of the Pascalian wager; not in the sense of faith as a wager on the existence of God, but in the sense of the absence of any teleology, certainty or safe ground. It is a conception that is at once tragic, in the sense defined by Goldmann, but also liberating and emancipating, offering a way to think the possibility of new encounters, new forms, and, in the last instance, new revolutionary projects. Althusser's apprehension of the crisis of Marxism, and of the Communist Movement, was indeed a tragic confrontation with defeats, mistakes and the absence of certainties. However, this tragic apprehension can open the way for a new beginning of revolutionary politics. In contrast to a historicist confidence in the course of history, this tragic conception of the world and history, this absence of any stable point of reference or ground, entails a different kind of optimism, arising not from certainty, but from the openness of the historical process, and the potentiality for new encounters and forms.

It is here where Althusser slightly diverges from Pascal. The Pascalian wager is always, in the last instance, about the agony of faith, the uncertainty and disbelief caused by a 'hidden God' that never comes forward, redemptively manifesting his existence. In contrast, Althusser's conception of an aleatory materialism is about actually existing elements, dynamics, and potentialities. In a sense, nothing is hidden.[90] What is contingent upon the dynamics of the conjuncture, and represents the challenge for political intervention (the 'dia-

---

88 Althusser 2006a, p. 175.
89 Althusser 1976a, p. 62.
90 It is interesting that Goldmann associated the whole tragic conception of the hidden God with the later emergence of structuralism. In this sense, we might say that Althusser's materialism of the encounter, as an actual negation of any form of 'latent structures', is exactly his eventual distancing from this conception of the tragic in Pascal.

lectic' of *fortuna* and *virtù* in Machiavelli that fascinated Althusser),[91] is the question of the encounter between all these elements. This, indeed, can also be tragic, in the sense of failed encounters and failed political projects. However, we can deal with this tragic aspect of revolutionary politics, not with an agonising wager, but with self-criticism, collective experimentation, and confidence in the creative character of popular movements. It is not a question of faith, but of political practice.

Pascal was a constant theoretical companion to Althusser in questions of religious faith initially, and of philosophy subsequently. From Althusser's theory of ideology, and the emphasis on material practices, bodily disciplines and material rituals, to Althusser's conception of epistemology and the possibility of an actual history of sciences, and his conception of an aleatory materialism of the encounter, one cannot properly understand his philosophical endeavours without taking into consideration his dialogue with Pascal.

---

91   See Althusser 2000.

CHAPTER 8

The Difficulties of being a Materialist in Philosophy: Assessing Aleatory Materialism

The answer to the question of the continuity of aleatory materialism in relation to Althusser's previous positions depends upon how one interprets his later writings. I think that the main element of continuity is that they remain inscribed in the politically inspired quest for a materialist practice of philosophy. Despite Althusser's refusal (and inability) in the 1980s to have any form of public political intervention, it is obvious that he remained a communist in philosophy, in sharp contrast to the theoretical and political anti-communism that marked other apprehensions of the crisis of Marxism, from the *nouveaux philosophes* onwards. Althusser's effort to rethink materialism does not originate from a general disillusionment with working-class politics and Marxism; on the contrary, it marks an effort to provide a left-wing alternative to communist politics, based on the centrality of the class struggle and the continuing relevance of the communist project.[1]

1 The Genealogy of Aleatory Materialism

Althusser's texts on *aleatory materialism* written during his forced isolation and public silence in the 1980s bear the mark of this difficult personal situation, tormented by serious health problems and periodic relapses of depression. They comprise extracts of a larger text written in 1982 which received the title *The Underground Current of the Materialism of the Encounter* by the French editors, an 'interview' he gave to F. Navarro, a Mexican philosopher,[2] in fact a collage made by Navarro from various texts, letters and discussions with Althusser,[3] which was published in Spanish in 1988[4] although not in French, parts of Althusser's correspondence on the Navarro 'interview' and other smaller texts. These texts, along with Althusser's autobiography,[5] constitute the main part of his post-1980 production that has been published.

---

1 On this see Althusser 1994a, pp. 253–69 and 508–26.
2 Althusser 1994b, in Althusser 2006a.
3 On the preparation of the 'interview', see Althusser 2006a, pp. 208–50.
4 Althusser 1988.
5 Althusser 1994a.

Althusser sets out to bring forward what he considers to be an *'almost completely unknown materialist tradition in the history of philosophy: the 'materialism' [...] of the rain, the swerve, the encounter, the take* [prise]',[6] a *materialism of the encounter* that had been 'interpreted, reversed and perverted into an *idealism of freedom*'.[7] This tradition is presented and explained in the form of a philosophical genealogy. The first figure is that of Epicurus. Althusser is fascinated by the image of the epicurean atoms moving in parallel directions in the void, leading a 'phantom existence'[8] until the moment of the *clinamen*,[9] the infinitesimal swerve that marks the beginning of the making of the world. Even though all the elements existed before the swerve, there is no formation of the world, no Meaning or Cause before it, the *'Swerve was originary'*.[10] Epicurus is presented as the archetypal figure of a radically anti-teleological philosophical stance:[11] the formation of the world is in itself purely accidental, any possibility of meaning, constant relations between things and causal relations are posterior to the contingent encounter. The second figure to be included in this genealogy of the materialism of the encounter is Heidegger. Althusser[12] refers with admiration to Heidegger's phrase *Es gibt*,[13] 'there is', 'this is what is given', as a rejection of questions of origin.

Derrida also occupies an important position in this genealogy of aleatory materialism, a pattern that we can also see in some of his manuscripts from the 1970s.[14] Althusser thinks that the necessary philosophical labour to free philo-

---

6   Althusser 2006a, p. 167.
7   Althusser 2006a, p. 168.
8   Althusser 2006a, p. 169.
9   On this notion, which comes from Lucretius's presentation of Epicurean philosophy in the *De rerum Natura*, see Long and Sedley 1987, pp. 46–52. It is also worth noting that although Althusser insists on distinguishing his reading of Epicurus from an 'idealism of freedom', the importance of freedom in the Epicurean swerve over the element of necessity in Democritus has been an important aspect of the history of Epicurean notions, including Marx's reading of Epicurean philosophy in his doctoral dissertation (Marx 1841). On this subject see also Suchting 2004, p. 11.
10 Althusser 2006a, p. 168.
11 'This is the negation of all teleology': Althusser 2006a, p. 260.
12 Althusser 2006a, p. 170, p. 261.
13 The phrase is from *Being and Time* and Heidegger himself comments upon it in a passage from the 'Letter on Humanism' (Heidegger 1994, p. 238): 'In Being and Time (p. 212) we purposely and cautiously say, *il y a l'Être, there is, it gives ("es gibt")* Being. *Il y a* translates "it gives" imprecisely, for "it" here "gives" is Being itself. The "gives" names the essence of Being that is giving granting its truth. The selfgiving into the open, along with the open region itself, is Being itself'.
14 Cf. Althusser 2015a.

sophy from metaphysics and teleology is a form of deconstruction,[15] insisting on an imagery of dispersion and disorder that he links to Derrida's *dissemination*.[16] He also stresses 'the primacy of "dissemination" over the postulate that every signifier has a meaning (Derrida)',[17] and 'the primacy of absence over presence'.[18] Moreover, the materiality of the gesture, as a *trace*, is also linked to the Derridean notion of the *trace*.

> Let me carry things to an extreme: it may be a mere trace, the materiality of the gesture which leaves a trace and is indiscernible from the trace that it leaves on the wall of a cave or a sheet of paper. Things go a very long way: Derrida has shown that the primacy of the trace (of writing) is to be found even in the phoneme produced by the speaking voice.[19]

Althusser then turns to Machiavelli as representing an important moment in the history of the materialism of the encounter. According to Althusser, the importance of the encounter can be found in the way in which Machiavelli describes the necessary encounter between a leader and a region in order to accomplish the project of Italian national unity and the equally necessary encounter between *fortuna* and *virtù* in the Prince himself. This encounter may or may not take place in the *void* of the existing political situation, a void that Althusser describes as a '*philosophical void*'[20] in the sense of a radical absence of any original Cause or necessity. In this sense we can say that Machiavelli is presented as the representative of a practical philosophy of the emergence of new political forms out of the inherently contingent and aleatory encounter of already existing elements, and at same time of the philosophy of the *political gesture* as a constitutive aspect of this encounter. If Althusser turned to Machiavelli in the 1970s in an effort to rethink the possibility of new political forms, now in his effort to come to terms with the recognition of the crisis of the Communist movement – in this sense repeating Gramsci's use of the Prince as an allegory for the emergence of a new conception of the Party – he turns to Machiavelli as the representative of the non-teleological nature of any political and social practice.

---

15 Althusser 2006a, p. 178. On deconstruction as a strategy see Derrida 1972 and Derrida 2001.
16 Althusser 2006a, p. 188. Cf. Derrida 1981.
17 Althusser 2006a, p. 189.
18 Althusser 2006a, p. 191.
19 Althusser 2006a, p. 262. Cf. Derrida 2011.
20 Althusser 2006a, p. 173.

The other important figure in Althusser's genealogy of aleatory materialism is Spinoza. The reference to Spinoza as an important philosophical 'detour'[21] and as an ally in the attempt to delineate an alternative non-metaphysical materialism is an integral part of Althusser's interventions since the 1960s.[22] But now, especially in the *Underground Current*, apart from the emphasis on the void, he first chooses Spinoza's notion of parallelism as what constitutes Spinoza's contribution to the tradition of aleatory materialism: 'The fact that they are *parallel*, that here everything is an effect of parallelism, recalls Epicurus' rain'.[23]

And on a more general level, one is tempted to note that this effort to include Spinoza in the genealogy of a philosophy of the aleatory and the contingent comes in sharp contrast to Spinoza's rejection of the notion of contingency, and his insistence that things appear as contingent because of inadequate knowledge.[24] On this point and in order to do justice to Althusser, we must say that some of his comments have great theoretical merit, such as his insistence on the gap separating Spinoza and any traditional theory of knowledge or traditional metaphysics in general and on Spinoza's rejection of any theory of the *cogito*. These points are also taken up in the fragment on Spinoza which was included in the second edition of *L'avenir dure longtemps*.[25]

The same effort to form a philosophical genealogy of the materialism of the encounter is also evident in Althusser's treatment of Hobbes and Rousseau. His reference to Hobbes is more reserved,[26] but he insists that Hobbes had arrived at the '*aleatory constitution of a world*'.[27] Concerning Rousseau, especially the second *Discourse*, Althusser treats the Social Contract as a form of constitutive encounter before which there was no society at all.

There are more figures included in this philosophical genealogy. Althusser makes references to Nietzsche,[28] Derrida, and Wittgenstein, since he seems to be fascinated by the first sentence of the *Tractatus Logico-Philosophicus* espe-

---

21 Althusser 1976a, p. 134.
22 Althusser and Balibar 1990, p. 102; Althusser 1976a; Althusser 1997a. On the relation of Althusser to Spinoza and a critical assessment of the true extent of Althusser's Spinozism, see Thomas 2002.
23 Althusser 2006a, p. 177.
24 Spinoza 2002, p. 234 (*Ethics*, Part I, proposition XXIX).
25 Althusser 1994a, pp. 467–87; Althusser 1997a.
26 '[In Hobbes] the "hold" of the atomized individuals was not of the same nature or as powerful as in Epicurus and Machiavelli' (Althusser 2006a, p. 183).
27 Althusser 2006a, p. 183.
28 Althusser 2006a, pp. 218 and 273.

cially in its German original: *Die Welt ist alles, was der Fall ist*,[29] and he believes that along with the Heideggerian *es gibt* it offers the possibility of thinking the world in terms of *encounters*.[30]

In a way, in these texts we are dealing with a reformulation of idealism. Whereas in Althusser's texts from the 1960s idealism was presented mainly in the form of the variations of empiricism and historicism (the latter being viewed as a variation of an empiricist conception of the theoretical object having the same – historical – qualities of the real object), here idealism is above all equated with all forms of teleological thinking, all forms of a philosophy of the Origin and the End: 'We can recognize idealism, I think, by the fact that it is haunted by a single question which divides into two, since the principle of reason bears not only on the *origin* but also on the *end*'.[31] This emphasis on the break with any form of teleological thinking is made even more evident by the recurring metaphor of the materialist philosopher catching a moving train without knowing where it comes from or where it goes.[32]

2 The Philosophy of the Encounter in the 1980s Texts

Here is how Althusser summarises the basic elements of a potential philosophy of the encounter. The first principle is the primacy of the encounter on being,[33] the primacy of the encounter on form and order. The second is that there are encounters only between series of beings that are themselves the results of series of causes. Althusser refers here to Cournot who had tried to present 'chance' as the encounter between two independent causal series.[34] The third

---

29   Althusser 2006a, p. 190. For a reading of Althusser's later writings that stresses the importance of this reference to Wittgenstein, see Suchting 2004.
30   Althusser 2006a, p. 191.
31   Althusser 2006a, p. 217.
32   Althusser 2006a, p. 290; Althusser 1969, p. 186.
33   'For a being (a body, an animal, a man, state or Prince) *to be*, an encounter has *to have taken place*' (Althusser 2006a, p. 192).
34   On this see Morfino 2005. On Cournot see also Raymond 1982, pp. 76–9. It also worth noting that Raymond in a way preceded Althusser in thinking of the aleatory character of political practice (Raymond 1982) and he has revealed that Althusser, with whom he remained in communication in the 1980s, did know about his researches (Raymond 1997). Althusser refers to Raymond in the texts on 'aleatory materialism' but only to his 1973 *Passage au Matérialisme* (Raymond 1973), not his later texts. See also André Tosel's comments on this issue (Tosel 2005, p. 169). François Matheron has suggested that Althusser's first encounter with Cournot, in the 1950s, is by means of his reading the references to Cournot in Raymond Aron's *Introduction à la philosophie de l'histoire* (Matheron and Ichida 2011, pp. 204–9).

principle is that '[e]very encounter is aleatory, not only in its origins (nothing ever guarantees an encounter), but also in its effects'.[35] Althusser insists that the aleatory nature of every encounter is its possibility not to have taken place and that the possible effects of any encounter cannot be prefigured, and this calls for a new thinking of the relation between necessity and contingency: 'instead of thinking of contingency as a modality of necessity, or an exception to it, we must think necessity as the becoming necessary of the encounter of contingencies'.[36] What we have here is the rejection by Althusser of any form of teleological thinking and teleological explanation. We can discern causal series and determinism, but only *after the fact has been accomplished*, not prior to it; we can work on them only *backwards*, in the same way that in biology we can trace the evolutionary path of a species only towards the past, with future evolutions depending only upon chance mutations.[37] According to Althusser, there is no meaning to history, in the sense of a teleological conception, there is meaning *in* history in the sense of the results of each encounter. This meaning comes only after the encounter 'has taken hold'[38] and it is only on this basis that we can try and provide explanations and even think in terms of laws and regularities, provided that we keep in mind the element of *surprise* in history, of new encounters taking hold.[39] By treating structural determinations as aleatory encounters, Althusser thought that he could avoid any danger of treating structures as 'latent meanings' of social reality. Structural effectivity is established only 'after the fact', after a Darwinian process of failed encounters.

> Every encounter is aleatory, not only in its origins (nothing ever guaranties an encounter), but also in its effects. In other words, every encounter might not have taken place, although it did take place; but its possible nonexistence sheds light on the meaning of its aleatory being. And every encounter is aleatory in its effects, in that nothing in the elements of the encounter prefigures, before the actual encounter, the contours and

---

35 Althusser 2006a, 193.
36 Althusser 2006a, pp. 193–4.
37 Althusser refers explicitly to Darwin (Althusser 2006a, p. 194). On the importance of the reference to Darwin as part of a non-teleological conception of history, see Morfino and Pinzolo 2005.
38 Althusser 2006a, p. 195.
39 Althusser 2006a, p. 196. Althusser here plays on the etymological relation in French between *prise* (take, taking-hold), which is crucial in the vocabulary of aleatory materialism and refers to the way an encounter becomes an accomplished fact, and *surprise* (surprise) as the contingent possibility of a new encounter.

determinations of the being that will emerge from it [...] This means that no determination of these elements can be assigned except by *working backwards* from the result to its becoming, its retroaction.[40]

Such a rethinking of historical materialism as a radical break with any form of teleology can be considered the closest Althusser ever came to an abandonment of any notion of structural determination. Social forms are presented as contingent encounters or as unstable conjunctions of societal elements, open to constant reorganisation and rearticulation. The conjuncture takes full precedence over the structure: 'Epicurus and Spinoza, Montesquieu and Rousseau range themselves in the same camp, on the basis, explicit or implicit, of the same materialism of the encounter or, in the full sense of the term, the same idea of the conjuncture'.[41] Historical materialism deals not with structural tendencies but *constants* and singular conjunctures themselves open to constant change.

> Here the materialist philosopher-traveller, who is attentive to 'singular' cases, cannot state laws about them, since such cases are singular/concrete/factual and are therefore not repeated, because they are unique. What he *can* do [...] is to single out '*general constants*' among the encounters he has observed, the 'variations' of which are capable for accounting for the singularity of the cases under consideration and thus produce knowledge of the 'clinical' sort as well as ideological, political and social effects.[42]

This radical break with any form of teleology leads Althusser to an attempt to rewrite the history of the emergence of capitalism in terms of the encounter of different historical elements. The different elements, social subjects and social forms that would form what could be described as 'social structures' and now as lasting encounters, had no predetermination to enter in this encounter and be part of a mode of production: 'The elements do not exist in history *so that* a mode of production may exist, they exist in history in *a "floating" state* prior to their "accumulation" and "combination", each being the product of its own history, and none being the teleological product of the others or their history'.[43]

---

40   Altusser 2006a, p. 193.
41   Althusser 2006a, p. 187.
42   Althusser 2006a, p. 278.
43   Althusser 2006a, p. 198.

This rejection of teleology is supplemented by an emphasis on the singular, the concrete and the factual. Althusser insists that in history and social reality we can only find constants, as the result of accomplished encounters, not laws.[44] There are even positive references to Hume and the construction of general concepts out of singular facts, cases and events, a reference that runs contrary to the anti-empiricist emphasis of Althusser's texts from the 1960s, where the trajectory from the concrete to the abstract is considered the essence of empiricism. Althusser combines this atomistic turn to the singular case, with a conception of history based on the distinction between History (*Historie*), the history of teleological conceptions and living history in the present (*Geschichte*), which has nothing to do with laws in the sense of the natural sciences.[45] This return to the singular case, the fact, the event is one of the most important aspects of Althusser's later writings and marks a divergence from the emphasis on structures and structural relations of his earlier writings. On this basis Althusser tends to reject any notion of the dialectic in his later writings. He considers it '*more than dubious* [...] *harmful*'[46] and proposes the replacement of dialectical materialism with aleatory materialism.

In order to provide an example of how the encounter works Althusser turns once again to the problem of the transition to capitalism. Althusser thinks that Marx and Engels oscillate between two different conceptions of the mode of production, one that is essentialist and presents history as a whole with an end that reproduces its elements, and a more aleatory conception according to which 'every mode of production comprises *elements that are independent of each other*'.[47] In this sense the encounter refers to how different historical elements, practices, even social groups, that had their own independent histories, without any predestination to become part of the capitalist mode of production, had to encounter and combine with each other, in a process that might or might not have taken place. The decisive encounter is the one Marx mentions in

---

44   Althusser 2006a, p. 278.
45   Althusser 2006a, pp. 263–4. Althusser thinks that the mistake made by Popper in his criticism of Marxism and psychoanalysis is that he neglected this distinction and that both Marxism and psychoanalysis belong to the realm of *Geschichte* (Althusser 2006a, p. 264). But in a curious twist this statement by Althusser actually reproduces the main point of Popper's criticism against Marx, that there can be no scientific explanation or prediction in history exactly because it is different from the object of the natural sciences! (Popper 1986). Althusser also deals with Popper in *How to be a Marxist in Philosophy* (Althusser 2017b).
46   Althusser 2006a, p. 242.
47   Althusser 2006a, p. 199.

Capital[48] between 'owners of money' and the 'free labourers' stripped of all but their labour power. In this sense Althusser thinks that there is no point in thinking of the bourgeoisie as the result of the decay and decline of the feudal mode of production, because this leads to a 'schema of dialectical production again, a contrary, producing its contraries'[49] and a conception of the bourgeoisie as the element that will provide the necessary unity of the totality.[50]

The last important aspect of the aleatory materialism texts concerns the redefinition of philosophy. Althusser here mainly follows the line he originated in the 1976 lecture on the transformation of philosophy.[51] According to this schema, traditional philosophy assigned itself the task of speaking the Truth, and in this sense philosophy plays an important part in the formation of dominant ideologies,[52] acting as a theoretical laboratory for the dominant ideologies.[53] Althusser also elaborates on the subject of the struggle between idealism and materialism as constitutive of philosophy. Althusser insists that every philosophy is tendentially materialist or idealist, at the same time incorporating elements of the opposite tendency, because in the course of the philosophical battle each philosophy tries to encircle and capture some of the position of its opponent, in this sense incorporating them.[54] This relation between philosophy and the mechanisms of ideological hegemony means that every philosophy in its traditional form is inherently idealistic, and that every 'materialism' that is pronounced as a philosophical system, as a system of philosophical truths, is also essentially idealist.[55] In contrast, what is opened as a theor-

---

48 Marx and Engels 1975–2005, Vol. 35. p. 705.
49 Althusser 2006, p. 201.
50 'And it is no accident that the theory of the bourgeoisie as a form of antagonistic disintegration of the feudal mode of production is consistent with the philosophically inspired conception of the mode of production. In this conception the bourgeoisie is indeed nothing other than the *element predestined* to unify all the other elements of the mode of production' (Althusser 2006a, p. 202). Althusser also insists on not treating the French Revolution as a 'capitalist' revolution and refers approvingly to Furet's 'revisionist' reading of the French Revolution (Althusser 2006a, pp. 237–8).
51 In Althusser 1990.
52 Althusser 2006a, pp. 286–7.
53 Althusser 1976a, pp. 259–60; Althusser 2006a p. 287.
54 The same point is also taken up in *Essays in Self-Criticism* (Althusser 1976a, pp. 142–50). In a letter to F. Navarro, Althusser also refers to Raymond's book (Raymond 1973) approving of the latter's emphasis on the existence of elements of idealism and materialism in every great philosophy (Althusser 2006a, p. 222). He also makes reference to Macherey as having been the first to have stated that there are idealist and materialist elements in all philosophy, possibly to Macherey's article on the history of philosophy as a struggle of tendencies (Macherey 1976).
55 Althusser 2006a, p. 272.

etical possibility by Marxism is not another philosophy but a new *practice of philosophy*,[56] it is a 'denunciation of philosophy produced as "philosophy"'.[57] The result of the importance of practices and the primacy of practice of theory is the affirmation that philosophy does indeed have an *outside*. But one must be careful not to see Practice as a substitute for Truth inside a philosophical system,[58] the materialist practice of philosophy being fundamentally asymmetrical to idealist philosophical systems.

3   Pierre Raymond on Aleatory Materialism

It is interesting to note that in a certain way Althusser was preceded in this confrontation with the question of the aleatory character of encounters by Pierre Raymond. Already in 1975, in *De la combinatoire aux probabilités* [*From the combinatory to probabilities*],[59] Raymond offered a concrete example of an history of mathematics, focusing on the emergence of combinatory analysis in the seventeenth century and the theory of probabilities in the eighteenth century. He traces the beginning of this tendency in Greek philosophy and in particular Carneades and then to the emergence after Galileo and the functioning of hypotheses in Galileo's system of a new conception of the probable. He stresses the importance of Pascal and Leibniz in the formation of this new conception of combinatory analysis. Regarding Hume and his problematic conception of probability, he stresses the fact that Hume refuses both '*real* experience' and '*theory*',[60] and in general the advances already made by the sciences. What is important is that the intrusion of the notion of probability in scientific discourse changes the traditional opposition between (scientific) determinism and (theological) indeterminism, leading to a new confusion between '*probabilism* (probabilist determinism) and *indeterminism*'.[61] In Bachelard's attempt to deal with this question he sees 'a materialism that is still dominated beginning

---

56   Althusser 1976a, p. 262. Althusser first introduced the notion of a new practice of philosophy in *Lenin and Philosophy* (Althusser 1971, p. 68).
57   Althusser 2006a, p. 275.
58   'Practice is not a substitute for Truth for the purposes of an unshakeable philosophy; on the contrary, it is what shakes philosophy to its foundations – whether in the form of the "variable" cause of matter or in that of class struggle – which philosophy has never been able to master' (Althusser 2006a, p. 275).
59   Raymond 1975.
60   Raymond 1975, p. 30.
61   Raymond 1975, p. 34.

to emerge in the heart of an idealism that is still dominant'.[62] For Raymond the challenge is exactly to think 'probabilities not as an image of a non dominated world, but as *a different type of causal apprehension*. To think a probabilistic causality *in place of an indeterminist philosophy*'.[63] This leads to a different kind of determinism, 'a theoretical organization of effects without causes, *a causality without causes*'.[64] However, there is still the danger of idealism especially in the sense of a conception of laws of chance that 'reveal a subtle harmony in the universe',[65] a position Raymond attributes to Poincaré, although in an ambiguous form. For Raymond, probability brings tensions both to mathematics and philosophy, because of the importance of experimentation and the way it affects the very notion of causality, despite the initial tendency of statistics to associate probability with state ideological strategies.

Raymond's *La résistible fatalité de l'histoire* [*The resistible fatality of history*] (1982) deals precisely with the question of history and the difficulty of a 'science of history', as envisaged in the Marxist tradition, especially if we think that in this tradition we have references to the inevitability of revolution or socialism. In contrast, Raymond wants to distance his position from any such dialectic of the 'inevitable'.

> Capitalism's contradictions are not revolutionary by themselves, only their exploitation is. In a different fashion to what goes on in Hegel there is no dialectic logic in Marx. Contradictions do not lead to anything but the mechanism of their enlarged return. A revolution can only come by the interplay of contradictions and not by their proper development. We are dealing with a struggle, not a destiny: and if we explain to the proletariat how capitalist crises function and how to organize in a different fashion society, it might be able to realize its unity beginning by its fundamental division and arrive at victory.[66]

This brings forward the difficulty of thinking the question of temporality, and in particular the articulation of different forms of temporality, and social becoming with reference to 'neither chance nor providence'.[67] Regarding this question, he suggests two answers, one materialist and one idealist. The materialist

---

62   Raymond 1975, p. 36.
63   Raymond 1975, p. 43.
64   Raymond 1975, p. 47.
65   Raymond 1975, p. 48.
66   Raymond 1982, pp. 17–18.
67   Raymond 1982, p. 31.

is what he calls the 'theory of the puppet',[68] in an analogy with how a theory of the functioning of a puppet requires all the combinations and interlaces of the string, along with an emphasis on the contradictions of the articulations. This means that we are not dealing with the 'state of things' but 'with the ensemble of the transformations of this state and its mechanisms. Namely, the practice of things, with the risk that this brings along regarding the exploitation of possibilities'.[69] The other idealist solution is to link the theory of history to eternity through the quest for regularity and order even in accidents. In contrast, for Raymond, the challenge is exactly to think, borrowing a notion from Macherey, in terms of a 'logic of the unforeseen',[70] and this is what comes out of political practice:

> [P]olitics instructs us in this way: clearing out the unforeseen is not the aim of theory, its existence is not a failure of theory. We experience in a very evident manner today: the success or failure of the union of the Left is not inscribed in history; nothing is decided in advance. No scientific formulation containing the word 'inevitable' can enable us to understand this.[71]

Consequently, what is needed is a thinking of causality as a calculus of chance, which was also Raymond's preoccupation in *De la combinatoire aux probabilités*, and he points towards both Machiavelli and Pascal as thinkers who attempted to confront this. At the same time, he insists that Kant is the first to stress the relation between political practice and theory of history: 'Kant is the first philosopher to say that the theory of history is not a theory like the others: we can surpass the limits of understanding, resolve all the mysteries that critique has left [...] on the condition of pracitising politics. Political practice is constitutive of the theory of history'.[72] A theory of history cannot be complete without political practice:

> Finally a science of history cannot be constituted without a political practice. We cannot do science of history in the office or in the laboratory, as is possible for physics. Historical theory would thus be incomplete, even mysterious, as Kant perceived, as Marx says: it is not theory that dissolves

---

68   Ibid.
69   Raymond 1982, p. 32.
70   Macherey 1964, p. 69.
71   Raymond 1982, p. 36.
72   Raymond 1982, p. 65.

mysteries but practice. Political practice does not only make use of history, it completes the theoretical aspect of history.[73]

This makes it rather urgent to rethink a theory of history as a theory of political action and transformation: 'A theory of political action as historical transformation, a theory of the fractures of history, here are two new urgencies'.[74] However, the main difficulty is how to reconcile the 'generality of a theory' with the 'indefinite continuity of singular dissimilar events'.[75] This dissimilarity and singularity of events, along with the unforeseen nature of their emergence is indeed an open question, and one which in the period of the non-repetition of May 68 took on an even greater significance, not only political but also theoretical. However, a 'historical theory cannot foresee the causality of political action',[76] and we must think of causality in terms of a relation of an event to its effects: '[i]t is the relation of an event to its effects that makes a cause out of it'.[77] Consequently, a 'historical causality is only theorizable a posteriori'.[78]

As a testing ground for this conception of historical causality, Raymond uses the theory of war, by means of a comparison between Clausewitz and (Vietnamese) General Giap. He chooses Clausewitz because he thinks that he introduced the 'calculus of chance into the theory of war'.[79] Moreover, Clausewitz thinks theory in its relation to practice, as a method for action, a way to take correct initiatives, a manner of producing correct judgements. In Clausewitz, Raymond thinks that he can discern the different form of causality induced by politics; one that discerns causes whose 'junction with their effects is only visible after their production'.[80] Therefore, it is an attempt to think history beyond both determinism and chance. However, the limit of Clausewitz's conception is the vague character of his references to the submission of war to politics.

On the question of the *just* war suggested by Giap, Raymond suggests that this points towards the conception of history as 'the possibility of transformation of things',[81] which also stresses the importance of politics and the articula-

---

73 Raymond 1982, p. 84.
74 Raymond 1982, p. 93.
75 Raymond 1982, p. 94.
76 Raymond 1982, p. 96.
77 Raymond 1982, p. 97.
78 Raymond 1982, p. 98.
79 Raymond 1982, p. 112.
80 Raymond 1982, p. 123.
81 Raymond 1982, p. 130.

tion of ideology and politics in revolutionary practice: 'The force of an ideology, its justness [*justesse*], is that it can draw values from the analysis of the possible transformations of reality'.[82] In this sense, winning a war is not about knowing in advance the outcome, but about 'mobilizing all the potentialities'.[83] Consequently, it is exactly the very labour of political practice that leads to a new conception of theory: 'there is causality, only by the thorough work, day by day, hour by hour, moment by moment, causality is only in the continuity of work and not at the level of determinism which would be historical'.[84] For Raymond, this offers the possibility of a radical renovation of historical materialism, as a new type of theory that insists on the singular event and the accident and on the relation between theory and transformative political practice.

> The essential in social history is the everyday, the accidental, the singular. What Cournot excluded from theory. This does not impede a general theory, on the other hand, or the attention in the long run. But to achieve theory, we have to engage practically in the everyday, the accidental, the singular. In distinction to classical theory, we have to engage in the transformation of reality in order to be able to theorize it.[85]

It is obvious that here we are dealing with an attempt towards a conception of historical materialism as above all a form of radical anti-teleology, a radical break with any conception of historical progress and destiny and a quest for the future that only struggle can construct:

> By nature the future belongs to neither progress nor communism. Not only is it possible to have returns of 'reaction' or of capitalism and 'social-democratic' advances, but above all every *description* of *the* communist society will be in vain in front of the *diversity* of communist societies that will be *possible* and, fortunately, dependent upon those that *will construct* it. The future does not belong to desk prophets but, and for the better, to those who *struggle* in order to render it 'inevitable'. In any case, this 'inevitable', which they transform in the struggle, qualifies only the abolition of fatality, the victory of liberty over the inevitable.[86]

---

82   Raymond 1982, p. 131.
83   Raymond 1982, p. 134.
84   Raymond 1982, pp. 148–9.
85   Raymond 1982, p. 153.
86   Raymond 1982, p. 155.

After Althusser's death and the editions of his texts from the 1980s, Raymond criticised Althusser's conception of aleatory materialism, insisting that he confuses the need for an anti-finalist position with a reference to the aleatory. Raymond insisted that 'non-necessitarianism is not essential chance, any more than anti-finalist chance excludes necessitarianism', and he insisted that such a conception of 'aleatory politics without any possible effectiveness' enabled Althusser to oppose the 'stifling Marxism of reproduction',[87] leading to an impasse and an inability of thinking and intervening in the openness of struggle:

> One point reveals well this ambiguity in Althusser: he slides from a conception, that of Clausewitz, according to which the theory of war does not have to foresee the outbreak of struggle but only the conditions of its engagement, leaving the struggle itself outside of theory, but not outside of every judgement, to the doctrine of the unforeseeable, the aleatory, in which anything can happen. He slides from the practical question of the future to the aleatory future. It is this specificity of the outside of theory, an outside that is neither necessary nor aleatory, but beyond theory, that Althusser did not succeed in thinking: that is to say a material outside, precisely about which concrete analyses can speak, in which they can intervene, but which they cannot replace. And if they wrongly pretend to do so, then chance is established illusorily in order to escape this aim.[88]

4 Contradictions of Aleatory Materialism

However, reading these texts as Althusser's *Kehre* does an injustice to Althusser's later writings and is more a projection than an actual reading. It would be better to think of an unresolved tension that runs through the theoretical core of the later writings. On the one hand, it is obvious that the notion of the encounter is a new attempt by Althusser to think the (non-)ontology of a relational conception of social reality in the sense of an absence of both a teleology of social forms and any form of social 'substance'. This is indeed a major question of any materialist social theory: how to think the effectivity of social relations, the way they combine social practices and their agents and reproduce themselves, while at the same time acknowledging that there is no 'deeper'

---

87   Raymond 2015, p. 184.
88   Ibid.

ASSESSING ALEATORY MATERIALISM   157

social substance that guarantees this process and its reproduction. This also leads to another important conclusion: modes of production and social forms are open to change, open to historical transformation, not because of any historical tendency towards progress but because of their inherent instability. On the other hand, we also have the linking of the encounter not only with *chance*, a certain randomisation of history, but also with a conception of a constant rearranging of the world through the endless movement of energetic social atoms, which might be considered to be close to an idealist conception of freedom of social agents.[89]

Therefore there are indeed also contradictory aspects in the whole conception of aleatory materialism. First of all we must deal with the problems at the centre of the notion of the encounter introduced by Althusser in the later writings. As Morfino and Pinzolo have stressed,[90] there is an oscillation in Althusser's conception of the encounter. On the one hand, it refers to a relational conception of social reality, to the 'ontology of the relation',[91] exemplified by Marx's notion of *Verbindung*.[92] We can say that this is the materialist instance of the notion of the encounter. On the other hand, we can say that the notion of the encounter (and the contingent swerve at its beginning) refers to a possible theory of the energetic character of singularities and it is close to the 'idealism of freedom' that Althusser himself tried to distinguish from aleatory materialism.

Consequently, it is necessary to pay particular attention to the open questions related to the notion of the encounter. What is primary, the atoms or the deviation that forms worlds, the parallel rain or the swerve? Is the rain of atoms a pre-existing world or state of affairs or the absence of any world and in this sense reality? It is obvious that from a theory of the non-teleological character

---

89   For a reading of the contradictions of aleatory materialism see Tosel 2013.
90   Morfino and Pinzolo 2005.
91   Balibar 1995, p. 32. See also Morfino 2010 on this.
92   'Welches immer die gesellschaftlichen Formen der Produktion, Arbeiter und Produktionsmittel bleiben stets ihre Faktoren. Aber die einen und die andern sind dies nur der Möglichkeit nach im Zustand ihrer Trennung voneinander. Damit überhaupt produziert werde, müssen sie sich verbinden. Die besondre Art und Weise, worin diese Verbindung bewerkstelligt wird, unterscheidet die verschiednen ökonomischen Epochen der Gesellschaftsstruktur' (Marx 1893). 'Whatever the social form of production, labourers and means of production always remain factors of it. But in a state of separation from each other either of these factors can be such only potentially. For production to go on at all they must unite. The specific manner in which this union is accomplished distinguishes the different economic epochs of the structure of society from one another' (Marx 1974, pp. 36–7). Although traditionally translated as 'unity' the French translation as 'combination' makes the relational character of the notion of *Verbindung* more evident.

of the encounter to a theory of the swerve as radical origin and beginning, the distance is small. If we have to remain within the limits of the encounter metaphor, and bring forward its materialist potential, then it is necessary to stress that what pre-exists any possible new encounter is not the 'original' rain (an image consistent with a conception of the swerve as origin) but other encounters (i.e. pre-existing modes and forms of production). In this reading the centrality of the encounter would not imply a theory of the radical origin but an attempt to theorise the constant repetition of both the encounter and the deviation.[93] Only if we break away from any reading of Althusser's texts that focus on the openly contingent character of social forms and of the energetic character of social atoms/singularities, then it is possible to treat the theoretical couple encounter/deviation as a materialist conception of the conjuncture in the open space of the articulation of social forms and relations, as a new non-teleological and non-mechanistic way to think the reproduction of social forms and relations. In this sense, encounter is not freedom materialised nor is deviation the trait of an emerging subjectivity, but the necessary dialectic of social reproduction.

There is always the danger of the notion of the encounter moving towards a conception of radical contingency, of chance. On the one hand, the primacy of the encounter can take the form of a refusal of any teleology and of an insistence on the necessarily provisional and tendential character of all our assertions regarding social reality. As André Tosel stresses:

> No necessary reason governs historical change and the production of structures. Beginning with floating elements a structure is born out of an encounter that allows these elements to be taken within an ensemble. Within this ensemble, that herein cannot be called a fixed totality, a conditional necessity is realized the laws of which we can research that are only tendential and therefore provisional. Everything – structure, elements, conjunctures – and submitted to refusals and the *aleas* of contingence. We have to affirm the primacy of the encounter and of its unconditional contingence over its forms and their conditional necessity.[94]

At the same time the very use of references to *aleas*, contingency, *clinamen* raises the question of whether we are dealing with a conception of radical contingency and chance, especially since it 'does not make a distinction between

---

93 On this see the reading in Morfino and Pinzolo 2005.
94 Tosel 2012, p. 27.

alea, aleatory and contingent'.[95] For André Tosel we must pay particular attention to the terminological tensions inherent in this theoretical direction

> The notion of the *alea* implies a calculus of hazards and probabilities which gives a totality of nodes of possible hazards in the infinite of time. The notion of the aleatory does not send back to this totality and does not function within a terrain [...] which presupposes [...] a relative constancy of the laws of hazard.[96]

It is based upon this idea that Tosel has raised the question of any possible analogies between this kind of radical contingency in Althusser and a Heideggerian conception of finitude and, at the same time, the dangers in such a theoretical direction.

> The question posed to the materialism of the encounter is therefore at least to know if it implies a philosophy of finitude of a Heideggerian type. It is the category of the necessity of contingency that we have to interrogate. Althusser has indeed affirmed it. If the rules have nothing that is necessary, what they allow us to learn from the in itself of the ordered world is not necessary. They could be different or not exist at all. But why not accept the possibility of other rules and other laws? Why must the miracle and the mystery be excluded? Relativism and scepticism wander around and it is impossible to resort to the principle of causality as an expression of the principle of reason. It becomes impossible for the impossible to be impossible. Pascal can be right against Spinoza and religious speculation can find again its rights beyond the critique of superstition and beyond the more moderate Kantian criticism regarding religion.[97]

This greater emphasis on contingency and chance also implies a redefinition of the reference to communism. André Tosel has suggested that we can talk about a '*Communismus absconditus*' [*absent communism*][98] in a similar fashion as Pascal's *Deus absconditus* [*absent God*]. In the case of Pascal we have faith in something that offers no sense of certainty whatsoever. In the case of Althusser and his conception of aleatory materialism, for Tosel we have the possibility of a '*clinamen* of the elements of the capitalist mode of production that could

---

95   Tosel 2012, p. 45.
96   Ibid.
97   Tosel 2012, p. 46.
98   Tosel 2012, p. 42.

inaugurate a series of transformations leading to a void of other elements, to form encounters giving place to another mode of production'.[99]

That is why it is necessary to read more carefully the metaphor of the rain (as an image of the parallel movement of atoms before the original swerve) and the problems related to its theoretical position and functioning. While Althusser had in many instances stressed the relation between the notions of the encounter and the rain, as Vittorio Morfino has stressed, the notion of the rain has less to do with the primacy of the encounter over form and more to do with the primacy of the non-encounter over the encounter:

> These rains are modelled on Epicurus's rain of atoms, the vertical and parallel fall of primal bodies that, with the *clinamen*, pile up and give birth to worlds. But this rain, it should be emphasised, is not a metaphor for the thesis of the primacy of the encounter over form, but rather of another thesis that is perhaps complementary to it, the thesis of the primacy of the *non*-encounter over the encounter: before the encounter that originates a world, atoms fall like raindrops without encountering one another, and their existence as elements that will make up a world is entirely abstract.[100]

To take one example: Althusser's treatment of Spinoza's parallelism[101] as an example of the *rain* is a rather strange theoretical choice, since parallelism in Spinoza is not an ontological proposition about the emergence of the world (such as Epicurus' rain of the atoms) and has much more to do with the relation between thought and extension (in fact the relation between thought and extension as part of the same ontological level, and the rejection of any form of dualism) and with the fact that the order and connection of ideas is the same as the order and connection of things.[102] In fact, the very notion of 'parallelism' comes from Leibniz, who tried to incorporate Spinoza into his own dualist perspective.[103] It seems as if Althusser is at this point trying to fit Spinoza into the whole imagery of the encounter, something made evident by his linking of the formation of 'common notions'[104] to the notion of

---

99   Ibid.
100 Morfino 2015b, pp. 100–1.
101 'The fact that [the attributes] are parallel, that here is an effect of parallelism, recalls Epicurus's rain' (Althusser 2006a, p. 177).
102 Spinoza 2002, p. 247 (*Ethics*, Part II, proposition VII).
103 Macherey 1997, pp. 71–81. See also Gueroult 1974, p. 64.
104 An important aspect of Spinoza's second kind of knowledge (Spinoza 2002, pp. 266–8, *Ethics*, Part II, proposition XL, scholia I and II).

the encounter. Furthermore, it is worth noting that Althusser takes a rather ambiguous position concerning imagination as the first kind of knowledge. Instead of considering it the prototype of a theory of ideology, as he emphatically did elsewhere,[105] he tends to view it as the only way to come to terms with the world in its dispersed and not totalised character.[106] This effort to include Spinoza in the genealogy of a philosophy of the aleatory and the contingent stands in sharp contrast to Spinoza's rejection of the notion of contingency, and his insistence that things appear as contingent because of inadequate knowledge.[107]

Althusser's use of the notion of the void is also contradictory.[108] On the one hand, he tends to treat the notion of the void as a reference to the absence of any philosophical object: '[a philosophy of the void] *begins by evacuating all philosophical problems*, hence by refusing to assign itself any "object" whatever'.[109] This brings us back to Althusser's redefinition of philosophy as having no object[110] and to his reference to the 'void of the distance taken' in *Lenin and Philosophy*,[111] as the description of how philosophical interventions, although deprived of an object in the sense of the sciences, can have real effects because of their retracing of the line of demarcation between materialism and idealism. Then, there is the possibility of reading the recurrence of the void in Althusser's writings as a metaphor for a relational conception of social reality according to which what exists are fundamentally relations,[112] a conception which was at the basis of his theoretical innovations of the 1960s (social totality as a decentred whole, structural causality, 'absent cause') and his search for a way to theorise historical causality in a way that would not be transitive-mechanical or expressive.

---

105   Althusser 1976a, pp. 135–6.
106   '[Spinoza] not only turns his back on all theories of knowledge, but also clears a path [...] for the recognition of the "world" as unique totality that is *not totalized, but experienced in its dispersion*, and experienced as a "given" into which we are thrown' (Althusser 2006a, p. 179).
107   Spinoza 2002, pp. 234 and 236 (*Ethics*, Part I, proposition XXIX and proposition XXXIII, scholium 1). On this point and in order to render Althusser some justice we must say that some of his comments have great theoretical merit, such as his insistence on the gap separating Spinoza and any traditional theory of knowledge or traditional metaphysics in general and on Spinoza's rejection of any theory of the *cogito*. See Althusser 1994a, pp. 467–87; Althusser 1997a.
108   On the importance of the void in Althusser's theoretical trajectory see Matheron 1997.
109   Althusser 2006a, p. 174.
110   Althusser 1990.
111   Althusser 1971, p. 62 (the original translation uses *emptiness* instead of *void*).
112   A position also expressed by Macherey (1979, p. 218).

On the other hand, a more 'ontological' conception of the void emerges in these texts, revealed by Althusser's understanding of the void pre-existing the formation of worlds in Epicurus, by his reading of Machiavelli and the possibility of the Italian national unity, by his return to Pascal's effort to elevate the void to the status of philosophical concept,[113] and by his position that the void must be at the centre of any materialist philosophy.[114] This notion of the void can be related to another important part of the later Althusser's imagery, the margin or the interstice,[115] which is exactly where the possibility of alternatives and new social and political forms arises,[116] with communist relations existing in the interstices of imperialism. The margin and the interstice are also where theoretical and social forms exist which are not conditioned by class struggle: *'not everything in life is class struggle'*.[117] André Tosel has stressed that the void in Althusser has both an epistemological and ontological sense. Regarding the epistemological and first ontological plane 'the void is some kind of a methodological operation which, on the interior of the fullness of theoretical world that is already occupied, it makes the void of these determinations'. On the second ontological plane 'the void sends us back to an absolute absence of determination. It signifies that no necessary reason pre-exists the world that is produced in the encounters'.[118]

However, this image of the void has more to do with an Epicurean rain of atoms, where new forms emerge only as swerves *ex nihilo*, and less with a historical materialist conception of social emancipation being possible because social relations and structures are inherently contradictory, always amidst uneven processes of reproduction and transformation, and therefore constantly open to change.

In this sense we can talk about a fundamentally unresolved tension that runs through the theoretical core of the later writings. On the one hand, it is obvi-

---

113 Contrary to traditional philosophical historiography Althusser also considers Spinoza to be a thinker of the void (Althusser 2006a, p. 178). François Matheron, in an editorial note (Althusser 2006a, p. 204) refers to a 1982 paper by Macherey (included in Macherey 1992) as supporting the same 'paradoxical' position. I think that Macherey is in fact more cautious and also stresses the differences between Pascal and Spinoza in what concerns the notion of the void.
114 On this notion of the void as the centre of any 'grand philosophy' see Althusser 2005a.
115 Which recalls Marx's references to trading nations of ancient times living in the intermediate worlds of the universe (Marx 1894, p. 225) or usury living in the space between worlds (Marx 1894, p. 412).
116 Althusser 1994, pp. 490–1; Althusser 2005a.
117 Althusser 2005, p. 191.
118 Tosel 2012, pp. 42–3.

ous that the notion of the encounter is a new attempt by Althusser to think the (non-)ontology of a relational conception of social reality in the sense of an absence of both a teleology of social forms and any form of social 'substance'. This is indeed a major question of any materialist social theory: how to think the effectivity of social relations, the way they combine social practices and their agents and reproduce themselves, while at the same time acknowledging that there is no 'deeper' social substance that guarantees this process and its reproduction. This also leads to another important conclusion: modes of production and social forms are open to change, open to historical transformation, not because of any historical tendency towards progress (and necessary historical stages) but because of their inherent instability. On the other hand, we also have the linking of the encounter not only with *chance*, a certain randomisation of history, but also with a conception of a constant rearranging of the world through the endless movement of energetic social atoms. As a result, the void acquires a new meaning: it refers to a necessary open space for this movement of social atoms, or the need to create this necessary free space.

It is here that the notion of radical beginning and commencement emerges. There has to be nothing in order for something radically new to emerge. The reasons why, at a time of major personal, political and philosophical crisis, Althusser opts for this image is more than obvious: Unable to confront the reality of both the extent of the crisis of the communist movement, a crisis that for many years he recognised and denounced, at the same time refusing to acknowledge its full extent (thus his insistence on a more or less imaginary communist movement to which he addressed his pleas for theoretical and political correction), he fantasises about a radically new beginning. But, as we all know, the fantasy of a new beginning – e.g. in personal relations – usually reflects a refusal to actually face reality.[119] As a result, the void acquires a new significance. It is as if Althusser insists that for something new to exist, there has to be a radical absence. But this is also another form of historicism and a philosophy of the origin, as if only from nothing can something emerge. It is exactly here,

---

119 That is why Ichida and Matheron's emphasis on the notion of beginning (*commencement*) in Althusser's later writings is a reading which is in sharp contrast to Althusser's rejection of both a teleological 'End' and an equally teleological 'Origin' and 'Beginning'. The following extract exemplifies the idealism of their position: 'This "non originary nature of the originary", which is for Logic its sure beginning, can we call it, despite whatever Althusser says here, otherwise than "pure beginning"? In its proper inaugural version, immediately discovered by the althusserian systematisation, the process without subject nor end(s), which has always begun, presents itself like the very problem of "a beginning from nothing": the process exists only in the pure beginning' (Ichida and Matheron 2005).

in this conception of radical absence as a prerequisite for something new to emerge, that the encounter/deviation couple tends more towards a notion of the chance and the random.[120]

There is no doubt that the question of historical novelty, of the possibility of *new social and political configurations* is crucial for any philosophical position attached to political projects of social emancipation. In order to challenge theoretically the existing social conditions, one must insist on the possibility of radical historical novelty. This has also been the line of demarcation between reformist and revolutionary conceptions of politics. Social and political change requires radically novel solutions. Answers to social contradictions must take the form of *ruptures*. That is why any truly materialist philosophy of history must be a philosophy of *events*, of the possibility of events. But any attempt to theorise the possibility of new events has to confront two theoretical temptations. The first is the temptation of teleology in the sense of treating the new as always already incorporated in the present situation as its inner truth or *telos*. The other is to treat the new as a *miracle*,[121] as something that was in no way foreseen in the contours of the situation and somehow just happens by a radically novel intervention. The question is therefore how to theorise the possibility of radically new configurations emerging through the existing conditions. In this sense one might say that a materialist position insists on radical novelty and beginning but not on *absolute* beginnings in a metaphysical sense.

What is missing in this second conception is that new social forms do not emerge *ex nihilo*. There is no 'void' in history, some form of societal configuration (or an articulation of modes and forms of production) is 'always – already – there'. What is radically new is exactly the possibility of new social forms and encounters. The void in this sense must be thought not in terms of nothingness but rather in terms of this absence of any essentialist, historicist form of an 'intrinsic' link between the preceding social forms and the ones that follow them, this absence of any Historical Design or prefigured Progress.

And this brings us to another contradictory aspect of Althusser's later writings, namely his turn towards the singular case, event, and fact, a turn that comes close to a kind of atomistic empiricism, leading even to a positive appraisal of Hume.[122] There is the possibility of treating these references as an expression of Althusser's conception of materialism as nominalism, a recurring theme in the later writings,[123] both in the sense of a radical distinction between

---

120 On such a reading of Althusser's reference to the aleatory, see Moulier-Boutang 2005.
121 On this see Bensaïd 2004.
122 Althusser 2006a, p. 278.
123 See for example Althusser 2006a, p. 265. On Althusser's nominalism see Montag 1998.

real objects and theoretical objects, and as an emphasis on singularity. But even though in the strict sense only singular historical formations and conjunctures exist, these must be viewed, to use Spinoza's terms, as singular essences, as complex relations, not atomistic facts or solitary cases, something that implies that we need a nominalism of relations, not of 'things'.[124] It is true that Althusser also speaks about constants, sequences and lasting encounters and tries to bring this atomistic conception close to the Marxist notion of the tendential law,[125] but the latter refers to the contradictory co-existence of tendencies and countertendencies as a manifestation of the contradictory nature of social reality[126] and not to the perception of sequences of relations between singular facts as a result of human imagination and reasoning,[127] a position quite far from the original conception of Althusser's materialism as anti-empiricism *par excellence*.

It is this emphasis, this search for some tangible form of facticity, which is at the basis of Althusser's inability to think, in these later writings, in terms of social forms. Although his insistence on the primacy of productive relations over productive forces and on the antagonistic character of class relations was very important and supported the theoretical break with forms of economism and technological determinism and facilitated the recognition of the importance of struggles and movements against the capitalist organisation of production, at the same time it tended to underestimate the importance of social forms, exemplified in his rejection of the theory of fetishism.[128] This emphasis on the antagonistic character of social practices tended to underestimate the fact that class struggle does not just take place within antagonistic class relations, but also under the weight of historical social forms that also induce their effects on the class struggle. In this sense capitalism must be defined not only

---

124 'The constitutive elements of an individual are thus themselves complex realities, composed of distinct parts that coexist within it and themselves are determined outside this relationship, and thus in an infinite sequence, because the analysis of reality is interminable, according to Spinoza, and can never lead to absolutely simple beings, from which a complex system of relations would be constructed. Not *existing*, strictly speaking, except as relations: this is why singular essences that are determined themselves are not affected by the exterior sequence of existence, and this is why they cannot be understood through an analysis that would discover the simple underneath the complex, as a terminal element, an irreducible unity' (Macherey 2011a, p. 178; Macherey 1979, p. 218). On the importance of the reference to Spinoza's singular essences for Althusser's self-correction of earlier theoreticist deviations, see Goshgarian 2003, p. xliii.
125 Althusser 2006a, p. 197.
126 Marx 1894.
127 This is the difference between a materialist position and Hume's empiricism (Hume 1964).
128 Althusser 2006a, pp. 126–35.

in terms of capitalist relations of production, but also in terms of the importance of the value form (as a historically specific result of the hegemony of capitalist relations of production without reference to some form of simple commodity production) and all the forms of social (mis)recognition and fetishistic representations it brings along with it, which is exactly the reason for the contradictory complexity of the first volume of Marx's *Capital*,[129] an aspect missed by Althusser.[130]

5 Contingent Encounter or Materialist Dialectic?

One of the most striking features of Althusser's later writings is his rejection of any notion of a dialectic, not only in the sense of his choice of theoretical vocabulary but also in a more profound sense: Althusser's use of the notion of the encounter (in its more general ontological sense) seems to reject the dialectical character of social contradictions. By dialectical character we mean that the primacy of the relation over its elements (and of the contradiction over its poles) implies that the contradiction is internalised in each element of the contradiction in a complex process of mutual determination, each pole of the contradiction being in a sense the result of the contradiction itself.[131] This leads to an underestimation of the 'labour of the negative', not as the self-development of a historical essence or *Weltgeist*, but as the recognition of the constant effectivity of social antagonism, which constantly prevents social reality from becoming a closed system and creates possibilities of social change. It also leads to the underestimation of the complex and uneven character of social contradictions and the way in which they are articulated and overdetermined. And this is important since, as Althusser himself showed, it is exactly this contradictory, uneven and overdetermined character of social real-

---

129 On this reading see Milios, Dimoulis and Economakis 2002. And although a great part of recent and important work on the theory of the value-form has been rather Hegelian in its philosophical debts (for example Arthur 2002), I think that only a reworking of these questions in terms of a non-metaphysical and non-historicist materialism such as Althusser's can help bring forward Marx's immense theoretical revolution.

130 This had consequences for theoretical trends influenced by him. The Regulation School's option of a 'middle range' descriptive theory of social forms is an example of such an empiricist approach. On the relation of the Regulation School to Althusser, see Lipietz 1993. This does not mean that Althusser is to be blamed for the Regulation School's shortcomings as some critics of Regulation maintain (see for example Mavroudeas 1999).

131 On the importance of the internalisation of the relation as the crucial aspect of a materialist conception of the contradiction, see Balibar 1997, pp. 298–9.

ity which also makes possible a 'labour on the "labour of the negative"', that is revolutionary politics as transformative social practice.

At a first reading this refusal of the dialectic seems to mark a theoretical retreat compared to his path-breaking earlier effort to rethink, in a non-metaphysical way, contradiction as the basis of a materialist conception of social causality. Althusser seems to be haunted by a very particular conception of the contradiction as the internal self-alienation and new unity of a substance and considers this to be the main problem of most classical definitions of the dialectic. As Yves Vargas has shown,[132] Althusser for many years had to combine two opposed necessities: on the one hand, to move beyond any metaphysical or historicist materialism, any traditional conception of the dialectic; on the other hand, to continue to be able to communicate with militants using classical Marxist terminology, even though he was distancing himself from this problematic. This can account for the discrepancy between his published texts and his unpublished manuscripts.

And although Althusser tries to distinguish between the aleatory and the contingent, in many cases he seems to opt for a conception of the chance encounter, an emphasis on historical contingency and surprise, a wait for the unexpected. But in his return to the contingent Althusser in a way forgets a basic theoretical premise of both Marx and Spinoza, namely their conception of the dialectic of freedom and necessity, of freedom as necessity.[133] Social change and the emergence of a just society are not the outcome of a chance encounter, but presuppose the intelligibility of social reality. It is the result of the society being determined and us being able to have a knowledge of this determination (especially if we view determinism in the open sense of the contradiction being the basis of social causality) and not indeterminate. In Spinoza's terms, freedom is a consequence of an intelligible necessity,[134] and in Marx's terms it is knowledge of the objective conditions of the class struggle that makes possible the political direction of the class struggle. That the process of knowledge is itself part of the social reality to be known, or that it is not possible to assume a neutral position, presents the difficult and dialectically contradictory nature of this process, not its negation or impossibility.

---

132 Vargas 2008.
133 It is worth noting that Slavoj Žižek has suggested that the classical position of freedom as conceived necessity (Hegel 1873, §147; Engels 1987, p. 129) must be complemented with its 'reversal': 'necessity as (ultimately nothing but) conceived freedom' (Žižek 1999, p. 44).
134 On the relation between knowledge and emancipation in Spinoza see Matheron 1988 and Tosel 1994.

This is why we must say, using Althusser's own metaphors, that although a materialist philosopher indeed jumps on a train on the move[135] and is always already within a particular historical conjuncture, she does not simply travel along: On the contrary, she tries to discern not only which way the train is going, but also how the train moves, what other routes are possible, and finally she tries to turn the train towards the direction she thinks best, something that Althusser, faced with a profound political, theoretical and personal crisis, thinks impossible.

But in order to do justice to Althusser, we can also say that his oscillations are a result of a contradiction which transverses any attempt to formulate a materialist practice of philosophy. On the one hand, we have the effort to bring forward the materiality of the social practices themselves as a rejection of any form of ontological dualism and any metaphysical beyond, an effort that runs the risk of empiricism, positivism and misrecognition of the mechanisms which produce social phenomena. On the other, there is the necessity of criticising ideological misrecognitions, of theoretically producing the real as opposed to the obvious of the ideological surface, an effort that runs the risk of theoreticism and a foundationalist approach to knowledge. In a sense there is no exit from this oscillation, only the successive bending of the stick to the opposite side.

---

135 'The materialist philosopher, in contrast, is a man who always "catches a moving train", like the hero of an American Western' (Althusser 2006a, p. 177).

CHAPTER 9

Spinoza in Althusser-as-Laboratory

The preceding analysis has shown that Althusser, from the beginning, set out to explore and at the same time challenge, in a highly original way, the main open questions regarding whatever had been termed materialism and dialectics in the Marxist tradition. His oscillations and his 'bending of the stick' stress the inherently contradictory and tendential character of this terrain. Yet there is one philosophical reference that remains constant in this entire trajectory: Spinoza.

Althusser's references to Spinoza have been an object of much scrutiny and study. This is due to the fact that, amongst other things, Althusser himself insisted on his Spinozism,[1] naming the group of his close collaborators, with whom he wished to wage war against idealist deviations in the theoretical scene in the second half of the 1960s, 'groupe Spinoza',[2] as well as the importance attributed to Spinoza in the lineage of aleatory materialism in the post-1980 texts. Moreover, the fact that some of Althusser's collaborators, such as Étienne Balibar and Pierre Macherey,[3] have been associated with the renaissance and new flourishing of Spinoza studies since the 1970s attests to the association of Althusserianism with Spinozism.[4] To this we must add that recent important studies of Althusser, such as Warren Montag's,[5] have shown how, at important turning points, such as the abandonment of 'structuralist' references to 'latent structures', this was related to discussions of Spinozist conceptions of singularity. More recently, Knox Peden has offered a magisterial survey of the influence of Spinoza within the French intellectual scene and how Spinozist references have been instrumental in the attempt to fight the influence of Phenomenology, and has also delineated the various phases of Althusser's engagement with Spinoza.[6] Other recent studies have attempted to problematise this relation, such as Peter Thomas's reading of Althusser's relation to Spinoza[7] and how this relation has been treated by commentators such as Perry Anderson.[8]

---

1 Althusser 1976a, p. 132.
2 Matheron 2012.
3 See *inter alia* Balibar 1998, Macherey 1994–98, Macherey 2011a.
4 It is also interesting that Althusser's interest in Spinoza coincides with a broader renewal in Spinozist Studies. On that see Macherey 2011b.
5 Montag 2013.
6 Peden 2014.
7 Thomas 2002.
8 Anderson 1976.

At the same time, we have from Althusser lots of references to Spinoza, and many analogies with Spinoza and obvious influences, but not the kind of extensive engagement he has with other philosophers such as Montesquieu, Rousseau, and Machiavelli.[9] In a certain way, Spinoza is like a constant companion to Althusser, a constant interlocutor.[10]

1   Spinozist Epistemology

In what follows, we will retrace some of the aspects of Althusser's confrontation with Spinoza. In *Montesquieu, Politics and History*, Spinoza is described as a precursor of a realist and naturalistic approach to human relations:

> Spinoza, too, intended that human relations should be treated in the same way as natural things, and by the same routes. For example, take the pages that introduce the *Political Treatise*: Spinoza denounces the pure philosophers who, as the Aristotelians do with nature, project into politics the imaginary of their concepts or ideals, and he proposes to replace their dreams with the real science of history. How then can we claim that Montesquieu opened routes which we find completely mapped out well before him?[11]

Spinoza is here is presented as a defender of the thesis that there can be a science of history, in contrast to moralistic concerns, in the same fashion as Hobbes, receiving the same accusation of atheism.[12] Moreover, Spinoza is presented as one of the first to signal the change in the very conception of law associated with the advent of modern science and Althusser refers to Spinoza's reference in the *Theological-Political Treatise* to the new 'metaphorical' meaning of 'law' in sciences, as opposed to the traditional meaning of 'command' in theology.[13]

In *For Marx*, references to Spinoza are scarce, even if the influence is more than obvious. Althusser refers to Spinoza in a footnote in *Marxism and Humanism*, where there is a reference to Spinoza's passage from the first to the second

---

9   On the relative paucity of Althusser's writings on Spinoza see Moreau 1993.
10   François Matheron (2012, p. 77) has indicated the existence of a large file of notes and commentary on Spinoza in Althusser's archive that suggests an extensive engagement with Spinoza's texts.
11   Althusser 1972a, p. 18.
12   Cf. Althusser 1972a, pp. 24–5.
13   Althusser 1972a, p. 32. Cf. Spinoza *TTP* IV (Spinoza 2002, p. 427).

kind of knowledge in order to support his position on the rupture between ideology and science and to refute the Hegelian position.

> Therefore science can by no criteria be regarded as the truth of ideology in the Hegelian sense. If we want a historical predecessor to Marx in this respect we must appeal to Spinoza rather than Hegel. Spinoza established a relation between the first and the second kind of knowledge which, in its immediacy (abstracting from the totality in God), presupposed precisely a radical *discontinuity*. Although the second kind makes possible the understanding of the first, it is not *its truth*.[14]

The second explicit reference to Spinoza in *For Marx* is in 'On the Materialist Dialectic' in a passage insisting upon the importance of the concept of overdetermination as the necessary condition for any real theoretical or political practice, in the sense that only within singular overdetermined conjunctures can we find the conditions for political intervention but also for theoretical production.

> Do we now need to repeat that unless we assume, think this very peculiar type of determination once we have identified it, we will never be able to think the possibility of political action, or even the possibility of theoretical practice itself [...] [D]o we need to add that unless we conceive this overdetermination we will be unable to explain theoretically the following simple reality: the prodigious 'labour' of a theoretician, be it Galileo, Spinoza or Marx, and of a revolutionary, Lenin and all his companions, devoting their suffering, if not their lives, to the resolution of these small 'problems': the elaboration of an *'obvious'* theory, the making of an *'inevitable'* revolution, the realization in their own personal 'contingency'(!) of the Necessity of History, theoretical or political, in which the future will soon quite naturally be living its 'present'?[15]

However, it would be an underestimation of the importance of Spinozist themes within *For Marx* if we limited ourselves to explicit references. Althusser's conception of knowledge production, exemplified in the whole schema of the three Generalities, is also of obvious Spinozist origin. As Peden has shown, we have here the influence of an entire tradition of a rationalist reading of Spinoza in France, as a philosopher insisting on the possibility of scientific knowledge. For Peden,

---

14   Althusser 1969, p. 78.
15   Althusser 1969, p. 210.

Althusser articulates his version of the theory of knowledge presented in Spinoza's *Treatise on the Emendation of the Intellect*, codifying it along the tripartite scheme of the 'Generalities'. Offering an alternative to dialectical accounts of knowledge, Althusser suggests a process of knowledge production wherein Generality II, the theory of a science at a given moment, works upon Generality I, the raw materials of scientific and ideological practice (i.e., lived experience), to produce the concrete, scientific Generality III.[16]

The origins of this position can be found in Spinoza's distinction between different kinds of knowledge both in the *Treatise on the Emendation of the Intellect* and *Ethics*. In the *Treatise* Spinoza distinguishes between four modes of perception and knowledge.

1. There is the perception we have from hearsay, or from some sign conventionally agreed upon.
2. There is the perception we have from casual experience; that is, experience that is not determined by intellect, but is so called because it chances thus to occur, and we have experienced nothing else that contradicts it, so that it remains in our minds unchallenged.
3. There is the perception we have when the essence of a thing is inferred from another thing, but not adequately. This happens either when we infer a cause from some effect or when an inference is made from some universal which is always accompanied by some property.
4. Finally, there is the perception we have when a thing is perceived through its essence alone, or through knowledge of its proximate cause.[17]

The distinction and hierarchy of different kinds of knowledge is even more evident in Spinoza's *Ethics*. Spinoza presents his distinction between three kinds of knowledge in Scholium 2 of Part II, Proposition 40.

> From all that has already been said it is quite clear that we perceive many things and form universal notions:

---

16 Peden 2014, p. 151. Gregory Elliott has presented the importance of Spinoza's position in the following way: 'Spinoza had rejected the Cartesian search for a priori guarantees of the possibility of knowledge as both unavailing (for condemned to an infinite regress) and unnecessary ("for we have a true idea": *habemus enim ideam veram*)' (Elliott 2006, p. 77).

17 Spinoza 2002, p. 7 (*TEI* I 19).

1. From individual objects presented to us through the senses in a fragmentary [*mutilate*] and confused manner without any intellectual order (see Cor. Pc. 29, II); and therefore I call such perceptions 'knowledge from casual experience.'
2. From symbols. For example, from having heard or read certain words we call things to mind and we form certain ideas of them similar to those through which we imagine things (Sch. Pc. 1 8, II).

Both these ways of regarding things I shall in future refer to as 'knowledge of the first kind,' 'opinion,' or 'imagination.'

3. From the fact that we have common notions and adequate ideas of the properties of things (see Cor. Pro 38 and 39 with its Cor., and Pro 40, II). I shall refer to this as 'reason' and 'knowledge of the second kind.'

Apart from these two kinds of knowledge there is, as I shall later show, a third kind of knowledge, which I shall refer to as 'intuition.' This kind of knowledge proceeds from an adequate idea of the formal essence of certain attributes of God to an adequate knowledge of the essence of things.[18]

Moreover, there are obvious analogies between Althusser's theory of ideology, especially in *For Marx*, and Spinoza's conception of imagination and of the tendency of human beings to view reality in a distorted and anthropomorphic fashion. In *For Marx* Althusser refers to ideology as an imaginary 'lived' relation into which humans actually live and experience reality.

> So ideology is a matter of the *lived* relation between men and their world. This relation, that only appears as '*conscious*' on condition that it is *unconscious*, in the same way only seems to be simple on condition that it is complex, that it is not a simple relation but a relation between relations, a second degree relation. In ideology men do indeed express, not the relation between them and their conditions of existence, but *the way* they live the relation between them and their conditions of existence: this presupposes both a real relation and an '*imaginary*', '*lived*' relation.[19]

In the *Appendix* of the first Part of *Ethics* Spinoza presents something close to a theory of ideology. This begins by the insistence that exactly because common men tend to think in terms of their own lived experience, they tend to

---

18   Spinoza 2002, p. 267 (*E* II, Pr40, Sch2).
19   Althusser 1969, p. 233.

have anthropomorphic and finalist conceptions of the world that do not correspond to the essence of things.

> I have thus sufficiently dealt with my first point. There is no need to spend time in going on to show that Nature has no fixed goal and that all final causes are but figments of the human imagination.[20]
>
> We see therefore that all the notions whereby the common people are wont to explain Nature are merely modes of imagining, and denote not the nature of anything but only the constitution of the imagination. And because these notions have names as if they were the names of entities existing independently of the imagination I call them 'entities of imagination' [*entia imaginationis*] rather than 'entities of reason' [*entia rationis*].[21]

Knox Peden has also linked Althusser's 'Spinozism of permanent incommensurability',[22] between concrete in thought and concrete in reality, the object of knowledge and the real knowledge, which is one of the cornerstones of Althusser's epistemology to Spinoza, by means of Martial Gueroult's particular reading of the parallelism between thought and extension.

> Following Gueroult, the parallelism thesis in the *Ethics* – 'The order and connection of ideas is the same as the order and connection of things' – is misleading and misnamed. The point, we argued, is not that there are two orders running in parallel and that an occasionalist faith à la Malebranche ensures their symmetry. It is that there is only *one* order, and thus it is the 'same' order. But within that order the two attributes never touch; they never coincide. For Gueroult, the radical noncoincidence between the attributes Thought and Extension was the precondition for the knowledge itself that could come to be within Thought. For Althusser, too, 'the problem of the relation between these two objects (the object of knowledge and the real object), [is] a relation which constitutes the very existence of knowledge' [...]. The relation must always remain a relation; it can never be 'resolved' in an original or an achieved unity.[23]

In *Reading Capital* Spinoza is credited with being the first to 'have proposed both a theory of history and a philosophy of the opacity of the immediate. With

---

20   Spinoza 2002, p. 240 (*E* I, App.).
21   Spinoza 2002, p. 243 (*E*I, App.).
22   Peden 2014, p. 158.
23   Peden 2014, pp. 158–9.

him, for the first time ever, a man linked together in this way the essence of reading and the essence of history in a theory of the difference between the imaginary and the true'.[24] Pierre-François Moreau has stressed that Althusser also searched in this reading of Spinoza for 'indications of the idea of a history without subject',[25] especially since the 'base of his [Spinoza's] anthropology is contained within this stunning formula: everyone ignores oneself'.[26] At the same time, we can also stress the fact that in Spinoza Althusser could also find a negation of any conception of substance as subject and thus of every teleology, be it of a Hegelian or an Engelsian variant. As Vittorio Morfino has stressed:

> The asymmetry of Engels's thought with respect to the symmetry of Spinoza's produces a radical difference in the two systems: the dialectical materialism of Engels, like Hegel's idealism, understands the process of the becoming subject of substance as the becoming liberty of necessity, while the Spinozist theory of substance as *causa sui* – identifying *ab origine* in the absoluteness of substance the concepts of essence and existence, of power and act, of free cause and necessary cause, of *in se esse* and *per se concipi* – bars any conception of nature and of history as a *Bildungsroman* of a subject (Hegel's Idea; Engels's humanity).[27]

Moreover, Spinoza is presented as the archetype of anti-empiricism through his insistence that there is a real difference between the object of knowledge and the real object.

> Against what should really be called the latent dogmatic empiricism of Cartesian idealism, Spinoza warned us that the *object* of knowledge or essence was in itself absolutely distinct and different from the *real object*, for, to repeat his famous aphorism, the two objects must not be confused: the *idea* of the circle, which is the *object* of knowledge must not be confused with the circle, which is the *real object*.[28]

However, Althusser insists that Spinoza has not received the attention he deserved and his intervention has been suppressed, despite being a theoretical revolution.

---

24 Althusser et al. 2016, pp. 14–15.
25 Moreau 1993, p. 83.
26 Ibid.
27 Morfino 2015, p. 44.
28 Althusser et al. 2016, pp. 40–1.

Spinoza's philosophy introduced an unprecedented theoretical revolution in the history of philosophy, probably the greatest philosophical revolution of all time, insofar as we can regard Spinoza as Marx's only direct ancestor, from the philosophical standpoint. However, this radical revolution was the object of a massive historical repression, and Spinozist philosophy suffered much the same fate as Marxist philosophy used to and still does suffer in some countries: it served as damning evidence for a charge of 'atheism'.[29]

The Spinoza evoked here is an anti-empiricist Spinoza insisting on the difference between the concept and the object. 'In view of this, we must clearly and unequivocally see and understand that the *concept of history* can no longer be empirical, i.e., *historical* in the ordinary sense, that, as Spinoza has already put it, *the concept dog cannot bark*'.[30] The reference here is to Spinoza's distinction in the *Treatise on the Emendation of the Intellect* on the difference between the idea and ideatum.

> A true ideal (for we do have a true idea) is something different from its object (ideatum). A circle is one thing, the idea of a circle another. For the idea of a circle is not something having a circumference and a centre, as is a circle, nor is the idea of a body itself a body. And since it is something different from its object, it will also be something intelligible through itself. That is, in respect of its formal essence the idea can be the object of another objective essence, which in turn, regarded in itself, will also be something real and intelligible, and so on indefinitely.[31]

André Tosel has suggested that at this phase Althusser's interest has been 'fundamentally gnoseologico-critical' in an attempt to 'think the dialectic under materialism'.[32] In a similar sense, Althusser suggests that the synchronic approach of the complex set of relations and determinations that define a whole, in the sense that only an adequate complex conceptual articulation can accomplish such a task, is analogous to Spinoza's conception of eternity.

> The synchronic is then nothing but *the conception* of the specific relations that exist between the different elements and the different struc-

---

29   Althusser et al. 2016, p. 250.
30   Althusser et al. 2016, p. 252.
31   Spinoza 2002, p. 10 (E I 33).
32   Tosel 1994, p. 205.

tures of the structure of the whole, it is the knowledge of the relations of dependence and articulation which make it an organic whole, a system. *The synchronic is eternity in Spinoza's sense*, or the adequate knowledge of a complex object by the adequate knowledge of its complexity.[33]

Consequently, Political Economy is presented as knowledge of the first kind, since its ignorance of its actual premises means that it is only the 'Imaginary in action'.

As an indication, let us adopt a famous thesis of Spinoza's: as a first approximation, we can suggest that Political Economy's existence is no more possible than the existence of any science of 'conclusions' as such: a science of 'conclusions' is not a science, since it would be the actual ignorance (*'ignorance en acte'*) of its 'premises' – it is only the Imaginary in action (the 'first kind').[34]

Moreover, Spinoza is presented as the first philosopher before Marx to have thought of the possibility of structural causality as opposed to any expressive conception of totality.

If the whole is posed as *structured*, i.e., as possessing a type of unity quite different from the type of unity of the spiritual whole, this is no longer the case: not only does it become impossible to think the determination of the elements by the structure in the categories of analytical and transitive causality, *it also becomes impossible to think it in the category of the global expressive causality of a universal inner essence immanent in its phenomenon*. The proposal to think the determination of the elements of a whole by the structure of the whole posed an absolutely new problem in the most theoretically embarrassing circumstances, for there were no philosophical concepts available for its resolution. The only theoretician who had had the unprecedented daring to pose this problem and outline a first solution to it was Spinoza.[35]

---

33 Althusser et al. 2016, p. 255. On the complexity of Spinoza's notion of eternity see Moreau 1994.
34 Althusser et al. 2016, p. 311.
35 Althusser et al. 2016, pp. 342–3.

A similar reference can also be found in *Essays in Self-Criticism* where structural causality is directly linked to Spinoza.[36] It is obvious that until here the influence of Spinoza is that of a highly original anti-empiricist and rationalist philosophy of the possibility of scientific knowledge in terms mainly of conceptual breaks and articulations that are in a position to reproduce, in terms of concepts and discursive practices, the complexity and interdependence of actual historical determinations, whilst at the same time maintaining a strict separation of concepts and real objects, of thought processes and real historical processes, of objects and ideas. It is at the same time an attempt towards a break with empiricism, defined here by Althusser in the broadest sense possible of any epistemological position that includes some sort of direct contact within theoretical practice with actual objects, and an insistence on the possibility of knowledge through conceptual transformation and production. In terms of the insistence on the possibility of knowledge, it is indeed reminiscent of the Spinozist insistence on the total intelligibility of things. Martial Gueroult captured this aspect of the Spinozist tradition in his assertion that 'absolute rationalism, imposing the total intelligibility of God, key of the total intelligibility of things, is therefore for Spinozism the first article of faith'.[37] In a similar manner one could also link Althusser's attempt towards a symptomatic reading of texts, and in particular Marx's *Capital*, as a variation of Spinoza's reading of the Scriptures in the *Tractatus Theologico-Politicus*.

At the same time, we know that Althusser in the end fails to present the 'protocols' of scientificity that would guarantee this process and this is the limit of his initial confrontation. Althusser is conscious that any attempt to seek guarantees would risk falling back into ideological illusions and thus he attempts to change the terrain from that of the guarantees of objectivity towards that of the conditions that produce scientific discourse as a differential form of conceptual transformation.

> Unlike the 'theory of knowledge' of ideological philosophy, I am not trying to pronounce some *de jure* (or *de facto*) *guarantee* which will assure us that we really do know what we know, and that we can relate this harmony to a certain connexion between Subject and Object, Consciousness and the World. I am trying to elucidate the *mechanism* which explains to us how a *de facto* result, produced by the history of knowledge, i.e., a given determinate knowledge, functions *as a knowledge*, and not as some

---

36   Cf. Althusser 1976a, p. 126.
37   Gueroult 1968, p. 12.

> other result (a hammer, a symphony, a sermon, a political slogan, etc.). I am therefore trying to define its specific effect: the knowledge effect, by an understanding of its *mechanism*. If this question has been properly put, protected from all the ideologies that still weigh us down, i.e., outside the field of the ideological concepts by which the 'problem of knowledge' is usually posed, it will lead us to the question of the mechanism by which forms of order determined by the system of the existing object of knowledge, produce, by the action of their relation to that system, the knowledge effect considered.[38]

And this differential nature of scientific discourse is in fact the presence of an absence, the absence of the constitutive order of its object, a point that Althusser has already linked to his insistence of the priority of the synchronic approach as opposed to a diachronic conception of 'becoming'. Scientific discourse produces a complex set of conceptual determinations, produces a theoretical object, produces reality in-thought and at the same time must – because this is exactly its claim to knowledge – make this presence absent.

> This last question confronts us definitively with the *differential* nature of *scientific discourse*, i.e., with the specific nature of a discourse which cannot be maintained as a discourse except by reference to what is present as absence in each moment of its order: the constitutive system of its object, which, in order to exist as a system, requires the absent presence of the scientific discourse that 'develops' it.[39]

It is exactly this conception of scientific practice as a process of conceptual transformation and displacement that indeed brings Althusser closer to the Spinozist tradition in French epistemology and in particular the work – and influence – of Jean Cavaillés and his insistence, presented in Spinozist terms, on a philosophy of the concept and not of consciousness in sharp contrast to Neo-Kantianism and phenomenology:

> There is not one consciousness generating its products or simply immanent to them; rather it is every time in the immediacy of the idea, lost in it and losing itself with it and only connecting with other consciences (which would be tempted to call other moments of conscience) through

---

38   Althusser et al. 2016, p. 72.
39   Ibid.

the internal links of the ideas to which they belong. The progress is material or between singular essences, its driving force the exigency that each one be surpassed. It is not a philosophy of conscience but a philosophy of the concept that can give a doctrine of science. The generating necessity is not that of an activity but of a dialectic.[40]

Warren Montag and Knox Peden have recently offered detailed accounts of the importance of Cavaillés for the French intellectual scene[41] and in particular for the articulation of a tendency that opposed the resurgence, in Phenomenology, of a philosophy of conscience. The passage quoted above includes not only the 'rationalist' epistemological appeal to a philosophy of the concept instead of philosophy of consciousness, a point that, if we could formulate it in Althusserian terms, also suggests that science is a process of transformation, a process 'without a subject'; it also includes both a Spinozist reference to singular essences and a rather cryptic opposition between activity and the dialectic that one could link to Althusser's insistence on the opposition between an idealist conception of praxis and a potential materialist dialectic.

However, Peter Thomas has challenged this conception of a homology between Spinozist and Althusserian conceptions. He has stressed the difference between Spinoza's conception of one substance (*Deus sive Natura*) and Althusser's insistence on social totalities as 'historically specific formations'.[42] Moreover, there is the problem of taking account of the efficacy of concrete social practices within a social totality, something impossible, according to Thomas, if we 'posit a social totality as bearing to its parts the same causal relationship as that of Spinoza's one substance to its modifications'.[43] To this Thomas adds the difference between Spinoza's assumption of a plenitude of being and the potentiality implied by the fact that a 'social totality is necessarily incomplete'.[44]

2   Spinoza and Singularity

However, there is an open question: what about the 'other' aspects of Spinoza's intervention, such as the insistence on singularity and the conception of com-

---

40   Cavaillés 1960, p. 78.
41   Montag 2013, Peden 2014.
42   Thomas 2002, p. 104.
43   Thomas 2002, p. 107.
44   Thomas 2002, p. 109.

plex bodies as the result of 'encounters' and articulation between singular essences? The presence of a strongly anti-metaphysical and anti-historicist philosophy of singular conjunctures in Althusser's work at the beginning of the 1960s is undeniable, exemplified in tests such as 'Contradiction and Overdetermination'. The very notion of overdetermination is an attempt at a theory of the singularity of conjunctures that could be combined with an insistence on the intelligibility of the social whole in terms of structural determinations. The interesting thing is that Althusser's explicit references to Spinoza in the texts up to 1965 mainly deal with the rationalist aspect of Spinozism and not with the – already present from the beginning – insistence on singularity.

Therefore it is interesting to revisit Althusser's self-criticism in the 1970s regarding his alleged structuralism and his insistence that what had been described as structuralism was in fact *Spinozism*.

> If we never were structuralists, we can now explain why: why we seemed to be, even though we were not, why there came about this strange misunderstanding on the basis of which books were written. We were guilty of an equally powerful and compromising passion: *we were Spinozists*. In our own way, of course [...] And by attributing to the author of the *Tractatus Theologico-Politicus* and the *Ethics* a number of theses which he would surely never have acknowledged, though they did not actually contradict him. But to be a heretical Spinozist is almost orthodox Spinozism, if Spinozism can be said to be one of the greatest lessons in heresy that the world has seen! In any case, with very few exceptions our blessed critics, imbued with conviction and swayed by fashion, never suspected any of this. They took the easy road: it was so simple to join the crowd and shout 'structuralism'! Structuralism was all the rage, and you did not have to read about it in books to be able to talk about it. But you have to read Spinoza and know that he exists: that he still exists today. To recognize him, you must at least have heard of him.[45]

What is interesting about this passage and its appearance within Althusser's self-criticism regarding his structuralism is that Althusser not only declares his intellectual debt to Spinoza, but also links his theoreticism/structuralism to aspects of his Spinozism. G.M. Goshgarian has insisted that Althusser's 'Spinozist' self-critical overtones after 1966 were a correction to aspects of his initial 'Spinozism'.

---

45   Althusser 1976a, p. 132.

Althusser would, in 1966–67, mobilize Spinoza against his theoreticism, which, however, his appeal to Spinoza also reinforced. Against the conception of knowledge as a shadowy reflection of a real lying outside it, *For Marx* and *Reading Capital* silently invoke the Spinozist principle that 'substance thinking and substance extended are one and the same substance', insisting that ideas, no less than their real objects, are *also* the real, albeit in the form of thought.[46]

The main form of this new interest in Spinozist themes had to do with singularity. Warren Montag has traced the importance of Macherey's discussions with Althusser,[47] his critique of the very notion of structure and his insistence on certain Spinozist themes, in particular those relating to a conception of the whole as an articulation of singular entities in relations of mutual determination as opposed to 'latent structures' treated as unified substances. This is evident in passages from Spinoza such as the following from a letter to Oldenburg.

> Now all the bodies in Nature can and should be conceived in the same way as we have here conceived the blood; for all bodies are surrounded by others and are reciprocally determined to exist and to act in a fixed and determinate way, the same ratio of motion to rest being preserved in them taken all together, that is, in the universe as a whole. Hence it follows that every body, insofar as it exists as modified in a definite way, must be considered as a part of the whole universe, and as agreeing with the whole and cohering with the other parts. Now since the nature of the universe, unlike the nature of the blood, is not limited, but is absolutely infinite, its parts are controlled by the nature of this infinite potency in infinite ways, and are compelled to undergo infinite variations. However, I conceive that in respect to substance each individual part has a more intimate union with its whole.[48]

We can see the same emphasis on singularity in Althusser's critique of Lévi-Strauss's structuralism:

> It would be easy to show that modern scientific thought sets out to think *singularity*, not only in history (Marx and Lenin: 'the soul of Marxism is

---

46 Goshgarian 2003, p. xv.
47 Cf. Montag 2013.
48 Spinoza 2002, p. 849.

the concrete analysis of a concrete situation') and psychoanalysis, but also in physics, chemistry, biology [...] Philosophers such as Spinoza (the 'singular essences') and Leibniz did not wait until our day to assign the non-savage mind the task of thinking singularity (that is, to register the *reality* of modem science in philosophy).[49]

In a letter to Franca Madonia from September 1966, sent along with the first of the 'Three Notes on the Theory of Discourse', Althusser links his new thinking of the relation between general theories and regional theories to the need to think in terms of singular essences. According to Althusser we need the intervention of the regional theories in order to have theoretical objects that correspond to real objects and these real objects have to be considered as singular essences: 'That which exists, in the narrow sense of the word "to exist", is real objects (which I today call, using a concept of Spinoza's, "singular essences")'.[50] At the same time, Althusser thinks that Spinoza's reference to a unifying substance is a way to think of the relation and articulation between General Theories without falling into the trap of a simple parallelism of attributes:

> In other words, if we do not think the possibility of an articulation between GTs, we will remain at the level of the *parallelism of attributes* and of the temptation that constantly accompanies it, the *conflation* of the attributes. The parallelism of the attributes is tempered and corrected in Spinoza by the concept of substance: the different attributes are attributes *of one and the same substance*. It is the concept of *substance* which plays the role of the concept of the articulation of the attributes (it plays other roles, too, but that is one of them). The *distinction* between attributes is possible only on condition that they are articulated. [...] [T]he distinction between the GTs (which are our attributes) is possible only on condition that they are *differentially articulated*.[51]

For Knox Peden, this is also an attempt by Althusser to rethink overdetermination: 'the "articulation between GTs," [is] an esoteric way of restating the figure of causality as the "overdetermined" convergence of disparate elements'.[52] It is

---

49 Althusser 2003, p. 30.
50 Althusser 1997b, p. 712.
51 Althusser 2003, p. 65.
52 Peden 2014, p. 170.

also interesting that in this entire period Althusser is also fascinated by Spinoza as a figure exemplifying intellectual commitment, something that can be found in all his work. This is also evident in this passage from a 1967 letter to Franca Madonia:

> I know very few things and I don't have the time to learn them. I am a political agitator in philosophy. We need this kind of figure, in order to open new roads. Others, younger and better armed with knowledge of all kinds will be *the* philosopher that I could not be. Being philosopher means being able to write the *Ethics* that we need. This will soon be *possible* (and it is indispensable). However, I will not write it.[53]

Moreover, the very choice to name the collective group he had formed and which offered the background for many of his interventions in the 1966–69 period 'Groupe Spinoza' offers an image of the significance of Spinozist themes in this period of self-criticism and correction. As François Matheron has shown, this group was formed at the end of spring 1967 and did not function after 1969. Althusser conceived of it in terms of a semi-clandestine group reminiscent of 'Marxist-Leninist' organisations of that time, but it was impossible to continue after Althusser's choice to remain in the Communist Party.[54] Matheron also makes interesting observations regarding Althusser's initial ambition to produce, through the collective work of the *Groupe Spinoza*, a philosophical work with a systematicity that would constitute their equivalent to the *Ethics*, as also mentioned in the above quoted letter to Franca Madonia. Matheron insists, based upon notes by Althusser in 1966, that what Althusser had in mind as the basis of a new *Ethics* was a 'general theory of the conjuncture'.[55] Moreover, Matheron suggests that if until then the Spinozist ontology of the attributes had been used as a means to refute pragmatism, the reference in 1966–67 to the need to write a new *Ethics* in fact refers to the need to stress the practical and political character of the theoretical practice.

> Until then the Spinozist ontology of the attributes had served as a support for the Althusserian conception of 'theoretical practice', of theory conceived as a specific practice, containing in itself the instruments of

---

53   Althusser 1997b, p. 750.
54   Matheron 2012, p. 79.
55   Matheron 2012, p. 81.

its proper validation; it is real battle horse against the all too famous 'criterion of practice' and the disastrous pragmatism with which it has always been associated. Althusser will never return to this position: in numerous texts and particularly in a big unpublished manuscript devoted to the 'Unity of theory and practice', he will even affirm that the grand characteristic of an ideological theory is to be always 'verified by practice' – because it is made for it. But after having defined as 'theory of theoretical practice' this specific theoretical practice that is philosophy, Althusser realizes rather quickly the risk of wanting to constitute by it a sort of 'science of sciences', of absolute knowledge, but also the concomitant risk of reducing political practice to a pure application of theory. From this, we have the effected progressive dissociation between science and philosophy; from this, the insistence, always problematic in his work, on the directly political dimension of theoretical practice; from this the project of writing an *Ethics*.[56]

I would like to suggest that the apex of this attempt towards a more Spinozist conception of singular essences in the complex and overdetermined articulation into 'wholes' can be found in *On the Reproduction of Capitalism*.[57] Here instead of thinking in terms of latent structures, we have Althusser thinking of practices and relations that depend upon the intervention of material apparatuses and the repetition of material practices and rituals that guarantee this process of reproduction. Here reproduction is not just the expression of the efficacy of a structure. Rather, reproduction is the attainment of *duration* for social relations and forms that are always contingent upon the dynamics of the conjuncture. In this new emerging conception, which has obvious Spinozist overtones, the notion of structure is transformed and becomes the notion of a lasting encounter of singular essences, of an encounter that can achieve duration. However, we can also say that apart from this attempt towards a 'Spinozist' correction of earlier 'Spinozist' positions, there was also another important encounter and detour, as Matheron has suggested: the encounter with Machiavelli. In a certain sense, Spinoza and Machiavelli 'incarnate the thinking of the conjuncture'.[58]

---

56   Matheron 2012, p. 82.
57   Althusser 2014b.
58   Matheron 2012, p. 91.

3   Spinoza and the Rejection of Classical Theories of Knowledge

Although we see in action this 'Spinozist' turn towards a thinking of singularity, most of Althusser's references to Spinoza in his early 1970s texts remain within the framework of Spinoza as a potentially materialist thinker of the relationship between ideology and knowledge and as a subversive intellectual figure. Perhaps this is due to the fact that the two main texts by Althusser on Spinoza in the 1970s, the chapter on Spinoza in the *Elements of Self-Criticism* and the 1975 *Soutenance d'Amiens* ('Is it Simple to be a Marxist in Philosophy'), are both formed as retrospective accounts of Althusser's theoretical and philosophical endeavour.

In *Elements of Self-Criticism* Althusser declares Spinozism as the position of the collective work they were performing: 'We were guilty of an equally powerful and compromising passion: *we were Spinozists*'.[59] It is interesting, however, that immediately afterwards the main subject is Althusser's conception of the need for theoretical detours; the detour via Spinoza was a way to think Marx's detour through Hegel. Peter Thomas has commented upon the Hegelian overtones in Althusser's conception of the necessary philosophical detours:

> Althusser's account of his detour via Spinoza seems performatively to confirm the most Hegelian of philosophic procedures: the phenomenological attempt to grasp the inner form of previous philosophies, as an element in understanding the organic relationships which composed them, recapitulating thought and in a condensed form the complex cognitive development which formed the prehistory and conditions of possibility of continuing philosophical practice.[60]

When Althusser returns to Spinoza he repeats his insistence that we can find elements of a theory of ideology in Spinoza: 'in the Appendix to Book I of the *Ethics*, and in the *Tractatus Theologico-Politicus*, we find in fact what is undoubtedly the first theory of *ideology* ever thought out, with its three characteristics: (1) its *imaginary* "reality"; (2) its internal *inversion*; (3) its "centre": the illusion of the *subject*'.[61] Moreover, Althusser insists that we can find in Spinoza a theory of the imaginary that is not based upon the centrality of the Cartesian Subject:

---

59   Althusser 1976a, p. 132.
60   Thomas 2002, p. 88.
61   Althusser 1976a, p. 135.

> But this theory of the imaginary went still further. By its radical criticism of the central category of imaginary illusion, *the Subject*, it reached into the very heart of bourgeois philosophy, which since the fourteenth century had been built on the foundation of the legal ideology of the Subject. Spinoza's resolute anti-Cartesianism consciously directs itself to this point, and the famous 'critical' tradition made no mistake here. On this point too Spinoza anticipated Hegel, but he went further. For Hegel, who criticized all theses of subjectivity, nevertheless found a place for the Subject.[62]

Moreover, Althusser insists that his initial proposition that the text of science includes in itself the protocols of its validity and scientificity, which he justified with reference to Spinoza's thesis *verum index sui et falsi*, did not entail a traditional gnoseological conception of criteria of truth. For Althusser this is the essence of Spinoza's conception, namely the refusal of any conception of the criteria of truth, in favour of a conception of science as a material practice that constantly reinstates the – never final – dividing line between science and ideology.

> I will however deal with one last theme: that of the famous '*verum index sui et falsi*'. I said that it seemed to us to allow a recurrent conception of the 'break'. But it did not only have that meaning. In affirming that 'what is true is the sign of itself and of what is false', Spinoza avoided any problematic which depended on a '*criterion of truth*'. If you claim to judge the truth of something by some 'criterion', you face the problem of the criterion of this criterion – since it also must be true – and so on to infinity.[63]

Althusser returns to this point in *Soutenance d'Amiens* where he insists that the crucial point in Spinoza's phrase is the reference to the fact of knowledge not to the criteria of knowledge, and this is a rejection of the premises of classical theories of knowledge:

> What does Spinoza in fact mean when he writes, in a famous phrase, '*Habemus enim ideam veram* ...'? That we have a true idea? No: the weight of the phrase lies on the '*enim*'. It is *in fact* because and only because we have a true idea that we can produce others, according to its norm. And it

---

62 Althusser 1976a, p. 136.
63 Althusser 1976a, p. 137.

is *in fact* because and only because we have a true idea that we can know that it is true, because it is '*index sui*'. Where does this true idea come from? That is quite a different question. But it is a fact that we do have it (*habemus*) [...] Thus Spinoza *in advance* makes every theory of knowledge, which reasons about the *justification* of knowledge, dependent on the *fact* of the knowledge which we already possess. And so every question of the Origin, Subject and Justification of knowledge, which lie at the root of all theories of knowledge, is rejected.[64]

Similar themes can be found in Althusser's *How to be a Marxist in Philosophy*, a manuscript that remained unpublished until 2015. There, Althusser repeats his well-known position that there was an audacity in Spinoza's conception of God, because if God existed in everything, this was equal to saying that he did not exist. He stresses the importance of infinite modes as an intermediary step in the passage from God to singular objects or individuals, and of Spinoza's notion of *facies totius universi* [figures of the total universe], 'figures which are, doubtless, the most general laws governing, on the one hand, the ensemble of bodies, and, on the other, the ensemble of minds'.[65] For Althusser in such a conception we move beyond a theory of knowledge, of truth criteria and of the subject. In contrast, Spinoza's theory of the three kinds of knowledge goes beyond any question of right and rejects the conception that we can think in terms of faculties. For Althusser, the movement from the first kind of knowledge, to the second of common truths culminates in the third kind, that of singular essences, 'the knowledge of human individuals and the singularity of their histories, or knowledge of the singularity of history, and even the moments and instants of a people's history, as we see in the case of the Jewish people in the *Theological-Political Treatise*'.[66] He also thinks that Spinoza opened up the continent of history in a certain manner and stresses the importance of Spinoza's conception of a causality existing only in its effects, a well-known theme even from the conceptualisation of structural causality in *Reading Capital*. However, he stresses that 'Spinoza lacked the idea of the dialectic he needed to confer a meaning on these intuitions of genius. It was not, however, Hegel, who rightly criticized him for this absence of the dialectic, who would truly answer this question, unspoken in Spinoza and posed by Hegel. It was Marx'.[67]

---

64 Althusser 1976a, p. 188.
65 Althusser 2017b, p. 107.
66 Althusser 2017b, p. 108.
67 Althusser 2017b, p. 109.

Althusser takes up this point again in his manuscript (unpublished during his lifetime) *Philosophy for Non-philosophers*, written after 1975. There he reminds readers of the importance of Spinoza's rejection of any psychological conception of faculty. The reference is to Spinoza's scholium at Proposition XLVIII of Book II of *Ethics*: 'In the same way it is proved that in the mind there is no absolute faculty of understanding, desiring, loving, etc. Hence it follows that these and similar faculties are either entirely fictitious or nothing more than metaphysical entities or universals which we are wont to form from particulars'.[68]

Moreover, in *Elements of Self-Criticism* Althusser insists that Spinoza can help us see knowledge as a material process and practice producing concrete knowledge of singular essences.

> But that does not prevent Spinoza from talking about knowledge: not in order to understand its Origin, Subject and Justification, but in order to determine the process and its moments, the famous 'three levels', which moreover appear very strange when you look at them close up, because the first is properly the lived world, and the last is specially suited to grasping the 'singular essence' – or what Hegel would in his language call the 'universal concrete' – of the Jewish people, which is heretically treated in the *Theologico-Political Treatise*.[69]

Althusser affirms his position that his conception of the three generalities was indeed indebted to Spinoza. What is also interesting is Althusser's discussion of nominalism and Spinoza, which he links again to the question of the difference between the real object and the object in knowledge.

> It is generally agreed that Spinoza fell into nominalism. But he did in any case take measures to protect himself from idealism, both in developing his theory of a substance with infinite attributes, and in arguing for the parallelism of the two attributes *extension* and *thought*. Marx protects himself in another way, more securely, by the use of the thesis of the *primacy of the real object over the object of knowledge*, and by the *primacy of this first thesis over the second: the distinction between the real object and the object of knowledge*. Here you have that minimum of generality, that is, in the case in question, of materialist theses, which, by drawing a line

---

68   Spinoza 2002, p. 272.
69   Althusser 1976a, p. 188.

between themselves and idealism, open up a free space for the investigation of the concrete processes of the production of knowledge.[70]

Althusser could also count Spinoza as an ally in his struggle against all forms of theoretical humanism, avoiding both an optimistic and a pessimistic conception of human nature, something that marks his particular conception of finitude. As André Tosel has stressed:

> Spinoza does not participate in the humanist rationalism that makes man the master of the exterior nature and of his proper nature, an empire in an empire. He does not validate [...] the project of subjectivity defined as a metaphysics of production for production, as he develops a thinking of the being as act. However, he also does not take up [...] the doleful vision of man founded upon the original sin; he does no more praise the obeying submission to the authority of sorrowful passions, than insist on the necessity to meditate death to attain the level of authentic life.[71]

It is interesting that while Althusser frequently refers to Spinoza as a subversive figure who could not easily fit with his historical and social contexts, as a theorist whose positions have been repressed, as a political intervention, there are relatively few references to Spinoza's thinking on politics. It is as if Althusser is always more at ease with the Spinoza of the rejection of any theory of knowledge and of the attempt towards an original theory of ideology, the Spinoza of the *Treatise of the Emendation of the Intellect*, of *Ethics* and of *Tractatus Theologico-Politicus*, rather than the Spinoza of the unfinished *Political Treatise*, the Spinoza that faces the complexity, unevenness and contradictory character of the politics of the Multitude. The following passage from *Philosophy for Non-Philosophers* exemplifies Althusser's treatment of Spinoza's conception of politics:

> If Spinoza discussed political power in terms of the concepts of natural law in order to criticize them, his critique was too shallow to allow him to get beyond a simple rejection of morality as the foundation of all political power, or to get beyond an abstract conception of force as the foundation of that same.[72]

---

70   Althusser 1976a, pp. 192–3.
71   Tosel 2008, pp. 9–10.
72   Althusser 2017a, pp. 174–5.

4 Spinoza in the Genealogy of the Materialism of the Encounter

After the second half of the 1970s and in particular in the texts on the potential genealogy of aleatory materialism, written after 1980, Spinoza is hailed as one of the most important thinkers in the long line of philosophers who thought in a radically anti-metaphysical and anti-teleological manner. Here the parallelism of the attributes is no longer considered an epistemological line of demarcation against any form of empiricism but acquires an ontological status, linked to the falling rain of atoms of the Epicurean rain.

> [T]his book is about another kind of rain, about a profound theme which runs through the whole history of philosophy, and was contested and repressed there as soon as it was stated: the 'rain' (Lucretius) of Epicurus' atoms that fall parallel to each other in the void; the 'rain' of the parallelism of the infinite attributes in Spinoza and many others: Machiavelli, Hobbes, Rousseau, Marx, Heidegger too, and Derrida.[73]

The same goes for Althusser's insistence that we have in Spinoza a philosophy of the void: 'I shall defend the thesis that, for Spinoza, the object of philosophy is the void'.[74] Althusser links this to Spinoza's well-known reference to Deus *sive* natura, which, according to Althusser, equates to the position that God is nothing but nature, an 'absolute, unique, infinite substance, endowed with an infinite number of infinite attributes'.[75] Althusser links his insistence on the void with his reading of the infinity of the attributes of the infinite substance with Epicurus's rain of atoms in the void conceived as an open space that enables in a non-teleological fashion new – potential – encounters (and non-encounters).

> The fact that there is an infinite number of them, and that they are unknown to us, leaves the door to their existence and their aleatory figures wide open. The fact that they are parallel, that here everything is an effect of parallelism, recalls Epicurus' rain. The attributes fall in the empty

---

[73] Althusser 2006a, p. 167. It is interesting to note that Spinoza himself refers positively to Epicurus, Lucretius and Democritus in Letter 56 (Spinoza 2002, pp. 905–6), where he presents his opposition to the existence of ghosts. See the comments by Moreau on the importance of Spinoza's emphasis on the conflict between different philosophical tendencies (Moreau 1975, pp. 173–84).
[74] Althusser 2006a, p. 176.
[75] Althusser 2006a, p. 177.

> space of their determination like raindrops that can undergo encounters [*sont rencontrables*] only in this exceptional parallelism, this parallelism without encounter or union (of body and soul ...) known as man, in this assignable but minute parallelism of thought and the body, which is still only parallelism, since, here as in all things, 'the order and connection of ideas is the same as the order and connection of things'. In sum, a parallelism without encounter, yet a parallelism that is already, in itself, encounter thanks to the very structure of the relationship between the different elements of each attribute.[76]

It is obvious that we are dealing here with a rather bold philosophical problem. Leaving aside the question of whether this emphasis on parallelism is loyal to the spirit of Spinoza's texts or whether it borders the Leibnizian conception, we are dealing with a more ontological reading of Spinoza that goes beyond the limits of any epistemology. The parallelism of the attributes becomes a more general reference to social and historical space of human practices, both as bodily movements and discursive practices. At the same time, Althusser does not underestimate the epistemological implications of parallelism, and in particular how in combination with the conception of God as nature as infinite substance, it leads to a refusal of the problem of knowledge as such and also of any problematic based upon a metaphysics of the knowing subject.

> The result of the fact that God is nothing but nature, and that this nature is the infinite sum of an infinite number of parallel attributes, is not only that there is nothing left to say about God, but that there is also nothing left to say about the great problem that invaded all of Western philosophy with Aristotle and, especially, Descartes: the problem of knowledge, and of its dual correlative, the knowing subject and the known object.[77]

Althusser also turns to the political implications of Spinoza's conception of the three kinds of knowledge and in particular of the knowledge of the first kind as a potential theory of ideology, of the role of the imaginary in political practice. Again Althusser reminds us that imagination is not a faculty, but the only way to actually experience reality in all its complexity and dispersion.

---

76   Althusser 2006a, p. 177.
77   Ibid.

> A strange theory, which people tend to present as a theory of knowledge (the first of the three kinds), whereas *the imagination is not by any means a faculty, but, fundamentally, only the only world itself in its 'givenness'*. With this slide [*glissement*], Spinoza not only turns his back on all theories of knowledge, but also clears a path for the recognition of the 'world' as that-beyond-which-there-is-nothing, not even a theory of nature – for the recognition of the 'world' as a unique totality that is not totalized, but experienced in its dispersion, and experienced as the 'given' into which we are 'thrown' and on the basis of which we forge all our illusions [*fabricae*].[78]

For Althusser it is in this conception of the imaginary and of the necessary political myths that we find the possibility of politics. 'For Spinoza, politics is then grafted on to the world's imaginary and its necessary myths'.[79] Althusser does not limit his approach to this relation between politics and the political imaginary. He links this to knowledge of singular essences, as knowledge of the third kind and also to his conception of the possibility (and non-possibility) of an encounter.

> But the theory of the imaginary as a world allows Spinoza to think the 'singular essence' of the third kind which finds its representation par excellence in the history of an individual or a people, such as Moses or the Jewish people. The fact that it is necessary means simply that it has been accomplished, but everything in it could have swung the other way, depending on the encounter or non-encounter of Moses and God, or the encounter of the comprehension or non-comprehension of the prophets.[80]

In another important text from the materials of Althusser's autobiography, he attempts to describe what he owes to Spinoza. Again he refers to Spinoza as a highly original and subversive theorist who, behind an image of strict rationalism, hides liberating and emancipating thinking:

> I discovered in him first an astonishing contradiction: this man who reasons *more geometric* through definitions, axioms, theorems, corollaries, lemmas, and deductions – therefore in the most 'dogmatic' way in the

---

78 Althusser 2006a, p. 179.
79 Ibid.
80 Ibid.

world – was in fact an incomparable liberator of the mind. How then could dogmatism not only result in the exaltation of freedom but also 'produce' it?[81]

Althusser links Spinoza's subversion of the Cartesian cogito with Hegel's subversion of the Kantian transcendental subject and thinks that dogmatism, in the sense of a rigorous logical demonstration, in both cases, is exactly to subvert the positions they were fighting.

> Thus I established a rather strict parallel between Spinoza against Descartes and Hegel against Kant, showing that in the two cases what was in play and in struggle was a *transcendental subjectivist* conception of 'truth' and knowledge. The parallel went quite far: no more *cogito* in Spinoza (but only the factual proposition *homo cogitate*, 'man thinks'), no more transcendental subject in Hegel, but a subject as process [...] In the two cases, Spinoza and Hegel managed – and little matter, or rather all the better, that their demonstration was rigorous and therefore apparently 'dogmatic' – to disentangle the mind from the illusion of transcendent or transcendental subjectivity as a guarantee or foundation of every meaning or every experience of possible truth.[82]

This reference of Althusser to the subversive 'dogmatism' of both Spinoza and Hegel in their respective philosophical strategies is also a way to describe and justify his own philosophical strategy, especially since he himself had been accused of dogmatism:

> I understood then, the reason for this apparent paradox, which, if I can say it, comforted me against the host of accusations of 'dogmatism' that had been thrown at my face. To know that a philosophy called 'dogmatic' and actually having the form of a dogmatic exposition can produce effects of freedom: I had never sought anything else.[83]

Althusser again returns to the importance of the theory of imagination in Spinoza and how it can be considered an archetype for a theory of ideology, a position that he has reinstated many times in his work. However, this time he also turns towards the third kind of knowledge, *amor intellectus Dei* and

---

81   Althusser 1997a, p. 3.
82   Althusser 1997a, p. 4.
83   Ibid.

beautitudo. According to Althusser, Spinoza offers an example of the third kind of knowledge in the *Tractatus Theologico-Politicus* and Spinoza's reference to the history of the Jewish people, which Althusser attempts to read as a reference to an object that is both singular and universal. Here Althusser returns to the problematic of the singularity of conjunctures and the problems it raises regarding the possibility of abstraction and consequently theory. If there are only singular cases, how can we think of something *in general*, especially since nothing exists *in general*, only singular – and overdetermined – conjunctures? Althusser's nominalistic answer is to search for constants and invariants instead of abstract generalities and thus include such a conception of 'universality' that avoids the dangers of a metaphysical abstraction.

> [I]t is only in the individual and singular life or singularities (nominalisms), really singular – but universal, for these singularities are as if traversed and haunted by repetitive and constant invariants, not by generalities but repetitive constants – that one can rediscover under their singular variations in other singularities of the same species and genus. Thus, Spinoza rediscovers quite naturally in the singular history of the Jewish people a *constant* that he has treated 'in general' in the appendix of part I regarding religion in general, and yet there never exists religion in general in Spinoza, no more than does production in Marx. He rediscovers generic constants or invariants, as one wishes, which arise in the existence of singular 'cases'.[84]

Consequently, in the third kind of knowledge we are not dealing with a new object but with 'a new form of relation of appropriation (the word is Marx's) of an object that is *always already there* since the first kind of knowledge'.[85] For Althusser this is the world as a 'concretion of universal singularities'.[86] Consequently, it is a question of a difference between singulars and universals, since in fact the universal is an interconnection and relation of singularities; it is question of a particular relation of appropriation. This, according to Althusser, was the meaning of moving from the abstract to the concrete in the knowledge process, leading to the distinction between the 'real concrete' as 'the universal singular (all the "cases" that constitute the world from the beginning of knowledge of the first kind) and the concrete-in-thought

---

84 Althusser 1997a, p. 9.
85 Ibid.
86 Ibid.

that constitutes knowledge of the first kind'.[87] This is what Althusser found in the singular history of the Jewish people in the *Tractatus Theologico-Politicus* along with a theory of the materiality of ideology. Althusser also returns to the Spinozist schema of an infinite substance effecting itself in infinite attributes and infinite modes, an infinite substance 'without exterior' and 'exteriority',[88] something that, according to Althusser, suggests a revolutionary strategy that recalls 'the theory of the urban guerrilla and the encirclement of cities by the countryside'.[89] Moreover, Althusser suggests that one of the keys to understand the importance of Spinoza is to think of his nominalism, in the sense of a factual conception of truth. For Althusser, this '*factual nominalism* was rediscovered [...] in the famous distinction, internal to any concept, between the *ideatum* and the *idea*, between the thing and the concept, between the dog that barks and the concept of the dog, that does not bark'.[90] This opened the way for the passage from the inadequate knowledge of the first kind to the knowledge of the third kind the 'intuition of the universal singularities' that are 'misrecognised in the imagination'.[91]

Althusser moves also toward a more ontological conception, through what he designates as an 'extraordinary theory' of the body. Althusser here refers to the conception of the body, through Spinoza's thinking of the *conatus* as *potentia* and *generositas*,[92] and also Spinoza's conception of the passions exemplified in an 'astonishing theory of ambivalence, since – to give a single example – *fear is the same thing as hope, its direct opposite*, and they are both "sad passions", passions of slavery under the imagination'.[93] This opens up the way for a philosophy of the body as a process of liberation and emancipation, through the emphasis on the power of thinking, also an attempt to think by one's body,

> to think liberation freely and strongly, therefore, to think properly with one's own body, in one's own body, with one's own body, better: that *to live*

---

[87] Althusser 1997a, p. 10.
[88] Althusser 1997a, p. 11.
[89] Ibid.
[90] Althusser 1997a, p. 12.
[91] Ibid.
[92] Spinoza (*E* III P59) defines *Fortitudo* as the combination of *Animositas* which is defined as 'the desire whereby every individual endeavors to preserve his own being according to the dictates of reason alone' and *Generositas* which is defined as 'the desire whereby every individual, according to the dictates of reason alone, endeavors to assist others and make friends of them' (Spinoza 2002, p. 310). Ted Stolze has stressed the importance of fortitude, courage, and generosity in Spinoza and suggested that they can be also the starting points for a Marxist ethics of struggle for liberation (Stolze 2014).
[93] Ibid.

freely within the thought of the conatus *of one's own body was quite simply to think within the freedom and the power of thought.*[94]

It is obvious that here Althusser moves much towards the direction of a Spinozist ontology, in the sense of an ontology, or non-ontology, of thinking bodies and their *potential* to get rid of both fear and simple hope and actually, in the materiality of their practice, think (and act) alternative configurations and ways toward emancipation. In a certain way, there is an analogy here between the *Communism of the spirits* invoked by Alexandre Matheron and Althusser's conception of liberation.[95] Such references also indicate that Althusser indeed moved beyond the mere epistemological use of Spinoza towards also an 'ethico-political' confrontation with the work of Spinoza.

It is interesting to read this alongside André Tosel's insistence that Althusser, in his reading of Spinoza, its importance notwithstanding, misses the importance of this ethico-political dimension (in a text written before the publication of *The Future Lasts Forever*). According to Tosel, Althusser's 'Spinozism remains aporetic in the measure that the theoretical revolution is condensed in an enterprise of deconstruction (of the triple myth of origin, of subject, of end) or of programmatic preparation, the lancing again historical materialism beginning from "structural causality, adequate to the complexity of modern capitalism"'.[96] Consequently, for Tosel, 'Althusser's Spinoza has lost any ethico-political dimension. It has remained critical and programmatic'.[97]

---

94 Althusser 1997a, p. 13. The reference that fear and hope cannot be good by themselves is to be found in *E* IV P47.

95 'Beyond the "bourgeois" liberal state and the transitory stage of reasonable inter-human life, he wants to establish the *Communism of Spirits*: make the entire Humanity exist as totality conscious of itself, a microcosm of infinite Understanding' (Matheron 1988, p. 612). In a footnote to this passage Matheron quickly adds (invoking Deborin) that '[Communism of the spirits] implies logically [...] a communism of goods'. Matheron has also offered another very convincing conception of a Spinozist 'road to Communism': 'Let's suppose that, if circumstances are favorable to us (which, of course, requires a good organization of political society, even if it is not enough), the determinism of our proper nature will be able to eventually end by importing it, in our body, upon the influences coming from outside. To this corresponds in our spirit the development of reason. Thus, step by step, we will stop alienating ourselves to things. And the relations of power, since they were derived in the last instance entirely from this alienation to things, will wither away progressively. The State would disappear, and with every form of domination, if people were reasonable: it would only be nothing but a community of free men, according spontaneously' (Matheron 2011, p. 79).

96 Tosel 1994, p. 209.

97 Ibid. Jean-Pierre Cotten on the other hand has suggested that we can see in the different approaches to Spinoza by Althusser an oscillation between a defence of the scientificity

For Tosel, going beyond this reading can be described as the challenge for a new materialism:

> [T]he next return of Spinoza could be that of theorist of the ethical transition, that of the constitution of subjectivities as transindividual effects, as liberation effects. Spinoza could well reappear as the moment of constitution of an explicitly novel thought, that will enlarge the theme of the formation of ethical individualities in the comprehension of our problems. Althusser used Spinoza in order to enlarge the interpretative model of Marxism and to ally Spinoza to negative thinkers of modernity, Heidegger and Nietzsche. The part of Spinoza that did not receive attention, which thinks the permanence of the thrust of the '*conatus*' to conquer more activity, more joy, more knowledge, still waits the hour of its return. This hour will simply be that of a new thinking, of another materialism.[98]

I think that we can conclude that Althusser's relation to Spinoza indeed represents a certain paradox. On the one hand, it is obvious that Althusser, in the entire trajectory of his work, confronted the full implications of Spinoza's intervention in the history of philosophy. Althusser moves beyond limiting his Spinozism to a mere rationalist anti-empiricist epistemology, however important this line of demarcation was. Althusser was fully aware of the importance of a materialism of singularities and encounters as what defines 'structures'. Althusser also realised the importance of a materialism of potentiality, in the sense of the need to have more confidence in the potential inscribed in the collective practices, initiatives and experimentations of the subaltern classes. On the other hand, Althusser never fully confronted the full extent of Spinoza's work, hence the fact that he mainly returns to certain specific textual references. Does this suggest some form of inadequacy of his reading? I think this would be unfair taking into consideration that all evidence points towards Althusser having a full apprehension of the work of Spinoza itself and of the relevant literature. I think that the answer to this reading has to do with the very strategy of Althusser's reading. It is a reading that is at the same time bold and careful, intuitive and strict to the letter. It is a reading that gives us an image of Althusser-as-laboratory. Althusser is a laboratory, never simply a reading process. By this, I mean that he never simply attempts a 'symptomatic' reading of a text in the sense of bringing forward its contradictions and dynamics. He

---

of Marxism and a critique of the subject, of teleology and of totalisation, which makes it more apophatic than aporetic (Cotten 1993).

98 Tosel 1994, p. 210.

also constantly attempts to construct elements of a new and original politically oriented materialism. Althusser always thinks the philosophy he attempts to construct through the philosophers he is reading. This can account for the uses he makes of certain philosophical references, for what appears in some cases to be a reluctance to discuss the full extent of texts. And this accounts for the creativity and originality of these readings and the way in which they articulate perspectives and different elements. In this sense, Althusser's Spinozism, as his confrontation with the 'heresy, that is, [Spinoza's] theoretical revolution'[99] along with his 'Machiavellism', along with his indebtedness to Pascal, his constant return to the materialism of Hobbes, his reading of Rousseau and, last but not least, the many intellectual debts to Hegel as a thinker of processes as contradiction, are all aspects of the same endeavour: to elaborate a materialism of (and in) politics, a philosophy that could incorporate the materiality (and potentiality) of struggles and popular initiatives, a philosophy for communism.

---

99   Montag 1993, p. 57.

CHAPTER 10

Structure and/as Conjuncture

So the question remains: Are we to abandon any notion of structural determinations (or any notion of more general historical tendencies as reproduced relations and social forms) in favour of a strictly conjunctural conception of social reality? I think that the price to be paid will be too high and there is the risk of a complete randomisation of social reality. This can lead to decisionism and/or a moralistic conception of politics as simple ethical choices, since there would be no way to think of political practices based upon social dynamics. By contrast, Althusser tried to theorise a different conception of politics which insisted on a certain intellectuality of politics (the articulation of a political process with a thought process) which tried to reconcile the intelligibility of social reality in the sense of discerning structural determinations and the open and always exceptional character of the conjuncture. It is here that notions of overdetermination and underdetermination of the contradiction prove their relevance. Of course, this would mean that we take a different approach towards the very notion of structure, avoiding any conception of structure as 'latent social meaning' and insisting upon treating social structures as inherently contradictory and therefore constantly open to transformation. It would also require a strictly immanentist conception, avoiding any kind of dualism and insisting that 'structural' and 'conjunctural' elements operate at the same level. It is obvious that we are dealing with a difficult and open question, the answer to which indeed involves critically rethinking all the main traditions of materialism, both in its immanentist, 'singular' versions and those with an emphasis on totalities, structured wholes and dialectical processes of transformation.

1   **Rethinking Singularity**

Yet, the question remains: How can we theorise a possible answer to the question of the relation of the structural and the conjunctural, even if we take this distinction and the very terms used as symptomatic of a theoretical challenge not yet posed in its proper terms? It is the question of rethinking singularity and attempting to combine or articulate it with a possible materialist dialectic. Gilles Deleuze has insisted on a thinking of singularities and their '*nomadic distribution*'[1] as the only way to avoid both referring to the bottomless abyss of

---

1   Deleuze 2004a, p. 118.

pure Being and taking individual persons as starting points.[2] Warren Montag has offered a defence of such a radical nominalism that stresses the importance of singular conjunctures, forms, bodies.[3] Michael Hardt and Antonio Negri return to the importance of singular struggles and their 'parallelism' in their recent *Commonwealth*.[4] Compared to historical teleology or metaphysics and an amorphic empiricism of individual 'choices', this turn towards the singular has been more than welcome, especially since it also recognises the importance of specific, concrete struggles in shaping social reality. However, how can we combine it with the Marxist emphasis on the intelligibility of broad historical tendencies?

One way can to be follow Althusser's own call for a Spinozist detour. Althusser himself acknowledged his debt to Spinoza's highly original conception of causality in *Elements of Self-Criticism*: '[Spinoza] in his effort to grasp a "non-eminent" (that is, non-transcendent) not simply transitive (á la Descartes) nor expressive (á la Leibniz) causality, which would account for the action of the Whole on its parts, and of the parts on the Whole – an unbounded Whole, which is only the active relation between its parts: in this effort Spinoza served us, though indirectly, as a first and almost unique guide'.[5] Alexandre Matheron had pointed to this direction of the relation between totality and singularity in his reading of Spinoza: 'The only thing that exists concretely is the self-productive Totality, both naturing and natured, which is articulated in an infinity of singular totalities'.[6]

Pierre Macherey has offered powerful readings of Spinoza that highlight the importance of singular essences, bodies and individuals as 'unities of bodies' in Spinoza and attempts to discern a theory of non-subjectivist and non-teleological relationality in Spinoza and his treatment of these encounters and articulations of singularities. According to Macherey's reading of Spinoza:

> The individual, or the subject, thus does not exist by himself in the irreducible simplicity of a unique and eternal being, but is composed in the encounter of singular beings, who agree conjuncturally within him in terms of their existence, that is, who coexist there but without this

---

[2] 'This is something neither individual nor personal, but rather singular. Being not an undifferentiated abyss, it leaps from one singularity to another, casting always the dice belonging to the same cast, always fragmented and formed again in each throw' (Deleuze 2004a, p. 122).
[3] Montag 1998; Montag 2003.
[4] Hardt and Negri 2009.
[5] Althusser 1976a, p. 141. On the relation of Althusser to Spinoza see the detailed exposition by François Matheron 2012.
[6] Matheron 1988, p. 21.

agreement presupposing a privileged relationship, the unity of an internal order at the level of their essences, which subsist identically, as they were themselves before being thus assembled and without in so being in any way affected.[7]

In Macherey's reading, singular things appear and disappear in a constant movement of causal determinations as extrinsic relations: 'the fact that singular things do not exist in eternity (but in the incessant and changing movement of extrinsic relations in the course of which they appear and disappear) has no effect at all on the eternity of their essence, that is, their immanent tendency to preserve their being'.[8] Equally important is Macherey's rejection of a metaphysical conception of potentiality, exemplified in his insistence on not treating the conatus as forces.[9] Existence and non-existence, appearance and non-appearance, perception and non-perception are the result of a whole chain of causal determinations, themselves belonging to the same ontic level, the same plain of immanence. In the same vein, Balibar has suggested that Spinoza reverses the 'traditional representation of the "real" and the "possible", by inscribing every thought of a possible in the order of the real, instead of making it either the anticipation of its actualization or the logical universe out of which it will pull its conditions of existence'.[10]

Moreover, with this emphasis on singularity there is always the danger of falling back on an image of society or historical development as just an agglomeration of singular essences. On this point, it would be necessary to think mainly in terms of a *nominalism of relations*, insisting on the relational character of singular entities or forms and also on the possibility of exactly a dialectical relational conception that would attempt to explain the necessity of these singular essences, their complex – and mutual – over- and underdetermination. Pierre Macherey's suggestion to treat social reality in terms of the relation between *singular essences*, with the emphasis laid upon their relational character, can offer a way toward this nominalism of relations.

> The constitutive elements of an individual are thus themselves complex realities, composed of distinct parts that coexist within it and themselves are determined outside this relationship, and thus in an infinite sequence,

---

[7] Macherey 2011, p. 176. See also Macherey's commentary on the second Part of Spinoza's *Ethics* in Macherey 1997.
[8] Macherey 2011, p. 173.
[9] Macherey 2011, p. 200.
[10] Balibar 1990b.

because the analysis of reality is interminable, according to Spinoza, and can never lead to absolutely simple beings, from which a complex system of relations would be constructed. Not *existing*, strictly speaking, except as relations.[11]

This thinking of structures not in terms of a social grammar but in terms of ensembles of social relations in the singularity of their encounter and articulation is also evident in Pierre Macherey's reading of Marx's 6th Thesis on Feuerbach. Macherey insists that Marx's definition of the essence of man as the '*ensemble of the social relations*'[12] can help us think the encounter of different social relations and the possibility of their relative 'structural' stability in modes of production and social formations.

> What is 'assembled' in the figure of a unity not simple but complex, are then 'social relations'. By this we understand the different social relations that constitute a multiplicity non totalisable a priori, because they form an 'ensemble', a totality of fact and not of right, which is kept only by their encounter, an encounter that is not fatally harmonious or convergent, but can take and more often takes violent and conflictual forms [...] That, in different moments in history these complexes of relations are not totally devoid of structure but take determinate forms, which stabilize them provisionally, what Marx would theorize by advancing the concepts of 'mode of production' and 'social formation', does not change the main point: these structures are not by right but by fact and nothing authorized us to identify them to *a priori* forms nor to return within the cadre of a logic where their place will be one time for all fixed.[13]

Therefore social structures are not a priori social forms, but relatively and provisionally stable complexes of social relations, in their singular, multiple and conflictual/antagonistic form. There is no teleology or deeper causality that guarantees this provisional stability; their tendency to be reproduced or transformed depends upon the balance of forces in their antagonistic relations.

---

11   Macherey 2011, p. 178.
12   Marx 1845.
13   Macherey 2008, pp. 151–2.

2   Contradiction and Antagonism

Such a conception also makes it imperative to rethink the importance of contradictions as materialised forms of social antagonism and the priority of contradictions over structures. This would require an attempt to reconceptualise, in non-idealist terms, the *labour of the negative*, the constant re-emergence of radical difference, alterity and antagonism at the centre of this constant rearticulation of singularities, both as the reason for of their potential rearrangement and as their condition of existence. It is here that the very notion of contradiction can be revisited. The problem with the concept of dialectical contradiction has to do with how the Hegelian legacy weighs upon it. In the Hegelian version, contradiction is *self-contradiction*, a contradiction that marks the division, internal opposition, sublation, and reconciliation of an essence,[14] and that is why it can easily be linked to some form of process, evolution or teleology. Such a conception of the contradiction and the dialectic is fundamentally incompatible with a materialist conception of singular practices and their articulation in concrete historical conjunctures marked by radical difference, antagonism, and struggle. In opposition to this, Althusser from the beginning in 'Contradiction and Overdetermination' insisted on the difference between the Hegelian and the Marxist concepts of the contradiction, stressing the unevenness, complexity, multiplicity, over- and underdetermination of social contradictions and refusing any conception of the contradiction as self-development. Does this mean that we should abandon the notion of contradiction altogether in favour of a notion of opposition?[15]

An attempt to deal with these questions can be found in Balibar's 1977 text 'Again on Contradiction. Dialectic of class struggles and class struggles in the dialectic'.[16] For Balibar the materialist dialectic is inextricably linked to class struggle: class struggle is its object and itself is a 'particular *form* of class struggle'.[17] Instead of a simple opposition between idealist and materialist dialectics, it is much better to think of a constant struggle of contradictory coexisting materialist and idealist tendencies. This conflict between materialist and idealist elements also takes place within the materialist dialectic leading to various forms of objectivist/naturalist and historicist/subjectivist deviations.

Regarding the question of contradiction Balibar thinks that the crucial question is the relation between contradiction and antagonism. The Marxist tradi-

---

14   Hegel 2010, pp. 374–85.
15   The solution suggested by Lucio Colletti, albeit in a neo-Kantian direction. See Colletti 1975.
16   Balibar 1977.
17   Balibar 1977, p. 21.

tion distinguishes between contradiction and antagonism (for example, in the contradiction between forces and relations of production as opposed to the antagonism between the bourgeoisie and the proletariat), but at the same time inscribes 'antagonism *within* the very definition of contradiction'.[18] The materialist dialectic refuses to identify contradiction and antagonism, but at the same time it does not approach contradiction independently of antagonism.

> [M]arxism studied *contradiction only under the specific form of class antagonism* and its *effects on social practice on its entirety*. And it is exactly *in relation* to this study and its effects that it seems essential to it to distinguish and articulate antagonism and contradiction. Not in order to (de)limit the position of antagonism within a 'general' theory of the contradiction, but in order to develop the analysis proper of antagonism.[19]

According to Balibar, the materialist dialectic has nothing to do with abstract general 'contradictions'. The materialist dialectic articulates class antagonism and specific *social relations* of exploitation and oppression that take analytical priority over the visible forms of class antagonism. The antagonism is inscribed in the capital–labour relation as an antagonistic social relation, and this antagonism is analytically more important than simply recording the conjunctural forms of the antagonism between the bourgeoisie and labour.

> The relation of the bourgeoisie to the proletariat is antagonistic only because the salaried labour is by itself an antagonistic social relation [...] [W]hat is determining in the antagonism between the bourgeoisie and the proletariat is not the autonomous existence of every term, every class – which can be transformed and are transformed profoundly in the course of their history in relation to the *conditions of reproduction* of the social relation of exploitation – *but the very existence of the relation itself*. What can express this by saying that in the historical antagonism of classes, there is a *primacy of the contradiction itself over the contradictory parts*.[20]

Balibar warns against any attempt to move towards a *formalism* of the relation, which would be another form of idealism. The crucial aspect is see how

---

18 Balibar 1977, pp. 43–4.
19 Balibar 1977. p. 46.
20 Balibar 1977, pp. 49–50.

these relations are *materialised* within specific historical conditions and conjunctures. It is obvious that we are dealing here with an important attempt to reformulate a potentially materialist conception of the contradiction in opposition to any idealism and teleology. This articulation between *relation* and *antagonism*, exemplified in the very notion of antagonistic social relation that stresses the efficacy of social antagonism and mass political practice, but at the same time points towards the reproduction of this relation, the historical, political, technological and institutional conditions that enable its repetition. Such a conception also enables a notion of *dialectical determination* in the sense of the determination/transformation of conflicting forces that enter into this antagonistic relation. Such a perspective also comes forward in Balibar's 1988 criticism of Foucault.

> [F]or Marx the condition for the development of a conflict is the *interiorisation of the relationship itself*, in such a way that the antagonistic terms become the functions or the bearers of the relationship. This is why it is not essential for the Marxist representation of the class struggle to describe empirically as characterized entirely by a 'binary and global opposition between the dominators and the dominated' [...] but it is absolutely essential for it to conceive of class relations as being internally irreconcilable, as relations from which the dominated can escape only by destroying the subjugating relationship itself and therefore transforming themselves into different individuals from those that 'constituted' that relationship.[21]

In such a perspective the concept of contradiction is not antagonistic to the emphasis on singularity and the contingency inherent within social structures as enduring encounters, but offers a way to theorise the effectivity of antagonism and antagonistic class relation. This is obvious in Balibar's self-critical rejection of his emphasis in *Reading Capital* on the primacy of the structure upon contradiction,[22] suggesting that a different conception of the priority of contradiction over structure can be found in the theorisation of the primacy of the social relations of production over the forces of production, when it is combined with acknowledging the fact that social antagonism is materialised within productive forces in the form of contradictions. This, in its turn, leads, to the following two theses:

---

21   Balibar 1992, p. 52.
22   'Contradiction is therefore not original, but derivative' (Althusser et al. 2016, p. 460).

1. that relations of production are themselves complexes of antagonistic social *strategies* [...] and not simply relations of distribution of men and things [...]
2. that the *antagonism* of the relations of production is historically realized *in* the contradictions of productive forces.[23]

However, Balibar is not content with simply acknowledging the primacy of contradiction and struggle over structure. He thinks that what is needed is a more thorough rethinking of the very notion of structure and the structured whole, in order to be able to think the contradictory and necessarily complex and uneven character of social reality.

> It is not the mode of production which *is* a 'structure', and neither is the 'whole' of the social formation (we can say that this is the *gestaltist* conception of the structure). It is the complex of the contradictions themselves, their 'unevenness', or, according to Althusser's expression, their overdetermination that can be considered 'structural', that is immanent in practice.[24]

Therefore, thinking about structures means exactly thinking about overdetermined complexes of contradictions and not about stable totalities. This is a crucial move away from any simple opposition between stable structures and contingent conjunctures. The effectivity of class antagonism, the constant unevenness of the balance of forces and the impossibility to avoid overdetermination, means that what we define as 'structures', namely relations that tend to be reproduced, materialised and interiorised, are also immanently contradictory because of the effectivity of class antagonism and antagonistic social relations. In such a perspective, this particular conception of the necessary contradictory character of 'structural' determinations, this recognition of the effectivity of struggle, conflict and antagonism not only within particular conjunctures but also within 'structural' forms also implies that Althusser's reference to the '*necessity of contingency*'[25] is not just a reference to the dynamics of overdetermined contradictions and the break with any teleology of reason, but also a more general position: contingency is a constitutive aspect of 'structural' determination, meaning that structures (and in general historical processes) are always open and non-totalisable.[26]

---

23   Balibar 1990a, p. 90.
24   Ibid.
25   Althusser et al. 2016, p. 45.
26   Balibar has based upon such a conception of the 'open and non-totalizable [...] complex-

We could also turn to Poulantzas for an example of such a relational conception of 'structural' social forms, which places antagonistic social relations at the centre of their materiality: 'The state is not an instrumental entity existing for itself, it is not a thing, but the condensation of a balance of forces'.[27] This inscription of social antagonism at the basis of the very materiality of state institutions offers precisely such an attempt towards a rethinking of the relation between 'structures' and social antagonism: 'If struggle always has primacy over apparatuses, this is because power is a relation between struggles and practices (those of the exploiters and the exploited, the rulers and the ruled) and because the State above all is the condensation of a relation of forces defined precisely by struggle'.[28]

3 Specific Historicities

Finally, such a rethinking of the relation between structural and conjunctural determinations within the contours of a singular conjuncture leads us back to Althusser himself. Despite all the criticism against *Reading Capital* as the summit of Althusser's structuralism, I think that we can find in it Althusser's most advanced attempt at a possible theorisation of the co-existence of different effectivities of 'structural' and 'conjunctural' determinations. In line with his later insistence on *durability* (in all his texts from *Sur la reproduction* to the texts on aleatory materialism), Althusser deals here with time, and more specifically *different historical times*. His insistence on different times and different *histories* for different levels, instances and structures of the social structured whole, the rejection of any common time reference and the inability to perform an 'essential section', the rejection of a schematic synchrony/diachrony dichotomy, the emphasis on unevenness, dislocation and non-correspondence, all these attest to Althusser's effort to define the very problem still facing social theory: how to theoretically make intelligible the complexity, the uneven unity of determinations, both 'structural' and 'conjunctural' within a specific historical conjuncture. The following passage from *Reading Capital* exemplifies this position:

---

ity of the historical process' (1994a, p. 174) his insistence on the importance of a theory of ideology that treats truth and knowledge within politics as an effect of the conjuncture produced by an encounter between the class struggle and the mass movement.

27   Poulantzas 1975, p. 98.
28   Poulantzas 2000, p. 151.

> [I]t is only possible to give a content to the concept of historical time by defining historical time as the specific form of existence of the social totality under consideration, an existence in which different structural levels of temporality interfere, because of the peculiar relations of correspondence, non-correspondence, articulation, dislocation and torsion which obtain, between the different 'levels' of the whole in accordance with its general structure. It needs to be said that, just as there is no production in general, there is no history in general, but only specific structures of historicity, based in the last resort on the specific structures of the different modes of production, specific structures of historicity which, since they are merely the existence of determinate social formations (arising from specific modes of production), articulated as social wholes, have no meaning except as a function of the essence of those totalities, i.e., of the essence of their peculiar complexity.[29]

Therefore to actually grasp these 'specific' forms of historicity and the differential durability of their reproduction in the 'peculiar complexity' of any given social formation, traversed as they are by social antagonism and therefore immanently contingent (in the sense of an open 'horizon of events' inscribed at the core of antagonistic class relations), remains the open challenge for radical social theory.[30] However, here we are also facing an open question: If the simple observation of the co-existence of different temporalities brings us back to an empiricism of the conjuncture that cannot account for their particular articulation, and if any suggestion about a deeper structure can lead us back to some form of surface/depth dualism, then we must rethink the effectivity of social antagonism and conflicting social and political strategies and dynamics upon complex, uneven and overdetermined reproduced social relations creates the possibility of a historical dialectic that is not the self-relationality of a Subject, but the radical difference of a process without subject and End.

---

29 Althusser et al. 2016, pp. 256–7.
30 Pierre Vilar in his dialogue with Althusser has suggested to think in terms of a 'three-fold dialectic' between (a) 'long times' and specific times of the mode of production, (b) the small spaces of ethnic groups and the large zones demanded by modern activity, and (c) between class struggles and the consciousness of groups (Vilar 1973, p. 95).

4   The Dialectic of Structure and Conjuncture and the Recurring Necessity of Philosophical Interventions

Althusser's theoretical trajectory, from the attempts at reformulating a properly scientific historical materialism to the emphasis on radical contingency in the texts on aleatory materialism, was in its very unevenness as an unfinished project one of the most fruitful confrontations with the question of the complex and necessarily contradictory relation between structural and conjunctural determinations. In the Althusserian endeavour, historical materialism emerges as a radically new way to think social reality, without resorting to law-like certainties, but as an open process, full of conflicting tendencies, with only relatively and provisionally stable points of reference, a process full of singular relations, collective non-subjects, antagonistic contradictions, of which we form part and which determine the ability to see events erupt, either as subtle changes or as abrupt ruptures, but also explain them in the necessity of their contingency as well as in the contingency of their necessity and even the contingency of their contingency. In this view we can find the theoretical potential and dynamics of historical materialism, but also the contradictions that necessarily traverse it as open questions and theoretical tensions that sometimes seem to remain unresolved.

One way to approach these issues would be to return to Althusser's own self-critical conception of philosophy. Althusser insisted on the need for new *materialist practice of philosophy*, not in the sense of a philosophical system, but in the sense of philosophical interventions as a constant redrawing of the line of demarcation with idealism, in all its forms, interventions that represent a form of politics in theory. If historical materialism as radical social theory can never be a closed, rigidified scientific system, but is instead a constant struggle with the complexity and conflictuality of social reality that necessarily leads to such tensions, then there is also a constant need for philosophical interventions as (self-)corrections in the form of constantly 'bending the stick to the opposite side', exactly because of the unevenness and conflictuality at the centre of historical materialism as a 'necessarily conflictual and scissionist science'.[31] Therefore, it is exactly this tension running through historical materialism that makes constantly necessary a new materialist practice of philosophy, tendentially representing the class position of the subaltern classes within theory, both as an attempt to deconstruct idealist tendencies (empiricist, historicist, objectivist)

---

31   Althusser 1999a, p. 109.

within historical tendencies but also as an attempt to devise new concepts, new theoretical vocabularies, new theoretical metaphors.[32]

Against the tendency to treat social structures as systems and self-reproducing totalities, an emphasis on the conjunctural and 'aleatory' aspect is always a necessary correction, but the same goes for the emphasis on the tendency of social forms and modes of production to be reproduced against any 'atomised' or randomised conception of social reality. Where the stick must be bent to is itself an aspect of the conjuncture, but surely Althusser has offered us – in the very multiplicity, unevenness and contradiction of his own philosophical trajectory – some potential ways of facing up to this challenge.

---

32 Althusser's text on the 'Transformation of Philosophy' offers some insights into such a conception of a new philosophical practice: 'the task assigned Marxist philosophy is not one for the distant future. It is an undertaking for the present, for which Marxists ought to be prepared. Marx was the first to show us the way by putting philosophy into practice in a new and disconcerting form, refusing to produce a philosophy as "philosophy" but practising it in his political, critical and scientific work – in short, inaugurating a new, "critical and revolutionary" relation between philosophy and the social practices, which are at one and the same time the stakes and the privileged site of class struggle. This new practice of philosophy serves the proletarian class struggle without imposing upon it an oppressive ideological unity (we know where that oppression has its roots), but rather creating for it the ideological conditions for the liberation and free development of social practices' (Althusser 1990, p. 265).

PART 2

A New Practice of Philosophy

∴

CHAPTER 11

Althusser's Struggle with the Definition of Philosophy

An important aspect of Althusser's theoretical endeavour has been his confrontation with questions pertaining to the status of philosophy as a particular theoretical practice. One could even make a periodisation of Althusser's work based on his different definitions of philosophy, from his first definition of – Marxist – philosophy as a potential Theory of theoretical practice, through to his later definitions of philosophy as political intervention and of philosophy as class struggle in philosophy. As Étienne Balibar once stressed, 'Althusser was never really a (Marxist) *social theoretician*; he is, rather, a *philosopher*, whose constant concern is the "transformation of philosophy" from a communist point of view'.[1]

1   The Aporias of Theoretical Practice

In Althusser's initial move, the specific status of philosophy as a Theory of theoretical practice was instrumental in his attempt to restore the scientific character of historical materialism. This attempt was politically motivated and related to Althusser's strategy of bringing about a change in the politics of the Communist movement. His initial conception was that since politics is determined mainly by theory, meaning that a correct theoretical starting point and knowledge of the balance of forces in the conjuncture can lead to the right political choices and a renewal of revolutionary strategy, then what was needed was a Theory that would guarantee this scientificity. This is made obvious in how Althusser treats the relation between revolutionary theory and revolutionary practice.

> One sentence is enough to answer this question: Lenin's 'Without revolutionary theory, no revolutionary practice'. Generalizing it: theory is essential to practice, to the forms of practice that it helps bring to birth or to grow, as well as to the practice it is the theory of. But the transparency of

[1] Balibar 1993c, p. 5.

this sentence is not enough; we must also know its *titles to validity*, so we must pose the question: what are we to understand by *theory*, if it is to be essential to *practice*?[2]

This phrase brings forward another tension in Althusser's schema: the relation between theory and practice. Althusser's solution is to present practice as a process of transformation. Consequently, theory can also be a practice, in the sense of being a 'process of *transformation* of determinate given raw material into a determinate *product*, a transformation effected by a determinate human labour, using determinate means (of "production")'.[3] This conception of theoretical practice is essential in the articulation of an anti-empiricist conception of knowledge production as epistemological break with ideology.

> By theory, in this respect, I shall mean a *specific form of practice*, itself belonging to the complex unity of the 'social practice' of a determinate human society. Theoretical practice falls within the general definition of practice. It works on a raw material (representations, concepts, facts) which it is given by other practices, whether 'empirical', 'technical' or 'ideological'. In its most general form theoretical practice does not only include *scientific* theoretical practice, but also pre-scientific theoretical practice, that is, 'ideological' theoretical practice (the forms of 'knowledge' that make up the prehistory of a science, and their 'philosophies'). The theoretical practice of a science is always completely distinct from the ideological theoretical practice of its prehistory: this distinction takes the form of a 'qualitative' theoretical and historical discontinuity which I shall follow Bachelard in calling an 'epistemological break'.[4]

If theory is a practice, a particular form of *theoretical practice*, then it is also possible to have a Theory of this practice, a Theory that has this practice as its object. This opens up the way for a potential Marxist epistemology, in the sense of a (scientific) Theory of theories.

> But Theory is also essential for the transformation of domains in which a Marxist theoretical practice does not yet really exist. In most of these domains the question has not yet been 'settled' as it has in *Capital*. The Marxist theoretical practice of *epistemology*, of the history of science, of

---

2 Althusser 1969, p. 166.
3 Ibid.
4 Althusser 1969, pp. 167–8.

> the history of ideology, of the history of philosophy, of the history of art, has yet in large part to be constituted. Not that there are not Marxists who are working in these domains and have acquired much real experience there, but they do not have behind them the equivalent of *Capital* or of the revolutionary practice of a century of Marxists. Their practice is largely *in front of them*, it still has to be developed, or even founded, that is, it has to be set on correct theoretical bases so that it corresponds to a *real* object, not to a presumed or ideological object, and so that it is a truly theoretical practice, not a technical practice. It is for this purpose that they need Theory, that is, the materialist dialectic, as the sole method that can anticipate their theoretical practice by drawing up its formal conditions.[5]

It was also important for this Theory not to be a construction or something added to Marx's theory, but something always existing in Marx's own theoretical texts, marking a rather peculiar moment where a theoretical revolution carries along its own protocols of scientificity. Hence, we have the insistence that this Theory can be found, albeit in a practical state, in Marx's own writing and in particular in *Capital*.

> This practical solution, this *dialectic*, exists in Marx's theoretical practice, and we can see it in action there. The method Marx used in his theoretical practice, in his scientific work on the 'given' that he transformed into knowledge, this method is precisely the *Marxist dialectic*; and it is precisely *this dialectic* which contains inside it in a practical state the solution to the problem of the relations between Marx and Hegel, of the reality of that famous 'inversion' which is Marx's gesture to us, in the Afterword to the Second Edition of *Capital*, warning us that he has settled his relations with the Hegelian dialectic.[6]

However, it seems that he soon realised that there are major problems with such a conception of philosophy. First of all, there was the problem with the very notion of a theory existing in a *practical state* within a theoretical practice. Since there was no explicit Marxian epistemology to be found in Marx's text, with the possible and partial exception of the introduction to the *Grundrisse*, this epistemology had to be reconstructed from its practical form in the scientific text of Marx's *Capital*. However, the very notion of a 'symptomatic read-

---

5 Althusser 1969, pp. 169–70.
6 Althusser 1969, p. 174.

ing' of Marx's philosophy within *Capital* raised a serious problem regarding this problematic. The 'symptomatic reading' of elements of value theory in the silences and gaps of classical political economy was, in the last instance, an expression of a theoretical miscognition, of an epistemological failure traversing the theoretical body of classical political economy. To tackle this problem Althusser was obliged to present a much more positive state of Marxian philosophy within Marxian science, especially since it was Marx himself who had attempted some form of symptomatic reading.

> We have simply tried to apply to Marx's reading the '*symptomatic*' *reading* with which Marx managed to read the illegible in Smith, by measuring the problematic initially visible in his writings against the invisible problematic contained in the paradox of *an answer which does not correspond to any question posed.* [...] [W]hereas in his text Smith produces an answer which not only does not answer any of the immediately preceding questions, but does not even answer *any* other question he ever posed anywhere in his work; with Marx, on the contrary, when he does happen to formulate *an answer without a question*, with a little patience and perspicacity we can find *the question* itself *elsewhere*, twenty or one hundred pages further on, with respect to some other object, enveloped in some other matter, or, on occasion, in Engels's immediate comments on Marx.[7]

Then, there was a dead-end regarding the very notion of a science of sciences and a philosophy offering the protocols of scientificity, taking into consideration that at the same time Althusser was proposing a highly original epistemology which was in rupture with traditional theories of knowledge, since his conception of a science offering its own criteria of validity and his anti-empiricist emphasis on truth being an internal aspect of the text of science and not a question of empirical validation, precluded in advance any notion of protocols of truth. This is most evident in the introductory text of *Reading Capital*, in chronological terms the last one written, where the question of what constitute the criteria of the 'knowledge effect' is never answered. Then there was the question of how a science of sciences is included in the text of a science. Towards the end of this text, the question of the definition of the knowledge effect as a theoretical object emerges:

---

7 Althusser et al. 2016, p. 27.

> How can we explain the mechanism of this knowledge effect? [...] We showed that the validity of a scientific proposition as a knowledge was ensured in a determinate scientific practice by the action of particular *forms* which ensure the *presence* of scientificity in the production of knowledge, in other words, by specific forms that confer on a knowledge its character as a ('true') knowledge. Here I am speaking of forms of scientificity – but I am also echoing this by thinking of the forms that play the same part (ensuring a different but corresponding effect) in ideological 'knowledge', and indeed in all forms of *knowing*. These *forms* are distinct from the forms in which the knowledge was produced, as a result, by the process of the history of knowledge: they deal, it will be remembered, with a knowledge already produced as a knowledge by that history. In other words, we consider the result *without its becoming*, ignoring any accusations of lese-Hegelianism or lese-geneticism, for this double crime is merely a single good deed: a liberation from the empiricist ideology of history. It is to this result that we put the question of the mechanism of production of the knowledge effect – exactly in the way Marx interrogated a given society, as a *result*, in order to pose it the question of its 'society effect', or the question of the *mechanism* which produces its existence *as a society*.[8]

Although Althusser attempts to describe the difference in form between the knowledge effect and the ideology effect, he does not offer any criteria that make possible the distinction or the judgement of objectivity. That is why the text ends with the declaration of the inability to offer any theory of the *guarantees* of knowledge and, in this sense, of the inability of any potential Theory of theories. There can be a theory of the differential form of scientific discourse as opposed to ideology, but not a theory of guarantees. This leads to a circle that Althusser attempts to present as virtuous whereas in reality it is the vicious circle of the impossibility of any theory of the foundations of knowledge:

> I shall leave the question in this last form, and merely recall its terms. Unlike the 'theory of knowledge' of ideological philosophy, I am not trying to pronounce some *de jure* (or *de facto*) *guarantee* which will assure us that we really do know what we know, and that we can relate this harmony to a certain connexion between Subject and Object, Consciousness and the World. I am trying to elucidate the *mechanism* which explains to

---

8   Althusser et al. 2016, p. 70.

us how a *de facto* result, produced by the history of knowledge, i.e., a given determinate knowledge, functions *as a knowledge*, and not as some other result [...] This last question confronts us definitively with the *differential* nature of *scientific discourse*, i.e., with the specific nature of a discourse which cannot be maintained as a discourse except by reference to what is present as absence in each moment of its order: the constitutive system of its object, which, in order to exist as a system, requires the absent presence of the scientific discourse that 'develops' it. [...] We have therefore not left the circle of one and the same question: if, without leaving it, we have avoided turning round in this circle, it is because this circle is not the closed circle of ideology, but the circle perpetually opened by its closures themselves, the circle of a well-founded knowledge.[9]

And finally there was the problem of how to incorporate class struggle and politics in this conception. Although Althusser had presented the contrast between ideology and science as, in the last instance, a political stake, in the end the class character of ideology seems to be underestimated in this initial phase of Althusser's work. Rather, he tends to present an image of a confrontation between science, or scientific practice as producing knowledge effects and ideology *per se* producing ideology effects.

Althusser's refusal to accept any form of traditional theory of knowledge guarantees, any form of epistemological substitute or version of a Kantian transcendental solution (perhaps as a result of his earlier confrontation with Hegel and his critical stance against Phenomenology), meant that he could not resort to any version of theory of knowledge.[10] It is this theoretical impasse that initiated a whole process of theoretical self-criticism and correction not only regarding any conception of 'latent structures' but also in respect of the very status of philosophy.

2 The Politics of the Epistemological Break

Was Althusser's conception of the epistemological break just 'a transformed, *marxisant* Bachelardian epistemology combined with certain Spinozist and structuralist theses, and with elements of Marx's own reflections'[11] as Gregory

---

[9] Althusser et al. 2016, p. 72.
[10] And this can also account for his break with the Della Volpe school that insisted upon a neo-Kantian theory of knowledge or epistemology.
[11] Elliott 2006, p. 49.

Elliott has suggested? I think that Althusser's strategy was more complex. First of all, his epistemological references were not simply anti-empiricist and rationalist. They represented a sharp break with the idealism of traditional philosophical theory of knowledge, thus enabling a different practice of philosophy. As Dominique Lecourt has insisted: 'Bachelardian epistemology refuses to pose the question of the foundations of knowledge or of the *guarantees* of knowledge (*savoir*) that traditional philosophy thinks within that of the duality of the Universe and the Mind'.[12] Moreover, this refusal of a theory of guarantees and of a classical realist theory is not a form of conventionalism or relativism as Ted Benton has suggested.[13] Instead, this conception of the scientific process as one that produces knowledge and does not simply bring forward the 'real' of reality, is also the only way to actually think of the historicity of sciences. As Lecourt has stressed:

> If scientific thought is a process for which neither its point of departure nor its point of arrival are that 'presupposed, deposited or projected' real which philosophy cannot do without, but an always-already-thought, organized real, it is clear that error is no longer an accident on the road, but an essential, necessary and driving moment of knowledge.[14]

Such a conception of the emergence of new theories implied the actual historicity of the epistemological break and also what was politically at stake. For Althusser, the radical discontinuity between Marx's theoretical revolution and pre-Marxist theories was indispensable in order to maintain the radical political and theoretical discontinuity of a renewed communist strategy and all forms of bourgeois or bourgeois-inspired forms of politics even within the working-class movement. It was, in this sense, a defence of the political and strategic autonomy of working-class politics, despite the fact that it was stated as an epistemological position. And at this more general level of a political rather than theoretical modality, we cannot say that 'Althusser's co-option of Bachelardian epistemology misfired',[15] as Gregory Elliott has suggested, not only because there was much more to Althusser than a simple reproduction of Bachelardian and Spinozist themes, but exactly because of the deeply political character of Althusser's endeavour.

---

12   Lecourt 1975, p. 41.
13   Benton 1985, p. 40.
14   Lecourt 1975, p. 55.
15   Elliott 2006, p. 122.

However schematic the notion of the break that was presented in Althusser's texts of the early 1960s was, it nevertheless had the merit of insisting that historical materialism was not just an inverted form or a continuation or a thematic variation of German Idealism or classical political economy. Although Althusser himself mainly used the notion of the epistemological break to refer to the rupture of Marx with theoretical humanism and ideology, the actual break that Althusser and his collaborators studied in a more systematic way was that between Marx's proposal for a *critique* of political economy and classical political economy. Althusser's (and Rancière's) initial insights and demarcations in *Reading Capital* offered indeed a line of reasoning that coincides with that of most critical theories of the value form, namely that Marx does not offer in *Capital* a radicalised 'socialistic' form of classical labour theory of value (the cornerstone of classical political economy) but rather a highly original theory of the value form emerging out of the social relations that became prevalent in capitalism.[16]

Consequently, the real question is not the philological validity of one or the other schematisation of the actual process of Marx's break, but rather whether or not we accept the radical originality of historical materialism and the antagonistic character of a theorisation of the possibility of a communist politics in relation to previous theoretical forms. Althusser never wrote a detailed analysis of the theoretical and political development of the work of Marx and Engels such as Georges Labica's monumental retracing of Marx and Engels's trajectory until the *Communist Manifesto*, a study that in all aspects indeed is compatible with Althusser's basic insights and offers a crucial presentation of the importance of the rupture inside philosophy and the search for a way out towards a highly original form of *historical materialism*.[17] However, this does diminish the importance of his insistence on the radical break between historical materialism and other varieties of political philosophy. Stathis Kouvelakis, in his own important contribution to the re-reading of the theoretical and political debates that formed the political and intellectual environment of the emergence of Marx's thinking, is justified in insisting not only on the fact that – as Althusser also accepted – Marx's 'political break preceded the epistemological break',[18] but also on the fact that certain forms of 'humanism' or even 'political liberalism' were not 'exterior' to the working class. However, I think that again this does not point towards some fundamental flaw in Althusser's conception of the break, exactly because the 'politics of theory' behind his propositions had

---

16   On this see Rubin 1973; Heinrich 1999; Milios et al. 2002.
17   Labica 1980.
18   Kouvelakis 2003, p. 298.

more to with the antagonistic character of historical materialism versus traditional philosophical idealism and consequently with historical materialism, rather than an exact presentation of the complex interplay of theory, politics and philosophy that marks Marx's theoretical trajectory.

3   Philosophical Self-Criticism

The June 1966 text on the philosophical conjuncture and Marxist research that marks the beginning of Althusser's gradual theoretical self-criticism is crucial. Althusser begins with a reference to the philosophical conjuncture and his attempt to draw the basic lines of struggle and confrontation within French Philosophy. On the one hand, there is the front against the '*religious-spiritualist* and *rationalist-idealist*' tendencies; on the other, the combination of alliance (against openly idealist tendencies) and confrontation with the '*rationalist empiricism* in its two forms, idealist and materialist',[19] exemplified in the French epistemological tradition which Althusser thinks offers the most interesting insights. What is important is not Althusser's definition of the dividing lines within French philosophy but the very conception of philosophy as a terrain of struggle, which marks a more political conception of philosophical confrontations than the one initially offered in the 1965 texts.

That is why Althusser moves on to make a self-critical reference to his earlier conception of philosophy, insisting on the difference in theoretical status – and not just object – between Marxist theory and Marxist philosophy. However, this 'strategic question number 1' for dialectical materialism[20] is the only one that is not answered, but merely mentioned. Other questions are dealt with in greater extent, such as the relation of the theory of structural causality to the theory of practice and the Theory of theoretical practice, the theory of ideology, the theory of subjectivity, the theory of individuality. Regarding the question of the theory of 'knowledge effect', the crucial question left unanswered in *Reading Capital* and the limit of the Theory of theoretical practice, Althusser suggests that this can be answered through a more general theory of discourse.

The *general theory of discourse* is Althusser's attempt, in this openly transitional period in his conception of philosophy, to think philosophical questions, such as a potential materialist theory of knowledge through some sort

---

19   Althusser 2003, p. 4.
20   Althusser 2003, p. 12.

of a scientific theory. In this sense, the theory of discourse(s) seems to emerge as a potential substitute for a theory of knowledge.

That is why we must turn to Althusser's 1966 *Three Notes on the Theory of Discourses*.[21] There he attempts to think different theories, such as psychoanalysis or the theory of ideology, as an aspect of a more general theory of discourse. This marks Althusser's turn away from a more abstract conception of theory. Knowledge presupposes not only theory, but a combination of a general theory, a regional theory and empirical knowledge in order to theorise real objects as Spinozean singular essences (a reference he also makes in his text on Lévi-Strauss). This is also in accordance with his move away from a structuralism of latent structures. However, it is worth noting that Althusser began a process of self-critical reflection on the concept of the Theory of Discourses while writing the three notes, something exemplified in the differences between the First Note, which mainly deals with the theory of the unconscious as a regional theory of the general theory of discourse, and the other two notes and Althusser's explicit reference that the first note must be revised. It is also worth noting that although the theory of knowledge is included, Althusser does not elaborate on it, marking his gradual coming to terms with the impossibility of proving a scientific theory of the knowledge effect.

Part of this question has also to do with Althusser's growing insistence that only real concrete objects exist (singular essences in Spinozean terms) – perhaps as a way to correct his earlier flirting with a theory of latent structures – but at the same time they can be known only though abstract theoretical concepts. Regarding the status of philosophy in his 1967 article 'On Theoretical Work: Difficulties and Resources' he still insists on the existence of Marxist philosophy in practical form within the texts of Marx's maturity and especially *Capital*. But he insists that this is not a simple 'extraction' or a matter of 'simply *identifying* an already adequate *content*, in order to provide it with the appropriate form'.[22] Therefore, what is needed is a work of theoretical elaboration, through an elaboration of Marx's mature works to themselves. Althusser finally leaves the question rather unanswered following the reference to a potential '*general* theory of the union of theory and practice'.[23]

---

21   In Althusser 2003.
22   Althusser 1990, p. 60.
23   Althusser 1990, p. 67.

4   Philosophy and/as Politics

The first major change is evident in a series of texts by Althusser from the fall of 1967 to the early spring of 1968 in which we find a completely different definition of philosophy. These texts are *Philosophy and the Spontaneous Philosophy of the Scientists* and *Lenin and Philosophy*, as well as *Notes on Philosophy* (unpublished during his lifetime) and part of a broader correspondence with his collaborators.

The 1967–68 *Notes on Philosophy* – most of them contemporaneous with the lectures later contained in *Spontaneous Philosophy and the Philosophy of the Scientists* – offer an image of Althusser's attempt to rethink philosophy beyond the conception of a 'Theory of theoretical practice'. For Althusser, what 'distinguishes philosophy, fundamentally, from science is the organic, intimate, interior, constitutive relation it has to politics'.[24] Its theoretical form facilitates the relation to the sciences, its political content the relation to class struggle.[25] Philosophy is related to scientific and theoretical breaks and ideological revolutions. Philosophy operates by way of *ruptures*; it is the theory of ruptures.[26]

> The break is an historical fact interior to the history of the sciences: it is an historical fact and at the same time a scientific fact.
>
>   The revolution is an historical, not theoretical, fact, but it is social-political and ideological.
>
>   'Rupture' is an historical fact that intervenes between philosophy and the sciences, on the one hand, and social ideologies, on the other hand. It is an historical-*theoretical* fact. It is a *philosophical* fact *par excellence*.[27]

Philosophy, for Althusser, thinks the difference between 'sciences and ideologies, breaks and ruptures' and is 'as rupture' a practice of '*intervention* in the conjuncture revolutions/breaks';[28] 'it *is* rupture as thought of this conjuncture'.[29] Consequently every scientific discovery brings about a philosophical revolution. Science precedes philosophy. Moreover, Althusser is more self-critical of his initial conception of the possibility of symptomatic reading of a philosophy existing in a practical form in Marx's *Capital*.

---

24   Althusser 1995a, p. 302.
25   Cf. Althusser 1995a, p. 304.
26   Althusser 1995a, p. 394.
27   Althusser 1995a, p. 309.
28   Althusser 1995a, p. 312.
29   Ibid.

In a certain manner, we had projected onto the original text of *Capital* a Marxist philosophy constituted in a later stage (Engels, Lenin and ... us), making it appear as if it already exists in a practical state in the scientific text of Marx. This conformed to the definition of philosophy that I gave in *For Marx* as the Theory of theoretical practice. The theoretical [*theorique*] of the science being the object of philosophy, Marxist philosophy was indeed, in our eyes, in a practical state in *Capital*, we could, then, read it there, on the condition that we could decipher it. The 'symptomatic lecture' thus hesitated between two definitions:

1. A lecture of the philosophical difficulties that *were not resolved* – which we could understand under the form: Marxist philosophy, is, at least to a great extent, absent from *Capital*.
2. A 'lecture' of the philosophy existing in a practical state in *Capital*.[30]

Althusser also chooses another way to mark the difference between science and philosophy: the difference between mode of production and practice. Science operates as a mode of production (a theoretical mode of production), which includes a combination of theoretical productive forces and theoretical relations of production. On the other hand, practice implies something different. A practice is always '*concrete*', it only exists in the 'concrete of a formation', it has structural determinations but it should not be confused with a production process, there is a 'diversity of practices' in every mode of production and any technique is 'subordinated to practice'.[31] In a certain way, the object of practice is the *concrete* of the 'conjuncture'.[32] In an analogy with political practice, this brings forward the importance of categories such as '*direction*', '*line*', '*strategy* and *tactics*', '*forms of action*'.[33] In light of this re-reading of the notion of practice, Althusser is more self-critical of his initial conception of theoretical practice, opting now for a distinction between scientific and theoretical practice.

> The expression 'theoretical practice', in its ambiguities 'covered' in a symptomatic but blind way a fundamental ambiguity, which I have designated in my self-critical essays as that of a 'theoreticist' tendency (or speculative or positivist). In fact, I have employed the expression 'theoretical practice' to designate at the same time 'scientific practice' (cf.

---

30 Althusser 1995a, p. 320.
31 Althusser 1995a, pp. 325–6.
32 Althusser 1995a, p. 327.
33 Althusser 1995a, p. 328.

the rectifications in what concerns the confusion between process and practice) *and* 'philosophical practice', therefore identifying *practically* by means of the functional use of the term 'theoretical practice', the scientific and the philosophical (in a state of equilibrium between the speculative and the positivist). That is why (conforming to Mao's expression in *On Practice*) I think that we have to restore the term 'scientific practice'.[34]

Althusser places particular emphasis on the importance of a *topography* [topique] in the theories of both Marx and Freud, namely the relation between structures and superstructures in Marx and the relation between the unconscious, ego and superego in Freud. For Althusser, this allows them to '*think* their proper *practice* [...] the specific practice (class struggle, therapy) that have as effect to trigger [*déclencher*]. Without topography we cannot "orient" ourselves in a *conjuncture*'.[35] Althusser also takes up this point in a very interesting letter to Franca Madonia in 1969. There, he makes a rather long reference to the notion of topography and its importance in both Marx and Freud. According to this, the particularity of both Marxism and psychoanalysis is that both sciences also have as their object the subject of their enunciation and this is the cause of their particular structure and their inclusion of the topography of the various instances of the social and psychic whole and their respective forms of determination. Moreover, Althusser does not limit his analysis to the fact that these disciplines have as objects also discursive practices, including their own scientific discourses; he sees this particular topography as offering the possibility of a theory of action.

> Marx's theory and Freud's theory present themselves as topographies. They are the only two sciences (along with philosophy that is not a science) that present this particularity, that no-one has observed. There is in Marx as in Freud a topography of instances doubled with a dialectic (Marx) and dynamics/economics (Freud). What does this strange structure correspond to? It seems to me to the following: Marxism and psychoanalysis alike are non-speculative disciplines, and therefore the 'subject' that enounces them must – like any scientific subject – disappear from this enunciations – but since this subject is part of the object in the field (topography) that we are dealing with, its place and its function are designated metaphorically by the 'dispositif' of the discipline under the form

---

34   Althusser 1995a, p. 330.
35   Althusser 1995a, p. 313.

of a topography. This is what permits these disciplines to avoid the 'world view', the 'interpretation of the world' and to inscribe in their structure their very particular character to be disciplines that cannot exist without integrating the moment of action in them: to be at the same time principle of intelligence (like all ordinary sciences) and principle of action. Lenin has insisted strongly on this in his first works opposing objectivism (passive, neutral, of bourgeois sociology) and objectivity (active, engaged, militant) of Marxist sociology.[36]

Returning to the *Notes on Philosophy*, Althusser thinks that it is imperative to think of the *place* that philosophy occupies in this terrain of struggle and even think of philosophy as *topography*, following the example of the sciences that are closer to it. The notion of the *topography* becomes crucial in order to comprehend the possibility of philosophy knowing '*what place* it occupies in the field of the conjuncture where it intervenes'; this implies also 'practical function', in the sense of '*putting in place* [*mise en place*]', of '*taking position* in a battle'.[37]

However, this gives rise to new problems, particularly in relation to the specific determination and efficacy of what Althusser designates as 'theoretical ideologies', and also the fact that the 'bearers' of these theoretical ideologies are not only scientists but also intellectuals in general, technicians, political oper-

---

[36] Althusser 1997b, p. 766. This elaboration on the notion of topography finally found its place in his theorisation of ideology in the manuscript *On Reproduction* and the article on Ideology and Ideological State Apparatuses: 'We can therefore say that the great theoretical advantage of the Marxist topography, i.e. of the spatial metaphor of the edifice (base and superstructure) is simultaneously that it reveals that questions of determination (or of index of effectivity) are crucial; that it reveals that it is the base which in the last instance determines the whole edifice; and that, as a consequence, it obliges us to pose the theoretical problem of the types of "derivatory" effectivity peculiar to the superstructure, i.e. it obliges us to think what the Marxist tradition calls conjointly the relative autonomy of the superstructure and the reciprocal action of the superstructure on the base' (Althusser 1971, pp. 135–6). A similar analysis can be found in *Essays in Self-Criticism* where Althusser insists that it is exactly the inclusion of the topography in Marx's conception of society and history that marks his break away from Hegel. Indeed, he insists that 'nowhere do you see Hegel thinking within the structure of a *topography*' (Althusser 1976a, p. 139). In the same text, he insists that 'The conclusion is obvious: *the position of the Marxist Topography protects the dialectic against the delirious idealist notion of producing its own material substance*: it imposes on it, on the contrary, a forced recognition of the material conditions of its own efficacy. These conditions are related to the definition of the sites (the "spheres"), to their limits, to their mode of determination in the "totality" of a social formation' (Althusser 1976a, p. 140).

[37] Althusser 1995a, p. 314.

atives.[38] At the same time, Althusser seems to be anxious about the efficacy of this notion of theoretical ideologies. Although it can account for the break, it does not help the theorisation of what it is that science breaks with.

Althusser proposes the thesis that philosophy has no history: 'I bring forward a triple thesis: philosophy has no history = philosophy is "eternal" = "nothing" happens in philosophy'.[39] The obvious analogy here is to the thesis that ideology in general has no history that Althusser would advance in the essay on Ideology and Ideological State Apparatuses.[40] However, there are effects of philosophy, there are *philosophy effects*. It is here that the conception of the topography acquires its significance. Within the topography, philosophy makes distinctions and differentiations and assigns places to different forms of being and knowing, introduces forms of *'hierarchisation'*,[41] and self-placement [*autoplacement*][42] in this topography. These operations constitute the philosophy effects and can be called the *'philosophical unconscious'*.[43] Althusser takes this analogy with psychoanalysis even further: the philosophical unconscious is described as being comprised of *philosophical phantasms*,[44] such as the philosophical conception of Subject, Object, and Truth in the theory of knowledge. In such an analogy, these philosophical phantasms lead in their combination to philosophical formations such as idealism, empiricism, and rationalism.[45]

Althusser then introduces the notion of a philosophical 'therapy'. For Althusser, the 'normal' philosophical practice is 'the repetition, that is, rumination, under the neurotic philosophy effect of the dominant formation of the philosophical unconscious [...] This practice-rumination leaves [...] intact the neurotic structure under which the philosophy effect is "repeated" compulsively'.[46] However, there is also the possibility of another practice of philosophy that can be defined as 'philosophical therapy' which aims, in a similar way to psychoanalytical therapy, to 'mak[e] something move ["*faire bouger*" quelque chose]'.[47] Consequently, for Althusser 'it is not question of "suppressing philosophy"'.[48] What is at stake for the philosophical practice-therapy (for Althusser practiced

---

38   Cf. Althusser 1995a, pp. 315–16.
39   Althusser 1995a, p. 333.
40   Althusser 1971, p. 159.
41   Althusser 1995a, p. 335.
42   Ibid.
43   Althusser 1995a, p. 336.
44   Althusser 1995a, p. 337.
45   Althusser 1995a, p. 339.
46   Ibid.
47   Althusser 1995a, p. 340.
48   Ibid.

by *dialectical materialism*) is to make this philosophical practice be heard. Here Lenin emerges as the practitioner of a 'savage therapy'.[49] In this analogy, traditional or idealist philosophy emerges as a form of theoretical neurosis.

For Althusser the topographical effect of *distinction* relates to the 'instance of sciences' (= epistemological breaks)', the topographical effect of *hierarchisation* relates to the 'instance of ideologies' (revolutions in ideological relations), and the 'topographical effect of putting in power [*mettre au pouvoir*] of philosophy by itself in the place of domination will be to relate in a dominant fashion to the *political* instance',[50] bringing forward the fundamentally political character of philosophy. In this sense, we can understand the actual functioning of philosophy and the particular efficacy of this 'nothing' that philosophy never ceases to repeat,[51] this nothing that he thinks justifies the thesis that philosophy has no history.

The *Notes on Philosophy* represent an important stage in Althusser's attempt to redefine philosophy as political practice and intervention. In a certain way, they offer us a way to take a view of Althusser's 'laboratory' of the new conception of philosophy that would emerge in the lectures on the *Spontaneous Philosophy and the Philosophy of the Scientists* and *Lenin and Philosophy*.

5   The Spontaneous Philosophy of the Scientists

Philosophy and the Spontaneous Philosophy of the Scientists is a crucial text. These lectures represented the first public pronouncement of Althusser's new definition of philosophy and one of his most extensive confrontations with the particular character of philosophy as a discourse.[52] He begins by insisting that philosophical propositions do not deal with truth but with their correctness in an obvious analogy with political practice (the reference is to the correct political line).

> Not being the object of scientific demonstration or proof, philosophical Theses cannot be said to be 'true' (demonstrated or proved as in mathematics or in physics). They can only be said to be 'correct' [*justes*].[53]

---

49   Althusser 1995a, p. 341.
50   Althusser 1995a, p. 342.
51   Ibid.
52   On the evolution of Althusser's circle and the circumstances that led to these lectures see Balibar and Duroux 2012.
53   Althusser 1990, p. 74.

This point is extremely important because Althusser acknowledges that philosophy is not a science and cannot claim some sort of 'knowledge effect'. Philosophy is presented as a particular discourse 'haunted by *practice*'[54] and does not have a real object in the sense of the sciences. Consequently philosophy does not produce propositions in the manner of the sciences, but rather philosophical Theses. These theses do not produce knowledge, but nevertheless have practical results, in the sense of the practice of drawing lines of demarcation.

> It will be noted that in so far as they are Theses, philosophical propositions are *theoretical* propositions, but in so far as they are 'correct' propositions, these theoretical propositions are haunted by *practice*. Let me add a paradoxical remark. An entire philosophical tradition since Kant has contrasted 'dogmatism' with 'criticism'. Philosophical propositions have always had the effect of producing 'critical' distinctions: that is, of 'sorting out' or separating ideas from each other, and even of forging the *appropriate* ideas for making their *separation* and its necessity visible. Theoretically, this effect might be expressed by saying that philosophy 'divides' (Plato), 'traces lines of demarcation' (Lenin) and produces (in the sense of making manifest or visible) distinctions and differences. The entire history of philosophy demonstrates that philosophers spend their time *distinguishing* between truth and error, between science and opinion, between the sensible and the intelligible, between reason and the understanding, between spirit and matter, etc. They always *do* it, but they do not say (or only rarely) that the practice of philosophy consists in this demarcation, in this distinction, in this drawing of a line.[55]

For Althusser, philosophical Theses have a different theoretical modality than that of scientific propositions. Philosophy does not have real objects in the sense that sciences have real objects, even if one can see 'philosophical objects'.[56] Althusser also distinguishes philosophy from any theory of interdisciplinarity; philosophy is 'neither an interdisciplinary discipline nor the theory of interdisciplinarity'.[57] But the question of philosophy's specific efficacy remains. Althusser's answer is that philosophy intervenes in order to support correct positions:

---

54 Althusser 1990, p. 75.
55 Ibid.
56 Althusser 1990, p. 77.
57 Althusser 1990, p. 79.

> [P]hilosophy is neither a science nor the science of the Whole, it does not provide the solution to these problems. It intervenes in another way: by stating Theses that contribute to *opening the way* to a *correct* position with regard to these problems.[58]

Therefore, philosophy is not a science; it intervenes and is in a certain relation to social and political developments by means of its specific relation to practical ideologies: 'philosophy is defined by a double relation – to the sciences and to practical ideologies'.[59] Practical ideologies are 'complex formations which shape notions-representations-images into behaviour-conduct-attitude-gestures'.[60] Althusser is particularly interested in *theoretical* ideologies as practical ideologies and how they influence the scientific practice. Although he insists on the difference in theoretical modality between Science and Ideology, it is obvious that this opposition is not between science in general and ideology in general, but between scientific practice and theoretical ideologies. As such, philosophy does not produce knowledge or truth, but intervenes in this complex and necessarily contradictory terrain. A materialist philosophy can play a crucial part in the drawing of a line of demarcation between the scientific and the ideological.

> A philosophy *capable* of discerning and criticizing them can have the effect of drawing the attention of scientists to the existence and efficacy of the epistemological obstacle that this spontaneous scientific ideology represents: the representation that scientists have of their own practice, and of their relationship to their own practice. Here again philosophy does not substitute itself for science: it intervenes, in order to clear a path, to open the space in which a correct line may then be drawn.[61]

In contrast, as the case of the human or the social sciences suggests, idealist philosophies in certain cases function as substitutes for the scientific foundations that these sciences in fact lack. In this case, 'philosophies serve as an ideological substitute for the theoretical foundations that the human sciences lack' and this 'holds for the majority of the human sciences',[62] and Althusser

---

58   Althusser 1990, p. 81.
59   Althusser 1990, p. 83.
60   Ibid.
61   Althusser 1990, p. 88.
62   Althusser 1990, p. 91.

insists that a great part of the so-called 'human sciences' in fact refers to techniques of social adaptation.

Althusser then turns his interest to the very notion of 'correctness' of the philosophical theses. He stresses that correctness has nothing to do with an idealised conception of justice. In contrast, it refers to the ability to have a correct assessment of the balance of forces in a certain conjuncture; it deals with intervening in terrains marked by contradictions and antagonisms.

> It is understood that *correct* [*juste*] is not the adjectival form of *justice* [*justice*]. When St Thomas Aquinas distinguished between just and unjust wars, he spoke in the name of *justice*. But when Lenin distinguished between correct and incorrect wars [*les guerres justes et les guerres injustes*], he spoke in the name of correctness [*justesse*]: of a correct line, of a correct assessment of the character of wars in the light of their class meaning. Of course, a politically correct war is waged by combatants who have a passion for justice in their hearts: but it is not only justice (an idealized notion under and in which men 'live' their relations to their conditions of existence and to their struggles) that made a war 'correct' for Lenin. A war is correct when it conforms to a correct position and line in the conjuncture of a given balance of forces: as a practical intervention in line with the class struggle, correct because it has been *aligned* with the meaning of the class struggle.[63]

This can account for a very specific discussion of philosophy as a very particular form of intervention in theory and also as a particular practice. Philosophy intervenes in theory in an attempt to separate the scientific from the ideological.

1. Philosophy functions by intervening not in matter (the mechanic), or on a living body (the surgeon), or in the class struggle (the politician), but *in theory*: not with tools or a scalpel or through the organization and leadership of the masses, but simply by stating *theoretical* propositions (Theses), rationally adjusted and justified. [...]
2. Philosophy intervenes in a certain reality: 'theory'. [...] Philosophy intervenes in the indistinct reality in which the sciences, theoretical ideologies and philosophy itself figure. What are theoretical ideologies? Let us advance a provisional definition: they are, in the last

---

63   Althusser 1990, pp. 102–3.

instance, and even when they are unrecognizable as such, forms of practical ideologies, transformed within theory.

3. The result of philosophical intervention, such as we have conceived it, is to draw, in this indistinct reality, a line of demarcation that separates, in each case, the scientific from the ideological. This line of demarcation may be completely covered over, denied or effaced in most philosophies: it is essential to their existence, despite the denegation. Its denegation is simply the common form of its existence.[64]

Although philosophy deals mainly with words and how they are arranged, this does not underestimate its importance: 'Yes, philosophy does act by modifying words and their order. But they are theoretical words, and it is this difference between words that allows something *new* in reality, something that was hidden and covered over, to appear and *be seen*'.[65] However, in order to think philosophy's particular kind of efficacy we must think the particular relation between philosophy, science, and ideology. It is here that the concept of the '*spontaneous philosophy of the sciences*' enters the frame. Here is Althusser's initial definition:

> In their scientific practice, specialists from different disciplines 'spontaneously' recognize the existence of philosophy and the privileged relation of philosophy to the sciences. This recognition is generally unconscious: it can, in certain circumstances, become partially conscious. But it remains enveloped in the *forms* proper to unconscious recognition: these forms constitute the 'spontaneous philosophies of scientists' or '*savants*'.[66]

Althusser uses the crisis in physics in the early twentieth century as an example of when scientists, faced with the collapse of an earlier conception of science, turned to various forms of philosophy. So it is obvious that the particular form that the relation between science and ideology (practical ideologies) takes is that of the emergence of *spontaneous philosophies of the scientists*. Therefore, philosophy becomes the particular terrain or form of appearance of the contradictory co-existence and interaction (or dialectic) between science and ideology. In most cases, this takes the form of varieties of idealism.

---

64 Althusser 1990, p. 106.
65 Althusser 1990, p. 107.
66 Althusser 1990, p. 109.

But if they recognize themselves in his philosophy, it is because they are *at home* there. And because *savant*-philosophers who believe they can extract their philosophy *purely* from their experience as scientists, and *purely* from their scientific knowledges, are simply *endorsing* a variation on the classical themes of the dominant philosophy, the 'philosophy of philosophers', in a language and with examples that appear to be new.[67]

Moreover, it is obvious that for Althusser scientists do not experience this contradiction as such, but in the form of philosophical questions. There is no scientific practice that is inseparable from some form of such spontaneous philosophy:

> all scientific practice is inseparable from a 'spontaneous philosophy' which may, depending upon which philosophy is involved, be a materialist aid or an idealist obstacle; that this spontaneous philosophy alludes, 'in the last instance', to the secular struggle that unfolds on the battlefield (*Kampfplatz*, Kant) of the history of philosophy between idealist tendencies and materialist tendencies.[68]

What is the relation of philosophy to the sciences? On the one hand, we have seen that in a certain way philosophy is unavoidable and therefore necessary. At the same time, the tendency of idealist philosophy is towards the *exploitation* of sciences by ideologies:

> the vast *majority* of known philosophies have, throughout the history of philosophy, always *exploited* the sciences (and not simply their failures) to the profit of the 'values' (a provisional term) of *practical ideologies*: religious, moral, juridical, aesthetic, political, etc.[69]

This means that philosophies are engaged in a struggle for domination and hegemony between old and new philosophies, a struggle in which the adversary is never defeated.[70]

> The history of philosophy is a struggle between tendencies realized in philosophical formations, and it is always a struggle for domination. But

---

67 Althusser 1990, p. 114.
68 Althusser 1990, p. 116.
69 Althusser 1990, p. 120.
70 On this see also Macherey 1976.

the paradox is that this struggle results only in the replacement of one domination by another, and not in the pure and simple elimination of a past formation (as '*error*': for there is no error in philosophy, in the sense that there is in the sciences) – that is, of the adversary. The adversary is never totally defeated and *therefore never totally suppressed*, totally *erased from historical existence*. It is only dominated and it lives on under the domination of the new philosophical formation that has overcome it after a very protracted battle: it lives on as a *dominated* philosophical formation, and is naturally ready to re-emerge whenever the conjuncture gives the signal and furnishes the occasion.[71]

Theories of knowledge, even in their more complex forms, in the end reproduce forms of idealism and in their search for guarantees of knowledge they also reproduce forms of ideology and in particular juridical ideology:

> It is necessary to unmask the subtle deceptions of this rationalist-critical idealist procedure, which does not invoke the rights of science but asks science a *question of right* external to science in order to *furnish* its rightful qualifications: always from the outside.
> What is this 'exterior'? Once again, a practical ideology. This time, *juridical* ideology.[72]

If the interaction between scientific practice and ideology, and ideological class struggle necessarily takes the form of *philosophical questions*, then it is also imperative to intervene in philosophy in favour of the sciences. Now historical materialism offers a way for philosophy to have an apprehension of its functioning and role of practical ideologies and this leads to dialectical materialism being a very peculiar political position in philosophy.

> [T]he philosophy to which we adhere – or, more exactly, the position we occupy in philosophy – is not unrelated to politics, to a certain politics, to Lenin's politics [...] There is no contradiction here: this politics is the politics of the workers' movement and its theory comes from Marx, *just as the knowledge of practical ideologies that finally permits philosophy to control and criticize its organic link with practical ideology, and therefore to rectify the effects of this link by taking a 'correct' line, comes from Marx.*[73]

---

71 Althusser 1990, p. 122.
72 Althusser 1990, p. 127.
73 Althusser 1990. pp. 130–1.

The possibility to intervene in a materialist fashion is based upon the very contradictory character of the spontaneous philosophy of the scientists which combines materialist and idealist aspects. According to Althusser 'in the spontaneous philosophy of scientists (SPS) the (materialist) Element 1 is, in the vast majority of cases, dominated by Element 2 (and the exceptions are therefore all the more noteworthy)'.[74] This means that a materialist philosophy can be an ally to the scientists in their attempt to reinforce the materialist element associated with scientific practice: 'This condition is *the alliance of scientists with materialist philosophy*, which brings to scientists the extra forces needed so to reinforce the materialist element as to dispel the religious-idealist illusions that dominated their SPS'.[75] However, this materialist philosophy cannot be a simple materialist version of mainstream idealist philosophies. It must be a radically different philosophy able to base itself upon knowledge of what it fights for and to understand its own relation to practical ideologies:

> For if it is to be able to serve scientific practice, this materialist philosophy must be prepared to combat all the forms of the idealist exploitation of the sciences; and if it is to be able to wage this combat *en connaissance de cause*, this philosophy must be capable of *mastering through knowledge and criticism* the organic link that binds it to the practical ideologies on which it, like any other philosophy, depends. We have seen under what conditions this critical control is possible: *only* in the case of a materialist philosophy connected to the discoveries through which Marx opened up the way to knowledge of the mechanisms of 'ideological social relations' (Lenin), and therefore a knowledge of the function of practical ideologies and their class antagonisms.[76]

Such a materialist philosophy can only be developed in the struggle itself:

> If philosophy is a struggle, and if, in this struggle, it is idealist philosophy that is dominant, this inevitably means that *dialectical materialist philosophy must itself be constituted in the struggle*, and that in the course of this struggle it must gradually win its own positions against the enemy simply in order to exist, to acquire the existence of a historical force.[77]

---

74 Althusser 1990 p. 134.
75 Althusser 1990, p. 137.
76 Althusser 1990, p. 142.
77 Althusser 1990, p. 143.

In this sense, philosophy is always intervention in a terrain of struggle, especially a potential new materialist practice of philosophy.

Philosophy and the Spontaneous Philosophy of the Scientists was originally pronounced as a set of five lectures in 1967. When Althusser edited them as a book, he left out the fifth lecture that was published in 1995. In it he stresses particularly the relation between philosophy and the sciences. Going back to Plato he stresses the fact that 'the determining element for the birth of philosophy was the existence of a mathematical science, therefore the existence of the first science that history had known'.[78] Thus, philosophy has a complex relation to the sciences; it recognises them and at the same time it attempts to subordinate them in terms of its own idealist representation of the sciences. One of the forms this process of exploitation-subordination takes is the representation of philosophy as a Theory of Science, as a theory of knowledge. In philosophy, the sciences exist in the 'form of a *dedoubling-redoubling*: under the form of the sciences situated in a limited and subordinate at the interior of philosophy; under the form of philosophy pretending to be science, the Science, understood at the limit the Science of sciences'.[79]

Althusser offers a categorisation of forms of idealism in their theorisation of the relation subject–object–truth, distinguishing between empiricism and formalism. The basic relation defined as *Subject = Object* leads to a second formulation which also includes truth: *(Subject = Object) = Truth*. For Althusser, this is a *speculary* relation, a speculary reflection, and here the point that initially was used against Feuerbach and – indirectly – phenomenology, is expanded to all theories of knowledge: 'every Theory of Science is therefore a specularly speculary Theory'.[80] For Althusser all theories of knowledge are variations of this theoretical invariant (Subject = Object) = Truth. Depending on the presence or the absence of a term we can have different variations: The suppression of the subject, (= Object) = Truth, leads to objective empiricism. The suppression of the object, (Subject =) = Truth, leads not only to subjective empiricism but also to formalism.[81]

The trait of formalism for Althusser is the position that truth 'is contained in the subject, in theory'.[82] Structuralist ideology is for Althusser a variety of formalism:

---

78   Althusser 1995a, p. 260.
79   Althusser 1995a, p. 264.
80   Althusser 1995a, p. 270.
81   See Althusser 1995a, pp. 274–8.
82   Althusser 1995a, p. 279.

> In our days, what I propose to be called the *structuralist ideology*: ideology of the combinatory, is directly in the line of Leibniz. The structuralist ideology considers that it operates within pure forms reconnecting the various elements into formal structures, a calculation that can be conscious, if it is practiced by the scientist [*savant*], but which is in essence unconscious. Here we can find the sense and importance of the theory of Lévi-Strauss on the unconscious, which – do I need to be more precise? – has no relation to Freud.[83]

Althusser also stresses the importance of neopositivism, which he describes as an 'assault of formalism within the ranks of empiricism'.[84] The characteristic form of positivism takes the form of the following invariant: (= facts) = Truth.[85] For Althusser the neopositivist conceptions of sciences and tendencies, such as calling metatheory the theory of theories, are just forms of '*philosophical exploitation*'[86] of the sciences. Moreover, neopositivism can be combined 'with a moral ideology, humanism and with a conservative politics: technocracy of what we can call neo-capitalism'.[87]

For Althusser a different practice of philosophy, which at this stage he still designates as dialectical materialism, is not just another philosophy, or philosophical system, but rather a particular form of self-criticism of philosophy, a 'critique of philosophy by philosophy' that 'does not depend only upon philosophy'.

> Fundamentally it depends upon the knowledge of the nature of philosophy, namely the knowledge of the nature 1) of the process of production of scientific knowledges, and 2) the conflicts of tendency between conceptions of the world.[88]

6   Philosophy as Class Struggle

In early 1968, in *Lenin and Philosophy* Althusser openly introduced his new conception of philosophy. Now the emphasis is not on philosophy emerging along

---

83   Ibid.
84   Althusser 1995a, p. 285.
85   Althusser 1995a, p. 283.
86   Althusser 1995a, p. 287.
87   Althusser 1995a, p. 285.
88   Althusser 1995a, p. 296.

with a science, but philosophy lagging behind science because only scientific revolutions can induce philosophical ruptures. 'Transformations of philosophy are always rebounds from great scientific discoveries. Hence *in essentials*, they arise *after the event*. That is why philosophy has lagged behind science in Marxist theory'.[89] It is through a fresh reading of Lenin's philosophical interventions that Althusser attempts to fully articulate his new conception of philosophy. Philosophy is a *Kampfplatz* in the Kantian sense, but without a particular object.

What is the result of this philosophical intervention? The constant redrawing of the line of demarcation between science and ideology, and more specifically between materialism and idealism as philosophical currents, is very important. The conception of philosophy as a constant struggle between idealism and materialism, which can be found in Engels's works from the 1880s, here is combined with its political repercussions. In a rather classical Marxist conception, materialism is identified in the history of philosophy with those positions representing the subaltern classes and idealism with those positions representing the ruling class.

However, what is important is not so much the content of this definition of philosophy, but the way the practice of philosophy is defined. Since philosophy does not have content or object in the proper sense, it is a practice, the practice of philosophy that produces results. These results have to do with changes in the relation of theoretical – and ideological – forces in given theoretical and in the last instance political conjunctures. Therefore philosophy is a very peculiar form of intervention that can be discerned only in its results, in how the theoretical and ideological conjuncture is developed.

What about traditional philosophical systems? For Althusser in the most part philosophy does not have any self-awareness of its role and that is the originality of Lenin who, although self-taught in philosophy, actually managed to grasp what is at stake in philosophical interventions. Marxism is not basically a philosophical revolution; it is a scientific revolution, the opening up of History as a scientific continent that induces the emergence of a new practice of philosophy. Marxist philosophy also reproduced the lag of philosophy in relation to sciences that Althusser thinks is characteristic of philosophical discourse. It is worth noting that in this definition of philosophical interventions, there is no positive conceptual content apart from the 'void' movement of intervention and consequently there can be nothing else in the history of philosophy.

---

89   Althusser 1971, pp. 15–16.

> We can thus understand why philosophy can have a history, and yet nothing occurs in that history. For the intervention of each philosophy, which displaces or modifies existing philosophical categories and thus produces those changes in philosophical discourse in which the history of philosophy proffers its existence, is precisely the philosophical nothing whose insistence we have established, since a dividing-line actually is nothing, it is not even a line or a drawing, but the simple fact of being divided, i.e. *the emptiness of a distance taken*.[90]

And it is on the basis of this conception of philosophy as intervention that Althusser insists on the relation between philosophy and politics.

> We can now advance the following proposition: philosophy is a certain continuation of politics, in a certain domain, *vis-à-vis* a certain reality. Philosophy represents politics in the domain of theory, or to be more precise: *with the sciences* – and, *vice versa*, philosophy represents scientificity in politics, with the classes engaged in the class struggle. How this representation is governed, by what mechanisms this representation is assured, by what mechanisms it can be falsified or faked and *is falsified as a general rule*, Lenin does not tell us. He is clearly profoundly convinced that in the last resort no philosophy can run ahead of this condition, evade the determinism of this double representation. In other words, he is convinced that philosophy exists somewhere as a third instance between the two major instances which constitute it as itself an instance: the class struggle and the sciences.[91]

If philosophy is not a theoretical practice producing knowledge effects, then Marxism, the first philosophy with an apprehension of its role, is not a new philosophy, nor is it a philosophical system; rather, it is a new practice of philosophy, a new way to intervene in philosophy. 'What is new in Marxism's contribution to philosophy is a new *practice of philosophy. Marxism is not a (new) philosophy of praxis, but a (new) practice of philosophy*'.[92]

Althusser takes up the question of the special status of philosophy in the big manuscript on *Reproduction*,[93] part of which he published in the form of the famous article on Ideology and Ideological Apparatuses of the State.

---

90 Althusser 1971, p. 62.
91 Althusser 1971, p. 65.
92 Althusser 1971, p. 68.
93 Althusser 2014b.

Here Althusser insists on the relation between different historical conjunctures, dominated by the *conjunction* between political-economic events and scientific events, and philosophy.[94] This is an elaboration on the position that philosophy comes after sciences and scientific revolutions, marking his distance from the initial insistence on philosophy being in practical form within the sciences, especially historical materialism, even at the cost of not being able to provide protocols of scientificity.

In the *Reply to John Lewis* Althusser elaborates more on the relation between an epistemological break and a philosophical break. It is worth looking at how Althusser here treats the question of time. In *Lenin and Philosophy* he insisted that philosophy lagged behind the sciences and that scientific revolutions provoke philosophical ruptures.

> If philosophy is to be born, or reborn, one or more sciences must exist. Perhaps this is why philosophy in the strict sense only began with Plato, its birth induced by the existence of Greek Mathematics; was overhauled by Descartes, its modern revolution induced by Galilean physics; was recast by Kant under the influence of Newton's discovery; and was remodelled by Husserl under the impetus of the first axiomatics, etc.[95]

However, in his *Reply to John Lewis* Althusser insists that in the case of Marx, the philosophical revolution was the necessary condition for the epistemological break. 'In the case of Marx it is the philosophical revolution which is *primary* – and this revolution is not a "break".'[96] This slight change in attitude has to do with two nodal points. The first is that for Althusser philosophy has no history in the strong sense, since it represents the recurring struggle between materialist and idealist tendencies. The second is that 'philosophy is, in the last instance, class struggle in the field of theory'.[97] This in turn is linked to the importance of what class positions one takes in politics and theory. If Marx's theoretical revolution was not a simply theoretical event, but also required Marx to move politically and ideologically towards proletarian positions, and this in turn was a stake in the class struggle, then philosophy is the necessary terrain on which this struggle is acted out. This justifies the difference in the conception of the timing between Marxism and Marxist philosophy.

---

94   Althusser 2014b, p. 16.
95   Althusser 1971, p. 41.
96   Althusser 1976a, p. 71.
97   Althusser 1976a, p. 72.

For if it is true that Marx had to pass over to proletarian class positions in theory in order to found the science of history, he did not make that leap all at once, once and for all, for ever. It was necessary to *work out* these positions, to take them up over and against the enemy. The philosophical battle continued within Marx himself, in his work: around the principles and concepts of the new revolutionary science, which was one of the stakes of the battle. Marxist science only gained its ground little by little, in theoretical struggle (class struggle in theory), in close and constant relation to the class struggle in the wider sense. This struggle lasted all of Marx's life. It continued after his death, in the labour movement, and it is still going on today. A struggle without an end.[98]

It is obvious that the new definition of philosophy as class struggle in theory seems like a less expansive conception of Marxist philosophy, since it is not there, according to Althusser, that one should look for the epistemological and political protocols of a revolutionary strategy. However, this does not mean that it is not important. Rather it stresses the social and political effectivity of philosophy. As William Lewis has stressed,

> Althusser's intervention made it clear that Marxist philosophy could no longer be understood as a dialectical formula for realizing political goals but must instead be understood as the articulation and deployment of a materialist critique that may have the effect of 'assist[ing] [in the transformation of the world]'. This is certainly a downgrading of the status of Marxist philosophy and one that puts it worlds away from a formula for revolution or from a theory of human liberation. In fact, it puts it much closer to the position of cultural critique. However, with its realism and concomitant ability to correct ideological errors, Althusser goes a long way to restoring or reconfiguring Marxist philosophy as a practice that is able to suggest, given present realities, what events are possible.[99]

Althusser elaborated further on this conception of philosophy as battlefield in the 1970s. The reference to philosophy as in the last instance class struggle in theory is not a simple radicalisation, nor is it a simple reproduction of an over-politicised conception of theory under the influence of Maoism and the Chinese Cultural Revolution. It is an attempt to re-think the particular charac-

---

98 Althusser 1976a, p. 71.
99 Lewis 2005, p. 198.

ter of philosophy. The crucial point is the relation of materialism and idealism with class tendencies. Here Althusser follows the suggestion, formulated by Engels but in a way already existent in eighteenth-century materialism, that objectivity and demystification of social reality is in the interest of the subaltern classes and that idealism is more on the side of Ideology and therefore of ruling ideologies. This conception, if taken in a schematic form, cannot explain what is the political or social role of idealist philosophies that expressed a desire for emancipation. It is here that the insistence on *philosophical tendencies* is important. Idealism and materialism are not simply antagonistic positions and systems; mainly they are antagonistic tendencies that can be found in every philosophical text. So the definition of philosophy as in the last instance class struggle in theory should not be read as implying that every class has its own philosophy, 'representing its interests'. What is implied in this definition is that as a result of class struggle in society (and in ideology), every philosophical text – and consequently every 'spontaneous philosophy of a scientist' – carries with it a certain balance of forces between these basic antagonistic tendencies.

> If it is true that philosophy, 'class struggle in theory', is, in the last instance, this interposed conflict between tendencies (idealism and materialism) which Engels, Lenin and Mao spoke about, then since this struggle does not take place in the sky but on the theoretical ground, and since this ground changes its features in the course of history, and since at the same time the question of what is at stake also takes on new forms, you can therefore say that the idealist and materialist tendencies which confront one another in all philosophical struggles, on the field of battle, *are never realized in a pure form in any 'philosophy'*. In every 'philosophy', even when it represents as explicitly and 'coherently' as possible one of the two great antagonistic tendencies, there exist manifest or latent elements of the *other* tendency.[100]

This contradictory co-existence of tendencies means that philosophical struggle is never a direct confrontation between well-defined conceptual armies. Rather, it is a complex and uneven process in which each tendency has to occupy the terrain of its adversary in order to take the initiative, thus interiorising the conflict.

---

100   Althusser 1976a, pp. 144–5.

And how could it be otherwise, if the role of every philosophy is to try to besiege the enemy's positions, therefore to interiorize the conflict in order to master it? Now this mastery may escape precisely whoever is trying to establish it. For a simple reason: the fate of philosophical theses does not depend only on the position on which they stand – because the class struggle in theory is always secondary in relation to the class struggle in general, because *there is something outside of philosophy* which constitutes it as philosophy, even though philosophy itself certainly does not want to recognize the fact.[101]

In light of this, it is obvious that the reference to class struggle in theory implies that for Althusser philosophy as class struggle in theory does not mean that dialectical materialism is a philosophy representing the class position of the proletariat, but that it is a practice that intervenes in the reproduction of the antagonism between materialism and ideology within philosophy, the spontaneous philosophy of the scientists and the multiple articulations of science and philosophy, in order to change the balance of forces in favour of materialism. However, there was also the danger that this new conception of philosophical confrontation could lead to a schematic conception of the battle between philosophical lines that could undermine the necessary creativity of Marxist theoretical research. As Pierre Raymond warned:

> The 'creativity' of Marxism, if it is not just a word, passes through the enrichment of the confrontations *between* Marxists, because materialism *and* the dialectic do not make dialectical materialism by means of a magical formula. The hypothesis of a *philosophical line* is a dangerous and sterilising fiction, whereas a political line is a necessity. 'Class struggle in theory' and 'theory in the class struggle' are far from suggesting a hypothesis, but, in contrast, imply that we define the *Marxist* terrain of the *philosophical* discussion between *Marxists*. Because no-one [...] keeps [*détient*] the philosophical line.[102]

---

101 Althusser 1976a, p. 145.
102 Raymond 1976, p. 148.

CHAPTER 12

Philosophy as Laboratory

1976 was an important year in terms of Althusser's confrontation with the question of the definition of philosophy and of a potential new materialist practice of philosophy. In the summer of that year, he prepared a manuscript, initially entitled *Introduction à la philosophie* [*Introduction to Philosophy*].[1] He later rewrote it as a different text in 1977–78 as *Initiation à la philosophie pour des non-philosophes* [*Initiation to Philosophy for Non-philosophers*][2] changing the title of the *Introduction* to *Être marxiste en philosophie* [*Being a Marxist in Philosophy*].[3] These two manuscripts, both meticulously edited by G.M. Goshgarian, which remained unpublished during the first wave of posthumous publications of Althusser's texts, offer us important insights into his conception of philosophy, the materialism of the encounter and the links between his quest for a new practice of politics and a new practice of philosophy.

Consequently, we are in a better position to understand Althusser's conception of philosophy after the attempt to redefine it in the late 1960s. Both texts belong, along with texts such as *Machiavelli and Us*, to Althusser's completed manuscripts that he decided not to publish. Thematically, they are close to the 1976 lecture on the Transformation of Philosophy,[4] delivered at the University of Granada, a text that coincides with their preparation. Althusser sort of announces these manuscripts in the first chapters of his 1969 manuscript *On Reproduction*.[5] However, they are broader in scope and address more questions.

1 Redrawing the Line of Demarcation with Idealism

How to be a Marxist in Philosophy is above all preoccupied with the question of the distinction between a materialist practice of philosophy and idealist philosophy. For Althusser one of the lines of demarcation refers to the question of the beginning of philosophy. He suggests that in contrast to idealist

---

1 Goshgarian 2015a, p. 40.
2 Althusser 2014a. The English translation has the title *Philosophy for Non-Philosophers* (Althusser 2017a).
3 Translated in English as *How to be a Marxist in Philosophy* (Althusser 2017b).
4 In Althusser 1990.
5 Althusser 2014b.

philosophies that search for an absolute beginning and 'board the train at the departure station, take their seats in it, and stay on board until the train reaches its terminus', materialist philosophies always 'board a moving train',[6] and this movement suggests a *'process without origin or end'* and consequently a 'process without a subject'.[7] This rejection of any absolute beginning in philosophy, any absolute origin or End, also implies that any materialist philosophy is necessarily atheist: 'materialism is necessarily an atheism'.[8]

This attempt towards a rethinking of philosophy brings up the question of what distinguishes philosophy from the sciences. For Althusser, every science has a finite object and a proper 'technical, material *experimental* set-up'[9] and he attacks Karl Popper's falsifiability thesis on the basis that it cannot account for the experimental processes of both historical materialism and psychoanalysis, or the epistemology of Mathematics. For Althusser what is the 'singular experimental set-ups' of both psychoanalysis and historical materialism is a particular *'conjuncture'*,[10] namely the particular relations between the unconscious of the analyst and that of the analysand and in historical materialism the relations of force in the class struggle. In contrast, *'philosophy has no object'* since 'there is no philosophical experimentation'.[11] There can be various forms of conceptual experimentation within philosophy but there is *'absence of any experimental set-up'*.[12]

Traditional idealist philosophy is preoccupied with a certain conception of the 'Whole' in contrast to the finite objects of the sciences (with the exception of philosophers who insisted on finitude and a radical absence of sense or destiny such as Nietzsche, Heidegger and Derrida). For Althusser the same idealist tendency towards a philosophy that claims to be able to 'utter the truth about the Whole'[13] is also evident in certain forms of structuralism preoccupied with order and classifications. He cites as examples of this tendency both Lévi-Strauss's conception of an 'order of orders',[14] but also Badiou and Foucault.

> Combined in this view of things, which outwardly resembles materialism (process without a subject), are the twin pretensions of functionalism

---

6   Althusser 2017b, p. 18.
7   Althusser 2017b, p. 19.
8   Althusser 2017b, p. 22.
9   Althusser 2017b, p. 27.
10 Althusser 2017b, p. 29.
11 Ibid.
12 Althusser 2017b, p. 30.
13 Althusser 2017b, p. 32.
14 Althusser 2017b, p. 33.

and structuralism, in which place and function go together like hand and glove – and it is not by substituting the logic of forces for that of places, à la Badiou, that one can escape the logic of Order, whoever happens to state it: whoever, that is, gives men this order, in the full sense of the word, on the strength of his own authority, whether he is a professor in the Collège de France or Secretary of a political organization.[15]

It is obvious that for Althusser any philosophy of classification, either in the sense of a mathematicised ontology or of a structuralist conception of social order, reproduces both the traditional role of idealist philosophy, namely the illusion that it can present the truth of the whole, and a political role of maintaining and reproducing the dominant social order. 'As they talk of order, they talk of authority, that is, of power, and since there is no power other than the established power, that of the dominant class, it is its power that they serve'.[16]

Althusser returns to his conception of philosophical theses, insisting that they are always in opposition and in struggle, each position always already in battle against philosophical enemies, a certain form of philosophical preventive war: 'in the horizon, there is always the presence of the Other, the philosophical Enemy, who not only watches but also dominates the situation and imposes upon our philosopher to put himself, as Hobbes wanted it, in a state of *preventive* war'.[17] Moreover, philosophy is more violent in its struggle than social life.

> Philosophy is much more radical than social life which has its moments of respite and its cease-fires, its Matignon Agreements and Grenelle Accords,[18] its popes who preach peace in the wilderness, its Vietnamese who pursue their Tet truce [...] Philosophy is a rather more serious business; it knows neither respite nor truce.[19]

For Althusser, this is a perennial war between opposing philosophical tendencies, with the antagonism between materialism and idealism structuring the 'field of philosophy' and the 'field of the history of philosophy' as an 'antagonistic fields'.[20] For Althusser, only a materialist 'reaction' to idealism can be truly

---

15   Ibid.
16   Althusser 2015a, p. 107.
17   Althusser 2017b, p. 37.
18   An allusion to the agreements signed by the Trade Unions during May 1968.
19   Althusser 2017b, p. 37.
20   Althusser 2017b, p. 38.

creative and revolutionary. However, idealist philosophies tend to mystify this violent philosophical war by a means of the '[f]eint that war does not reign between philosophers'.[21]

Althusser moves to a discussion of his conception that, in contrast to scientific propositions, philosophical theses can only be just, insisting that this conception of correctness has nothing to do with justice, but how to adjust reasons and means in practice.

> It is plain that nothing in this practice of correctness recalls the legal-moral idea of justice. Quite the contrary: correctness points in the direction of the most realistic, concrete, materialist practice (material or not). To return to our classic example, it is in this sense that politicians as well as materialists will, using the same terms, call a war 'correct': correct not in the sense of justice, but in that of correctness and of the adjustment of motives and means – taking account, accordingly, of the relation of forces in the struggle of the classes, and the general tendency that dominates this relation.[22]

In contrast to this notion of correctness, the notion of Truth is idealist. Althusser reminds us that Spinoza always spoke about the *verum*, the true, never about Truth. This brings forward the idealism inherent in traditional theories of knowledge. 'For the theory of knowledge is nothing other than a philosophical theory that claims to explain what truth is'.[23] Althusser takes up again the questioning of the variations of idealism regarding the relations between subject and object already explored in the fifth lecture of the '*Cours de philosophie pour scientifiques*'.[24] In particular Althusser stresses a certain reduplication of truth, depicted in the formula $T(S=O)=T$, which he explains as '*it is indeed true that the adequation of subject and object produces a truth*'.[25] Moreover, this reduplication 'registers, reproduces and thinks *an intellectual division of labour* which [...] exists between the scientists who produce scientific knowledge and the philosophers who think about it, thinking and stating its philosophical truth'.[26] This conception of truth, and in particular of the philosophical absolute truth, leads to the conception of philosophy as being able to discern the *ratio rationis*

---

21   Althusser 2015a, p. 119. This phrase does not appear in the English translation.
22   Althusser 2017b, p. 42.
23   Althusser 2017b, p. 46.
24   In Althusser 1995a.
25   Althusser 2017b, p. 48.
26   Althusser 2017b, pp. 48–9.

and the 'radical origin of things'.[27] The result is an idealist philosophy not only of absolute truth but also of Origin and of End, since the '*the ultimate, radical End of things is identical with the primary, radical Origin of things*' expressed in the equation 'O=(V=(S=O)=T)E'.[28]

The fact that idealist philosophy assumes the role of guaranteeing truth leads not only to a certain conception of the distinction between scientific knowledge and practical knowledge, but also to the certain 'self-justification'[29] of idealist philosophy. This does not preclude the fact that there are also materialist elements in idealist philosophies, as an expression of the preventive character of philosophical war:

> For, since every philosophy is in a state of war, at the limit, with the other philosophical tendency, materialist or idealist, it must necessarily take preventive action against the enemy in order to get the better of him; in other words, it must preventively occupy its adversary's positions, even if that means cloaking itself in its adversary's arguments.[30]

For Althusser, such a tendency can be discerned not only in classical idealist theories of knowledge, but also in more recent forms of '*logical neo-positivism*'[31] and the influence of positivism in functionalism and structuralism in the human sciences.

The conclusion of Althusser's insistence on the idealist character of any theory of knowledge is that there can be no materialist theory of knowledge. However, there is the open question about the reality that is in action in the theory of knowledge. For Althusser the materialist tendency would be to think the equation of subject and object as an identity, at the same time respecting the difference between subject and object. He points to the direction of the '*Leninist theory of reflection*' as a 'scandalous form of the suppression of the problem'.[32] However, even this solution leaves many philosophical questions unanswered. Althusser suggests that a much more complex answer is offered by the Spinozist conception of *parallelism* as a way to think of the unity (and) difference between an object and its knowledge. He insists that what is important is the play and dialectic between the three kinds of knowledge in Spinoza, the

---

27 Althusser 2017b, p. 53.
28 Althusser 2017b, p. 53. O for Object, V for Truth, S for Subject, and E for End.
29 Althusser 2017b, p. 57.
30 Althusser 2017b, p. 59.
31 Althusser 2017b, p. 62.
32 Althusser 2017b, p. 65.

first and 'purely practical', the second kind with the 'common notions' as the general laws of all objects, and the third kind of knowledge, which 'produces knowledge of the singular', the 'individual or a given historical conjuncture'.[33] He also acknowledges that Hegel's conception of the dialectic and of the 'labour of the negative' points in the same direction, although he thinks that Hegel also retreats toward a metaphysical/religious conception. In contrast, Marxist materialism tends towards 'neither the abstraction of difference (Spinoza) nor the teleology of the labour of the dialectic (Hegel)'.[34] Marx's materialism rejects any 'juridical' question regarding the theory of knowledge at the same time as affirming '*the primacy of practice over theory*'.[35] However, this position is 'less a line drawn once for all, than *the constantly recurring demand to return to and redraw this line of demarcation on the occasion presented by each theoretical or concrete case*'.[36] For Althusser knowledge begins from the sensible and he refers to the *Theses on Feuerbach*:

> Thus when Lenin declares that all knowledge has its origin in *the senses*, he finds himself in a direct line of descent from Marx. Doubtless we can criticize him, at most, for trailing slightly behind the 'Theses on Feuerbach', which talk about not the senses, but human 'sensuous practical activity', since the senses are passive only at the limit and when abstractly considered; in fact, they come into play in the 'whole' of a sensuous practice, which orients and guides them in accordance with not just human individuals' needs, but the 'interests' of the primitive social group, intent (unawares) on maintaining a favourable equilibrium with the nature from which it draws its subsistence.[37]

Conceptual and theoretical knowledge follow after this original form of sensible practice. In this conception, there is no room for the centrality of the subject as in idealist philosophy. What we have is an 'agent [...] in a "process without subject or end"'.[38] Moreover, in scientific practice '[t]*he object is reduplicated*'[39] since we do not work theoretically on the object itself but upon its 'provisional representation'.[40] That is why Althusser insists that knowledge of

---

33 Althusser 2017b, p. 66.
34 Althusser 2017b, p. 67.
35 Althusser 2017b, p. 68.
36 Althusser 2017b, p. 69.
37 Ibid.
38 Althusser 2017b, p. 71.
39 Althusser 2017b, p. 72.
40 Ibid.

an object does change the object although it 'adds something to a society's culture: superior knowledge of this object that is determined and determinable as a function of this knowledge'.[41]

In this sense, Althusser distances himself from any traditional conception of gnoseology and also of any conception of ontology. He criticised Heidegger for his ontological turn. Althusser insists that any conception of Being as a foundation of ontology is based upon a metaphysics of presence: because Being is present we can assert the existence of finite beings. This omnipresence of Being guarantees that any finite being is in the manner that it is. Moreover, it is here that teleology can also be founded. For Althusser, any theory of Being leads not only to a theory of origins but also to a theory of Nothing, even in the sense of a dialectic that includes it as the moment of the labour of the negative. Moreover, Althusser is particularly critical of the tendency of Soviet philosophers to think in terms of ontology.

> These authors take the idealist thesis of the primacy of Being over beings and even of Being over thought – and also, as we have seen, of the primacy of Nothingness over Being, at the limit – to be identical to Marx's materialist thesis of the primacy of matter over thought.[42]

Consequently, the Soviet philosophers' emphasis on ontology also leads to an emphasis on the theory of knowledge despite Marx's and Lenin's caution against any such gnoseology. Althusser, in one of his most critical references to 'actually existing socialism', insists that this kind of materialist ontology and gnoseology is an expression of the evolution of class struggle in the USSR and the fact that it is no longer a socialist country.

> Yes, Marxism has 'disappeared' in the USSR; yes, bourgeois ideology largely holds sway there, disguised, for the time being, in Marxist terminology. The reason is that the USSR, although it is not a classic capitalist state, is nevertheless not a socialist state either, although it claims to be. But, at all events, it is a state; and, like any other state, it needs the help and support of an ideology suited to the prevailing relation of forces in the class struggle. Marxist philosophy, interpreted as a gnoseology and an ontology, finally performs, and rather well – at its own level, of course – the role expected of it: because it took more than thirty years for Soviet

---

41 Althusser 2017b, p. 75.
42 Althusser 2017b, p. 81.

philosophers to make up their minds at last to produce what was expected of them, what the state of the class struggle expected of them: this deformation of Marx's and Lenin's thought in philosophy. The fact that the product has been exported to foreign countries, like any other commodity, does not find its sole explanation in the contagion of ideas or the power of the Soviet state, and certainly not in the prestige of a philosophy of a rare mediocrity. It finds its explanation in the state of the class struggle in our countries, where the class struggle is waged, with the help of well-known practices, by Communist parties that need this philosophy in their turn in order to maintain their domination over their rank-and-file.[43]

It is obvious that for Althusser Soviet Marxism is not simply a philosophical deviation towards a metaphysical historical-natural ontology, along with a theory of knowledge. For Althusser this kind of philosophy is a strategy to legitimise a social and political regime that is no longer socialist and the politics of Western communist parties that have also moved away from a revolutionary conception of politics.

2   The Margin and the Encounter

For Althusser any ontology also entails a conception of Order or even of an 'Order of order', a 'taxonomy that has been haunting ontologising Western thought since Aristotle and even Plato, the great classifiers, to Leibniz and modern logical neo-positivism'.[44] This stresses the centrality of Order in this conception of ontology and metaphysics. Kant's conception of a round Earth is the basis for his conception of private property, his social contract theory and his conception of social order. This order can be combined with a reference to disorder – Althusser refers to Machiavelli, Hobbes, Marx and Rousseau as thinkers who have brought forward this conception of disorder – in the sense of a reference to human passions. However, in such a conception, in the end the emphasis is on order, in the sense of social and political order, something evident in Kant's conception of limits, especially in respect of the danger of Terror, as experienced in the French Revolution. In contrast, Hegel begins with the assumption that there are no limits.

---

43   Althusser 2017b, p. 82.
44   Althusser 2017b, p. 83.

> If there are no limits, it is, firstly, because one is no longer in the finite, as Kant would have it, but in the infinite. Secondly, it is because *the outside isn't outside, but inside*; you have to look for and find your own limits in yourself, finite-infinite man, for they're nowhere but inside you.[45]

For Althusser the question of the relation between the conception of Order and the affirmation of the absence of a limit – this limit that can be a non-limit – expressed in the image of a circle without an outside, acquires a much broader significance.

> We must accordingly find the means, and it is not easy, to think, simultaneously, the Order which is round, and thus limited by its curve, and the not-outside, that is, the absence of curves and limits. A limit that is, in sum, a non-limit, a circle that is a circle, but with no outside. One thinks of Rousseau again, of those islands that have surged up out of the sea and are connected to no other land mass; one thinks of those scientific continents that have surged up in the sea of practical ignorance. One thinks of the appearance of a saint in a world torn asunder by egoism: one thinks of the impossible love that Géraldy sings: 'if you loved me, if I loved you, how I would love you!'; one thinks of a chief-of-state who would put cultivating the family's eggplants in command, as Cato did; one thinks of a scientist who would look for women with sorrel-shaped ears, a bird that would make redcurrant jam on André Breton's head, and what else? We all know enough about such things to know, in any case, that this question is damned serious, that it may even be the question of questions, and that we must treat it as it deserves, even if it is handed to us on a platter by, first and foremost, our friends the idealist philosophers.[46]

It is obvious that what is at stake here is the question of how to account for radical novelty and the possibility of events without going into some form of metaphysics or teleology, how to think of the emergence of new forms and new practices, without falling into some dualism or finality. Therefore, we are dealing here with one of the most important questions regarding not only social ontology but also the very possibility of revolutionary politics. For Althusser, Heidegger attempted to think this ontological question, but as a spiritualist he

---

45 Althusser 2017b, p. 86.
46 Althusser 2017b, pp. 86–7.

assigned 'Being primacy over beings'.[47] In contrast, he finds more convincing Derrida's conception of the *margin*.[48] Althusser insists that

> one suddenly realizes that interesting things go on in the vicinity of the margin: on the margin of official society, where the exploited workers and the immigrant workers are, together with children, from whose mouths the truth has long come, and artists, from the greatest to the humblest, with Breton and his friends in-between, and the poor in spirit when they are saints, even if they don't know it, and the mad, and certain prisoners, Soviet and Latin American prisoners in particular and so on. The margin is also the beach, the one on which everyone will alight to enjoy the sun after we have at last crossed this terrible river of socialism in the boat of the dictatorship of the proletariat. And then we shall have the free reign of the margin on the beach of communism: there will be no more written texts, no more written right, no more written law, no more written orders, no more writing, nothing but living traces, traces of the spoken word, exchanges of words and goods without money, without (written) accounts, exchanges of looks and voices, of love or hate, with no dishonest descriptions of the merchandise. This will be the end of the dictatorship of writing, the end of the dictatorship of language, the reign of the universal margin and the universal family, I tell you, the reign of whiteness, which one will see in the whites of people's eyes, the universal reign of whites, that is, of the white race, but all the races will be white [*blanc*], that is, all colours, and only the wise guys [*blancs-becs*, literally, white beaks] will have to watch their behaviour, unless they turn into Prince Charmings [*merles blancs*, literally, white blackbirds]. What is more, all blackbirds will be white: black will be suppressed, along with all the mourning and suffering it is possible to avoid.[49]

Althusser here offers a powerful reference to the image of the margin that would also return in the 1980s texts, as one of the central categories of aleatory materialism: 'the void, the limit, the margin, the absence of a centre, the displacement of the centre to the margin (and vice versa), and freedom'.[50] It is

---

47   Althusser 2017b, p. 87.
48   Cf. Derrida 1982.
49   Althusser 2017b, p. 88.
50   Althusser 2006a, p. 261. It is also interesting that we can see the same reference to the margin in a letter to Fernanda Navarro from 1985: 'in connection with the conflicts that philosophy has provoked in the course of its history, there appear margins or zones that

also in those texts that we see a certain conception of the margin as the place where we can identify practices that escape the determination by class struggle:

> in connection with the conflicts that philosophy has provoked in the course of its history, there appear *margins* or zones that can escape unequivocal determination by class struggle. Examples: certain areas of reflection on linguistics, epistemology, art, the religious sentiment, customs, folklore, and so on. This is to say that, within philosophy, there exist islands or 'interstices'.[51]

We can also see the same reference to the margin in the *Thèses de Juin* from 1986, here in the context of Althusser's conception of a new movement of liberation and liberty.

> In order to do this, we must follow the example of Marx. Marx used to say that the proletariat *camps in the margins* of bourgeois society. And he put it in the centre, in the heart of class struggle. What did Marx do? *He made the margin into the centre. Formally*, the problem is the same. We must make the margin into the centre. However, the margin is not united, it is very divided, into multiple alternative groups, and the vast majority of youths, of unemployed, of the poor remain beyond the conscience of the necessity of union.[52]

Concerning this use of forms as part of the vocabulary of philosophy, Althusser makes the point that this conception of the limit and the margin suggests that when we discuss forms in the sciences we usually see a certain poverty in comparison 'to the forms observable in human relations, in "inter-subjectivity" or the unconscious where the Formless [*L'Informe*] of phantasies holds sway'.[53]

Althusser reminds us that contrary to the traditional conception of the subject as indivisible, when we move towards the unconscious, things become more fragmented. At the same time, the category of the subject 'is obviously indispensable to every philosophy'.[54] In Plato, this is organised around the

---

can escape unequivocal determination by class struggle. Examples: certain areas of reflection on linguistics, epistemology, art, the religious sentiment, customs, folklore, and so on. This is to say that, within philosophy, there exist islands or "interstices"' (Althusser 2006a, p. 236).

51   Althusser 2006a, p. 271.
52   Althusser 1986, p. 12.
53   Althusser 2017b, p. 89.
54   Althusser 2017b, p. 92.

notion of participation in the Idea. Aristotle in turn attempted a theory that could combine a 'theory of substance, essence, and individuality'.[55] Moreover, Aristotle's conception of nature suggests a certain conception of Order. This means that there was something political in both his conception of nature, in the sense of an attempt to maintain the established order. At the same time, Aristotle is for Althusser an example of the ability of philosophy to produce concepts and categories, thus playing an important role in the terrain of scientific practice. Althusser stresses the importance of the Stoics and their hypothetical reasoning, which he considers an important advance in comparison to the philosophy of the Idea, since they are based upon a conception of the world with 'neither origin nor end',[56] something that does not prevent them from adding knowledge, 'but they can hope for nothing from either Nature, which exists, or the gods, who, if they exist, are perfectly impassible'.[57] For Althusser, '[t]his is how the Stoics dealt with the gods: by exiling them, the way the new tyrants exiled their opponents'.[58]

Epicurus has a distinct place in Althusser's genealogy of philosophy. For Althusser, Epicurus not only insisted on radical contingency and rejected any sense of origin and end, but also had an atomistic conception. Moreover, he insists that the most important aspect is the imagery of the rain, as described by Lucretius in *De rerum natura*, and in particular the reference to the *clinamen* as the beginning, in the sense of an infinitesimal deviation at the beginning of world. The notion of the encounter is here presented as a central concept. First of all it offers a new way to think of a singular subject, in a rather Spinozist conception of singularity: 'the different atoms, encountering each other and aggregating produce the singular entities that we know and that constitute our world'.[59] Moreover, the encounter is a 'developed concept of contingency',[60] in the sense that no encounter is predetermined, and also brings us to the notion of the conjuncture. Consequently, for Althusser the fact that 'everything is an encounter', and that 'every encounter is [...] necessarily contingent'[61] opens the possibility of events, of time and of history. An encounter can happen, or not happen; it can also be undone, and Althusser cites the case of the Italian bourgeoisie of the fourteenth century as an example. What is important is how an

---

55 Althusser 2017b, p. 94.
56 Althusser 2017b, p. 99.
57 Althusser 2017b, p. 100.
58 Ibid.
59 Althusser 2017b, p. 101.
60 Ibid.
61 Ibid.

encounter 'takes', which means that we can define its conditions only after the fact, since before it rests a 'relatively aleatory possibility'.[62] This also offers a conception of the emergence of a subject.

> What I wish to say, however, is that, with his thesis about *deviation*, *encounter*, and the *take*, Epicurus has provided us with the means of understanding precisely what the idealists had aimed at and missed: namely the irruption of a subject, *this* particular subject and no other.[63]

In contrast, after the emergence of capital a new model of the subject emerges, that of the subject of law, especially since the modern conception of law and right is related to the realities of capitalism: *'Right is a matter of fact, and expresses nothing but fact*. The fact it expresses is doubtless the fact of commercial law [*droit marchand*], but, in this case, right [*droit*] and fact coincide, a property whose mirage idealist philosophy had pursued in vain'.[64] Moreover, it is through the emergence of legal ideology, which is 'partway between pure law and moral-religious ideology', that we have a displacement and the subject of law becomes *'human subject'*.[65] This centrality of legal ideology can account for the evolution of bourgeois philosophy exemplified in the philosophy of Kant and a conception of the subjects that are 'subjects of not just knowledge but also of law, morality, politics, taste, and religion'.[66] This brings Althusser to Spinoza and, as we have already stressed, for Althusser Spinoza enables us to move beyond a theory of knowledge, of truth criteria and of the subject.

In this genealogy there is also a place for Hegel. Althusser insists that the very notion of the dialectic and of the labour of the negative was something that was missing from Spinoza. However, even this conception was not free from idealism, in the form of teleology and a certain apology for the social and political configuration of the bourgeois era.

> The affirmation that history has ended has been misunderstood. It does not mean that time has been suspended, but that the time of political events is over and done with. Nothing more will happen: you can go home and go about your business, you can 'enrich yourselves', and all will be

---

62 Althusser 2017b, pp. 100–1.
63 Althusser 2017b, p. 101.
64 Althusser 2017b, p. 103.
65 Althusser 2017b, p. 104.
66 Althusser 2017b, p. 106.

well; your property is guaranteed. This whole history of the guarantee, this long, painful conceptual history of the guarantee thus culminates, pathetically, in a guarantee of private property. With it culminates, in the same way, the whole long history of the guarantee of the proprietorship [*propriété*] of things, the properties [*propriétés*] of things, the specificity [*propre*] of things and of everyone, hence of the subject, whose hands are always clean [*propre*], for there are no bad apples or, if there are, there are courts and there are hospitals for the mad to take them in and rehabilitate them. Everyone can sleep in peace, decent folk in their homes, thieves in the prisons, the mad in the hospitals: the state of reason watches over them, this state that is, as Gramsci said, borrowing a phrase from I-don't-know-whom, a 'night watchman'. In the daytime, the state slips away, since the citizens keep watch. An excellent economy: the economy of bourgeois exploitation.[67]

On the other hand, for Marx the most urgent challenge was to '*assure within philosophy itself, the primacy of practice over theory*', which means to ascertain that philosophy is above all '[s]truggle, a combat that is perpetual and preventive because it is universal'.[68] Philosophy is a battlefield between the great warring camps, idealism and materialism, a battlefield where there 'is no possible neutrality' and in which every philosophy in the end must '*choose one's camp*'.[69] Every philosophical side must know not only its own territory, but also the territory of its opponent, since the frontline is always changing during the course of the battle.

> So it is that, depending on the course of the battles, nominalism changes camps, as does empiricism, and realism, and even the names 'idealism' and 'materialism'; for, in this war as in any other, one tries to trick the enemy with ruses and feints. Thus Spinoza takes God by surprise and by storm and, from the divine heights, dominates the whole battlefield: from then on, no one can drive him from it. Thus, again by surprise, even if we saw him coming a long way off, Heidegger captures the Thing and turns it against Hegel. Thus Marx wrests thought from idealism in order to subordinate it to the primacy of matter, or to that of the (nominalist) difference between the real object and the object of thought and so on.[70]

---

67   Althusser 2017b, pp. 110–11.
68   Althusser 2017b, p. 113.
69   Ibid.
70   Althusser 2017b, p. 114.

Turning to Marx, Althusser thinks that the conception of the dialectic as a method is an idealist position and he is very critical of Soviet philosophers and their 'caricatural idea' that 'the dialectic is something other than materialism'.[71] Althusser also opposes any notion of laws of the dialectic and is critical of Engels's attempt to think of the dialectic in terms of laws: '*There are no laws of the dialectic, but only dialectical theses*'.[72] For Althusser, we are dealing with philosophical theses that are at the same time materialist and dialectical. These dialectical theses do not take the form of an ontology; rather they are the affirmation of the 'primacy of the contradiction over the contraries',[73] which is echoed in historical materialism in the 'scientific concept of the determination of classes by class struggle'.[74]

3 Philosophy and Ideology

Regarding some basic tenets of historical materialism, Althusser insists on the importance of reproduction and the role of the state and of State Ideological Apparatuses. He also insists that he places greater emphasis on the 'state character of the ideological apparatuses and on their objective attachment to the dominant class', in contrast to Gramsci, who according to Althusser tended to 'underestimate the force of the state, and, therefore, the force of the domination of the class in power'.[75] Althusser thinks that such a conception can lead to a reformist strategy of politically investing in the intervention within the ideological and political apparatuses and try to occupy them from within. For Althusser, this is not a strategy that could prove successful even though it reflects a certain 'weakness of the bourgeois state',[76] because in the end there is always the extra force of imperialism.

Althusser stresses the importance of ideology and its relation to class struggle, since ideology is divided not only according to different practices or regions but also according to 'the tendencies of political and economic class struggle'.[77] What is more important is that the 'dominant ideology' is the result of processes of unification of diverse ideological elements. At the same time, the very

---

71 Althusser 2017b, p. 116.
72 Ibid.
73 Althusser 2017b, p. 117.
74 Althusser 2017b, p. 120.
75 Althusser 2017b, p. 123.
76 Ibid.
77 Althusser 2017b, p. 126.

'forms of capitalist class struggle [...] contribute directly to the constitution of the ideology of the working class as a class ideology'.[78]

Regarding the existence of philosophy Althusser thinks that since the emergence of a science faces resistance in the ideological terrain and creates ruptures in the forms of ideological domination, 'philosophy can accordingly be regarded [...] as [...] a means of "patching up" this tear in the unified tissue of the dominant ideology'.[79] If philosophy plays such an important role in the unification of the dominant ideology as an answer to the ideological ruptures induced by both the emergence of scientific discoveries and the evolution of class struggle, then we can say that it is 'ideological and political by virtue of its function'.[80] There is a double determination of philosophy, on the one hand by the sciences that offer to philosophy their model of theoretical abstraction, and on the other by the dominant ideology and its contradictions. In light of the above, the main political challenge was how to constitute the unity of the dominant ideology. For Althusser, the determinant role is played by '*legal ideology*'[81] and the dominant role by philosophy: 'In the labour of centuries that was required to constitute and, consequently, unify the dominant bourgeois ideology, *legal ideology was determinant* and *philosophy was dominant*'.[82] At stake in the philosophical debates and in the potential refutation of a philosophical thesis are 'the practices [...] *what happens in these practices*'.[83] Therefore, only through this unification of the dominant ideology is it possible to dominate practices and their agents. And it is here that philosophy plays its role:

> It is here that philosophy plays its part, since it works, as in a laboratory, on legal ideology's orders, to elaborate questions, theses, and categories that the dominant ideology adopts and carries to the heart of the ideological forms dominating the practices and their agents.[84]

Consequently, the systematic form that most philosophies take is the result of this effort to overcome the contradictions the dominant class faces 'in constituting its dominant ideology'.[85] At the same time, there is a complex relation

---

78 Althusser 2017b, p. 127.
79 Althusser 2017b, p. 129.
80 Althusser 2017b, p. 130.
81 Althusser 2017b, p. 133.
82 Ibid.
83 Althusser 2017b, p. 134.
84 Althusser 2017b, p. 135.
85 Ibid.

between philosophy and scientific practice. Every scientist works under the influence of some ideological forms which also include philosophical categories that can 'either constitute obstacles to research, to researchers' theoretical practice or can facilitate it'.[86] The research practice itself and the production of scientific knowledges enhance a materialist perspective, but every scientist is also vulnerable 'to ideology's ready-made ideas'.[87] This is the mechanism for the re-introduction of the dominant bourgeois ideology. Consequently, the role of materialist philosophy is exactly to avert and explain these mechanisms of ideological mystification. Moreover, through this mechanism philosophical categories 'after being elaborated in the laboratory of the philosophy of the erudite [...] penetrate the ideologies that dominate human practices'.[88] And it is here that we find 'the need for philosophy in the class struggle'.[89] In this terrain of struggle, Marxist materialist philosophy 'takes sides' in the philosophical class struggle, in favour of the 'materialist camp and takes proletarian positions'.[90] Consequently, 'it fights'.[91] However, a Marxist philosopher battles by practicing philosophy, by '*a new practice of philosophy*' that avoids 'the pitfalls of idealism':[92]

> He does not lapse into the inanity of drawing distinctions between materialism and the dialectic, or into the theory of knowledge, or into ontology. Nor does he mistake the so-called human sciences, which are merely bourgeois ideology's theoretical formations, for sciences. He knows that this domain, occupied by the adversary, has to be conquered for scientific knowledge, thanks to the principles and concepts of historical materialism, the science of the laws of class struggle.
>
> Finally, he does not succumb to one last bourgeois illusion: the belief that there exists a 'Marxist philosophy'.[93]

For Althusser, Marx was not the founder of a new philosophy, '[h]e simply practiced existing philosophy in a revolutionary way, by adopting theses that expressed the proletariat's revolutionary class positions'.[94] This means that we

---

86   Althusser 2017b, p. 136.
87   Ibid.
88   Althusser 2017b, p. 137.
89   Ibid.
90   Ibid.
91   Ibid.
92   Ibid.
93   Althusser 2017b, p. 138.
94   Ibid.

are not just dealing with another philosophy, but with a different and revolutionary practice of philosophy. Therefore, it cannot take the traditional form of a philosophical system: *'there can exist no Marxist philosophy in the classic sense of the word philosophy'*.[95] This new practice of philosophy has to be openly politically motivated, it has to be a 'new avatar of the "handmaiden of politics – of proletarian politics"',[96] and Althusser compares this conception to what he considers as the idealism of Lukács's emphasis on the universality of proletarian subjectivity. In contrast, Althusser insists that in his conception philosophy can serve the 'liberation of the social practices'.[97]

The fact that Althusser chose to end the manuscript with Marx's 11th Thesis on Feuerbach is significant. It signals that this conception of a new practice of philosophy is not simply a materialist deconstruction of idealism. It is also a transformative and emancipating theoretical and political practice aiming at liberating the political and social potential of proletarian struggle.

In the case of *How to be a Marxist in Philosophy*, we are dealing with an important contribution to the evolution of Althusser's thinking on philosophy. The emphasis on the radical break with any form of teleology and with any theory of origin and end, the conception of philosophy as a complex antagonistic terrain of struggle between philosophical tendencies, the highly original genealogy of the emergence of the subject and also of its absence from any materialist philosophy, the elaboration on the imagery of the margin as the political and historical space of new encounters along with the full conceptualisation of a materialism in the encounter, and, last but not least, the emphasis on the liberating character of a new Marxist materialist practice of philosophy in opposition to any form of philosophical 'system', all attest to the importance and the theoretical fecundity of this manuscript. Its publication offers a much clearer insight in the development of Althusser's theoretical – and political – project in the 1970s.

4   Different Practices of Philosophy

The *Philosophy for Non-Philosophers* is also presented as an introductory manual in philosophy for people with no special training in philosophy. Althusser begins by enumerating the different attitudes towards philosophy in order

---

95   Althusser 2017b, p. 139.
96   Althusser 2017b, p. 140.
97   Althusser 2017b, p. 143.

to conclude that many people think of philosophy only as something that is taught, that '*the one purpose philosophy serves is the teaching of philosophy*'[98] something attested by the common image that philosophy is mainly a preoccupation for philosophy professors. For Althusser, the common trait of philosophers is that 'they live in a world apart, in a *closed world*, constituted by the great works in the history of philosophy'. They are in the process of an '*endless re-reading*', because 'a philosophical work does not yield up its meaning, its message, on a single reading. It is overloaded with meaning: it is by nature inexhaustible and, so to speak, infinite, and it always has something new to say to someone who knows how to *interpret* it. The practice of philosophy is not just reading, or even demonstration. It is *interpretation, interrogation, meditation*'.[99] Consequently, 'this world without outside is *a world without history*',[100] in the sense of philosophers being in a constant dialogue with other philosophers despite the distance in terms of historical time. This reference to this 'world without history', the 'eternity' of philosophy, is similar to Althusser's well-known reference to ideology *in general* having no history.[101] Consequently, philosophers do not teach any piece of actual knowledge; they only teach how to '*philosophize*'.[102]

In contrast to idealist philosophers, there are other *materialist* philosophers, for whom philosophy is 'above all *practical*'.[103] For Althusser the perpetual struggle between idealism and materialism is not a fight between two different philosophies; it is a struggle between two '*contradictory practices of philosophy*'[104] that are not symmetrical. One refers to the practice of teaching *idealist* philosophy by specialised *professors* of philosophy. In contrast, materialist philosophers '(like Diderot, Lenin, and Gramsci)' insist that '*every one is a philosopher*'.[105] It is interesting that Althusser uses here a well-known phrase from Gramsci, from a passage from the *Prison Notebooks* that had been the target of Althusser's critique of historicism in *Reading Capital*.[106]

For Althusser, the philosophy of ordinary people includes knowledge and ideas and has both a practical and theoretical aspect. These have to do with

---

98 Althusser 2017a, p. 19.
99 Althusser 2017a, pp. 19–20.
100 Althusser 2017a, p. 20.
101 Althusser 2014b, p. 253.
102 Althusser 2017a, p. 20.
103 Althusser 2017a, p. 21.
104 Althusser 2017a, p. 22.
105 Althusser 2017a, p. 23. Cf. Q12, § 3; *SPN*, p. 9.
106 Cf. Althusser et al. 2016, p. 278.

'a certain conception of the *necessity* of things, the order of the world, and a certain conception of human *wisdom* in the face of the course of the world'.[107] However, Althusser thinks that this 'natural' philosophy can be paradoxical and contradictory. Unless it is 'educated' by political struggles it can be 'profoundly *passive* and *conformist*',[108] especially when it thinks of a necessity that surpasses human powers. For Althusser, Gramsci was the only one who thought of these contradictory tendencies and the danger of passivity unless this 'natural' philosophy of ordinary people is educated by class struggle and an encounter with revolutionary theory, in order to avoid resignation.

> Here I am simply summarizing the thought of the Italian Marxist philosopher Gramsci on this point. You can see, from this example, how a materialist philosopher reasons. He doesn't 'tell himself stories'; he doesn't make lofty speeches; he doesn't say that 'everyone is a revolutionary'. He lets people talk and he tells things the way they are. There is no denying the fact: in the broad masses of people *who have not yet been awakened to the struggle*, or even in the case of those who have fought, but were defeated, there is an underlying resignation. It goes all the way back to the earliest periods of history, which has always been the history of class societies, hence of exploitation and oppression. Men of the people, shaped by this history, may have revolted; but, since their revolts were always put down, they had no choice but to resign themselves to the *necessity* to which they were subjected and to accept it 'philosophically'.[109]

Religion represents this philosophy of resignation, '*uncontrollable* nature'[110] of this necessity, in the sense of a feeling of helplessness against 'the power (nature's, the State's)'.[111] Consequently, God becomes a metonymy for this power and the centre of this philosophy of resignation. For Althusser idealist philosophy has been a 'daughter of religion'.[112]

Idealist philosophy inherits the preoccupation with the question of the Origin of the World. For Althusser philosophical notions like Plato's Idea of Good, Aristotle's primary motor, Descartes' first cause, Spinoza's infinite substance, or

---

107   Althusser 2017a, p. 24.
108   Ibid.
109   Althusser 2017a, p. 25.
110   Althusser 2017a, p. 26.
111   Ibid.
112   Althusser 2017a, p. 27.

Leibniz's infinite calculator, are examples of how philosophy gives an abstract, conceptual content to the question of God as the question about the origin of the world. One of the main achievements of materialist philosophy is to prove that questioning why there is something instead of nothing is exactly one of those *'meaningless questions'*.[113] In contrast, for Althusser a materialist philosophy like that of Epicurus 'talks about not the Origin of the world (a meaningless question), but the *beginning* of the world'.[114] The materialist thesis is that '[t]here is [...] *always already something, always already matter*',[115] and he describes the Epicurian theme of the rain of atoms falling that encounter each other after a deviation:

> The *slightest [un rien de] deviation, the slightest 'deviance'*, is enough for the atoms to *encounter each other* and agglomerate: there we have the beginning of the world, and the world. Neither God nor Nothingness at the Origin: no Origin, but the beginning and, to account for the beginning, pre-existent matter, which becomes a world thanks to the (contingent, arbitrary) *encounter* of its elements.[116]

At the same time, Althusser links religion to teleology, the question of the '*End of the world*',[117] but also to the conception of a Sense or Meaning of history. In contrast, Marx's materialist philosophy 'denounced the theoretical imposture involved', following 'a long tradition in which Epicurus, Machiavelli, Diderot and others all figure'.[118] Any reference to the Meaning or Sense of the world or history is a meaningless question that represents the connection between idealist philosophy and religion, by means of the reference to an omnipotent god that can assign '*every being in the world a purpose and function*'.[119] In contrast, materialism offers a vision of the world where there is no need to search for meaning in everything, an affirmation that can offer the only possibility to actually act upon the world.

> [W]hy not frankly admit that the surest condition for acting in the world, modifying its course and thus investing it with *meaning* through work,

---

113   Althusser 2017a, p. 28.
114   Althusser 2017a, p. 29.
115   Ibid.
116   Althusser 2917a, pp. 29–30.
117   Althusser 2017a, p. 30.
118   Ibid.
119   Althusser 2017a, p. 31.

discovery and struggle, is to admit that *the World has no Meaning* (no pre-established meaning determined by an all-powerful Being, who is a pure fiction)?[120]

The tradition of materialist philosophy rejects *'questions devoid of meaning'*.[121] Althusser pays particular attention to how religion attempts to answer the question of death, with the promise of an afterlife 'making what was unbearable in this life bearable with the promise of recompense in a life to come'.[122] For Althusser it is not simply about fear of death in terms of personal survival and existence. It has more to do with facing loss and death and destruction in all aspects of historical existence. In contrast, knowing how to face death is 'a tragic theme of popular wisdom and materialist philosophy'.[123] Althusser thinks that the answer of eighteenth-century materialists, namely death as retuning to a previous material state, cannot answer the question of fear before death. Moreover, he insists that on the question of death we can find distance between not only religion and philosophy, but also between idealism and materialism, insisting that the materialist position is something like Spinoza's dictum that philosophy is not about learning to die but about learning to live.

In the spontaneous philosophy of the people, we can also find another conception referring to people, namely *'this finite condition of destitution and need that makes people work, transform nature and search painstakingly – a task religion spares them – for a little truth about the world'*.[124] It is exactly this effort, in most parts collective, to transform the world and act upon it that inscribes the 'conviction that there are reasons for things, comprehensible and controllable reasons, since one succeeds in producing defined results by respecting the laws of their production, which are laws of nature and society. Production and action are thus proof of the truth of these laws'.[125] This produces a *'philosophy of work and struggle, an active philosophy'*,[126] a 'philosophy of *practice*' in contrast to idealism as a 'philosophy of *theory*'.[127]

Althusser also includes in this text his well-known insistence that philosophy begins in Ancient Greece, exactly because it is there that we have the

---

120 Ibid.
121 Althusser 2017a, p. 32.
122 Althusser 2017a, p. 34.
123 Althusser 2017a, p. 35.
124 Althusser 2017a, p. 37.
125 Althusser 2017a, p. 38.
126 Ibid.
127 Ibid.

emergence of the first scientific continent, that of mathematics.[128] He distinguishes between simple practical observations of numbers and proportions and mathematics proper, whose emergence he associates with Thales. With Thales people stopped '*observing* combinations of concrete numbers and transformations of concrete figures in order to reason about *abstract* objects considered as such: pure numbers and pure figures, abstracted from their content or from concrete representations of them'.[129] The emergence of such a science, based upon abstraction and stating 'incontestable truths',[130] was a challenge to religion. Plato's effort was to submit mathematics as a science to his philosophy, '*to put it back in its place* in the established order – the order, that is, of the moral and political values that mathematics had momentarily threatened or might threaten'.[131] For Althusser this was a 'gigantic political-ideological operation' that needed a 'new discourse', and with 'a new method, *rational* and *dialectical demonstration*'.[132] Althusser here elaborates on the theme of philosophy as a reaction to the effects of the emergence of the sciences and in particular the way in which scientific truths can have an effect of rupture on dominant ideological forms. Idealist philosophy is a form of reaction, an attempt to cover this rupture. Moreover, idealist philosophy is a philosophy in the service of power, a philosophy dedicated to maintaining social order.

> For the kings and priests, and all those holding any sort of power whatsoever, *have a stake in this philosophy*; it is the only one capable of putting things in order and reinforcing the order of things so that everyone stays in his place and performs his social function: so that the slave remains a slave, the craftsman, a craftsman, the merchant, a merchant, the freemen, freemen, the priests, priests, the warriors, warriors and the king, a king. Idealism talks about Truth, but, behind Truth, it is power that appears on the horizon, and, with power, Order. Philosophers seem to withdraw from the world: they do so to set themselves apart from the ignorant, from common men and materialists. But they withdraw from the world only to intervene in it and dictate the Truth to it: the Truth of power and Order.[133]

---

128   Cf. Althusser 1971; Althusser 1995a, pp. 299–343.
129   Althusser 2017a, p. 40.
130   Althusser 2017a, p. 41.
131   Ibid.
132   Ibid.
133   Althusser 2107a, p. 43.

PHILOSOPHY AS LABORATORY 269

Althusser then makes a *big detour*. The notion of detour plays an important role in Althusser's conception of philosophy. Philosophers often make a *detour* through other philosophers in order to formulate their own positions. However, Althusser here is not simply interested in this dialogical character of philosophy. He insists on another form of big detour, not in philosophy, but towards *non-philosophy*, towards the outside of philosophy, a potential '*History of non-philosophy*', that would take account of the materiality of concrete social practices and antagonisms outside philosophy, exactly those aspects of social reality that had been '*neglected, rejected, censored, or abandoned*'[134] by idealist philosophy.

> Above all, *matter*, its ponderousness and power; above all, *labour* and its conditions, exploitation, slaves, serfs, proletarians, women and children in the hell of the factory, and slums and disease, and the attrition due to usury and also physical attrition; above all, the *body* and the desire that comes to it from its sex, that suspect part of man and woman which countless authorities have surveyed and still do; above all, *woman*, long man's property, and *children*, monitored from earliest infancy and in the stranglehold of an elaborate system of controls; above all, *madness*, condemned to the 'humanitarian' prison of the asylums; above all, *prisoners*, hunted down by law and Right, and all the exiles, the condemned and the tortured; above all, *the Barbarians* for the Greeks and the 'wogs' or 'foreigners' or 'natives' for us; above all, *state power* and all its apparatuses of coercion and 'persuasion', concealed in seemingly neutral institutions, the family, the School System, the Health Care System, the Administration, the Constitution; above all, class struggle; above all, war. *No more than that*.[135]

Here materialism is presented as a detour through the very materiality of labour, exploitation, class struggle, sexual difference, madness, state power. This makes even more clear the need for materialist philosophy to focus on this material and conflictual outside of philosophy. Idealist philosophy is usually silent about its responsibility, along with religion and dominant politics, in censoring or remaining silent about these aspects of social reality.

---

134 Althusser 2017a, p. 47.
135 Althusser 2017a, pp. 47–8.

5   Philosophy and Abstraction

Althusser moves to another crucial aspect of the functioning of philosophy, namely *abstraction*. Abstraction is not about abandoning the concrete terms of our existence or talking about non-existent things: *'every specific practice* (labour, scientific research, medicine, political struggle) *abstracts from the rest of reality in order to concentrate on transforming one part of it'*.[136] But one cannot think of abstraction without talking about language. Althusser offers a didactic presentation of a classical Saussurian conception of the arbitrary relation between words and their meaning and of the relation between phonological elements in the system of differences that is a language. Language itself is a mechanism of abstraction that makes possible to point towards the concrete. Using the syntagm 'the cow' as an example, referring to the specific cow of a peasant, he thinks that *'the most abstract, the most general of forms, namely the two words "the cow", unfailingly designates the most concrete of objects* [...] *the abstraction of language serves to designate the most concrete of concrete things'*.[137] The concrete does not properly exist without language: 'Hegel quite rightly concludes not that concrete immediacy does not exist, but that the language whose function it is to designate it as concrete is itself *abstract, general*'.[138] It is interesting that Althusser here uses the reference to the necessity of the abstract as a necessary starting point for the production of the concrete, not just in terms of epistemological process, a position also evident in the 1965 texts, but also in terms of the functioning of language. At the same time, there is another *'appropriation of the concrete that proceeds by way of not language, but the human body'*.[139] However, this kind of appropriation requires some form of communication and social recognition, consequently some form of *law*, as an abstract system of relations.

> Even the most 'concrete' kind of appropriation thus has to have the social sanction of the *language of law*, that is, of an abstract system of relations, if it is to be accomplished without risk – and not just without risk, but with all possible guarantees. When the concrete appropriation of the concrete does not submit to this abstraction and this sanction, it runs the risk,

---

136   Althusser 2017a, p. 50.
137   Althusser 2017a, p. 54.
138   Ibid.
139   Althusser 2017a, p. 55.

at the limit, of not being socially recognized, hence of violating the law, hence of being qualified as theft or crime.[140]

For Althusser there is a certain '"dialectical" circle'[141] between the abstract and the concrete. The concrete practices, in labour or in love, cannot be understood without some reference to ideological relations that make people repeat the same 'gestures which the tradition established'.[142]

> [T]here also exists an infinite number of *abstract gestures* that are linked to concrete practices, yet exist independently of them, and this makes it possible for them to have general value and *serve these concrete practices*.[143]

Here, Althusser's emphasis (well-known from his 1969–70 texts) on ideology as deriving from practices and being expressed in practices is related to this conception of abstraction. Abstraction refers to this tendency for the reproduction of practices, offering a link between the abstract and the concrete. The crucial aspect is that of relations. Althusser here brings forward the full force of his relational conception of social reality. What has been defined as the abstract is in reality not something that is cut off or separated from the concrete but something that *adds* something to the concrete. It adds a certain aspect of generality, or of repetition to the concrete. Therefore what we tend to define as concrete is something that is produced as such, by its 'social appropriation'. It cannot be taken as a starting point:

> [Abstraction adds] [t]*he generality of a relation* (linguistic, legal, social, ideological) that concerns the concrete. Better: *this relation dominates the concrete without the latter's knowledge, and it is this relation that constitutes the concrete as concrete* [...] without language and law, without the relations of production and ideological relations, nothing in the world is concrete for man. For I can neither name it, nor attribute it, nor produce it, nor make my intentions known to it.[144]

Regarding abstraction, Althusser stresses the specificity of each particular practice. In productive practices, one can see not only the technical know-how

---

140 Ibid.
141 Ibid.
142 Althusser 2017a, p. 56.
143 Althusser 2017a, p. 57.
144 Ibid.

invested in the reality of each practice but also an 'abstract, relatively coherent body of knowledge [*savoir*]'.[145] The importance of technical know-how and practical knowledge does not imply the empiricist myth of a '*direct contact*' with things; knowledge is not 'simple seeing' or 'extracting'[146] and pure empirical knowledge is an idealist myth. For Althusser practical-technical knowledge is a 'blind spot' of idealist philosophy that 'does not want to see the practical knowledge' coming from concrete practices in social production and work. At the same time this practical knowledge is also not 'pure'[147] since it is always thought within ideological representations, although few philosophers attempted to think of these preconceived ideas as a *system* and in a *positive* manner, with the exception of Spinoza and his emphasis on imagination as a *necessary illusion*[148] and of course Marx's conceptualisation of ideology. This relation between technical-practical knowledge and ideological relations is indispensable in order to understand the emergence of scientific knowledge. Sciences emerge 'on the basis of pre-existing body of practical knowledge and a particular ideological, philosophical [...] and scientific conjuncture'.[149] Scientific practice does not only add an element of abstraction and generality, like practical-technical knowledge; its abstraction points towards not '*generality, but universality*'.[150] Science is not limited to particular cases and '[s]cience's concrete is the *experimental* concrete, the 'purified' concrete, defined and produced as a function of the problem to be posed'.[151] Therefore its concrete character is not primary, but it is produced as a result of theoretical operations as an experimental dispositif. Therefore we have a '*concrete – abstract – concrete*' cycle or a '*practice – theory – practice*'[152] which represents a correction in relation to Althusser's insistence on the centrality of theory in the 1960–65 texts. However, this should not lead us towards a conception of a simple primacy of practice over theory, since the 'pair theory-practice designates not two distinct objects, but a variable relationship between two inseparable terms'.[153]

Turning to philosophical abstraction, Althusser stresses the tendency of idealist philosophy to think about everything that exists and everything that is possible to exist; philosophy has to do not with generality but with totality. This

---

145 Althusser 2017a, p. 60.
146 Althusser 2017a, p. 62.
147 Althusser 2017a, p. 63.
148 Ibid.
149 Althusser 2017a, pp. 63–4.
150 Althusser 2017a, p. 64.
151 Althusser 2017a, p. 65.
152 Ibid.
153 Althusser 2017a, p. 66.

forces philosophy to think in terms of non-existent 'supplements'[154] to actually existing things. One such example is the void in Democritus and Epicurus as 'the condition of possibility of the encounter of atoms'.[155] Another example is the notion of 'nothingness' in Plato, Hegel and Sartre. Philosophical abstractions are not 'universalising' but 'totalising'[156] and in contrast to science, which 'is always left to confront its finite object', philosophy ends up facing 'its infinite project'.[157]

Althusser turns to the myth of the State of Nature, which is similar to the religious myth of paradise. In contrast to the religious myth, the fall is not the result of a moral deviation, but '*private property*, the physical appropriation of the earth, fruit, animals and money, which, as it is generalized, spawns conflicts over boundaries and a war that tends to be general: the state of war'.[158] For Althusser, in the myth of the State of Nature, as with all other myths, there is an element of truth. The 'fall' is in reality the real condition of men and women who live their social relations and sexual relations under the need to work for a living and to undertake the labour of intellectual research.[159] Althusser sees in the myth of the State of Nature a form of imaginary ideological abstraction which we need to exit in order to have another sense of abstraction, namely the necessary labour to produce and know.

> We discover in them, in short, that people have left behind the *imaginary 'abstraction'* (forged for reasons that, obviously, reflect the interests of established religion) in which they have an immediate, direct relation with things that immediately deliver up their truth, in order to enter the world of real life, in which one must work to produce and know. In this world, the meaning of abstraction changes. It is no longer this simple 'reading' or 'picking', this simple, immediate '*extraction*' of the truth of things from things. It becomes, rather, a veritable *labour* in which one needs, in order to know, not just raw material, but also labour-power (human beings) as well as know-how and instruments of labour (tools, words).[160]

---

154   Althusser 2017a, p. 69.
155   Ibid.
156   Ibid.
157   Althusser 2017a, p. 70.
158   Althusser 2017a, p. 74.
159   Althusser 2017a, p. 75.
160   Ibid.

Both religious and philosophical myths aim at creating a sort of unity; therefore, they have to include the existence and the practical experience of the masses themselves. A myth aims at disarming their opposition to the 'conception of the world presented to them, which serves not their interests, but those of very different human groups: a priestly caste, the Church, the social class in power'.[161] Consequently philosophy, in reality, deals less with the knowledge of existing and possible beings, and more so with *'the conflicts of which they may be the stakes'*, making every philosophy '[...] haunted by its opposite'.[162] As a result, philosophical abstractions are active, polemical, and divisive, referring not only to 'objects' but also to 'positions' that have to be affirmed in their very contradictory co-existence with opposite positions. Philosophy constantly tries to master conflictual tendencies that come from outside, from the very materiality of social practices, of class struggles and of ideological formations, which determine philosophy and which philosophy is obliged constantly to interiorise. Philosophical abstraction becomes the site and the form of this interiorised conflict.

> It is a very strange abstraction indeed, for it aims not to produce knowledge of things that exist in the world, as science does, but, rather, to speak about all that exists (and even all that does not) in a mode that implies *a previous conflict*, still present, involving the place, meaning and function of these beings, a conflict which commands philosophy *from without* and which philosophy has to bring *within itself* in order to exist as philosophy. It is, then, an *active* and, as it were, *polemical abstraction*, divided against itself, which concerns not just its ostensible 'objects', inasmuch as these can exist or not, but also its own positions, its own 'theses'. For these theses can be affirmed only on the paradoxical condition that they are simultaneously negated by contradictory theses which, to be sure, are relegated to the margins of the philosophy in question, yet are present in it nonetheless. It is, obviously, this very surprising characteristic of philosophical abstraction which distinguishes it from the abstraction of both technical-practical and scientific knowledge. At the same time, this feature of philosophical abstraction is what makes it, as we have already noted, strangely similar to ideological abstraction.[163]

---

161 Althusser 2017a, p. 76.
162 Ibid.
163 Althusser 2017a, p. 77.

6   Practice Revisited

The recurring references to practice require a theoretical clarification of this concept and whether it is better to think of it in terms of *poiësis*, in the Aristotelian sense of production or of *praxis* in the sense of the subject transforming itself through practice. In the first case there is an '*exteriority*' and in the second an '*interiority*' of the object.[164] The concept of practice indicates an '*active contact with the real*' and an '*active contact with the real that is peculiarly human*'.[165] Practice should not be easily opposed to theory, not only because in a certain manner '*everyone is a theorist*',[166] but also because what we tend to define as 'conscience' in reality has more to do with language and social practice and should not be viewed as contemplation. The most important aspect is that practices are not individual but *social*: '[t]*hus every practice is social*'.[167] Therefore it is better to describe practice as a *social process*: We call practice '*a social process that puts agents into active contact with the real and produces results of social utility*'.[168] Idealism insists on the determining in the last instance character of ideological practices, materialism on 'the *practice of production*, namely the unity of relations of production and the productive forces'.[169] This implies the importance of the '*social relation of production*' that determines, 'in the last instance', the other relations and practices, thus explaining the importance of a certain form of *topography*[170] in Marxism as a way to indicate relations and degrees of determination and efficacy. However, there is one problem: '*scientific practice figure nowhere in this topography*',[171] the reason being exactly the complexity of its efficacy and its relation to particular conjunctures that oblige us to study it in its particularity without attaching it one-sidedly either to production or to the superstructures. This is an interesting point because Althusser refuses to treat science as a simple variation of ideology.

Regarding the *practice of production*, Althusser insists on its determination by *abstractions*, both in the form of technical relations of production and of social relations of production. Any production practice and process requires that workers are obliged to work by a '*class relation*'.[172] This social relation is

---

164   Althusser 2017a, p. 79.
165   Ibid.
166   Althusser 2017a, p. 80.
167   Althusser 2017a, p. 81.
168   Ibid.
169   Althusser 2017a, p. 83.
170   Ibid.
171   Althusser 2017a, p. 84.
172   Althusser 2017a, p. 87.

a *relation of production* an '*abstract relation* [...] has nothing to do with the concrete movements that the workers make in performing their tasks'.[173] What Althusser defines as an abstraction is in reality a reference to social relations that are reproduced. Moreover, it is exactly because of the dominance of these relations of production that we can arrive at the concrete social practices of workers.

> Thus the 'immediate and concrete' relation between the worker and his work, far from being immediate and concrete, is concrete only because it is dominated, that is, established and determined, by the all-powerful abstractions known as the relation of production and the social relations flowing from it.[174]

Althusser insists on rejecting the reference to production as *praxis*, insisting that 'at the limit'[175] *poiesis* is a better definition than *praxis* regarding the practice of production because of the exteriority of nature in relation to social relations. At the same time, laws of nature and social 'laws', the abstract 'laws' that govern social relations, are not the same. Social 'laws' include conflict, struggle, and tendential dynamics, elements that we cannot find in laws of nature.

> *The laws of nature are not 'tendential', that is, they are not conflictual and not subject to revolutions*, whereas the laws that govern the relation of production are laws that pit one class against another. As such, they are premised on conflict, and either the perpetuation or the overthrow of the established order.[176]

For Althusser, the main form of idealism is *empiricism*, which treats truth as something that is 'extracted' from an object. There is sensualist empiricism, either subjective 'if everything that is given about an object is reduced to its perception', or objective 'if sensation gives the properties of the object perceived by itself'. On the other hand, if 'the object is revealed in intellectual intuition, empiricism is *rationalist* (as in Descartes)'.[177] It is in interesting to note that Althusser, adopting a position similar to the one adopted in the 1960s texts, insists on refusing the traditional dichotomy between empiricism

---

173　Ibid.
174　Althusser 2017a, p. 89.
175　Althusser 2017a, p. 90.
176　Ibid.
177　Althusser 2017a, p. 91.

and rationalism, incorporating within empiricism traditional empiricism, subjective rationalism but also philosophical realism. For Althusser empiricism defines all philosophies that insist on *finding* or *extracting* truth and knowledge as a property of things (or of our intellect), whereas materialism insists on knowledge and truth being something that 'is not there' but, in contrast, is the product of a knowledge process.

Although the varieties of idealism indeed point towards the fact that an object has an existence 'independent of its knowledge',[178] they also underestimate the work of the scientist and the transformation process through which we arrive at knowledge. For Althusser the dominant form of idealism at his time was logical neo-positivism[179] whose idealism lies in the combination of formalism and empiricism. Both empiricism and formalism are presented as offering scientists some form of *'guarantee of their own practice'*.[180] Althusser links this notion of knowledge guarantees to the role of guarantees in commercial practices, where the important role is that of the person who offers a guarantee for a contractual transaction. 'The idealist philosophies are the Third Party who provides him with this guarantee. They guarantee the validity of his statements, the conditions and forms of his experimentation, and the accuracy of his results, as long as he carefully follows all the rules'.[181] This relation of idealist philosophies to science and social practices can be in certain cases positive and progressive as was the case with bourgeois idealist philosophy during the period of the ascendancy of the bourgeoisie. It offered a 'certain notion of science *to guarantee the future of the bourgeoisie's political struggles*'.[182] Since at that time the bourgeoisie was a revolutionary class, this could have a liberating effect on science and all social practices. However, after the end of the bourgeois revolutionary era, the attempt of positivist or logical-positivist philosophy to offer guarantees to science is also an attempt to *'control'* people working in science in the name of a certain 'idea of Order'[183] that comes from the 'the practice of the class struggle of a bourgeoisie now forced *to impose its Order*, because that order was being challenged by the workers. The bourgeoisie imposed it in the name of a philosophy guaranteeing that Order is necessary, and that the bourgeois Order is the true Order'.[184] Consequently, idealist philo-

---

178   Ibid.
179   Althusser 2017a, p. 92.
180   Althusser 2017a, p. 94.
181   Ibid.
182   Althusser 2017a, p. 96.
183   Althusser 2017a, p. 97.
184   Ibid.

sophies 'exploit' a certain idea of science in order to safeguard the established social and political order.[185]

What is the relation between materialism and scientific practice? Althusser points towards the fact that scientific practice resembles a production process, with its own given material, labour force and instruments of production. At the same time there are differences with a typical production process because both scientific and non-scientific (ideological representations) enter this process. Even if we leave aside the fact that scientific practice also deals with already given scientific propositions, science always faces as its raw material 'abstractions' that are present and come from concrete social practices, 'practices in production, social practices of reproduction, [...] practices of class struggle'.[186] Althusser links these to what he had defined in *For Marx* as *Generalities I*[187] emerging from social practices and ideologies. There is an objective material element to be studied but it 'cannot be recorded without this entire experimental apparatus, which represents a considerable mass of abstractions and knowledge, realized in the apparatus itself'.[188] Science does not begin from the concrete; it moves towards it as the 'result of the combination of the multiple abstractions or knowledge constituting it'.[189] Consequently,

> *On the contrary, science proceeds from the abstract to the concrete*; it gradually refines abstraction, the existing abstractions, moving from ideological abstractions to the abstractions of technicalpractical knowledge and, ultimately, scientific abstractions, and, after exactly combining them, to a definite abstraction bearing on a concrete object.[190]

Coming to the question of the subject of scientific practice, Althusser insists on the priority of the process itself. Scientific practice is dominated by the process itself, by the confrontation with the materiality of the object of knowledge and of the experimental apparatus.

> [The researcher] is an agent of a process that goes beyond him, not its subject, that is, its origin or creator. The process of the practice – that is to say, of scientific production – is thus a 'process without a subject'. This

---

185   On the notion of the exploitation of the sciences by idealist philosophy see Althusser 1990.
186   Althusser 2017a, p. 100.
187   Althusser 1969, pp. 183–4.
188   Althusser 2017a, p. 101.
189   Ibid.
190   Ibid.

does not mean that it can dispense with the researcher's labour-power or his intelligence, talent, etc.; it means that this process is subject to objective laws which also determine the agent's – the scientific researcher's – nature and role.[191]

Scientific production is not isolated; it is determined, to a large extent from the outside, by the exigencies of production but also of class struggles. Consequently, there are strong links between politics and science. For Althusser, 'it is not science or knowledge that commands politics, but politics that command the development of science and knowledge'.[192] This is an interesting point if we consider that Althusser's initial theoretical intervention, in the early 1960s, was based exactly on the possibility of Marxist theory being able to command communist politics.

In this process of scientific production, scientists always work with theoretical instruments and upon a theoretical 'raw material' comprised of previous theories, previous knowledge and instruments as materialised theories, with Althusser explicitly referring to Bachelard. These represent what Althusser had defined in the 1960s texts as *Generalities II* as a 'complex set of abstractions and instruments'[193] that work upon the 'raw material' (Generalities I) in order to produce *Generalities III* as new knowledge. Scientific knowledge never implies a complete break with ideology, it is always subject to the pressure of ideology 'which contaminates and can contaminate the way it poses scientific'.[194]

Consequently, the process of scientific production is dominated by *a complex ensemble of relations*, relations of existing theory and technique, but also philosophical and ideological relations. Philosophical relations are constituted by 'certain arrangements of philosophical *categories* and *theses*'[195] and Althusser cites the example of the new concept of causality that was indispensable for Galilean physics. At the same time, 'on the front of scientific practice, philosophy takes into account *the ensemble of the stakes of its combat*',[196] which is not limited to sciences but includes the other human practices. For Althusser this importance of philosophical and ideological relations contrasts with the positivist conception of science. The positivist insistence on the neutrality and power of science is part of the 'bourgeois ideology of science'.[197] Philosophical

---

[191] Althusser 2017a, p. 102.
[192] Ibid.
[193] Althusser 2017a, p. 103.
[194] Althusser 2017a, p. 104.
[195] Althusser 2017a, p. 105.
[196] Althusser 2017a, p. 106.
[197] Ibid.

and ideological relations are therefore crucial as 'conditions of reproduction'[198] of scientific production. Notions of substance and of causality or of natural law played an important role in the political and ideological battles of the seventeenth and eighteenth centuries, forming a *theoretical matrix*.[199] As a result of this relation between philosophy and the sciences, this constant struggle, linked 'in the last instance, to class struggle', this part of philosophy 'serves the interests of science and another that exploits them in the dominant ideology's interests'.[200] Only a handful of scientists realise this particular efficacy of philosophy, 'by the instinct of their practice', 'Materialist philosophers' and Marxist activists 'by the theory of historical materialism'.[201]

What about ideological practice? For Althusser, ideology is not just a system of ideas but a '*system of social relations*'.[202] The important point for Althusser is that human subjects do not recognise themselves in systems of ideas; rather, systems of ideas interpellate and dominate them:

> That is how the ideas making up an ideology forcibly impose themselves on people's free 'consciousnesses': by interpellating people in forms such that they are compelled freely to recognize that these ideas are true – in forms such that they are compelled to constitute themselves as free *subjects*, capable of recognizing the truth where it resides, namely in the ideas of ideology.[203]

Consequently, '*the mechanism of the ideological interpellation* [...] *transforms individuals into subjects*'.[204] Ideologies have a social function, in favour of social cohesion or social struggle, thus '*ideologies in class societies always bear the mark of a class*, that of the dominant class or that of the dominated class'.[205] However, this should not be viewed in terms of a simplistic confrontation. In reality there are ideological tendencies that co-exist, 'we would do better to talk, rather than about a dominant ideology and a dominated ideology, about *the dominant and the dominated tendency in each* (local and regional) *ideology*'.[206] Ideologies are reproduced within ideological apparatuses, which had

---

198　Althusser 2107a, p. 107.
199　Ibid.
200　Althusser 2017a, p. 108.
201　Ibid.
202　Althusser 2017a, p. 110.
203　Althusser 2017a, p. 112.
204　Ibid.
205　Althusser 2017a, p. 113.
206　Ibid.

to be conquered by the dominant classes '*after a very long and very bitter class struggle*'.[207] For Althusser, 'class struggle does not come to a halt at the frontier of the state apparatuses or the ideological state apparatuses'.[208] Consequently, the 'Marxist theory of the Ideological State Apparatuses' avoids every functionalism and structuralism.[209] This is how Althusser sums up his conception of the relation between practice, class struggle, and ideology:

1. There is no practice except under the domination of an ideology.
2. There are local and regional ideologies.
3. Ideology is tendentially unified as a dominant ideology as a result [*sous l'effet*] of the dominant class's struggle to constitute itself as a ruling, hegemonic class.
4. The dominant ideology tends to integrate into its own system elements of the dominated ideology, which thus finds itself absorbed by the dominant ideology.
5. Ideology operates by interpellating individuals as subjects.
6. Ideology is double: cognition-miscognition, allusion-illusion.
7. Ideology has no outside and is nothing but outside.
8. Ideology commands philosophy from without, in the forms of its struggle.
9. Ideology is among the theoretical relations of production constitutive of all science.
10. A science can be 'practised' as an ideology and pulled down to its level.
11. Proletarian ideology is a special ideology resulting from the fusion of the proletariat's spontaneous ideology with the Marxist theory of class struggle.[210]

Althusser then moves towards political practice. He insists that despite attempts to think political practice as encounter and antagonism, Machiavelli being the main example, bourgeois philosophy could not theorise the rooting of political practice in the *mode of production*. Althusser refuses any narrative that would naturalise the emergence of capitalism. Instead, Althusser, in a line similar to both some of his 1967 texts and his post-1980 texts on aleatory materialism,[211] insists on capitalism being the result of a historical *encounter* between

---

207   Althusser 2017a, p. 114.
208   Althusser 2017a, p. 121.
209   Althusser 2017a, p. 122.
210   Althusser 2017a, pp. 129–30.
211   Cf. Althusser 2003 and Althusser 2006a.

the '*owners of money*', the '*free workers*' and the '*scientific and technical discoveries*'.[212] Finality or teleology are absent from this process, '*the capitalist mode of production was born and died several times in history*'.[213] From the outset, exploitation marks the political practice of the bourgeoisie, even if against the feudal state the bourgeoisie had to make '*an alliance with the very workers it exploited against the feudal lords' dictatorship*'.[214] For Althusser this kind of political practice through '*through intermediaries, very precisely, by way of the action of the class, or a segment of the class, that it exploits and dominates*' is an integral part of bourgeois politics and requires state power: 'maximum use out of the forces of the popular masses it dominates, by dominating them through state repression and the state ideology'.[215] It is exactly the bourgeois political ideological state apparatus and in particular the electoral apparatus that creates this illusion of a submission based upon free will. 'Just as the bourgeoisie does not work, but makes others work – that is why it dominates those it exploits – so *it does not act for itself, but makes others act: the others whom it exploits*'.[216]

In contrast, the proletarian political practice must be '*utterly different: "a new practice of politics*" (Balibar)'.[217] For Althusser the proletariat finds itself in a condition of domination by the ideas of dominant class. The people realise that these ideas are wrong and the look '*for ideas of their own, ideas specific to them*'.[218] It finds the ideas of revolutionaries belonging to the labour movement, from Owen to Marx. The crucial 'encounter' is with Marxist theory, an encounter of a 'relatively contingent character'.[219] In contrast to the 'bourgeoisie's political ideas' which are '*ideas for others*', proletarian ideas 'born of *struggle*, could not but be translated into acts'.[220] Proletarian political practices are direct, without intermediaries, avoiding both 'putschism' and 'spontaneism', and tend towards the 'greatest possible democracy of discussion, decision and action', since 'history is no longer made by individuals or ideas,

---

212 Althusser 2017a, p. 134.
213 Althusser 2017a, p. 135.
214 Ibid.
215 Althusser 2017a, p. 136.
216 Althusser 2017a, p. 137.
217 Ibid. The explicit reference is to Balibar's text on the 'rectification' of the *Communist Manifesto* where Balibar elaborates this conception of a new practice of politics. See Balibar 1974.
218 Althusser 2017a, p. 137.
219 Althusser 2017a, pp. 137–8.
220 Althusser 2017a, p. 138.

but by the self-organized masses'.[221] Moreover, the '*does not have a scientific theory of the laws of class struggle and does not want to acknowledge the existing theory of them*'.[222]

Political practice is also about abstractions, because 'the absolute condition for its existence is constituted by relations – economic, political and ideological relations – that mark it in all its determinations'[223] and because 'under the domination of these social relations, *it produces abstractions in its turn*, practical to begin with, then abstract and theoretical abstractions, which modify its own field of action and field of verification'.[224] Finally these abstractions 'encounter' those of a science, namely historical materialism, 'forged, it is true, by intellectuals' but based upon the 'theoretical (philosophical) positions of the proletarian class'.[225] For Althusser, in the last analysis, political practice is a practice that is not so much oriented toward an exterior object, but concerns '*the process itself*'.[226] And it is interesting that Althusser stresses that in this sense political practice is closer to 'Aristotle's second definition (transformation of the self by the self)',[227] since it has more to do with a process in which the agents involved are transforming themselves. That is why, in contrast to some of his earlier polemics against the notion of *praxis* and certain 'humanist'–'historicist' readings of Marx, here Althusser seems to endorse a version of Marx's reference to '*revolutionäre praxis*' in the *Theses on Feuerbach*:

> It is a peculiar feature of proletarian political practice consciously to assume this condition, and to *realize the unity of transformation of the objective situation with self-transformation*. Marx came up with the earliest formulations of this identity in his 'Theses on Feuerbach', where he speaks of revolutionary 'praxis' as the identity of the transformation of the object (the balance of power) and the subject (the organized revolutionary class). Here, what subsists of externality in bourgeois political practice, between those who lead and those who act, or between ideas and action, disappears in favour of a dialectic of unification and reciprocal transformation of the objective situation and the revolutionary forces engaged in the combat […]

---

221 Ibid.
222 Ibid.
223 Althusser 2017a, p. 141.
224 Ibid.
225 Ibid.
226 Ibid.
227 Ibid.

> This new relation, this new concrete abstraction, confers, this time, its full significance on the Marxist-materialist thesis of the primacy of practice over theory.[228]

Psychoanalytic practice represents for Althusser an attempt to end 'the bourgeois idealist representation of man as an entirely conscious being, as a sentient, juridical, moral, political, religious and philosophical subject, as a transparent being "without a backside"'.[229] For Althusser, psychoanalysis goes beyond simply pointing towards the 'outside' of consciousness, the materiality of the body or towards the social determination of consciousness; the important thing is that Freud 'talked about an outside *inside thought itself*'.[230] Psychoanalytic theory also deals with particular 'abstractions' that also take the form of 'topographies',[231] either the first topology (unconscious – preconscious – conscious) or the second topology (id – ego – superego). Althusser follows a line similar to the observations made in the 'Discovery of Dr Freud' (the text of the infamous 'Tbilisi Affair'),[232] namely that psychoanalysis, even its Lacanian version, is not a proper science, being still in a pre-scientific state, 'a prudent state of scientific *incompletion*',[233] without underestimating the importance of psychoanalytic abstractions.

> At all events, the experience of the history of psychoanalytic theory demonstrates that objective abstractions which are not ideological, but are not yet scientific, can and must remain in this state for as long as the neighbouring sciences have not reached a level of maturity that makes it possible to re-unify neighbouring scientific 'continents'.[234]

For Althusser, psychoanalytic theory is not yet a scientific theory and consequently it is not yet possible to go towards the direction of a general theory unifying different theories (a question that preoccupied Althusser in the 1960s, when he contemplated the idea of a general theory of discourse, of which psychoanalytic theory would be a regional theory[235]). What is particular about psychoanalysis is its special 'relation to practice', especially because of the

---

228 Althusser 2017a, pp. 141–2.
229 Althusser 2017a, p. 143.
230 Ibid.
231 Althusser 2017a, p. 145.
232 In Althusser 1999b.
233 Althusser 2017a, p. 147.
234 Ibid.
235 In Althusser 2003.

particularity of the analytical cure as both an 'experimental situation' and a 'practical situation'.[236] At the same time, the analyst is not the subject of that analytical cure, since in reality an analytic cure is a process without subject.

> Psychoanalytic practice is the most serious questioning of, and challenge to, *medical practice* that has ever existed – indeed, of *any* practice involving 'a subject supposed to know' (Lacan) capable of healing and counselling by virtue of the authority of his knowledge and social power. *The psychoanalyst is not a physician, moral or practical counsellor, confessor or priest; he is not even a friend.* He is simply the mute agent of a process without a subject in which fantasies (his own) confront, silently but concretely, someone else's fantasies (the analysand's) in an effort to re-equilibrate them until they are in a state that puts an end to the troubles affecting his psyche.[237]

At the same time, analytic practice can also be considered a form of praxis: 'psychoanalytic practice further enriches Aristotle's ancient intuition about *praxis*, for it is the subject himself who produces his own transformation through the intermediary of the psychoanalyst'.[238] And this has a limited analogy with revolutionary practice: 'psychoanalytic practice is similar to revolutionary practice, with the difference that the two practices obviously do not have the same object, inasmuch as psychoanalysis changes only the internal configuration of an individual's unconscious, whereas revolutionary practice changes a society's class structure'.[239]

Regarding artistic practice Althusser begins with a reference to the *uselessness*[240] of the work art as a social object that is similar to a Kantian 'purposiveness without purpose'.[241] Artistic pleasure, as the result of a social process that attributes to objects of art their beauty and inutility, is the product of '*a new form of abstraction*', that presents itself as a '*concrete object*'.[242] Althusser insists on this dimension of artistic pleasure referring both to Aristotelian catharsis and to Freud's conception of art as realisation of a desire. Both the production and the consumption of artistic objects is subject to the ideological class

---

236 Althusser 2017a, p. 148.
237 Althusser 2017a, pp. 149–50.
238 Althusser 2017a, p. 150.
239 Althusser 2017a, pp. 150–1.
240 Althusser 2017a, p. 152.
241 Cf. Kant 2007.
242 Althusser 2017a, pp. 152–3.

struggle: 'aesthetic practice too, far from being a pure act that creates beauty, unfolds *under the domination of abstract social relations*, which are not just norms defining the beautiful, but also ideological relations of class struggle'.[243]

Althusser attempts to recapitulate his definition of the importance of abstractions in all social practices. What Althusser defines as *abstractions* has to do exactly with the relational character of social reality, the importance of the constant effectivity of social relations and consequently of class struggle. That is why he maintains that there is no *abstraction in general*, although there are general abstractions.

> We may say, firstly, that *people live in abstraction, under the domination of abstract relations* that command all their practices. We may say, secondly, that there is no *abstraction in general*, but that there are different types and levels of abstraction, depending on the different practices and different types of practices. We may say, thirdly, that while there is no abstraction in general, *there are general abstractions* that command the ensemble of the different practices and more or less profoundly influence their specific abstractions. These *general abstractions are the social relations*: relations of production, circulation and distribution, political relations and ideological relations – all of them organized in relation to [*ordonnées aux*] class relations and the class struggle.[244]

Abstraction refers precisely to social relations that are '*rooted in the materiality of social practices*' and are abstract 'to the extent that they make possible the *final production of the concrete*'.[245] These abstract relations exist only to the extent that they are rooted in concrete practices. And it is exactly this contradictory articulation of concrete practices and abstract relations, traversed as they are by the constant effectivity of class struggles, which produces what we tend to define as human history:

> It is the contradictions of this immense cycle which produce, in the form of class struggle, that which is called human history and which makes this history *human* – makes it, that is, not a disembodied history, but one fraught with weight, materiality and finitude, with human suffering, discoveries and joys.[246]

---

243   Althusser 2017a, p. 154.
244   Althusser 2017a, p. 156.
245   Ibid.
246   Ibid.

7   Philosophy and Practice

For Althusser, this entire detour regarding all forms of practices (and the relations that determine them and the relevant abstractions) aims at defining the object that philosophy transforms, namely the ideologies related to these social practices: *'what philosophical practice transforms is the ideologies under the domination of which the various social practices produce their specific effects'*.[247] Practices, ideologies, philosophy become the three sides of a conceptual triangle. Althusser attempts first of all to define philosophical propositions and to distinguish them from scientific propositions. He insists on the 'performative' character of philosophical propositions with a direct reference to Austin's theory of speech acts,[248] and he offers as an example the functioning of Descartes' declaration that God exists, which for Althusser 'inaugurates'[249] the world of Descartes' idealist philosophy, although in reality it offers no objective knowledge. Althusser insists on the position, first introduced in the 1967–68 texts, that philosophy *'does not produce knowledge of a real object, but it posits Theses'*.[250] In this sense philosophy '*philosophy has no object* (in the sense in which scientific practice and productive practice have objects), but has something else in view: *objectives or stakes*'.[251] Philosophical theses are 'abstract terms' but should be viewed as '*categories*' instead of scientific concepts.[252] Philosophical objects, although purely 'internal to philosophy' and 'not real', are '*a means of occupying ground held by a philosophical adversary*'.[253] The aim of philosophical interventions is not to produce knowledge; rather it is a 'strategic and tactical war against the adversary's theoretical forces, a war that, like all others, has *stakes*'.[254] However, there is a particularity in the philosophical *Kampfplatz*: philosophy is by nature contradictory; there is always a question of which tendency prevails, the materialist or the idealist one. Moreover, in every philosophy one can find both tendencies in their contradiction: '[w]*hat is realized in every philosophy is not the tendency, but the antagonistic contradiction between the two tendencies*'.[255] It is in the nature of philosophical warfare to always attempt to enter the 'enemy's country', to 'occupy the adversary's posi-

---

247   Althusser 2017a, p. 157.
248   Althusser 2017a, p. 158.
249   Ibid.
250   Althusser 2017a, p. 159. Cf. Althusser 1990; Althusser 1995a.
251   Ibid.
252   Ibid.
253   Althusser 2017a, p. 160.
254   Ibid.
255   Althusser 2017a, p. 161. On this see also Macherey 1976.

tions'.[256] The particularity of philosophical battles is that although they refer to real stakes, in the sciences or in other social practices, at the same time these stakes do not appear 'in person' in the terrain of philosophy.

> [T]*he philosophical war shifts this way and that on its own battlefield* in obedience to a course of events which, albeit absent from that field, have so profound an impact on it that they can precipitate such shifts: events in the history of scientific discoveries, events in the history of politics, morality, religion and so on. Thus there are *real stakes* in this makebelieve war, serious stakes in this semblance of a war. We do not see them as such on the battlefield, however, because *they are found outside it*.[257]

In a way, philosophy attempts to answer the major ideological repercussions caused by scientific discoveries but also from antagonistic political practices. But this requires a return to the question of the relation between philosophy, dominant ideology and the state. To deal with this issue Althusser reminds us that dominant ideology does not aim simply at the subjection of the exploited but also at the ideological unification of the dominant class. The reason is that what we define as dominant ideology is the result of a process of unification of 'regional' or 'local' ideologies, which themselves are 'ultimately grouped together in two grand political tendencies that stand over against each other: the ideology of the dominant class (or classes) and that of the dominated classes'.[258] Without taking into consideration this 'counter-power of rebellion and revolution',[259] we cannot understand the extent of this effort to unify the dominant ideology. For Althusser, Plato, who wanted to wage war against the 'Friends of the Earth', namely materialist philosophies, in reality attempted to restore 'the old aristocratic ideology'.[260] It is an 'implacable law' that every philosophy in the last instance finds itself 'in one of these two camps or in its margins (by mistake or by manoeuvre)'. This does not require an explicit adhesion to a camp but only a certain perspective or even some silences that 'are sometimes quite as eloquent as certain declarations'[261] and Althusser refers to Descartes' silence on politics (which is coupled with his reference to God as a sovereign and King which for Althusser is expression of his support of Absolute

---

256   Ibid.
257   Althusser 2017a, p. 162.
258   Althusser 2017a, p. 165.
259   Ibid.
260   Althusser 2017a, p. 166.
261   Althusser 2017a, p. 167.

Monarchy) as an example. Consequently, Althusser's provisional conclusion is that philosophy plays an important role within the whole process of the unification of 'existing ideological elements as a dominant ideology'.[262]

For Althusser, philosophy is a 'theoretical laboratory',[263] an interesting metaphor that can be compared to Gramsci's use of the 'laboratory' and 'elaborator' metaphors regarding the formation of hegemony and forms of mass intellectuality. Althusser talks about philosophy and philosophers as 'adjustors' or 'machinists'[264] in order to describe the role philosophy plays in unifying diverse ideological elements into a dominant ideology, a role that in the past was mainly played by religion, but now because of the emergence of scientific knowledge and the 'materialist threat' it brings to 'established authority',[265] that task falls upon philosophy. In order to accomplish this task, philosophy had to incorporate certain elements of scientific discourse, such as the logical vigour of mathematics, in order to make them serve the dominant ideologies. '*To domesticate one's adversary by stealing his language*: that is the whole secret of ideological struggle, even when, for determinate historical reasons, it takes the form of philosophical struggle'.[266] This response of philosophy is not limited to the ideological effects of the emergence of the sciences. Philosophy has also reacted to – and has been influenced by – other historical events and developments that are 'far more dangerous', such as 'the great social upheavals, the revolutions in the relations of production and in political relations'.[267] Sometimes this reaction of philosophy comes with a certain delay, the time needed 'for the transition from an economic revolution to a revolution in politics and then in ideology'.[268] It can even come before the event and Althusser refers to the long process of the transition to the dominance of capitalist relations of production, a large part of which took place before the full emergence of new forms of the bourgeois state, although bourgeois ideology was effective during all this process. And this complex and uneven articulation of temporalities also affects proletarian ideology, which also has 'a lead on the revolution',[269] and which evolves under the influence of the socialisation of production and by the education in struggle and discipline, offered by everyday capitalist reality. For Althusser, the 'surprising phenomenon of the ideological anticipation

---

262 Althusser 2017a, p. 168.
263 Althusser 2017a, p. 169.
264 Ibid.
265 Althusser 2017a, p. 170.
266 Althusser 2017a, p. 171.
267 Ibid.
268 Ibid.
269 Althusser 2017a, p. 172.

of history' also leads to every ideology having to develop under the 'domination of the class in power',[270] and this also means incorporating some of the themes of the existing dominant ideology. Althusser cites as examples the inability of bourgeois ideologues to fully reject god but also the way in which even the proletarian struggles had to be waged in the name of fraternity and liberty, before 'endowing themselves with an ideology of their own: that of socialism and communism'.[271]

Althusser insists that it is impossible for dominant ideologies not to take notice of the importance of sciences and in particular their materialist effectivity. Consequently, philosophy has to take the form of a theory which includes existing forms of scientific demonstration, in order to 'participate'[272] in this process of ideological unification which is not limited to philosophy. Philosophy as a *'theoretical adjustor'* may even find itself in need of '"serial production" of multi-purpose parts' which can be used in all cases where such an 'ideological connection is called for'.[273] Moreover, 'the philosopher-adjustor's work consists in *forging categories that are as general as possible, capable of unifying the different domains of ideology under their theses'*.[274] Consequently, philosophy imposes its 'theoretical rule' not only upon actually existing objects but also upon the 'ensemble of ideologies' in order to 'overcome the contradictions in existing ideology, in order to unify this ideology as the dominant ideology'.[275] The example that Althusser gives of such philosophical categories that are imposed upon all practices is that of the subject in the modern era:

> Originating in legal ideology (the ideology of the law of commercial relations, in which every individual is the rightful subject of his legal capacities, as the owner of property that he can alienate), this category invades, with Descartes, the domain of philosophy, which guarantees scientific practice and its truths (the subject of the 'I think'). With Kant, it invades the domain of moral ideology (the subject of 'moral consciousness') and religious ideology (the subject of 'religious consciousness'). It had long since, with the natural law philosophers, invaded the domain of politics, by way of the 'political subject' in the social contract.[276]

---

270 Ibid.
271 Althusser 2017a, p. 173.
272 Ibid.
273 Althusser 2017a, p. 174.
274 Ibid.
275 Ibid.
276 Althusser 2017a, p. 175.

At the same time, each philosophy has to take consideration of the material constraints imposed upon it by existing ideologies. That is why philosophies often 'advance masked',[277] that is, accepting these constraints, albeit at a price. 'The dominant philosophy goes as far as it can in its function of unifying ideology, but it cannot leap out of its time, as Hegel said, or out of its class character, as Marx said',[278] and Althusser reminds us that bourgeois philosophy was not only anti-feudal but also against wage workers. This function of philosophy in the ideological class struggle – or in the articulation of hegemony, to use Gramscian terms – can explain the traditional form of the philosophical system.

> The system thus confirms the existence of the unity that is the product of its unification; it is unity exhibited and demonstrated by its very exhibition – visible proof that philosophy has truly encompassed and mastered 'the whole', and that there is nothing in existence that does not fall under its jurisdiction.[279]

In contrast, philosophers who have refused this kind of systemic form, such as Kierkegaard or Nietzsche, waged in the 'paradoxical form' of their philosophy a sort of 'battle formation, as it were, of philosophical guerrilla warfare' [...] attacking 'by surprise, by aphorisms, in an effort to hack the enemy's front to pieces'.[280]

For Althusser, all past philosophies were subjected to the mechanism of reproduction and unification of dominant ideologies; they were dependent upon this *class 'subjectivity'*.[281] The question that arises is how to make sure that 'philosophy is not the theoretical delirium of an individual, or a social class in search of guarantees or rhetorical ornament'.[282] Philosophies that attempt to help the unification of dominant ideologies are affected by the 'dynamics of class exploitation'.[283] The important difference of a potential materialist philosophy related to the political ideology of the proletariat is exactly the special relation to a historical materialist scientific knowledge of the ideology. This is a point that Althusser had already taken up in other texts: Marxist philosophy differs from idealist philosophy because it is inscribed in the background of a sci-

---

277 ibid.
278 Althusser 2017a, p. 176.
279 Ibid.
280 Ibid.
281 Althusser 2017a, p. 180.
282 Ibid.
283 Althusser 2017a, p. 181.

ence, which can offer a scientific explanation of the mechanism of ideological domination. This can lead to a particular form of philosophical adjustment. *'This scientific knowledge of the ideology commanding the philosophy charged with unifying proletarian ideology will make it possible to create the conditions for a philosophical adjustment that is as objective as can be'.*[284] This particular form of adjustment is linked to 'Marxist category of *correctness'*.[285] This correctness is not the result of something like Lukács's conception of 'the "universal" nature of the proletarian class'; in contrast, it avoids *'subjectivity'*, because *'it is under the control of an objective science'*.[286] Althusser draws a sharp line of demarcation with the 'evolutionary economism' of Stalin's Marxism and his conception of the science of 'the "laws" of class struggle'.[287] However, beginning with Marx's relative silence regarding philosophy after *The German Ideology*, the relatively few writings and notes of Lenin on philosophy, the fact that 'Gramsci likewise devoted nothing of importance to philosophy',[288] just as Mao merely offered some interventions, one confronts the paradox that there has not been such an expression of the proletarian class position in philosophy to 'unify proletarian ideology'[289] apart from the Stalinist deviation. For Althusser, the difficulty lies exactly in the character of a system that usually idealist philosophy assumes which *'is directly bound up with the state'*.[290] Idealist philosophy, when it takes the form of a system, in order to help the unification of diverse ideological elements, is reproducing 'the form of the state within itself: its unity, stronger than all diversity'.[291] If a strategy for communism requires a new practice of politics, it also requires a new practice of philosophy, not another philosophical system, a practice of philosophy in a sharp break from the state.

> It is still the strategy of communism that is at work in these perspectives, which are philosophical and, equally, political. It is a matter of preparing, here and now, the revolutionary communist future; it is therefore a matter of putting in place, here and now, completely new elements, without yielding to the pressure of bourgeois ideology and philosophy – on the contrary, by resisting it. And, since the question of the state commands

---

284 Ibid.
285 Ibid. Note the play on words in the French original between *ajustement* (adjustment) and *justesse* (correctness).
286 Althusser 2017a, p. 182.
287 Ibid.
288 Althusser 2017a, p. 183.
289 Ibid.
290 Althusser 2017a, p. 184.
291 Ibid.

everything, it is necessary to break, here and now, the subtle, yet very powerful bond that binds philosophy to the state, especially when it takes the form of a 'system'.[292]

For Althusser, philosophy is about power, the power 'of ideas over ideas'.[293] Idealist philosophy leads to a relation of exploitation of other practices and ideologies, an attempt to incorporate them in the reproduction of relations of domination and exploitation. This means that there can be another emancipatory relation between philosophy and social practices and in particular the political practices of the proletariat: 'we can imagine a completely different relationship between philosophy and the ideologies and practices: a relationship that is one not of servitude and exploitation, but of emancipation and freedom'.[294]

The problem is that the question of such a new practice of philosophy in the history of Marxism has been seen as the question of a new philosophy, either in the form of a philosophy that could 'absorb [...] the science of history', a position he attributes both to young Hegel and to Labriola and Gramsci, but also to Stalin, a position which 'made philosophy a science that incorporated the Marxist theory of history'.[295] It is interesting that Althusser still thinks of Gramsci's references to philosophy as suggesting an historicist conception of a philosophy of historicised social praxis, a variation of a philosophy of history, as a reaction to the economism of the Second International, a position similar to the one he held in *Reading Capital*, despite describing Gramsci's position as the most 'discerning'.[296] The problem, according to Althusser, was that all these attempts at thinking about Marxist philosophy were still inspired by the existing model of bourgeois philosophy, defined in the form of a 'system' or a 'theory', and he self-critically admits that he made the same mistake when in his earlier texts he had modelled his description of philosophy 'on of science'.[297] A new philosophy cannot take the form of an epistemological break; it is 'not marked by the same discontinuity'.[298] Even a philosophy that aims at representing 'the worldview of a revolutionary class in philosophy' will have to intervene in the same philosophical terrain of struggle, even when it chooses

---

292 Ibid.
293 Althusser 2017a, p. 185.
294 Ibid.
295 Althusser 2017a, p. 186.
296 Ibid.
297 Ibid.
298 Althusser 2017a, p. 187.

to refuse traditional rules of combat, such as the reference to a 'system', and imposes its own. For Althusser, this can define a 'new practice, a Marxist practice, of philosophy'.[299] And it is interesting that he still feels the need to again repeat his respectful but critical position regarding Gramsci's conception of a 'philosophy of praxis'. It is as if he realises that Gramsci is his main intellectual interlocutor regarding the question of this new practice of philosophy.

> I would not describe Marxism as a 'philosophy of praxis', as does Gramsci, who may have been forced to by the censorship of his jailers. This is not because I consider the idea of praxis (transformation of the self by the self) to be out of place in Marxism – quite the contrary – but because this formulation can commit us to the old idealist form of the 'philosophy of ...', which enshrines a particular determination, here praxis, as the essence or 'meaning' of the ensemble of things.[300]

The final difficulty Althusser wants to confront is the 'idealist distinction *between theory* (or science) *and method*',[301] because this makes method a truth before truth and he refers to the Hegelian conception of the dialectic as 'an absolute method, the dialectic, superior to any truth content', a conception that makes method an 'an absolute given which one need only apply to any object at all in order to extract knowledge of it'.[302] The problem was that Marx and Engels inherited this method and Althusser points towards Engels's conception of the dialectic in *Dialectics of Nature*, which in turn was taken up by Stalin, leading to the conception of the laws of the dialectic. This meant that Marxist philosophy was in 'insoluble contradiction of submitting to a philosophy from which it claims to be emancipating itself'.[303] There are no 'dialectical laws' but only dialectical and materialist *theses*. Moreover, the thesis of the primacy of the contradiction over the opposites is at the same time *dialectical* and materialist because the 'primacy of conditions of existence over their effects'.[304] Philosophical theses can be infinite in number, because they must answer the concrete questions 'posed by the development of practices, which is infinite'.[305] Therefore the task of a new practice of philosophy that would serve as an 'arm

---

299 Ibid.
300 Ibid.
301 Althusser 2017a, p. 188.
302 Ibid.
303 Althusser 2017a, p. 189.
304 Althusser 2017a, p. 190.
305 Ibid.

of the revolution' is difficult. On the one hand, it has to affirm constantly 'the primacy of practice over theory', but at the same time it must be something more than a simple 'handmaiden of proletarian politics'.[306] Rather it is

> an original form of existence of theory, turned wholly towards practice and capable of enjoying genuine autonomy if its relation to political practice is constantly controlled by the concrete knowledge produced by the Marxist science of the laws of class struggle and of its effects. Doubtless the most extraordinary thing about this conception is the profound unity which inspires all its determinations, even as it liberates the practices that are the stakes of its struggle from all the forms of exploitation and oppression exercised by bourgeois ideology and philosophy.[307]

8 How Can Anybody be a Philosopher?

Althusser insists on the positive and liberating role that philosophy, as a relatively autonomous theoretical intervention, can play regarding social practices, in their emancipation from the constraints imposed by bourgeois ideology and its philosophical forms. This particular relation to social practice also implies that Marxist philosophers cannot live isolated from social reality and struggle. In contrast, a Marxist philosopher is 'theorist who acts as a militant not just in philosophy, but in political practice as well'.[308]

In the final pages Althusser returns to the question he posed at the beginning of the manuscript, namely whether every man is a philosopher. For Althusser we can say that every man is 'virtually, a philosopher'[309] in the sense that he could have conscience of philosophical questions in a spontaneous way. However, philosophy requires also the study of works of philosophy, but above all a certain practice of philosophy; we must 'learn philosophy in practice, in the different practices and, above all, in the practice of class struggle'.[310] Consequently, one can become a philosopher, but this apprenticeship in philosophy requires that one has a theoretical formation not only in terms of theory and scientific practice, but also in terms of political practice and class struggle. This combined philosophical education by both theory and militant practice

---

306 Althusser 2017a, p. 191.
307 Ibid.
308 Ibid.
309 Althusser 2017a, p. 192.
310 Ibid.

renders a completely different modality, both theoretical and political, to a materialist practice of philosophy in the service of the proletariat, at the same time offering the only possible way to revitalise philosophy as such, facing the decline of bourgeois philosophy in a time of capitalist technocracy as an aspect of the crisis of the bourgeoisie's ability to offer a hegemonic narrative:

> If I were asked: but what, finally, is a philosopher?, I would say: *a philosopher is a man who fights in theory*. To fight, he has to learn to fight by fighting, and to fight in theory, he has to become a theorist through scientific practice and the practice of ideological and political struggle.
>
> In a time in which the bourgeoisie has given up all notion of producing even its eternal philosophical systems; in a time in which it has given up the guarantee and the perspectives held out by ideas and entrusted its destiny to the automatism of computers and technocrats; in a time in which it is incapable of offering the world a viable, conceivable future, the proletariat can take up the challenge. It can breathe new life into philosophy and, in order to free the world from class domination, make it 'an arm for the revolution'.[311]

Philosophy becomes vital again only through the development of a radically different practice of philosophy and a new figure of the philosopher, this 'militant theoretician', trained both in theory and in class struggle. It is a more positive image of philosophy than one of simply drawing lines of demarcation and intensifying contradictions. In particular this emphasis on an active relation to social practices and militancy is, in a certain yet distant way, close to Gramsci's conception of the 'democratic philosopher', who 'is a philosopher convinced that his personality is not limited to himself as a physical individual but is an active relationship of modification of the cultural environment'.[312]

All these attest to the importance of the *Philosophy for Non-Philosophers*. It sheds new light on the development of Althusser's thinking on philosophy. In particular, the theoretical schema he proposes, that is centred upon the importance of practices and relations and consequently abstractions in all aspects of social life, is not only an important contribution to a relational conception of social practices, it is also a way to rethink how philosophical reflection is linked to ideology and social practice. It offers the possibility to rethink both the role of idealist philosophy in forging and establishing forms of ideological

---

311   Ibid.
312   Gramsci 1971, p. 360.

and political domination, and the possibility of a materialist practice of philosophy aiming not only at defending the materialist potential of the sciences (their 'scientificity') but also at liberating the collective social and political practices of the subaltern classes. If philosophy is the theoretical laboratory of forms of hegemony of the dominant classes, a materialist practice of philosophy can also help the collective elaboration of forms of a potential hegemony of the subaltern. Not in the sense of revolutionary 'philosophical systems' and not only in the sense of responding to the constant re-emergence and reproduction of idealist tendencies, but in the sense of enabling practices of collective critical intellectuality, of facilitating new forms of collective elaboration of theories and political practices, of helping the establishment of new vocabularies and metaphors, in the service of social emancipation.

The 1976 lecture on the 'Transformation of Philosophy' elaborates more on this theme of – idealist – philosophy as an attempt to impose a certain conceptual violence in the sense of imposing a certain Truth that is an aspect of an attempt towards Hegemony.

> In both cases it is a question of reorganizing, dismembering, recomposing and unifying, according to a precise orientation, a whole series of social practices and their corresponding ideologies, in order to make sovereign, over all the subordinate elements, a particular Truth that imposes on them a particular orientation, guaranteeing this orientation with that Truth. If the correspondence is exact, we may infer that philosophy, which continues the class struggle as befits it, in theory, responds to a fundamental political necessity. The task which it is assigned and delegated by the class struggle in general, and more directly by the ideological class struggle, is that of contributing to the unification of the ideologies within a dominant ideology and of guaranteeing this dominant ideology as Truth. [...] Philosophy produces a general problematic: that is, a manner of posing, and hence resolving, the problems which may arise. In short, philosophy produces theoretical schemas, theoretical figures that serve as mediators for surmounting contradictions and as links for reconnecting the different elements of ideology. Moreover, it guarantees (by dominating the social practices thus reordered) the Truth of this order, enunciated in the form of the guarantee of a rational discourse.[313]

---

313   Althusser 1976b, p. 259.

In light of the above-mentioned definition of idealist philosophy and its political character, Althusser elaborates more on the notion of a new practice of philosophy, which is presented as a non-philosophy mainly aiming at undermining and deconstructing traditional philosophical systems and philosophical idealism in general and thus opening up the way for emancipatory and transformative social and political practices.

Althusser's successive redefinitions of philosophy after the abandonment of any possibility of a 'Theory of theoretical practice', the importance attached to the political character of philosophical interventions,[314] the distinction between scientific propositions and philosophical positions and in general the emphasis on philosophy not having an object in the sense of the sciences,[315] the linking of philosophy, ideology and the class struggle in the definition of philosophy as 'class struggle in theory in the last instance',[316] all attest to a theoretical effort to think philosophy as both inescapable (the interconnection of ideological class struggle and theoretical practices leads inevitably to philosophical conflicts) and necessary (we have to intervene in a specifically philosophical way if we want to battle the influences of dominant ideologies both in the theoretical and the political field). The same goes for his insistence on the recurring opposition between idealism and materialism, internalised in any philosophical intervention, as the specific form of the effects of class antagonism on the theoretical plane. Althusser's references to a new materialist practice of philosophy, radically incommensurable with traditional idealist philosophy, a practice that can only work as an intervention, an effort to change the balance of forces in theoretical and political practices, and in no way as a philosophical system, have to be considered as the starting points for any critical evaluation of the possibility of a materialist philosophy.[317] This conception of a political – and philosophical – practice that liberates collective potentialities is evident in the 'Transformation of Philosophy'. In this text, he elaborates upon the different modality between this practice of philosophy and the idealism inherent in the traditional form of the philosophical system. It is also linked to Althusser's distancing from the politics of communist reformism, stressing the need for a

---

314   Althusser 1971.
315   Althusser 1990.
316   Althusser 1973.
317   It is worth noting that Fredric Jameson has also suggested a similar description of philosophical materialism: 'Rather than conceiving of materialism as a systematic philosophy it would seem possible and perhaps more desirable to think of it as a polemic stance, designed to organize various anti-idealist campaigns' (Jameson 1997, p. 36). On the same point of the materialist philosophy being possible only as a materialist practice of philosophy and not as a materialist philosophical system, see Macherey 1999, pp. 35–73.

PHILOSOPHY AS LABORATORY

distance of proletarian politics from the state. The emphasis is on the need for new mass organisations, new forms of 'free associations' emerging through the experience of the popular masses in struggle, making sure that the revolutionary state is a 'non-state'. In this sense, the philosophy of the encounter, or the 'new materialist practice of philosophy', emerges as a 'non-philosophy' not in the sense of a 'negation' of philosophy but as the challenge of an antagonistic theoretical and philosophical laboratory in the struggle for communism.

> To support our argument by comparison with the revolutionary State, which ought to be a State that is a 'non-State' – that is, a State tending to its own dissolution, to be replaced by forms of free association – one might equally say that the philosophy which obsessed Marx, Lenin and Gramsci ought to be a 'non-philosophy' – that is, one which ceases to be produced in the form of a philosophy, whose function of theoretical hegemony will disappear in order to make way for new forms of philosophical existence. And just as the free association of workers ought, according to Marx, to replace the State so as to play a totally different role from that of the State (not one of violence and repression), so it can be said that the new forms of philosophical existence linked to the future of these free associations will cease to have as their essential function the constitution of the dominant ideology, with all the compromises and exploitation that accompany it, in order to promote the liberation and free exercise of social practices and human ideas.[318]

One point is of particular importance. Althusser is aware of the various ways in which philosophy does have a more positive role. This is evident in the reference in *Lenin and Philosophy* to philosophy as 'a theoretical laboratory in which the new categories required by the concepts of the new science are brought into focus'.[319] But generally Althusser tends to see this 'positive' role only in relation to the elaboration of ideological motives, or only as a form of helping sciences in their conceptual innovations. Althusser until the end insists that philosophy and the sciences represent different theoretical and discursive modalities. Moreover, despite his growing coming to terms with the unfinished and inherently contradictory character of Marxist theory, he never seems to abandon the view that revolutionary theory must have the form of a *scientific* theory and not a philosophy.

---

318 Althusser 1976b, pp. 264–5.
319 Althusser 1971, p. 42.

However, texts like the *Philosophy for Non-Philosophers* or the 'Transformation of Philosophy' offer a way to rethink exactly this possibility of a liberating role for a different materialist practice of philosophy. The main role of such a practice is not to systematise and elaborate, as is the case with traditional philosophy, but to liberate, to emancipate social practices. If proletarian political practice aims at liberating collective practices of transformation from the coercive constraints of bourgeois politics and the state, a materialist practice of philosophy, aligned to the working-class movement, aims also at liberating collective practices, of resistance, transformation and creativity, from the forced ideological unification imposed by the dominant ideology. This in turn is directly related to the conception Althusser had about communism being not a 'project' or an 'ideal', but a process of collective resistance and experimentation with alternative social configurations. That is why he insisted on communism emerging at the margins of capitalism, in practices and resistances that oppose the commodity form. This position was exemplified in the answers that Althusser gave to Rossana Rossanda some months after the 1977 Venice Conference and his intervention on the crisis of Marxism. There Althusser makes reference to *communism* as a material tendency emerging from the contradictions of capitalism and to the *virtual forms of communism* existing in the interstices of capitalist social forms.[320]

Therefore, we might say that the role of a different materialist practice of philosophy is exactly this liberation of relations, practices and imaginaries coming from the terrain of the autonomous class struggles of the working classes, their resistances, their collective experimentations, in an attempt to bring them from the 'margins' to the centre of social life.

Dominique Lecourt also tried to offer such a reading of an alternative materialist practice of philosophy. The epilogue to his 1981 critique of logical positivism, *L'ordre et les jeux*[321] titled 'For a philosophy without feint. Towards a surmaterialism', follows exactly such a conception of a practice of philosophy and was then further expanded in the 1982 *La philosophie sans feinte*.[322] Beginning with a reading of Wittgenstein's *Philosophical Investigations*, Lecourt insists on the need to 'transform profoundly the very notion of "materialism"'.[323] For Lecourt, we must oppose 'every philosophy of "unification", of cement' because it is 'a language game' that has the effect of balancing and absorbing differences.

---

320 Althusser 1998, p. 285.
321 Lecourt 1981.
322 Lecourt 1982. It is probable that Lecourt had access to Althusser's texts such as *Philosophy for Non-Philosophers*.
323 Lecourt 1981, p. 211.

Therefore, 'another practice of philosophy'[324] aims at helping the emergence of differences within social practices and cannot be a 'theory' or a 'doctrine'.

> It will not be the putting in place of a 'theory' or a 'doctrine' which will be the agency [...] of another 'linguistic machine' destined at proceeding to an opposing ideological unification. Rather, it will be an 'anti-machine' which by practicing philosophy in a radically dissymmetrical mode, will systematically dismantle the gears of the former [idealist philosophy].[325]

Lecourt chooses to describe this philosophy as a sur-materialism, in a play on words following Bachelard's 'sur-rationalism'. He is highly critical of references to 'dialectical' materialism, insisting that 'materialist' positions are also 'dialectical' in exactly the sense of a refusal of 'ontology'.[326] In *La philosophie sans feinte* Lecourt elaborates on this point. In a line similar to Althusser, he insists that lived experience is determined by abstraction, the first abstraction being language. Moreover, the emergence of dominant ideologies implies a mechanism by means of which 'local' ideologies or 'micro-ideologies', which by themselves are 'anchored' to particular social practices, are reabsorbed and unified. Philosophy and its 'language machine' attempts to give 'to this unification a systematic and *total* form'.[327] Therefore we need to 'practice [philosophy] without feint'.[328] This is necessary if we take into consideration the effectivity of philosophical abstractions once they have been inscribed into ideological representations and language games. For Lecourt, philosophy can never stop being 'abstract' but at least it can stop being an obstacle to the development of collective practices.

> Surely, philosophy will never stop being 'abstract', but it will be answering the exigency of those that reproach it [...] by putting in movement, by means of a play of displacements, the abstractions in their concrete existence, it could contribute to the concrete deployment of social practices, without being an obstacle to them.[329]

---

324   Lecourt 1981, p. 214.
325   Lecourt 1981, p. 215.
326   Ibid.
327   Lecourt 1982, p. 78.
328   Lecourt 1982, p. 93.
329   Lecourt 1982, pp. 94–5.

CHAPTER 13

A Philosopher Always Catches a Moving Train

As we have already seen, Althusser's writings in the 1980s include an attempt to offer a fuller version of his conception of the materialism of the encounter as an aleatory materialism along with his presentation of a genealogy of this particular version of a materialist practice of philosophy. Moreover, as we will see in this chapter, there is also here a move forward in his redefinition of philosophy, or, to be more precise, of the new *materialist* practice of philosophy.

1   The Return of Philosophical Metaphors

One of the most striking features of the 1980s texts is Althusser's increased use of philosophical metaphors and philosophical images. The very reference to the image of the rain of atoms in Lucretius's rendition of Epicurus's atomistic philosophy is such an example. An ontological statement about the origin of the Cosmos and the absence of any telos is transformed into a profound theme running through the history of philosophy as an underground current and as an image that can account for the persistence of a materialism of the encounter; it is about a

> profound theme which runs through the whole history of philosophy, and was contested and repressed there as soon as it was stated: the 'rain' (Lucretius) of Epicurus' atoms that fall parallel to each other in the void; the 'rain' of the parallelism of the infinite attributes in Spinoza and many others: Machiavelli, Hobbes, Rousseau, Marx, Heidegger too, and Derrida.[1]

Althusser insists that we are dealing here with an '*almost completely unknown materialist tradition in the history of philosophy: "materialism"* (we still have to find a word to distinguish it as a tendency) *of the rain, the swerve, the encounter, the take [prise]*'.[2] We shall not dwell here on the philosophical importance of this position, but on the conception of philosophy it suggests. We are not

---

1   Althusser 2006a, p. 167.
2   Ibid.

dealing with a complex and sophisticated attempt towards an epistemology that approaches the problems of traditional theories of knowledge with their juridical conception of guarantees, as was the case with the texts until 1965. Nor are we dealing here with simply an attempt to draw lines of demarcation with forms of idealism in both politics and the sciences, in an operation that is inherently political in character, as was the case with the second definition of philosophy as politics and – in the last instance – class struggle in theory. In both these definitions of a potential Marxist materialist practice of philosophy we are still within the contours of a philosophy that is in a certain relation or dialogue with the sciences, with the conceptual and ideological breakthroughs and subversions brought on by the emergence of the sciences. Although neither a philosophy of knowledge nor a philosophy of the sciences, Althusser's endeavour, even in the second definition of politics or class struggle in theory, remains in a specific relation to the sciences, their discourses, their mode of reasoning. This is also evident in Althusser's attempt to show how a new materialist practice of philosophy, capable of articulating positions that can help draw lines of demarcation with the ideological in both sciences and politics, draws from the 'special relationship' it has with historical materialism as a science. It is a philosophy that while not claiming to be a science or a science of sciences ('Theory of theoretical practice'), is nevertheless more informed, more educated with its relation with the sciences; it is a philosophy or a philosophical practice that is in knowledge of itself and its role. In *Lenin and Philosophy* this is stated in the following manner:

> only the scientific knowledge of the mechanisms of class rule and all their effects, which Marx produced and Lenin applied, induced the extraordinary displacement in philosophy that shatters the phantasms of the denegation in which philosophy tells itself, so that men will believe it and so as to believe it itself, that it is above politics, just as it is above classes.[3]

Of course, we know that Althusser, at the same time, was a very attentive reader of philosophical images, returning to them continuously in his École Normale Superieure lectures, something that we tried to present in our reading of his lectures on Rousseau's *Discourse on Inequality* and in particular his constant rereading of the whole imagery of the forest. We also know the importance

---

3   Althusser 1971, p. 67.

that he attributes already in 1966 to the imagery of the *clinamen*, the swerve. However, until the 1980s Althusser refrained from the use of more 'ontological' images, at least in his published works.

This also has to do with the fact that until the 1970s his preoccupation is more with the politics of theory and the attempt towards a theoretical correction of the political line. We can even say that both definitions of philosophy in a sense point in the same direction: how to liberate the scientific potential of Marxism as historical materialism and consequently the political correction of the political line based upon better knowledge of the dynamics of the conjuncture and the potential of the masses. However, from the 1970s onwards, along with the increased apprehension of the depth and extent of the crisis of the communist movement and the attempt to rethink the relation or, more precisely, the encounter between the initiatives and creativity of the masses, the 'traces of communism', with political projects and political organisation, we can see an increased emphasis on anti-teleology.

Of course, the emphasis on anti-teleology was there from the beginning, exemplified in the polemics against historicism in the 1965 books. However, in those texts, the enemy was the conception of Marxism as philosophy (or *anti-philosophy*) of History and the identification of philosophy, science, politics and social practice. In the 1970s and in a stronger sense in the 1980s, Althusser seems to look for an anti-teleological conception that can account for the possibility of the encounter not to happen, for the possibility of missed encounters, for the uneven, contingent, always at risk, even aleatory character of the (im)possible encounter between the elements that constitute revolutionary politics (the masses and their struggles, Marxism as antagonistic theory, forms of political organisation). It is here that anti-teleology and a theory of the aleatory character of encounter acquire a greater importance.

Moreover, it is here that images or more general philosophical lines of demarcation take on a new level of interest. The philosophy of the encounter can no longer be simply a 'philosophy of the concept', as the one evoked by Cavaillés, even though it still deals with concepts and conceptualisations. It has to be broader conception of philosophical conceptual tools that can include quasi-ontological images, a non-ontology of the encounter.

And this can account for the more 'poetic' kind of writing of Althusser and his use of such categories. However, it would be wrong to treat them as simply images or as metaphors that can be translated into more theoretical statements. On the one hand, they are also 'lines of demarcation', expressed in a negative way, about the contingent and aleatory character of any social relation, and the (im)possibility of social relations as lasting encounters. On the other, the particular images invoked here, the Epicurean rain of atoms or Rousseau's forest or the loneliness of the New Prince, can be treated as *examples* or *paradigms* in an *analogical* reasoning in the sense suggested by Giorgio Agamben.[4] In analogy as reasoning, an example is different from an encapsulation of all the determinations of the genus. Rather it is just one possibility in a whole series of distinct individual cases that have similar characteristics. In this sense, it is neither a metaphor nor a simple substitution in a metonymic series. Each in its particularity is a particular case that is not simply an expression of a more general trend but of a series, itself aleatory, of concrete manifestations and of the absence of teleology, articulating this not in terms of generalisations but of constant analogical determinations of the particular from the particular, seeking to constantly deduce similarities in the singularity of each case that can account not for the expression of a common substance but for the recurrence of a theme.

2   The New Practice of Philosophy Revisited

In light of the above it is interesting to see how Althusser revisits the theme of the new practice of philosophy in the 1980s. First of all, he draws a line of demarcation with any conception of materialism as positive ontological determination.

> [T]he evocation of materialism is the index of an exigency, a sign that idealism has to be rejected – yet without breaking free, without being able to break free, of the speculary pair idealism/materialism; hence it is an index, but, at the same time, a trap, because one does not break free of idealism by simply negating it, stating the opposite of idealism, or 'standing it on its head'. We must therefore treat the term 'materialism' with suspicion: the word does not give us the thing, and, on closer inspection, most materialisms turn out to be inverted idealisms. Examples: the materialisms of the Enlightenment, as well as a few passages in Engels.[5]

---

4 'A paradigm is a form of knowledge that is neither inductive not deductive but analogical. It moves from singularity to singularity' (Agamben 2009, p. 32). This has been a recurring theme in Agamben's work. In the *Coming Community* he stressed that 'One concept that escapes the antinomy of the universal and the particular has long been familiar to us: the example [...] [The example] is one singularity among others, which, however, stands for each of them and serves for all' (Agamben 1993, pp. 9–10).

5 Althusser 2006a, p. 272.

Althusser also returns to the question of practice, one of his main preoccupations, as we have seen in *Philosophy for Non-Philosophers*. The primacy of practice over theory, or *logos* in general, is presented as the crucial point that necessitates a new practice of philosophy.

> Practice, which is utterly foreign to the *logos*, is not Truth and is not reducible to – does not realize itself in – speech or seeing. Practice is a process of transformation which is always subject to its own conditions of existence and produces, not the Truth, but, rather, 'truths', or *some* truth [*de la vérité*]: the truth, let us say, of results or of knowledge, all within the field of its own conditions of existence. And while practice has agents, it nevertheless does not have a subject as the transcendental or ontological origin of its intention or project; nor does it have a Goal as the truth of its process. It is a process without a subject or Goal (taking 'subject' to mean an ahistorical element).[6]

Consequently, it is the centrality of practice that leads to the 'denunciation of philosophy produced as "philosophy"':

> It categorically affirms – in the face of philosophy's claim to embrace the entire set of social practices and ideas, to 'see the whole', as Plato said, in order to establish its dominion over these same practices – it categorically affirms, in the face of philosophy's claim that *it has no outside*, that philosophy *does indeed have an outside*; more precisely, that it exists through and for this outside.[7]

This means that a materialist practice of philosophy attempts to avoid the role played by traditional or idealist philosophy, namely to act as a laboratory for the unification of ideological elements into coherent dominant ideologies.[8]

---

[6] Althusser 2006a, pp. 274–5.
[7] Althusser 2006a, p. 275.
[8] Althusser more or less repeats in his 1984 interview to Fernanda Navarro the conception of idealist philosophy as a laboratory that we can find also in the *Philosophy for Non-Philosophers*: 'Again, philosophy may be likened to a laboratory in which the ensemble of ideological elements are unified. In the past, religion played this unifying role; even earlier, the myths of primitive societies did. Religion contented itself with grand (ideological) Ideas such as the existence of God or the creation of the world; it used them to order all human activities and the corresponding ideologies, with a view to constituting the unified ideology that the classes in power needed to ensure their domination. There is, however, a limit: the dominant philosophy goes as far as it can in its role of unifier of the elements of ideology and the diverse

Althusser in a certain way links philosophy and ideology exactly through this process of unification since he attributes to ideology exactly this tendency towards unity and coherence that in his view only philosophy can provide:

> My main idea can be summed up in a few words: philosophy is, as it were, the theoretical laboratory, solitary and isolated, despite all the links tying it to the world, in which categories are developed that are appropriate for [*propres à*] thinking, and, above all, unifying/diversifying – appropriate for thinking the various existing ideologies in unitary/unifying forms. Engels utters, somewhere, a great piece of foolishness: about the 'eternal need of the human spirit' to 'overcome contradiction', and therefore to think the real in the form of unity, or even a non-contradictory system.[9]

For Althusser it was exactly this negation of this traditional role of idealist philosophy that makes some philosophies *interesting*, as he states in a 1984 letter to Fernanda Navarro.

> That is why I would say that if certain philosophies escape this materialism/idealism pair, which is dominated by idealism right down to its very 'opposite', they can be recognized by the fact that they escape, or attempt to escape, questions of origin and end, that is, in the final analysis, the question of the End or Ends of the world and human history. These philosophies are 'interesting', for, in escaping the trap, they express the exigency to abandon idealism and move towards what may be called (if you like) materialism. There are not many of them, of these non-apologetic, truly nonreligious philosophies in the history of philosophy: among the great philosophers, I can see only Epicurus, Spinoza (who is admirable), Marx, when he is properly understood, and Nietzsche.[10]

---

ideologies, but it cannot "leap over its time", as Hegel said, or "transcend its class condition", as Marx said' (Althusser 2006a, p. 279).

9 Althusser 2006a, p. 231. Althusser attributes this need for unity to the very contradictory character of 'dominant' ideologies: 'Similarly, be careful with the term dominant ideology. Historical periods marked by a dominant ideology that is truly one and truly unified are rare: the dominant ideology is always more or less contradictory, tending toward a controlling [*dominateur*] unity, but attaining itonly very rarely and with great difficulty. It would be preferable to speak, as you do elsewhere, in terms of the (contradictory) tendency of an ideology which seeks to constitute itself as a (non-contradictory) uniry and aspires to domination over ideological elements inherited from the past, elements which it never succeeds in truly unifying as a unique, dominant ideology' (Althusser 2006a, p. 239).

10 Althusser 2006a, p. 218.

This means that a philosophy has to be judged mainly by its effects. These effects can be either the elaboration/reproduction of the dominant ideologies as hegemonic projects or the undermining of such projects and the potential opening up of new possibilities for initiatives of the subaltern classes in their struggle for social transformation.

> It follows that in order to be able to characterize a philosophy (leaving its self-conception to one side), we have to consider it in its effects on practices: does it exploit them or does it respect and help them, etc. This is what I tried to show, a bit, in *The Spontaneous Philosophy of the Scientists*. The closer a philosophy comes to the practices – the more it respects them, the more it assists them through the relay of the ideologies – the more it tends towards materialism, a materialism other than the one inscribed in the idealism/materialism pair, which is a speculary pair. (Dominique [Lecourt] has tried to break out of this pair by using the term sur-materialism, bearing in mind that Bachelard talks about the 'sur-rationalism' of modern physics, and doubtless thinking of Breton's 'sur-realism' as well.)[11]

3 Portrait of a Materialist Philosopher

Here Althusser puts forward his image of a materialist philosopher, in contrast to an idealist philosopher, as someone who always catches a moving train:

> [T]he idealist philosopher is a man who, when he catches a train, knows from the outset the station he will be leaving from and the one he will be arriving at; he knows the beginning [*origine*] and end of his route, just as he knows the origin and destiny of man, history and the world.
>
> The materialist philosopher, in contrast, is a man who always catches 'a moving train', like the hero of an American Western.[12]

---

11   Althusser 2006a, p. 221.
12   Althusser 2006a, p. 277. In another text of the same period Althusser describes the materialist philosopher in an analogy with American Westerns: 'The man's age doesn't matter. He can be very old or very young. The important thing is that he doesn't know where he is, and wants to go somewhere. That's why he always catches a moving train, the way they do in American Westerns. Without knowing where he comes from (origin) or where he's going (goal). And he gets off somewhere along the way, in a four-horse town with a ridiculous railway station in the middle of it' (Althusser 2006a, p. 290).

The materialist philosopher avoids thinking in terms of absolute origins or of absolute principles. In contrast, he just records a multitude of aleatory encounters and sequences of events and just attempts to draw generalisations out of these aleatory sequences.

> He witnesses, without having been able to predict it, everything that occurs in an unforeseen, aleatory way, gathering an infinite amount of information and making an infinite number of observations, as much of the train itself as of the passengers and the countryside which, through the window, he sees rolling by. In short, he records sequences [sequences] of aleatory encounters, not, like the idealist philosopher, ordered successions [consequences] deduced from an Origin that is the foundation of all Meaning, or from an absolute First Principle or Cause.[13]

Althusser quickly draws a distinction between those sciences where experiments can lead to statements that can claim universality and those fields in which we are dealing with singular cases and consequently can only have general constants, thus opposing universality to generality, the latter being the kind of abstraction suitable for singular cases. It is obvious that what Althusser has in mind is how to theorise the social, hence the references to singularity, or the need for a 'clinical' approach.

> Here the materialist philosopher-traveller, who is attentive to 'singular' cases, cannot state 'laws' about them, since such cases are singular / concrete/ factual and are therefore not repeated, because they are unique. What he can do, as has been shown by Lévi-Strauss in connection with the cosmic myths of primitive societies, is to single out 'general constants' among the encounters he has observed, the 'variations' of which are capable of accounting for the singularity of the cases under consideration, and thus produce knowledge of the 'clinical' sort as well as ideological, political and social effects. Here we again find not the universality of laws (of the physical, mathematical or logical sort), but the generality of the constants which, by their variation, enable us to apprehend what is true of such-and-such a case.[14]

---

13   Althusser 2006a, p. 278.
14   Ibid.

In this imagery of the philosopher we are not dealing with the philosopher who intervenes in complex ideological/philosophical contradictions arising out of the practice of sciences. Rather, we have a more general conception of the *theorist* or the researcher. Not that Althusser abandons his distinctions between philosophy and the sciences, but it is obvious that he also considers the philosopher to be a theorist of aleatory encounters. In this sense, and in sharp contrast to his earlier description of materialist philosophy as a potential scientific theory of scientificity or even his conception of a rigorous form of intervention that could draw lines of demarcations in very complex theoretical/ideological contradictions, Althusser now even suggests that the materialist philosopher/traveller mainly attempts to work upon 'true philosophy' which is the contradictory philosophy that people already have in their minds, even as a contradictory form of 'common sense'.

> From time to time, he catches the moving train in order to see, talk, listen – like Gorbachev in the streets of Moscow. Besides, one can catch the train wherever one happens to be!
>
> More popular than anyone else, he could be elected to the White House, although he started out from nothing. But no, he'd rather travel, go out and walk the streets; that's how one comes to understand the true philosophy, the one that people have in their heads and that is always contradictory.[15]

In a strange turn of a complex and unique philosophical trajectory, Althusser's latest definition of philosophy is indeed a philosophy not only of singular cases and of aleatory encounters, but also one that attempts to listen and enhance the very thinking, the very discourses, and the very experiences of the masses in all their contradictions. In a similar manner to his increased reliance upon the initiatives of the masses and the 'traces of communism' arising in the struggles and the interstices of capitalist social reality, we have here a renewed reliance upon the very thinking of the masses. Consequently, a new practice of philo-

---

15   Althusser 2006a, p. 291. As Peter Thomas has stressed (2009, p. 429) Althusser here moves to the opposite direction of his condemnation in 1965 in *Reading Capital* of Gramsci's conception of the relation of philosophy and common sense. 'As we have seen, for him [Gramsci], a philosopher is, in the last instance, a "politician"; for him, philosophy is the direct product (assuming all the "necessary mediations") of the activity and experience of the masses, of politico-economic praxis: professional philosophers merely lend their voices and the forms of their discourse to this "common-sense" philosophy, which is already complete without them and speaks in historical praxis – they cannot change it substantially' (Althusser et al. 2016, p. 284).

sophy is not an attempt from above to dictate what is (not) materialist. Rather, the materialist practice of philosophy becomes itself an encounter with the contradictory philosophy of the masses, with collective forms of intellectuality that a new practice of philosophy must not only encounter but also liberate and emancipate. It is only by liberating and at the same time transforming this 'spontaneous philosophy of the masses' that philosophy can play a role in broader projects of social and political emancipation. From philosophy as a privileged field or vanguard in the battles over the politics of theory, we have here philosophy as an attempt to intervene in a struggle where the major role is played by the masses, their initiatives, their aspirations and – last but not least – their thoughts, conceptions, and worldviews, which materialist philosophy attempts to discern, listen to, and elaborate as part of broader counter-hegemonic social and political movements.

CHAPTER 14

Althusser and Gramsci on Philosophy

Louis Althusser's critique of Antonio Gramsci's concept of the 'philosophy of *praxis*' is one of the most important cleavages in the history of Marxism and one of the supposedly definitive dividing lines between different theoretical traditions, one more associated with an emphasis on structural determinations and theoretical anti-humanism, and the other associated with an emphasis on historical praxis, human agency and praxis. Beginning in *Reading Capital* and despite positive references to Gramsci in other texts and his personal correspondence, Althusser openly accused Gramsci's references to a potential absolute historicism as a threat to the very scientificity of Marxism. Althusser seems particularly suspicious of any philosophy that would attempt to include any reference to historicity or human praxis as determining factors, opting instead for a redefinition of scientificity as strictly intra-theoretical, proposing the distinction between scientific discourse and actual historical reality as the foundation of any potential knowledge. Knowledge is a result, not a starting point. Althusser's long self-criticism of his initial theoreticist conception of (Marxist) philosophy as Theory of theoretical practice, a non-foundational yet scientific in its aspiration theory of the production of knowledge, and his turn towards a definition of philosophy as intervention in the political contradictions of knowledge production and theoretical production, represented by his two subsequent redefinitions of philosophy – philosophy as representing politics within theory and philosophy as in the last instance class struggle in theory – did not, seemingly at least, alter this distrust of any 'positive' conception of philosophy. Rather, philosophical intervention and the attempt to put forward 'correct' (*juste*) philosophical positions in order to answer the attempts toward idealist exploitation of sciences (and ideological miscognition of the effectivity of class struggle) seemed more like a 'negative' or even 'deconstructive' practice, with the more positive aspects left to historical materialism as a science of class struggles, and of course to proletarian politics as such. Do all of these simply lead to the observation of the irreconcilable divergence between Althusser and Gramsci? I would try to suggest that despite the differences in their problematics, both Gramsci and Althusser shared a certain conception of the role of philosophy as a theoretical and conceptual laboratory for the development of forms of hegemony. They apply it not only to idealist philosophy and its relation to bourgeois hegemony, but also to a potentially different and antagonistic philosophical practice related to a potential proletarian hegemony, a *new materialist practice* of philosophy for Althusser or a philosophy of *praxis* according to Gramsci.

1   Gramsci and the Philosophy of Praxis

First of all, let us return to Gramsci's elaborations upon philosophy in the *Prison Notebooks*. In Gramsci's work the question of the theoretical status of philosophy is always related to his more general project of a theory of hegemony.[1] One can see it in the interplay between Gramsci's confrontation with the notions of ethico-political history, coming from the work of Croce, of hegemony and of a philosophy of praxis.

> One can say that not only does the philosophy of praxis not exclude ethico-political history, but that, indeed, in its most recent stage of development it consists precisely in asserting the moment of hegemony as essential to its conception of the state and in attaching 'full weight' to the cultural factor, to cultural activity, to the necessity for a cultural front alongside the merely economic and merely political ones.[2]

For Gramsci, historical materialism and what he defines as philosophy of praxis are the result of an entire process of historical development from the Reformation onwards and especially of the emergence of popular culture in its dialectical relation to high culture: 'Historical materialism, in its dialectic of popular culture-high culture, is the crowning point of this entire movement of intellectual and moral reform. It corresponds to Reformation + French Revolution, universality + politics'.[3] At the same time, Gramsci insisted on the very origin-

---

[1] On the articulation between philosophy, politics, and hegemony in Gramsci, see Buci-Glucksmann 1980, Frosini 2003, Thomas 2009, and Burgio 2014.
[2] Q10, §7; *FSPN*, p. 345. Following the standard in references to Gramsci's *Quaderni*, we use Notebook number (Q) and paragraph (§) to refer to the critical Italian edition (Gramsci 1975) and abbreviations to refer to the English translations: *SPN* for *Selections from Prison Notebooks* (Gramsci 1971) and *FSPN* for *Further Selections from the Prison Notebooks* (Gramsci 1996), *PN* for *Prison Notebooks* (Gramsci 2007).
[3] Q4, §3; *PN*, vol. 2, p. 142. It is interesting to note also the rephrasing of this in Q16: 'The philosophy of praxis is the crowning point of this entire movement of intellectual and moral reformation, made dialectical in the contrast between popular culture and high culture. It corresponds to the nexus Protestant Reformation plus French Revolution: it is a philosophy which is also politics, and a politics which is also philosophy' (Q16, §9; *SPN*, p. 395).

ality of Marxism as a theoretical form. 'The affirmation that Marxism is a new, independent philosophy is the affirmation of the independence and originality of a new culture in incubation that will develop with the development of social relations'.[4] Gramsci is fully aware of the relation between philosophy and worldviews in a particular era, the relation between philosophy and mass ideological practices, when he refers to 'the "philosophy of the age", that is, of the mass of sentiments [and conceptions of the world] prevalent among the "silent" multitude'.[5] That is why Gramsci insisted upon the relation of 'common sense' to philosophy.[6] Common sense 'is the "philosophy of nonphilosophers" – in other words, the conception of the world *acritically* absorbed from the various social environments in which the moral individuality of the average person is developed. [...] It is the "folklore" of philosophy'.[7] Only when a theory or a worldview manages to remain in contact with people does it become actually effective: 'Only through this contact does a philosophy become "historical", cleanse itself of elements that are "individual" in origin, and turn itself into "life"'.[8] This is linked to Gramsci's insistence that 'all men are philosophers'.[9] Philosophy becomes a synonym for a certain form of intellectuality that accompanies all forms of human activity and social practice and is itself one of the stakes of social antagonism.

> There is no human activity from which every form of intellectual participation can be excluded: *homo faber* cannot be separated from *homo sapiens*. Each man, finally, outside his professional activity, carries on some form of intellectual activity, that is he is a 'philosopher', an artist a man of taste, he participates in a particular conception of the world, has a conscious line of moral conduct, and therefore contributes to sustain a conception of the world or to modify it, that is, to bring into being new modes of thought.[10]

---

4   Q4, §3; *PN*, vol. 2, p. 144.
5   Q5, §54; *PN*, vol. 2, p. 313.
6   On the importance of the relationship between philosophy and common sense as part of the broader 'pedagogical' role of the communist party in the attempt towards a new form of mass intellectuality and civility, see Frosini 2003, pp. 170–6. See also Liguori 2006, pp. 79–82.
7   Q8, §173; *PN*, vol. 3, p. 333.
8   Q8, §213; *PN*, vol. 3, p. 360.
9   Q8, §204; *PN*, vol. 3, p. 352.
10 *SPN*, p. 9.

Consequently, 'philosophy cannot be separated from the history of philosophy, nor can culture from the history of culture'.[11] At the same time, the extent of the actual historical effectivity of any new emerging philosophy and conception of the world is to be judged by the extent to which it affects mass ideological practices, especially when we are talking about the worldview of the subaltern classes.

> For a mass of people to be led to think coherently and in the same coherent fashion about the real present world, is a 'philosophical' event far more important and 'original' than the discovery by some philosophical 'genius' of a truth which remains the property of small groups of intellectuals.[12]

For Gramsci, common sense is not simply a reference to ideological miscognition or to spontaneous forms of popular ideology; at the same time, the transformation of common sense is one of the aims of a new hegemony. This creates a dialectical relation between philosophy and common sense.

> Perhaps it is useful to make a 'practical' distinction between philosophy and common sense in order to indicate more clearly the passage from one moment to the other. In philosophy the features of individual elaboration of thought are the most salient: in common sense on the other hand it is the diffuse, uncoordinated features of a generic form of thought common to a particular period and a particular popular environment. But every philosophy has a tendency to become the common sense of a fairly limited environment (that of all the intellectuals). It is a matter therefore of starting with a philosophy which already enjoys, or could enjoy, a certain diffusion, because it is connected to and implicit in practical life, and elaborating it so that it becomes a renewed common sense possessing the coherence and the sinew of individual philosophies. But this can only happen if the demands of cultural contact with the 'simple' are continually felt.[13]

And this relation between philosophy and 'common sense', theoretical abstraction and mass ideological practices is itself a part of the political process. 'The relation between common sense and the upper level of philosophy is assured

---

11   Q11, §12; *SPN*, p. 324.
12   Q11, §12; *SPN*, p. 325.
13   Q11, §12; *SPN*, p. 330.

by "politics";[14] although this does not imply a symmetry between different philosophies as class conceptions of the world: 'The philosophy of praxis does not tend to leave the "simple" in their primitive philosophy of common sense, but rather to lead them to a higher conception of life'.[15] The emergence of a new conception and practice of philosophy is by itself an aspect of the emergence of a new hegemonic project, which also means that philosophy is transformed by the emergence of proletarian hegemony. 'This is why it must be stressed that the political development of the concept of hegemony represents a great philosophical advance as well as a politico-practical one'.[16]

Gramsci's identification between philosophy and history should not be seen as an identification of theory with its subject matter (one of the targets of Althusser's critique in 1965[17]), but as an acknowledgement of the importance of the relation of politics and theory, and a conception of theory as being part of a historical process and its dynamics. This is also important since ideology and discourse practices are part of the historical process and its dynamics. That is why Gramsci did not limit himself to the Crocean assertion about the identity of history and philosophy, but also insisted on the relation of history and politics and of philosophy and politics, as well as that between philosophy and mass ideological practices.

> Croce's proposition regarding the identity of history and philosophy is richer than any other in critical consequences: 1) it remains incomplete if it does not also arrive at the identity of history and politics [...], and 2) thus also at the identity of politics and philosophy.
>
> But if it is necessary to admit of this identity, how can one any longer distinguish ideologies [...] from philosophy? That is to say, the distinction is possible, but it is only of degree (a quantitative distinction) and not qualitative. Ideologies, rather, are the 'true' philosophy since they are then those philosophical 'popularisations' that lead the masses to concrete action, to the transformation of reality. In other words, they are the mass aspect of every philosophical conception, which in the 'philosopher' assumes the characteristics of an abstract universality, divorced from time and space, the characteristics peculiar to a literary and anti-historical origin.[18]

---

14   Q11, §12; *SPN*, p. 331.
15   Q11, §12; *SPN*, p. 332.
16   Q11, §12; *SPN*, p. 333.
17   Althusser et al. 2016.
18   Q10II, §2; *FSPN*, pp. 382–3.

When Gramsci chose to refer to the philosophy of praxis, this was neither a metonymy for historical materialism nor an attempt to avoid prison censors.[19] Gramsci consciously chose the reference to philosophy instead of science in an effort to distinguish the philosophy of praxis from a simple sociological scientism. This is not an underestimation of the importance of theory or of a scientific approach to political economy and social relations in general. The elaboration of a new proletarian hegemonic apparatus requires also the elaboration of a new conceptual apparatus, an elaboration that is not simply theoretical, but also historical and political, translating historical and political dynamics. That is why for Gramsci the realisation of a hegemonic apparatus, to the extent that it creates a new ideological terrain, determines a reform of consciences and methods of knowledge, constitutes a knowledge fact, a philosophical event: 'The realization of a hegemonic apparatus, in so far as it creates a new ideological terrain, determines a reform of consciousness and of methods of knowledge: it is a fact of knowledge, a philosophical fact'.[20]

For Gramsci, 'philosophy in general does not in fact exist',[21] only different and antagonistic philosophies and conceptions of the world exist. Consequently, what prevails in each particular era is a balance of forces between different philosophical tendencies but also between different ideologies and theoretical practices. 'Therefore the philosophy of an epoch cannot be any systematic tendency or individual system. It is the ensemble of all individual philosophies and philosophical tendencies, plus scientific opinions, religion and common sense'.[22] And every philosopher is in a constant and dialectical relation to their social and political environment: 'One could say therefore that the historical personality of an individual philosopher is also given by the active relationship which exists between him and the cultural environment he is proposing to modify'.[23] That is why the history of traditional philosophy, the history of the philosophies of the philosophers, is the history of the attempt to correct, transform, and perfect existing worldviews.

> The history of philosophy as it is generally understood, that is as the history of philosophers' philosophies, is the history of attempts made and ideological initiatives undertaken by a specific class of people to change,

---

19 On this I am following Peter Thomas's arguments against treating the language and terminology of the *Quaderni* as Gramsci's way to avoid prison censors (Thomas 2009).
20 Q10II, §12; *SPN*, pp. 365–6.
21 Q11, §12; *SPN*, p. 326.
22 Q11, §16; *SPN*, p. 455.
23 Q10II, §44; *SPN*, p. 350.

> correct or perfect the conceptions of the world that exist in any particular age and thus to change the norms of conduct that go with them; in other words, to change practical activity as a whole.[24]

One of the tasks of a philosophy of praxis is to historicise philosophies and conceptions of the world. 'The intention of the philosophy of praxis, in contrast, is to justify [...] the historicity of philosophies, a historicity that is dialectical because it gives rise to struggles between systems, to struggles between ways of seeing reality'.[25] Idealist philosophy is for Gramsci a philosophy that attempts to organise consent in favour of the dominant classes. Gramsci links modern idealism to the process of bourgeois state formation, the role of intellectuals in this process and the transformation of hegemony in an era of passive revolution.

> The problem can be formulated as follows: since the State is the concrete form of a productive world and since the intellectuals are the social element from which the governing personnel is drawn, the intellectual who is not firmly anchored to a strong economic group will tend to present the State as an absolute; in this way the function of the intellectuals is itself conceived of as absolute and pre-eminent, and their historical existence and dignity are abstractly rationalised. This motive is fundamental for an historical understanding of modern philosophical idealism, and is connected with the mode of formation of the modern States of continental Europe as 'reaction-national transcendence' of the French Revolution (a motive which is essential for understanding the concepts of 'passive revolution' and 'revolution/restoration', and for grasping the importance of the Hegelian comparison between the principles of Jacobinism and classical German philosophy).[26]

It is obvious that for Gramsci the question of the specific definition of philosophy cannot be simply theoretical, nor can it be thought in terms of a traditional theoretical division of labour between science and philosophy (as theory of knowledge, ontology and ethics). On the contrary, the theoretical efficacy of a philosophical proposition has to do with how it affects the popular masses. 'Mass adhesion or non-adhesion to an ideology is the real critical test of the

---

24   Q10II, §17; *SPN*, p. 344.
25   Q10II, §41i; *FSPN*, p. 413.
26   Q10II, §61, *SPN*, p. 117.

rationality and historicity of modes of thinking'.[27] This is what leads Gramsci to the identification of philosophy and history that Althusser considered the epitome of historicism.

> The philosophy of an historical epoch is, therefore, nothing other than the 'history' of that epoch itself, nothing other than the mass of variations that the leading group has succeeded in imposing on preceding reality. History and philosophy are in this sense indivisible: they form a bloc.[28]

In contrast, a philosophy of praxis is an attempt towards a philosophy that is not a 'walking anachronism', a 'future philosophy which will be that of a human race united the world over',[29] a philosophy *for communism*. Philosophy of praxis is a philosophy of historical contradiction and a form of struggle of the subaltern classes to gain social and political power.

> The philosophy of praxis, on the other hand, does not aim at the peaceful resolution of existing contradictions. It is not the instrument of government of the dominant groups in order to gain the consent of and exercise hegemony over the subaltern classes; it is the expression of these subaltern classes who want to educate themselves in the art of government and who have an interest in knowing all truths, even the unpleasant ones, and in avoiding the (impossible) deceptions of the upper class and – even more – their own.[30]

However, it is necessary that a philosophy of praxis first begins as critique and as a polemical theoretical activity. 'A philosophy of praxis cannot but present itself at the outset in a polemical and critical guise, as superseding the existing mode of thinking and existing concrete thought (the existing cultural world)'.[31] Philosophy of praxis is 'materialist' in the sense of a break with any form of metaphysical dualism and Gramsci insists on the polemical character of the very term materialism. 'The term "materialism" in the first fifty years of the nineteenth century should be understood not only in its restricted technical philosophical sense but with the more extended meaning that it acquired polemically in the debates that grew up in Europe with the rise and victori-

---

27 Q11, §12; *SPN*, p. 341.
28 Q10II, §17; *SPN*, p. 345.
29 Q11, §12, *SPN*, p. 324.
30 Q10II, §41xii; *FSPN*, pp. 395–6.
31 Q11, §12; *SPN*, p. 330.

ous development of modern culture'.[32] At the same time, Gramsci distinguishes the philosophy of praxis from any form of metaphysical materialist ontology. In his polemic against Bukharin's manual he is highly critical of any 'philosophical alias metaphysical or mechanical (vulgar) materialism'.[33] For Gramsci the question of the emergence of this highly new and original form of materialism should be seen in light of the contradictory relation of a historical materialism to previous forms of materialist tendencies in the complex terrain of philosophical tendencies in their 'overdetermination' by historical conjunctures and theoretical exigencies. It is this complex and uneven history of the emergence of Marxism that can account for the contradictory character of Marxist materialism. The following passage from Q8 exemplifies this point.

> One of the reasons, and perhaps the most important reason, for the reduction of historical materialism to traditional materialism resides in the fact that historical materialism could not but represent a primarily critical phase of philosophy, whereas there is a perennial demand for complete and perennial systems. Complete and perfect systems, however, are always the work of individual philosophers. The historically relevant respect of these philosophical systems – namely, the aspect that corresponds to contemporary conditions of life – is always accompanied by an abstract component that is 'ahistorical', in the sense that is tied to earlier philosophies [thought that generates thought abstractly] because of external and mechanical system requirements (internal harmony and architecture of the system) and personal idiosyncrasies. But the philosophy of an epoch is not the philosophy of an individual or a group. It is the ensemble of the philosophies of all individuals and groups [+scientific opinion] _ religion + common sense. Can such a philosophy be created 'artfully'? Through the work of an individual or a group? The only possible way is through critical activity and specifically through posing and critically resolving specific philosophical problems. In the meantime, though, one must start with the idea that the new philosophy is different from any previous philosophy.[34]

It is obvious from this passage that for Gramsci historical materialism, or in more general terms, a philosophy and theory in favour of proletarian hegemony, enters the theoretical stage in a contested terrain, ridden with conflicts

---

32   Q11, §16; *SPN*, p. 454.
33   Q11, §22; *SPN*, p. 434.
34   Q8, §211; *PN*, vol. 3, pp. 358–9.

and problems, conditioned by a certain idealist conception of the philosophical system and has to achieve its necessary originality through a long and necessarily contradictory process, which also includes dealing with the relative weight of already existing idealist and metaphysical philosophical systems, in terms of both content but also form. However, this does not diminish the necessity to start with the premise that what is needed is a new philosophy or – if this anachronism is permitted – a new practice of philosophy.

Because of all the metaphysical connotations associated with materialism as a potential 'philosophical system', Gramsci in many instances prefers to refer to immanence and what he describes as an immanentist tradition in philosophy. As Frosini[35] and Thomas[36] have shown, the emergence of the importance of immanence is related to Gramsci's attempt to confront crucial aspects of a non-metaphysical and non-deterministic conception of social practices, expressed in crucial notions such as 'homo oeconomicus', 'determinate market' and 'tendential law' that Gramsci uses in his attempt to theorise social relations and forms in the economy.

> The discovery of the formal logical principle of the 'law of tendency' which leads to the scientific definition of the fundamental economic concepts of homo oeconomicus and of the 'determined market', was this not also a discovery of epistemological value as well? Does it not precisely simply a new 'immanence', a new conception of 'necessity' and of freedom, etc.?[37]

One might say that for Gramsci the reference to immanence is an attempt to think the materiality of social practices, the absolute earthliness of thought and social practices in general, in sharp break with any metaphysical conception of reality.

> The philosophy of praxis continues the philosophy of immanence but purifies it of all its metaphysical apparatus and brings it onto the concrete terrain of history. The use is metaphorical only in the sense that the old immanence has been superseded – that it has been superseded but is still assumed as a link in the process of thought out of which the new usage has come.[38]

---

35   Frosini 2009.
36   Thomas 2009.
37   Q10II; *SPN*, p. 401.
38   Q11, §28; *SPN*, p. 450.

However, this does not mean that the philosophy of praxis is a simple extension of existing philosophies. Rather, the philosophy of *praxis* is an 'integral and original philosophy which opens up a new phase of history and a new phase in the development of world thought',[39] which opens a way to rethink philosophy in general.

> At the level of theory the philosophy of praxis cannot be confounded with or reduced to any other philosophy. Its originality lies not only in its transcending of previous philosophies but also and above all in that it opens up a completely new road, renewing from head to toe the whole way of conceiving philosophy itself.[40]

As a new and original way to conceive of philosophy as a theoretical activity, philosophy of praxis should not be seen through the lens of a traditional distinction between pure philosophy on the one hand and economics and politics on the other. In contrast, it is a complex theoretical approach to historical reality.

> It will be asked whether the philosophy of praxis is not precisely and specifically a theory of history, and the answer must be that this is indeed true but that one cannot separate politics and economics from history, even the specialised aspects of political science and art and of economic science and policy. This means that, after having accomplished the principal task in the general philosophical part, which deals with the philosophy of praxis proper – the science of dialectics or the theory of knowledge, within which the general concepts of history, politics and economics are interwoven in an organic unity.[41]

And if objectivity is the goal of an immanentist philosophy, in the sense of emancipation from ideological miscognition, then the objectivity as aim and communism as a political goal are part of the same historical process. Objectivity as emancipation from ideology is at the end of the process that leads to communism.

> Objective always means 'humanly objective' which can be held to correspond exactly to 'historically subjective': in other words, objective would

---

39 Q11, § 22. *SPN*, p. 435.
40 Q11, § 27; *SPN*, p. 462.
41 Q11, § 33; *SPN*, p. 431.

> mean 'universal subjective'. Man knows objectively in so far as knowledge is real for the whole human race historically unified in a single unitary cultural system. But this process of historical unification takes place through the disappearance of the internal contradictions which tear apart human society, while these contradictions themselves are the condition for the formation of groups and for the birth of ideologies which are not concretely universal but are immediately rendered transient by the practical origin of their substance. There exists therefore a struggle for objectivity (to free oneself from partial and fallacious ideologies) and this struggle is the same as the struggle for the cultural unification of the human race.[42]

Objectivity requires a change in social conditions, requires a new development of humanity, communism and the transformed social consciousness associated with it, the new forms of mass intellectuality associated with communism but also with the advance of technology. Objectivity is a relation between humanity and reality mediated by technology and social relations; it is much more that simply asserting the existence of reality.

> [W]hat is of interest to science is then not so much the objectivity of the real, but humanity forging its methods of research continually correcting those of its material instruments which reinforce sensory organs and logical instruments of discrimination and ascertainment (which include mathematics): in other words culture, the conception of the world, the relation between humanity and reality as mediated by technology. [...] Without humanity what would the reality of the universe mean? The whole of science is bound to needs, to life, to the activity of humanity. Without humanity's activity, which creates all, even scientific, values, what would 'objectivity' be a chaos, i.e. nothing, a void.[43]

This is also related to the role of intellectuals, intellectuals being the crucial organisers, and the elaboration of a new proletarian hegemony implies a dialectical relation between intellectuals and masses. That is why a crucial aspect of proletarian hegemony is the formation of a new stratum of intellectuals. And that is why political parties can be laboratories for new mass critical intellectualities. Gramsci has a conception of philosophy as a contested terrain, a terrain of struggle, a necessarily contradictory co-existence of antagonistic tenden-

---

42   Q11, §17; *SPN*, p. 445.
43   Q11, §37; *FSPN*, p. 292.

cies and philosophical currents. The 'philosophy of an epoch cannot be any systematic tendency or individual system. It is the *ensemble* of all individual philosophies and philosophical tendencies, plus scientific opinions, religion and common sense'.[44]

If philosophy is linked to forms of social and political intellectuality, the many ways in which ordinary people deal with the realities of life and social antagonism, and if mass intellectuality is one of the main stakes of the struggle for hegemony, then a philosophy of praxis is an integral part of this attempt towards mass critical intellectuality, an attempt that is also integrally linked to the elaboration of new forms of mass politics and in particular the emergence of the mass party (and of course the proletarian party). The following passages, coming from one of Gramsci's most dense notes on philosophy (Q11, §12), exemplifies this complex articulation between philosophy, mass intellectuality and collective political organisations:

> One should stress the importance and significance which, in the modern world, political parties have in the elaboration and diffusion of conceptions of the world, because essentially what they do is to work out the ethics and the politics corresponding to these conceptions and act as it were as their historical 'laboratory'. The parties recruit individuals out of the working mass, and the selection is made on practical and theoretical criteria at the same time. The relation between theory and practice becomes even closer the more the conception is vitally and radically innovatory and opposed to old ways of thinking. For this reason one can say that the parties are the elaborators of new integral and all encompassing intellectualities and the crucibles where the unification of theory and practice, understood as a real historical process, takes place.[45]

---

44   Q11, §16; *SPN*, p. 455.
45   Q11, §12; *SPN*, p. 335. I have slightly altered the translation. Hoare and Nowell-Smith translate it as 'elaborators of new integral and totalitarian intelligentsias'. However, in the Italian original, Gramsci refers to political parties as '*elaboratori delle nuove intelletualità integrali e totalitarie*', so I choose to translate *intelletualità* as intellectualities. Regarding *totalitarie*, I choose not to translate as totalitarian, but as all-encompassing, in order to avoid any identification with the notion of 'totalitarianism' and the connotations it acquired after WWII, especially since Gramsci uses the adjective *totalitario* as a more general term referring to the emergence in modernity of non-partial and all-encompassing 'conceptions of the world' and political projects. On the meaning of *totalitario* in Gramsci see the entry *totalitario*, by Renato Caputo in the *Dizionario Gramsciano* (Liguori and Voza (ed.) 2009, pp. 851–3).

The relation of philosophy to hegemony is exemplified in Gramsci's insistence that any relation of 'hegemony' is also an 'educational relation'.[46] It is on the basis of this conception of the relation between philosophy and hegemony that Gramsci suggests the need for a different practice of philosophy that leads to the need for a new type of philosopher, the 'democratic' philosopher, a type of philosopher that is itself the result of a historical process and a certain dialectic between theory and practice.

> The environment reacts back on the philosopher and imposes on him a continual process of self-criticism. It is his 'teacher'. This is why one of the most important demands that the modern intelligentsias have made in the political field has been that of the so-called 'freedom of thought and of the expression of thought' ('freedom of the press', 'freedom of association'). For the relationship between master and disciple in the general sense referred to above is only realised where this political condition exists, and only then do we get the 'historical' realisation of a new type of philosopher, whom we could call a 'democratic philosopher' in the sense that he is a philosopher convinced that his personality is not limited to himself as a physical individual but is an active social relationship of modification of the cultural environment. [...] The unity of science and life is precisely an active unity, in which alone liberty of thought can be realised; it is a master-pupil relationship, one between the philosopher and the cultural environment in which he has to work and from which he can draw the necessary problems for formulation and resolution. In other words, it is the relationship between philosophy and history.[47]

The figure of the democratic philosopher suggests the need for a new form of intellectuals who are aware of the limits of their subjectivity and the need for them to engage in collective political practices and knowledge practices that are the necessary conditions for their critical intellectual activity. This is a highly original conception of a non-subjective or post-subjective condition of intellectuality which also allows for a more precise articulation of the relation between philosophy and history than some of the criticisms about 'historicism' tend to suggest.

Therefore, it is obvious that Gramsci is treating philosophy of *praxis* as a rather broad theoretical practice, more precisely a range of theoretical prac-

---

46   Q10II, § 44; *SPN*, p. 350.
47   Q10II, § 44; *SPN*, pp. 350–1.

tices, dealing with social reality and the politics of social emancipation. It is indeed a theoretical laboratory of alternative intellectualities. That is why philosophy of praxis is a creative activity. And that is why Gramsci links philosophy of practice to the notion of the historical bloc and complex dialectic of passion and understanding and passion in a relation of hegemony. This complex articulation between philosophy, ideology and politics, including the use of a strategic concept such as the 'historical bloc', offers an insight into the depth of Gramsci's confrontation with the historical and political modalities of theory. In this sense, Gramsci's 'historicism' is exactly this apprehension of the historicity and political dynamics of theory, its actual effectivity in the politics of proletarian hegemony and communist emancipation.

> If the relationship between intellectuals and people-nation, between the leaders and the led, the rulers and the ruled, is provided by an organic cohesion in which feeling-passion becomes understanding and thence knowledge (not mechanically but in a way that is alive), then and only then is the relationship one of representation. Only then can there take place an exchange of individual elements between the rulers and ruled, leaders [*dirigenti*] and led, and can the shared life be realised which alone is a social force with the creation of the 'historical bloc'.[48]

2 Althusser and Gramsci: A Missed Encounter?

Althusser's encounter with the work of Gramsci in the early 1960s was an important event in his theoretical development. Althusser discovered Gramsci along with Machiavelli[49] and was initially enthusiastic about these discoveries. We know from his correspondence with Franca Madonia that he read Gramsci during the summer of 1961[50] and that he returned to Gramsci during the preparation of his 1962 course on Machiavelli.[51] On January 1962 during the preparation of the course on Machiavelli, the 'forced writing' as he describes it, he again remembers 'that ease [*aisance*] that I had found in Gramsci'.[52] This first course on Machiavelli was intense for him, both on a philosophical and on a personal level, with Althusser insisting that 'it was about me that I had

---

48 Q11, § 67, *SPN*, p. 418.
49 Morfino 2015a, p. 62.
50 See the reference in his 28 November 1961 letter (Althusser 1997a, p. 122).
51 Althusser 2006b.
52 Althusser1997b, p. 161.

spoken: the will of realism (will of being someone real, to have something to do with real life) and a "de-realising" [*déréralisante*] situation (exactly my present delirium)'.[53] Althusser maintained this respect for Gramsci's reading of Machiavelli, making positive references to Gramsci in *Machiavelli and Us*, his 1970s manuscript on Machiavelli, in which he basically accepts Gramsci's position that the theoretical and political challenge Machiavelli faced was that of the formation of a national state in Italy.[54] The importance of this initial encounter with Gramsci is evident in 'Contradiction and Overdetermination'.

> [T]he *theory of the specific effectivity of the superstructures and other 'circumstances' largely remains to be elaborated*; and before the theory of their effectivity or simultaneously (for it is by formulating their effectivity that their *essence* can be attained) there must be elaboration of *the theory of the particular essence of the specific elements of the superstructure*. Like the map of Africa before the great explorations, this theory remains a realm sketched in outline, with its great mountain chains and rivers, but often unknown in detail beyond a few well-known regions. Who has *really* attempted to follow up the explorations of Marx and Engels? I can only think of Gramsci.[55]

In a footnote in the same passage, Althusser opposes the originality of Gramsci to the Hegelianism of Lukács:

> *Lukács*'s attempts, which are limited to the history of literature and philosophy, seem to me to be tainted by a guilty Hegelianism: as if Lukács wanted to absolve through Hegel his upbringing by Simmel and Dilthey. *Gramsci* is of another stature. The jottings and developments in his *Prison Notebooks* touch on all the basic problems of Italian and European history: economic, social, political and cultural. There are also some completely original and in some cases genial insights into the problem, basic today, of the superstructures. Also, as always with true discoveries, there are

---

53 Althusser 1997b, p. 163.
54 Althusser 1999a, p. 11.
55 Althusser 1969, pp. 113–14. One could also see the reference that Althusser makes to Gramsci in a letter to Hélène Rytman in August 1962, during the preparation of 'Contradiction and Overdetermination'. Althusser there refers to his need to proceed with real '*discoveries* [...] in the line of what Gramsci had started to make' (Althusser 2011, p. 411). For a reading of Gramsci in relation to the analysis of the conjuncture see Juan Carlos Portantiero 'Gramsci y el análisis de coyuntura (algunas notas)', in Portantiero 1981. For a reading of Althusser's references to Gramsci in *For Marx* see Frosini 2006.

> *new concepts*, for example, *hegemony*: a remarkable example of a theoretical solution in outline to the problems of the interpenetration of the economic and the political. Unfortunately, at least as far as France is concerned, who has taken up and followed through Gramsci's theoretical effort?[56]

I think that this reference to Gramsci is very important. At the moment that Althusser presented a highly original anti-teleological and anti-metaphysical reading of historical materialism, based upon the singularity of conjunctures and the complexity of determination, he thought of Gramsci and hegemony as a crucial conceptual innovation to deal with these questions. The same line of reasoning regarding the importance of Gramsci as a thinker of the superstructures is evident in Althusser's elaboration on the concept of the Ideological State Apparatuses (with its analogy with the concept of hegemonic apparatuses). Althusser cites Gramsci as an important influence in the development of the concept of Ideological State Apparatuses.

> To my knowledge, Gramsci is the only one who went any distance in the road I am taking. He had the 'remarkable' idea that the State could not be reduced to the (Repressive) State Apparatus, but included, as he put it, a certain number of institutions from '*civil society*': the Church, the Schools, the trade unions, etc. Unfortunately, Gramsci did not systematize his institutions, which remained in the state of acute but fragmentary notes.[57]

On the other hand, early on Althusser launches an open attack on Gramsci in the 'Marxism is not a historicism' section of *Reading Capital*, where he presents Gramsci as a proponent of a historicist conception of philosophy.[58] Therefore Gramsci was to be considered an important theoretician of the superstructures and of questions of state ideological apparatuses, but his observations would be seen as lacking the necessary theoretical rigour and as being tainted with ideal-

---

56   Althusser 1969, p. 114.
57   Althusser 1971, p. 142.
58   Althusser et al. 2016, pp. 268–94. In a letter to Franca Madonia dated 2 July 1965 (Althusser 1997b, pp. 623–4), Althusser is even more aggressive towards Gramsci. He thinks that Gramsci's writings have 'profound weaknesses', that Gramsci had never read Marx's *Capital*, that he held the Catholic Church as the model for philosophy as worldview, and that his theory of ideology is purely formal. On Althusser's reading and misreading of Gramsci, see Thomas 2009 and Thomas 2013.

ist and historicist elements. Althusser's reference to 'practical concepts'[59] – as opposed to proper theoretical concepts in the sense of what he termed Generalities III – helped this critical inclusion of certain Gramscian notions without excluding the necessary philosophical polemic.[60] Moreover, Gramsci's conception of the emergence of the modern nation-state, as expressed in his reading of Machiavelli, was praised by Althusser.[61] However, the second half of the 1970s Althusser became even more critical of Gramsci.[62] The target now was not Gramsci's historicism but his conception of hegemony. As Vittorio Morfino has stressed, '[i]n 1965, he [Althusser] attacks historicism as a paradoxical [...] form of justification of Stalinism. In 1977–78 he attacks the concept of hegemony as the inspiring concept for Eurocommunism'.[63] An entire section of his 1978 *Marx in his Limits* is devoted to criticism of Gramsci.[64] Althusser accuses Gramsci of over-generalising the notion of hegemony, of underestimating the economic infrastructure, of downplaying the role of force, of tending towards an idealist conception of the state as educator. This criticism is overdetermined by political considerations. Althusser's interventions in the late 1970s were his last efforts to fight against what he perceived as a right-wing Eurocommunist turn away from a revolutionary politics of smashing the state apparatus.[65] This critique was intensified in another unpublished text by Althusser from the same period, entitled *Que faire?*, in which Althusser accuses Gramsci's concepts, such as the historical bloc or the passive revolution, as being tainted by an idealist and normative conception of the state and the different political forms.[66]

However, the question remains. Why did Althusser choose such an open attack on Gramsci especially in *Reading Capital*, taking into consideration that

---

59 Althusser 2005, pp. 243–5.
60 However, other members of the Althusserian School chose the road of silence regarding Gramsci. Balibar's *Cinque études du matérialisme historique* (Balibar 1974) contains only a single reference to Gramsci!
61 Morfino 2015a, p. 72.
62 Even though there were still positive appreciations such as the one found in his 1976 text on the 'Transformation of Philosophy' (in Althusser 1990) or his positive references to Gramsci in *Machiavelli and Us* (Althusser 1999a).
63 Morfino 2015a, p. 81.
64 Althusser 2006a, pp. 139–49. Aspects of this criticism can also be found in other texts of the same period. See for example his 1977 intervention on the Crisis of Marxism (Althusser 1998, pp. 267–80).
65 For Althusser's political and theoretical considerations of that period, see Goshgarian 2006.
66 Althusser 2018b. See also Morfino 2015a, pp. 77–81. I return to this text in Chapter 18.

other Marxist thinkers of 'historicist' tendencies, such as Lukács and Korsch do not have the privilege of such an attack (even though *History and Class Consciousness* seems like the 'absent opponent' in many instances in *Reading Capital*)? I think that there are two reasons for this insistence. The first is actually Althusser's interest in Gramsci, which is contemporary with his own attempt to theorise a break with idealism and economism.[67] The second has to do with Althusser's particular political and theoretical strategy in the early 1960s, which we discussed earlier. Althusser's initial project was to induce a left-wing correction of the political line of the communist movement, during a period of right-wing reformist de-Stalinisation, through a theoretical turn towards a much more scientific version of Marxism. The scientific character of this redefined Marxism would guarantee, in its fusion with political leadership, the making of correct political decisions. This scientific character would itself be guaranteed by the development of a Marxist materialist philosophy, including a Marxist materialist epistemology, which would provide the necessary protocols of scientificity, what Althusser termed the 'Theory of theoretical practices'. In its turn, this Marxist 'science of sciences' was not to be considered an arbitrary theoretical construction, but it was already existing in a practical, latent form in Marx's mature works and especially *Capital*, hence all this insistence on a return to Marx. Gramsci posed an important challenge to this endeavour. While Gramsci did not by any means support a typical historicist-metaphysical conception of a messianic Subject of history, or an all-encompassing substance at the centre of a historical dialectic, which seemed to be the main targets of Althusser's attack on Hegelian Marxism, he did insist on Marxism being not a science in the positivist sense of the term. Instead, he insisted – especially in his polemic against Bukharin, as we saw – on the need for a different theoretical modality for historical materialism. This was expressed in his call for a philosophy of praxis. As Peter Thomas correctly points out:

> The philosophy of praxis therefore insists upon its necessarily partial and incomplete nature, as the theoretical expression of an historical subjectivity that wants to help create the conditions of a genuinely human objectivity, that is, a 'universal subjectivity'. Its truth, in other words, is located in the world rather than transcending it. As a mode of knowing the world from within it, 'immanently', it challenges both the meta-

---

67   See for example his insistence, in a 1962 Letter to Hélène Rytman, that new research in historical materialism must be 'in the line of what Gramsci started doing' (Althusser 2011, p. 411).

physical materialism of Bukharin and the idealist traditions of Western Philosophy by offering a radically alternative conception of the relation between thought and Being.[68]

This was something that Althusser thought posed a challenge to his strategy of a scientific correction of a political line. In addition, Althusser was highly sceptical of any attempt to historicise both social reality and the concepts used to theorise it, despite his insistence on the co-existence of different historical times and their specific structures of historicity,[69] which, at least in my opinion, opens the way for a highly original conception of historicity. Here Althusser's negative position is also overdetermined by his identification of any reference to historicity with a historicist conflation of real history and theory and with a humanist vision of human actors as the authors of their destiny.[70] This aversion towards historicisation marks both his conception of science and of a potential scientific 'Theory of theoretical practice'. Even his more political conception of 'philosophy as in the last instance class struggle in the field

---

[68] Thomas 2009, p. 306.
[69] '[I]t is only possible to give a content to the concept of historical time by defining historical time as the specific form of existence of the social totality under consideration, an existence in which different structural levels of temporality interfere, because of the peculiar relations of correspondence, non-correspondence, articulation, dislocation and torsion which obtain, between the different "levels" of the whole in accordance with its general structure. It needs to be said that, just as there is no production in general, there is no history in general, but only specific structures of historicity, based in the last resort on the specific structures of the different modes of production, specific structures of historicity which, since they are merely the existence of determinate social formations (arising from specific modes of production), articulated as social wholes, have no meaning except as a function of the essence of those totalities, i.e., of the essence of their peculiar complexity' (Althusser et al. 2016, pp. 256–7).
[70] 'It must be said that the union of humanism and historicism represents the gravest temptation, for it procures the greatest theoretical advantages, at least in appearance. In the reduction of all knowledge to the historical social relations a second underhand reduction can be introduced, by treating the *relations of production* as mere *human relations*. This second reduction depends on something "obvious": is not history a "human" phenomenon through and through, and did not Marx, quoting Vico, declare that men can, know it since they have "*made*" all of it? But this "obviousness" depends on a remarkable presupposition: that the "actors" of history are the authors of its text, the subjects of its production. But this presupposition too has all the force of the "obvious", since, as opposed to what the theatre suggests, concrete men are, in history, the actors of roles of which they are the authors, too. Once the stage-director has been spirited away, the actor-author becomes the twin-brother of Aristotle's old dream: the doctor-who-cures-himself' (Althusser et al. 2016, pp. 290–1).

of theory'[71] is presented more as a negative turn towards a materialist deconstruction of idealist positions than as a positive construction of concepts and theories.

3   The Open Question of Marxist Philosophy

However, the question remains. How are we to conceive of a possible materialist practice of philosophy? What does it mean to practice philosophy in Marxist terms? Is it simply an attempt to deconstruct and subvert idealist tendencies and bring forward the radical and materialist element in theoretical practices, a constant bending of the stick to the opposite side, an attempt to intervene and change the theoretical and in the last instance political balance of forces, as Althusser has suggested? Or is it a much more positive attempt to rethink philosophy or – to be more precise – an attempt simultaneously at realising and historicising philosophy as a highly original historical social theory, as Gramsci has suggested?

It would be too easy to simply say that Althusser and Gramsci dealt with different conceptions of philosophy or sought to answer different sets of questions. One reason is that there are also common elements. They both stressed that philosophy should be conceived not as a spiritual system, but as a particular practice of philosophy. They both insisted on the close links between philosophy, ideology, and politics and the deeply political character of philosophical debates and confrontations. They both linked philosophy to a particular conception of intellectuality of politics (exemplified in Althusser's insistence that philosophy represents scientificity in politics[72]).

Both Gramsci and Althusser shared the same apprehension of the historical and political dynamics traversing theory in general and also of the historical and political effectivity of theory in its articulation to social and political movements and dynamics. In particular, they both paid attention to the dialectical relation between ideology and theory and how mass ideologies can be transformed and at the same time how the social dynamics and aspirations associated with the political struggles of the subaltern classes can transform theories. Both Gramsci and Althusser had the same apprehension that philosophy is the crucial theoretical terrain for the emergence between this dialectic of theory, ideology, and politics. They both understood that philo-

---

71   Althusser 1976a, p. 72.
72   Althusser 1971, p. 65.

sophy is a sort of a laboratory of new ideas, metaphors, notions, conceptual frameworks, and that it is within philosophy that new ideas and theories can be forged and adjusted according to the exigencies and dynamics of the historical conjuncture. And they were both fully aware of the role of philosophy in the formation and elaboration of hegemony, in the sense that it is within philosophy where the ideologies and worldviews of potentially hegemonic classes are transformed into theory and strategic ideology. At the same time, they both realised that the philosophical practice for a new potential proletarian hegemony cannot be symmetrical to an idealist philosophical system, since the traditional philosophical form is determined not only by idealism but also by its relation to dominant ideologies and the reproduction of relations of domination and exploitation. In this sense, and despite Althusser's repeated opposition between his call for a new practice of philosophy and Gramsci's philosophy of praxis, both Althusser's insistence on a new practice, a new way to intervene in philosophy, and Gramsci's quest for a new and original philosophy of praxis, immanence, and historicity are referring to the same challenge.

Moreover, it is also important to stress certain affinities between Gramsci's notion of praxis (and its origins in Marx's reference to '*revolutionäre Praxis*') and Althusser's references to the centrality of practices. Especially in the *Initiation to Philosophy* Althusser articulates his argument about the role of philosophy through references to the centrality of practices, the fact that wherever there are practices one can also see 'abstractions', namely relations that determine concrete social practices, and the role of philosophy in dealing with abstractions. For Althusser, the particular role of philosophy has exactly to do with the encounter between science, class politics, and ideology and also with the reflection in theoretical terms of this relational 'abstract' character of social relations. Wherever there are practices, one can find social relations that determine them, relations that represent the 'abstract' aspect of reality, the relations that in their reproduction lead to the reproduction of these concrete 'singular' practices. And wherever there are these abstractions one can see theories and ideologies, in the last instances determined by social struggles and antagonisms, and this can account for the constant re-emergence of philosophy as a specific form of theoretical practice, as a battlefield for hegemony. And this intervention in theory and the balance of forces within ideology and science, this struggle of words against words, this forging of new metaphors and new concepts, this form of collective theoretical creativity (another common trait of Gramsci and Althusser is this emphasis on the creative character of philosophical interventions) is itself a practice, as Althusser himself admits when he refers to the Aristotelian distinction between *poiësis* and *praxis*, a form of praxis, namely the 'identity of the transformation of the object (the balance of power) and the subject (the organized revolutionary class)'.[73]

The other reason is that we can see both positions as useful in any attempt to rethink Marxist philosophy as militant materialist practice of philosophy. I think that some of Althusser's questions concerning the theoretical status of Marxist theory, especially his insistence that a potentially *scientific* theory of history cannot be articulated in traditional philosophical terms, but needs a novel theoretical apparatus, are still of value, despite Althusser's own shortcomings in answering them. I am not suggesting a return to Althusser's early scientism and his idealised conception of science as rigidly separated from ideology, which is in fact a reprise of the idealist distinction between truth and falsity. Nor do I suggest that we must think critical social theory only in terms of an 'ideal type' of science, or treat all forms of philosophically inspired social theorising as some form of non-theory. However, I insist that Marxist theory of history represents a theoretical modality that is different from traditional philosophy, requires a different conception of theory and a strong claim to the intelligibility of social reality as at the same time 'historical-practical' and 'objective', even though any actual attempt at such theorising would be necessarily uneven and inherently contradictory. As a result, Gramsci's effort to rethink a radically novel *historical* materialism through the vocabulary of classical Marxism and historicist philosophy, as well as his insight that post-Renaissance philosophy has to be studied as the theoretical expression of a more general historical movement, need to be considered as *starting points* rather than definitive answers.

And indeed I think that today, faced with the limits (as well as the importance and insights) of much of current post-historicist and post-humanist radical theorising with its refusal of any claims to scientificity and its return to a more philosophical drawing of lines of demarcation, we still need to elaborate and produce an adequate conceptual apparatus for a Marxist theory that would be at the same time historical, critical, and reflexive, but also with a strong claim at producing some sort of 'knowledge effect'. In this effort it is obvious that Marxist philosophy can indeed play an important role, not as the guarantor of scientificity or as a simple deconstructing of idealist tendencies, but rather as a crucial theoretical laboratory. And to deal with this challenge we need both Althusser's warnings against the inherent idealism of philosophical elaborations as well as Gramsci's insight that philosophy still has a positive role to play in the development of Marxist theory.

---

73   Althusser 2017a, p. 141.

Consequently, philosophy is both unavoidable (the contradictions emerging at the intersection of science, ideology, and class struggle necessarily take a specifically philosophical form[74]) and necessary: we need a new materialist and historical practice of philosophy as a theoretical laboratory as a way to forge not only new concepts but also new forms of mass critical political intellectuality. And we need philosophy in order to be able to experiment with new ways of thinking precisely in order to be able to think about how to experiment with new social forms and relations, new practices and terrains of experimentation. We need a philosophy for communism.

74 As Balibar has noted: '*every practice is philosophical*, or, to put it another way, there is philosophy *everywhere*, that is, in every practice' (1994a, p. 173).

PART 3

Is There an Althusserian Politics?

CHAPTER 15

Althusser 1960–65: Attempting a Theoretical Correction of a Political Strategy in Crisis

In one of his most famous quotes, Louis Althusser insisted that there can be no Hegelian politics.[1] Althusser linked this to his reading of Hegel as presenting an image of social reality that leads to the homogenous presence of all the determinations of the whole with the essence that makes the present the '*absolute horizon*'[2] of knowing, leaving no space for thinking the future and its specific dynamics. This was part of a broader critique by Althusser of what he saw as the inherent idealism of Hegelian philosophy. In general, Althusser was aiming at a critique of the Hegelian dialectic and what he described as an expressive conception of social totality, where all development is at the level of the economy as social essence with politics and ideology being simple surface phenomena or expressions of deeper tendencies. Such a conception of the dialectic of social totality could only lead either to an economistic emphasis on inexorable economic laws leading to the decline and collapse of capitalism or to a historicist emphasis on the proletarian will as the social subject (or the subject/object unity) that forms this substance. In such a conception there is no room for politics as an active and transformative intervention, except for some form of conformity with historical laws and tendencies (the classical deterministic conception of the Second International), or of identification of spontaneous beliefs with historical tendencies.[3] Contrary to this conception,

---

1 'And that is why the ontological category of the present prevents any anticipation of historical time, any conscious anticipation of the future development of the concept, any *knowledge* of the *future*. [...] The fact that there is no knowing the future prevents there being any science of politics, any knowing that deals with the future effects of present phenomena. That is why no Hegelian politics is possible strictly speaking, and in fact there has never been a Hegelian politician' (Althusser et al. 2016, p. 242).

2 Ibid.

3 'Paradoxical as this conclusion may seem – and I shall doubtless be attacked for expressing it – it must be drawn: from the standpoint of its *theoretical problematic*, and not of its political style and aims, this humanist and historicist materialism has rediscovered the basic theoretical principles of the Second International's economistic and mechanistic interpretation. If this single theoretical problematic can underlie policies of different inspiration, one fatalist, the other voluntarist, one passive, the other conscious and active – it is because of the scope for theoretical *"play"* contained in this ideological theoretical problematic as in every ideology. In this case, this kind of historicism can be opposed politically to the theses of the Second

Althusser insisted that only a more open conception of determination and causality within the social whole can make room for politics. Particularly, it can make room for that kind of contradiction and conflict that destabilises social totality, alters the relation of forces and opens a crucial space for radical political intervention. Althusser's theorisation of overdetermination, of the relative autonomy of the political and ideological instances, and of the conjuncture as a singular condensation of contradictions[4] aims at grounding exactly this possibility of politics.

But the question is: did Althusser manage to offer a conception of Althusserian politics? To answer this, we must look at Althusser's own political interventions, strategies and suggestions, but also what we can deduce, as political recommendation, from his own writings.

1 Althusser's Political Engagement

The story of Althusser's own political engagement is well known. A devout Catholic he found himself engaged in the Catholic Left after WWII, during which he had the experience of a POW camp.[5] Althusser maintained an interest in Catholic politics, even after he had formally joined the French Communist Party.[6] Even in 1949 he would still insist that: '[a]*lthough the objective conditions for a social emancipation of the Church through the proletarian struggle already exist, the conditions for a collective reconquest of religious life have not been created* [...] *The future of the Church depends on the number and the courage of those Christians who, day by day, are developing an awareness of the necessity of struggle*'.[7] Althusser accused the Church of being supportive of reactionary governments, of being overly influenced by the bourgeois strata that were turning towards it and of being dominated by conservative ideological and philo-

---

    International by conferring on the infrastructure the most active qualities of the political and ideological superstructure, in a compensating crossed connection. This transfer of qualities can be conceived in different ways: e.g., by endowing political practice with the qualities of philosophy and theory (spontaneism); by attributing to economic practice all the active and even explosive virtues of politics (anarcho-syndicalism); or by entrusting to political consciousness and determination the determinism of the economic (voluntarism)' (Althusser et al. 2016, p. 289).

4 'Are we not always in exceptional situations?' (Althusser 1969, p. 104).
5 Althusser 1993b; Moulier-Boutang 2002.
6 See Althusser's writings on matters of the Church in Althusser 1997a.
7 Althusser 1997c, p. 195.

sophical currents.[8] In a way, the Church was accused by Althusser, in the same manner as the PCF 30 years later, of being an institution unable to come into contact with, represent, and fulfil the expectations of the masses of the faithful in a situation of social and political polarisation.

He finally found himself in the Communist Party, which he formally entered in 1948, a political engagement he described in the introduction to *For Marx* as the only possible choice:

> History: it had stolen our youth with the Popular Front and the Spanish Civil War, and in the War as such it had imprinted in us the terrible education of deeds. It surprised us just as we entered the world, and turned us students of bourgeois or petty bourgeois origin into men advised of the existence of classes, of their struggles and aims. From the evidence it forced on us we drew the only possible conclusion, and rallied to the political organization of the working class, the Communist Party.[9]

Until the theoretical and political debates that his texts triggered in the early 1960s, there is little evidence that he openly criticised the political line of the Party and the international communist movement,[10] although he had an experience of the workings of bureaucratic power within the PCF through his attempts to reinstate his companion, Helen Rytmann in the Party.[11] He considered the Communist Party to be the main political formation of the working class and that there can be no revolutionary politics outside the Party. Althusser's more open political intervention begins with his entrance onto the stage of postwar Marxist debate with his early 1960s texts.

Consequently, Althusser's terrain of political intervention was to be the French Communist Party. Especially in the 1950s and 1960s French Communism was Althusser's basic reference point with the exception of his interest in the developments within Italian Communism. Retracing and evaluating the historical trajectory of French Communism is beyond the scope of this book, yet it is important to stress some points. The politics of the PCF that formed the

---

8   Althusser 1997c, pp. 185–96.
9   Althusser 1969, p. 21.
10 In most instances, especially in the early phase of his membership in the Party, he seemed rather loyal to the official positions, exemplified in his support for the 'official' narrative on the Stalinist purges such as the Rajk Trial (Althusser 1997c, p. 202).
11 A militant in the Party from the 1930s and active in the Resistance, Hélène Rytmann was the victim of various accusations and was not accepted back into the Party after the war. Althusser made a great effort to have her name cleared. See the detailed account in Moulier-Boutang 2002.

background of Althusser's initial philosophical engagement and also the starting point of his theoretical and political interventions in the 1960s represented an explosively contradictory combination of the potential of the communist movement in its mass appeal to the working class and other subaltern strata and of the strategic deficiencies of postwar communist reformism.

Emerging out of the Resistance having captured the moral and political high ground in contrast to the collective guilt of 'collaboration' in the Vichy regime and having managed to expand the appeal of the Popular Front period, the PCF was in reality representing a dynamic that could initiate a political process with a revolutionary potential. Yet following the basic line of USSR foreign policy, it opted for a strategy of national unity government and respect for parliamentary procedure that, after a brief participation in government, led it to the forced withdrawal into opposition and a missed opportunity of a broader revolutionary rupture in Western Europe.[12] The inability of the PCF leadership to articulate a political strategy in the 1950s that could make the Communist movement the catalyst for a broader hegemonic bloc, a strategy that could be substituted neither by the logic of the party as tribune of the grievances and aspirations of the subaltern classes,[13] nor by the debates on the terms of a potential alliance with the Socialists, opened up the political space for De Gaulle to make an impressive come-back, incorporate some elements of the rhetoric of the Left, such as the emphasis on an independent foreign policy and set the terms of the political debate. This led in the early 1960s to an even greater strategic unease on the part of the leadership of the PCF, despite the improvement of the electoral results and the organisational expansion. It is exactly this period and the urgent need to mount a credible challenge to De Gaulle's dominant role in the political scene that led to the renewed emphasis on the dialogue with non-Communist forces (from Socialists to progressive Christians) and finally to the choice of supporting a socialist, François Mitterrand, as common candidate of the Left in the 1965 presidential election.[14] The same year that Althusser rose to prominence after the publication of *For Marx* and *Reading Capital* is also the year that the leadership of PCF opted for the support of the candidate who 16 years later brought the French Left to power but also initiated the open crisis of the French Communist movement.

Of particular importance was the emphasis given by the French Communist Party to the question of culture and intellectuals. It was considered to be not only an important front for the Party to exercise its influence, but also

---

12   Claudin 1975.
13   On the notion of the party as tribune see di Maggio 2009.
14   On the politics of the PCF in the 1950s and 1960s see Raymond 2005.

one of the terrains where the Party could forge broader alliances, something that could account for the seemingly disproportional impact of intellectual and even philosophical debates inside the PCF, exemplified in the debates around Althusser's interventions. Moreover, this led to an increasing importance of the Party's student sectors, with the debates inside the UEC (Union of Communist Students), the various tendencies emerging (from the 'Italians' to Althusser's Maoist disciples and the Trotskyists), and the interventions of the Party leadership forming an important part of the background of Althusser's interventions in the 1960–65 period.[15]

The polarisations that Althusser refers to in the preface to *For Marx* and the need to make choices were real, exemplified in the various major confrontations that marked France in the 1940s and 1950s from various forms of anticommunism, the rehabilitation of important segments of the Vichy collaborators and the establishment of workplace discipline in industry to the struggles against French colonial rule. Choosing sides in various instances, as Althusser himself did, was indeed a forced choice. However, in a certain way, the PCF of the first half of the 1960s was a party that could see at the same time its influence rise, attracting larger segments of the population and having an impressive appeal in intellectual circles, and establishing its role as a main force of opposition to Gaullism both on the political scene but also in the streets, and at the same time finding it even more difficult to affect the course of events especially in response to De Gaulle's authoritarian leanings and his ability to maintain leadership of a broader alliance of bourgeois and traditional petty bourgeois strata. Yet it was a political party that was growing bigger, attracting large segments of the youth and creating not just a political movement but an entire social milieu with a distinct and common identity, a society within society, from the red suburbs around Paris to the rising fame of communist writers, actors and intellectuals.

The beginning of the 1960s was an important period of open rifts in the international communist movement. If the opposition of minorities of communist intellectuals to the Soviet invasion of Hungary in 1956 marked an important turning point, it did not seem to halt the organisational expansion of West European Communism. In contrast, the open split between the USSR and China seemed like a rupture of much greater proportions.[16] Coming at a period of intensified anti-colonial and anti-imperialist struggles, exemplified in the victories in Vietnam and Cuba, the fact that China, itself the biggest

---

15   On the PCF's politics regarding intellectuals and the divisions inside the UEC see di Maggio 2013. On the evolution of the PCF's relation to Marxism see Lewis 2005.
16   On the Soviet-Chinese rift see Communist Party of China 1965.

example of the possibility of a new revolutionary wave in the 'Third World', openly accused the Soviet Union of opting for a conciliatory strategy of cooperation with the imperialist camp, resonated with the aspirations of many militants, even if at that period, before the Cultural Revolution, the Chinese 'difference' mainly took the form of the defence of a more aggressive stance against the West and of a refusal to fully accept the post-1956 repudiation of Stalinism.

Next to France, the Italian Communist Party seemed to offer an alternative to Soviet or Soviet-inspired orthodoxy without openly challenging the leadership of the Soviet Union. Itself the result of a conscious choice to avoid a direct confrontation with the bourgeois forces after the Liberation and with an impressive rooting in Italian society, Italian Communism, with its more open political and theoretical dialogue and a more sophisticated and elaborated approach towards a democratic and peaceful road to socialism, seemed to offer an alternative especially in the early 1960s.[17] For Althusser, Italy also presented an example of a country with a more open communist culture and a richer Marxist theoretical debate.

This insistence on the importance of the developments inside the 'official' communist movement in relation to Althusser's interventions does not underestimate the importance of other forms and currents of communist and socialist dissidence, either from the tradition of the Fourth International or other currents. Later developments stressed the importance of groups like *Socialisme ou Barbarie*,[18] yet for someone like Althusser these seemed perhaps marginal in relation to the communist movement. At the same time, France seemed to lack the emergence of currents such as early Operaismo in Italy which coming from the trade-union Left could at the same time maintain a dialogue with the Communist intelligentsia, although the postwar French theoretical explosion in the humanities and philosophy indeed offered, at a different level, the possibility of a different dialogue.

It is inside this political and ideological climate that we must place Althusser's intervention in order to account for its political character and how, from the start and despite the absence of more open references to questions of political strategy, it was a political endeavour, a philosophical work towards a political correction.

---

17   On the evolution of postwar Italian Communism see Rossanda 2010 and Magri 2011.
18   Castoriadis 1988a; 1988b; Hastings-King 2014.

2 The Politics of the 1960–65 Texts

What is the conception of revolutionary politics offered in Althusser's early writings? Here we must make a distinction between three different aspects: (1) Althusser's own political positions at that time; (2) his theoretical conception of politics; and (3) Althusser's theoretical and political strategy at that time.

Regarding Althusser's own political positions, although there are few explicit references to his published texts in the early 1960s, it is obvious that he was critical of the dominant line within the international communist movement of that time. This is particularly evident in his criticism of the 'humanist' turn in Marxist theoretical circles. In the first paragraphs of the 1961 article 'On the Young Marx', Althusser warns about the dangers associated with the turn towards Marxist Humanism:

> First of all, any discussion of Marx's Early Works is a *political* discussion. Need we be reminded that Marx's Early Works, whose history and significance were well enough described by Mehring, were exhumed by Social-Democrats and exploited by them to the detriment of Marxism-Leninism?[19]

This is even more evident in the 1963–64 article on 'Marxist and Humanism', where the debate on Humanism is clearly linked to the contradictions of the process of socialist construction and of the fight for communism, even though Althusser tactically accepts the official line of the USSR that it is a socialist country *en route* to overcoming the dictatorship of the proletariat towards communism. 'Humanism' in these texts is in many cases not only the description of a theoretical deviation, but also a metonymic reference to the contradictions and the right-wing turn of the communist movement. In the introduction to *For Marx*, written in early 1965, a political position is more clearly spelled out, albeit still in a rather ambiguous form. According to Althusser, the problem facing communist philosophers and intellectuals was how to deal with the heavy burden of Stalinism, both theoretically and politically. However, the precise nature and contradictions of Stalinism is not offered, apart from the insistence on the disastrous consequences of the 'leftist' conception of a 'proletarian science'.[20]

---

19   Althusser 1969, p. 51.
20   Althusser 1969, p. 23. As William Lewis has stressed: 'Although before 1965 Althusser never really criticizes the Communist Party directly, this intervention can be recognized as an attempt to suggest to the party that its Stalinism is a deeper tendency than it might be

In a way, what we can retroactively reconstruct as Althusser's political position in the early 1960s, based also on his subsequent self-critical references, is the apprehension that the main bulk of the political answers to Stalinism offered in the post-1956 period within the international communist movement was a *right-wing* answer, in terms of theory, strategy and tactics (especially *alliance* tactics). The following passage from the 'Preface for my English Readers' in *For Marx* summarises this position:

> If this ideological reaction, characteristic above all of Communist intellectuals, has, despite some resistance, been capable of such a development, it is because it has benefited from the direct or indirect support of certain *political* slogans laid down by the Communist Parties of the U.S.S.R. and the West. On one side, for example, the Twenty-second Congress of the C.P.S.U. declared that with the disappearance of the class struggle, the dictatorship of the proletariat had been 'superseded' in the U.S.S.R., that the Soviet State is no longer a class State but the 'State of the Whole People'; and that the U.S.S.R. has embarked on the 'construction of communism', guided by the 'humanist' slogan, 'Everything for Man'. On the other, for example, Western Communist Parties have pursued policies of unity with socialists, democrats and Catholics, guided by certain slogans of related resonance, in which the accent is put on the 'peaceful transition to socialism', on 'Marxist' or 'socialist humanism', on 'dialogue', etc.[21]

This is a position that obviously searches for a left-wing answer to Stalinism. This can explain why, for Althusser and the small group of communist students that were attracted to his positions, the initial political strategy was to counter the right-wing tendencies, especially those that openly called for a turn towards a peaceful democratic road to socialism – the various 'Italian' fractions in Western communist parties that took their inspiration from the PCI politics of that time – without falling back into some sort of Stalinist orthodoxy.[22]

Althusser follows a rather classic Marxist tradition in insisting that revolutionary politics must be based on a scientific knowledge of the terrain of social

---

willing to admit and that some of its most fundamental assumptions about what Marxism is need to be questioned in order to purge Party theory and practice of these residues' (Lewis 2005, p. 165).

21   Althusser 1969, p. 11.
22   For a description and criticism of Althusser and his circle in the early 1960s see Rancière 2011.

struggle. Marxist theory, as historical materialism, is a scientific theory with claims to objectivity. A revolutionary movement cannot be victorious without this kind of objective knowledge of social dynamics. This is at the basis of Althusser's insistence on the *scientific* character of Marxist theory, his full acceptance of the position that only through a correct and scientifically valid Marxist theory do we have the possibility of a correct political strategy and tactics and of course his opting for a strategy of theoretically (and in the last instance *philosophically*) correcting the political line of the communist movement, to which we will return later. In a 1965 manuscript entitled 'Theory, Theoretical Practice and Theoretical Formation: Ideology and Ideological Struggle', he summarised this position:

> Marxist doctrine, by contrast, is *scientific*. This means that it is not content to apply existing bourgeois moral and juridical principles (liberty, equality, fraternity, justice, etc.) to the existing bourgeois reality in order to criticize it, but that it criticizes these existing bourgeois moral and juridical principles, as well as the existing politico-economic system. [...] It rests on the knowledge of this ensemble, which constitutes an organic totality of which the economic, political, and ideological are organic 'levels' or 'instances', articulated with each other according to specific laws. It is this *knowledge* that allows us to define the objectives of socialism, and to conceive socialism as a new determinate mode of production which will succeed the capitalist mode of production [...] It is this knowledge that permits us to define the appropriate *means of action* for 'making the revolution', means based upon the nature of historical necessity and historical development, on the determinant role of the economy in the last instance on this development, on the decisive role of class struggle in socioeconomic transformations, and on the role of consciousness and organization in political struggle [...] It is the application of these scientific principles that has allowed the definition of a revolutionary tactics and strategy whose irreversible first results are henceforth inscribed in world history, and continue to change the world.[23]

On the other hand, another question seems to haunt these early texts, especially the texts on the Marxist dialectic. Although presented in terms or searching for the break between Hegelian and Marxist conceptions of the dialectic, it is also a search for a theory and dialectic that would bridge the gap between

---

23 Althusser 1990, p. 4.

abstract theory and political practices, and bring forward a Marxist theory (and dialectic) of the dynamic of singular historical moments and conjunctures. This creates a tension in the very concept of scientific knowledge that was supposed to condition politics, since it is dealing not only with knowledge of general 'abstract' tendencies, but also with specific social and political dynamics within the historical moment. That is when the notion of the conjuncture enters the stage. Politics for Althusser, in the sense of political intervention, has mainly to do with the dynamics of the conjuncture as a singular condensation of contradictions in complex forms of determination, overdetermination and underdetermination.[24] Politics, especially revolutionary, transformative politics, has to do not with the direct manifestation of structural tendencies – although it seems that these can account for the formation of opposing social classes and the delineation of the main forms of social antagonism – but with the much more complex determination of the specific historical moment. It is exactly the conjuncture that offers the conceptual possibility of politics as transformative intervention. Consequently, revolutionary politics, have not to do with simply enhancing objective structural tendencies, nor with a voluntarist intervention in contrast to these tendencies; it has to do with the unevenness, exceptionality and singularity of the conjuncture, the possibilities for action opened through the interplay of contradictions, the potential to reach crucial tipping points. Although the working-class movement is the result of structural tendencies of the capitalist mode of production, the possibility of action emerges at the level of the conjuncture.[25]

---

24 'How is it possible, theoretically, to sustain the validity of this basic Marxist proposition: "*the class struggle is the motor of history*", that is sustain theoretically the thesis that it is by *political* struggle that it is possible to "*dissolve the existing unity*", when we know very well that it is not politics but the economy that is determinant in the last instance? How, other than with the reality of the complex process with structure in dominance, could we explain theoretically the real difference between the economic and the political in the class struggle itself, that is, to be exact, the real difference between the economic struggle and the political struggle, a difference that will always distinguish Marxism from any spontaneous or organized form of opportunism? How could we explain our necessity to go through the distinct and specific level of *political* struggle if the latter, although distinct, and because it is distinct, were the simple phenomenon and not the real *condensation*, the nodal strategic point, in which *is reflected the complex whole* (economic, political and ideological)? How, finally, could we explain the fact that the Necessity of History itself thus goes in decisive fashion through *political practice*, if the structure of contradiction did not make this practice possible in its concrete reality? How could we explain the fact that even Marx's theory which made this necessity comprehensible to us could have been *produced* if the structure of contradiction did not make the concrete reality of this production possible?' (Althusser 1969, p. 215).

25 On Althusser and political practice see Lahtinen 2009.

This is a very interesting theory of *political practice and action* in Althusser's early texts. Of course, there are also many questions left unanswered. Although Althusser offers an image of a politics of the conjuncture – and *in* the conjuncture – and especially the revolutionary conjuncture, the revolutionary moment, the question of the political organisation of the working class, of the collective subject of this intervention and transformative practice is dealt with in very classical terms: the working class and its Party. One can say that this was an obvious tactical choice on the part of Althusser. Since he thought that there could be no politics outside the Communist Party and its relations with the working class, he could not offer some other conception of politics. However, taking the Party as granted limited Althusser's conception of both the extent of the crisis of the communist movement and of the potential answers to this crisis. Therefore, he opted for a strategy of theoretical correction of a strategic crisis, based on a theoretical and philosophical reconstruction of Marx's own theoretical authority. In the words of Jacques Rancière:

> Althusser's theoretical and political project, the one that begun with the publication of 'On the Young Marx' in 1961, is staked on the bet that it is possible to effect a *political* transformation inside the Communist Party through a theoretical investigation aimed at restoring Marx's thought.[26]

This is also based on a classical Marxist conception of politics based on objective scientific knowledge. This leads to a conception of the correct political line as the result of a scientific reading of objective social determinations. This makes theory the crucial point and explains Althusser's emphasis on Marxist philosophy as a Theory of theoretical practice. If theory is the most crucial determinant with regard to revolutionary politics, then a philosophical practice that can offer a guarantee of scientificity is the main vector of a political correction. In this sense, Althusser's early political strategy ends up being mainly a philosophical strategy. If the political line is determined by scientific knowledge of the terrain of struggle, and in turn this scientific knowledge is conditional upon a philosophical practice that is close to a science of sciences, then philosophy becomes the main determinant factor in this process of political correction. But by doing this we are abandoning the image of a politics of the conjuncture articulated around the intervention in complex ensembles of political and social dynamics and mutual determination, and opting instead for a rationalist even neo-platonic emphasis on philosophy determining politics.

---

26   Rancière 2011, p. 24.

And this conception of theory (and scientific philosophy determining politics) is the core contradiction of the initial Althusserian move which is also enhanced by Althusser's ambivalence regarding the relation between structure and conjuncture. A certain over-emphasis on 'deep structures' as hidden scripts for social reality also helps this conception of philosophical and theoretical politics.[27]

This does not mean that Althusser's theoretical intervention did not have political motivations.[28] As noted above, of particular importance was his criticism of Marxist humanism (and humanist Marxism), since it targeted not only a theoretical turn but also the reformist-electoralist turn of the PCF leadership, who, keen on creating an electoral alliance for a left-wing government with the Socialists and progressive Catholics, openly used humanist overtones as proof of its readiness to move in such a direction. This was also evident in the tone many opponents to Althusser adopted within the intra-Party debate. Althusser was accused of undermining through his anti-humanist intervention the Party's line for a broad progressive alliance. However, we are still within the limits of a politics of theory and within theory, and of debates that remained restricted to Party intellectuals and students, not to the broader base of the party and its militants. In this sense, although G.M. Goshgarian is right to insist that Althusser's intervention was 'a call to break the Stalinist-humanist stranglehold on the Party's intellectual life',[29] at the same time this represented the limits of his initial intervention, his inability to think in terms of a unity of theory and practice.

Althusser at that time was thinking indeed in terms of being part of a group that would attempt to alter the theoretical and political balance of forces within the PCF. That is why he treats the small group of students that were gathered around him as some form of theoretical and political vanguard within the Party. In a letter to Franca Madonia he even refers to them as his 'theoretical shock troopers'.[30]

---

27 See for example the references to the 'latent structure of the whole' in the first edition of *Lire le Capital*, which were omitted from subsequent editions (Althusser et al. 1996, p. 646).

28 In 1975, in 'Is it Simple to be a Marxist in Philosophy?', he referred to the political character of his 1960s interventions as follows: 'this philosophical intervention was the work of a member of the Communist Party, acting – even if I was at first isolated, even if I was not always listened to, even if I was then and still am criticized for what I said – within the Labour Movement and for it, thus the work of a militant trying to take politics seriously in order to think out its conditions, limits and effects within theory itself, trying in consequence to define the line and forms of intervention' (Althusser 1976a, p. 169).

29 Goshgarian 2003, p. xxviii.

30 Althusser 1997b, p. 583.

3   The Debate on 'Student Problems'

In light of the above we can revisit the debate on Althusser's text regarding student problems. In 1964, Louis Althusser made an intervention in *Nouvelle Critique* that was to become notorious mainly because of Jacques Rancière's subsequent attack some years later. It was an intervention in the debates in the UEC (Union of Communist Students) regarding the demands of students. In the early 1960s important segments of the UEC openly called for 'transformations of the institutional and pedagogical function of the university',[31] including new forms of organisation of the courses, searching for alternatives to exams, etc. Here is how Rancière described these initiatives:

> These initiatives, for the most part the work of the UEC's 'syndicalist left', drew attention to the following topics: the ends of academic knowledge, which seemed to be to educate future auxiliaries of the bourgeoisie; the forms for the transmission of knowledge – the 'pedagogic relation' – tied to this objective (lecture courses which inured students to being docile); individualism (which the UNEF had opposed with its proposal for research groups, the GTUs); and the arbitrary nature of exams. Students saw their overall situation within the university through the categories of student alienation and dependence (the financial dependence on the family, compounded by the pedagogical dependence on professors). And it was to offset this situation of assistance that the students demanded *student wages*, a demand that clashed with the PCF's advocacy of scholarships for underprivileged students.[32]

Althusser's opposition to these demands was based on the distinction between the technical and the social division of labour, the need not to underestimate technical aspects of the social division, and consequently the need to support 'traditional' university liberalism as opposed to modern technocracy. In his own words 'university liberalism is today a real *political value* in the struggle against the transformation of the educational organization into an instrument subject to the objectives of the ruling technocracy – that is, to the objectives of the monopolistic bourgeoisie'.[33] To violate these traditions would be a 'political mistake'[34] for Althusser. Moreover, he insists that we cannot avoid

---

31   Brown 2011, p. 18.
32   Rancière 2011.
33   Althusser [1964] 2011, p. 12.
34   Ibid.

the fact that 'the pedagogic situation is based on the absolute condition of an *inequality between a knowledge and a lack of knowledge*',[35] and that is why he opposes demands of a pedagogic equality between teachers and students. For Althusser, such demands, however democratic they might sound, end up in 'half-knowledge'. In contrast, the *'revolutionary cause* is always indissolubly linked with knowledge, in other words *science*'.[36] It is obvious that Althusser remains within the limits of his initial strict distinction between science and ideology and within his strategy of a theoretical correction of political deviations. He fears that any attack on knowledge and science, even in the name of radical positions, undermined his strategy of a correction of a political line through theoretical and scientific rigour, and he opposed any notion of a primacy of politics over science. However, by doing this Althusser contradicts his own political strategy by negating a priori any possibility of direct political intervention. What is surprising, however, is how he identifies the question of revolutionary theory with the technical division of labour and with the strict limits of a bourgeois hegemonic institution like the university.

35   Althusser [1964] 2011, p. 14.
36   Althusser [1964] 2011, p. 15.

CHAPTER 16

The Politics of Theoretical Anti-humanism

Of all the elements of Althusser's initial intervention, theoretical anti-humanism was the more openly political, since socialist humanist overtones had been a cornerstone of Communist politics in the conjuncture after the 20th Congress of the CPSU and were linked to a line of alliance with progressive forces, including socialists and Catholics. Although in reality this 'frontist' and electoralist strategy was ridden with contradictions and was far from answering the open questions for a revolutionary strategy in the West, at that time this entrance into national politics and the possibility of toppling bourgeois governments, along with electoral advances and the entrance of a mass of new militants to the Party – in reality a result of the growing 1960s militancy and radicalism – seemed to provide ample justifications for this strategy.[1] Such a strategy was dominant in most Western communist parties. As the leadership of the *Il Manifesto* group in Italy commented in what was perhaps the most coherent strategic document of the 1968 Left, the *200 Theses on Communism*, this line could combine a mainly parliamentary political practice, a trade-unionist line in the movement and an emphasis on alliances with classical Third International forms of organisation and support for Soviet foreign policy.[2]

1　Theoretical Anti-humanism as a Theoretical and Political Strategy

Althusser was well aware of the political consequences and dimensions of the debate on humanism. This is evident in the 1967 English preface to *For Marx* where the turn towards socialist humanism is presented as an important aspect of the theoretical and political conjuncture and is linked to the developments after the 20th Congress of the CPSU.[3] Although political considerations

---

1　For a criticism of the politics of the PCF in that period see Goshgarian 2003.
2　*Il Manifesto* 1970, p. 6.
3　'The critique of Stalinist "dogmatism" was generally "lived" by Communist intellectuals as a "liberation". This "liberation" gave birth to a profound ideological reaction, "liberal" and "ethical" in tendency, which spontaneously rediscovered the old philosophical themes of "freedom", "man", the "human person" and "alienation". This ideological tendency looked for theoretical justification to Marx's Early Works, which do indeed contain all the arguments of a philosophy of man, his alienation and liberation. These conditions have paradoxically turned the tables in Marxist philosophy. Since the 1930s Marx's Early Works have been a war-

alone cannot fully account for the theoretical displacement towards socialist humanism, since they also had to do with the theoretical modalities of modern humanism as a more general theoretical tendency, they nevertheless played their role.

Theoretical anti-humanism has been one the most controversial aspects of Althusser's theoretical endeavour.[4] In a certain way it resonated with a broader theoretical climate exemplified in Lévi-Strauss's dialogue with Sartre,[5] in Foucault's declaration of the death of man as a theoretical category,[6] and Derrida's famous lecture on the 'Ends of Man'.[7] It was also, theoretically and politically, a crucial cornerstone of Althusser's attempt at a theoretical correction of what he perceived as the crisis in the political strategy of the PCF and the international communist movement in general.[8] It was also an aspect of his theoretical work that was from the beginning perceived as politically contentious. The attacks he earned, the wide discussion of his interventions and the fact that the session of the CC of the PCF in Argenteuil in 1966[9] was mainly preoccupied with the question of theoretical humanism and anti-humanism provide ample evidence of the extent of the debate. Although today, after many years of widespread acceptance in academic circles of postmodern theories reproducing some form of theoretical anti-humanism, the bitterness of the debates might seem out of

---

horse for petty bourgeois intellectuals in their struggle against Marxism; but little by little, and then massively, they have been set to work in the interests of a new "interpretation" of Marxism which is today being openly developed by many Communist intellectuals, "liberated" from Stalinist dogmatism by the Twentieth Congress. The themes of "Marxist Humanism" and the "humanist" interpretation of Marx's work have progressively and irresistibly imposed themselves on recent Marxist philosophy, even inside Soviet and Western Communist Parties' (Althusser 1969, pp. 10–11).

4 E.P. Thompson (1995) offered one of the harshest criticisms of Althusser, although it was basically based upon a misapprehension of Althusser's work. Norman Geras (1977; 1983) attempted to defend the core of a humanist-anthropological conception of human nature as a response to theoretical anti-humanism. Paul Ricœur (1986) attempted to criticise Althusser's conception of the break and consequently his underestimation of human praxis.
5 Lévi-Strauss 1966. On the importance of Lévi-Strauss in that particular theoretical conjuncture see Keck 2011, Franchi 2011, Montag 2013.
6 Foucault 2002.
7 In Derrida 1982.
8 On the political character of Althusser's confrontation with theoretical and in particular Marxist humanism, see Benton 1984 and Elliott 2006. On the relation between Althusser's theoretical anti-humanism and the anti-psychologism of his reading of Lacanian psychoanalysis, see Gillot 2009.
9 The interventions were published in the *Cahiers du Communisme* – the theoretical review of the Central Committee of the French Communist Party. On this see also Althusser 2003, pp. 222–7; Geerlandt 1978; Di Maggio 2013.

hand, nevertheless at that time it was perceived as a challenge to the core of the political appeal of the communist movement.

Althusser insisted that theoretical humanism was 'idealist' and alien to Marx's mature work. In 1960, in the text on Feuerbach, Althusser insisted that 'all the expressions of Marx's idealist "humanism" are Feuerbachian'.[10] In the 1962 text on Marx's *1844 Manuscripts* he referred to concepts such as humanism, alienation, social essence of man as examples of a problematic that was later abandoned.[11] But in most of the texts of 1960–63 the references to theoretical humanism have more to do with Althusser's attempt to theorise the 'break' than with actually dealing with the question of humanism.

It was the 1963 text on 'Marxism and Humanism' that opened the controversy, beginning with Erich Fromm's decision not to include the text in his collection of texts on humanism, despite the fact that he had actually commissioned the text.[12] Althusser from the beginning thought of this intervention as not just a theoretical elaboration but also as an intervention in the political and theoretical conjuncture. This is made evident by the initial phrase: 'Today, Socialist "Humanism" is on the agenda'.[13] Althusser attributes this to the evolution of the construction of socialism. He seems as if he is fully accepting the dominant conception offered by the CPSU that the USSR had reached the end of the dictatorship of the proletariat and was moving towards communism, whilst China was still going through the phase of the dictatorship of the proletariat. That is why, according to him, the dominant ideological form is different respectively: socialist humanism in the USSR and class humanism in China.

Although Althusser does not openly criticise this conception, he nevertheless avoids actually endorsing it. All the references to the absence of antagonistic class relations and the transition from the class state of the dictatorship of the proletariat to the State of the whole people are preceded by the phrase 'The Soviets say'.[14] Althusser also stresses the affinity of socialist humanism with bourgeois 'liberal' humanism and his quest for the 'reign of Man'.[15] However, Althusser insists that his aim is not to dispute the realities to which socialist humanism refers, i.e. the transformation of the USSR into a classless society, but to consider the theoretical concepts involved in this conception. That is why humanism is treated as an ideological symptom par excellence: 'while it

---

10   Althusser 1969, p. 45.
11   Althusser 1969, p. 156.
12   Fromm (ed.) 1965. Althusser 2003, pp. 222–4.
13   Althusser 1969, p. 221.
14   Althusser 1969, p. 222.
15   Ibid.

really designates a set of existing relations, unlike a scientific concept, it does not provide us with a means of knowing them'.[16] Althusser does not choose to elaborate more on this in this initial criticism of socialist humanism. Rather he returns to the question of the 'break'. For the first time in such clear terms 'Young' Marx is presented as the *humanist* Marx and anthropology as the basic problematic of Young Marx's works: 'The "Essence of Man" (whether freedom – reason or community) was the basis both for a rigorous theory of history and for a consistent political practice'.[17] He stresses Marx's references to human nature and the essence of Man in the Early Writings and suggests a periodisation of Marx's humanism, with the first phase being 'liberal-rationalist' and closer to Fichte and Kant and the second phase dominated by the influence of Feuerbach. Feuerbach's theory of alienation is for Althusser the theoretical basis of Marx. Even Marx's criticism of political emancipation and his insistence on social emancipation, the main point of *On the Jewish Question*, is for Althusser fully inscribed in a humanist anthropological problematic.

By contrast, the emergence of Marx's actual scientific discovery is marked exactly by the break with this anthropological conception, the 'rupture with every *philosophical* anthropology or humanism'.[18] For Althusser even the sixth thesis on Feuerbach represents an anthropological problematic based on two basic premises: Firstly, that there is a universal essence of man. Secondly, 'that this essence is the attribute of "*each single individual*" who is its real subject'.[19] Althusser's criticism is not limited to the socio-theoretical dimension and the inadequacy of the any reference to human essence to theoretically account for the history of social formations. He also draws an important methodological and epistemological conclusion, insisting that the reference to concrete empirical human beings is not the opposite of an idealism of Man in general, but its necessary counterpart: '*an empiricism of the subject always corresponds to an idealism of the essence (or an empiricism of the essence to an idealism of the subject)*'.[20]

Althusser uses humanism as an ideal type of ideology and as the first major example he offers of what constitutes ideology. For Althusser ideology is inescapable. There can never be a society without ideological forms and practices. '[H]uman societies could not survive without these *specific formations*, these

---

16   Althusser 1969, p. 223.
17   Ibid.
18   Althusser 1969, p. 227.
19   Althusser 1969, p. 228.
20   Althusser 1969 p. 228.

THE POLITICS OF THEORETICAL ANTI-HUMANISM   357

systems of representations (at various levels), their ideologies'.[21] If no human society can exist without ideology, then even a classless communist ideology could exist without its proper ideological forms.[22] This reference is serves two purposes. On the surface it serves Althusser's purpose to base an openly critical conception of the USSR upon the 'official' assumption that it was a classless society. On the other hand, it represents Althusser's more profound theoretical insight that ideological mystification and misrecognition are not contingent historical facts, which would have implied that the advent of communism would also lead to full transparency, an assumption in sharp contrast to his conceptualisation of a potential Theory of theoretical practice and the constant re-emergence of the need for a break with ideology.

Althusser's initial conception of ideology of imaginary relation to real relations, conditioned by the exigencies of each historical society, is projected upon a classless society where the main exigency is for the development of a communist society. The contradictions in this process are being lived in the form of socialist humanism. According to Althusser, through socialist humanism, an ideology that rejects all forms of discrimination, exploitation, and oppression, the Soviet Union is living the transition from the abuses of the Stalinist era to 'mature' communism, a transition that ought not to have happened and therefore is experienced as a contradiction.[23]

Althusser's overall criticism is that socialist humanism, even in the form of 'real humanism' suggested in Jorge Semprun's 1964 article that sparked the debate on humanism (and to which Althusser replies in the 'Complementary note on real humanism'),[24] remains an ideological notion, symptomatic of contradictions and pointing to open theoretical questions, but it cannot be considered a theoretical notion or part of a scientific discourse.

---

21   Althusser 1969 p. 232.
22   'And I am not going to steer clear of the crucial question: *historical materialism cannot conceive that even a communist society could ever do without ideology*' (Althusser 1969, p. 232).
23   'Socialist humanism, in its internal use, deals with the historical reality of the supersession of the dictatorship of the proletariat and of the "abusive" forms it took in the USSR. It deals with a "dual" reality: not only a reality superseded by the rational *necessity* of the development of the forces of production of socialist relations of production (the dictatorship of the proletariat) – but also a reality which *ought not to have had to be superseded*, that new form of *"non-rational existence of reason"*, that part of historical *"unreason"* and of the "inhuman" that the past of the USSR bears within it: terror, repression and dogmatism – precisely what has not yet been completely superseded, in its effects or its misdeeds' (Althusser 1969, p. 237).
24   Althusser 1969, pp. 242–7.

2   Marx's *Sixth Thesis* Revisited

For Althusser, Marx's Sixth Thesis on Feuerbach, taken literally, '*means nothing at all*'[25] and just marks the need for a theoretical and terminological displacement. However, one can raise an important question. Does the Sixth Thesis on Feuerbach represent the culmination of a humanist anthropological problematic, or the break with it, the exit from anthropology towards a relational–materialist conception of human social practices, representing the complete decentring (or immanent critique) of the anthropological problematic?

That is why it is worth looking at other readings of the Sixth Thesis, suggested within the framework of the Althusserian tradition. For Georges Labica in his timely reading of the *Theses*, the Sixth Thesis 'in its brutal concision [...] marks its proper rupture with Feuerbachian anthropology'.[26] According to Labica, even though Marx seems to be making an equation between 'human nature' and 'the ensemble of social relations', the insertion of the phrase *in its reality* shakes things and marks the impossibility of such an equation. In Marx's move from 'human essence' to 'real essence' a transmutation takes place, the result being that this 'real essence' cannot be conceived as a genus.[27]

Étienne Balibar has suggested that although Marx seems to not be rejecting a question that would have been in line with the then recent problematic of philosophical anthropology and theoretical humanism, at the same time he 'attempts radically to displace the way in which it has until now been understood, not only where "man" is concerned, but also as regards "essence"'.[28] For Balibar, what emerges is a highly original *ontology of relations* that stresses the importance of transindividuality and transindividual relations and the multiplicity of interactions involved in them. And this leads to a radically different conception of the very notion of *essence*. For Balibar, Marx rejects both a conception of the essence as a genus that precedes social reality and the empiricist/nominalist conception of an abstraction. The emphasis on *relations* is exactly the crucial point in transcending the realist/nominalist divide.

> We can see, then, the meaning of the strange equation made by Marx. At bottom, the words 'ensemble', 'social' and 'relations' all say the same thing. The point it to reject both of the positions (the *realist* and the *nominalist*) between which philosophers have generally been divided: the one

---

25   Althusser 1969 p. 243.
26   Labica 1987, pp. 79–80.
27   Labica 1987, p. 87.
28   Balibar 1995, p. 29.

arguing that the genus or essence precedes the existence of individuals; the other that individuals are the primary reality, from which universals are 'abstracted'. For, amazingly, neither of these positions is capable of thinking precisely what is essential in human existence: the multiple and active *relations* which individuals establish with each other (whether of language, labour, love, reproduction, domination, conflict etc.), and the fact that it is these relations which define what they have in common, the 'genus'. They define this because they constitute it at each moment in multiple forms. They provide the only 'effective' content applied to the human being (i.e. to the human being).[29]

Pierre Macherey, in his very attentive and close reading of the *Theses*, argues that Marx attempts to 'explore the open camp'[30] between the two different problematics, the one offered by the emphasis on the unique individual, the other on the multiplicity of individuals. The theoretical exit from the divide is exactly Marx's reference to the *ensemble* of social relations. Both Balibar and Macherey insist on Marx's choice of the French Word *ensemble* instead of any potential German synonyms referring to the *Whole* (*das Ganze, die Ganzheit, die Totalität*). For Balibar, Marx uses the French term consciously in order to avoid the connotations of the German ones[31] and for Macherey it is evidence of Marx's attempt at an original conception of relational multiplicity.

> What is 'assembled' in the figure of a unity, which is not simple but complex, are therefore 'social relations'. By these we must understand the different social relations [*rapports*] that constitute a multiplicity that is not totalisable *a priori*, because they form an 'ensemble', a totality of fact and not right, which is being held by their encounter, an encounter which is not fatally harmonious or converging but can take, and indeed takes, more often, violent and conflictual forms.[32]

For Macherey, all this reference to a human essence historically conditioned and relatively destabilised equates to a reference to a *non-essence* that cannot be considered like a genus.[33] In the light of readings such as those proposed by Labica, Balibar, and Macherey, it is obvious that Althusser, preoccupied with

---

29　Ibid.
30　Macherey 2008, p. 142.
31　Balibar 1995, p. 30.
32　Macherey 2008, p. 151.
33　Macherey 2008, p. 153.

the need to draw a line of demarcation with any conception of the human essence, failed to read the very complexity and richness of Marx's formulations in the *Theses on Feuerbach*. Particularly, he failed to grasp the fact that Marx was not offering just another case of a definition of a human essence, but something closer to an immanent critique of philosophical anthropology and theoretical humanism. Marx is not offering a definition in the form of a classical conception of the relation between a term and its predicates or attributes. The very syntax of the phrase, the break before the 'predicate', the insertion of the phrase 'in its reality' mark something close to a terminological inversion and reversal. The result is not a phrase about what 'human essence' is, but a theoretical displacement towards *the ensemble of social relations*. Marx does not refer to 'essence' in the sense that he wants to go back to a predefined conception of it, but in order to offer a terminological starting point to be transcended in order for a radically novel conception to emerge, one in which what actually exists, in all its multiplicity and constant transformative potentiality, are neither essences nor individuals, but conflictual social relations. Althusser failed to see that what preoccupied Marx was not a variation of philosophical anthropology but a conception of social reality as being in a constant process of transformation that entails the possibility of revolutionary change, and this is exemplified by all the references to *praxis*.[34] It is this interlinking of a relational conception and of the possibility of transformative social and political practices that is missing from Althusser's reading.

3   The Combination of Historicism and Humanism as the Main Danger

In the evolution of Althusser's conception of theoretical anti-humanism, *Reading Capital* also represents a major step. It is there that Althusser elaborated on the relation to humanism and the relation between humanism and historicism. It is there that he insisted that in the strict sense Marxism is an 'a-humanism'[35] in the sense of the radical absence of a humanist anthropological problematic

---

34   'Let us risk the expression, then, and say that social relations as designated here are nothing but an endless transformation, a "permanent revolution" (the term was doubtless not invented by Marx, but it would play a decisive role in his thinking up to around 1850). For the Marx of March 1845, it is not enough to say with Hegel that "the real is rational" and that the rational, of necessity, becomes reality: one has to say that the only thing which is real or rational is revolution' (Balibar 1995, p. 33).

35   Althusser et al. 2016, p. 268.

from Marx's mature theory. For Althusser the emergence of the revolutionary humanist and historicist problematic was the result of a more general 'leftist' turn following the 1917 revolution. Althusser insisted on the possibility of a humanist historicism, where the historicist problematic would be coupled with emphasis on human nature.

> It must be said that the union of humanism and historicism represents the gravest temptation, for it procures the greatest theoretical advantages, at least in appearance. In the reduction of all knowledge to the historical social relations a second underhand reduction can be introduced, by treating the *relations of production* as mere *human relations*.[36]

Althusser is particularly sceptical of any conception of history as a simple product of human practice as if concrete persons can be the authors of the script of their own history and destiny, and are in a position to actually 'make' their own history.

> This second reduction depends on something 'obvious': is not history a 'human' phenomenon through and through, and did not Marx, quoting Vico, declare that men can know it since they have '*made*' all of it? But this 'obviousness' depends on a remarkable presupposition: that the 'actors' of history are the authors of its text, the subjects of its production. But this presupposition too has all the force of the 'obvious', since, as opposed to what the theatre suggests, concrete men are, in history, the actors of roles of which they are the authors, too. Once the stage-director has been spirited away, the actor-author becomes the twin-brother of Aristotle's old dream: the doctor-who-cures-himself; and the *relations of production*, although they are the real stage-directors of history, are reduced to mere *human relations*?[37]

It is obvious from the above that Althusser feared that instead of a theory of modes of production and social formations we would end up with a theory of concrete men making history and changing themselves in the process. Althusser does not consider classical ethical and metaphysical anthropologies as the main opponent. It is the coupling of humanism and historicism that Althusser feared. He thought that such a coupling might appear as the answer

---

36   Althusser et al. 2016, p. 290.
37   Althusser et al. 2016, pp. 290–1.

to the dangers of classical, a-historical, 'ethical' humanism. He wanted to stress that his theoretical opponent is not only the references to some transhistorical human essence, what we might designate as a 'naïve' humanism that would ignore historicity and historical change. The adding of the historicist problematic might lead us to mistakenly identifying historical materialism with a historicised humanist conception, where the object of a theory of history would have been a theory of human beings constantly making history and remaking themselves.

> Once this human nature has been endowed with the qualities of 'concrete' historicity, it becomes possible to avoid the abstraction and fixity of theological or ethical anthropologies and to join Marx in the very heart of his lair: historical materialism. This human nature will therefore be conceived as something produced by history, and changing with it, while man changes, as even the Philosophers of the Enlightenment intended, with the revolutions of his own history, and is affected by the social products of his objective history even in his most intimate faculties (seeing, hearing, memory, reason, etc). [...] History then becomes the transformation of a human nature, which remains the real subject of the history which transforms it. As a result, history has been introduced into human nature, making men the contemporaries of the historical effects whose subjects they are, but – and this is absolutely decisive – the relations of production, political and ideological social relations, have been reduced to historicized *'human relations'*, i.e., to inter-human, inter-subjective relations. This is the favourite terrain of historicist humanism.[38]

However, despite all the references to concrete men and historicity and materialism Althusser feared that in the end the central concept would still be an ideological and not scientific theory of human nature, therefore a theoretical ideology preceding Marx's theoretical breakthrough. In such a case, what distinguishes Marx's theoretical revolution is at stake, namely a highly original conception of history as a non-linear and non-predetermined succession of modes of production where causal priority is attributed to relations and social forms and not 'concrete men'. It also seems as if for Althusser the terminological displacement from Man to Men does not change much. Concrete men without the social relations and forms of which they are the bearers (*träger*) will eventually lead to a reproduction of the basic anthropological problem-

---

38 Althusser et al. 2016, p. 291.

atic concerning the historical actualisation of some common human 'essential' characteristics. This would mean that historical materialism would have been seen as just a continuation of an earlier problematic, that of the Philosophers of Enlightenment. In contrast, theoretical anti-humanism is the necessary theoretical defence of the originality and scientificity of Marxist historical materialism.

4 The Debate at Argenteuil

1966 was a crucial year in the development of Althusser's theoretical and political interventions. The two 1965 books had brought Althusser and the group around him to the centre of theoretical and political debates and offered him a new visibility in a period of rising interest in new theoretical directions. It was the year that the political repercussions of theoretical debates were at the centre of the debate within the PCF. Garaudy's aggressive defence of his version of socialist humanism, that seemed to contradict aspects of Party orthodoxy in a trajectory that would lead him from being the Party's semi-official philosopher to exiting the Party, and the impact of Althusser's anti-humanism, forced the Party leadership to have an extensive debate, first in a meeting in January 1966 of the Party's philosophers and intellectuals at Choisy-le-Roi and then in a plenary of the Central Committee at Argenteuil.[39]

The PCF opposition to both Garaudy and Althusser was not so much theoretical as it was political. If one reads the interventions presented at 1966 session of the CC of the PCF at Argenteuil, one is struck by the lack of theoretical depth. The main question raised by the humanist debate – namely the question of whether a reference to human essence can be a theoretical foundation for historical materialism – is cast away or answered through a cursory reference to the Sixth Thesis on Feuerbach or an equally hasty distinction between idealist and materialist conceptions of humanism. The main fear seems to be the identification of socialist humanism with all the turns in the line of the PCF in the post-1956 period and the 'frontist' line of alliances with Socialists and Catholics. The fear and the political calculation that any move away from such a humanist rhetoric might alienate allies is evident, even though at the same time there is a fear that also Garaudy's tendency to go 'too far' in the direction

---

[39] For the interventions at the meeting in Argenteuil see the texts compiled in *Cahiers de Communisme* 5–6. See also Geerlandt 1978 and Di Maggio 2013. Althusser was absent from these meetings.

of the dialogue with the Catholics might also endanger the Marxist theoretical core of the Party's theoretical line, and consequently its hegemony within the Left, especially against the rise of the Socialists and particularly F. Mitterrand. As G.M. Goshgarian has noted, 'at stake in this campaign was [...] the post-Stalinist reformism for which humanism and a vulgar Hegelianism provided ideological cover'.[40]

This conception of the polemic against humanism as an attack against the alliance policy of the PCF towards Catholics, socialists, and in general non-communists, is evident in Garaudy's intervention in Argenteuil.[41] His main aim is to defend his position on the need for a theoretical foundation for the dialogue with the Catholics, a sort of philosophical defence of the famous Maurice Thorez line of the '*main tenue*' (extended hand) towards Christians, in an attempt to present Christianity as an expression of desperation in face of oppression. The polemic against theoretical anti-humanism takes second place. For Garaudy, who had been the main theoretical proponent inside the PCF of the position that Marxism is a real humanism, Marxist humanism has nothing to do with bourgeois humanism because it offers a conception of human nature and human essence that is materialist, non-individualist, dialectical, and historical, an 'integral humanism'.[42] The political consideration is also evident in interventions such as the one by Henri Krasucki who insisted that it is necessary to take into consideration the 'theoretical and political consequences of any conclusions that would have rejected the idea of a Marxist humanism. They would lead to narrow positions and to isolation'.[43]

However, there were also other positions more critical of Garaudy.[44] For example, Lucien Sève openly accused him of misinterpretating Marx's *On the Jewish Question*,[45] and of underestimating the importance of science,[46] but also insisted that Althusser borrowed concepts from non-Marxists without convincing that they could supersede classical Marxist references.[47] There were also voices more favourable towards Althusser, like Michel Simon.[48] Guy Besse also

---

40 Goshgarian 2003, p. xxx.
41 Garaudy 1966.
42 Garaudy 1966, p. 40.
43 Krasucki 1966, p. 170.
44 On Sève's criticism of Garaudy at Argenteuil see Di Maggio 2013.
45 Sève 1966, p. 95.
46 Sève 1966, pp. 97–8.
47 He also complains of Althusser that in his writings Marx or Lenin are being treated as naïve, whereas non-Marxists like Lacan, Foucault, and Canguillhem receive privileged treatment (Sève 1966, p. 107).
48 Simon 1966.

attempted to present the merits of Althusser and his collaborators and was critical of aspects of Garaudy's interventions.[49]

However, it is important to note that despite its final decision to take a position in favour of a Marxist humanism, through affirming that there is a Marxist humanism, that is distinct from bourgeois humanism, a humanism that is based upon a scientific conception, the Central Committee nevertheless refrains from openly condemning theoretical anti-humanism and does not take a position in defence of *theoretical* humanism. The following phrase epitomises this careful approach:

> The affirmation of such a humanism does not signify the rejection of an objective conception of reality for the benefit of a vague élan of the heart. In contrast, Marxism is the humanism of our time because it founds its demarche upon a rigorously scientific conception of the world.[50]

However, this did not mean that the apparatus of the Party actually had a conception of open political and theoretical research and debate, befitting a party that could act as a collective intellectual. Rather the debate was thought of in terms of making sure that there were no challenges to the political line of the leading group. As Marco di Maggio stresses:

> In fact, facing the debate that included the communist philosophers, the leading group does not favour the research of a synthesis that would be capable of reinforcing the structure of the Party as a 'collective intellectual' but remains upon the only plan that its political culture permits it to conceptualize and master, that of a Marxist-Leninist doctrine and of the total equivalence between theoretical elaboration and ideological production, where the Marxist-Leninist ideology is an instrument of justification of the politics of the Party and of the power of the leading Group.[51]

Althusser's reaction to the Central Committee resolution was an attempt to defend his position. In a letter to the PCF Central Committee, that he probably never actually sent, he insisted that there were errors in the final resolution. First, he stressed the importance of theoretical anti-humanism and the fact

---

49 Besse 1966.
50 CC du PCF 1966, p. 273; Geerlandt 1978, p. 129.
51 Di Maggio 2013, p. 140.

that it was an essential aspect of Marx's theoretical revolution.[52] Secondly, he urged for caution in the use of the 'humanist-socialist' rhetoric, because there is the danger that such a 'practical ideological' use in terms of mass propaganda can have theoretical repercussions, because 'our theory *runs real risks* if we *systematically* employ these formulae and if we conceive our own theory in humanist terms'.[53] Thirdly, he considered the Central Committee resolution a compromise with the positions advanced by Garaudy. Fourthly, he criticised the way in which the Central Committee resolution refused the existence of the break in the evolution of Marx's thought and tended to treat Marxism not as a theoretical resolution but as an aspect of the creative movement of the human spirit. In the same line, he criticises the resolution's references to art as being influenced by an idealist, spiritualist conception. Finally, Althusser did not deny the need to pursue an alliance with the Christian Left but insisted that this alliance requires that the Communist Left stands firmly on its principles. Again Althusser chose not to oppose the main aspects of the dominant line of the PCF, even if in theoretical terms he was indeed touching upon a nodal point in the right-wing strategy of the PCF. Again we are confronted with an element that would mark Althusser's interventions: raising the level of theoretical criticism and at the same time remaining more or less silent about political questions.

5   *The Humanist Controversy* Revisited

Althusser's 1967 text *The Humanist Controversy* is important because it represents Althusser's thinking on the subject after the main debate within the ranks of Communist intellectuals. It is also written after his 1966 'encyclical' 'The Philosophical Conjuncture and Marxist Theoretical Research', which marks the beginning of the second phase of the intervention. Initially conceived as an introduction to a book on the controversy surrounding Althusser's theoretical anti-humanism, it begins by recuperating the circumstances under which 'Marxism and Humanism' was written and the debates that followed. He then proceeds to clarify his position, beginning by invoking again the importance of Feuerbach both in the development of philosophical debate in Germany in the mid-nineteenth century and the evolution of Marx's thought. Althusser

---

[52]   'To say that Marxism is, *theoretically* speaking, an anti-humanism or a-humanism, is quite simply to *observe* that, in Marx's mature thought, theoretical-humanist concepts are absent and are *replaced* by new *scientific* concepts' (Althusser 2007, p. 157).

[53]   Althusser 2007, p. 159.

insists that Feuerbach represents a very important turning point. For Althusser, Feuerbach's philosophical anthropology, his reference to Man, Nature, and *Sinnlichkeit*, attempted to answer and at the same time transcend all the major questions posed by Kant, German Idealism, and Hegel, even though it is basically incoherent and constitutes a retreat compared the philosophers before him.

> Thus, with Feuerbach. Man is the unique originary and fundamental concept, the *factotum*, which stands in for Kant's Transcendental Subject, Nooumenal Subject, Empirical Subject and Idea, and also stands in for Hegel's Idea. The 'end of classical German philosophy' is then quite simply a verbal suppression of its solutions by heteroclite philosophical notions gathered from here and there in the philosophy of the eighteenth century (sensualism, empiricism, the materialism of *Sinnlichkeit*, borrowed from the tradition of Condillac; a pseudo-biologism vaguely inspired by Diderot; an idealism of Man and the 'heart' drawn from Rousseau) and unified by a *play on theoretical words* in the concept of Man.[54]

For Althusser theoretical humanism is the foundation upon which Feuerbach's philosophy is based and is 'overtly at work in the *1844 Manuscripts*'.[55] What marks in his opinion the retreat of Feuerbach in relation to Hegel is the former's conception of history as a process of alienation with a subject, with the subject being man. For Althusser this is alien to Hegel's thought, because there is no anthropological problematic in Hegel.[56] On the contrary, a common thread in Hegel and Marx is the conception of history as a '*process without a subject*',[57] a point that Althusser is going to bring forward in all his interventions from 1967 onwards (being also an important theoretical node in 1968 *Lenin and Philosophy*). For Althusser, in Hegel there is no proper Subject except from the process itself, and this provides the basis for the teleological character of Hegelian dialectic. In contrast, for Althusser, Feuerbach marks a theoretical retreat

---

54 Althusser 2003, p. 236.
55 Ibid.
56 '[N]othing is more foreign to Hegel's thought than this *anthropological* conception of History. For Hegel, History is certainly a process of alienation, but this process does not have Man as its subject. First, in the Hegelian history, it is a matter not of Man, but of the Spirit, and if one must *at all costs* (which in respect of a "subject" is false anyway) have a "subject" in history, one should talk about "nations", or, more accurately (we are approaching the truth), the *moments* of the development of the Idea become Spirit' (Althusser 2003, pp. 238–9).
57 Althusser 2003, p. 239.

compared to Hegel exactly in his attempt to recognise Man as the subject of this dialectical process of alienation. That is why 'the Feuerbachian concept of alienation should in its turn be a pathetically contracted version, and a caricature, of the Hegelian concept of alienation'.[58] The result is a theory of the alienation of Human Essence '*without a process*'.[59] The absence of the notion of process reduces alienation to 'the speculary equation "subject = object", to the *mode of meaning/direction* [sens] of this identity – to be precise, to a *reversal of meaning / direction*'.[60] The result is that alienation is not treated as a historical process but as an 'abstraction involving only *significations*'.[61] Therefore the disalienation of Man is considered to be only an act of reversal, the emergence of a new disalienated consciousness, and this can explain Feuerbach's political silence during the revolutions of 1848–49.

> Thus Theoretical Humanism showed, in practice, what it had 'in its head': a petty-bourgeois ideology dissatisfied with Prussian despotism and the imposture of established religion, but frightened by the Revolution that its moral concepts had disarmed in advance.[62]

For Althusser this theoretical humanism is the theoretical basis for Marx's early writings. He is aware that Marx is not concerned with the critique of religion, but with the critique of politics and the state, but he insists that there is no change in the underlying theoretical problematic: 'Marx merely *extends one and the same theory from religion to politics*: the Feuerbachian theory of Man and alienation'.[63] The encounter with Political Economy in the *1844 Manuscripts* does not change the theoretical problematic. The theory of alienated labour is being treated by Althusser as a variation on the Feuerbachian equation 'Essence of Man = Essence of his objects as objectification of his Essence'.[64] However, there is an important development in the *1844 Manuscripts*, namely the *'intervention of Hegel in Feuerbach'*.[65] For Althusser, Marx reintroduces Hegelian notions, especially the emphasis on *labour*, the dialectic, but without leaving the terrain of a basically Feuerbachian anthropological problematic.

---

58 Althusser 2003, p. 241.
59 Althusser 2003, p. 242.
60 Ibid.
61 Althusser 2003, p. 243.
62 Ibid.
63 Althusser 2003, p. 245.
64 Althusser 2003, p. 248.
65 Ibid.

> With history and the dialectic, the Hegelian conception of *labour* enters the schema as well, realizing, as Marx sees it, the miraculous theoretical encounter between Hegel and Political Economy with the blessing of the Feuerbachian Essence of Man. Marx celebrates the harmony prevailing at this Summit Conference of the Concept in terms that are touching in their naivety [...] What has modern Political Economy [...] accomplished? It has, says Marx, reduced all the economic categories to their *subjective* essence: labour. What extraordinary exploit has Hegel achieved ('in the *Phenomenology*')? He grasps, says Marx, '*labour* as the *essence* of man'. Subject, Man, Labour. Subject = Man = Labour. Labour is nothing other than the act of objectification of the Essential Forces of Man in his products. The process of alienation of man externalizing his essential forces in products by means of labour is History. Thus everything enters into Feuerbach again, for a very good reason: we have not left Feuerbach for a single second.[66]

For Althusser, Alienation, Subject, and Man represent, as concepts, the main epistemological obstacles, in the Bachelardian sense, that Marx had to clear away. That is why the three-way encounter between Hegel, Feuerbach, and Political Economy in the 1844 manuscripts ends in a theoretical crisis, leading to a theoretical rupture. For Althusser the insistence on the notion of a generic human essence is fundamentally incompatible with the reference to social relations and social structure, a reference that for Althusser marks a new problematic. Marx's insistence on the human essence not being an abstraction inherent in each individual is not enough for Althusser, since the notion of human genus is present in its theoretical – idealist – results.

> The world of man is not the objectification of his essence; it is not mere Objects; it consists of altogether astounding realities: *relations*, taken in their 'ensemble'. However something of Feuerbach remains even in this innovation: namely, that which Feuerbach called the *generic* essence of man, the 'ensemble' of men [...] It is on account of this concept, which is *absent* from the sentence (the human *genus*), that Marx can write this impossible sentence [...] The 'human essence' clearly *aims at* (since it avoids the individual) the problem of the structure of society, but by way of the Feuerbachian concept of *human genus*. Unless this concept of *human genus* (which is itself a fine example of an epistemological

---

66   Althusser 2003, pp. 249–50.

obstacle) has been eliminated, it is only possible to produce contorted sentences that are literally incomprehensible.[67]

For Althusser this attempt towards a realignment of Feuerbachian and Hegelian themes is evident in the introduction of the notion of historical praxis, 'the transformation of the Subject into praxis, and the *historicization of this subject* as subject',[68] leading to the historicism of the subject in the *German Ideology*. Stirner's distinction between the concrete individual and the religious idea of Man, according to Althusser, dealt a blow to the ideology of Man and brought forward a different set of problems and questions: the problem of a theory of individuality, the problem of a theory of society, the problem of a theory of ideology.[69] However, even in the *German Ideology* we can find traces of the original Feuerbachian problematic in the conception of the relations of production as inter-individual relations, but also in the echoes of the theory of alienation in Marx's initial conception of the division of labour along with a Hegelian emphasis on teleology. That is why he insists that the emergence of new concepts in the *German Ideology* does not imply a complete break with previous philosophical categories. 'In all of this, with the modification effected by a radical historicist empiricism which declares that Man is mere ideology, and that ideology is *nothing*, we are still within the philosophical legacy of Feuerbach'.[70] The evolution of Marx's thought according to Althusser is marked by the disappearance of humanist references[71] and the emergence of the problematic of a science of history, a science of social formations and modes of production. Therefore the break is not just a singular event but also a 'process of very long duration'.[72]

Instead of the 'epistemological obstacles' posed by theoretical humanism, such as the notion of Man, the notion of the human species or Human Genus, the notion of the concrete individual, the notion of the subject, the notion of consciousness, the notion of labour as the essence of man, the notion of alienation, the notion of the dialectic as teleology, which for Althusser are 'theoretical transcriptions of actually existing social *solutions*',[73] he suggests dealing with real problems:

---

67   Althusser 2003, p. 255.
68   Althusser 2003, p. 256.
69   Althusser 2003, p. 258.
70   Althusser 2003, p. 263.
71   'These notions of Theoretical Humanism have been eliminated from Marx's scientific theory' (Althusser 2003, p. 264).
72   Althusser 2003, p. 269.
73   Althusser 2003, p. 274.

1. The problem of the definition of the *human species* – or of the specific difference that distinguishes the forms of existence of the *human species* from those of animal species [...]
2. The problem of the structure of *social formations* [...]
3. The problem of the dialectic of *history* as a process without subject [...]
4. The problem of the forms of *individuality* [...]
5. The problem of the nature of the *ideological*.[74]

Althusser elaborates only the first question, trying to insist why it is ideological to think in terms of a notion of the Human Genus in general. He begins by refusing the sharp distinction between Man and Nature exemplified in the position that there is a privileged position of Man in respect of Nature. He insists on the inadequacy of the position that only a human 'historical' dialectic exists. For Althusser Hegel's insistence on the existence of a Dialectic of Nature marked his refusal of an anthropological conception. He also reminds us that the thesis that there is a Dialectic of Nature came to the fore during Engels's battle against Dühring's attempt to bring forward a religious conception of the privileged position of the human species. He also insists that this revival by Engels of the Dialectic of Nature also served epistemological ends and is closely bound to the category of the process without subject. Therefore, it is not, according to Althusser, a thesis on the actual existence of a dialectic in nature, which is an open question, but a thesis concerning the science of History. This brings him to a discussion of what he designates as the 'Recent Discoveries' in Human Palaeontology[75] and what he perceives as a tendency by some Marxists to treat them as a justification for a Humanist problematic, where Labour would be equated with the Human Essence and the creation of Man by Man. Althusser seems to fear such a conception of labour as a transhistorical ontological foundation of a humanist problematic. That is why he insists that in Marx's mature work and the criticism of Classical Political Economists, the category of labour 'explodes'[76] and a whole array of scientific notions emerges: labour process, labour power, concrete labour, abstract labour, etc. A transhistorical conception of labour can lead to the idealism of the conception of the 'Origin of Man' and an historicist–geneticist conception of History, in the sense of seeing the Man in the ape that is going through labour to become Man.[77] In contrast, Marx's mature theory

---

74 Althusser 2003, p. 275.
75 Althusser 2003, p. 284.
76 Althusser 2003, p. 289.
77 Althusser 2003, p. 295.

of History is not an historicist theory of the genesis of capitalism, and as we already discussed it is here that the notion of the encounter becomes central.

> To put it plainly, capitalism is not the result of a *genesis* that can be traced back to the feudal mode of production as if to its origin, its 'in-itself', its 'embryonic form', and so on; it is the result of a complex process that produces, at a given moment, the encounter of a number of elements susceptible of constituting it in their very encounter. Evolutionist, Hegelian or geneticist illusions notwithstanding, mode of production does not contain 'potentially', 'in embryo', or 'in itself', the mode of production that is to 'succeed' it.[78]

6   Theoretical Anti-humanism in the 1970s

The *Reply to John Lewis* also represents an important aspect of Althusser's polemic against theoretical humanism. Here the enemy is the conception of Man as the species that makes its own history, having the ability to be at the same time within history and outside of it. Humanism is linked to a historicist and voluntarist perspective.

> John Lewis's man is a little lay god. Like every living being he is 'up to his neck' in reality, but endowed with the prodigious power of being able at any moment to step outside of that reality, of being able to change its character. A little Sartrian god, always '*en situation*' in history, endowed with the amazing power of 'transcending' every situation, of resolving all the difficulties which history presents, and of going forward towards the golden future of the human, socialist revolution: man is an essentially revolutionary animal because he is a *free* animal.[79]

In its turn this is attributed mainly to a perspective such as Sartre's, whom he accuses of expressing a certain petty-bourgeois revolt. Althusser opposes the insistence on class struggle as the motor force of history. Whereas in the 1960–65 writings Althusser opposed to theoretical humanism the emphasis on social structures, here the line of demarcation has to do with the question regarding

---

78   Althusser 2003, p. 296.
79   Althusser 1976a, p. 44.

the motor force of history in opposition to the 'who makes history' question, emblematic in his opinion of a humanist-historicist problematic.

> It is precisely the Thesis of the *Communist Manifesto* – 'the class struggle is the motor of history' – that *displaces the question*, that brings the problem into the open, that shows us how to pose it properly and therefore how to solve it. It is the masses which 'make' history, but 'it is the class struggle which is the motor of history'. [...] The question is no longer posed in terms of 'man'. That much we know. But in the proposition that 'the class struggle is the motor of history', the question of 'making' history is also eliminated. It is no longer a question of *who* makes history.
> Marxism-Leninism tells us something quite different: that it is the *class struggle* (new concept) which is the *motor* (new concept) of history, it is the class struggle which moves history, which advances it: and brings about revolutions. This Thesis is of very great importance, because *it puts the class struggle in the front rank*.[80]

This reference to the class struggle as the motor force of history also covers another necessity in Althusser's theoretical edifice. One of the strong points of the humanist-historicist conception is that it gives the impression that it can account for political practice and emancipatory, transformative struggle, since it is based upon a conception of the *political subject*. And this has to be put into perspective. Regarding humanism, we are not only dealing with a question about alliances. It is also a debate upon the ability to have a revolutionary political subject. Althusser's own periodisation in the 1960s of humanism and historicism as the results of revolutionary zeal and enthusiastic voluntarism following the October Revolution marks an apprehension of this problem, even though the then dominant communist reformism and gradualist frontism could also apply to a classical Stalinist conception of the 'laws of history'. However, in 1972, just a few years after May 1968 and the emergence of a new emphasis on the possibility of a revolutionary subjectivity, Althusser has to answer a different challenge and this can be done only though a reappraisal of class struggle and an emphasis on what this implies for political action.

> If the question of 'man' as 'subject of history' disappears, that does not mean that the question of *political action* disappears. Quite the contrary! This political action is actually given its strength by the critique of the

---

80 Althusser 1976a, p. 48.

> bourgeois fetishism of 'man': it is forced to follow the conditions of the class struggle. For class struggle is not an individual struggle, but an *organized* mass struggle for the conquest and revolutionary transformation of state power and social relations. Nor does it mean that the question of the revolutionary *party* disappears [...] But it does mean that the 'role of the individual in history', the existence, the nature, the practice and the objectives of the revolutionary party are not determined by the omnipotence of 'transcendence', that is, the liberty of 'man', but by quite different conditions: by the state of the class struggle, by the state of the labour movement, by the ideology of the labour movement (petty-bourgeois or proletarian), and by its relation to Marxist theory, by its mass line and by its mass work.[81]

Althusser cannot avoid dealing with the question of the subject, especially since he had insisted on history as a process without a subject in contrast to humanist voluntarism and historicist teleology. The question he has to face is how to reconcile this thesis with the realisation that political practice is possible only through the existence of subjects, individual and collective, and that the subject as the result of ideological interpellation is an inescapable social form. As an analytical category, with regards to historical explanation, the subject is an ideological form. History has no Subject and no subject can master or direct history. At that level of explanation one can only speak of agents of social practices, conditioned by social structures and social relations. However, at a different level of explanation, one cannot avoid the observation that human beings can be agents of practices and bearers of social relations only if they are also subjects.

> No human, i.e. social individual can be the agent of a practice if he does not have the *form of a subject*. The 'subject-form' is actually the form of historical existence of every individual, of every agent of social practices: because the social relations of production and reproduction necessarily comprise, as an *integral part*, what Lenin calls '(juridico-) *ideological social relations*', which, in order to function, impose the subject-form on each agent-individual. The agent-individuals thus always act in the subject-form, as subjects. But the fact that they are necessarily subjects does not make the agents of social-historical practices into the *subject* or *subjects* of history (in the philosophical sense of the term: *subject*

---

81   Althusser 1976a, pp. 53–4.

of). The subject-agents are only active *in* history through the determination of the relations of production and reproduction, and in their forms.[82]

However, the main thrust of Althusser's polemic remains philosophical and has to do with the centrality of the category of the subject and how it is related mainly to an idealist and historicist conception. It is worth noting that Althusser seems to avoid the question of the political subject, of how to create an effective form of political subjectivity, preferring instead to focus on the question of the inadequacy of any 'grand theory' centred upon the concept of the Subject, insisting upon the centrality of the reference to the class struggle as motor of history.

> In advancing the Thesis of a 'process without a Subject or Goal(s)', I want simply but clearly to say this. To be dialectical-materialist, Marxist philosophy must break with the idealist category of the 'Subject' as Origin, Essence and Cause, *responsible* in its internality for all the determinations of the external 'Object', of which it is said to be the internal 'Subject'. For Marxist philosophy there can be no Subject as an Absolute Centre, as a Radical Origin, as a Unique Cause. [...] In reality Marxist philosophy thinks in and according to quite different categories: determination in the last instance – which is quite different from the Origin, Essence or Cause *unes* – determination by Relations (*idem*), contradiction, process, 'nodal points' (Lenin), etc.[83]

There remains another point that Althusser has to answer. From the beginning, as Althusser himself stressed, socialist humanism had to do with the contradictions of 'actually existing socialism'. For Althusser socialist humanism was an ideological, and therefore fundamentally inadequate, attempt to deal with all the problems associated with the construction of socialism. This debate was even more heated after the end of the hopes created by de-Stalinisation, after the Sino-Soviet break and finally after the traumatic experience of the 1968 invasion of Czechoslovakia. 'Socialism with a human face' became the reference of all those within the communist movement that wanted a different road. Althusser feels obliged to enter this debate, fearing that the main tone of the debate moved to the right. The criticism of the deformation of socialism

---

82 Althusser 1976a, p. 95.
83 Althusser 1976a, p. 96.

by the dominant Soviet strategy and the philosophical and theoretical criticism of theoretical humanism are of equal and interrelated importance for Althusser.

> The humanist reactions of western Communist theoreticians, and even of some from eastern Europe, are one thing. It would however be an extremely serious political mistake, for example, to claim to judge and condemn – on account of an adjective ('human') – something like the slogan *'socialism with a human face,'* a slogan under which the Czech masses let everyone know – even if the form was sometimes confused – about their class and national grievances and aspirations. [...] What the Czech people wanted was socialism, and not humanism. It wanted a socialism whose face (not the body: the body does not figure in the formula) would not be disfigured by practices unworthy both of itself (the Czech people: a people of a high political culture) and of socialism. A socialism with a human face. The adjective is in the right place. The national mass movement of the Czech people, even if it is no longer to be heard of (and the struggle is nevertheless still going on) merits the respect and support of all Communists. Exactly as the 'humanist' philosophies of western intellectuals (at ease in their academic chairs or wherever), the philosophies of 'Marxist humanism', whether they are called 'true' or 'scientific,' merit the criticism of all Communists.[84]

In the 1975 *Soutenance d'Amiens*, Althusser insists that theoretical anti-humanism marks a break with any historicist conception of the Origin and the Subject.

> I would say that Marx's theoretical anti-humanism is above all a *philosophical* anti-humanism. If what I have just said has any truth in it, you only have to compare it with what I said earlier about Marx's affinities with Spinoza and Hegel in their opposition to philosophies of the Origin and the Subject to see the implications.[85]

For Althusser theoretical anti-humanism marks an important theoretical displacement: from the emphasis on human nature (either as generic essence or as multiplicity of individuals) to the causal primacy of social relations.

---

84   Althusser 1976a, pp. 76–7.
85   Althusser 1976a, p. 200.

> The effects can be seen in *Capital*. Marx shows that what in the last instance determines a social formation, and allows us to grasp it, is not any chimerical human essence or human nature, nor man, nor even 'men', but a *relation*, the production relation, which is inseparable from the Base, the infrastructure. And, in opposition to all humanist idealism, Marx shows that this relation is not a relation between men, a relation between persons, nor an intersubjective or psychological or anthropological relation, but a double relation: a relation between groups of men concerning the relation between these groups of men and things, the means of production.[86]

Theoretical anti-humanism also represents for Althusser a clear break with bourgeois ideology and is politically effective in any attempt to combat bourgeois influence within the labour movement, and especially the ideology of 'freedom'.

> For when you begin with man, you cannot avoid the idealist temptation of believing in the omnipotence of liberty or of creative labour – that is, you simply submit, in all 'freedom', to the omnipotence of the ruling bourgeois ideology, whose function is to mask and to impose, in the illusory shape of man's power of freedom, another power, much more real and much more powerful, that of capitalism.[87]

There is an important point here. One cannot offer any plausible theory of history by simply referring to people being the same in the entire human history. This can only lead either to a tragic conception of history, human history as inescapably bound to relations of oppression and exploitation, or to a quasi religious conception: exploitation and oppression as a Fall from an original state of grace and classless society as a fulfilment of a prophecy of emancipation.

---

86   Althusser 1976a, p. 201.
87   Althusser 1976a, p. 205.

CHAPTER 17

Althusser's Self-Criticism

This intensification of theoretical intervention in the politics of theory (and especially the politics of philosophy and the relation of philosophy and politics) marked Althusser's first wave of self-criticism after 1966. It includes a changed conception of both philosophy and of the relation between structure and conjuncture. Althusser gradually abandoned any notion of a Theory of theoretical practice, especially after he abandoned his attempt to suggest a general theory of discourse in place of the Theory of theoretical practice, leading to the second definition of philosophy as a political intervention in philosophy and as in the last instance class struggle in theory. He paid more attention to the singularity of conjunctures and of social practices, gradually moving towards a definition of structures as lasting encounters and relations.

1   1966: The Turning Point

His June 1966 talk on 'The Philosophical Conjuncture and Marxist Theoretical Research'[1] marks the beginning of the effort. Althusser offers a description of the main dividing lines within the theoretical and particularly philosophical battlefield against all forms of idealism. Regarding Marxist theory, Althusser begins to move away from the earlier conception of philosophy as Theory of theoretical practice: 'Strategic question number 1: *The difference in theoretical status between Marxist science and Marxist philosophy*'.[2] This offers a series of questions for historical materialism: from the general stratus of historical materialism as theory to specific questions about social classes, political and ideological superstructures, political practice, transitional forms and a new emphasis on singular historical forms through a 'theory of the forms of historical individuality (including the social formation)'.[3] As a renewed strategy for a political intervention in theory it manages to incorporate most of the open questions and indeed one can see in this text the analogies between such a project and the actual flourishing of Marxist theoretical production in the late 1960s and 1970s. But as a theoretical and political intervention it is far

---

1   In Althusser 2003.
2   Althusser 2003, p. 12.
3   Althusser 2003, p. 15.

from answering open political questions. Althusser, despite the beginning of his process of self-criticism, remained in this text loyal to a strategy of theoretical correction of political deviations, or of the importance of theory as a way to answer the right-wing turn of the communist movement, even though this strategy refrains from the philosophical arrogance of the initial conception of Marxist philosophy as a Theory of theoretical practice. Moreover, we are still within a conception of identification of the working class with the Party and consequently of Marxism with the debates and the theoretical balance of forces within the Party. This can explain the silence on questions of politics that he admitted in a July 1966 letter to Franca Madonia, in which Althusser attempts to articulate a tactic that will make possible the break with the reformism of the European Communist Parties.

> If you read the text that I have sent you on the philosophical conjuncture, you would be aware that it has an important *silence*: it refers to the philosophical conjuncture, but there is not a single word on the *political* conjuncture, which, however, commands everything, including the philosophical conjuncture itself. This silence was *politically* voluntary, it was reflected upon, necessary and I wait for its philosophical results that have *already* been produced: a certain number of those that I invited to the conference came *afterwards* to see me to talk about what I couldn't yet talk publicly about, namely *politics*. Talking about politics today means analysing the political conjuncture, confirming the French and Italian communist parties, following the soviet communist party, are objectively engaged in a reformist and revisionist politics, that they have become social-democrat parties, that they have stopped being revolutionary parties and that *essentially*, and despite its often dogmatic form, the critique from the part of the Chinese is justified. Following the consequences of these, means waging theoretical and political struggle [...] against the revisionism and opportunism of our parties, so that we can arrive, *when the moment comes*, on something other than actually exists. And this we must accomplish practically *alone*, without the help of our elders, without the help of our parties (because they are in their present state practically lost) [...] I say: we must do this practically *alone*.[4]

Here Althusser presents the need for a complete political break with the politics of communist reformism, makes a very negative assessment of the present

---

4 Althusser 1997b, pp. 693–4.

state of communist parties, and conveys the difficulty – and perhaps tragedy – of such an endeavour: the *loneliness* that comes from the need to think in highly original and novel terms without the possibility of resorting to either experience or the collective resources of the Party. It is the same loneliness that he would later invoke in his reading of Machiavelli, the loneliness when faced with the task of thinking of a radically *new* social and political sequence, in a process open and without any prior guarantees.

Some of the people who were close to Althusser took that step. In December 1966, the UJCML (*Union des jeunesses communistes marxistes-léninistes*) was formed, combining in its first public interventions political criticism and theory, exemplified in UJCML documents such as the 1966 text entitled *Must we Revise Marxist-Leninist theory? Marxism is not a Humanism*.[5] But Althusser, in the end, decided that it was not the time for such a break. In March 1967, following yet another bout of depression, he admitted to Franca Madonia:

> I had to define my line and my position, and conform to the consequences of this. I stay in the Party. I have reflected on this for a long time: there is no other solution for me at the moment. I only hope that they will let keep to this decision, and they will not make me face impossible alternatives. But I do not think so. [...] Moreover, I have the liberty to write in my collection. In short, a certain space in front of me.[6]

2   Althusser on the Cultural Revolution

In the initial phase of the Sino-Soviet Split, China appeared to represent more of an continuation of Cold War communist tactics and rhetoric rather than a strategic alternative, especially since the official Chinese rhetoric insisted on not condemning Stalin, despite Mao's actual criticism of aspects of Stalinist politics. In contrast, the Cultural Revolution seemed to offer a much more profound alternative to 'actually existing socialism', by presenting socialism as a period of intensified class struggles during which it is possible to see the re-emergence of capitalist social forms and relations and by practicing what seemed to be, and to a large extent indeed was, a revolution inside a revolution. From the rebellious challenge of the authority of the Party Apparatus to the critique of the social division of labour, which could remain capitalist even under nominally 'socialist' relations of ownership, and the need for a constant

---

5   UJCML 1966.
6   Althusser 1997b, p. 738.

revolutionising of culture and mass ideology, the Cultural Revolution became a reference point for intellectuals and militants alike.[7]

In light of the above, it is interesting to read Althusser's anonymous article on the Chinese Cultural Revolution.[8] Although he treats the Cultural Revolution as an *ideological revolution*, in line with the initial rhetoric of the Chinese Communists of that time, and avoids any direct criticism of the USSR, he nevertheless insists that the problem facing socialist countries is indeed the regression towards capitalism,[9] although he cites only Yugoslavia as an example.[10]

Althusser insists that the central trait of the Cultural Revolution is that we must have 'confidence in the masses', who act through their own organisations.[11] He opposes the economistic position that it suffices to abolish the economic bases of social classes in order for classes to disappear. For Althusser, classes can also be defined in terms of social and political relations.[12] Consequently, his schema for the continuation of class struggle within socialist countries underestimates the contradictions in the economic field and the emergence and reproduction of an original form of state capitalism and stresses instead political and ideological relations, and a contradiction between 'a socialist infrastructure and bourgeois ideological superstructure'.[13] That is why he accepts the premise that there can be a '*dominant* role of the ideological in a political conjuncture of the history of the labour movement'.[14] Consequently, a revolution in the ideological is needed in order to 'reverse the process' and lead to 'revolutionary road'.[15] Althusser insisted that the ideological in the end has to do with *practical* attitudes,[16] a reference to the relation of ideology and practice. This resonates with his emphasis on theory and ideology as the crucial terrains of struggle for the correction of the political line of the party. So Althusser's insistence that the ideological can be decisive is also a justification of his own tactics in terms of theory as a correction for the right-wing line of the PCF. For Althusser, the Cultural Revolution reminds us that 'the domain

---

7   On the significance of the Cultural Revolution, see Bettelheim 1974; Badiou 2005c; Jiang 2014.
8   Anon. [Althusser] 1966. On Althusser's references to the Cultural Revolution, see Cavazzini 2009; Sibertin-Blanc 2009; Girval-Pallota 2009.
9   Anon. [Althusser] 1966, p. 8.
10 Anon. [Althusser] 1966, p. 11.
11 Anon. [Althusser] 1966, p. 9.
12 Anon. [Althusser] 1966, p. 12.
13 Anon. [Althusser] 1966, p. 13.
14 Anon. [Althusser] 1966, p. 12.
15 Anon. [Althusser] 1966, p. 13.
16 Anon. [Althusser] 1966, p. 14.

of ideology is one of the terrains of class struggle, and it can become a strategic terrain [...] there is an extremely profound connection between the theoretical conception and the ideological class struggle'.[17] Again, we are facing the same emphasis on political intervention as theoretical correction, from class struggle, to ideology as the terrain of the struggle to theory as what determines the ideological terrain. This still seems to be Althusser's line of reasoning as well as a tactic within the PCF, avoiding direct attacks on the party line and opting instead for theoretical interventions.

3 May 1968 and the New Challenges

It is on these grounds that we must see the many forms of Althusser's subsequent self-criticism. There was a radicalisation of his position, which is made evident in the evolution of his definitions of philosophy. Although it was not an open challenging of the politics of the Communist movement, it nevertheless referred to a different conception of the politics of theory and of politics in general, stressing the importance of movements, the priority of class struggle over the authority of theory or of the party, and laying the theoretical ground for a more open confrontation with political questions. In *Lenin and Philosophy* one can find not only a more militant conception of the *partisanship* in philosophy and the definition of philosophy as what 'represents politics in the domain of theory',[18] but also a very interesting reference to philosophy representing 'scientificity in politics',[19] interesting in the sense that it links the knowledge aspect of politics not only to science (and the guarantees it can provide) but also to a more open theoretical and political practice: philosophy. That is why we must combine this position on philosophy representing scientificity in politics with Althusser's insistence that philosophy has no proper object, in contrast to scientific knowledge, but operates through philosophical propositions and theses that intervene in given theoretical (and ideological) contradictions drawing lines of demarcation. If we combine these two positions, then it becomes obvious that the relation of philosophy to politics in terms of 'scientificity' is not one of offering knowledge or scientific guarantees for strategic and tactical political choices. It refs more to a highly original conception of a political practice that requires not only knowledge of a changing terrain but also an ability to draw

---

17   Anon. [Althusser] 1966, p. 16.
18   Althusser 1971, p. 65.
19   Ibid.

lines of demarcation (and to make choices) in contradictory circumstances without the benefit of full knowledge.

A crucial moment in Althusser's political development was his confrontation with May 1968. Although he did not have any direct participation in the events and despite the fact that some of his students had already broken ranks with the PCF, having formed their own Maoist group (UJCML), these events had a tremendous significance for Althusser. This is obvious in the texts he wrote in early 1969. On the one hand we have his criticism of Michel Verret's article on the 'Student May'.[20] In contrast to Verret's sharp criticism of the limits of student radicalism as opposed to proper working-class politics, Althusser saw in May 1968 the encounter between 'a general strike [...] without precedent in western history, in terms of number of participants and duration'[21] and an expression of the 'world revolt of scholarized youth [...] a profoundly progressive revolt that historically has a non negligible historical role in the world wide class struggle against imperialism'.[22] And although Althusser praised the attempts of the PCF to get in touch with youth revolts, he nevertheless stressed the fact that the PCF had lost touch with large segments of youth. Moreover, he avoided all the usual polemics against 'leftists' and considered May 68 to be an event of very important proportions. But it is also obvious that he still thought that it was the Communist Party that represented the working class and consequently that revolutionary or radical politics could only be built through the Communist Party, especially since he did not share the assumption, common to many leftists, that France had already reached some sort of pre-revolutionary situation.

Althusser returned to the question of how something could change in the Party in an unpublished small text from 1970.[23] Althusser insists that change cannot come from the pressure of the various Maoist or Trotskyst groups. On the other hand, he thought that change cannot come simply from inside the Party, and he refers to the way the PCF sought to 'integrate in its traditional line'[24] the events of May 1968. His suggestion was that change in the Party could be something happening inside the Party but as a result of an event happening outside the Party, especially something that could question the reference of the

---

20 Verret 1969. It is worth noting that Verret's article is an attempt towards a criticism of the Student Revolt that tries to avoid traditional PCF rhetoric and instead attempts to articulate a criticism of the limits of the aristocratic and phantasmatic aspects of youth revolt.
21 Althusser [1969] 2006, p. 75.
22 Althusser [1969] 2006, p. 81.
23 In Althusser 2018a, pp. 87–90.
24 Althusser 2018a, p. 88.

Party to the USSR. He thinks that the 'Czech crisis'[25] offered such an example, even though the Party managed to deal with it, and suggests that a more serious crisis of this kind could create an opposotion inside the Party which would lead to a more open crisis of its unity.

4 *On the Reproduction of Capitalism* as a Political Statement

This influence of May 1968 is also evident in Althusser's large manuscript *On the Reproduction of Capitalism*.[26] The preface to this manuscript, which is presented as the first part of a two-volume book on the reproduction of the relations of production and on class struggles, provides evidence of Althusser's insistence on the possibility of revolutionary change and consequently on the importance of Marxist philosophy as a *revolutionary weapon*.

> Let there be no mistake: we need only become aware of the unprecedented crisis into which imperialism, beleaguered by its contradictions and its victims and assailed by the people, has now plunged, in order to conclude that it will not survive it. We are entering an age that will see the triumph of socialism across the globe. We need only take note of the irresistible course of popular struggles in order to conclude that in a relatively near future, despite all the possible twists and turns, the very serious crisis of the international communist movement included, the revolution is already on the agenda One hundred years from now, perhaps only fifty years from now, the face of the world will have changed: the revolution will have carried the day from one end of the earth to the other.[27]

On the Reproduction of Capitalism is the first major manifestation of Althusser's break with any conception of deep structures regarding social reality. Instead of 'deep structures' we have a theorisation of lasting relations, and of practices and relations being reproduced by the interventions of the ideological apparatuses of the state through the material embodiment of practices and the repetition of social rituals.

---

25 Althusser 2018a, p. 89.
26 Althusser 1995; Althusser 2014b.
27 Althusser 2014b, pp. 5–6. See also the 1969 interview with M.A. Macciochi 'Philosophy as a Revolutionary Weapon' (in Althusser 1971).

> It is easy to see that, if a mode of production lasts only as long as the system of state apparatuses that guarantees the conditions of reproduction (reproduction = duration) of its base, that is, its relations of production, one has to attack the system of the state apparatuses and seize state power to disrupt the conditions of the reproduction (= duration = existence) of a mode of production and establish new relations of production. They are established under the protection of a new state and new state apparatuses which ensure the reproduction (= duration= existence) of the new relations of production, in other words, the new mode of production.[28]

It is a text that represents a break with important aspects of the Communist orthodoxy, echoing the radicalism of both the 1968 movements and the Cultural Revolution, such as the insistence on the primacy of relations of production over forces of production. Especially this reference to the primacy of the relations of production, as opposed to the traditional economism of the communist movement, which was centred upon the primacy of the forces of production,[29] is also used for Althusser as a justification for Lenin's and Mao's revolutionary tactics in contrast to Second International and Stalinist evolutionism and finalism.[30]

On the Reproduction of Capitalism is also filled with references to the need for a new conception of radical politics that should avoid the dangers of treating ideological apparatuses of the state as socially and politically neutral institutions. This is more evident in those chapters dealing with the political and trade union Ideological Apparatuses of the State. For Althusser the existence within the Ideological Apparatuses of the State of proletarian parties and trade unions can only be explained in terms of a long history of class struggle that imposed the presence of the Party and its trade union within these apparatuses. However, the very choice of treating trade unions and left-wing parties as parts of Ideological Apparatuses of the State is of particular political and theoretical significance, since it draws a line of demarcation against any identification of proletarian politics with the limits set within bourgeois Ideological Apparatuses, making sure that proletarian politics does not limit itself to parliamentary procedures and traditional 'legal' trade union operations. For

---

28 Althusser 2014b, p. 151.
29 '[T]he productive forces of society change and develop, and then, *depending* on these changes and *in conformity with them*, men's relations of production, their economic relations, change' (Stalin 1976, p. 859).
30 Althusser 2014b, p. 213.

Althusser proletarian politics should always go beyond these limits, exactly because proletarian organisations were born outside the ideological apparatuses of the state:

> Created by a class struggle external to the ISAs, sustained by it, charged with furthering and sustaining it by all available legal means, the proletarian organizations that figure in the ISAs concerned would betray their mission if they reduced the external class struggle, which merely finds a reflection in very limited forms in the class struggle carried out in the ISAs, to this class struggle internal to the ISAs.[31]

Of particular interest is the section on the relation of proletarian parties to the political Ideological Apparatus of the State. Althusser insists, in contrast to the prevailing strategy of European Communist Parties, that there can be no parliamentary road to socialism, since the important factor is mass action and not parliamentary action.

> Since, today, everyone is thinking about the 'transition' to socialism, it must be recalled that there is no parliamentary road to socialism. Revolutions are made by the masses, not by parliamentary deputies, even if the communists and their allies should fleetingly, by some miracle, attain a majority in the parliament.[32]

Althusser does not deny the possibility or the necessity of an attempt towards gaining parliamentary majority, but he insists that it is '*the actions of the popular masses*, assuming that they are educated, mobilized and committed to a struggle based on a correct line, would determine the nature of the transitional period thus initiated'.[33] Moreover, he insists that without a confrontation with state apparatuses, without smashing state apparatuses, it is not possible to have a revolutionary process. This calls for a different practice of politics that must be based on the '*deep, irreversible implantation of the political class struggle in the economic class struggle*'.[34] This is also based on the importance and primacy of the relations of production, since for Althusser a proper revolution is one that in the end opens up the way, through a long class struggle, for the

---

31   Althusser 2014b, p. 96.
32   Althussser 2014b, p. 107.
33   Althusser 2014b, p. 109.
34   Althusser 2014b, p. 135.

destruction of the State Apparatuses that guarantee the prevailing relations of production in order for them to be replaced by new relations of production. This gives a particularly political and strategic tone to *On Reproduction*. The question of reproduction is no longer purely theoretical; it is from the point of view of reproduction that questions of revolutionary strategy can be dealt with.

> If our interpretation is on the mark, we have to rise to the standpoint of reproduction not only in order to grasp the function and functioning of the superstructure, but also so as to have the concepts that will allow us to understand the concrete history of revolutions a little better (so that we can at last found the science of their history, which is at present still much more like chronicle than science): the history of revolutions that have already been made and of others that must still be made. This will also enable us to understand a little better the conditions that must be realized if we are to establish, under the dictatorship of the proletariat, the Ideological State Apparatuses required concretely to prepare the transition to socialism – that is, the gradual disappearance of the state and all its apparatuses – instead of floundering around in 'contradictions' that are more or less successfully camouflaged under 'policed' designations, of which contemporary history offers us all too many examples.[35]

Althusser's 1976 'Note on the ISAs' expands his conception of the Political Ideological Apparatus of the State. Of particular importance is his position that it is not a particular political party that acts as an Ideological Apparatus of the State but the entire political Ideological State Apparatus.[36] Consequently, a communist party, even if it participates in a government, '*cannot, on any grounds, be defined as a "party of government"*'.[37] This is in sharp contrast to the electoralism of the European Communist Parties that prevailed at the time. Moreover, Althusser offers in this text a more dialectical conception of 'proletarian ideology', which for Althusser must be distinguished from simple spontaneous proletarian elements, since it can include elements of bourgeois ideology and also the influence of Marxist theory, along with the historical experience of the labour movement, in a fusion that creates a new form of mass ideology, which

---

35   Althusser 2014b, pp. 161–2.
36   Althusser 2014b, p. 221.
37   Althusser 2014b, p. 225.

is transformed by historical experience and scientific elements.[38] That is why for Althusser ' "proletarian ideology" is by itself stake of a class struggle'.[39]

5   Balibar and the New Practice of Politics

Étienne Balibar's 1971 'La rectification du Manifeste Communiste'[40] is an important text in the same line of reasoning. Balibar uses his reading of the changes or additions brought to the *Communist Manifesto* by Marx and Engels as a way to trace the emergence of a radically antagonistic form of revolutionary politics. For Balibar, in the *Communist Manifesto* 'the revolution is not conceived simply as an act, but as an *objective* process',[41] a process which is based on class struggle; it is a series of class struggles. For Balibar the initial references of the *Communist Manifest* to the state, the revolutionary process, and the possibility of an 'end of politics' after the victory of the revolution are not deprived of contradictions, open questions and theoretical absences regarding the dictatorship of the proletariat, the revolutionary process, the actual process of dismantling the existing state apparatuses.[42] Marx came to terms with some of these contradictions after the experience of the Paris Commune, which can explain why he and Engels referred in their 1872 preface to the *Communist Manifest* to changes they would have made in light of the experience of the Commune, especially regarding the inability of the working class to simply take up the existing state apparatus.[43] For Balibar, the measures taken by the

---

38   'It is therefore a very special kind of ideology. It is an ideology, because, at the level of the masses, it functions the way any ideology does (by interpellating individuals as subjects). It is, however, steeped in historical experiences illuminated by scientific principles of analysis' (Althusser 2014b, p. 228).
39   Ibid.
40   In Balibar 1974.
41   Balibar 1974, p. 79.
42   Balibar 1974, pp. 88–9.
43   'However much the state of things may have altered during the last twenty-five years, the general principles laid down in this Manifesto are, on the whole, as correct today as ever. Here and there some detail might be improved. The practical application of the principles will depend, as the Manifesto itself states, everywhere and at all times, on the historical conditions for the time being existing, and, for that reason, no special stress is laid on the revolutionary measures proposed at the end of Section II. That passage would, in many respects, be very differently worded today. In view of the gigantic strides of Modern Industry in the last twenty-five years, and of the accompanying improved and extended party organisation of the working class, in view of the practical experience gained, first in the February Revolution, and then, still more, in the Paris Commune, where the prolet-

Commune and its attempt to do away with parliamentary democracy and bureaucracy represented an actual process of dismantling the State Apparatus, which – in contrast to twentieth-century communist reformism and its conception of 'stages of the revolutionary process' – was not at the end but at the beginning of the revolutionary process. Moreover, according to Balibar, there were important changes in the definition of state power and the apparatuses of the state, which necessarily lead to the conclusion that the proletariat cannot simply conquer and then use the old bourgeois state apparatus.

> [T]he *exploiting classes* and the *exploited class*, which for the first time in history and because of its role in production, is in the position to take power for itself, *cannot exercise their power* (and even their absolute power, their 'dictatorship') *with the same means and thus in the same forms*. They cannot, not in the sense of a moral impossibility but in the sense of a material impossibility: the machine of the State does not function 'for the sake of' the working class; either it does not function at all, or it does function, but for the sake of someone else, who can be no other than the class adversary. It is impossible for the proletariat, to conquer, safeguard and use political power by using an instrument analogous to the one used by the dominant classes; otherwise it will *lose* it, in one form or the other, 'violent' or 'peaceful'.[44]

This makes necessary a new practice of proletarian politics. This new practice of politics, this revolutionary transformation of politics includes the emergence of new forms of mass political organisation exterior to the state, and the penetration of politics within the realm of production, putting an end to the bourgeois separation of economics and politics.

> It is the penetration of political practice in the sphere of 'work', of production. In other words it is the end of the absolute separation, which was developed by capitalism itself, between 'politics' and 'economics'.[45]

---

ariat for the first time held political power for two whole months, this program has in some details become antiquated. One thing especially was proved by the Commune, viz., that "the working class cannot simply lay hold of the ready-made state machinery, and wield it for its own purposes." (See *The Civil War in France; Address of the General Council of the International Working Men's Association*, London, Truelove, 1871, p. 15, where this point is further developed)' (Marx and Engels 1970, p. 2).

44 Balibar 1974, pp. 95–6.
45 Balibar 1974, p. 96.

That is why revolutionary transformation cannot have as an end the 'end of politics' and its replacement by the 'administration of things', which for Balibar represented a bourgeois distinction between persons and things. What is needed is a new form, a new practice of proletarian politics. One can find in Balibar's intervention echoes not only of the criticism of the Cultural Revolution, but also of the need for a new form of communist politics that would go beyond communist reformism and opportunism, along with an insistence that the attempt to smash the state and transform social and political relations is a constant political battle that cannot wait for after the revolution. It must be at the beginning of any emancipatory and transformative politics.

6   The Left-Wing Critique of Stalinism

As many commentators have suggested, one of the crucial aspects of Althusser's interventions was an attempt towards a left-wing critique of Stalinism. This was important because Althusser had mainly refrained in the 1960s from openly criticising socialist construction in the USSR. This was more evident in his conception of socialist humanism mainly as a way to deal with the internal contradictions of socialism. Althusser's references to most of his public interventions in the 1960s remained within the limits of a criticism of errors and Stalinist excesses that was repeated in many instances in Western European communist parties. As we have already noted, even his 1966 unsigned text on the Cultural Revolution treats only Yugoslavia as a case of a return to capitalist social forms. At the same time and under the influence of the Cultural Revolution there was especially in France an attempt to actually criticise Soviet socialism in terms of class analysis and class struggle (instead of traditional leftist criticisms of 'bureaucracy' and right-wing criticisms of 'totalitarianism'). This is especially evident in the work of Charles Bettelheim.[46]

In the Appendix of *On Reproduction*,[47] Althusser offers his arguments in favour of the primacy of the relations of production over the forces of produc-

---

46   Bettelheim 1974; Bettelheim 1974–76; Bettelheim 1975. In my opinion Bettelheim's books remain an indispensable reference for anyone attempting a Marxist analysis and critique of Stalinism, and that is why Gregory Elliott's reference to 'Bettelheim's effective apologia for Stalin' (Elliott 2006, p. 236) totally misses the essence of Bettelheim's endeavor.
47   Althusser 2014b, pp. 209–17.

tion. This is not just a theoretical or analytical choice, but a political criticism of the Soviet model for the construction of socialism. For Althusser the policies adopted by Stalin can only be explained by the primacy of the forces of production thesis.

> Incontestably, we can characterize Stalin's politics (inasmuch as, from the 1930–32 'turn' onwards, Stalin was, in the last resort, the only one to take political decisions) by saying that it was the *consistent politics of the primacy of the productive forces over the relations of production*. It would be interesting to examine, in this regard, Stalin's policies [*politique*] in connection with planning and the peasantry; the role he assigned the party; and even certain stupefying formulas such as the one which, defining 'man' as 'the most valuable capital', obviously treated man with regard to labour power alone, in other words, as nothing more nor less than a component of the productive forces (consider the related theme of Stakhanovism).[48]

For Althusser the changes after the 20th Congress of the CPSU did not fundamentally alter this conception of the primacy of the productive forces and consequently. In this sense *Reply to John Lewis*[49] is a particularly important text regarding Althusser's attempt at a left-wing critique of Stalinism that cannot be reduced to 'violations of Soviet legality alone'.[50] Althusser offers here a profound critique of Soviet 'socialism' that stresses the importance of the couple economism/humanism as both an explanation of the re-emergence of capitalist social relations within 'socialism' and the ideological/mystifying functioning of humanist ideology. Althusser insists on the need for a *left-wing* critique of Stalinism, as opposed to a *right-wing* critique that would target 'only certain aspects of the *legal* superstructure, and of course can then invoke Man and his Rights, and oppose Man to the violation of his Rights (or simple "workers' councils" to the "bureaucracy")'.[51] The combination between economism and humanism of the Stalinist deviation can explain what seems like a '*posthumous revenge of the Second International*'.[52] For Althusser economism is an ideological mystification of the relations of production and the

---

48   Althusser 2014b, p. 215.
49   In Althusser 1976a.
50   Althusser 1976a, pp. 91–2.
51   Althusser 1976a, p. 82.
52   Althusser 1976a, p. 89.

material forms they take which is instrumental for bourgeois hegemony but also dangerous if it is reproduced within a process of transition to socialism.

> The fact that the bourgeoisie, in its own ideology, keeps *silent* about the relations of production and the class struggle, in order to exalt not only 'expansion' and 'productivity' but also Man and his liberty – that is its own affair, and it is quite in order, in *bourgeois order*: because it needs this silence, which allows economism/humanism, expressing *the bourgeois point of view*, to work at the concealment of the relations of production while helping to guarantee and reproduce them. [...] Because, unless it is only a question of words or of a few speeches, if it is really a question of a consistent political line and practice, then you can bet – as Lenin did, when he spoke about the pre-1914 Second International – that this bourgeois point of view is a contaminating agent which can threaten or even overcome the *proletarian point of view* within *Marxism itself*.[53]

In contrast he insisted that in the history, practice, and experience of the Chinese Cultural Revolution, however uneven and unfinished, we could find the only left-wing critique of Stalinism:

> If we look back over our whole history of the last forty years or more, it seems to me that, in reckoning up the account (which is not an easy thing to do), the only *historically existing* (left) 'critique' of the fundamentals of the 'Stalinist deviation' to be found – and which, moreover, is *contemporary* with this very deviation, and thus for the most part precedes the Twentieth Congress – is a concrete critique, one which exists in the facts, in the struggle, in the line, in the practices, their principles and their forms, of the Chinese Revolution. A silent critique, which speaks through its actions, the result of the political and ideological struggles of the Revolution, from the Long March to the Cultural Revolution and its results. A critique *from afar*. A critique 'from behind the scenes'.[54]

---

53 Althusser 1976a, p. 88.
54 Althusser 1976a, pp. 92–3.

This marks Althusser's explicit break with not only the conception of the construction of socialism developed by Soviet Marxism, but also with any hope that there could be some form of 'reform' of it. At the same time it is a break with the politics of Communist Parties in Western Europe.[55] Althusser offers a way to think of the contradictions and shortcomings of Soviet 'socialism' not in terms of a 'bureaucratic deformation' or of 'totalitarianism', but in terms of a history of class struggles, in all instances of the social whole, including theory, which led to the eventual reproduction of bourgeois economic, political and ideological forms within 'socialist' formations. In light of this reference to the critique of Soviet Socialism by the Cultural Revolution,[56] we can understand that 'economism' for Althusser is not simply an ideological deviation but the condensation of contradictions and displacements in communist strategy as a result of a complex history of class struggle. Moreover, this helps to avoid the danger of seeing this evolution as the simple result of a betrayal of principles, since the question was – and still is – how to explain the tragedy of 'soviet socialism' as the result of choices and practices of people that perhaps thought that they were constructing socialism.

This left-wing critique of Stalinism, absent in the formulations of Althusser's 1960s texts, was an important aspect of his theoretical and political self-criticism and his attempt to more openly intervene in the debates on the politics and tactics of the communist movement. It was also a break with the political and theoretical traditions of the PCF.[57] At a time when to the already traumatic experience of the Stalinist purges new traumas had been added, especially by the Soviet invasion of Czechoslovakia in 1968, it was imperative for any attempt to rethink communist strategy to take a stand regarding the evolution of soviet socialism. That is why Althusser attempted now this critique of Stalinism.

However, it has been suggested, mainly by Gregory Elliott, that the *Reply to John Lewis* does not offer a genuine left-wing critique of Stalinism.[58] This is based on Elliott's rather schematic rejection of the experience of the Cultural

---

55 On Althusser's attempt towards a left-wing critique of communist reformism see Goshgarsian 2006 and 2015.
56 On a recent evaluation of the importance of the Cultural Revolution and its radical dynamics, see Jiang 2014.
57 We should bear in mind, as William Lewis has stressed, that '[w]ith the [Stalin's] *Short Course*, the French Communist Party found its primer to teach the algebra of revolution' (2005, p. 74).
58 In a similar vein, Alex Callinicos has insisted on Althusser's 'ambiguity' towards Stalinism (see Callinicos 1976).

Revolution as an actual left-wing critique of Stalinism, based on a 'to the letter' reading of pro-Stalin statements of the Chinese Communist Party.[59] It is also based on Elliott's preference for an explanation of Stalinism based on the 'primordial sin' of a strategy for 'socialism in one country' being the inevitable result of the isolation of the Soviet Union.[60] Elliott's preference for 'socialism in one country' as the root of Stalinism may be in line with a more traditional 'left-opposition' critique of Stalinism but in my opinion it falls short of providing an explanation. The Soviet Union's isolation was not a political choice but a historical fact, based in the very unevenness of the development of the revolutionary project, something made painfully evident in the defeat of the 'revolution in the West'. It did pose an important constraint, but the evolution of social and political forms inside the USSR and the reproduction of capitalist forms of production, hierarchy and organisation (in the sense of treating social relations as technical relations), as a result of a process of class struggles was surely a contributing factor. Althusser's insistence on economism is justified, if we take economism as a metonymic reference not simply to a theoretical 'deviation' but to an entire process of the persistence and later endorsement of a capitalist division of labour that could act as the material social matrix for the re-emergence of state capitalist forms of exploitation and consequently of a state capitalist class. Therefore, Althusser's reference to 'economism' as the root of the Stalinist deviation retains its validity, at least as the basis for an explanation, that itself would require a much broader study of the history of class struggles in the Soviet Union as a complex and uneven history that was far from being predetermined.

Elliott's criticism of Althusser's interpretation of Stalinism is also based on his criticism of Althusser's positive references to the Cultural Revolution. Although Elliott justifies Althusser's 'indulgence'[61] in the sense of the allure of the Cultural Revolution for Western intellectuals, he still considers its actual legacy to be one of obscurantism and voluntarism. Yet Elliott is missing exactly the fact that the Cultural Revolution was crucial not in the sense of a well

---

59   Elliott 2006, p. 232.
60   'A plausible hypothesis is that the very project of "socialism in one country" was a product of the isolation of a post-revolutionary state which, crippled by backwardness, devastated by war and ravaged by scarcity, was the epitome of the kingdom of necessity; that it contributed to the reinforcement of the isolation until the changed correlation of forces in the end of World War II; and that after 1945 "socialism in one zone" (Eastern Europe) was established by Stalin at the price of the salvation of Western Europe from communism' (Elliott 2006, p. 237).
61   Elliott 2006, p. 242.

defined strategic alternative to Stalinism but in the sense of the full eruption of both the contradictions of 'socialist construction' and the initiative of the popular masses, thus offering a kind of radical critique of Stalinism that was missing from the Marxist debates until now.[62]

---

62 Alain Badiou summarised the importance of the Cultural Revolution in a 1980 article in *Le Monde*: '[L]ike every other revolution, the Cultural Revolution combined the exceptional with the worst; it witnessed dramatic reversals, tortuous maneuvers. Obscure confrontations, major repressions. All of this matching the scale of an unprecedented endeavor: to block the process of emergence of a bureaucratic bourgeoisie [...] Behind the enormous confusion about its various stages, the lines of force of the Cultural Revolution, the entrance on the stage of tens of millions of actors, and the blockage of its goal, all bear in what is essential: the reduction of the gap between intellectual and manual labor, between town and country; the subordination of the productive impetus to the institution of new social relations; the end of university elitism; the reduction of the insolence of cadres; the end of wage systems of inequality and stratification; the ideological opposition to the degenerate "Marxism" that rules in Moscow and in the "communist" parties pledging allegiance to it, and so on' (Badiou 2005c, p. 660).

CHAPTER 18

Althusser in the 1970s: Break and Open Critique of Communist Reformism

In the second half of the 1970s Althusser attempted a criticism of the Eurocommunist turn of most European communist parties and especially of their realignment towards a peaceful, democratic, and parliamentary road to socialism. In the mid-1970s it seemed that a possibility had opened up for the Left to gain governmental power. The combination of the economic crisis, the crisis of imperialism exemplified in the US defeat in Vietnam, the persistence of elements of the 1968 social and political radicalism, and the electoral rise of Communist Parties seemed to offer this possibility, especially in Italy and France. This was combined with political and theoretical shifts. The road to socialism was presented as a mainly peaceful and democratic parliamentary road, with respect to formal liberties, avoiding violence and even including (as in the case of the Italian 'Historical Compromise'[1]) tactical alliances with bourgeois mass parties. In line with this shift, references to the dictatorship of the proletariat were abandoned, in highly publicised debates, such as the one within the PCF, and even parties traditionally loyal to Soviet Union, opted for criticisms of Stalinism. Moreover, many Marxist intellectuals that until then were more or less critical of European communist parties' politics now rallied to the new strategy of *democratic road to socialism*, Nicos Poulantzas[2] being perhaps the most notable case.

1 **The French Debate on the Abandonment of the Dictatorship of the Proletariat**

In France this entire debate was articulated around the tactics of the Union of the Left, an alliance with the Socialist Party, after the latter's supposed radical turn in the 1971 Congress, which was expressed in the 1973 *Programme Commun* (Common Programme). At the same time, the second half of the 1970s

---

1 Berlinguer 1973.
2 On Poulantzas's theoretical and political trajectory, see Jessop 1985 and Martin 2008. See also the texts in Poulantzas 2008.

was also a period of crisis for the revolutionary Left in Europe. The exhaustion of the post-1968 radical surge, the end of the Cultural Revolution and the right-wing turn of the Chinese Communist Party and the inability to have an actual alternative strategy to communist reformism, contributed to this. This was made evident in the problems facing the varieties of Trotskyism, the open crisis of Maoist organisations, the inability of the massive Italian organisations of the revolutionary left to challenge the hegemony of the PCI in the Italian Left.[3] This created an intense contradiction between the euphoria for the electoral successes of the Left and the actual strategic impasse of the European Left. The inability of a Left majority in the 1976 Italian elections, the crisis in the French Union of the Left, the inability of the Greek communist Left to challenge the rising hegemony of PASOK, marked the beginning of a period of an open crisis for European Communist Parties. In the early 1980s the electoral victories of Socialist parties and their rapid turn towards policies of austerity and capitalist restructuring put an end to the hopes about potential 'progressive governments'.

Althusser gradually chose a more openly political manner to intervene. In sharp contrast to his early opposition of the political deviation of the communist movement to the correct line embedded in Marxist theory, now he stressed the crisis within Marxism itself, not only in the form of deviations from the original but also in the sense of open contradictions, lacunae and unanswered questions in the works of the classics themselves. So the necessary correction of the political line could no longer be the theoretical correction but a new elaboration both of theory but also of politics. That is why he hailed the open crisis of Marxism – especially in what concerned questions of the state – as a salutary event. However, even this new emphasis on struggles outside the state seemed rather schematic, as some of his critics stressed even at the time, especially regarding this inside/outside the state dialectic. In what follows we take a close look at his interventions in the second half of the 1970s.

The political conjuncture of that period is marked by the debates in the French Left around *Le Programme Commun*, and the possibility of forming a government in collaboration with the socialists. Of particular importance, regarding the debates within French Communism was the 22nd Congress of the French Communist Party, itself marked by the debates around the abandonment of the dictatorship of the proletariat from Party statutes, a move that

---

[3] On the strategic crisis of the Italian Left in the 1970s, see Abse 1985 and Magri 2011. See also Harman 1979 for an overview of the impasse of most organisations of the European revolutionary left in the late 1970s.

was openly presented as a correction that could draw in to the PCF voters who were appalled by what was happening in the Soviet Union and other countries of actually existing socialism. For Althusser and some of his collaborators, this was the crucial point from which to launch a much more open polemic against the party line.

This took the form first of all of a book by Balibar on the question of the dictatorship of the proletariat.[4] In this, Balibar attempts to criticise the main position of the leadership of the PCF, which is based upon the distinction between two 'revolutionary' roads, one that was violent, undemocratic, and based upon a fraction of the popular classes, and another that would be based upon peaceful means, democratic legality, and the union of the people, with implicit references to the need to avoid the mistakes of the Soviet Union. For Balibar this conception tends to view the dictatorship of the proletariat as simply a political regime or a set of institutions:

> Now this idea of the dictatorship of the proletariat as a simple 'political régime' directly determines the terms in which the problem of the political power of the working class, or of the working people, is posed. The dictatorship of the proletariat becomes *a special form of the political power of the working people*, and a narrow form at that (since not all working people are proletarians). In fact, this amounts to saying that the dictatorship of the proletariat is a *form of government* (in the legal, constitutional sense), that it represents a particular *system of institutions*. To choose between a number of paths of transition to socialism, for or against the dictatorship of the proletariat, is – according to this idea – to choose between a number of systems of institutions, notably between institutions of a parliamentary or so-called 'pluralist' type (containing several political parties) and institutions of a non-parliamentary type, in which the power of the working people is exercised through a single party. Socialist democracy differs from the dictatorship of the proletariat, in this view, as one political regime differs from another; it is conceived of as another form of the political power of the working people, in which other institutions organize in a different way the choice of the 'representatives' of the working people who run the government, and the 'participation' of individuals in the functioning of the State.[5]

---

4 Balibar 1977b. For the French debate on the question of the dictatorship of the proletariat, see Balibar et al. 1977.
5 Balibar 1977b, p. 46.

Balibar attempts to see the dictatorship of the proletariat as an attempt to theorise the transition to *communism*, to see socialism as the period of transition to socialism. It is only under these terms that the very notion of the dictatorship of the proletariat can be conceived, and not as simply the political regime of socialism.

> But when Marx discovered the historical necessity of the dictatorship of the proletariat, he did not refer simply to socialism: he referred to the process which, within the very heart of the existing class struggles, leads towards the *society without classes, towards communism*. Socialism, alone, is a half-way dream house, where everyone can choose his own menu, where the demarcation line between proletarian politics and bourgeois or petty-bourgeois politics cannot be drawn in a clear way. The classless society is the real objective whose recognition characterizes proletarian politics. This 'shade of meaning' changes everything, as we shall see. By defining the dictatorship of the proletariat in terms of 'socialism', one is *already* trapped within a bourgeois framework.[6]

Balibar attempts to answer these challenges by going back to Marx's and Lenin's conception of state forms, including democratic forms as forms of class dictatorship:

> For the Marxist theory of the State, which involves a class standpoint diametrically opposed to that of bourgeois legal ideology, *every democracy is a class dictatorship*. Bourgeois democracy is a class dictatorship, the dictatorship of the minority of exploiters; proletarian democracy is also a class dictatorship, the dictatorship of the immense majority of working and exploited people.[7]

Balibar in a rather provocative way returns to a conception of the state as 'instrument':

> State power is not the power of an individual, of a group of individuals, of a particular stratum of society (like the 'bureaucracy' or 'technocracy') or of a simple, more or less extensive fraction of a class. State power is always *the power of a class*. State power, which is produced in the class

---

6 Balibar 1977b, pp. 48–9.
7 Balibar 1977b, p. 70.

struggle, can only be the instrument of the ruling class: what Marx and Engels called the *dictatorship* of the ruling class.[8]

However, Balibar is very far from a traditional instrumentalist conception of the state. The reference to the *production* of state power in class struggle refers to a relational conception of state power. State power as 'instrument' refers to the materialised condensation of a class balance of forces. That is why Balibar opposes any conception of state power as a neutral instrument or as an instrumental that can be used or bent at will.

> Opportunism therefore consists in the belief and the argument that the State apparatus is an instrument which can be bent according to the will, the intentions and the decisions of a given class. It consists in the argument that the government is the master of the State apparatus. And of the actions which follow from this belief.[9]

Balibar seems particularly critical of recent attempts to offer a supposedly enlarged version of the state, apart from class domination, fearing that this would lead to an underestimation of the class character of the state, the reproduction of bourgeois legal ideology, and, in the end, a reformist struggle for the reform of the state:

> In fact, if the State 'in the broad sense' could not be reduced to class domination, if this domination only affected its operation after the event, pulling it and deforming it 'in the direction' of the reproduction of such domination, and sooner or later coming into contradiction with the 'needs of society', then the revolutionary struggle would not be a struggle against the existing State, but more fundamentally a struggle *for* that State, for the development of its universal functions, a struggle to rescue it from the abusive 'stranglehold' maintained on it by the ruling class [...] this definition of the State quite simply adopts the traditional image provided for it by bourgeois legal ideology. The Marxist thesis says: it is *because* the social relations of production are relations of exploitation and antagonism that a special organ, the State, is necessary for their reproduction [...] But what we are now being offered, on the contrary, is the bourgeois thesis (whose value has, it seems, not been 'suf-

---

8 Balibar 1977b, p. 66.
9 Balibar 1977b, p. 90.

ficiently attended to' by the classics of Marxism) that the State is *something other* than the class struggle.[10]

All these have also to do with the question of a progressive or democratic government. For Balibar, it is impossible to have a profound social change by a simple change of government without a change in the state apparatuses regarding the actual class relation of forces within the state: 'it is obviously not sufficient for this purpose to *change the government*, without touching the structure of the State: historical experience shows that every government, whether it likes it or not, is always subject to the relation of class forces; it does not stand above the State apparatus of which it is a part, but in a subordinate relation to that apparatus'.[11] These questions were not simply theoretical; they also had some political urgency, especially after the traumatic experience of the *Unidad Popular* government in Chile, and the failure of the revolutionary process in Portugal. For Balibar this has a more general importance: the possibility of progressive governance can only be the beginning of a process of revolutionary process. Without a revolutionary confrontation with the question of political and state power there is always the possibility of defeat:

> Those Frenchmen who have lived through the Popular Front government of 1936 and the Liberation will in this connexion recall not only the victories of these periods but also what we must accept (in order to draw the objective lessons) as a fact: that they were, for the time being, defeated, for they were unable to move forward from a popular government acting in favour of the working people, and in support of its demands, to the revolutionary seizure of State power. And if we look for a moment at the history of other countries, the examples of Chile with its Popular Unity alliance and Portugal with its Armed Forces Movement are more recent reminders, among others, of the *existence of this critical threshold*, below which all the victories won by the masses in struggle, however many and however heroic these victories may be, can always be reversed, and worse. But this is also the lesson of the Russian Revolution.[12]

In contrast, a different process of revolutionary change would require working upon and expanding the tendency towards new forms of political institutions

---

10   Balibar 1977b, p. 75.
11   Balibar 1977b, p. 82.
12   Ibid.

that emerges during the intensification of the class struggle: 'Their importance – the importance of the Soviets – is that they *proved* the reality of this tendency. All subsequent revolutions, even if they were defeated by a more powerful enemy, even if they were only 'dress rehearsals', have provided in their own way illustrations of this tendency: from the Italian "factory councils" and the Chilean "workers' cordons" to the Chinese "People's Communes".'[13] The dictatorship of the proletariat does not represent a 'model' but a strategic question: 'The dictatorship of the proletariat does not provide Communists with a ready-made answer, with a clearly marked road; it only provides them with the possibility of posing an unavoidable problem. But well-posed problems will always be more valuable than dozens of imaginary answers'.[14] Moreover, the dictatorship of the proletariat must be viewed from the standpoint of communism, as part of the struggle for communism, as a process of liberating social and political potentialities.

> The proletarian revolution already entails, right from the beginning, the *development of communist social forms*, in particular in the shape of the political intervention and organization of the masses themselves, without which it would never have been possible to make the transition from the bourgeois State to proletarian democracy. In other words, proletarian democracy is not the realization of full liberty for the working people, but it is the struggle for liberation, it is the process and concrete experience of liberation as materialized in this very struggle.[15]

Consequently, for Balibar is utterly wrong to oppose the dictatorship of the proletariat to the democratic demand. Rather, the dictatorship of the proletariat represents the radical democratic drive inherent in the communist project. The fear of the dictatorship of the proletariat is essentially not the fear of its supposed undemocratic character; rather it is the fear of the radical, liberating, and egalitarian character of mass proletarian and popular democracy. This is one of the boldest condemnations of the right-wing turn of the communist movement in the 1970s: the abandonment of the dictatorship of the proletariat is not a democratic advance; it is a fear of democracy, a fear of the masses and of their own struggles, initiatives, and demands; it is the expression of the inability of communist parties to base themselves upon the social and political dynamics of the social classes and forces they supposedly represented.

---

13   Balibar 1977b, p. 99.
14   Balibar 1977b, p. 110.
15   Balibar 1977b, p. 123.

From this point of view it is possible to explain why the dictatorship of the proletariat is feared or rejected. The reason does not lie in a principled bringing about socialism by democratic means. On the contrary, it lies in the *fear of democracy*, the fear of *the mass forms* of democracy which overshoot and explode the extraordinarily narrow limits within which every bourgeois State confines democracy. Or perhaps in despair that history will ever make it possible for these forms to develop.[16]

Therefore, for Balibar the dictatorship of the proletariat is a '*historical tendency*',[17] not just a political programme. It is a historical tendency – and not certainty – towards the escalation of class struggle and the opening of communism as possibility. That is why Balibar provides a necessary reminder that socialism is not a mode of production but a historical process of intense struggles towards communism as a non-exploitative mode of production. And this means that socialism, the period of the dictatorship of the proletariat, is a period of experimentation with new social forms and of transformation of the forms of organisation of social production.

That is why it produces nothing but confusion to picture socialism in terms of the simple 'rationalization' of the organization of social labour, the parasitic capitalist class having been eliminated (even if this process is supposed to be accompanied, at the social level, by a fair distribution of the products of labour, and at the political level by greater liberty and increased 'participation' for the masses). [...] [S]ocialism, as an historical process, can only develop on the basis of a profound, progressive transformation of the division of labour, on the basis of a conscious political struggle against the division of manual and intellectual labour, against 'narrow' specialization, for what Marx called 'all-round competence'. Socialism cannot consist in the permanent *association*, in the service of their common interest, of the various social strata and categories of 'working people' existing in capitalist society: it cannot perpetuate, or even 'guarantee' the distinctions in function and status which divide them, as if there always had to be engineers on the one hand and unskilled

---

16   Ibid. Balibar would later return to this conception of the fear of the masses in his reading of Spinoza: '*It is the fear that the masses feel. But it is also a fear that the masses inspire* in whoever is placed in the position of governing or acting politically, hence in the state as such' (Balibar 1994b, p. 5).
17   Balbar 1977b, p. 134.

workers on the other, professors, lawyers and labourers [...] It can only be the continuous process of the *transformation* of these divisions.[18]

We have here an important attempt to offer a left-wing critique of communist reformism and an attempt at confronting what he defined as the 'crisis of Leninism'.[19] Although it might sometimes seem like a traditional 'dogmatic' defence of the 'letter' of the classics of Marxism, in fact it is a continuation of the thematic of the 'new practice of politics' and the need to think of the transition to communism as a process of constant struggle and transformation. It is also a political intervention, not only in relation to the debate within the PCF but also – and mainly – in relation to the open political question of how to expand the dynamic of the 'global 1968'.

2 Althusser's Confrontation with the Crisis of the Communist Movement

Balibar's text on the dictatorship of the proletariat was part of a broader attempt at a critique of what was perceived by the Althusserian current as the right-wing turn by the leadership of the PCF, of which the abandonment of the concept of the dictatorship of the proletariat was but one expression. In 1976 Althusser prepared a lengthy manuscript on this subject, entitled *Les vaches noires. Interview imaginaire*.[20] This manuscript, written in the form of an 'auto-interview', was intended to be Althusser's more direct and critical public intervention regarding the politics and strategies of the PCF and the communist movement in general. However, after receiving various criticisms by people to whom he had sent the manuscript, he decided not to publish it.[21]

The manuscript begins with Althusser attempting to explain that although a member of the Party since 1948 he had faced many difficulties in his relation to it, both in the sense of harsh criticism and false accusations regarding his work. Situating the 22nd Congress in the broader conjuncture of a '*serious crisis of the international communist movement*',[22] exemplified in the problems relating to the USSR and the difficulty of maintaining a classical version of 'proletarian internationalism' and made evident in the 'wobbly compromise' [*compromis*

---

18   Balibar 1977b, p. 149.
19   Balibar 1977b, p. 155.
20   Althusser 2016.
21   On the history of the manuscript of *Les vaches noires* see Goshgarian 2016.
22   Althusser 2016, p. 90.

bancal]²³ in the declaration of the meeting of the European Communist Parties in Berlin in June 1976, Althusser proceeds to a critique of the way the PCF leadership handled the debate. In particular, he points towards the fact that it was not an attempt just a using new wording for a revolutionary strategy,²⁴ but an abandonment of the concept and insists that 'words' cannot be treated separately from the political practice to which they are related, since after a certain point 'they have become forces, objective realities that we cannot reduce to the simple form of words'.²⁵ For Althusser the problem is that the Party, instead of liberating the concept by dissociating it from Stalinist practices, opted to abandon it. For Althusser this leads to very serious problems regarding the entire ideological and theoretical edifice of the Party, in a period marked also by a crisis in Marxist theory.

> [T]he party that abandons a key concept of the doctrine is obliged by the same inescapable law, either to completely revise the doctrine (what we can call, using a word that is perfectly correct, the theological revisionism of the Reformation), that is to produce another doctrine, itself formally coherent yet profoundly different in its theoretical orientation, and [...] in its practical effects; or to resolutely preserve the old concepts, *with the exception* of the abandoned concept [...] that is to replace the abandoned concept by a pseudo-concept.²⁶

Althusser then takes up the theme of the dictatorship of the proletariat *per se*. It is interesting that reworking the manuscript of *Les vaches noires* he used the text of a lecture he gave in Barcelona in July 1976,²⁷ in a very particular conjuncture marked on the one hand by the contradictions of the transition period in Spain and on the other by the evolution of the debate on Eurocommunism.²⁸ Althusser begins by insisting that the dictatorship of the proletariat is still part of the order of the day of communist parties all over the world. He attacks Stalin for his 1936 declaration that for the Soviet Union attaining socialism means that the dictatorship of the proletariat is not relevant, a position Althusser criticises, in a line similar to Balibar's, as being in contrast to Marx's

---

23 Althusser 2016, p. 117.
24 Althusser refers to Jean Kanapa's phrase that the document of the Congress 'spoke the language of everyone' (Althusser 2016, p. 128).
25 Althusser 2016, p. 103.
26 Althusser 2016, p. 160.
27 Althusser 2014c; Althusser 2015b.
28 On the conjuncture of the lecture see Montag 2015.

and Lenin's insistence on the dictatorship of the proletariat coinciding with the entire phase of socialism. Abandoning the dictatorship of the proletariat in the name of a 'State of the entire people', as was the case with Stalin's 1936 declaration, for Althusser 'makes no sense from the standpoint of Marxist theory',[29] since there are always forms of class struggle and class antagonism even in the context of socialism.

Turning his attention to the abandonment of the dictatorship of the proletariat by Western Communist Parties, Althusser criticises the tradition of Italian Communism of abandoning the dictatorship of the proletariat, in the name of the concept of hegemony, and in particular the conception that there could be hegemony of the proletariat over society (and not just its allies) before taking power. For Althusser this leads to a 'vicious circle', since it implies that hegemony could exist *'before the historical conditions – meaning the economic, political and ideological conditions – for its own existence [...] even before the seizing of state power'*.[30] However, Althusser has to confront the absence of the concept of the dictatorship of the proletariat in Gramsci's *Quaderni*. For Althusser, if Gramsci had the full liberty of expression he would have used the notion of the dictatorship to refer to the dictatorship of the proletariat and not hegemony.

For Althusser the concept of the dictatorship of the proletariat is 'a scientific concept', within the science of *'the laws of class struggle'*[31] that Marx founded, and as a scientific concept it brings real knowledge. However, it can also have other ideological usages or even false forms, but this does not alter its scientific character. Althusser even treats it as an 'eternal' truth in the sense defined by Spinoza but he insists that although it exists as a truth, there is a difference between its truth and its application, since its application depends upon the existence of its object.

> Concretely, this means that the dictatorship of the proletariat is true for us even when the dictatorship of the proletariat – that is, socialism – does not exist in our countries. When the proletariat has already taken power, the truth of the dictatorship of the proletariat exists in another way, since its object has an actual existence to which this truth is thus directly applicable, strategically. Furthermore, when communism reigns over the world, the truth of the dictatorship of the proletariat will continue to exist, as the truth of what took place under socialism, even though it will not be

---

29   Althusser 2016, p. 198; Althusser 2015b, p. 156.
30   Althusser 2015b, p. 154.
31   Althusser 2016, p. 200; Althusser 2015b, p. 158.

applicable to what is going on under communism, since, with classes and the class struggle having disappeared, the dictatorship of the proletariat will have become superfluous.[32]

Althusser describes his position as being in opposition to historicism, which is 'with neo-positivism, which is one of the forms of bourgeois philosophical ideology most dangerous to the international communist movement'.[33] For Althusser, the very choice of words in the syntagm 'dictatorship of the proletariat' is of theoretical and political significance:

> [Marx] took a word from the language of politics: *dictatorship*. He took a word from the language of socialism: *proletariat*. And he forced them to co-exist in an explosive formulation (dictatorship of the proletariat) in order to express, with an unprecedented concept, the necessity of an unprecedented reality.[34]

The originality of Marx was this conception of a dictatorship of a class, and not just a person or an assembly, or any other legal entity. For Althusser, dictatorship does not simply imply political power; it refers to the necessarily absolute in the last instance and all-encompassing character of the power exercised by a dominant class.

> [Marx] tore the word 'dictatorship' from the terrain of political power in order to force it to express a reality that radically different from any form of political power. Namely, that type of absolute power, not previously endowed with a name, which every ruling class (feudalist, bourgeois, proletarian) necessarily exercises, not only at the political level but much more so beyond it, *in the class struggle that spans the whole of social life, from the base to the superstructure, from exploitation to ideology, passing – but only passing – through politics*.[35]

For Althusser, simply speaking in term of class domination or of class hegemony cannot account for this idea of an 'absolute power', beyond any law, that the notion of dictatorship implies. Consequently, the dictatorship of the proletariat entered explosively into the theoretical and the political stage 'as violent

---

32   Althusser 2016, p. 203; Althusser 2015b, p. 159.
33   Althusser 2016, p. 204; Althusser 2015b, p. 159.
34   Althusser 2016, p. 205; Althusser 2015b, p. 160.
35   Althusser 2016, p. 206; Althusser 2015b, p. 161.

language, as a violent language to express the violence of class rule'.[36] But since the notion of class dictatorship does not limit itself to the proletariat, we must turn to the dictatorship of the bourgeoisie in order to understand the dictatorship of the proletariat. This will help us understand the distinction between class dictatorship and the political forms it would take, forms that, in the case of the dictatorship of the bourgeoisie, could even be democratic. For Althusser, this brings us to the fundamental Marxist position that

> because class relations are, in the last instance, extra-juridical (with a force distinct from right and laws), and these are thus 'above the law', and because they are, in the last instance, relations of force and violence (whether openly so or otherwise), the rule of one class in the class struggle must 'necessarily' be thought as 'power above the law': dictatorship.[37]

According to Althusser, thinking of classes independently of class struggle runs the danger of thinking about a potential collaboration between classes which is the essence of reformism within the workers' movement. In contrast, Marx 'gave primacy to class struggle over classes'.[38] Class struggle is not something derived from the existence of classes. Class struggle and the existence of classes is the same. This can be seen within the capitalist relation of production, which despite its juridical appearance is not a juridical relation.

> Formally speaking, the capitalist production relation appears to be a juridical one: buying and selling labour power. However, it is not reducible to a juridical or a political relation, neither to an ideological one. The capitalist class's ownership of the means of production (which stands behind each individual capitalist) can be sanctioned and regulated by juridical relations (the application of which presupposes the state) but it is not itself a juridical relation – rather, it is a relation of uninterrupted force, from the overt violence of the period of primitive accumulation up to the contemporary extortion of surplus-value. The working class's sale of its labour power (which stands behind each productive worker) can be sanctioned by juridical relations, but it is a relation of uninterrupted force, violence against the dispossessed, who pass back and forth between work and the reserve work force.[39]

---

36   Ibid.
37   Althusser 2016, pp. 209–10; Althusser 2015b, p. 162.
38   Althusser 2016, p. 212; Althusser 2015b, p. 164.
39   Althusser 2016, pp. 213–14; Althusser 2015b, p. 164.

Therefore, in the centre of the capitalist relation of production, in the centre of class division and antagonism, there is violence. 'The dictatorship of the bourgeoisie is a dictatorship because, in the last instance, it is a violence stronger than any law'.[40] But he insists on 'in the last instance', since without juridical and political forms, this violence cannot be exercised. All these lead to the need for a different form of politics; this is exactly the theme of the *new practice of politics* that we have also seen in *On the Reproduction of Capitalism*, but also in Balibar's texts. This conception 'shapes another type of politics, different to that of bourgeois or the social-democratic conception'.[41] This new antagonistic form of politics is based exactly upon the special character of the state, which, in a line similar to the one he will later elaborate in *Marx in his Limits*, is described as a special 'machine', that transforms 'the relations of force of the class struggle into juridical relations'.[42] According to Althusser both this conception of the state as 'machine' but also an 'apparatus' dependent upon the forms of class struggle, imply, contrary to any instrumentalist position, that no class can be dominant without transforming the existing state apparatus:

> As such, when the new class has made itself the ruling class, conquering state power, it is obliged – whether it wants to do so or not – to transform the state apparatus that it has inherited, in order to adapt it to its own forms of exploitation and oppression.[43]

Althusser warns against reducing the concept of the dictatorship of the proletariat to the mere 'violent seizing of state power'.[44] He insists that the concept of the dictatorship does not permit to determine any concrete forms of taking power; rather it defines the character of class power. In this sense, we can even conceive of a potentially peaceful process of taking power without abandoning the dictatorship of the proletariat. However, the main question refers to how we can think of what in the Marxist tradition has been defined as the destruction of the state. For Althusser the main point is to remember that 'the question of the destruction of the bourgeois state apparatus can only be understood if we start out from the extinction of the state, that is, *the position of communism*. This is an absolute condition'.[45] The reason is that the working class cannot just use

---

40   Althusser 2016, p. 214; Althusser 2015b, p. 164.
41   Althusser 2016, p. 215; Althusser 2015b, p. 164.
42   Althusser 2016, p. 219; Althusser 2015b, p. 166.
43   Althusser 2016, p. 222; Althusser 2015b, p. 168.
44   Althusser 2016, p. 224; Althusser 2015b, p. 169.
45   Althusser 2016, p. 228; Althusser 2015b, pp. 170–1.

the existing state apparatus and transform it. Its objective is 'the end of exploitation, the classless society, communism'.[46] 'Smashing' the state refers to the difference between the bourgeois and the communist standpoint, and to the necessary ruptures within state apparatuses, both ideological and repressive.

> I will simply say this: between the bourgeois world and the communist world there is, somewhere, a rupture, between bourgeois ideology – which rules, structures and inspires the whole apparatus of the state and its various (repressive and ideological) apparatuses (the political, trade-union, school, information, 'cultural' and family system, and so on), its mechanisms, its division of labour, its behaviour and so on – and the ideology of communism. To 'break' the bourgeois state apparatus means finding the right form of this rupture for each time, for each apparatus, including every branch of this apparatus, and carrying this through precisely in the bourgeois apparatus itself.[47]

However, there is another important question regarding the dictatorship of the proletariat, namely its identification with dictatorial forms of governance. Althusser insists that this a dangerous misunderstanding since the dictatorship of the proletariat does not refer to particular political forms but the potential for the working class to be dominant. Moreover, Althusser insists that we must never forget that socialism is not a mode of production and that there are no socialist relations of production; rather it is a period of transition, a 'period defined by the contradiction between capitalism and communism, by the contradiction between capitalist "elements" and communist ones'.[48] This is evident in the appropriation of the means of production, a process which means 'that the old (capitalist) relation has submitted to the new (communist) form'.[49] Althusser, expanding here the Marxian theme of the distinction between real and formal subsumption of labour, insists that, in the beginning, we are dealing with a new *form*, not an established new relation, and this means that there is class struggle in the entire period of the dictatorship of the proletariat.

> I say communist form because the transformation of production (collective property, planning) is only formal, since it does not affect the relations of production (wage labour) or the division and organisation of labour.

---

46   Althusser 2016, p. 229; Althusser 2015b, p. 171.
47   Althusser 2016, pp. 229–30; Althusser 2015b, p. 172.
48   Althusser 2016, p. 237; Althusser 2015b, p. 173.
49   Althusser 2016, p. 240; Althusser 2015b, p. 174.

> But at the same time, I say communist form because it has, nonetheless, already been set in motion, a subsumption tending towards its future and waiting for this future to give it reality and existence. And everything is at stake in this indecision, this crossroads: either the old capitalist relation will prove more powerful than the new communist form, or else the new communist form will become real and impose itself as the new relation.[50]

Regarding the political forms of the dictatorship of the proletariat, Althusser follows Lenin in insisting that it implies the 'fullest democracy', of the masses in sharp contrast to the hypocrisy and limitations of bourgeois democracy.

> 'Mass democracy' incorporates and transforms parliamentary democratic forms, the grip of whose division of labour it must necessarily break. But it also 'breaks' the grip of the two other great divisions of 'labour' before which bourgeois parliamentary democracy is blind: one realised in production, and another realised in ideology.[51]

This, in its turn, is based upon a conception of communism as a real material tendency, a trace, in contemporary struggles.

> Communism is an objective tendency already inscribed in our society. The increased collectivisation of capitalist production, the workers' movement's forms of organisation and struggle, the initiatives of the popular masses, and – why not? – certain bold initiatives by artists, writers and researchers, are outlines and symptoms of communism that exist even today.[52]

Althusser insists that some 'concrete forms of are already realized; for example in every human association where commodity relations no longer reign'.[53] Consequently, the working class '*must forge a strategy for communism*'.[54] It is really interesting that in contrast to the dominant discourse of the communist movement of the time, which was centred upon varieties of a progressive and democratic reform of capitalism in crisis, Althusser insisted on the need to think of a strategy for communism. And for Althusser such a strategy should begin by

---

50 Ibid.
51 Althusser 2016, p. 242; Althusser 2015b, p. 175.
52 Althusser 2016, p. 248; Althusser 2015b, p. 178.
53 Althusser 2016, p. 253.
54 Althusser 2016, p. 259.

restoring proletarian internationalism and *'real democratic centralism* which ends the arbitrary domination of the leaders [*dirigeants*] over militants and gives militants full rights of initiative'.[55]

Since one of the main aspects of the insistence of the PCF and other European communist parties was the acknowledgement of the need for formal liberties under socialism, Althusser dedicates an important part of *Les vaches noires* to a critique of bourgeois formal liberties. After recalling the violence of primitive accumulation, he insists that the bourgeois conception of liberty mainly referred to enabling 'the free circulation of the labour force' and therefore 'to create a labour market that was indispensable to free enterprise, namely capitalist exploitation'.[56] In this sense the equality of bourgeois law in fact abstracts from real inequality in capitalist production and exploitation. For Althusser a strategy of communism is not a political struggle for equality, which will 'reinforce along with bourgeois juridical ideology the force of the bourgeois class struggle';[57] rather communism is the end of any political right, the end of any political freedom 'in order to liberate the real liberty of individuals'.[58]

However, this brings forward the question of democratic centralism. Althusser paints a very negative image of the absence of democracy inside the PCF. He attributes that to the 'fear of *factions*'[59] to which he opposes the right to recognise tendencies and the need to constantly 'listen to the masses'.[60]

However, any discussion of the relation between democracy and a communist strategy necessarily brings us to the question of the situation in the USSR. This is one of the most extensive elaborations on the history of the Soviet Union that we find in the work of Althusser. He attributes some of the problems that occurred after the early 1920s to the fact that the proletarian vanguard of the pre-revolution days had disappeared because of the Civil War and their appointment to positions in the state or political positions. Althusser overviews the dramatic history of the Soviet Union, the mass executions by the Stalinist regime, the mistakes of Stalin before WWII, the 'patriotic' references the latter chose when the Soviet Union entered WWII. He is particularly critical of the developments after WWII and the creation of 'popular democracies' and he refers to a 'durable political blockage [...] of the development of socialism

---

55   Althusser 2016, p. 265.
56   Althusser 2016, p. 291.
57   Althusser 2016, p. 308.
58   Althusser 2016, p. 309.
59   Althusser 2016, p. 347.
60   Althusser 2016, p. 357.

in the "popular democracies".[61] Althusser overviews the situation of the working class in the Soviet Union. He stresses the real gains made by the working classes and enhanced access to education, but also notes the contradictions of the working classes in the Soviet Union, such as the appeal of anti-Semitic remarks. For Althusser all these attest to the persistence of class struggles inside the Soviet Union.

Althusser then moves on to some important theoretical questions associated with the discussions inside the PCF. He offers a rather negative criticism of the then dominant economic theory inside the PCF, namely the theory of State Monopoly Capitalism, developed by P. Boccara. For Althusser this theoretical construction around the devaluation of capitals by means of state intervention cannot stand the test of criticism and it points to a conception of the state as an apparatus in the hands of 'handful of capitalists',[62] which reduces the state to the political apparatus and underestimates the ideological and repressive apparatuses.

For Althusser, the working class has changed, especially by means of the influx of young peasants and employees, who, despite being more 'parcelised', 'learn and adopt new forms of struggle'.[63] Consequently, the party must also change not only in terms of internal democracy but also 'in the exterior political practices'.[64] This also implies the need to think of social alliances and Althusser stresses the shortcomings of the politics of the PCF, for example the fact that it said nothing about the 'crisis of immigrant workers',[65] showing that Althusser could understand important challenges, such as the fight against racism. Moreover, he is critical of thinking in terms of 'needs' of workers, since 'needs' 'are not the cause, but an effect of the relations of production'.[66] Continuing the confrontation with communist economism that we have also seen in texts such as *On the Reproduction of Capitalism*, he also attacks the theory and notion of scientific-technological revolution, which at that time was a cornerstone of communist reformism.

Althusser thought that such an intervention would help to avoid both the danger of reproducing Stalinist practices and the possibility of 'right wing exit'.[67] His idea was to open up the debate, to help others also take positions,

---

61 Althusser 2016, p. 376.
62 Althusser 2016, p. 402.
63 Althusser 2016. p. 407.
64 Althusser 2016, p. 408.
65 Althusser 2016, p. 410.
66 Althusser 2016, p. 417.
67 Althusser 2016, p. 454.

and to make them speak. He uses the phrase 'It is the turn of the Communists to speak' [*La parole est aux communistes*]. However, in the end he opted not to publish it, although many of the thematics of the texts can be found in later texts. Perhaps, he felt too weak to proceed with the entire process of rupture, yet this text reveals a much more profound and extensive critique of the reformist and anti-democratic functioning of the PCF, of the limits of Eurocommunism, and of the fact that the 'popular democracies' and the Soviet Union represented the crisis and defeat of the revolutionary project.

In the end Althusser's public intervention in the debates around the 22nd Congress took the form of a speech at a discussion organised by the Sorbonne Philosophy Circle of the Union of Communist Students on 16 December 1976. Althusser begins with the assumption that '*never* has the mass movement, despite serious local defeats and despite the problems raised by the socialist countries, been so powerful in the world'.[68] For Althusser, the combination of a mass strike with a student and petty-bourgeois revolt in May 1968, the new forms of struggle that include 'conditions of labour and life, housing, transport, health education, the family, the environment'[69] and the movements in the Third World along with the defeat of American Imperialism in Vietnam proved the strength of the people's movement. At the same time he points to the crisis of the Communist Movement and the resources still left to imperialism, especially the '*threat of a substitute imperialist solution of a social-democratic type*'.[70]

On the basis of these premises Althusser proceeds with his criticism of the PCF's position. First of all he opposes the simplistic conception of monopolistic capitalist power residing in the hands of 'twenty-five great trusts + 500 auxiliaries + 500,000 big bourgeois',[71] since it cannot account for the dominant power bloc and its functioning and the ways it will still oppose the initiatives of the popular forces even after it was defeated electorally. Regarding the abandonment of the reference to the dictatorship of the proletariat, which was the highlight of the Congress, Althusser accepts the need to elaborate a new road to socialism that will combine liberty with revolution and the need to openly discuss Stalinist practices in the USSR and other socialist countries, but insists that the dictatorship of the proletariat is a scientific concept that cannot be abandoned, since 'it will be rediscovered as soon as we come to speak of the state

---

68   Althusser 1977, p. 4.
69   Althusser 1977, p. 5.
70   Althusser 1977, p. 6.
71   Althusser 1977, p. 8.

and socialism',[72] and of questions regarding the dictatorship of the bourgeoisie, the destruction of the bourgeois state and the withering away of the state. This also calls for new forms of autonomous organisation of the subaltern class apart from traditional party forms. This is one of the first of such interventions by Althusser on the need to go beyond the traditional Party-Form and to use these new forms of organisations as exactly the means for a process of revolutionary 'withering away' of the state. Again, the emphasis is on a new practice of politics, and in particular of *mass* politics autonomous from the state.

For Althusser, the dictatorship of the proletariat refers to the class rule of the working class and the mass democratic forms this can take. He accepts the possibility that in particular conjunctures the mass action of the proletariat can be peaceful and democratic and lead to the broad alliance most proponents of Eurocommunism supported, but he also warns of the possibility of violence in case the counter-revolutionary forces remain strong. Moreover, he links the abandonment of the theoretical concept of the dictatorship of the proletariat to a certain conception of socialism that is presented not '*as a contradictory period of transition* between capitalism and socialism [but] *as a stable mode of production*'.[73] For Althusser, '*there is no socialist mode of production*',[74] and socialism is a period of intensified class struggle, in a position that follows not only the line of reasoning from Marx's *Critique of the Gotha Program*[75] to Lenin's *State and Revolution*,[76] but also the critique of the Chinese Communists against Soviet socialism during the Cultural Revolution and the writings of Marxists such as Bettelheim. Consequently, Althusser insists that the question is not to add the adjective 'democratic' to existing state apparatuses, but instead to initiate processes that revolutionise them.[77]

Regarding democratic centralism in the Party, Althusser argues that the internal unity of the Party must not be a means in itself, but must serve the struggle of the masses and he laments the fact that because of the '*filtration*

---

[72] Althusser 1977, p. 10.
[73] Althusser 1977, p. 15.
[74] Ibid. Althusser had already elaborated his posistion regarding the absence of a socialist mode of production in a 1973 manuscript entitled *Livre sur l'impérialisme* (in Althusser 2018a).
[75] 'Between capitalist and communist society there lies the period of the revolutionary transformation of the one into the other. Corresponding to this is also a political transition period in which the state can be nothing but *the revolutionary dictatorship of the proletariat*' (Marx 1875).
[76] Lenin [1917] 1974, pp. 469–79.
[77] Althusser 1977, p. 17.

system'[78] through which the Party leadership controlled the election of delegates, 'there was no real discussion at the 22nd Congress'.[79] Moreover, there is a need for real discussion that would enable party members to 'think for themselves'.[80]

3 Facing the Crisis of the Party

Althusser's criticism of the politics and practices of the communist movement became even more intense after the political and electoral defeat of the Left in 1978. The break-up of the Union of the Left and the absence of an open debate of Party politics and tactics led to public interventions by Party militants.[81] Some of these criticisms were directed at the contradictions of the Party political line and functioning and demanded a left-wing turn as opposed to the Eurocommunist turn and a more democratic culture.[82] Others tried to enter into a dialogue with the Eurocommunist turn, demanding a more left-wing turn, exemplified in the positions of Poulantzas and Buci-Glucksmann in favour of a left-wing Eurocommunism.[83]

Of particular importance is Althusser's open criticism of the PCF's policies in his *Le Monde* articles collected in *What Must Change in the Party*.[84] Written in the aftermath of the defeat of the Left in the 1978 elections, following the dissolution of the Common Program of the Left, the failure to obtain a Left majority in the 1978 elections and the rise of the Socialists as the biggest party of the Left, it is an intervention in a period of crisis for the French communist movement and of intense debate regarding the causes of this failure. Regarding the need for an open debate, in the preface to the publication of these articles as a small book, Althusser chastises the culture of secrecy and false unanimity in the PCF and insists on the need for an open debate, refusing the opposition between internal debate and public debating and insisting that an open internal debate can also have public aspects. Although one of the major texts

---

78   Althusser 1977, p. 20.
79   Ibid.
80   Althusser 1977, p. 21.
81   For an overview of the debates within the PCF, see Duhamel and Weber (eds) 1979. On the crisis of the strategy of the PCF, see Bensaïd 1978.
82   Labica 1979; Molina and Vargas 1979.
83   Buci-Glucksmann 1979.
84   Althusser 1978b; Althusser 1978c. The French book version of the original *Le Monde* articles (which are translated in the *New Left Review* article) also includes a preface commenting on the post-election debate in the CC of the PCF (Althusser 1978b, pp. 5–30).

in which Althusser openly criticised the Party's line and tactics – and not just the theoretical deviations – it is still a form of critique within the limits of the PCF, a critique that considers the PCF to be the inescapable terrain of political intervention and attempts a certain dialogue with the positions of the leadership. Moreover, it is obvious that for Althusser at the time it seemed like there could be no venue for political intervention other than the PCF, even though it was more than obvious by that time that it was not possible to think in terms of simply theoretically correcting the political line and/or 'theoretically tutoring' the Party's leadership back to a correct revolutionary line (a fantasy which Althusser alludes to in various instances, especially in his positive references to Valdeck-Rochet).[85]

It is interesting how much Althusser is distancing himself from a traditional version of the injection of consciousness from the outside and criticising G. Marchais's choice to talk about the need to 'impregnate workers' with the necessary ideas,[86] which for Althusser is a conception in contrast to 'every materialism, every dialectic'.[87] Althusser called for an open debate and a concrete Marxist analysis of the Party's practices and organisation. To this end, 'mouths should open'.[88]

What are the main points of Althusser's criticism of the line of the Party? The internal debate was organised in a way that forbade open discussion. The Party had failed to offer an explanation of the changes in the political line during the years of the Common Program and the obvious differences between the line of collaboration with the Socialists, which was adopted initially, and the line of confrontation. Althusser opposed the way the PCF handled the differences with the Socialists accusing the Party leadership of designating the socialists as the main enemy instead of fighting the most reactionary Right. For Althusser most alarming is not the very fact of a political error but the way this error was treated. The worst way to treat an error is to ignore it and insist that the 'Party is always right'. On the contrary, he insists on the possibility of a Marxist treatment of a political error.

> In this Marxist method of handling errors, they are alarm-signals coming from practice. They always point to a lacuna or failure, either in the structure of thought or in the structure of organization. [...] According to the Marxist conception, the really important thing is *what the mistake con-*

---

85 See for example Althusser 1993b, p. 198.
86 Althusser 1978b, p. 20.
87 Althusser 1978b, p. 26.
88 Althusser 1978b, p. 30.

ceals: namely structural contradictions of which it is but manifestation. As a precise 'event' an error eventually passes by: but unless the causes are tackled and reduced, *they will always persist*.[89]

Althusser has a lot of criticism regarding the way the Party leadership handled these changes in the party line without making militants part of the decision-making process. He is very critical of the abandonment of class analysis in favour of a line opposing the 'poor' to the 'rich', but above all he is critical of the way the question of unity of the Left was handled. For Althusser, the Unity of the Left represented, for the first time in many decades, the possibility of victory and a break with the dominance of the Right. Confidence in the Unity was rooted in the 'revolt against exploitation and daily oppression'.[90] That is why he opposes the way the Party leadership decided the break-up of the Union of the Left, a decision taken by a small group around the leadership without any open discussion.

For Althusser the problem lies with the way the party is organised, especially its parliamentary aspects in terms of organisation, exemplified in the treatment of the party members as a 'sovereign people',[91] according to which the base is there simply to legitimise the choices made by the party leadership, but also a 'military aspect'[92] in the sense of a vertical hierarchy and partitioning and also of an isolation of militants within their cell without any possibility of a 'horizontal' communication between different Party cells and branches in the name of refusing 'factional activity'.[93] Moreover, he accuses the PCF of a '*bourgeois mode of politics*',[94] in the sense of reproducing a bourgeois parliamentary mode of internal functioning: 'just as the bourgeoisie succeeds in having its forms of domination reproduced by "free" citizens, so does the Party leadership have its forms of domination reproduced by the militants'.[95] Consequently, instead of an open discussion, what they had was the collective unity of the leadership as a refusal of any responsibility. Party unity is not an end in itself, since the '*Party is the provisional organization of working-class struggle* [...] its unity is required only to serve action'.[96] If the party is really a part of the struggle, it will be necessarily a *contradictory unity*.

---

89 Althusser 1978b, p. 54; Althusser 1978c, p. 25.
90 Althusser 1978b, p. 66; Althusser 1978c, p. 28.
91 Althusser 1978b, p. 73; Althusser 1978c, p. 30.
92 Althusser 1978b, p. 75; Althusser 1978c, p. 31.
93 Althusser 1978b, p. 75; Althusser 1978c, p. 31.
94 Althusser 1978b, p. 77; Althusser 1978c, p. 32.
95 Althusser 1978b, p. 77; Althusser 1978c, p. 32.
96 Althusser 1978b, p. 89; Althusser 1978c, p. 34.

> If the party is withered and hardened, its unity may yet remain intact; but it will then be formal and unreal, and the party itself will be 'cemented', namely *paralyzed* by a withered and hardened ideology. If, however, a party is alive its unity will be contradictory; and the party will be united by a living ideology, which, while it is bound to be contradictory, is yet open and fertile. Now, what is that gives life to a party. *Its living relation to the masses*: to their battles, discoveries, and problems, in a class struggle traversed by two major trends of which one points towards superexploitation, the other towards the liberation of the exploited.[97]

For Althusser the problem with the PCF's ideology was not only the theoretical poverty of the discussions within the Party, especially during the Cold War, a criticism that Althusser also made in the preface to *For Marx*, but also its current analysis and the French version of State Monopoly Capitalism. Althusser was particularly critical, analytically and politically, both of the position that the current form of the state is the antechamber of socialism and of the assumption that France was dominated by a handful of monopoly capitalists.

> The ante-chamber of socialism and the 'single mechanism' of monopolies/State *change the question of the State*; the State tends to assume a form that will render it capable of being directly utilized be people's power; there is no longer any question, then, of 'destroying' the State; and already on the horizon appears the 'abandonment' of the dictatorship or the proletariat.[98]

This conception of a handful of monopoly capitalists dominating the whole of France leads to the abandonment of concrete analysis of both the conjuncture and the Party line. It leads to the position that socialism is the 'objective interest' of the French people and every discussion is turned to questions of whether the people have conscience of that and whether the effort of the Party is strong enough. As a result, the Party's ideology assumes the 'caricatural function: to "cement" Party unity at any price'.[99]

For Althusser the solution is to *leave the fortress*.[100] The decisive question is the relation of the Party to the masses. He insists that the Party deliberately

---

97 Althusser 1978b, p. 89; Althusser 1978c, pp. 34–5.
98 Althusser 1978b, p. 94; Althusser 1978c, p. 36.
99 Althusser 1978b, p. 102; Althusser 1978c, p. 39.
100 Althusser 1978b, p. 103, Althusser 1978c, p. 39.

cut itself off from the student masses and petty-bourgeois strata in May 1968, forgetting the importance of alliances in communist politics. For Althusser alliances and forms of unity between different strata also imply the need to struggle to expand the influence of the working class. But in the case of the PCF this was substituted by unity as a contract between the leadership of parties and combat between these parties, leading to results such as the break-up of the Unity of the Left. Faced with these contradictions the Party opted for a strategy of 'withdrawal', with the leadership 'presenting this unmotivated withdrawal, as a sign of strength, prudence and even political far-sightedness'.[101]

This *exit from the fortress* demands a new political line. For Althusser this should comprise: a new conception of Marxist theory, able to confront 'its proper contradictions',[102] that could 'nourish itself' with the initiative and the experiences of the masses;[103] a rigorous criticism of the forms of Party organisation; a concrete analysis of the conjuncture and the class situation in France, including the internal contradictions of the working class and the political parties of the Left; a new political line, a '*line of popular union* (free of sectarianism or reformism), for active mobilization of the masses and unfettered development of their initiative'.[104]

Along with the texts on the crisis of Marxism, this text represents Althusser's more open criticism of the politics of the official communist movement in sharp contrast to his earlier insistence that Western communist parties remain the basic venues for working-class politics provided that they make the necessary theoretical corrections to their political line. Now, it is no longer a question of a simple correction of theoretical errors. The very essence of the Party's internal mode of organisation, the absence of internal democracy, the lack of contact with the masses is put into question along with the hegemony of aspects of bourgeois ideology regarding the Party line and ideology. Althusser called for an opening of the party to the masses and their contradictions, for a party openly contradictory if it wants to be a party of the masses, in a way reminiscent of Luxemburg's conception of the Party as an openly contradictory process.[105] However, what is missing from Althusser's narrative are two import-

---

101 Althusser 1978b, pp. 118–19; Althusser 1978c, p. 44.
102 Althusser 1978b, p. 122. This phrase does not appear in the English translation.
103 Althusser 1978b, p. 123; Althusser 1978c, p. 45.
104 Althusser 1978b, p. 124; Althusser 1978b, p. 45.
105 Some of Althusser's formulations are in a way reminiscent of Luxemburg's formulation in texts like *Organizational Questions of Russian Social Democracy*: 'The nimble acrobat fails to perceive that the only "subject" which merits today the role of director is the collective "ego" of the working class. The working class demands the right to make its mistakes and learn the dialectic of history. Let us speak plainly. Historically, the errors committed

ant aspects. One has to do with the very question of whether the Party is still the sole terrain of struggle for proletarian politics, or a break away from the Party was necessary either in the form of new party formation (the Leninist line of the decisive break) or in the form of experimenting with non-party forms of political organisation. The other refers to Althusser's reluctance to talk not only in terms of the party as militant organisation but also a knowledge process, in the sense of the Party as collective intellectual and a laboratory of new militant intellectualities. It seems as if Althusser, confronted with what he also perceived as the open theoretical crisis of Marxism, stressed more the question of organisation and the hope that a new open relation to the masses will facilitate discussion and a more correct line than the question of how the party can actually produce theory, analysis, and ideology. In a way, using one of Althusser's favourite metaphors, he bends the stick more to the side of political process and organisation instead of theory and knowledge production. Moreover, all these references to the initiatives of the masses pose an important question: how will these initiatives emerge? Do they not also depend on some sort of political line and intervention? Was Althusser coming close to some form of spontaneism, in the long line of such positions in the history of the labour movement? I think that all these open questions represent exactly Althusser's struggle to come to terms with the deep strategic crisis of the Left.

4 The Confrontation with the Crisis of Marxism

Althusser's more open criticism of the politics of the Communist movement is also reflected in his much more open confrontation with the crisis of Marxism. This is based on Althusser's abandonment of the strict dichotomy between science and ideology, which led him to a new theoretical schema based on class perspective and bias as an epistemological prerequisite for any objective theorisation of social reality.[106] The contradictions in the politics, the strategy and

---

by a truly revolutionary movement are infinitely more fruitful than the infallibility of the cleverest Central Committee' (Luxemburg 1904).

106 'It will be admitted that Marxist theory is necessarily enlisted in the class struggle, and that the conflict that pits it against bourgeois ideology is irremediable, but it will be more difficult to admit that the *conflictuality* of Marxist theory is *constitutive* of its *scientificity*, its *objectivity*. One will retreat to positivist and economist positions, and the conflictual conditions of the existence of the science as *contingent* will be distinguished from its scientific results. This amounts to not seeing that Marxist science and the Marxist investigator are obliged to *take a position* in the conflict whose object is Marxist theory, are obliged to occupy (proletarian) class theoretical positions, which are opposed to every theoretical

tactics of the labour movement and the Marxist-inspired Left are also internalised within Marxist theory. The class struggle and the balance of class forces actually transverse Marxism. Consequently, the crisis in the movement will also lead to a crisis in theory.

In 1977, on the occasion of a Congress organised by *Il Manifesto*, Althusser chose to openly insist on the crisis of Marxism as a manifestation of the crisis of the International Communist Movement. It is important to note that Althusser's references to the crisis of Marxism do not limit themselves to open theoretical questions but also to open strategic conceptions, especially since Marxism is theory organically linked to the practices, strategies, and tactics of the labour movement. That is why this open crisis of Marxism can be a liberating event in the sense of 'obliging us to change our relation to Marxism and consequently Marxism itself'.[107] Althusser's assessment of the state of Marxism is highly critical, insisting on important lacunae in most aspects of Marxist theory: the theory of value and the articulation of abstract theories of the value form to the concrete historicity of class struggle, the absence of a theory of the state, the absence of a theory of the forms of organisation. This marks an important reversal in Althusser's conception of the ways to correct the political line of the Party. Whereas in the 1960s he proposed the theoretical correction of political deviations in the communist movement through a 'return' to the theoretical core of Marxism, now he insists that gaps, contradictions, lacunae, 'weak links', exist even in this theoretical core. Moreover, he insists that these theoretical and strategic lacunae and weak links mark the problems facing contemporary communist parties. The list of the open questions he lists is revealing.

> What is the nature of the State, and in particular of the type of State found in present-day imperialist societies? What is the nature, what is the mode of functioning of the parties and trade unions? How can we escape the risk of an eventual fusion of the State and Party? How can we grasp now, in order to spur on the process, the need for the 'destruction' of

---

position of the bourgeoisie, in order to be able to constitute and develop their science. What are those proletarian class theoretical positions indispensable to the constitution and development of Marxist theory? They are materialist and dialectical *philosophical positions* allowing one to *see* what bourgeois ideology necessarily *conceals*: the class structure and class exploitation of a social formation. Now those philosophical positions are always and necessarily antagonistic to bourgeois positions' (Althusser 1999b, pp. 110–11). On the importance of this conflictuality of Marxism, see Baltas and Fourtounis 1994.

107   Althusser [1977] 1998, p. 274.

the bourgeois State, and prepare the 'withering away' of the revolutionary State? How can we review and modify the nature and functioning of the organisations of class struggle? How can we transform the traditional Communist image of the Party, whether as 'the party of the working class' or as 'the leading party', how can we transform its ideology in order to allow it to recognise in practice the existence of other parties and of other movements. And above all – the most important of questions for past and future – how can relations be established with the mass movement which, transcending the traditional distinction between trade union and party, will permit the development of initiatives among the people, which usually fail to fit into the division between the economic and political spheres (even 'added together')?[108]

Althusser does not suggest some form of solution, of political initiative or of concrete change in the political line other than a call to rely on the initiative of the masses and the strength of the movement. For Althusser it was possible – albeit difficult – to overcome this Crisis of Marxism because 'the Labour Movement and the movement of the people, even if it is divided, even if it seems here or there to have reached an impasse, has in fact never been so powerful, so rich in resources and initiatives'.[109] In light of the subsequent change in the relation of forces, this rather schematic distinction between political parties in crises and movements in full power seems like ungrounded optimism. However, it is important that Althusser was not only abandoning his earlier conception of a theoretical correction, but also suggesting a much more open process of political transformation through the interaction of theory and the movement, where the experience and initiative of the masses is becoming the catalyst for the necessary change in the political line and where there is no longer question of a simple battle inside the Party, but of the full eruption of the necessarily contradictory relation between the Party and the Movement.

In the spring of 1978, following the repercussions of his Venice intervention, he made his position clearer in a series of answers to questions posed by Rossana Rossanda.[110] In this Althusser insists on the finite character of Marxist theory and its limits. That is why it is not a 'total' theory but an open theory. Regarding the theory of the state Althusser fears that a certain reading of Gramsci can lead to the position that all politics is inscribed within the limits of the

---

108 Althusser 1978a, p. 220.
109 Ibid.
110 For the reactions to his positions, see Ph. de Lara (ed.) 1978.

state. '*The fact that the class struggle (bourgeois and proletarian) has the State as a stake (hic et nunc) does not simply mean that politics must be defined by its relation to the state*'.[111]

Althusser relates this position to questions facing the European Left and especially the PCI. He agrees with positions such as the one adopted by Ingrao in relation to the growing politicisation of the popular masses, but he disagrees that this means a politics centred on the state. Moreover, he relates this position to questions of revolutionary strategy. For Althusser the problem lies in the identification of the Party and the state in post-revolutionary societies: 'The Party must be *outside the State*, not only under the bourgeois State, but for a stronger reason under a proletarian State'.[112] This also marks Althusser's much more open criticism of 'socialist construction' in the USSR and other 'socialist republics': the identification of the Party and the state, the becoming state of the Party, along with economism and an inability to transform relations of production, are the main traits of Stalinism.

5 Marx in His Limits

The theoretical background to these political interventions and the condensation of Althusser's thinking about this relation between politics, theory, and strategy can be found in *Marx in his Limits*, a 1978 manuscript. Althusser here presents in its full form an argument that he repeated on many occasions, namely that Marxism is internal to the workers' movement: '*Marx's thought was formed and developed not outside the workers' movement, but within the existing workers' movement, on the political basis provided by that movement and its rectified theoretical positions*'.[113] This argument is crucial for Althusser, since it helps him stress the possibility of overcoming the political crisis of the communist movement and the theoretical crisis of Marxism through the force of the workers' movement and of current struggles. For Althusser, especially in the Second International a *bourgeois* conception of knowledge and political expertise was dominant within the working-class movement, especially in respect of the relation between the Party and the masses, exemplified in the conception of socialist theory 'introduced from without into the workers' movement':

---

111   Althusser 1998, p. 287.
112   Althusser 1998, p. 290.
113   Althusser 2006a, p. 33.

> In the last, this representation could not but reproduce bourgeois forms of the production and possession of this knowledge on the one hand, and, on the other, bourgeois forms of the possession and exercise of power, all these forms being dominated by a *separation* between knowledge and non-knowledge, between the informed and the ignorant, between the leaders, the guardians of knowledge and the led reduced to receiving it from without and from on high because they were naturally ignorant of it.[114]

In contrast, the transformation of Marx and Engels into '"organic" intellectuals of the working class [...] was played out in their *encounter* with – that is to say, their direct and practical, or in a word, personal experience of – the exploitation of the working class'.[115] Moreover, *'Marx never once, from his initial commitment of 1843 on, left the terrain of working-class struggle'*.[116]

Moreover, this position helps Althusser to suggest that it is through its full engagement with the practices and struggles of the working classes that Marxist theory can actually evolve and become critical and revolutionary. This is reinforced by Althusser's reassessment of the positive role of proletarian ideology in his 1970s texts. Instead of the simple opposition between ideology and science, proletarian ideology is presented as forming the basis of a different politics and strategy. The following passage from the 1976 'Note on the ISAs' exemplifies this position:

> The conditions of existence, the (productive and political) practices and forms of the proletarian class struggle have nothing to do with the conditions of existence, the (economic and political) practices and forms of the capitalist and imperialist class struggle. This gives rise to antagonistic ideologies, which, like the (bourgeois and proletarian) class struggles themselves, are unequal. This means that proletarian ideology is not the direct opposite, inversion, or reversal of bourgeois ideology – but an altogether different ideology that is the bearer of different, 'critical and revolutionary' 'values'.[117]

This is one of most interesting and yet contradictory positions of Althusser in the late 1970s. It is a necessary reminder of the epistemological importance of

---

114   Althusser 2006a, pp. 26–7.
115   Althusser 2006a, p. 27.
116   Althusser 2006a, p. 32.
117   Althusser 2014b, p. 231.

class partisanship in Marxist theory, for which class partiality is the prerequisite of objectivity. It is also an important contribution in any to attempt to understand why Marxism is a necessarily conflictual and scissionist science[118] in the sense that it opens up breaks in dominant ideology and at the same time is always a stake of class struggle. Not only is Marxism based on the adoption of a class position, but it is also traversed by class struggle 'subject to a dialectic of resistance – attacks – revision – scissions'.[119] This can also be read not only as a warning for Marxism but also as a way to rethink the strategy of the communist movement, offering a way for a theory of the crisis of communist strategy that defines it as an inability to counter the many forms of influence of bourgeois politics which are always already internalised in the labour movement, in contrast to the simplifying idealism of any references to revisionism as betrayal.

However, what is missing here is a questioning of the very concept of proletarian ideology as the necessary ground for both Marxist theory and communist strategy. Although a useful reminder of the importance of class positions, it seems like a search for a positive, always already inherently anti-capitalist proletarian ideology, as the necessary ontological grounding (in the form of a powerful popular movement) that would lead to the re-emergence of the communist movement. As Balibar has shown, if it is impossible to theorise 'dominant ideology' as the 'ideology of the dominant classes', it is equally impossible to theorise the pre-existence, in an almost messianic form, of proletarian ideology as proletarian worldview.[120] What is missing in Althusser's references to proletarian ideology is a reflection on the many ways in which proletarian ideological practices are themselves traversed by class struggle and tend to internalise the class relation of forces, but also to how 'dominant ideology' itself is, at a given conjuncture, not the simple projection of the worldview of dominant class, but the result of a complex process that includes the re-appropriation and transformation of elements of the discourses, demands, and aspirations of the subaltern classes.[121] Revolutionary theory and strategy is not a simple enhancement

---

118 Althusser 1999b, p. 109.
119 Ibid.
120 On the open questions regarding a Marxist theory of ideology, see Balibar 1994b; Balibar 2002.
121 'In Marxist terms this would be the problem of how dominant ideologies are constituted with respect to the "consciousness" of dominant and dominated people. Marx's original formulation (in the *German Ideology*), asserting that "the dominant ideology is always the ideology of the dominant class" is hardly tenable: not only does it make ideology a mere duplicate or reflection of economic power (thus making it impossible to understand how "ideological" domination can contribute to "real" domination, or add something to it), but precludes the possibility of explaining how any social *consent* or *consensus* except

of proletarian class instinct, but a process of collective elaboration emerging out of the necessary contradictions traversing the ideological plane, the conflictual representations and recognitions/misrecognitions of reality, the experiences and practical knowledge emerging from struggle. But Althusser seems to be more interested in constantly 'bending the stick to the other side' than in attempting some sort of dialectical synthesis.

Returning now to *Marx in his Limits* it is obvious that for Althusser Marx's engagement with the proletarian movement did not prevent him from being influenced by idealist positions as part of a constant ideological struggle. This was evident in the 'idea of a philosophy of history, of an Origin and an End, in short of a Meaning [...] embodied in the sequence of epochs making progress',[122] culminating in the 'mythical idea of communism as a mode of production *without relations of production*'.[123] This idealism was also evident, in a more subtle form, in the problem of the order of exposition of *Capital*, especially in Marx's insistence that to start from the abstraction of value, that in fact meant 'bracketing out' the concrete conditions and histories of exploitation and oppression.

> For paradoxically, in order to propose such a theory, he has to take into account what the *order of exposition* requires him to *bracket out*: the productivity of labour in all its forms; labour power as something other than a simple commodity; and quite simply, the history of the conditions under which capitalism arose, which necessitates, among other things, reference to primitive accumulation. Whence the long chapters on the working day, the labour process, manufacture and big industry, and the extraordinary chapter on primitive accumulation.[124]

For Althusser, this was the result of a philosophical conception of science, inspired by Hegel and his idea of Science (*Wissenschaft*). However obliged

---

by trick, mystification, deception and so on – that is categories borrowed from a fantasmatic psychology. The alternative seems to be to reverse the pattern and propose the (only apparently) paradoxical idea that the necessary condition for an ideology to become dominant is that it should elaborate the values and claims of the "social majority", become the discourse of the *dominated* (distorted and inverted as it may appear). "Society" or the dominant forces in society can speak to the masses in universalistic language (rights, justice, equality, welfare, progress ...), because in this language a kernel remains which came from the masses themselves, and is returned to them' (Balibar 2002, p. 164).

122   Althusser 2006a, p. 36.
123   Althusser 2006a, p. 37.
124   Althusser 2006a, p. 39.

Marx was to abide by such a conception of theoretical exposition, he was also obliged to acknowledge all the concrete forms of exploitation beyond a simple extraction of surplus value in arithmetical terms, that is, the concrete realities and struggles of the labour process but also of the concrete conditions of the reproduction of the labour power. Moreover, this battle between a former idealist conception and new emerging materialist one turns Marx's own text into a terrain of struggle:

> For – as goes without saying – the battle is also a battle over concepts and even words, whenever they sum up the stakes of great conflicts, great uncertainties, or silent, obscure contradictions. Witness the most profound hesitations in *Capital*, in which the word, theme, notion, or even concept of alienation continues to haunt not only the theory (which is one-hundred-per-cent Feuerbachian) of fetishism, but also the theatrical opposition between dead and living labour, the domination of workers' conditions over the worker, and the figure of communism, that free association of 'individuals' who have no social relations other than their freedom – alienation, an old word, an old idealist concept that can be put to any use you like (including that of making felt what is still inadequately thought) and is manifestly there to think something else: something which is unthought, and has remained so.[125]

However, the contradictions that led to the open crisis of Marxism were not the result solely of idealist elements 'surviving' between the lines of Marx's mature text. There was also the problem, which Marx himself could not foresee, of how the theoretical propositions of Marxism could turn into mass ideological forms even in the sense of a deformation. For Althusser the problem begins with Marx's own inability, at the time of the Paris Commune, to actually produce a more insightful analysis of the politics and ideology of both the bourgeois state and the Commune. The same contradiction is evident in the actual inability of Marx to actually intervene against what he and Engels perceived as the shortcomings of German Social Democracy, exemplified in the decision to publish their criticism of the Gotha Programme, but also of his own inability to think the use of his own theory by the Party.

> Here too we are reduced to making negative hypotheses, but only after duly noting that Marx felt helpless in the face of realities like the *Party*,

---

[125] Althusser 2006a, p. 46.

with its structure, mechanism, effects and decisions, and that he may have felt even more helpless in the face of certain *ideological misunderstanding-effects* – above all, in the face of the *ideological status of his own theoretical persona*, and so on.[126]

For Althusser, the absolute limit of Marx's thinking were the superstructures, the ideologies and the state, beginning with all the ambiguities surrounding Marx's 1859 Preface to the *Critique of Political Economy*. Althusser reaffirms his insistence that 'Marx never upheld the primacy of the productive forces over the relations of production [...] [h]e simply upheld the thesis of the primacy, "in the last instance", of the infrastructure (the base) over the superstructure'.[127] However, this does not mean that he had a theory of the relation between base and superstructure. In contrast there is a *'theoretical lacuna concerning the relation between the base on the one hand and the superstructure on the other'*.[128]

Althusser insists that the crucial turn in Marx's thinking was when he abandoned his earlier conception – under the influence of Feuerbach – of the state as alienation of civil society, in favour of a conception of the state as a separate material apparatus or 'machine'. He even insists on the conception of the state as an instrument which for him exemplifies this conception of the necessary separation of the state from class struggle and especially the *bourgeois class struggle*:

> Of course *the state is separate from class struggle, since that is what is made for*, that is why it is an instrument. Can you imagine an instrument used by the dominant class that would not be 'separate' from class struggle? It would be in danger of exploding in the hands of this class at the first opportunity! And I am not talking about the 'traversal' of the state by the class struggle *of the masses* [...], a mass struggle that has doubtless 'traversed' the state in history only to culminate in bourgeois politics (as in 1968). I am talking, above all, about the bourgeois class struggle itself. If the big state apparatuses were at the mercy of the 'traversal' of the state by the bourgeois class struggle, the upshot might well be the end of bourgeois domination [...] It almost came to that during the Dreyfus affair and the war in Algeria, to cite no other examples.[129]

---

126 Althusser 2006a, p. 53.
127 Althusser 2006a, p. 59.
128 Althusser 2006a, p. 60.
129 Althusser 2006a, pp. 70–1.

In this sense, the separation of the state is the condition for its ability to defend the general interests of the bourgeoisie as the dominant class, even 'against the will of a part or even a majority of the bourgeoisie'.[130] Consequently, this text is also an attack on those who supported some form of politics within the state or through the state. One of the targets is also Poulantzas and his relational theorisation of the state as the condensation of class relations. In contrast, for Althusser, 'to leap to [...] the conclusion that the state "is by definition traversed by class struggle" is to engage in wishful thinking'.[131] It is in light of this conception of the necessary separation that Althusser insists that '[t]here can be no question of abandoning it'.[132] However, the conceptual couple that Althusser wants more to underline is that of apparatus/'machine'. For Althusser the notion of the state of Apparatus refers to its status as a *machine* transforming social class power into political power and law. Althusser bases this on a reading of the evolution of the conceptualisation of the 'machine' from the seventeenth century onwards, stressing the importance of a process of transformation of energy, which is exactly the reason why the state is not simply an instrument, since

> 'machine' adds something essential to 'apparatus': to the idea of the simple utilization of a great amount of energy, it adds that of the *transformation of energy* (of one type of energy into another: for example, of caloric into kinetic energy). In the case of an apparatus, one kind of energy is sufficient; *in the case of a machine we have to do with at least two types of energy, and, above all, the transformation of one into the other.*[133]

Althusser insists that the important aspect, which was in a certain manner underestimated by even Marx and Lenin, was that of the relation between the state and *reproduction*, something that he attempted to answer by his elaborations on the notion of the Ideological State Apparatuses. That is why the 'body' of the state is comprised by an 'apparatus of public force'. The '*political apparatus*' and the '*Ideological State Apparatuses*'.[134] It is on this basis that the state can be considered a power machine and in particular a '*machine for producing*

---

130 Althusser 2006a, p. 77.
131 Althusser 2006a, p. 80.
132 Althusser 2006a, p. 81.
133 Althusser 2006a, p. 85.
134 Althusser 2006a, p. 101.

legal power'.¹³⁵ However, at the beginning of this process of transformation of energy, there is always class force:

> In the case of the state-machine, if the state-machine is a power machine, that is because it transforms one form of already existing energy, that of Force or Violence, into another, the energy of Power. What, then, is this energy A, which we are here calling Force or Violence? It is, quite simply, the force or Violence of class struggle, the Force or Violence that has 'not yet' been transformed into Power, that has not been transformed into laws and right [droit].¹³⁶

It is interesting that although Althusser insists on this conception of the state as a machine as an answer to Poulantzas's theorisation of the state as a condensation of class forces and as constantly traversed by class struggle, Althusser's conception is also rather relational, although he insists on the fact that what is the energy of the state is the excess force of the dominant class in class struggle, in its *confrontation* with the oppressed classes.

> The relatively stable resultant (reproduced in its stability by the state) of this *confrontation* of forces (*balance* of forces is an accountant's notion, because it is static) is that *what counts is the dynamic excess of force* maintained by the dominant class in the class struggle. It is *this excess of conflictual force, real or potential, which constitutes energy A*, which subsequently transformed into power by the state-machine: *transformed into right, laws and norms*.¹³⁷

For Althusser, it is such a conception that legitimises a strategy for the destruction of the state, in the sense of a destruction of the '*forms of domination and subordination* in all state apparatuses [...] [and] *the forms of the division of labour between the various apparatuses*'.¹³⁸ This is the only way to avoid the danger that the existing body of the state, its personnel and the strategies inscribed in it ultimately neutralise any attempt towards a more radical politics. That is why *Marx in his Limits* also includes a defence of the strategic significance of the notion of the dictatorship of the proletariat as a referent to the

---

135   Althusser 2006a, p. 107.
136   Althusser 2006, p. 108.
137   Althusser 2006a, p. 109.
138   Althusser 2006a, p. 115.

means by which the proletariat imposes its politics on the '*old dominant exploiting class*', in the form of a domination that

> must exist *in the forms of production* (nationalizations combined with a more or less extensive market sector, self-management, workers' control over production, and so on), *in political forms* (councils, represented in a National Council by their delegates) and *in ideological forms* (what Lenin called cultural revolution).[139]

However, this rejection of any reformist conception of the state as a class-neutral institution also requires dealing with positions within the Communist movement that insisted on the progressive role of the state and especially the 'public services' it can offer. For Althusser there is nothing progressive in this; rather, it is a form of mystification of the role of the state. That is why he is highly critical of the French version of the theory of 'State Monopoly Capitalism' represented especially by the work of Paul Boccara and his conception of the role of the state in the 'devalorisation' of capital as part of his conception of the tendency of the profit rate to fall, to which Althusser opposes his insistence on a '*theory of the tendential rise in the class struggle*'.[140] It is necessary to stress the role of the state in social reproduction, the complexity of its mechanisms and consequently the *ideological* role of the state as a result of this complexity. This is the actual 'circle of the State':

> If I may be allowed to charge the term 'circle' with the weight of everything I have just said, then it is *'the circle of the reproduction of the state in its functions as an instrument for the reproduction of the conditions of production, hence of exploitation, hence of the conditions of existence of the domination of the exploiting class' which constitutes, in and of itself, the supreme objective mystification.*[141]

And it is exactly this emphasis on the ideological role of the state that makes Althusser rather sceptical regarding the theory of fetishism or in general any form of ideology emerging from social practice itself. For Althusser the problem with the theory of fetishism is that it remains the prisoner of an opposition between persons and things that in fact remains 'trapped in the categories of

---

139   Althusser 2006a, p. 90.
140   Althusser 2006a, p. 123.
141   Althusser 2006a, p. 126.

the law or in the notions of juridical ideology'.[142] Moreover, it remains within the contours of a conception of labour as substance as opposed to its phenomenal appearances. For Althusser, this is also the result of Marx's own order of exposition that began from the simplest 'abstraction'.

> Here he pays the price, for the first but not the last time, for having set off on an analysis of the capitalist mode of production (*Capital*) with a certain idea of the order of exposition that compelled him to 'begin' with the prescribed beginning: the simplest abstraction, value.[143]

For Althusser the problem with any theory of fetishism is that it underestimates the concrete reality of the ideological role of the state, what he designates as the 'state's political-economical-ideological function as a machine for transforming the force that emanates from class struggle into power'.[144] Two points have to be made here: One is that Althusser seems to underestimate the fact that 'commodity fetishism' is in fact not the basic form of fetishism in Marx, this being mainly the fetishism of value and capital, explored by Marx mainly in the 1861–63 manuscripts,[145] in the form of a fetishistic belief in the ability of value for self-valorisation, which, as a form of a socially necessary miscognition, is necessary for the reproduction of capitalism.[146] In contrast to Balibar's position that a theory of fetishism based upon the market is structurally incompatible with a theory of ideology based upon the role of the state,[147] this fetishism of capital, although 'emanating' at the point of economic practices themselves is also dependent upon certain ideological features regarding the role of the state, the legal guarantees of contracts, credit and money, and so on.

It is obvious from the above presentation that for Althusser a position such as that proposed by Poulantzas, and his relational conception of the state as the condensation of class relations or a class balance of forces, would lead to a gradualist and reformist position. On the contrary, he insists on the state being separate to the class struggle as an apparatus serving the interests of the dominant classes and consequently on the necessary externality of the revolutionary movement to the state and the need to insist on smashing the state.

---

142   Althusser 2006a, p. 129.
143   Althusser 2006a, p. 133.
144   Althusser 2006a, p. 135.
145   Marx and Engels 1975–2005, vols. 30–34.
146   On such a reading of fetishism see Milios, Dimoulis and Economakis 2002.
147   Balibar 1995.

However, compared to the complexity of texts such as Poulantzas's *State, Power, Socialism*, Althusser's notion of the state as a machine transforming social force into political power – in a certain analogy to Foucault's 'technology of power' might seem rather schematic, although we have tried to show that there is a certain relational perspective in Althusser's 'mechanical' metaphor. It is more like a warning about the dangers of reformism, and a refusal of the reformist fantasy about a potential use of bourgeois state apparatuses for socialist construction, rather than a coherent theorisation of the new extended forms of state intervention in all aspects of social life.

As mentioned above, one of the main premises of Althusser's positions in the 1970s regarding the necessary exteriority of the Party and the movements to the state, but also of his hope that there could a radical refoundation of the communist project, had to do with his insistence on the strength of popular movements. This is not only an estimate of the actual balance of forces and how favourable they were for such a radical reorientation; it is also an epistemological premise for the possibility of the elaboration of such a strategic reorientation. This is evident in a recurring theme in Althusser's writings in the 1970s, namely his insistence that Marxist theory was not external but internal to the labour movement. It is on the basis of this position that Althusser distances himself from Kautsky's reference to Marxism being introduced to the workers' movement from without and his position that Marxist theory could not have been possible if Marx and Engels had adopted very specific class positions in theory.

Perhaps attempting to answer all these questions was beyond Althusser's powers. *Marx in his Limits* was never published, Althusser never actually left the PCF, nor did he take any other more open initiative. The personal tragedies in 1980 put an end to any possibility of public intervention. By then it was obvious that Althusser could not conceive of politics outside the Party despite all references to the need to 'exit the fortress'. In his autobiography Althusser makes an analogy of his decision not to leave the Communist Party despite his disagreements with the escape strategy he had devised while in captivity in a German POW camp. This strategy – which Althusser never actually used – consisted in creating the impression of an escape, simply by hiding within the camp and waiting until the alert and the search were over in order to actually escape. For Althusser it was a strategy to remain 'a prisoner in order to escape'.[148] Here is how he justified, in his autobiography, his insistence to remain in the Party.

---

148   Althusser 1993b, p. 108.

> Can you think of any other organization, whether the PSU, the Communist League, or any of the tiny left groups, which would have enabled a militant to gain equivalent social, political and ideological experience of the class struggle to that which could be gained by those who belonged for a while to the Party?

Althusser's final move was an attempt to rethink a politics based on movements and their strength – as opposed to the crisis of the communist movement. In his autobiography, he refers to an attempt in 1979–80 to set up a Centre for the Study of Popular Movements, their Ideologies and Theoretical doctrines which would follow this line of research.[149] Unfortunately, the tragedy of late 1980 put an end to this effort.

6   Traces of Communism

One of the most important aspects of Althusser's endeavour in this period was a recurring insistence on the potential of popular initiatives and on the possibility of communism emerging as a trace, or an actual virtuality in the interstices of contemporary societies. Traces of communism can be found already in struggles, popular initiatives, forms of organisation and democratic struggle, in artistic creation, scientific research and also in the very fact of the increasingly collective character of capitalist production itself.

> And since I am speaking of communism, the concept of the dictatorship of the proletariat also reminds us, above all else, that communism is not a word, not a dream for who knows what vague future. Communism is our unique strategy and, like every real strategy, not only commands today, but it also starts today. Even better, it has already started. It repeats to us the old saying by Marx; for us communism is not an ideal, but the real movement that is produced in front of our eyes. Yes, real. Communism is an objective tendency already inscribed in our society. The increased collectivisation of capitalist production, the initiatives of the popular masses, and, why not?, certain bold initiatives by artists, writers and researchers, are from today the outlines and traces of communism.[150]

---

149   Althusser 1993b, p. 246.
150   Althusser 2014c; 2015b, p. 178. Translation altered.

It is interesting that we have three different versions of this part of Althusser's text. The Spanish version of the text, which was a talk given by Althusser at the Catalan College of Building Engineers and Technical Architects, on 6 July 1976, as it appeared in a 1978 collection, refers to 'esbozos y sintomas de comunismo'[151] (outlines and symptoms of communism) and this is the version of this phrase in the English translation.[152] However we do not know whether this was an arbitrary choice of the person responsible for the translation into Spanish, since we do not know which text his translation was based on. When Althusser incorporated parts of this text in *Les vaches noires* he referred to 'esquisses et promesses du communisme'[153] (outlines and promises of communism). There is also in the archive another French version of the text that refers to 'esquisses et traces du communisme'[154] (outlines and traces of communism). The use of different words suggests both a tension but also an experimentation with different concepts to suggest this virtual emergence of communism in collective practices.[155]

This means that we are dealing with not an ideal to be attained but an active tendency emanating from class struggles themselves, a material tendency that we must enhance and elaborate upon. Communist politics is not about working upon a plan towards communism. Rather, it is about liberating possibilities and potentialities that have already emerged in the very materiality of class struggles and forms of popular organisation. Communist politics therefore has to be fundamentally emancipating and liberating from the beginning, with confidence in the collective ingenuity of the working classes. In a similar line, Althusser describes in his manuscript on the *Initiation to Philosophy* the actuality of communism in this manner:

> The proletariat knows that these perspectives are not utopian, for communism is not a dream, but a necessity, a tendency, inscribed in the his-

---

151 Althusser 1978d, p. 54.
152 Althusser 2015b, p. 178.
153 Althusser 2016, p. 247.
154 Althusser 2014c.
155 This conception of the emergence of communist elements within capitalist society was a constant reference point for Althusser in the 1970s. In the 1973 *Livre sur l'impérialisme* he refers to their multiplication because of the 'proletarian inventions in the class struggle' (Althusser 2018a, p. 131), but he warns they cannot alone lead to socialism: 'They are elements for communism. Communism will adopt them, unite them, accomplish them, and develop their virtualities, integrating them into the revolution in the relations of production which commands everything and which is absent from our world. But communism will not come about by itself [*le communisme ne se fera tout seul*]. It has to be constructed, during a long march, one stage [*étape*] of which is called socialism, which is not a mode of production' (Althusser 2018a, p. 132).

> tory of the present. Yes, communism already exists in our midst and has for a long time now, not just in embryo, but in actual fact: for example, in communist organizations and other communities (even religious communities) or activities – on one absolute condition: *that no commodity relations reign in them, but only the free association of individuals who desire the emancipation of humanity and act accordingly*.[156]

Consequently, communists aim at putting an end to any politics '*bound up to the State*',[157] but they know that the most difficult period is socialism, as a period of *transition*, which can easily 'lapse back into capitalism' if an 'economistic and idealist line'[158] is followed. At the same time, it is exactly in that period that Althusser dealt with the question of what a *new practice of communist politics* implies. Although most presentations of this debate centre upon the question of the *state* and whether the working class and its Party is (or should be) inside or outside the state, we think that the actual stake of the debate is mainly the question of a new form and new practice of politics in opposition to communist parties embracing a bourgeois practice and form of politics.

This is evident in the first of Althusser's major interventions, his lecture on the problems associated with the strategic turn of the French Communist Party in its 22nd Congress. Althusser's intervention is not simply a criticism of the abandonment of the notion of the dictatorship of the proletariat. It is also a call for new forms of autonomous organisation of the subaltern class apart from traditional party forms. This is one of the first such interventions of Althusser on the need to go beyond the traditional Party-Form and use these new forms of organisations as exactly the means for a process of revolutionary 'withering away' of the state.

> [T]he slogan 'union of the people of France', is not synonymous with the slogan of the Union of the Left. It is broader than it, and different in nature; for it does not designate just the union or united action of the political organizations of the Left, parties and trade unions. [...] Why address the popular masses in this way? To tell them, even if still only as a hint, that they will have to *organize* themselves autonomously, in original forms, in firms, urban districts and villages, around the questions of labour and living conditions, the questions of housing, education, health, transport, the environment, etc.; in order to define and defend

---

156 Althusser 2017a, p. 139.
157 Ibid.
158 Althusser 2017a, p. 140.

> their demands, first to prepare for the establishment of a revolutionary state, then to maintain it, stimulate it and at the same time force it to 'wither away'. Such mass organizations, which no one can define in advance and on behalf of the masses, already exist or are being sought in Italy, Spain and Portugal, where they play an important part, despite all difficulties. If the masses seize on the slogan of the union of the people of France and interpret it in this mass sense, they will be re-establishing connections with a living tradition of popular struggle in our country and will be able to help give a new content to the political forms by which the power of the working people will be exercised under socialism.[159]

At the same time, this requires a new form of politics with the masses and within the masses, along with an ability to bring forward their own autonomous forms of politics, their proper inventiveness and ingenuity. Above all this means giving back the masses their own voice.

> Something may come to fruition in the union of the people of France, something which has been destroyed by Stalinist practices but which is central to the Marxist and Leninist tradition, something which concerns the relationship between the Party and the masses: *restoring their voice to the masses* who make history. Not just putting oneself 'at the service of the masses' (a slogan which may be pretty reactionary), but *opening one's ears to them*, studying and understanding their aspirations and their contradictions, their aspirations in their contradictions, learning how to be attentive to the masses' imagination and inventiveness.[160]

This linked to rethinking of socialism as the transition to communism, as a 'real movement', therefore as an attempt to *revolutionise* social forms and the state.[161] In opposition to the reformist turn of the French Communist Party

---

159   Althusser 1977, p. 140.
160   Ibid. See also the comments by Sara Farris (2013) and her observation that it is exactly this emphasis that distinguishes Althusser's conception of the primacy of class struggle from positions such as Mario Tronti's 'autonomy of the political' (see the 1971 postscript in Tronti 2006).
161   '[C]ommunism is not an ideal but *"the real movement unfolding beneath our eyes"*. Very concretely this means: the strategy of the workers' movement must take this dialectic into account: *it cannot be merely the strategy of socialism*, it is necessarily the strategy of communism, or else the whole process is in danger of marking time and getting bogged down at one moment or another (and this must be foreseen). Only on the basis of the strategy of communism can socialism be conceived as a transitory and contradictory phase, and

and its strategy of 'democratising' the state, Althusser insists on the need for a *revolutionary approach*.

> Truly, and I ask that these words be carefully weighed, to 'destroy' the bourgeois state, in order to replace it with the state of the working class and its allies, is *not to add the adjective 'democratic' to each existing state apparatus*. It is something quite other than a formal and potentially reformist operation, it is to revolutionize in their structures, practices and ideologies the existing state apparatuses; to suppress some of them, to create others; it is *to transform the forms of the division of labour* between the repressive, political and ideological apparatuses; it is *to revolutionize their methods of work* and *the bourgeois ideology* that dominates their practices; it is to assure them *new relations with the masses* in response to mass initiatives, on the basis of a new, *proletarian* ideology, in order to prepare for the 'withering away of the state', i.e. its replacement by mass organizations.[162]

This same emphasis on the mass initiatives is also a cornerstone of Althusser's November 1977 intervention on *The Crisis of Marxism* in the *Il Manifesto* Venice Conference. For Althusser the crisis of Marxism is the result of an inability to come to terms with the theoretical and strategic question facing us, especially in light of the open crisis of the Soviet social formations. And this means how to think the question of the Party and mass organisations and their relation to the state not just as theoretical questions but as a revolutionary practice and politics that start today. For Althusser the process that can lead us to an actual withering away of the state starts from now, must be a defining aspect of our political practice long before the revolutionary process. The question is: 'How can we grasp now, in order to spur on the process, the need for the "destruction" of the bourgeois State, and prepare the "withering away" of the revolutionary State?'[163] Therefore, the open questions coming from the crisis of 'actually existing socialism' along with the new dynamics of the movements become at the same time the potential explanation for the crisis of Western communism and Marxism and the testing ground for any proposition to exit

---

a strategy and forms of struggle be established from this moment that do not foster any illusions about socialism (such as "We've arrived: everybody out" – Lenin's ironic comment) but treat socialism as it is, without getting bogged down in the first 'transition' that happens to come along' (Althusser 1977, p. 16).

162 Althusser 1977.
163 Althusser 1978a, p. 220.

this crisis. A new practice of mass politics is necessary both for the recomposition of the revolutionary movement but also for the transition process. That is why, noting the emergence of new mass popular movements that emerge outside the limits of the traditional party-form but also of the trade unions, Althusser insists that 'the most important of questions for past and future – how can relations be established with the mass movement which, transcending the traditional distinction between trade union and party, will permit the development of initiatives among the people, which usually fail to fit into the division between the economic and political spheres'.[164]

In the answers that he gave to Rossana Rossanda some months after the Venice Conference, Althusser makes a reference to *communism* as a material tendency emerging from the contradictions of capitalism and to the *virtual forms of communism* existing in the interstices of capitalist social forms.

> Marx thinks of communism as a *tendency* of capitalist society. This tendency is not an abstract result. It already exists, in a concrete form in the 'interstices of capitalist society' (a little bit like commodity relations existing 'in the interstices' of slave or feudal society), virtual forms of communism, in the associations that manage [...] to avoid commodity relations.[165]

This conception of a political – and philosophical – practice that liberates collective potentialities is also evident in the *Transformation of Philosophy* (1976), another crucial text in the development of Althusser's self-critical conception of a materialist practice of philosophy in the 1970s. In this text, he elaborates upon the differences between this practice of philosophy and the idealism inherent in the traditional form of the philosophical system. It also marks Althusser's distancing from the politics of communist reformism, being one of the first texts by Althusser to stress the need for a distance of proletarian politics from the state. The emphasis is on the need for new mass organisations, new forms of 'free associations' emerging through the experience of the popular masses in struggle, making sure that the revolutionary state is a 'non-state'.[166]

---

164   Ibid.
165   Althusser 1998, p. 285.
166   Althusser 1990, p. 264.

7   The Debate on the State

Althusser's intervention was part of a broader debate regarding the role of the state and the relation of the proletarian party-form to the state. This debate, on the one hand, was an attempt to deal with the political questions (and traumas) originating from the evolution of Soviet socialism and the identification of ruling communist parties in 'people's democracies' with the state in a very authoritarian version. On the other hand, the question of the state and its extended role, of the possibility for Communist Parties to find themselves managing the state, through left-wing governments, raised serious theoretical and political issues regarding the role of the state and the relation of communist parties to the state and led to conflicting positions: Either in the form of an attempt to rethink the potentially positive role of the state and the Party along to new forms of democracy in civil society and a effort towards the socialisation of politics, a position evident for example in Pietro Ingrao's interventions in the second half of the 1970s.[167] Or it took the form of an attempt to think of a politics beyond (and against) the state. Alain Badiou's insistence from the 1970s on a communist politics openly antagonistic and external to the state, which evolved into his call for a politics at a distance from the state,[168] is an example of this tendency. And it is interesting that in the 1970s there are certain analogies between Althusser's calls for the exteriority of the Party to the state and similar statements by Badiou.[169]

However, apart from this polarisation there were also other interventions in those debates that attempted a more dialectical approach. Of particular interest are those interventions that came from people who, in one way or another, had been theoretical interlocutors of Althusser. Poulantzas took up the challenge to answer Althusser. Poulantzas opposed the exteriority thesis on the basis of the fact that 'the state is already *present* in the very *constitution* of production relations and not only in their reproduction'.[170] Moreover, for Poulantzas all the new movements that Althusser referred to as proof of the exteriority of popular movements '*are necessarily positioned on the stra-*

---

167   Ingrao 1977a; 1977b; 1978. Althusser makes many references to the Italian debates of that time in his texts in the second half of the 1970s. On the positions of the Left in Italy in the 1970s, see Abse 1985.
168   Badiou 2005a.
169   It is interesting to read how in a 1978 text included in *Theory of the Subject* Badiou refers to 'anticommunist fusion of the State and the masses, under a "proletarian" class name that is henceforth absolutely imaginary. This entity has a name: the new bourgeoisie, born from within the party itself' (2009b, p. 230).
170   Poulantzas 1980, p. 166.

tegic terrain that the State is. A proletarian *politics* cannot be situated outside the State'.[171] Theoretically, Poulantzas grounds his opposition to Althusser on his relational conception of the state.[172] Consequently, for Poulantzas a revolutionary politics can be neither an attempt to destroy the institutions of representative democracy, nor its simple reform. It must be an attempt to deal with these contradictions in a combination between the transformation of the state and movements from below. Poulantzas also deals with these matters in *State, Power, Socialism*, where he offers an even clearer conception of a struggle both 'inside' and 'outside' the state:

> The choice is not, as is often thought, between a struggle 'within' the state apparatuses (that is, physically invested and inserted in their material space) and a struggle located at a certain distance from these apparatuses. *First*, because any struggle at a distance always has effects within the State: it is always there, even if only in a retracted manner and through intermediaries. *Secondly*, and most importantly, because struggle at a distance from state apparatuses whether within and beyond the limits of the physical space traced by the institutional *loci*, remains necessary at all times and in every case, since it affects the autonomy and the struggles and organizations of the popular classes. [...] The question of *who* is in power *to do what* cannot be isolated by these struggles for self-management and direct democracy. But if they are to modify the relations of power, such struggles and movement cannot tend towards centralization in a second power, they must rather seek to shift the relationship of forces on the terrain of the State itself.[173]

However, the problem with Poulantzas's intervention was that in contrast to the early formulation of his relational theory of state and state power, he had already shifted towards a thinking of the left-wing politics mainly as *parliamentary* politics, or, to be more precise, he thought in terms of the superiority of this kind of struggle for parliamentary representation and left-wing governance within the contours of a parliamentary democracy. In this perspective, mass struggles outside the state objectively took a secondary place in relation

---

171 Poulantzas 1980, p. 171.
172 Poulantzas's relational conception emerges fully first in *Classes in Contemporary Capitalism*: 'The state is not an "entity" with an intrinsic instrumental essence, but it is itself a relation, more precisely the condensation of a class relation' (1975, p. 26).
173 Poulantzas 2000, pp. 259–60. On the question of struggles 'inside' and 'outside' the state, see Brand and Heigl 2011.

to electoral campaigns. Moreover, this shift by Poulantzas makes it impossible to rethink a new practice of politics. As Andrea Cavazzini notes, Poulantzas's positions 'make it impossible to pose the questions regarding *a transformation of politics*, which will not limit itself to modifying existing structures, but will dare question the place of its "production", the status of its agents and which will finally propose a change even *at the level of its definition*'.[174]

Balibar's response to Althusser, initially pronounced during a conference in January 1979 and subsequently published as an article in *Dialectiques*, is of particular interest and marks the beginning of a rich and profound confrontation with the question of the relation of class, politics, and the state. Balibar begins by stressing the importance of Althusser's opposition to the then dominant position within communist parties that they should be 'parties of government', but he also stresses that in the 'logic of Althusser's argument the idea of a "party of opposition" will be equally erroneous as that of "party of government"',[175] since both will be inscribed in the same form and practice of politics. Balibar also insists that this symmetry in political practice was a manifestation of the crisis of the historical communist movement.

> Despite the virtualities and the real revolutionary tendencies that gave a thrust to the Popular Fronts and the resistance movements, we had a perfect symmetry between the communist parties 'of government' (in the East) and the communist parties 'of opposition' (in the West) having in common the same model of organization, a common ideology and 'line'.[176]

For Balibar, the problem lies exactly in Althusser's call for the party to be fundamentally outside of the state returning to the masses and in autonomy to the state. Balibar thinks that this brings us back to an 'ideal (and idealist) conception of a party that would be nothing but the effect of the (revolutionary) will of its members, the product of the rules that it imposed itself as a function of the final end to which it tendentially moves (communism = the withering away of the State)'.[177] For Balibar such a conception leads to contradictions that cannot be easily solved. The party is presented at the same time as the expression of the class conscience of the masses and as the centre of organisation and education of the masses. He also finds the same tension evident in Marx's own writings,

---

174 Cavazzini 2009, p. 92.
175 Balibar 1979, p. 81.
176 Balibar 1979, pp. 81–2.
177 Balibar 1979, p. 82.

in the 1848 writings as a tension within the conception of a class organised as Party that does not take into consideration the transformation of the state but also in the writings on the Paris Commune where the question of the party is not posed in detail. For Balibar the main question is exactly the problem of the relation between the Party and the state, even though they are presented in the Marxist tradition as offering two 'incompatible "points of view"',[178] as if the 'revolutionary Party' and the 'proletarian State' represented two contrasting solutions for the transition to communism, 'one of which is always *in excess*, despite the fact that the experience of class struggle imposes both the one *and* the other'.[179] And this contradiction emerges whenever the question of the model of the Paris Commune is evoked, in Soviet Russia in 1917–18 and in China during the Cultural Revolution.

For Balibar, Althusser's critique of communist parties being modelled on the state and its apparatuses did not offer *per se* a way to theorise the problem because the open question remained how to theorise the state. Moreover, he thought that an opposition between a 'good' democratic state and a 'bad' corporatist state and between a 'good' party freeing the initiative of the masses and a 'bad' party repressing this initiative, is 'an abstract and moral opposition that shows [...] the incapacity to analyze the genesis and historical results of real contradictions that "work through" workers' parties today, thus, in the last instance, the working class itself'.[180] That is why for Balibar there was no point in treating the masses as being outside the state; on the contrary, they are conditioned in many respects by their relation to state apparatuses.

> The masses are not, in any case, 'outside the State'. In contrast, they are always *already* taken within a network of state relations, namely institutional divisions (the code of professional 'qualifications' and the code of national membership) with a functioning of repression and ideological subjection which, within given historical conditions, are simply indispensable for their existence and form the material condition of all politics.[181]

For Balibar it was exactly that which led to Lenin's polemics against spontaneity at the same time that he recognised the importance of the initiative of the masses. This also implies that the revolutionary worker's movement cannot be

---

178   Ibid.
179   Balibar 1979, p. 83.
180   Balibar 1979, p. 84.
181   Ibid.

conceived as being outside the constraints imposed by the state. This requires a different approach: '[we must] not think in terms of interior/exterior of the State, namely the "purity" of antagonistic positions (this old idealist temptation already denounced by Lenin), but in terms of *contradictions internal* to the system of State relations'.[182] Consequently, the problem with the European Communist Parties' position is not their reference to internal contradictions, but how they tended to underestimate the inequality inherent in the balance of forces between classes and the effects on state practices upon the workers' movement.

For Balibar there was a problem with how the distinction between proletarian and bourgeois politics was conceived in the Marxist tradition. Initially it was conceived as a 'distinction between *politics* (bourgeois) and *non-politics* (proletarian)'.[183] With Lenin this distinction was displaced in an opposition between different institutional forms of politics, but it also had the cost of treating the Party as the locus where the contradiction between these different forms of politics was resolved (underestimating the extent that the Party internalises this contradiction) and of thinking in terms of antagonistic *juridical* forms. For Balibar this led to '*new forms* of "parliamentary cretinism" and "antiparliamentary cretinism"'.[184] Political domination should not be confused with the juridical form it takes (as modality of representation, etc.); on the contrary, the juridical form 'in reality draws its efficacy from the cumulative effect of all the underlying apparatuses of ideological and political domination (school, family, Law etc.)'.[185]

Balibar then turned his attention to the Chinese Cultural Revolution, the way it stressed that class struggles continue throughout the 'transition process' and the opportunity it offered to rethink the question of the Party. First by criticising the 'evolutionist and in fact apologetic Kautskist motif, conserved by communist parties, according to which the *party* represents the "final" form of the integration of struggles and of the theory/practice synthesis',[186] and then by insisting that the party is itself a site of class struggle. However, Balibar wants to move forward and pose the question of what was also missing from the Cultural Revolution in terms of revolutionary theory. For Balibar, Althusser's conception of the Ideological Apparatuses of the State can help us rethink how the relation of forces between the initiative of the masses and their subjection, which

---

182 Balibar 1979, p. 85.
183 Balibar 1979, p. 86.
184 Ibid.
185 Balibar 1979, p. 87.
186 Balibar 1979, pp. 87–8.

is exactly the meaning of proletarian politics taking precedence in relation to bourgeois politics. At the same time, it can help us understand how we have missed encounters between the masses and the communist movement, such as May 1968 and even forms of *break* between the Party and the masses. That is why it is important to analyse the '*contradictory place of the revolutionary party itself* within this "play" of the ISAs [...] and the transformations of the revolutionary party as antagonistic *tendency* within the ISAs'.[187] This calls for a rethinking of all the ideological constraints and effects that offer the material ground for the inherently contradictory character of revolutionary parties, beyond a schematic opposition within/outside the state. Moreover, this thinking of the Party as *antagonistic tendency* manages to capture the force of class antagonism and the fundamental opposition between potentially proletarian and bourgeois politics, without into a schematic conception of the Party as a political and organisational entity immune to the material constraints of the state, thus going beyond the inside/outside opposition. For Balibar this calls exactly for thinking the historical significance and the contradiction of the party form. Therefore for Balibar the problem with Eurocommunism was that it believed that it could resolve the contradictions of the party-form without profoundly positing and confronting them.[188] This entails a necessary break within this form, not in the sense of liquidating the organisational forms of the workers' movement but in the sense of coming to terms with the limits and contradictions of the party-form. As Balibar puts it:

> It is a structural fact, that affects the interior of the 'party-form' as an historical form, that Marxism is today a mass revolutionary ideology only within certain countries of Latin Europe, the Far-East and perhaps Cuba [...] in the end it has not permitted, under its current form, the concentration and the centralization of class struggles in the majority of 'developed' imperialist countries (thus the dominant poles of imperialism), or the continuation of the revolution in the countries of 'realized socialism', or the real fusion of the worker's movement and national liberation movements (with some rare and 'precious' exceptions), or the proletarian answer to 'multinational' enterprises. It is a structural fact that the 'party-form', as it functions today, is not the form of *unity* of the international communist movement, but has become the form of its crisis and division, within which what prevails is not the solidarity of

---

187   Balibar 1979, p. 88.
188   Ibid.

struggles, but (especially after the end of the Vietnam War) the opposition between national State interests, namely, in the last instance of the *subordination* to the tendencies of imperialism and its 'rules of game'.[189]

At the same time Balibar insisted that European Communist Parties of this time were organising only a fragment of the working class and working-class struggles, unable to organise immigrants, unemployed, and new sections of the working class and also unable to deal with actual divisions within the working class.

For Balibar this called for a profound transformation of the party-form, well beyond rethinking it within the contours of the relation between party and trade union defined by both the Second and the Third Internationals. Such a transformation posed the challenge of *'the "pluralism" of the Party but also of "movements" – namely the organisations – of the masses*, which is much more fundamental than the *pluralism – only – of parties*, which by itself does not contribute to the undermining of the subjection of the masses to the forms of bourgeois politics'.[190] Balibar's conclusion was that we cannot separate the history of working-class organisations from the history of the state and the history of class struggles, if we want to study how new tendencies within the class struggle were internalised as contradictions within the communist movement, overdetermining the effects of the 'crisis latent since the 1930s'.[191]

This was an important intervention, part of a series of interventions that would also continue into the 1980s in an attempt to rethink politics under a class perspective. The crucial aspect of Balibar's intervention was the way it attempted to problematise the distinctions upon which Althusser's intervention was based – exemplified in the inside/outside the state imagery – not in the sense of trying to negate its importance but of bringing forward the complexity of the question and the contradictory relation between class movement, party, and the state. In a way, Balibar actually attempts to think the consequences of Althusser's conception of the Ideological State Apparatuses, as a way to think the extent, depth, and contradictions of the capitalist state, in a manner that Althusser himself did not dare to, trapped in a thinking of State Apparatus in terms of inside/outside. In Balibar's reading the entire conception the Ideological Apparatuses of the State stops being simply a more complex thinking of state functions. It becomes a thinking of the state as a broader network and field of material practices, constraints and antagonisms that creates, in its

---

189 Balibar 1979, pp. 90–1.
190 Balibar 1979, p. 91.
191 Balibar 1979, p. 92.

complexity and unevenness – traversed as it is by class struggle – the material ground and the possibility of politics, including proletarian politics as antagonistic politics.

This does not mean that Balibar denied the political significance of Althusser's call for autonomy of the Party and movements from the state, as a line of demarcation with reformism and bourgeois politics. He was attempting to think of this necessary demarcation in its actual terms and the confrontation with both the complexity of state intervention and the limits of the historically determined relation between the party-form and other forms of proletarian mass politics.

Althusser's call for the externality of the Party to the state was an attempt at a left-wing criticism of communist politics. However, the schematic character of the inside/outside metaphor brought forward the limits of his position. In this sense, many of Althusser's observations regarding the crisis of the PCF and the communist movement in general are accurate. Missing was a broader confrontation with the crisis of revolutionary strategy; especially since in the 1970s we witnessed another defeat of the revolution in the West (the first one occurring in the aftermath of the October Revolution and the second with the national unity governments after WWII in Italy and France). The combined inability of both the post-1968 revolutionary Left and the Communist Parties in Western Europe to articulate a coherent strategy that would enable the confrontation with the question of political power contributed to this. On the one hand, the tendencies of the revolutionary Left, even in their most advanced form, such the Italian Far Left, never managed to challenge the hegemony of the communist parties (and/or social-democratic parties) in the labour movement, nor did they conceive of an actual revolutionary process, despite their undeniable contribution to the radicalisation of the movements. This led them to an impasse and having to choose between political marginalisation, becoming a Left opposition or even Left 'pressure group' with regard to communist reformism, and following the even more tragic road of armed struggle. On the other hand, the embedded reformism and deep-rooted electoralism of the Communist Parties made them unable to understand the combined dynamics of post-1968 radicalism, the capitalist crisis and the various forms of an evolving crisis of hegemony. Consequently, they engaged in various forms of right-wing turns and lost momentum, paving the way for the neoliberal turn of the 1980s (which in some cases was initiated by the social-democratic parties that were considered allies for the government of the Left). Thus, the 1970s made obvious the crisis of both the insurrectionist strategy and the 'government of the Left' position.

In such a conjuncture, what was missing was a theoretical and strategic confrontation with the forms of bourgeois hegemony, the complexity of capitalist power, the extent of hegemonic apparatuses, in order to articulate a revolutionary strategy that would have combined the slow and arduous preparation within society in order to transform 'common sense' the building of counter-hegemonic apparatuses, the experimentation with forms of self-management and radical struggle as potential modern forms of 'dual power', plus a strategy for political power that even if it could have an electoral victory and governmental power as a starting point, it could never be limited to simply 'managing the state' demanding instead a strategy of transformation and struggle within the state and outside of it.[192] This would have required the transformation of political parties into collective elaborators of new intellectualities, into laboratories of new projects and tactics, in the line of Gramsci's thinking about the 'Modern Prince', instead of treating them as simple electoral mechanisms. It would also have required a non-instrumentalist conception of movements and forms of collective organisation as actual experiments in new forms of power and collective organisation and as terrains for experimentation with new social forms. It would also mean confronting the political implications of what Balibar described as 'Marx's theoretical short-circuit', the interconnection between the labour process and the political sphere that bourgeois thinking tends to negate.[193]

Regarding such questions it is obvious that Althusser offered important lines of demarcation and necessary forms of 'bending of the stick to the other side' (the emphasis on the Party as an open process, the insistence on the non-identification of the Party and the state, social movements in their autonomy, the need to 'smash the State') and an important left critique of communist reformism, but he could not answer the question of a politics of hegemony. Perhaps, it was too big a challenge for someone who despite his strong political conviction always remained an intellectual and never a political leader; or

---

192   Henri Weber attempted to articulate this challenge in 1979 as follows: 'The advanced capitalist countries of Western Europe are the terrain of specific contradictions whose condensation can precipitate pre-revolutionary crises, perfectly exploitable by the workers' movement. [...] But this transition to socialism must take full account the specificities of capitalist domination in the West. As Gramsci has stressed, but before him Karl Radek, Paul Levy and many others, the transition to socialism in these countries will be the outcome of a long work of gestation, of political preparation, where the workers' movement must consciously and systematically contribute to the production of the conditions for the revolutionary conquest of power. [...] It is possible only on the terrain of self-organization – unitary and democratic – of the popular masses for the defense of the interests and the taking up of the affairs directly in their own hands' (Weber 1979, p. 36).
193   Balibar 1994b, p. 136.

we can also say that this task could only have been a *collective effort*, a *collective process of experimentation and elaboration*. Even those thinkers who tried to confront the complexity of these questions, such as Poulantzas in *State, Power, Socialism*, describing the democratic road to socialism as the process of a '*sweeping transformation*'[194] of the state as a process of withering away of the state through an increased intervention of the popular masses, had to acknowledge the risks of failure and 'social-democratization'[195] of this process.

8   Confronting Gramsci

Part of the contradictions and the limits of Althusser's late 1970s writings on the state and politics have to do with a missed theoretical encounter with Gramsci. Although Gramsci has been one of main theoretical interlocutors of Althusser, and this is manifest both in the concept of the Ideological Apparatuses of the State and in Althusser's reading of Machiavelli, at the same time in many instances Althusser chose Gramsci as a theoretical opponent. In *Reading Capital* he insisted that Gramsci's positions are historicist, fearing that Gramsci's attempt at a theorisation of the actual historicity of social forms (including theoretical and political positions) would undermine his own project of bringing back scientific rigour to Marxism.[196]

---

194   Poulantzas 2000, p. 261.
195   Poulantzas 2000, p. 264.
196   'Gramsci constantly declares that a scientific theory, or such and such a category of a science, is a "superstructure" or a "historical category" which he assimilates to a "human relation". [...] To make science a superstructure is to think of it as one of those "organic" ideologies which form such a close "bloc" with the structure that they have the same "history" as it does! But even in Marxist theory we read that ideologies may survive the structure that gave them birth (this is true for the majority of them: e.g., religion, ethics, or ideological philosophy), as may certain elements of the politico-legal superstructure in the same way (Roman law!). As for science, it may well arise from an ideology, detach itself from its field in order to constitute itself as a science, but precisely this detachment, this "break", inaugurates a new form of historical existence and temporality which together save science (at least in certain historical conditions that ensure the real continuity of its own history – conditions that have not always existed) from the common fate of a single history: that of the "historical bloc" unifying structure and superstructure. Idealism is an ideological reflection of the temporality peculiar to science, the rhythm of its development, the kind of continuity and punctuation which seem to save it from the vicissitudes of political and economic history in the form of a historicity and temporality; in this way it hypostasizes a real phenomenon which needs quite different categories if it is to be thought, but which *must be thought* by distinguishing between the relatively autonomous

Moreover, in *Marx in his Limits* Althusser accuses Gramsci of not being able to provide a coherent theory of the state and of offering a simplistic theorisation of state power as a combination of consent and coercion. Gramsci is accused of not understanding the importance of force: '*in Gramsci, the "moment" of Force is ultimately swallowed up by the moment of hegemony*'.[197] Moreover, Althusser seems to treat Gramsci as being extensively overdetermined by the open political exigencies of his time, in the sense *of 'a political examination of the "nature", hence of the "composition" or internal arrangement [dispositif] of the states of the day*, undertaken with a view to defining a political strategy for the workers' movement after all hope that the schema of 1917 would be repeated had faded'.[198] Althusser criticises Gramsci not for insisting on the need for a long-term strategy for the hegemony of the working class over its allies – a position he considers part of the Marxist tradition – but exactly for using hegemony as the central concept.

> The novelty that Gramsci introduces is, rather, the idea that Hegemony can, as it were, be *representative of the whole constituted by* (1) *civil society* (which is its domain); (2) *the state as Force or coercion*; and (3) *the effect, also called Hegemony*, that results from the functioning of the state as a whole, comprising, be it recalled, Force and Hegemony.[199]

Althusser thinks that there are in Gramsci three different notions of hegemony. One is hegemony as the complement of force regarding the role of the state. Second, there is the hegemony exercised by the state. Third, there is the hegemony of the party of the working class. The danger in such a conception of hegemony for Althusser is that it can underestimate the importance of force leading to an idealist conception, the 'absolute idealism of a *Hegemony lacking a material basis*, with no explanation of the Coercive Apparatuses which nevertheless play an active part in engendering the Hegemony-effect'.[200] Consequently, Althusser insists that *contra* Gramsci it is impossible to '*to decipher everything that happens* not just in the infrastructure, reproduction and the class struggle, but also in law and the state (Force + Hege-

---

and peculiar history of scientific knowledge and the other modalities of historical existence (those of the ideological and politico-legal superstructures, and that of the economic structure)' (Althusser et al. 2016, pp. 283–4).
197 Althusser 2006a, p. 141.
198 Ibid.
199 Althusser 2006a, p. 143.
200 Althusser 2006a, p. 144.

mony), *exclusively at the level of what Gramsci calls Hegemony*'.[201] For Althusser this '*process of the sublimation of the state into Hegemony*'[202] is the basis for a certain idealistic conception of communism as a 'regulated society' with the political Party in a quasi-Hegelian role as educator. The danger is both the underestimation of class struggle but also of the role of the state as a special 'machine'.

> The specific reality of the state clearly does disappear in a formula in which Hegemony = Force + consensus, or political society + civil society, and so on. When the realities of class struggle are treated in the guise of Hegemony-effects alone, it is obviously no longer necessary to scrutinize either the nature or the function of the state as a 'special machine'.[203]

Althusser is afraid that such a conception of Hegemony will not allow thinking of the specific materiality of the state and its role in class reproduction. Moreover, he thinks that Gramsci's conception of culture will make it impossible to have a theory of ideology and a replacement of ideology with culture will underestimate class struggle and reproduce an elitist conception of cultural hegemony.

> For if ideology rather quickly comes to mean ideological struggle, hence an inevitable, necessary form of class struggle, the notion of culture leads straight to the ecumenism of the notion that an elite (in the Party as well as in bourgeois society) is the guardian of culture's own values of 'production' ('creators') and consumption ('connoisseurs', 'art-lovers', and so on).[204]

Althusser also fears that such a conception of Hegemony could also lead to a variation of the 'thesis of the autonomy of the political or of politics'[205] position, which he thinks cannot offer a way to conceive of politics. This refers to the debates within the Italian Communist Party during the period of the historical compromise, when the 'autonomy of the political' thesis was also used as a means for a distancing from class politics and as justification for policies such the 'Historical Compromise'. It is also interesting that it is exactly here, on the

---

201 Althusser 2006a, p. 145.
202 Althusser 2006a, p. 146.
203 Althusser 2006a, p. 147.
204 Althusser 2006a, p. 149.
205 Althusser 2006a, p. 150.

question of politics, that Althusser's manuscript ends. The final phrase seems like a confrontation with the main open question of communist politics: 'For to ask what politics might be implies that one state one's views on the Party. But what does one do in the Party, if not politics?'[206]

The text that presents Althusser's most comprehensive critique of Gramsci is *Que faire?* [*What is to be done?*], a 1978 manuscript, and it is here that we find not only a critique of Gramsci's theory of hegemony, but also a critique of Gramsci's reading of Machiavelli. We also know from the archive that these texts were based on Althusser's extensive reading of Gramsci in the Gerratana critical edition that appeared in 1975, but also of books on Gramsci.

Que faire? begins with what it means to offer a concrete analysis of a concrete situation, with Althusser insisting that this requires a '*minimum mastering of Marxist theory*',[207] in order to understand the determination of complex conjunctures and the particular situation of workers themselves. Althusser stresses the inability of even the most militant workers to fully understand their situation not only within a particular corporation in the context but also of national and international developments and reminds readers that this terrain is traversed by ideologies. For Althusser the problem lies in the fact that although we must insist on the 'primacy of masses upon classes and the primacy of masses and classes on the organisations of class struggle, the trade union and the party', at the same time workers are not outside ideological class struggle. It is here that the question *What is to be done?* emerges in every conjuncture, in the form of a '*political line*' and at the same time of the 'theoretical, organisational, ideological and practical means'[208] needed for the realisation of such a political line. However, developing such a political line requires indeed a concrete analysis of a concrete situation, and Althusser laments the fact that the French Communist Party did not produce such concrete analysis, opting instead for the simple application of a 'theory' which for Althusser was artificial, arbitrary, inexact and insufficient,[209] referring to the particularly French version of the theory of 'State Monopoly Capitalism'. For Althusser the problem was that this conception of a theory was applied to the concrete of the conjuncture without taking into account its changing character. However, he also believes that in this attempt to deal with the relation between a changing con-

---

206 Ibid.
207 Althusser 2018b, p. 31.
208 Althusser 2018b, pp. 39–40.
209 Althusser2018b, p. 44.

crete conjuncture and theory lies the danger of treating this theory as being itself 'historical' in character, hence the danger of *historicism* and he refers to Gramsci as the principle example.

Althusser attributes Gramsci's historicism to his 'antidogmatism'.[210] In contrast to the historicist conception he presents his own position on how to think the relation between stability and change within capitalist socialist reality. For Althusser the stable aspect refers to the *'capitalist relation of production'*,[211] but this can be stable only on the condition that it can *'produce the change of its proper antagonistic terms as means to perpetuate its stability'*,[212] suggesting that this enables a 'history of the capitalist mode of production'.[213] Althusser opposes this conception to the position that 'everything is historical', suggesting that *'historicism is a bicycle without wheels'*. Althusser repeats here his criticism of historicism from *Reading Capital*, namely that theory is reduced to philosophy, philosophy to politics and politics to history.[214] Althusser accuses Gramsci of disregarding the distinction of structure and superstructures and leading to a 'phantom' [*fantômale*] existence of the superstructures,[215] and an empiricist conception. He thinks that the Gramscian notion of the 'historical bloc' tends to replace the notion of the mode of production, which *'realizes* the profound tendency of historicism: everything is history, everything changes'.[216] Althusser accuses Gramsci of having a theory of the State as educator, a theory of an ethical State. Consequently, Althusser appears here much more critical of the notion of hegemony, suggesting that it refers to such a conception of an *'ethical unity'*.[217] He also is very critical of the notion of *passive revolution* and its use for a variety of historical situations, and he thinks that this relates to Gramsci's refusal to use the notion of *'counter-revolution'*.[218] Althusser believes that the problem with this use of the notion of revolution to characterise such a vast array of historical phenomena has to do with Gramsci thinking mainly in terms of *activity*, with history being categorised on the basis of the presence or absence of activity, revolution or passive revolution. The result is that Gramsci cannot have a theory of history, only a description of historical events: '*Gramsci*

---

210   Althusser 2018b, p. 52.
211   Althusser 2018b, p. 53.
212   Althusser 2018b, p. 54.
213   Ibid.
214   Althusser 2018b, p. 59.
215   Althusser 2018b, p. 60.
216   Althusser 2018b, p. 67.
217   Althusser 2018b, p. 69.
218   Althusser 2018b, p. 72.

is not a theorist of history, he is a reader of history.[219] Moreover, such an emphasis on activity can explain, according to Althusser, the very notion of the *philosophy of praxis* and why Gramsci insists that '*every philosophy is political*'.[220]

Althusser's preoccupation is not just theoretical; it is also political. In particular, as is the case with other texts of that period, his target is Eurocommunism and how Gramsci is becoming the main reference of the Eurocommunist current. Althusser thinks that Gramsci is substituting the distinction between structure and superstructures with the distinction between State and civil society, the latter being conceived as the ensemble of 'private associations, which exist outside the state'.[221] Althusser is critical of Gramsci using the notion of hegemonic apparatus to describe such associations since the very notion of apparatus refers to the state. Above all, in a line similar to the critique we find in *Marx in his Limits*, Althusser thinks that the very notion of hegemony hinders the necessary thinking of the 'materiality of ideologies'[222] and leads to thinking the '*State as hegemony*',[223] without any reference to either class domination or class dictatorship.[224] Althusser insists that he accepts the definition of hegemony of the 'classics of Marxism'[225] as increased influence and alliance building by the working class, but he is critical of Gramsci's position that the 'working class must become hegemonic in the entire society "before taking power"'.[226] Althusser thinks that this is what leads to Eurocommunism and also suggests that the theoretical problem is Gramsci's underestimation of capitalist exploitation, the fact that Gramsci '*never enters* into the reality, the detail, the mechanism and the role ("determinant in the last instance") of this immense white zone'.[227]

Althusser believes that all these can account for Gramsci's admiration of Machiavelli and that everything that Gramsci suggests is 'already in Machiavelli', in the latter's theory of the state as '"beast" (force) and human (consensus)', although for Althusser there is more in Machiavelli:

> because the beast in his work *is separated in tout*, being at the same time lion (brutal force) and fox (fraud and deceit) and that finally the fox is

---

219 Althusser 2018b, p. 79.
220 Althusser 2018b, p. 86.
221 Althusser 2018b, p. 90.
222 Althusser 2018b, p. 94.
223 Althusser 2018b, p. 96.
224 Althusser 2018b, p. 97.
225 Althusser 2018b, p. 100.
226 Ibid.
227 Althusser 2018b, p. 103.

virtù, or capacity to use force and consensus (hegemony) according to its will, according to the exigencies of the conjuncture [...] and something more, since this capacity of fraud is definitely reduced to the power to deceive, to the capacity to make an appearance [*puissance de faire semblant*] (to appear virtuous when they are not and above all, which is much more difficult, to appear virtuous when they are).[228]

Althusser thinks that in this way Machiavelli shows how ideology is 'constitutive of all State power',[229] and also how military forms and practices also induce ideological transformation. Althusser thinks that Machiavelli in contrast to Gramsci insists on the 'primacy of the "moment" of force (the army) over "hegemony" in the State'.[230] Moreover, Althusser criticises Gramsci for failing to take account of the theory of ideology that we can find in Machiavelli:

> Gramsci never understood that deception was consubstantial to the State, and also to the political strategy of the Prince and that above all it had as effect to produce this representation, this 'image' of the Prince at the use of people, without which there is no power of the State.[231]

That is why for Althusser Machiavelli goes beyond Gramsci's silence on the question of ideology by recognising 'the organic necessity of a State ideology in order for the State to exercise its hegemony'.[232] Althusser insists on the materialist character of Machiavelli, that 'he thinks in politics and as materialist' [*pense en politique et en matérialiste*],[233] realising the need to destroy previous forms of State in order to lay the foundations of a new State with a new Prince. Moreover, for Althusser the Prince 'is not an individual who would be a human *subject* [...] The Prince is a system of instances without central subject, without subjective unity [...] The Prince is a political strategy, a "process without subject"'.[234] For Althusser the crucial question is that of ideology, because it is 'indispensable not only for the existence and functioning of the State, but for the presentation of this strategy to the people, its popular representation'.[235] It is here that he finds the problem of a construction of hegemony before the

---

228 Althusser 2018b, p. 106.
229 Ibid.
230 Althusser 2018b, p. 107.
231 Althusser 2018b, p. 108.
232 Ibid.
233 Althusser 2018b, p. 111.
234 Althusser 2018b, p. 112.
235 Althusser 2018b, p. 114.

emergence of the New State, a problem that Gramsci attempts to solve 'with the thesis of the realisation of hegemony before taking State power',[236] and with his conception of Communist Party as the Modern Prince.

However, Althusser disagrees with Gramsci's solution and insists that the 'party is not a Prince',[237] and that it represents something completely different from the bourgeois strategy for the destruction of feudalism. Moreover, Althusser criticises Gramsci for not paying enough attention to the distinctions that Machiavelli makes with regard to the strategy of the Prince as *man, lion and fox*. Althusser elaborates more on the particular significance of fraud or deception [*feinte*] in the *Prince* insisting that Machiavelli *'had discovered in ideological matter an absolutely original [inédite] deceit, that is a form of discourse that produces ideological effects without precedent: which consists on not deceiving on anything [...] The ideological representation* of known reality appears in his work under the paradoxical form of the *simple representation of known reality'*.[238] And it is here, Althusser thinks, that we can find Machiavelli's true materialism:

> He knows that he can only say the true [*dire le vrai*], and he knows well that this cannot go far, because other conditions are necessary for the true to penetrate the masses: political conditions that are not in the power of an isolated intellectual [...] Machiavelli is a materialist: at the same time that he chooses to say the true without ever deceiving, he never falls into the delirium of the omnipotence of ideas.[239]

What is missing in Machiavelli according to Althusser is a conception of class struggle not around relations of property but around the question of exploitation. According to Althusser exploitation is for both Machiavelli and Gramsci an 'immense white zone': '*What Machiavelli could not see and understand, Gramsci, in fact, simply erased and suppressed*'.[240] For Althusser, this poses an absolute limit: 'Which Marxist does not understand [...] *that it is absolutely impossible to follow in his "conclusions", someone like him who has erased, in all this reasoning, what is "determinant in the last instance" in the eyes of Marxism: that is exploitation, its conditions, reproduction and their incalculable con-*

---

236 Althusser 2018b, p. 115.
237 Ibid.
238 Althusser 2018b, p. 119.
239 Althusser 2018b, p. 122.
240 Althusser 2018b, p. 125.

sequences?'[241] The problem for Althusser is that Gramsci makes a conceptual construction while ignoring *'two or three elementary truths of Marxism'*.[242] He attributes this to Gramsci's specific prison condition, where his only pleasure was to '"look" at things directly [...] to consume the object, that is history, *as a delicacy'*.[243]

All these can account, according to Althusser, for how Gramsci was being used as part of the Eurocommunist strategy. He believes that the crucial point is the conception of the State of hegemony that leads to the class struggle being substituted by the 'struggle of hegemonies', which means that *'the question of the state finds itself practically and theoretically evacuated'*.[244] For Althusser, here is the problem, namely the entire conception of the relation between civil society, State and hegemony that in his eyes in the end justifies a reformist conception of a 'war of position' and instead of a Leninist communist party of something close to Togliatti's 'partito nuovo'.[245]

I believe that in the case of Althusser's relation to the work of Gramsci we have an important 'missed encounter'. What is missing is a confrontation with the depth of hegemony as a theorisation of the complex modalities of power in capitalist social formations. Moreover, lacking a concept close to Gramsci's *integral state*, that would offer a much more dialectical conception of the relation of social movements to the state, through a theorisation of the expansion of both the state and of the forms of organisation of the subordinate classes and the 'mutual interpenetration and reinforcement of "political society" and "civil society"',[246] Althusser is pushed to a rather schematic distinction between the state as a machine for political power and the space of social movements and consequently to the theoretical and political limits of his externality to the state position. What is missing in Althusser is exactly this insight that subordinate classes and their movements are already always within and outside the state, exactly because the state is neither a fortress nor simply a machine but a complex and expanded network of relations, practices, and apparatuses that is traversed by class struggles. So the question is not one of simple externality; what is needed is a political strategy that would make this necessarily contradictory and uneven relation antagonistic and transformative. Such a conception of the *integral state*, which was beginning to emerge in the

---

241 Althusser 2018b, p. 126.
242 Ibid.
243 Althusser 2018b, p. 127.
244 Althusser 2018b, p. 136.
245 Althusser 2018b, p. 137.
246 Thomas 2009, p. 137.

series of readings of Gramsci that followed Valentino Gerratana's critical editions of the *Quaderni di Carcere* such as Christine Buci-Glucksmann's *Gramsci and the State*,[247] could have helped Althusser answer both the question of the defeats of the Left (the actual extent and depth of bourgeois hegemony even in a period of social radicalisation), and the challenges for Left strategy. These challenges could not be answered simply by a combination of a turn towards the strength of the popular movement. They demanded a (counter-)hegemonic project, a strategy to transform radicalism into a coherent strategy both at the level of civil society (emerging new social forms and forms of organisation) and the state (new political forms) beyond simply taking up governmental power. Instead Althusser offered lines of demarcation but the theoretical choices he made regarding the theory of the state, however welcome they were as a criticism of electoralism and reformism, fell short in terms of providing answers.

---

247   Buci-Glucksmann 1980.

CHAPTER 19

The Politics of the Encounter: Machiavelli and Beyond

Althusser's preoccupation with the notion of the encounter was in fact a way to rethink the possibility of a politics of emancipation and social transformation and a potential re-enactment of revolutionary politics.[1] It was also an attempt to rethink the possibility of a theory of the political event under the primacy of class struggle.[2] One of the main forms through which Althusser attempted to deal with this question was by means of a constant confrontation with the work of Machiavelli. Althusser's encounter with Machiavelli was one of the most defining moments in his theoretical and political trajectory. A constant reference point, it provided Althusser, especially in the 1970s the terrain upon which Althusser attempted to rethink a novel conception of a politics of the encounter, of a politics *under* the conjuncture, with the figure of the *new Prince* haunting the imagery of a potential new practice of politics. That is why it is important to retrace this encounter.

1   The First Confrontation

Machiavelli had been a reference point for Althusser since the 1960s.[3] We have his 1962 course notes on Machiavelli.[4] He announces his intention to make

---

[1] The importance that Althusser attributed to the notion of the encounter can be seen in the following phrase that he added to the manuscript of his 1977 lecture on 'Machiavelli's Solitude': 'a "philosophy of the encounter", the only materialist philosophy of all the history of philosophy' (Althusser 1998, p. 324).
[2] Bourdin 2008, p. 201.
[3] Here is how Althusser himself described his discovery of Machiavelli: 'I discovered Machiavelli for the first time in August [1961] in Bertinoro, in an extraordinary old and large house on a hill dominating the whole plain of Emelia. Franca lived there, and I had known her for hardly a week. A woman of dazzling Sicilian beauty, black-haired (in Sicily it is called "mora") who had been introduced to me by her sister-in-law Giovanna, the companion of Cremonini, the great painter, who was one of my old friends. [...] I was dazzled by her, by her love, by the country, the marvel of its hills and towns. I became an Italian, easily as always, and we often went down to Casena, a large plain at the foot of the hills. One day after she taught me that Casena was the little town from which Césare Borgia had left for his great adventure.

a course on Machiavelli in a January 1962 letter to France Madonia,[5] and in another letter he refers to his anxiety about the course on Machiavelli he was about to deliver the following day,[6] a course he later refers to as 'mediocre'.[7] Nevertheless, he was excited about this experience, even though he called it a 'forced' work,[8] because there was something that 'spoke' to him in Machiavelli's text along with the richness that he found in Gramsci's text.[9]

Althusser begins by presenting the classical interpretations of Machiavelli (Croce's interpretation, the tradition of treating Machiavelli as Machiavellian, the 'democratic' interpretation, the interpretations offered by Gramsci and Hegel). For Althusser the paradox of Machiavelli is that although his thought does not find its place in the recognised space of political theory, at the same time he has theoretical value. That is why he insists on the 'theoretical solitude'[10] of Machiavelli. After a reading of the *Prince* Althusser moves to his conclusions (which are the closest to a complete text). He confronts the problem of the theoretical status of the *Prince*, insisting that Machiavelli's theory is 'disarmed' in the same manner that his 'realist project' is disarmed.[11] The problem Althusser faces is how to deal with the question of whether Machiavelli is based upon anthropology, a theory of human nature. Althusser insists that all the examples Machiavelli gives 'are always political examples, taken from concrete political situations' and one can talk about 'reversals of this anthropology'.[12] In a similar manner, he rejects all references to Machiavelli's cyclical conception of history as evidence of anthropology. In contrast, he insists on Machiavelli's solitude.[13] Althusser insists on Machiavelli's singularity in his thinking of the problem of the constitution of a national state, an absolute novelty, 'a radical

---

I began to read a little Gramsci (on the intellectuals) but quickly interrupted my reading in order to engage myself in reading Machiavelli' (Althusser 1997a, p. 14; I have corrected the date to 1961 from the 1964 of the original following the edition of this text in the second edition of Althusser's autobiography [Althusser 1994a, p. 481]).

4   In Althusser 2006a. For a detailed account of Althusser's relation to Machiavelli, see in particular Lahtinen 2009.
5   Althusser 1997b, p. 151.
6   Althusser 1997b, p. 155.
7   Althusser 1997b, p. 156.
8   Althusser 1997b, p. 161.
9   Ibid.
10 Althusser 2006b, p. 200.
11 Althusser 2006b, p. 235.
12 Althusser 2006b, p. 239.
13 Althusser 2006b, p. 244. He also makes a reference to Machiavelli's theoretical solitude in a letter to Franca Madonia (Althusser 1997b, p. 169).

beginning, a new form of organization and of political existence'.[14] Althusser in a certain way was recognising himself in Machiavelli, even in his first confrontation. During the preparation of the courses he repeatedly makes to Franca Madonia the same observation that he is talking not about Machiavelli but about himself.

> I attempted a description of Machiavelli's conscience, of his will of realism which contradicted his 'de-realising' situation [...] and then, rethinking this formulation I was extraordinarily and ironically hit by the fact that under the guise of the supposed conscience of Machiavelli it was about me that I was talking: will of realism (will to be someone real to have something to do with real life) and 'de-realising' situation (exactly my present delirium ...).[15]

He expands this point in a September 1962 letter where he insists that the delirium of the course is in reality his own delirium. He thinks of his course on Machiavelli as being 'double strange, triple strange', that it was being done

> outside of me, in an absolutely phantasmagoric and *delirious* manner, without [...] being able to *control* or *verify* what I was saying [...] finally, I could find but *a single means* to convince me that it was indeed *me* that was making the course: and this means was to *note* [*constanter*] that the delirium of this course was nothing else but *my own proper delirium*.[16]

The main point of this 'delirium' was in reality the problem of this radical beginning, 'the central problem of an *absolutely indispensable and necessary beginning from nothing* of a new State'.[17] Althusser insists that he had to immerse himself in the *void* in order 'to finally reach the solution of this beginning from nothing which had become the form of my problem'.[18] It is obvious that Althusser feels a certain affinity with Machiavelli in the sense of dealing with the need to think in terms of radical novelty, both in politics and in theory.

---

14   Althusser 2006b, p. 247. For Negri even in the 1962 course Althusser was considering that 'Machiavelli is not a thinker *of* politics but a thinker *in* politics' (Negri 1997, p. 142).
15   Althusser 1997b, p. 163.
16   Althusser 1997b, p. 224.
17   Ibid.
18   Althusser 1997b, p. 225.

2   The Founder of a Theory without Precedent

If in the 1960s the challenge is the beginning of a new theoretical philosophical and – in the last instance – political research project, the first tentative steps of 'Althusserianism', and Althusser's realisation of the radical novelty of what he was trying to accomplish in the void of the Marxist discussion of the early 1960s, in the 1970s the challenge is more openly political; it is the challenge of a left critique of the right-wing and reformist turn of the Communist movement, the open crisis of Marxism as theory and the new possibilities emerging from mass popular radicalisation. Therefore the challenge is now the radical beginning of new politics.

Althusser praises Claude Lefort's *Le Travail de l'oeuvre*[19] which indeed is not only one of the most important readings of Machiavelli but also one of the best commentaries upon the evolution of the various readings of the Florentine thinker and also of the various theories of 'Machiavellism'. He also refers to the surprise Machiavelli causes, citing De Sanctis's phrase that Machiavelli 'takes us by surprise, and leaves us pensive'.[20]

Althusser insists on a philosophical reading of Machiavelli along the same line as his attempt to 'read *Capital* as philosophers'[21] that is declared at the beginning of *Reading Capital*. For Althusser, 'Machiavelli confronts philosophy with a singular and singularly difficult question: that of his comprehension'.[22] And this difficulty is exactly the problem of the radical beginning that was also the problem in the conclusions of the 1962 course. The importance and also the difficulty of Machiavelli consist in his being a theorist of beginnings.

> Machiavelli is the theorist of something new solely because he is the theorist of beginnings [...] – of *the* beginning. Novelty can only repose on the surface of things; it can only affect an aspect of things, and fades with the moment that induced it. In contrast, the beginning is, so to speak, rooted in the essence of a thing, since it is the beginning of *this* thing. [...] The novelty of the beginning thus grips us for two reasons: because of the contrast between the after and the before, the new and the old; and because of their opposition and their impact, their rupture.[23]

---

19   Lefort 1986.
20   Althusser 1999a, p. 3.
21   Althusser et al. 2016, p. 12.
22   Althusser 1999a, p. 6.
23   Althusser 1999a, pp. 6–7.

Therefore, for Althusser, 'Machiavelli considered himself the founder of a theory without any precedent',[24] he represents a radical beginning towards the rupture that brings something new, 'a path still untrodden'.[25] For Althusser, Machiavelli's reference to the actual truth (*la veritá effetuale della causa*) refers to a politics of ruptures and new beginnings, because this actual truth is opposed to the '*imaginary representation*'[26] of things. Between this actual truth of things and their imaginary representation 'there is an abyss, the emptiness of a distance taken', and condemning this falsity can 'pave the way for truth'.[27] Althusser mixes his conception of the radical beginning expressed in Machiavelli's work with references that come from other aspects of his work, namely his description of the effectivity of philosophical interventions and displacements in *Lenin and Philosophy*,[28] and his endorsement of Spinoza's dictum that '*verum index sui et falsi*'.

Althusser then turns towards Hegel and his 'emotive eulogy of Machiavelli',[29] in his 1802 essay on the German Constitution,[30] which depicts him as the man of the state par excellence. He insists that Machiavelli 'speaks' to Hegel in the present 'of the German political situation', and his quest for the 'question of the constitution of a state, in this country suffering from its absence',[31] a divided and fragmented Germany reminiscent of the fragmented Italy whose unification Machiavelli envisaged.

Althusser then turns to Gramsci. 'If Machiavelli speaks to Gramsci, it is not in the past tense, but in the present: better still, in the future'.[32] For Althusser, Gramsci finds in Machiavelli a profound thinking of the question of Italian national unity and in particular of the role of class struggle on the constitution of it: 'Class struggle is at the heart of the constitution of nations: the nation represents the form of existence indispensable to the implantation of the cap-

---

24 Althusser 1999a, p. 8.
25 Althusser 1999a, p. 7, quoting Machiavelli from the *Discourses*.
26 Althusser 1999a, p. 7.
27 Althusser 1999a, p. 8.
28 'For the intervention of each philosophy, which displaces or modifies existing philosophical categories and thus produces those changes in philosophical discourse in which the history of philosophy proffers its existence, is precisely the philosophical nothing whose insistence we have established, since a dividing-line actually is nothing, it is not even a line or a drawing, but the simple fact of being divided, i.e. *the emptiness of a distance taken*' (Althusser 1971, p. 62).
29 Althusser 1999a, p. 9.
30 In Hegel 1999.
31 Althusser 1999a, p. 9.
32 Althusser 1999a, p. 10.

italist mode of production, in its struggle against the forms of the feudal mode of production [...] [the nation] is the stake of class struggle'.[33] For Althusser, Gramsci in his attempt to think, following Machiavelli, the very history of the Italian Unification realises the 'dual aspect of the power of the absolutist state [...] [I]t involves violence and coercion, but at the same time consent, and hence "hegemony"'.[34] But Gramsci sees something else in his confrontation with Machiavelli, 'what grips Gramsci in Machiavelli is the future inherent in the past and the present'.[35] Faced with fascism and at the same time the historical rupture and possibility opened up by the Bolshevik Revolution, Gramsci sees in the figure of the Modern Prince the possibility not of national unity but of proletarian revolution.

> Gramsci's Modern Prince is likewise a specific political form, a specific means enabling modern history to execute its major 'task': revolution and the transition to a classless society. Gramsci's Modern Prince is the Marxist-Leninist proletarian party. It is no longer a single individual and history is no longer at the mercy of this individual's *virtù* [...] To take up Lenin's expression, what is 'on the agenda' is no longer national unity, but proletarian revolution and the institution of socialism. The means to this end is no longer a superior individual, but the popular masses equipped with a party that rallies the avant-garde of the working and exploited classes. Gramsci calls this avant-garde the Modern Prince. This is how, in the dark night of fascism, Machiavelli 'speaks' to Gramsci: in the future tense.[36]

Althusser stresses the importance of this characterisation of the *Prince* as a revolutionary utopian manifesto, in the sense that this describes 'a quite specific dispositive [*dispositif*] that establishes particular relations between the discourse and its "object", between the discourse and its "subject"'.[37] The *singularity* of Machiavelli is that although he declared that he wanted to discuss the objective and universal laws of politics, in the end he presents texts that possess 'a mode of existence quite different from the statement of "laws of history"'.[38] Machiavelli is presented as a thinker of *singularities* and con-

---

33   Ibid.
34   Althusser 1999a, p. 12.
35   Althusser 1999a, p. 13.
36   Althusser 1999a, p. 13.
37   Althusser 1999a, p. 14.
38   Althusser 1999a, p. 15.

crete cases, a thinker of *encounters* and specific *conjunctures*, of the contingent particularity of a given conjuncture:

> [T]he main thing about Machiavelli [...] is not universal history, or even politics in general. Rather, it is a definite concrete object, and a very peculiar 'object' (but is it still an object?) – the *formulation* of a political problem: the political problem of the concrete practice of the formation of national unity by a national state.[39]

In Althusser's reading – and through Gramsci's reading, in a strange reversal from other instances of criticism of Gramsci by Althusser – Machiavelli becomes a thinker of *singular* political questions instead of totalising discourses. The key lies exactly in the particular theoretical *dispositive* deployed and a radically new relationship between theory and political practice, where political practice intervenes and transforms a theoretical dispositive.

> We must therefore bring to light a new determination, hitherto passed over in silence – political practice – and say that the theoretical elements are focused on Machiavelli's concrete political problem *only because this political problem is itself focused on political practice*. As a result, political practice makes its sudden appearance in the theoretical universe where initially the science of politics in general, and then a particular theoretical problem were at issue. Obviously, it is a question of a sudden appearance *in a text*. To be more precise, a theoretical text is affected in its modality and dispositive by political practice.[40]

3   Thinking under the Conjuncture

Machiavelli did not think about national unity in general, but in terms of a *singular conjuncture*, that of Italy of his time.[41] Therefore, for Althusser, Machiavelli is someone who thinks '*in* the conjuncture: that is to say, in its concept of an aleatory, singular case'.[42] To think *in* the conjuncture means to think within the conjuncture and its determinations, to think *under* the con-

---

39   Ibid.
40   Althusser 1999a, p. 17.
41   Ibid.
42   Althusser 1999a, p. 18. Here, as in other instances in the text, 'singular' and 'aleatory' are handwritten addenda.

juncture and its determinations, and to submit oneself to its tendencies and dynamics. It also means to think *objectivity* as *singularity*, as *singular case* and as urgent exigency dictated not by abstract theory but by the questions posed by *political practice*.

> To think *in terms of* the category of conjuncture is not to think *on* the conjuncture, as one would reflect on a set of concrete data. To think under the conjuncture is quite literally to submit to the problem induced and imposed by its case: the political problem of national unity and the constitution of Italy into a national state. [...] Machiavelli merely registers in his theoretical position a problem that is objectively, historically posed by the case of the conjuncture: not by simple intellectual comparisons, but by the confrontation of existing class forces and their relationship of uneven development – in fact by their aleatory future.[43]

This theoretical attempt to think the centrality of the category of the conjuncture for any potential *materialist* conception of history and politics is, of course, not something new for Althusser. This is the guiding thread from Althusser's book on Montesquieu onwards and the main point of 'Contradiction and Overdetermination'. As Mikko Lahtinen has stressed, Althusser's approach to Machiavelli as a thinker of the conjuncture *par excellence* has many analogies to his approach towards Lenin as a thinker of political practice within a singular conjuncture.[44] Balibar insists that what we have in this thinking under the conjuncture is exactly 'a notion of the under-determination or of the contingence of events which is correlative to the over-determination or the complexity of practices'.[45]

It is a new dialectic of the singular and the universal. This is a universalism of singularities and singular conjunctures, a new way to think both of singularity, which never becomes a chaotic plurality of 'cases', and of generality, which

---

[43] Althusser 1999a, p. 18.
[44] Cf. Lahtinen 2009, pp. 83–7. For Lahtinen this conception of the 'man of action' facing the aleatory dynamics of the conjuncture also implies a certain form of subjectivity: 'If a man of action takes into account the subjectivity of the aleatory, it means that he strives be means of his situational analysis to map out as far as possible the *factual* conditions and circumstances of the case and his actions. In this endeavour, it is also useful for him to have knowledge of these constants that are repeated in some form or other from one case to the next. In other words he attempts to lessen the degree of his subjective ignorance or the degree of *subjective* randomness' (Lahtinen 2009, p. 164).
[45] Balibar 2009, p. 14.

never takes the form of an all-encompassing self-repeating 'structure', while at the same time insisting on the possibility of objectivity and of actually theorising the conjuncture.[46]

> We are no longer dealing with the mythical pure objectivity of the *laws* of history or politics. Not that they have disappeared from Machiavelli's discourse. Quite the reverse: he does not cease to invoke them and track them in their infinite variations, so as to make them declare themselves; and this hunt has some surprises in store. But the theoretical truths thus produced are produced only under the stimulus of the conjuncture; and no sooner are they produced that they are affected in their modality by their intervention in a conjuncture wholly dominated by the political problem it poses, and the political practice required to achieve the objective it proposes.[47]

And this is how such a thinking of the conjuncture enables political practice: 'the present space of an analysis of the political conjuncture [...] makes sense only if it arranges or contains a certain place, a certain *empty space*: empty in order to be filled, empty so as to have inserted it in the action of the individual or group who will come and take a stand here, so as or to rally to constitute the forces accomplishing the political task assigned by history empty for the future'.[48] Here we have again Althusser's preoccupation with that empty space, that *void* that enables political intervention as practice. Althusser acknowledges that in reality this space 'is always occupied',[49] and insists that there are no fixed points in the space of politics. The emptiness of the political space is never given in advance; in fact, we can say that this emptiness is constituted by the very attempt to cover this space with a new political configuration and dispositive. This notion of the empty space does not refer only to the 'subject' of political practice (the Prince or the party) but also to another empty space: that

---

46 Althusser's 1977 lecture on 'The Solitude of Machiavelli' encapsulates in the following manner the originality of Machiavelli's approach as an important aspect of his 'solitude': 'This is perhaps the ultimate point in Machiavelli's solitude: the fact that he occupied a unique and precarious place in the history of political thought between a long moralizing, religious and idealist tradition of political thought, which he radically rejected, and the new tradition of the political of natural law, which was to submerge everything and in which the rising bourgeoisie found its self-image' (Althusser 1999a, p. 124). Cf. the comments in Lahtinen 2009, pp. 146–7 and in Terray 1996.
47 Althusser 1999a, pp. 19–20.
48 Althusser 1999a, p. 20.
49 Ibid.

of the place of political *text* that stages this political practice. It is obvious that here we have also a new thinking not only of the determination of political theory by the exigencies of political practice, but also of what it means to produce theory and *texts* 'under the conjuncture', texts that can actually be *politically effective*:

> As we can see, the question concerns a dual place or space, or a double encirclement. For Machiavelli's text to be politically effective – that is to say for it to be, in its own fashion, the agent of the political practice it deploys – *it must be inscribed somewhere in the space of this political practice.*[50]

Consequently for Althusser the question is not only one of the dynamics of a singular political conjuncture. Nor is it simply about the politics of theory and theoretical practices in general. It is about the very dialectic or articulation of theory and politics, of theory as political intervention that opens a political space for the political practice it invokes. Therefore the question is: 'how does the written text, which mobilizes and deploys this political problematic and this new dispositive, *deploy itself in the space of the problematic of the political practice* laid out by it?'[51] This gives a new meaning to the actuality of the truth.

> Machiavelli knows that there is no truth – or rather, nothing true – other than what is *actual*, that is to say borne by its effects, nonexistent outside them; and that the effectivity of the true is always merged with the activity of men; and that, politically speaking, it exists only in the confrontation between forces, the struggle between parties.[52]

It is in this sense that Althusser treats the character of Machiavelli's text as a *manifesto*: 'it is a text that belongs to the world of ideological and political literature, which takes sides and a stand in that world [...] [with] a new format [...]

---

[50] Althusser 1999a, p. 22.
[51] Ibid. On this see also Lahtinen's comment: 'The text itself is the tool of Machiavelli's own political action or intervention, with which he positions himself in his own conjuncture. Furthermore it is on the basis of his own text that he sets forth the political problem of his conjuncture to be solved by a possible political actor within that conjuncture, that is, a new prince. Using terminology from literary theory, one could say that *The Prince* is one of those works that lie on the border between text and context, particularly in this case where the difference between them is negligible' (Lahtinen 2009, pp. 112–13).
[52] Althusser 1999a, p. 22.

and a new style: lucid, compact, vigorous and impassioned'.[53] Consequently the text becomes a means in the struggle waged, is itself part of the political and ideological battle, Machiavelli makes the text 'serve as a means in the struggle he announces and engages [...] it is a *political act*'.[54]

To accomplish this kind of writing that is itself a *political act* does not mean only that it is a 'passionate' text; what matters is the *viewpoint* from which the text is written. For Althusser it would seem normal to adopt '*the viewpoint of the one who is to revolutionize the historical conjuncture: the Prince*'.[55] Surprisingly, Machiavelli insists there that one has to be 'of the people' in order to understand the characters of rulers and the functioning of leadership. For Althusser this delineates exactly the '*space* of political practice', 'the place [...] that [the text] must occupy in this space for it to be politically active therein, for it to constitute a political act – an element in the political transformation of this space'.[56]

In these opening sections of *Machiavelli and Us* Althusser is more preoccupied with the political efficacy of the text than of the New Prince himself. This preoccupation with the conditions that turn a political text into a political act is also his way to think of the effectivity of his own theoretical interventions, given that the 1970s are the period *par excellence* of Althusser's interventions as a public communist intellectual. Althusser finds in Machiavelli a conception of the politics of theory that actually links the theoretical and political exigencies, a form of a *political gnoseology*. True knowledge of the terrain of social and political antagonism can only come from the viewpoint of the subaltern classes.

> Now, what is quite remarkable is that the place fixed upon by Machiavelli for this text, the place of the *viewpoint, is not the Prince,* who is nevertheless determined as the 'subject' of the decisive political practice, *but the people* [...] This means not only that rulers are incapable of knowing themselves, but that *there can be no knowledge of rulers except from the viewpoint of the people.*[57]

This is a point that has to be linked to one of the major preoccupations of Althusser in the 1970s, namely his insistence that in class antagonism a cer-

---

53 Althusser 1999a, p. 23.
54 Ibid.
55 Althusser 1999, p. 24.
56 Ibid.
57 Ibid.

tain degree of class partiality is indispensable in order to reach some form of objective knowledge of the terrain of class struggle. This how he formulated this in 1976:

> It will be admitted that Marxist theory is necessarily enlisted in the class struggle, and that the conflict that pits it against bourgeois ideology is irremediable, but it will be more difficult to admit that the *conflictuality* of Marxist theory is *constitutive* of its *scientificity*, its *objectivity*. One will retreat to positivist and economist positions, and the conflictual conditions of the existence of the science as *contingent* will be distinguished from its scientific results. This amounts to not seeing that Marxist science and the Marxist investigator are obliged to *take a position* in the conflict whose object is Marxist theory, are obliged to occupy (proletarian) class theoretical positions.[58]

For Althusser this is an affirmation of class partisanship that is necessary for Machiavelli's theoretical and political enterprise: 'to speak of the Prince as he does, one needs to be a man of the people. This is what Gramsci says: in his manifesto, Machiavelli "becomes the people"'.[59] That is why for Althusser Machiavelli is not just a thinker of the state, but of the *'national state', 'of national unity by means of the popular state'*.[60] The *Prince* is not written in the form of offering counsel to an individual; it is a manifesto that is being addressed to the people, to the masses. However, there is a difference with another famous manifesto, namely Marx and Engels's *Communist Manifesto*. Marx and Engels call for a class party, and consequently a '[c]lass viewpoint and class party pertain to one and the same class: the proletariat'.[61] In contrast, in Machiavelli 'there is an irreducible duality between the *place* of the political *viewpoint* and the *place* of the political force and practice; between the "subject" of the political viewpoint – the people – and the "subject" of the political practice: the Prince'.[62] For Althusser this is exactly what turns the *Prince* into a *utopian* text, since the Prince is a 'pure aleatory possibility'.[63]

For Althusser this insistence on *the Prince* as the 'subject' of political practice and transformation in a certain way also marks the theoretical and political

---

58 Althusser 1999b, p. 110.
59 Althusser 1999a, p. 25.
60 Ibid.
61 Althusser 1999a, p. 26.
62 Ibid.
63 Ibid.

limit of Machiavelli. Machiavelli cannot offer an answer as to how to 'transform this consciousness into *a political force capable of producing this event, or participating in its production*'.[64] One is tempted to observe that although Althusser opposes the declaration of workers' self-emancipation to Machiavelli's duality of viewpoint and 'subject', this reference to the inability to *produce the – revolutionary* – event sounds also like a criticism addressed to the communist parties of the 1970s and their deep crisis of strategy. How to build a political force capable of producing this event was indeed Althusser's own political preoccupation at that time. Such an approach also enables us to locate *Machiavelli and Us* within the broader context of Althusser's confrontation with the strategic and political crisis of the communist movement and his attempt towards offering a way out of this impasse. The questions Machiavelli posed – namely, how to make possible a *political act* that actually accomplishes a change in the social and political configuration – are in fact also Althusser's own.

One is also tempted to read here Althusser's own difficulty with articulating his political preoccupations with his theoretical work, with his own attempt not simply at a theoretical/political correction but towards a new form of political effectivity of theory, or, in more traditional terms, a new dialectic of theory and practice, a 'double reflection' of politics into theory and of theory into politics. Confronted with Machiavelli's 'utopian manifesto' Althusser is trying to think if and how a manifesto for a different course of the communist movement might be possible, with what content, and under what conditions of production.

> If all these remarks are not unwarranted, we can appreciate why Machiavelli is simultaneously gripping and elusive. It is precisely because he is gripping that he cannot be grasped by traditional philosophical thought. He is gripping because – as much as any writing can – his text practically, politically implicates and involves us. He hails us from a place that he summons us to occupy as potential 'subjects' (agents) of a potential political practice. This effect of captivation and interpellation is produced by the shattering of the traditional theoretical text, by the sudden appearance of the political problem as a problem and of the political practice in it as a practice; and by the double reflection of political practice in his text and of his text in political practice. Gramsci was the first to appreciate this. It is no accident that Gramsci, having grasped the elusiveness

---

64   Althusser 1999a, p. 28.

of Machiavelli, could understand him, and that he discusses him [...] In fact, Gramsci, too, is elusive for the same reasons that render Machiavelli elusive to us.[65]

4   A Philosophical Reading of Machiavelli

Althusser's reading of Machiavelli is a philosophical reading, with an emphasis on the *theoretical dispositive* deployed in Machiavelli's text. Althusser is aware that his initial presentation of Machiavelli as a thinker *par excellence* of singular conjunctures seemingly contradicts the Florentine thinker's references to *general laws of history*, especially in the *Discourses on the First Ten Books of Titus Livy*. For Althusser this has to be combined with the fact that Machiavelli introduces in fact an *experimental* method, an 'experimental comparison' between ancient and modern events.[66] How can these different positions be reconciled? One is again tempted to think of this question as a metonymy for a similar problem regarding the question of general historical determinations in historical materialism as opposed the concrete analysis of concrete conjunctures. Althusser deploys the distinction between scientific propositions and philosophical theses he had already developed since *Spontaneous Philosophy and the Philosophy of the Scientists*.[67] Machiavelli's insistence that the course of human things is basically immutable is presented as a philosophical thesis about the general objectivity of scientific propositions that permits the deployment of the experimental method of comparing different events. It is

> on the one hand, a thesis about the objectivity and universality of the forthcoming scientific propositions; on the other hand, a thesis founding the possibility of the experimental comparisons between 'cases'.[68]

Without this reference to something constant it would be impossible for Machiavelli to actually compare different conjunctures and events. The second thesis of Machiavelli moves to the opposite direction and stresses the continual and unstable motion of things and their unpredictable nature. This is exemplified in the importance attached to *Fortune*, whose 'law is change, and this law

---

65   Althusser 1999a, p. 32.
66   Althusser 1999a, p. 33.
67   Althusser 1990.
68   Althusser 1999a, p. 34.

sums up the law of historical time, hence of history: times change, conjunctures change, men change'.[69] This is presented as 'the equivalent of a "dialectical" or, rather, "*aleatory*" thesis'.[70]

For Althusser, Machiavelli's synthesis of these two theses, immutable reality and continual change, is his *cyclical* theory of history, which represents the third thesis. Althusser underscores the point made by Machiavelli that at the 'origin of all governments (and, before them, every society) we find *chance*'.[71] This emphasis on dispersion and chance as origin is a rejection of 'any anthropological ontology of society and politics', and consequently of any theory of man as 'by nature' a political animal and also of 'any *contractual* theory of the origin of society and government',[72] making Machiavelli a political theorist without a theory of the social contract.

As is well known, Machiavelli seemingly opts for the classical cyclical conception of forms of government and their corruption (monarchy degenerating into tyranny, to be replaced by aristocracy which degenerates into oligarchy, to be replaced by democracy, degenerating into anarchy). However, for Althusser, Machiavelli is not simply repeating this classical schema, there is a different 'modality' at work here.[73] This is evident in Machiavelli's assertion, in contrast to the writers of antiquity that all forms of government are defective, the 'bad' ones because they are bad, and the 'good' ones because they have a brief duration. Consequently, duration becomes an important factor and this can explain Machiavelli's preference for Lycurgus of Sparta over Solon of Athens, because the Spartan laws and form of government lasted longer. For Althusser, Machiavelli abandons the terrain of typology of forms of government and moves in the direction of another terrain and problem. Moreover, 'Machiavelli is interested not in governments as governments pure and simple – hence in simple *forms* giving rise to typological treatment – but in governments as governments of *states*'.[74] This emphasis on *duration* undermines the thesis of cyclical continual change: '*Machiavelli's position on the duration of the state contradicts the thesis of the endless cycle of revolutions in forms of government*'.[75] Althusser stresses the importance of *duration*, which is also one of his own major preoccupations: how to have lasting encounters and social forms.

---

69   Althusser 1999a, p. 35.
70   Ibid.
71   Althusser 1999a, p. 36.
72   Ibid.
73   Althusser 1999a, p. 38.
74   Althusser 1999a, p. 39.
75   Althusser 1999a, p. 40.

Consequently, we can see Machiavelli's theses under a new light: 'the formulation of the first thesis functions in Machiavelli's discourse as a materialist thesis of objectivity; and it is solely on against its background that the formulation of the second thesis can function as an aleatory *dialectical determination* of this objectivity'.[76] Moreover, Machiavelli's third position on the endless cycle of revolutions is not just a synthesis but a *displacement* by means of the emphasis on the '*state that lasts*'.[77] And this for Althusser is Machiavelli's position, in which 'there is a significant space, a vacuum, a leap into the theoretical void, an anticipation', and Machiavelli 'must leap into the void'.[78] The state that lasts is not just a theoretical concept; it is also an absent reality and a crucial political objective, albeit in 'unchartered space'.[79] The question of the duration of a state is not just a theoretical problem, the answer of which can be deduced from theoretical premises; it is an open political problem. Consequently, the theoretical void within Machiavelli's discourse is not simply theoretical, it is the void created by the intrusion of a political problem that involves a necessarily novel social and political form. This is what happens when 'what is involved is not the natural order of things (an existing permanency) but an order to be instituted, a duration to be fashioned, a permanency to *be established* – in short a political undertaking and innovation'.[80] That is why he refers to this kind of duration not as the negation of the negation (negation of the endless cycle of revolutions as negation of the immutable nature of human things) but as the 'negation of the negation of the negation'.[81] Machiavelli does not apply his general theses, he '*determines* them in negating them by one another [...] in order to make them produce [...] concepts that it is strictly impossible to *deduce* from these theses'.[82] Althusser thinks of the relation between general theses and concrete objects in its contradictory and inconsistent way, but insists that 'if they are considered in their *arrangement*, their dispositive and their interplay, their inconsistency becomes productive of a new theoretical space and precise conceptual effects'.[83]

Again there are analogies with the question that communism poses within the theoretical dispositif of historical materialism, as both a material tendency

---

76   Althusser 1999a, p. 41.
77   Ibid.
78   Althusser 1999a, p. 42.
79   Ibid.
80   Althusser 1999a, p. 43.
81   Althusser 1999a, pp. 42–3.
82   Althusser 1999a, p. 44.
83   Ibid.

already inscribed and an unchartered territory, leading to necessary inconsistencies between general concepts and concrete conjunctures. It is here that *virtù* enters the stage. If *'there is no longer a cycle, but displacement and distribution'*, then '[i]t is no longer a question of the various *forms* of government, but of *virtù* and its opposite'.[84] *Virtù* as an ability to achieve duration of state forms offers Machiavelli the necessary legitimisation to seek in the past, and especially Rome, 'the exemplary historical *rehearsal* of those laws of political practice to be observed to ensure the triumph of Italian unity'.[85] Consequently, we are not dealing with the traditional ideological celebration of antiquity, but with a return to 'the antiquity of *politics* [...] the concrete history and practice of politics'.[86] It is exactly this antiquity that nobody speaks about and in reality represents the terrain to draw examples for his experimental conception of politics. Rome is not the mythical Rome, but *'the example par excellence of the duration of a state'*.[87]

For Althusser, all these offer a novel relation to theory and antiquity, but they do not avoid a certain *utopian* dimension: 'Machiavelli, who seeks the future solution to Italy's political problem in Rome, does not escape the illusion of utopia'.[88] The utopian illusion lies exactly in this attempt to seek the future in the examples of the past. To this Althusser counterposes Marx's opposition in the *Eighteenth Brumaire* between proletarian revolutions creating 'their poetry from the future' to the bourgeois revolutions' tendency to present themselves under the guise of historical examples. For Althusser these historical references are a 'necessary illusion',[89] because

> without these mythical examples of the Roman accomplishment of liberty, equality and fraternity, without the ideology of Roman political virtue, the leaders and protagonists of the bourgeois revolution would not have been able to mobilize the masses, *would not have been able to mobilize themselves*, to carry out the revolution and bring it to completion [...] they needed the *excess* of the past relative to the present, in order to disguise the *narrowness* of the *actual content* of the bourgeois revolution [...] when bourgeois revolution could *only* liberate men from feudal relations

---

84 Althusser 1999a, p. 44.
85 Althusser 1999a, p. 45.
86 Ibid.
87 Althusser 1999a, p. 46.
88 Althusser 1999a, p. 49.
89 Althusser 1999a, p. 50.

of exploitation, and then solely so as to subject to bourgeois-capitalist relations of exploitation.[90]

Machiavelli does not invoke an imaginary Rome, he sees in Rome 'the *guarantee* of the political existence of a state that endures',[91] the proof 'that his theory of the aleatory invariant is *true*', and as the '*rehearsal* for a *necessary* task, whose concrete conditions of possibility are, however, *impossible* to define'.[92] Althusser redefines the very notion of utopia. We are not dealing, according to his reading of Machiavelli, with the utopian projection of the idealised version of a political project to the past. Rather, in Machiavelli's '*theoretical* utopia' we are treating the past as an experimental terrain for the possibility of achieving a historical task that because of its very novelty and originality is in fact unthinkable. This leads to a discrepancy between a '*necessary* political task' and the '*impossible* and *inconceivable*, because aleatory conditions of its possibility'.[93] The analogy is obvious: the attempt to 'think the unthinkable'[94] is not only a description for the task of national unity of the fragmented Italy of that era, it is also a way to think the possibility of socialist revolution and social transformation and a new turn in the international communist movement. Althusser, again, is thinking through Machiavelli the challenges he is facing.

5   The Encounter and the New Prince

When Althusser moves on to Machiavelli's theory of the New Prince, he stresses that the problem he faced was 'the constitution of Italian national unity',[95] which he treats as Machiavelli's actual stance and not just an interpretation coming to us by De Sanctis through Gramsci. He reminds us that Machiavelli exhorted Lorenzo de' Medici to liberate Italy from the 'barbarian yoke' and to 'make a nation *of the Italians*, to make a nation of Italy under a *new Prince*'.[96] The form will be a '*New Principality*' and the '*matter*' the particular Italian conjuncture and Machiavelli stresses three aspects:[97] 1. the 'extreme misery of Italy' and

---

90 Althusser 1999a, p. 50.
91 Ibid.
92 Althusser 1999a, p. 51.
93 Althusser 1999a, p. 52.
94 Ibid.
95 Althuser 1999a, p. 53.
96 Ibid.
97 Althusser 1999a, p. 54.

its political 'emptiness'; 2. this 'political vacuum' is in fact 'an immense aspiration to political *being*' which means that the people is *already ready* within the void of the conjuncture to accept and embrace the new Prince; 3. there is political matter that waits to take form, a political 'raw material: the *virtù* of *individual* Italians'.[98] It is exactly the combination of these elements that sets everything ready for the 'intervention of the *liberator* Prince'.[99]

This conception of *intervention* must be read alongside Althusser's preoccupation with the question of the encounter and the question of how an encounter can actually take hold and *last*. Political intervention is neither some messianic creation of a new political configuration *ex nihilo*, nor simply the bearer of a historical teleology. It is that political act or intervention that enables an encounter between elements already existing. And this encounter is by definition aleatory; it can also not happen or even if it happens it may not last.

It is exactly within this emphasis on the encounter and on the radical anti-teleology and anti-finalism of the position that an encounter might not take place that the possibility of politics emerges. It is the political intervention that helps an encounter take place, the absent aspect that enables the encounter of the elements that give rise to a new social and political configuration. This gives a new meaning to revolutionary politics. The politics of transformation and emancipation can never simply be about 'accelerating' existing historical dynamics – or even worse simple waiting for them to reach their critical points. Revolutionary politics is never simply about 'expressing' an existing dynamic or an irreversible historical tendency: it is an active intervention that creates conditions, produces results, constitutes. The void of the conjuncture does not suggest emptiness, since in reality the elements of the conjuncture already occupy their proper space, but the absence of the encounter, the absence of the aleatory yet constitutive intervention. The 'political raw materials' are there, what is absent is exactly this defining political intervention, or, to be more accurate, there is an inability to have the encounter with that political intervention, with the bearer of possibility of a new form that would turn all the elements of the encounter into a lasting encounter. And in 1982, in his text on the 'Underground Current of the Materialism of the Encounter', here is how Althusser theorises the philosophy of the encounter active in Machiavelli's work:

---

98   Althusser 1999a, pp. 54–5.
99   Althusser 1999a, p. 55.

The reader may object that this is merely *political philosophy*, overlooking the fact that a philosophy is simultaneously at work here too. A curious *philosophy which is a 'materialism of the encounter' thought by way of politics*, and which, as such, does not take anything for granted. It is in the political *void* that the encounter must come about, and that national unity must 'take hold.' But this *political void is first a philosophical void*. No Cause that precedes its effects is to be found in it, no Principle of morality or theology [...] As in the Epicurean world, all the elements are both here and beyond [...] but they do not exist, are only abstract as long as the unity of a world has not united them in the Encounter that will endow them with existence [...] in this philosophy [...] the encounter may not take place [...] A successful encounter one that is not brief, but lasts, never guarantees that it will continue to last tomorrow.[100]

The reason Althusser is preoccupied with this question is more than obvious. Althusser from the mid-1960s onwards was fully aware of the important social and political dynamic emerging, of the radicalisation of popular movements, and of the crisis of imperialism. At the same time he was aware that Western Communist Parties, despite their organisational strength and important electoral appeal, lacked the political line that would enable the encounter with these dynamics, and the creation of a popular unity able to initiate processes of socialist transformation. The new Prince was also absent in the particular conjuncture of the advanced capitalist social formations in the 1970s, despite the 'political raw material' of the crisis of imperialism and the advance of radical mass social movements. The crucial intervention of a communist movement acting as new Prince forging a popular unity for socialism was absent, representing the absence of a determining political intervention.

This explains why Althusser insisted on the *difficulty* of the emergence of a new Prince and a new Principality (Althusser insists also on seeing the pair of these tasks): 'for Machiavelli there is no solution other than this *very difficulty*'.[101] Why this insistence on difficulty? Because we are talking about limit cases, about tasks that are almost impossible to accomplish, tasks that test the very limits of possibility. For Althusser, Machiavelli 'is condemned to thinking the possible at the boundary of the impossible'.[102] That is why Machiavelli refuses the fantasy of a pure beginning. That is why Althusser turns to Chapter 1

---

100   Althusser 2006a, pp. 173–4.
101   Althusser 1999a, p. 55.
102   Althusser 1999a, p. 56.

of Book 1 of the *Discourses*, where Machiavelli deals with the beginnings of cities. There, Machiavelli begins by suggesting that it would be better to start with a new city in a poor area, because people will be more virtuous there, only to reject this by insisting that poverty will make the city unable to expand. Consequently, Machiavelli refuses to think of the beginning of a new state in terms of the 'utopia of an ideal city, uncultivated and pure'.[103] Therefore, it is better to start in a richer site, despite the danger of corruption. Political *virtù* is not something to be searched at the beginning, rather it is necessary to 'impose *laws* on them, so as to induce something quite distinct from moral virtue: military and political *virtù*'.[104] And this also means that the new state, the new principality must include its own laws and its own beginning, by itself, without foreign intervention, it must be a national state. Or, in more general terms, in the politics of radical novelty and duration, it is exactly the political act that induces the necessary new forms not some pre-existing configuration. Moreover, there is a radical break with any anthropology here. The successful establishment of a new Principality cannot be based upon the supposed 'good nature' of people but upon the effectivity of the new forms and the *virtù* inscribed in them.

For Althusser this emphasis on laws has also to do with the explicit assumption that a city is a social and political terrain traversed by antagonistic social practice, because of the existence of antagonistic social groups. That is why good laws arise from situations when the people rebel against the noble, adopting even here 'the viewpoint of the people'.[105] 'Machiavelli's thesis is that in the conflict between nobility and people, the king takes the people's side by decreeing laws'.[106]

For Althusser there is an obvious 'partisanship' in Machiavelli's positions: the challenge is not about having a peaceful state but how to have a strong and expanding state, and this makes acceptable the price of '*class struggle* between people and nobility [...] in this struggle the Prince must rely on the people; the class struggle is indispensable to impart to the state not only *duration* but also the capacity to expand, that is to say, become a national state'.[107] Althusser stresses particularly Machiavelli's point that a Prince must be *alone* if he wishes to establish a new principality. This solitude becomes a necessity; only under its terms can a new principality be established.

---

103 Althusser 1999a, p. 57.
104 Althusser 1999a, p. 57.
105 Althusser 1999a, p. 59.
106 Ibid.
107 Althusser 1999a, p. 62.

> This thesis is fundamental in Machiavelli: that 'it is necessary to *be alone* to found a new republic or completely reform it'. The foundation of a state, the beginnings of a state, or the complete reformation that is also an absolute (re)commencement in the course of history – in short *every absolute beginning requires the absolute solitude of the reformer or founder*. The Prince's solitude is the precise correlate of the *vacuum* of the conjuncture.[108]

This is reminiscent of Althusser's initial insistence that we are always in the exception, the exceptional circumstances that demand original and profoundly novel forms of intervention, forms of intervention that induce a certain sense of loneliness. The reference to the necessary loneliness of the new Prince is a metonymy for the necessary *singularity* and *originality* of every conjuncture, a point that marked Althusser's entrance to the theoretical scene ever since 'Contradiction and Overdetermination'. However, singularity and originality are not enough. The crucial question is *duration* and *reproduction*; this is the challenge for every political project.

> We are at the point where he reaches a decisive conclusion, distinguishing *two moments* in the constitution of a state. (1) The first moment is that of the absolute *beginning*, which is necessarily the deed of one man alone, 'a single individual'. But this moment is itself unstable, for ultimately it can as readily tip over into tyranny as into an authentic state. Whence (2) the second moment, that of *duration*, which can be ensured only by a double process: the settlement of laws and emergence from solitude – that is to say, the end of absolute power of a single individual. Now we know that laws are linked to the existence of contending classes, and that they above all establish recognition of the people. Duration obtains, then, exclusively through laws, be which the Prince can 'take root' in his people.[109]

Althusser attempts to think through Machiavelli one of the major questions and challenges he was facing, a challenge both 'theoretical and methodological' and 'political': *how can we have lasting encounters*, social and political forms that initiate new – revolutionary – sequences, forms that *can last*, forms that can surpass and exceed their initial moments? The reference to loneliness at

---

108   Althusser 1999a, p. 64. On Althusser's constant confrontation with the possibility of an absolute beginning, see Fourtounis 2013. On the thematic of solitude in the work of Althusser, see Elliott 1993.
109   Althusser 1999a, pp. 64–5.

the beginning of such processes refers to the singularity and originality of such conjunctures, but also to the fact, observed in history, that usually the possibility of such a sequence is not immediately visible, since the common tendency is to see that things follow their 'usual path', leading also to the loneliness and singularity of the leaders that actually have this insight, Lenin on the eve of the Russian Revolution being the obvious example.

For Althusser the *Prince* deals with the first moment, the moment of absolute commencement, whereas in the *Discourses* the emphasis is on what causes a state to expand and endure. This can explain why during the Enlightenment intellectuals saw Machiavelli as a representative of republicanism even though he has Rome as an example. For Machiavelli 'Rome is the successful conversion of the absolutist form of the state's beginnings into the *durable* form of its legal – that is popular – functioning under kings, whether they bear the title of consul (as in Rome) or king (as in France), who ensure its *expansion*'.[110] For Althusser, both the *Discourses* and the *Prince* can only be understood on the basis of the political problem they try to answer. The key towards which Machiavelli points is how to create the space of a state that 'endures and constantly enhances its strength – that of the people – in order to be capable of expanding'.[111] This necessarily leads not only to the solitary founding moment but also to the importance of a rooting in the people, because the 'single individual', who founds a new state,

> if he wishes to found a state that endures and grows strong, the one who is alone in order to found it must emerge from the solitude of the founding moment, and '*become many*', precisely so as to root the state in the people by means of laws an derive from them a popular, that is – Machiavelli's ultimate objective – a national strength.[112]

As Emmanuel Terray has noted, Althusser saw that in order 'to create a new principality, it is necessary to effect a radical and complete rupture with the legacy and influence of the past'.[113] Althusser agrees with Gramsci that Machiavelli wants to get rid of feudal forms, wants to make '*a clean sweep of existing feudal forms as incompatible with the objective of Italian unity*'.[114] Machiavelli, according to Althusser, treats even the existing republics, for Althusser the '*urban*

---

110   Althusser 1999a, p. 66.
111   Althusser 1999a, p. 67.
112   Ibid.
113   Terray 1996, p. 284.
114   Ibid.

forms of feudalism', as 'incapable of the economic transformation and expansion, and political conversion, that would make them suitable for the task of unifying the national state'.[115] This gives a new dimension to the need to conquer them:

> For they are inscribed in the configuration of the Italian conjuncture, and if nothing can be expected of them as regards constitution of the national state, it is imperative to conquer them. If it is impossible to construct the national state on the basis of feudal forms, that state must subordinate those forms to itself, conquer and transform them. They are its raw material.[116]

And here is where the actual difficulties begin, the difficulty of trying to think a political form that goes beyond the existing configuration, beyond the existing social and political 'raw material'. Machiavelli attempts to answer this challenge by the image of the archer who in order to strike the target aims at a much a higher point. For Althusser,

> to aim at a much higher point has a further sense, not spelt out, but practised, by Machiavelli: to aim at a much higher point = to aim *beyond what exists*, so as to attain a goal *that does not exist* but must exist = to aim above all existing principalities, beyond their *limits*.[117]

All these attest to the difficulty of a new beginning. Because this beginning includes both 'becoming-the-Prince' and 'becoming-the-new-Principality', since the 'Prince does not pre-exist the New Principality' and the 'New Principality does not precede the Prince'.[118] That is why Machiavelli refers to this process as an *adventure*, which for Althusser is the adventure of the transition towards the national state. What are the necessary conditions for this 'adventure'?

The first condition is a favourable encounter between the objective conditions of the conjuncture, *fortuna*, and the 'subjective conditions of an equally

---

115   Althusser 1999a, p. 71.
116   Ibid.
117   Althusser 1999a, p. 73.
118   Ibid. Mikko Lahtinen has argued that this conception of the founding of a state stresses 'the *processual* and *aleatory* nature of founding and maintaining a state [...] Althusser's interpretation emphasizes that the state is not a static organization, but a complex *process*' (Lahtinen 2009, p. 209).

indeterminate individual Y – *virtù*.[119] This condition can take three forms: The '*limit-form*' is *correspondence* between *fortuna* and *virtù*. The negative form is *non-correspondence*, in which '*fortuna* does everything – as regards conjuncture and individual alike – but *the individual is not endowed with corresponding virtù*'.[120] There is also *deferred correspondence*, when thing begin with a good *fortuna*, without any intervention from the individual, who, if in a position to '*recapture this sheer fortuna by his virtue*',[121] can achieve duration. The second condition refers to the individual who at the beginning has to resort to the *power of others*, for example in the case of relying on foreign armies. If the individual lacks *virtù* he will not be able to found an enduring state. If he has *virtù*, then he can '*master his beginnings* and found a state that endures'.[122] The third condition is the 'conversion of *fortuna* into *virtù*'.[123] In this case *virtù* is the ability to 'to transform the instant of *fortuna* into political duration, the *matter* of *fortuna* into political form'.[124] Although this sounds like a general and rather abstract theory, Althusser insists that it refers to the concrete Italian conjuncture. This abstraction marks the distance between Machiavelli's project and the existing states and political protagonists in Italy. We might say that this anonymity is a metonymy for the radical novelty of the project and the necessary political act, of the rupture with all pre-existing political configurations and forms. Consequently, for Althusser,

> this anonymity is in no way an effect of theoretical abstraction but, on the contrary, a political condition and objective, inscribed in the theory. In other words, the *abstract form* of the theory is the index and effect of a *concrete* political stance.[125]

It is interesting to note here the analogies but also the differences between this conception of 'anonymity' in Althusser's and Badiou's references to the *unnameable* of the truth of a situation. The *unnameable* is the element that 'remains inaccessible to truthful nominations',[126] that exceeds the possibility of naming it within a truth-process, and that 'is the symbol of the pure real

---

119 Althusser 1999a, p. 74.
120 Ibid.
121 Ibid.
122 Althusser 1999, p. 75.
123 Ibid.
124 Ibid.
125 Althusser 1999a, p. 77.
126 Badiou 2001, p. 85.

of the situation'.¹²⁷ There is analogy in the sense of a common reference that goes beyond existing social and political forms and their discourses articulated about them. However, whereas for Badiou the *unnameable* is some sort of a limit, and any attempt to name the *unnameable* can lead to political Evil, as was the case with Nazism's attempt to force a name upon the community, for Althusser this condition of anonymity is *positive*, it implies the radical novelty of an actual possibility.

Althusser then turns to the main example Machiavelli had in mind: Cesare Borgia. For Machiavelli, Cesare Borgia was able to make a state, a new Principality out of a 'politically *shapeless* site and material',¹²⁸ he was able to combine *fortuna* and the use of another's forces with his own *virtù*, but could not deal with the situation when *fortuna* turned against him. For Althusser this specific reference to Cesare Borgia does not contradict the emphasis on anonymity because it is a case of starting from nowhere.

> Far from contradicting this anonymity, the example of Cesare, who sets out from the Romagna, is proof of its correctness. For who could have foreseen that it would be Cesare, and that he would set out from the Romagna? What the example of Cesare proves is that *the New Prince can start from anywhere, and be anyone: ultimately start from nothing and be nothing to start with*. Once again, nothingness – or, rather, the aleatory void.¹²⁹

This combination of specific conditions and elements of the conjuncture with a totally unspecified site and subject of the necessary political practice rep-

---

127   Badiou 2001, p. 86.
128   Althusser 1999a, p. 78.
129   Althusser 1999a, p. 79. Here how Althusser refers to the same point in the 1980s: 'What is most astonishing in Machiavelli, in the theory that he made of the new prince before founding a new principality, is that this new man is a man *of nothing, without past, without titles or burdens*, an anonymous man, alone and naked (that is, in fact free, without determination – again the solitude, first of Machiavelli, then of his prince – that bears down on him and could impede the free exercise of his *virtù*). Not only is he like a naked man, but he finds himself intervening in one place as anonymous and as stripped of every outstanding social and political determination, which could impede his action. Whence the privileged example of Cesare Borgia. Of course he was the son of a Pope, but, one who did not love him and, in order to extricate himself from him, bequeathed to him a plot of land in Romagne, really in Cesena – a part of the papal estates. Yet [...] the church estates [...] it was the total political void, another nakedness, in short an empty space without genuine structure able to obstruct the exercise of *virtù* of the future new prince' (Althusser 1997a, p. 14).

resents for Althusser a contradiction, a 'theoretical disjuncture'[130] to which Machiavelli refuses to offer some form of resolution. In contrast, Althusser insists that 'Machiavelli not only formulates, but thinks this problem *politically* – that is to say as a contradiction in reality that cannot be removed by thought, but only by reality'.[131] It is obvious that Althusser's thinking about Machiavelli and a potential materialist conception of an aleatory materialism is far from Antonio Negri's insistence that Althusser thinks in terms of liberation and the 'constitution of the subject';[132] Althusser thinks in terms of practices and processes not of constituting subjects.

The contradictions induced by the intrusion of a political problem within a theoretical text cannot be resolved or reconciled theoretically, only through concrete political practices. It is this kind of disjuncture and discrepancy that actually makes room in theory for political practice.

> In this theory that ponders and preserves the disjuncture, room is thereby made for political practice. Room is made for it through this organization of disjoined theoretical notions, by the discrepancy between the definite and indefinite, the necessary and the unforeseeable. This discrepancy, thought and unresolved by thought, is the presence of history and political practice in theory itself.[133]

Althusser then turns his attention towards Machiavelli's political practice. He begins by stressing the main points upon which Machiavelli bases his positions: (1) The Prince is a leader of a *popular state*. (2) The political practice of the Prince refers to the state defined in the narrow sense of the state apparatus. (3) The state can be divided in three elements: 'at one extreme the apparatus of force, represented by the *army*; at the other, the apparatus of *consent*, represented by religion and the entire system of ideas that the people forms of the Prince; and, between the two, the *politico-juridical* apparatus represented by the "system of laws"'.[134]

Althusser stresses Machiavelli's references to the army and praises them for their 'incisiveness and political acuteness' since they 'anticipate not only the Jacobin positions of the French Revolution, but also the well-known theses of

---

130   Althusser 1999a, p. 80.
131   Ibid.
132   Negri 1997, p. 158.
133   Ibid.
134   Althusser 1999a, p. 82.

Clausewitz, Engels and Mao Zedong'.[135] For Machiavelli, the army is the state apparatus *par excellence* since a Prince without an army is just an 'unarmed prophet', and this implies a 'primacy of force: *the primacy of the army as state apparatus over ideology and laws*'.[136] This reference to the importance of coercive force can also be related to Althusser's polemics against the right-wing Eurocommunists' tendency to underestimate the role of force in favour of a more 'consensual' vision of politics.

However, this does not suggest a militarisation of politics, or a conception of politics in terms of military force. In contrast, Machiavelli is presented as 'the first, conscious, explicit and consistent theorist of the *primacy of the political over the military* [...] the first theorist [...] to subordinate technical questions regarding armies and war to the primacy of politics'.[137] The primacy of force over consent is subordinated to the primacy of politics. This expressed Machiavelli's insistence that the real citadels are the people. The duality 'force/consent, army/ideology' is not antagonistic, the 'duality realizes two necessary forms of state power under a single rule: that of the Prince's popular and national politics'.[138] Machiavelli adds a fourth thesis that 'the Prince must *rely on his own forces*' and that the 'Prince's forces are those of his people';[139] the only good armies are the '*purely national armies*'.[140]

For Althusser, Machiavelli's quest is for an army that is intrinsically compatible with his political project for Italian national-popular unity, an army that, consequently, cannot be external to the target. That is why he makes a distinction between three moments in Machiavelli's thinking. In the first moment, the army is presented as simply a means to the ends of national and popular unity, but we are still within the limits of a relation of exteriority. In the second moment, the emphasis is on the importance of the Prince recruiting a national army, an army of his own forces, which in its generality remains within the limits of the exteriority relation. The most important moment is the third moment which refers to the forms of organisation of the army that actually are *internal* to the end of national and popular unity, an army that is already, by itself, the realisation of a political strategy.

Althusser also finds elements of a theory of political ideology in Machiavelli. This is evident in the latter's insistence that what 'could be of concern to the

---

135   Ibid.
136   Althusser 1999a, p. 83.
137   Ibid.
138   Althusser 1999a, p. 84.
139   Ibid.
140   Althusser 1999a, p. 86.

Prince's political practice is the opinion of the people in its mass: "*il volgo*".[141] It is also evident in Machiavelli's conception of religion as a necessary 'support' in safeguarding popular consent, especially since it is based upon fear, 'fear of gods' that 'has the immense advantage over fear of the Prince that it is *constant*'.[142] But the role of ideology is not limited to religion. The Prince and his representation in popular opinion play an important ideological role:

> In effect it can be said that in Machiavelli the representation of the Prince in popular opinion is a veritable *means* of state power, and that on his account it may be regarded as part of state ideology, not to say *ideological state apparatus*.[143]

This has to do with the particular features of the Prince as a political personality that personifies *political virtù* and that is dedicated to a historical task. The political *virtù* is also a moral virtue of a different order, since it is based upon the goal of founding an enduring state. The morality of virtue is related to this goal and this can account for why the Prince might even use in certain cases 'immoral' means. And in this sense *virtù* is not an individual quality, it 'is not the *intrinsic essence* of individuality; it is merely the reflection, as conscious and responsible as possible, of the objective conditions for accomplishment of the historical task of the hour in a Prince-individual'.[144]

Althusser proceeds to a reading of Machiavelli's description of the nature of the political practice of the Prince, exemplified in the well-known of the Prince combining the force (the animal side) and consent (the human side). However, Althusser points to the importance of the division of the animal side (force) into the two images of the lion (force) and the fox (fraud). For Althusser, 'what is astonishing in the division, this dual personality, of the beast is precisely that the *beast*, which is force, is divided into force (the lion) and fraud (the fox); whereas fraud – the art of deception – apparently has nothing to do with force, is not a division of force, but something quite different'.[145] For Althusser this reference to fraud does not refer to a mode of government but to '*a manner of governing the other two forms of government*: force and laws'.[146] Althusser elevates this to a question of political ontology: fraud (the fox) 'is the capacity to

---

141 Althusser 1999a, p. 89.
142 Althusser 1999a, p. 91.
143 Althusser 1999a, p. 92.
144 Althusser 1999a, p. 94.
145 Althusser 1999a, p. 95.
146 Ibid.

govern government by laws immorally [...] the necessity and understanding of non-being under the guise of being, and vice versa'.[147]

In Althusser's reading Machiavelli's infamous references to fraud and deception are not a description of the inherent immorality of cynical power – the classical narrative of Machiavellianism – but of the need for a concrete ideological policy, that 'must be subject to the primacy of politics *tout court*', with the goal of establishing 'a correct ideological *relation* between Prince and people, via the representation of the figure of the Prince'.[148] Because the Prince must not, at any cost, '*find himself in the position of having the people against him*'.[149] But his does not mean that the people love the Prince, the 'most reliable bond' is fear, but a 'fear without hatred',[150] which means that the Prince does not ally with the hated nobles but sides with the people. This 'fear without hatred' 'closes down one political space and opens up another, specific space: the minimal political space from which the people's friendship [...] becomes the decisive political objective'.[151] For Althusser all these account for the fact that this formula of 'fear without hatred' is the resolution to the political problem of constituting a national state, in the conditions that led to absolute monarchy as a form of transition from feudalism to capitalism:

> it is the mandatory resolution of a political problem linking the constitution of the national state to a twofold imperative: that the Prince's absolute power is 'popular' (not that the people are in power, but that out of fear initially, and then friendship, they recognize themselves in the Prince's popular politics and in his figure); and that by means of his power the popular Prince circumscribes the class struggle between nobles and people, to the advantage of the latter. Utopia? But it suffices to know the history of the constitution of national states in broad outline to appreciate that Machiavelli does nothing but *think* the conditions of existence, and the class conditions, for that form of transition between feudalism and capitalism which is *absolute monarchy*.[152]

---

147 Althusser 1999a, p. 96.
148 Althusser 1999a, p. 99.
149 Althusser 1999a, p. 100.
150 Ibid.
151 Althusser 1999a, p. 101.
152 Althusser 1999a, p. 103. In 1982, he encapsulated Machiavelli's importance for philosophy as follows: 'I would like to suggest that it is less to politics than to his "materialism of the encounter" that Machiavelli basically owes the influence he has had on people who do not give a damn about politics' (Althusser 2006a, p. 175).

Althusser ends the text with a reference to Machiavelli as being 'not the least utopian', but rather as an exemplary case of a materialist philosopher:

> Machiavelli is not the least utopian: he simply thinks the conjunctural *case* of the thing and goes *dietro alla verità effetuale della cosa*. He asserts it in concepts which are *philosophical* and no doubt make him, in his temerity, solitude, and scorn for the philosophers of the tradition, the greatest materialist philosopher in history – the equal of Spinoza, who declared him '*acutissimus*', most acute. He would appear not to have suspected that Machiavelli was also most incisive in materialist philosophy. I shall attempt to demonstrate this in a subsequent work.[153]

According to Emmanuel Terray, the materialism Althusser sees in Machiavelli is a materialism of the irreducible plurality of reality, of diversity, and of overdetermination.

> [A]ccording to Althusser, Machiavelli is an authentically and deeply materialist thinker. What must we understand here by materialism? In the form in which Althusser defended it, the materialist thesis asserts, first of all, that reality is irreducibly plural: differences are real, insurmountable, and every effort to abolish them into an artificial and arbitrary unity or conformity, is inevitably idealist. The notion of overdetermination means precisely that differences can come together and combine but that this combination is never a fusion, a suppression, or a reduction to unity or simplicity. In other words, each instance of the real possesses its own nature and effectivity: no instance is the phenomenal form of another; none is the truth of another.[154]

Machiavelli and Us is one of Althusser's most important political and theoretical statements. It is a confrontation with both the crisis of the communist movement and the need for a politics of the encounter. His own search for a *New Prince* is the search for a new collective political and ideological subject, a new practice of politics of popular unity in sharp break with the organisational, political, and ideological premises of the existing communist movement and of course in a sharp break to the Soviet experience. It is his own *utopian manifesto* that in the end, faced with his own political and personal crisis, he chose not to publish.

---

153   Ibid.
154   Terray 1996, p. 273.

6 Throwing the Dice: Machiavelli in the 1980s Texts

Althusser also deals with Machiavelli in the texts from the 1980s. In his manuscript from the 1980s on the 'Underground Current of the Materialism of the Encounter', Althusser treats Machiavelli as the thinker who confronted the question of the decisive political intervention that creates the conditions for the swerve, the *clinamen* that is at the origin of all social and political form:

> All the circumstances favourable to imitating France or Spain exist, but without connections between them: a divided and fervent people, the fragmentation of Italy into small obsolete states that have been condemned by history, a generalized but disorderly revolt of an entire world against foreign occupation and pillage, and a profound, latent aspiration of the people to unity, an aspiration to which all the great works of the period bear witness, including that of Dante, who understood nothing of all this, but was waiting for the arrival of the 'great hound'. In sum, an atomized country, every atom of which was descending in free fall without encountering its neighbour. It was necessary to create the conditions for a swerve, and thus an encounter, if Italian unity was to 'take hold'.[155]

We have a juxtaposition of a 'classical' cataloguing of conjunctural dynamics and conditions in their singular and overdetermined relations, something close to the themes of 'Contradiction and Overdetermination', and the reference to the Lucretian rain of atoms and the need for a swerve, the initiating political act. The tension evident in this passage, that is suggestive of a great part of his theoretical trajectory, is the definition of the conjuncture and whether it can be considered simply a rain of atoms, an agglomeration of non-connected singular and topical dynamics without any articulation prior to the constitutive political intervention of the Prince; or whether we must see the conflicting dynamics and interconnections and interrelations of the conjuncture as the terrain of intervention; not in the sense of an 'originary act' but rather as an attempt to enhance dynamics to their transformative potential. It is interesting that Althusser returns here to the emphasis on the 'void' of the conjuncture, in the sense of the need for that kind of intervention that could actually enable the encounter of the elements of the conjuncture. This brings him to the necessary anonymity, in the sense of not bearing any relation to the existing social and

---

155 Althusser 2006a, p. 171.

political configuration, of whoever takes up the task of initiating this process, but also to a much greater emphasis on the aleatory character of this encounter.

> Once all the states and their princes – that is, all the places and people have been rejected, Machiavelli, using the example of Cesare Borgia, moves on to the idea that unification will be achieved if there emerges some nameless man who has enough luck and *virtù* to establish himself somewhere, in some nameless corner of Italy, and, starting out from this atomic point, gradually aggregate the Italians around him in the grand project of founding a national state. This is a completely aleatory line of reasoning, which leaves politically blank both the name of the Federator and that of the region which will serve as starting point for the constitution of this federation. Thus the dice are tossed on the gaming table, which is itself empty (but filled with men of valour).[156]

For Althusser, Machiavelli is the thinker *par excellence* of the encounter, the encounter between *fortuna* and *virtù*, and the thinker of encounters that last, of social forms (and political projects) that take hold, linking this form of encounter with Marx's reference to the encounter between the man with money and the free labourer. In his autobiography he describes this linkage between the notion of the encounter in Marx and in Machiavelli in the following way:

> I came to Machiavelli by means of a word, ceaselessly repeated, of Marx's, saying that capitalism was born out of the '*encounter between the man with money and free labourers*', free, that is, stripped of everything, of their means of labour, of their abodes and their families, in the great expropriation of the English countryside (this was his preferred example). *Encounter*. Again, a '*casus*', a 'case', a factual accident without origin, cause, or end. I would rediscover the same formula in Machiavelli when he speaks of the 'encounter' between the good occasion (*fortuna* or good conjuncture) and the man of *virtù*, that is, a man having enough intelligence (intuition) to comprehend that the good occasion presents itself, and above all, having enough energy (*virtù*) or excess vigorously to exploit it for the success of his vital project.[157]

---

156   Althusser 2006a, p. 172.
157   Althusser 1997a, pp. 13–14.

This leads to much greater emphasis on contingency. Here the materialism of the encounter is not defined mainly in terms of a negation of teleology but as an emphasis on contingency. It is also here that Althusser also insists of the philosophical importance of Machiavelli's political thinking, hence the reference that the political void is also a philosophical void:

> The reader may object that this is merely political philosophy, overlooking the fact that a philosophy is simultaneously at work here too. A curious philosophy which is a 'materialism of the encounter' thought by way of politics, and which, as such, does not take anything for granted. It is in the political void that the encounter must come about, and that national unity must 'take hold'. But this political void is first a philosophical void. No Cause that precedes its effects is to be found in it, no Principle of morality or theology (as in the whole Aristotelian political tradition: the good and bad forms of government, the degeneration of the good into the bad). One reasons here not in terms of the Necessity of the accomplished fact, but in terms of the contingency of the fact to be accomplished.[158]

It is obvious that we are dealing here with something that is beyond a simple reference to the complexity of determination and overdetermination, or the openness of the conjuncture, or to the possibility that something might not happen. Increasingly it becomes a reference to chance and randomness:

> In other words, nothing guarantees that the reality of the accomplished fact is the guarantee of its durability. Quite the opposite is true: every accomplished fact, even an election, like all the necessity and reason we can derive from it, is only a provisional encounter, and since every encounter is provisional even when it lasts, *there is no eternity in the 'laws' of any world or any state.*[159]

It is this reference to the dice, the *alea*, that is thrown on an empty place along with the insistence on the provisional character of any encounter, and the apprehension of the revocability of any accomplished fact that marks Althusser's confrontation with the (im)possibility of politics. It combines the openness of the historical terrain, the endless possibility for new encounters,

---

158 Althusser 2006a, pp. 173–4.
159 Althusser 2006a, p. 174.

with the tragic apprehension of a radical instability, of the possibility that no encounter can last, of the radical randomness inherent in any social practice.[160] In a certain sense, this is the limit of aleatory materialism.

Althusser's dialogue with Machiavelli presents all the questions Althusser faced both philosophical – in all his attempts towards a materialism of the conjuncture and the encounter – and political – his confrontation with the crisis of the communist movement: How can we think of a dialectic of general determinations and singular conjunctures and encounters? How can avoid both complete randomisation while avoiding a metaphysics of historical 'laws'? How can we combine all this with a conception of political intellectuality and knowledge? How can politics, and especially revolutionary politics, think this dialectic of the aleatory and the encounter, both in the sense of the singularity of the conjuncture but also of the possibility to have lasting encounters? How can we face the urgency and the difficulty of establishing new practices, new relations, new institutions, new 'structures'? How can a revolutionary intervention establish the necessary open space for its intervention, the necessary void, which is at the same time so empty with the absence of a revolutionary political form, and so full with all the elements and determinations of the conjuncture? How can the revolutionary movement fight to bring together social strata, ideological representations and collective practices in a unity that has to be radically new and original, at the same time dealing with all the historical and political weight of existing ideologies, political forms, alliances? How can this new politics – that has to be necessarily alien to the existing situation, social and political configuration, and common sense – manage to 'take hold' so as to root itself in the concrete social and political forces of the conjuncture and articulate them in a new popular unity and hegemony?

What is particularly interesting insofar as it reflects Althusser's quest for radical novelty as the trademark of any really revolutionary politics, is his emphasis on *absolute beginnings* that make necessary the solitude of the New Prince. This emphasis on absolute beginnings marks Althusser's fuller apprehension of the extent of the crisis of the communist movement. It was no longer a question of theoretically 'correcting' a political line, of changing the theoretical balance of forces within a Party that it is taken as given that it represents the working class, or even of forcing the dynamics of the movements to enter

---

160 As Emmanuel Terray recently noted, there is a line in Althusser's confrontation with Machiavelli that 'ends up defying all kinds of necessity and making Marxism a thinking of risk, a thinking of bet' (Terray in Wald Lasowski 2016, p. 297).

the 'fortress' of the Party in order for its politics and tactics to move towards a more radical and revolutionary direction. Althusser seems to lose hope with a communist movement in crisis and calls for something radically new, the communist version of the 'New Prince', not so in the sense of Gramsci's call for a complex and uneven process of hegemony, but more like the solitary and uneven political act (or even gesture) that inaugurates a new political and social sequence.

Although Althusser seems in *Machiavelli and Us* to 'bend the stick' towards a conception of radical and emancipatory politics as pure novelty, as a radically novel political gesture, the solitary political act that initiates a new political sequence, I think that there are many references also to the opposite, namely the importance of the existing balance of forces and the singular political dynamics of the conjuncture. However, Althusser insists on the radical novelty, exactly because he has in mind the crisis of the communist movement and the need for something radically new – rooted in the dynamics of the popular movements and the revolutionary heritage of the workers' movement, but, nevertheless, new. By then Althusser was fully aware that it was not possible to have some sort of self-reform of the existing communist movement and its political forms and strategies. What was needed was indeed a *New Prince*, a new collective political and ideological figure, a new politics of popular unity in sharp break with the organisational, political, and ideological premises of the existing communist movement and of course in a sharp break to the soviet experience. It is interesting to note here how in his treatment of Machiavelli's references to annexations (good annexations are the ones that enhance unity[161]), Althusser in a way is also thinking about how a new political point of reference could manage to expand its political and ideological influence and help the emergence of a new popular unity, a new 'principality' of the subaltern classes in the road to socialism.

In this sense, this text that attempts to deal with Machiavelli's 'utopian manifesto' is also Althusser's boldest statement about revolutionary politics, his own 'utopian manifesto' about the need and possibility of new forms of revolutionary politics, even in the metonymical terms of his close reading of Machiavelli. However, this is also the limit of Althusser, the inability to think what could constitute the *New Prince* that could do away with the crisis of the communist movement, 'sweep it away' and establish a new hegemony. He only manages to point – in his 1976–78 interventions – to the potential inscribed in the force and ingenuity of the popular movements.

---

161   Cf. Althusser 1999a, pp. 72–3.

It is in light of this reading that we can see the changes Althusser made when he revisited the manuscript of *Machiavelli and Us* after 1980. He made corrections, adding phrases that refer to the void of the conjuncture, to the aleatory conditions of the conjuncture, the importance of the singular case. These additions do not fundamentally alter the structure of the arguments. One might say that the ease with which these additions work within the whole architecture of the text exemplifies the fact that *Machiavelli and Us* already contains elements of the problematic of aleatory materialism. This can also account for the continuity between the manuscript of *Machiavelli and Us* and the texts on Machiavelli that he wrote in the 1980s.

In this sense, we can think the importance of *Machiavelli and Us*, its centrality in Althusser's endeavour in the 1970s, and the difficulty he had in deciding to publish it. If we discern two parallel and interwoven tendencies in Althusser's thinking of the materialism encounter, one more oriented towards the challenge of 'organizing good encounters', in the sense suggested by Deleuze[162] to 'transform the event into duration',[163] and one towards the aleatory character of any encounter, *Machiavelli and Us* entails both. On the one hand, it deals with the *political and organisational* question *par excellence*, namely the *New Prince*, the challenge of *lasting encounters*, and, on the other, it deals with the open and aleatory character of the conjuncture and the necessity of contingency. This was perhaps Althusser's difficulty with this text, a text that calls for a *new* communist movement, *a new political form*, while at the same time insisting on its contingency, on its possibility of it not happening.

7 Althusser's Solitude

And this is exactly the specific *political solitude* of Althusser himself. Perhaps this can explain why Althusser chose ultimately not to publish this text, despite the fact that it was worked on even to a final form and could easily stand as a book. Perhaps he thought that calling for a New Prince and a new political form for the communist movement, without being able to determine it or its conditions, was an unbearable contradiction. In a way the publishing silence offers a very audible revelation of a political impasse.

Althusser's preoccupation with politics as radical novelty in the 1980s text can also account for the emphasis on the *void* as a necessary condition. Politics

---

162   See the discussion in section 9 of this Chapter.
163   Negri 1997, p. 146.

as an *aleatory encounter* that 'holds' cannot be conceived without a reference to the void: 'on one hand as absence of cause, principle, essence, origin etc., absence of ontological and ethical principles, as we well know. But also the real void, factual and conjunctural'.[164] For Althusser the void here seems to represent not only the inherent instability and contingency of any politics, in the sense of an absence of any metaphysical or ontological ground, but also the need for an open space and a radical absence that enables the new politics and the new political forms to actually hold. However, the question remains: is there ever a void in politics or in social life? And consequently: is there a possibility of an absolute beginning? Or are we always already within the conjuncture and a history of social and political dynamics and forces that make absolute beginnings – in politics as in life in general – a fantasy? I do not want to suggest that new beginnings are not possible – this would amount to a denial of the possibility of revolutionary change and social transformation – but that the dialectic of the existing and of the absent, of the weight of things and of the void, of what already exists (as struggle, movement, collectivity, political forms) and of what is not here and needs to be constructed, is always much more complex.

8 *A Convergence for Liberation*: Althusser in the 1980s

In the fragments on Machiavelli and the concrete analysis of the political situation that have been included in the second French edition of *The Future Lasts a Long time* this feeling of a crisis of radical and revolutionary politics in all the forms it took in the twentieth century is more than evident. For Althusser the world in the 1980s was considerably different from that in the 1960s. Processes of globalisation led to a situation in which capitalist power was more diffused than ever, there was mass depoliticisation creating a 'political desert'[165] and consequently because of the crisis of the communist movement, there was no '"strategic centre" capable of designing historical perspectives for action'.[166] But the tone is not simply one of desperation; there is also hope:

> Marx never stopped repeating: 'History has more imagination than us' [...] if we dare and know '*to think by ourselves*' and exactly the aleatory and unpredictable element in history [...] we have a chance in front of us.[167]

---

164 Althusser 1994a, p. 490.
165 Althusser 1994a, p. 520.
166 Althusser 1994a, p. 506.
167 Althusser 1994a, p. 526.

In the 1980s texts, Althusser insists on the 'autonomous reality'[168] of the workers' movement and its relative strength, despite the open crisis of the communist movement and the independence of Marxist theory from the workers' movement, following a line of reasoning also evident in the late 1970s texts. This gives a certain political dimension to imagery of the encounter. It is not only a reference to the aleatory and non-teleological character of social reality in general, but also to the relation between social dynamics and revolutionary politics. The relation between the workers' movement and Marxist theory and revolutionary politics is not an 'organic' one: it is also an encounter, an encounter that can fail or take many forms, that can start and never 'hold', and that can be missed. Reconstructing the possibility of revolutionary politics means creating the conditions for lasting encounters, but also looking for *the surprise* in history when 'the cards are dealt out again without warning',[169] which for Althusser is the marking point of the revolutionary event.

This is even more evident in the 1986 *Théses de Juin* [June Theses], a philosophical manifesto that was never circulated that recapitulates the basic premises of aleatory materialism, in a line similar to other texts from the same period, and presents Althusser's conception of politics. Althusser no longer speaks of a crisis of the communist movement, but more about reaching the end of class struggle and of social classes and at the same time of the displacement of class struggle towards ideology. Consequently, it is this ideological class struggle that will determine the general direction that class struggle will take. Although Althusser admits that the main strategic point of that period was to move social democracy to the left, at the same time he is more optimistic regarding the possibility of communism. For Althusser 'there is communism in those places where neither exploitation, nor state domination, nor ideological mystification reign'.[170] It is on the basis of this potentiality that he suggests a 'centre of ideological convergence for liberation and liberty' as a 'centre of information and not direction', open to all groups and enabling the 'exchange of information'.[171] There is also a certain optimism based upon the 'youth movement'. In the end, Althusser declares his return to silence but in the hopeful tone that 'finally, soon, bread and roses'.[172]

Although most of Althusser's later texts seem to be more like philosophical notes, especially those relating to the non-ontology of the materialism of the

---

168   Althusser 2006a, p. 212.
169   Althusser 2006a, p. 196.
170   Althusser 1986, p. 11.
171   Althusser 1986, p. 12.
172   Ibid.

encounter, and despite their fragmentary, uneven, and unfinished character, their political motivation is more than obvious. In this sense, as Emilio de Ípola has suggested, this conception points towards the encounter between 'a *thinking of the social* renewed and redefined as *theory of collective intervention*, with Marxism (or rather, *aleatory materialism*) as philosophy of politics'.[173] Étienne Balibar has recently insisted exactly on this deeply political character of the notion of the encounter.

> The 'encounter' that Althusser spoke of and the 'deviation' that he placed at its origin (not a punctual origin, but a virtual origin, always disposable) take here a more concrete and historical significance, very far from the 'naturalism' of the habitual lucretian references and also radically foreign to any dialectic of the subject of history [...]. The encounter is the *crystallisation of collective unities* (themselves conjunctural, aleatory, contradictory, but in no way indeterminate as it would have been with a pure 'multitude') that *make situations deviate* beginning from their internal instability, or 'counter-tendencies' that are inherent in their 'tendencies'.[174]

Althusser's insistence on the aleatory character of social reality in the sense of the absence of any teleology or strong structural determination is also an expression of Althusser's confrontation with the crisis of the communist movement, much more evident in the 1980s than the late 1970s, when there was still hope for some form of left-wing governance. Since all of Althusser's initial reference points – the leading role of communist parties in the popular masses, the ability of Marxist theory to provide strategic references and guidelines, the possibility of a mass self-correction of the communist parties from within – were put into question, he was in need of a new conception of materialism that would ground philosophically the possibility of political and historical novelty. That is why the theme of the encounter, that had preoccupied him since 1966, as a rejection of teleology, took on renewed importance in the 1980s texts. It is no longer simply a metonymic reference to the non-teleological articulation of different historical elements in highly original configurations; nor is it simply a reformulation of the contingent nature of 'structures' as lasting encounters. It is a new conception of politics, which includes both the possibility of historical failure, in the sense of missed encounters between the working classes and revolutionary politics, and historical surprise and hope, in the sense of new

---

173   de Ípola 2012, p. 116.
174   Balibar 2012, p. xix.

encounters between struggling masses and emancipatory political projects. It is at the same time a more tragic conception of revolutionary politics, since failure is an imminent potentiality, and a more open vision of the political and historical field that could entail the possibility of new collective practices. Despite the obvious overdetermination of Althusser's own painful confrontation with his trajectory and the realisation of the limits of many of his own certainties, and despite the recurring tendency of an 'over-correction' of earlier positions, it is still an attempt towards a redefinition of the possibility of revolutionary politics.

It is obvious that in the 1980s Althusser thought that the main theoretical danger came from a metaphysical conception of the historical possibility of communism, a conception that could not account for the crisis of the communist movement. The emphasis on the aleatory or even contingent character of social and political practices, including radical politics, was a form of a necessary 'bending of the stick to the other side'. However, faced with neoliberal ideology's pre-emptive denial of any form of intelligibility of history apart from social reality as an aggregation of individual choices and atomised social transactions, the task ahead of us is how to make lasting encounters that would enable again the possibility of a politics of transformation and not simply resistance.

9   How to Organise Good Encounters?

In his 1976 lecture in Barcelona on the dictatorship of the proletariat, Althusser insists on communism being an objective tendency in the sense of being re-enacted in the very struggles and the collective creativity of the popular masses, in material practices that in certain way bring forward the 'traces of communism'[175] in contemporary societies. In his intervention after the 22nd Congress of the PCF, Althusser insists on the importance of the autonomous practices and collectivities of the working masses as an important and indispensable aspect of any process of revolutionary renewal of the communist movement and of an actual process of withering away of the state.[176] Moreover, in the preface to the answers he gave to Rossana Rossanda after his 1977 intervention to the Venice Congress, Althusser introduces another important thematic, that of 'virtual forms of communism' emerging at the 'interstices of contemporary

---

175   Althusser 2014c.
176   Althusser 1977, p. 11.

society'.[177] Althusser in these interventions moves with the assumption that it was possible – albeit difficult – to overcome this crisis of Marxism because 'the Labour Movement and the movement of the people, even if it is divided, even if it seems here or there to have reached an impasse, has in fact never been so powerful, so rich in resources and initiatives'.[178] It is exactly this strong belief that there was a strong movement, there were 'traces of communism', communist virtualities and forms of collective ingenuity, that was one of the foundations of his new conception of communist politics as lasting encounters between collective practices of the working and popular masses – expressed in autonomous social movements – and new forms of political organisation of communist and Marxist inspiration.

The centrality of the notion of the encounter in this context is an attempt to rethink communist politics and the relation between politics and the masses in a way that is completely hostile and opposed to Kautsky's call for an insertion of Marxist politics and class consciousness from without. At the same time, Althusser attempts to avoid a spontaneist fantasy of politics arising only out the practices of the masses, refusing to either underestimate or idealise the collective practices of the masses. The crucial point is that in Althusser's schema of an encounter between the collective practices of the masses, there is politics on both sides, and they are both expressions of class struggles (and the result of histories – in the plural – of class struggles), representing at the same time the very unevenness, complexity, and overdetermination of class struggles, the encounters and non-encounters within the scope of the practices of the masses. In this sense, the notion of the encounter is exactly the attempt towards thinking the necessity and the contingency of constantly recomposing forms of communist politics in a period of crisis and also potential. In this sense we can see how – in their very unevenness – the elaboration of the materialism of the encounter ever since the second half of the 1960s and the renewed attempt to counter the crisis of the communist movement, by means of a left critique of communist reformism, are parts of the same theoretical and political effort to rethink the possibility of a movement of transformation. In this sense, despite Althusser's own personal distrust of what he considered as Gramsci's historicism, he is in fact much closer to the challenge of how to recompose a 'Modern Prince' out of the 'molecular' practices and aspirations of the subaltern classes in an attempt to create conditions for a new historical bloc.

---

177   Althusser 1998, p. 285.
178   Althusser 1978a, p. 220.

As already mentioned, another way to rethink the politics of the encounter is to go back to Deleuze. It is really interesting to see the emphasis Deleuze places in his reading of the centrality of experimentation in Spinoza's *Ethics*, which in a certain way presents Deleuze's version of a potential *Spinozist* politics, articulated around the question of how to form common notions, which for Deleuze is exactly the production of collective practices of emancipation and transformation. For Deleuze this also means the question of *how to organise good encounters*, or the challenge of communist politics that attempts to grasp the dynamics of singular conjunctures and their radical contingency, not the in the sense of a metaphysics of contingency and fidelity to the miraculous advent of the event, but in the sense of *organising* and *experimenting*, a position reminiscent of both the Leninist version of politics, of Gramsci's conception of the political party as laboratory, and of Althusser's search for 'lasting encounters':

> So it appears that the common notions are practical Ideas, in relation with our power; unlike their order of exposition, which only concerns ideas, their order of formation concerns affects, showing how the mind 'can order its affects and connect them together.' The common notions are an Art, the art of the Ethics itself: organizing good encounters, composing actual relations, forming powers, experimenting.[179]

It is only in the sense of a constant attempt towards experimentation that any notion of criteria for political action can be conceived, or as Sibertin-Blanc has stressed, the necessary *prudence*[180] that is necessary to deal with experimenting in a plane of singular multiplicities, what Deleuze referred to as the 'prudence of the experimenter':[181]

> Schizoanalysis, or pragmatics, has no other meaning: Make a rhizome. But you don't know what you can make a rhizome with, you don't know which subterranean stem is effectively going to make a rhizome, or enter a becoming, people your desert. So experiment.
>
> That's easy to say? Although there is no preformed logical order to becomings and multiplicities, there are *criteria*, and the important thing is that they not be used after the fact, that they be applied in the course of events, that they be sufficient to guide us through the dangers.[182]

---

179   Deleuze 1988, p. 119.
180   Sibertin-Blanc 2006, p. 239.
181   Deleuze and Parnet 1987, p. 139.
182   Deleuze 1987, p. 251.

I think that we can discern two parallel and interwoven tendencies in Althusser's thinking of the materialism of the encounter, one more oriented towards the challenge of 'organising the encounters', as an attempt to make them lasting, to 'transform the event into duration',[183] and one towards the aleatory character of any encounter. In this sense, we might even suggest that the passage from the materialism of the encounter to the aleatory materialism of the 1980s texts, although in no sense a 'break', perhaps under the effects of both Althusser's own personal crisis and a greater apprehension of the depth of the crisis of the communist movement, expresses to a greater extent an emphasis on the contingent political gesture in the void of the crisis of the movement and the capitalist counteroffensive instead of the stronger emphasis on the possibility of lasting encounters. In the 1970s and especially the texts and interventions around the 'crisis of Marxism' problematic, the emphasis, despite the references to the crisis, still tends more towards the possibility of 'organising the encounters' based upon popular initiatives and a Marxist theory with apprehension of the crisis, using the autonomous organisations of the masses as 'medium term'. In the 1980s the full 'intensity' of aleatory materialism emerges. Not that Althusser loses hope in the possibility of emancipation; rather in the 1980s he is thinking it more in terms of a 'flux' of emancipatory and liberating movements for communism, like a parallel rain of atoms (in this case communist singularities), something evident in texts like the 1986 'Theses de Juin'.[184]

That Althusser never managed to produce in the end a more coherent strategy should not be seen in terms of personal limitations. Rather it is an expression of the unevenness and difficulty of a dialectic of tentative encounters that, in the last instance, depend upon actual collective practices in their singular dynamics, not simple theoretical constructions. The philosophy of the encounter, consequently, was never simply an attempt towards deconstructing idealism. It was also an attempt towards a new practice of philosophy that would facilitate a new practice of politics, a new practice of politics for communism.

183   Negri 1997, p. 146.
184   Althusser 1986.

CHAPTER 20

Ideology and Political Subjectivity

When thinking about the question of Althusserian politics, the question of Althusser's theory of ideology comes to the fore. By itself one of Althusser's most important – and most discussed – contributions to Marxism and social theory in general, it moved from an initial conception of ideology as the 'other' of science, towards a highly original theory of the relation between ideology and social practices plus a conceptualisation of the relation between ideological interpellation and subject formation. Leaving aside other aspects, it is necessary to see its importance as opening the question of political subjectivity, the question of political practices and its agency.

1 The Subject as Problem and Not Answer

In his theory of ideology and particularly in his theorisation of how ideology constitutes human beings as subjects, Althusser was obviously trying to avoid the traditional metaphysics of beginning with the subject. He attempted to rethink the possibility of subject formation and political action while remaining within the contours of theoretical anti-humanism. What marks Althusser's originality of thought on subject formation and, consequently, on political subjectivity is his insistence that the subject is a *problem to be tackled* and not a starting point. In this sense, the very complexity of the social whole, suggested by his conception of a decentred and overdetermined whole, is the condition of possibility for subject formation. The bearers (*träger*) of conflictual and antagonistic social relations (economic, political, and ideological) necessarily take the form of subjects, with ideological social relations rather than the particular human beings in question being the causal mechanism. The crucial aspect is thus ideology. It is ideology that actually interpellates people as subjects, the subject being the ideological formation par excellence.

But at the same time this seems like Althusser's limit. In his elaborations on ideology and ideological interpellation, Althusser always treats processes of subjectivation in a negative way: being interpellated as a subject almost necessarily leads to the subject being dominated by an ideology – and consequently being in a state of misrecognition of actual social reality – that is instrumental to the reproduction of forms of social domination. In this conception of ideology, alternative forms of subjectivity are only limit cases. 'Bad subjects'[1] seem to be relatively rare and are dealt with by repressive mechanisms.

If we treat the subject only as the result of ideological interpellation and as a form of misrecognition, however, I think that we will simply be reproducing a crucial line of anti-humanist demarcation. We will not be making any advances toward answering the question of how political practices, collectivities, and (consequently) forms of subjectivity emerge. The open question is how to link the question of the subject with the possibility of action.

Scholars such as G.M. Goshgarian[2] have suggested that one crucial aspect of Althusser's attempt to overcome his initial difficulty to think on politics and collective political action was his thought concerning the concept of the encounter. As mentioned already, we should treat the notion of the encounter as an aspect of a broader theoretical problematic and not in the narrow sense of an identification of the encounter with contingency and the aleatory. From the mid-1960s onward Althusser was trying to reconfigure forms of causal determination within the social whole in a non-teleological and non-essentialist way, refusing any conception of latent structures as 'deeper' causal mechanisms. This is exemplified in his turn from a thinking of structures toward a thinking of practices and the apparatuses that guarantee their reproduction. This is particularly evident in *On the Reproduction of Capitalism*. This is a conception of the social whole that is more open and more dialectical and that entails the possibility of action, in the sense of an encounter between conditions and determinations.

I think that this reference to lasting encounters also has to do with the question of transformative, emancipatory politics. There is symmetry at least between the questions of a lasting social form and that of a lasting form of political organisation and of political transformation (or a *sequence* of social transformation). The emergence of a political collectivity in position to actually affect and change the social balance of forces can also be thought of in terms of an encounter between different elements and circumstances. The emergence of a proper political subject – one who is *faithful* to a process of social transformation, to borrow Badiou's term – is also a condition of a lasting encounter. So we have the challenge of lasting encounters and the question of the political subject at both sides of the relation. Are we then encountering here the limits of Althusser's thinking on the subject?

---

1 Althusser 1971, p. 181.
2 Goshgarian 2006.

2 Return of the Subject?

Althusser's emphasis on the subject being a result of social processes of misrecognition that are instrumental for the reproduction of power relations was part of a broader theoretical tendency that challenged the traditional metaphysics of the subject. The self-conscious, self-reflexive, and sovereign subject that epitomises the thinking of the Enlightenment was put into question both by the Marxist theory of ideology and by the Freudian topography of the psychic world, which in turn led to a variety of postwar 'anti-humanist' theories insisting that societal trends are processes without subjects. As Balibar has suggested, the new emphasis on structures referred to '*a mechanism of reversal of the constituting subject into constituted subjectivity*, based on a deconstruction of the "humanist" equation of the subject'.[3] Along similar lines, Mladen Dolar suggests,

> The general strategy promoted by structuralism could, in a very simplified way, be outlined as an attempt to put forward the level of a 'nonsubjective' structure as opposed to the subject's self-apprehension. There is a nonsubjective 'symbolic' dimension of which the subject is but an effect, and which is necessarily overlooked in the subject's imaginary self-understanding.[4]

At the same time, in most traditions of radical and emancipatory political thinking – including most varieties of Marxism, despite all the references to social transformation being the result of objective processes – there is always a reference to political collectivities emerging in the historical scene more or less as *subjects*, even if we consider them 'bad' subjects.

In light of the above, it is necessary to consider critical readings of Althusser's theory of the formation of the subject through ideological interpellation. These readings not only refer to the complexity of processes of subjection and subjectivation but also challenge the tendency to treat the subject as only an ideological formation.

Judith Butler's exploration of the question of the subject and her critical confrontation with Althusser's theory of the subject is indeed very interesting and brings forward contradictions and overlooked aspects of Althusser's the-

---

3 Balibar 2003, p. 11.
4 Dolar 1998, p. 13.

ory of ideology. One can see it, for example, in the way she locates the relation between subject formation, the law, and guilt in Althusser's process of interpellation.

> 'Submission' to the rules of the dominant ideology might then be understood as a submission to the necessity to prove innocence in the face of accusation, a submission to the demand for proof, an execution of that proof, and acquisition of the status of the subject in and through compliance with the interrogative law. To become a 'subject' is thus to have been presumed guilty, then tried and declared innocent. Because this declaration is not a single act but a status incessantly *reproduced*, to become a 'subject' is to be continuously in the process of acquitting oneself of the accusation of guilt [...] Yet because this guilt conditions the subject, it constitutes the prehistory of the subjection to the law by which the subject is produced. Here one might usefully conjecture that the reason there are so few references to 'bad subjects' in Althusser is that the term tends toward the oxymoronic. To be 'bad' is not yet to be subject, not yet to have acquitted oneself of the allegation of guilt.[5]

Moreover, Butler has brought forward the problems surrounding the very notion of the subject and the fact that it refers to both the subject that is subjected to power relations and the subject that is capable of challenging these relations. '"Subjection" signifies the process of becoming subordinated by process as well as the process of becoming a subject'.[6] In Butler's reading of the dialectic of subjection and subjectivation in Althusser's theory of interpellation, the problem lies exactly in this process of the interpellation of a subject that must always already have been a subject in order to be interpellated. For Butler one of the main problems of Althusser's theory is a certain circularity in the whole schema of interpellation, which is symptomatic of a 'failure' inherent in the process, a circularity that is evident in the fact that the subject is simultaneously a prerequisite and a result of the process of ideological interpellation and subject formation.

> Is it a failing of Althusser not to provide the subject prior to the formation of the subject, or does his 'failure' indicate only that the grammatical requirements of the narrative work against the account of subject form-

---

5   Butler 1997, pp. 119–29.
6   Butler 1997, p. 2.

ation that the narrative attempts to provide? To literalize or to ascribe an ontological status to the grammatical requirement of the 'subject' is to presume a mimetic relation between grammar and ontology which misses the point, both Althusserian and Lacanian, that the anticipations of grammar are always and only retroactively installed. The grammar that governs the narration of subject formation presumes that the grammatical place for the subject has already been established. In an important sense, then, the grammar that the narrative requires results from the narrative itself. The account of subject formation is thus a double fiction at cross-purposes with itself, repeatedly symptomatizing what resists narration.[7]

At the same time, Butler's discussion of mourning and melancholia – and their relation to processes of subjection – also has a political dimension. According to Butler the 'state cultivates melancholia among its citizenry precisely as a way of dissimulating and displacing its own ideal authority'.[8] For Pierre Macherey this position means that the only way out of melancholia is political, which implies that power 'has found the means to coil up in the most intimate part of ourselves and our private being',[9] leading to a fear of power as 'the fear of the power buried within us'. Consequently, what is needed is liberation from fear through understanding of the mechanisms that condition processes of subjection, and subjectivation is therefore necessary in any attempt for a politics of emancipation.

I think, however, that rather than a theory of collective political agency, Butler is concerned with how to develop a highly original performative theory of critical and ethical subjectivity. Indeed, she is trying to reintroduce a notion of critical self-reflection without falling back into a form of traditional idealist conception of self-consciousness. She brings forward Althusser's contradictions and shortcomings but does not offer a way to reconfigure a non-metaphysical conception of collective political agency.

A new emphasis on critical and ethical subjectivity, however welcome it might be compared to neoliberal postmodern cynical egoism, can lead to circularities of a different kind. It is true that, in Althusser's case, the problem is the gap separating radical political action and subjectivity as ideological subjection – and consequently the difficulty in presenting the conditions for the

---

7   Butler 1997, p. 124.
8   Butler 1997, pp. 190–1.
9   Macherey 2004, p. 17.

emergence of collective 'bad subjects' in some really plausible way other than a simple reference to an encounter with Marxism as science. The same problem persists, however, in any attempt to ground the possibility of collective political action in some form of ethical subjectivity. How is such subjectivity possible? Is it a question of individual enlightenment, decision, and ascesis? Is it the result of an encounter with a correct theory or with an ethics having strong foundations, either formal (Kantian) or more naturalistic? It is obvious that we are still facing open questions.

Another line of reasoning comes from the Lacanian tradition, especially from the reading of the *cogito* and consequently of the *subject* by thinkers such as Žižek and Dolar. Here one can find a new emphasis on the centrality of the subject, not in the sense of a self-conscious and self-reflexive, sovereign and ethical subject but in the more 'algebraic' sense of Lacan's distinction between the subject and the 'I'.[10] But although this is a useful reminder of the centrality and inescapability of the subject as form, both in what concerns the psychic world and the terrain of ideology, nevertheless it does not offer an answer to the questions surrounding the emergence of political subjects as collectivities engaged in the politics of emancipation. Moreover, this reading tends to suggest something close to a 'subject before the subject' in the process of interpellating an individual as subject, whereas in Althusser's schema, as Won Choi has stressed, this presupposition is exactly the retroactive effect of interpellation: 'The illusion of the *eternity* of the subject [is] an essential effect of ideological interpellation'.[11]

There is also Alain Badiou's long preoccupation with the question of the subject – a preoccupation that has as its origin the very question of the political subject par excellence, the political party. Beginning with the *Theory of the Subject* and then proceeding to the cycle of works on *Being and Event*, Badiou has offered a highly original conception of the political subject as an aspect of the situation and the evental site rather than a 'subjective' stance.[12] Other aspects

---

10   Žižek 1998. Patrice Maniglier has recently insisted on the centrality of a certain conceptualisation of the subject in both Lévi-Strauss and Lacan. According to Maniglier, Lacan 'was aware that the concept of structure offered by Lévi-Strauss, far from formalizing this projecting but immanent and self-sufficient symbolic order from which subjects were excluded, implied the elicitation of an entity which at one and the same time belonged to the system but forced it out of itself, a term which was nothing other than an endless (self-)displacement: the subject is constituted by these elements which cannot be actualized as such, but which are still necessary to the very completion of the system' (Maniglier 2012, p. 45).
11   Won Choi 2013, p. 17.
12   See Badiou 2005a; 2009a; 2009b.

of his more general ontological schema, however, can be read as an overemphasis on *subjective decisions* at the beginning of a political sequence.[13]

3 A Non-subjectivist Theory of Political Subjectivity

The question therefore remains open. How can we conceive the political subject in a non-subjectivist way without resorting to a reformulation of the classical metaphysical conception of the sovereign subject, and at the same time how can we avoid treating antagonistic politics as simply an expression of impersonal structural tendencies?

One way to treat such a question would be to rethink Althusser's conception of the break with ideology. Althusser's insistence that science is the opposite of ideology can be read as a reference to a potential form of discourse or enunciation that is a sharp contrast to the modalities of the ideological. Although Althusser abandoned his initial – and philosophically arrogant – conception of a complete break and of the possibility of a theoretical practice capable of providing the protocols for this break, he nevertheless insisted on science and ideology having different discursive modalities. Moreover, he suggested that the very process of producing the text of science – science's engagement with the process of research and confrontation with the materiality of the object – also produces a particular type of discourse. This is evident in his defence of a spontaneous materialist position related to scientific discourse. According to Althusser, in the spontaneous philosophy of scientists we can find an 'intrascientific' materialist element.

> In its most 'diffuse' form, this element represents 'convictions' or 'beliefs' stemming from the experience of scientific practice itself in its every immediacy: it is 'spontaneous'. If it is elaborated philosophically, this element can naturally take the form of Theses. These convictions-Theses are of a materialist and objectivist character. They can be broken down as follows: (1) belief in the real, external and material existence of the *object* of the scientific knowledge; (2) belief in the existence and objectivity of the *scientific knowledges* that permit knowledge of this object; (3) belief in the correctness and efficacy of the procedures of scientific experimentation, or *scientific method*, capable of producing scientific knowledge.[14]

---

13 On this see Sotiris 2011.
14 Althusser 1990, pp. 132–3.

We can therefore say that Althusser points toward the possibility of a discourse that, although it is the product of a particular subject (the scientist or the group of scientists), nevertheless takes the form of a discourse without a subject. Although subjects are the mark of the ideological, there are certain 'discursive conjunctures' when these subjects become the subject of enunciation of a discourse that is not centred on a subject.

Michel Pêcheux has suggested that Althusser's work marks the quest for a 'non-subjectivist theory of subjectivity',[15] a point that has also been made by Alain Badiou who has suggested that the challenge for Althusser was that of a subjectivity without a subject.[16] His reading of Althusser's theory of ideology is important, especially in the way he links the subject form to ideology and consequently to idealism. 'Idealism is not first an epistemological position, but above all the spontaneous operation of the *subject form*'.[17] Pêcheux has offered powerful support for the position that scientific discourse is at the same time the result of a process without a subject – in the sense that it is *produced* by a process of concept formation and experimentation – and of a discourse that refers to natural or social phenomena as 'processes without subjects'. It is

> the 'paradox' [...] of *a thought from which any subject is absent as such*, so that the concepts of science as such do not strictly speaking have a *meaning*, but rather a function in a process. 'Paradox' of a discourse and a construction (experimental devices) without a subject which [...] results in the realization that in the conceptual process of knowledge, the determination of the real (the 'exterior') and its necessity, a necessity independent of thought, is materialised in the form of an articulated body of concepts which at once *exhibits* and *suspends* the 'blind' action of this same determination as subject-effect (centring-origin-meaning), i.e., as interior without exterior – or to which the exterior is subordinate – produced by the determination of the real ('exterior') and specifically by the determination of interdiscourse as real ('exterior').[18]

For Pêcheux, the same goes for historical materialism, the *'experimental science of history'*[19] that transforms the very notion of political practice and the effectivity of the subject form. The effect of the subject form does not simply

---

15 Pêcheux 1982, p. 91.
16 Badiou 2005a.
17 Pêcheux 1982, p. 114.
18 Pêcheux 1982, p. 137.
19 Pêcheux 1982, p. 148.

disappear but 'is transformed and displaced.' In this sense, proletarian politics are not simple subjective positions. 'In other words, the empirical and spontaneous – subjective – forms of political practice operate differentially as a function of the class positions to which they correspond, and constitute the point of application of a political practice of a new type (non-subjective practice of experimentation-transformation of history developed by the masses through their organizations)'.[20]

A similar line of reasoning can also be found in Jack Amariglio's reading of Althusser's treatment of knowledge production, in which he insists that Althusser treated knowledge as a process without a subject. For Amariglio, 'Althusser reserves the term science, like Marxism (maybe *only* Marxism) for those discourses for which knowledge is not a "process with a Subject"'.[21] In similar terms, Ceren Özselçuk has suggested that Althusser's critique of the empiricism of classical political economy is also a critique of the theoretical humanism and the anthropological presuppositions of both classical political economy and humanist-historicist Marxism that 'privileg[e] a notion of the subject as origin and goal'.[22]

So if we try to expand this from the perspective of transformative political practice, we have to assume particular knowledge practices from which a non-ideological discourse and, consequently, a non-ideological view of social reality emerge. The important element is that this is a *process* involving particular subjects, individual and collective, and not a 'subjective state'. The same line of reasoning has also been suggested by Balibar in his reading of Marx's theory of revolution:

> The proletarian revolution is not conceived as an *act*, the act of the proletariat realizing its own programme or project, even though it is indeed the proletariat's political practice that accomplishes the revolution [...] The revolution is not conceived simply as an act, but as an objective *process*.[23]

Althusser himself makes an important distinction in the *Reply to John Lewis*. He insists that we should not treat the masses as a subject, with all of its idealist connotations, but as something completely different:

---

20 Pêcheux 1982, p. 150.
21 Amariglio 1987, p. 188.
22 Özselçuk 2013, p. 188.
23 Balibar 1974, p. 79.

The masses are actually *several* social classes, social strata and social categories, grouped *together* in a way which is both complex and *changing* (the positions of the different classes and strata, and of the fractions of classes within classes, *change* in the course of the revolutionary process itself). And we are dealing with huge numbers: in France or Britain, for example, with tens of millions of people, in China with hundreds of millions! Let us do no more here than ask the simple question: can we still talk about a 'subject,' identifiable by the *unity* of its 'personality'? Compared with John Lewis's subject, 'man,' as simple and neat as you can imagine, the masses, considered as a subject, pose very exacting problems of identity and identification. You cannot hold such a 'subject' in your hand, you cannot point to it. A subject is a being about which we can say: 'that's it!' How do we do that when the masses are supposed to be the 'subject'; how can we say: 'that's it'?[24]

Emilio de Ípola has commented on this point and has insisted that the basic argument of Althusser's text is that it is impossible to 'subsume under the category of the "subject" collectivities (classes, fractions of classes and social strata) composed by tens or even hundreds of millions of persons as it is the case of Europe and Asia'.[25] The very size, diversity, and heterogeneity of such collectivities renders any use of the category of the subject impossible.

For Althusser it is important never to forget that, although the masses make history, the class struggle is the motor force of history. This displacement from the centrality of the subject to the centrality of an antagonistic and inherently contradictory process marks, in my opinion, the importance of the notion of a 'process without a subject', a crucial theoretical and terminological innovation. It is not a simple reproduction of the functionalist and structuralist insistence on the systemic character of social reality. On the contrary, it suggests that what we find at the centre of the social whole is neither a simple causal mechanism nor the decision of a subject, individual or collective, but rather an open form of antagonism. This antagonism does not preclude the formation of collective subjects, but they are not self-sufficient entities since they are constantly conditioned and transformed by the terms of the struggle. In this sense, whatever collectivities engage in the struggle – political or social, and which have been described by various terms in the history of Marxism – are not 'subjects' but are particular collective 'non-subjects.'

---

24   Althusser 1976a, p. 48.
25   de Ípola 2012, p. 111.

Another important point is Althusser's elaboration on the question of Marxism's influence on proletarian ideology. In the 1970s Althusser insisted that the emergence of Marxism does not only lead to a new science but also has repercussions for mass ideological recognition. It is possible to have ideological interpellations – that is, interpellations of intellectuals as subjects – that are informed and transformed by a scientific and non-ideological discourse, such as historical materialism. This can lead to collective non-subjects endowed with a transformed subjectivity or subjective awareness of social reality.

In the 1976 'Note on the ISAs', Althusser insisted on '*the primacy of class struggle over the dominant ideology* and *the Ideological State Apparatuses*'[26] and on the possibility of proletarian ideology being a different ideology because of its infusion with elements of Marxism as scientific knowledge and because of the concrete historical experiences of struggle. For Althusser, proletarian ideology after the emergence of Marxism is a special form of ideology. It is an ideology in the sense of an interpellation of individuals as subjects – to be precise, as '*militant*-subjects'[27] – but it is informed both by the historical experiences of proletarian struggles and also by Marxist theory. '*It is therefore a very special kind of ideology*. It is an ideology, because at the level of the masses, it functions the way any ideology does (by interpellating individuals as subjects). It is, however, steeped in historical experiences illuminated by scientific principles of analysis. It presents itself as one of the forms of the fusion of the worker's movement with Marxist theory'.[28]

Althusser, however, did not elaborate much on how this conception of ideology, Marxist theory, and the primacy of class struggle in theory and ideology were related to the question of the political party apart from an appeal to opening up the party to contradictions and the opinions of the rank and file.[29]

4   Political Organisations and Collectivities as Knowledge Processes and Forms of Collective Intellectuality

In order to deal with this question we must go back to Lenin's and Gramsci's conceptions of the political party. I suggest that one can find in their writings a relational and procedural conception of the party, in the sense of the party as a knowledge process.

---

26   Althusser 2014b, p. 220.
27   Althusser 2014b, p. 227.
28   Althusser 2014b, p. 228.
29   Althusser 1978c.

In one possible reading of Lenin's classic texts on the need for a break with economism and spontaneism (such as in *What Is To Be Done?*), I think that we can see elements of a certain political theory of knowledge, or of a theory of political knowledge. The emphasis on the party and on the need for a separate organisation of 'professional revolutionaries' is not a proto-Stalinist conception of a party with iron discipline. It is not primarily an elitist conception of revolutionary theory injected into the workers' movement from the outside. It is mainly a conception of political strategy as informed by correct knowledge of the terrain of the struggle – this knowledge being itself a stake of class struggle because of the constant and recurring influences of dominant ideology. The response to this is not just a subjective stance; that would be exactly *Stalinism* in the sense of a bureaucratic conception of the political line. The response is to understand that the party is a particular apparatus, a mechanism, and a process. Adherence to the party, the exigencies that implies, and the way political strategies and choices are developed within the party all mark the possibility to counter bourgeois ideology and put in practice a revolutionary form of politics. In this sense the party is not a subject; it is an apparatus and a process that *produces* knowledge, strategy, and informed forms of subjectivity.

An even more advanced conception of the political party not as a 'subject' but as a *collective* knowledge process can be found in Gramsci's work, the thinker par excellence of intellectuality in politics. Gramsci's conception of the political party as a modern Prince marks exactly his distance from a traditional conception of political subjectivity: 'The protagonist of the new Prince could not in the modern epoch be an individual hero, but only the political party'.[30] I would like to insist that in Gramsci's discourse the party is always something more than a subject or a collectivity. It is always an apparatus, a mechanism, and a complex process, even if the phrasing of his discourse might seem to suggest that a party is a subject.

Gramsci's conception of intellectuality as an integral aspect of all forms of human practical activity is very important in my opinion. For Gramsci, '[t]here is no human activity from which every form of intellectual participation can be excluded [...] The problem of creating a new stratum of intellectuals consists therefore in the critical elaboration of the intellectual activity that exists in everyone'.[31] That is why the political party is exactly the apparatus that enables this kind of critical mass intellectuality.

---

30   Q13 § 21; *SPN*, p. 147.
31   Q12, § 3; *SPN*, p. 9.

> The political party for some social group is nothing other than their specific way of elaborating their own category of organic intellectuals directly in the political and philosophical field [...] it is responsible for welding together the organic intellectuals of a given group – the dominant one – and the traditional intellectuals [...] That all members of a political party should be regarded as intellectuals is an affirmation that can easily lend itself to mockery and caricature. But if one thinks about it nothing can be more exact.[32]

Gramsci stresses the importance of this critical mass intellectuality and the need to see the importance of the dialectic of theory and praxis. The political party is a critical *laboratory* of new forms of intellectuality:

> One should stress the importance and significance which, in the modern world, political parties have in the elaboration and diffusion of conceptions of the world, because essentially what they do is to work out the ethics and the politics corresponding to these conceptions and act as it were as their historical 'laboratory'.[33]

Gramsci is very concerned with mass critical intellectuality as an important stake in the politics of emancipation. The mass character of this intellectuality refers both to the process of its formation and also to the results it produces in the sense of a change in the ideological, 'moral', and intellectual balance of forces. 'For a mass of people to be led to think coherently and in the same coherent fashion about the real present world is a "philosophical" event far more important and "original" than the discovery by some philosophical "genius" of a truth which remains the property of small groups of intellectuals'.[34] This, in turn, is related to Gramsci's conception of political practice and political agency. His emphasis is on collectivities, on historical blocs instead of political 'subjects' in the more traditional conception:

> An historical act can only be performed by 'collective man,' and this presupposes the attainment of a 'cultural-social' unity through which a multiplicity of dispersed wills, with heterogeneous aims, are welded together with a single aim, on the basis of an equal and common conception of the world, both general and particular, operating in transitory bursts (in

---

32   Q12, §1; *SPN*, pp. 15–16.
33   Q11, §12; *SPN*, p. 335.
34   Q11, §12; *SPN*, p. 325.

emotional ways) or permanently (where the intellectual base is so well rooted, assimilated and experienced that it becomes passion).[35]

This makes necessary a new form of intellectual. The important distinction in these new intellectuals has to do with their awareness of the limits of their own subjectivity and their need to engage in collective political practices and knowledge practices, which are the necessary conditions for their critical intellectual activity. This conception of a non-subjective or postsubjective condition of intellectuality is made evident in Gramsci's elaborations on the figure of the *democratic philosopher*:

> The historical personality of an individual philosopher is also given by the active relationship that exists between him and the cultural environment he is proposing to modify. The environment reacts back on the philosopher and imposes on him a continual process of self-criticism. It is his 'teacher.' This is why one of the most important demands that the modern intelligentsias have made in the political field has been that of the so-called 'freedom of thought and of the expression of thought' [...] For the relation between master and disciple in the general sense referred to above is only realised where this political condition exists, and only then do we get the 'historical' realisation of a new type of philosopher, whom we can call a 'democratic philosopher' in the sense that he is a personality not limited to himself as a physical individual but is an active social relationship of modification of the cultural environment.[36]

It is exactly this notion of the intellectual as 'an active social relationship of modification of the social environment' that marks the crucial originality of Gramsci's conception of intellectuality and its relation to mass political practices and processes of political organisation. As Peter Thomas notes:

> As an historical experimenter in philosophy, as much educated as educator, the figure of the democratic philosopher represents the maximum concentration and intensification of the determining coordinates of a proletarian intellectuality capable of absorbing and providing direction to the experiences of its class.[37]

---

35 Q10II, § 44; *SPN*, p. 349.
36 Q10II, § 44; *SPN*, p. 350.
37 Thomas 2009, p. 435.

A similar conception of the party as a knowledge process occurs in Mao's writings on the need to return constantly to the masses – their ideas and experiences – as a way to actually produce political knowledge.

> In all the practical work of our Party, all correct leadership is necessarily 'from the masses, to the masses.' This means: take the ideas of the masses (scattered and unsystematic ideas) and concentrate them (through study turn them into concentrated and systematic ideas), then go to the masses and propagate and explain these ideas until the masses embrace them as their own, hold fast to them and translate them into action, and test the correctness of these ideas in such action. Then once again concentrate ideas from the masses and once again go to the masses so that the ideas are persevered in and carried through. And so on, over and over again in an endless spiral, with the ideas becoming more correct, more vital and richer each time. Such is the Marxist theory of knowledge.[38]

Also of great importance here is Mao's conception of self-criticism. It is not a simple instrumental practice of the correction of the political line. I think it is a profound thinking about the limits of political awareness in the terrain of the struggle amidst conditions of ideological class struggle, of the inevitability of deviation, and of the impossibility of finding 'Archimedean' points in a particular social and political conjuncture. Consequently, it is necessary to act as if one is always in the possibility of error, and therefore one is in constant need of being open to criticism and self-criticism. This is a particular ethics of political subjectivity that insists on the need to always remember its own limits and attempt to overcome them, and it incorporates the displacements that are always inherent in a political process traversed by social antagonism.

I think that what emerges from a critical reading of Lenin's, Gramsci's, and Mao's writings on the political party is a novel way to think political agency and subjectivity. In this conception it is the very process of creating forms of political agency and intervention that conditions political subjectivity, in a non-linear manner that includes constant confrontation with the terrain of the struggle, the continuous production of new knowledge, and recurring processes of self-criticism and correction. It is a collective process of producing militant subjectivities, based not on a variation of the 'sovereign' reflexive subject of the Enlightenment tradition but on the constant apprehension of the

---

38   Mao 1967, p. 119.

limits and displacements of political subjectivity and of the need to subject oneself to processes of collective engagement and intervention.

It is interesting to note that in the history of philosophy a certain conception of democratic collective critical intellectuality can also be found in the work of Spinoza as part of his broader conception of human sociability. First of all Spinoza in fact had a complex and relational conception of individuality. As Vittorio Morfino has stressed, 'for Spinoza the individual is neither substance nor subject (neither *ousia* nor *hypokeimenon*): the individual is a relation between an outside and an inside paradoxically constituted by this very relation (for Spinoza, there is no absolute interiority of the *cogito* opposed to the absolute exteriority of a world in which my own body is included)'.[39]

André Tosel has also stressed that in Spinoza we move beyond both methodological individualism and methodological holism. Spinoza also insisted on dealing with singular political forms, themselves complex and composed. Consequently the there is a 'relational ontology' in politics[40] that leads to a 'permanent process of politicisation of the social and socialisation of politics'.[41]

Pierre-François Moreau has shown the importance of the affective dimension in his reading of the role of the passions in the constant forming and reforming of social relations. According to Moreau's reading, the passions for Spinoza are both 'intra- and interindividual',[42] their force 'constitutes the effective reality of [natural] law',[43] and (contra Hobbes) their effectivity is not suspended after the establishment of the social contract. This can account for the very complexity of the state, of its institutions and their practices, in the sense of 'complex parts united' by complex relations.[44] For Moreau the same affective dimension is necessary in order to understand the symbolic order that makes citizens adhere to their communities.[45] In a similar line, Hadi Rizk has stressed, in his comparative reading of Spinoza and Sartre, the role of common passions in the formation of social forms.[46] In this sense we are dealing not with a simple *opposition* between the passions and reason within society and the state but with a much more complex conception of social and political *praxis* that can account for the possibility of new 'lasting encounters' as new social

---

39 Morfino 2015a, p. 63.
40 Tosel 2008, p. 114.
41 Tosel 2008, p. 117.
42 Moreau 1994, p. 382.
43 Moreau 1994, p. 411.
44 Moreau 1994, p. 454.
45 Moreau 1994, p. 459.
46 Rizk 1992.

configurations based on emancipation and justice, positive common passions, and new forms of collective intellectuality.

This complex and relational conception of both social praxis and political form makes up the basis of Spinoza's well-known insistence on established political power (*potestas*) being nothing other than an alienated form of the actual and effective power of the masses (*potentia*) conceived as collective potential and productivity.[47] And this can account for Spinoza's insistence that, in the democratic politics of the multitude, judgements can be produced that isolated individuals would otherwise have been incapable of making. Warren Montag has suggested that 'because the power of thought of the many is necessarily greater than that of the few', for Spinoza 'it is correspondingly more likely for the multitude to follow the course of reason than for the few'.[48] This is most obvious in the following passage from the *Political Treatise*: 'The fact is that men's wits are too obtuse to get straight to the heart of every question, but by discussing, listening to others, and debating, their wits are sharpened, and by exploring every avenue they eventually discover what they are seeking, something that meets with general approval and that no one had previously thought of'.[49]

In a similar vein, Balibar has shown the importance of knowledge as political praxis within Spinoza's conception of democracy, exactly because 'communication is structured by relationships of ignorance and knowledge, superstition, and ideological antagonism'.[50] The sequence of social forms and arrangements can also be thought of as a sequence of different '*regime[s] of communication* (affective, economic and intellectual)'.[51] Consequently, the 'democratisation of knowledge' can be identified as the 'decisive mechanism' for the creation of new forms of social emancipation. This gives a new dimension to the need for new forms of mass critical intellectuality.

Likewise, Hasana Sharp has drawn our attention to the importance of Spinoza's theory of affects as a way to rethink human agency and collective practice in a much more complex way, avoiding the problems associated with traditional conceptions of the 'subject'.

> With Spinoza's theory of affect, we have a comprehensive redefinition of human agency. More than an affirmation of our corporeality, Spinoza's

---

47   Matheron 2011, pp. 67–9.
48   Montag 1999, p. 81.
49   Spinoza 2002, p. 746.
50   Balibar 1998, p. 98.
51   Balibar 1998, p. 124.

theory of affect gives rise to a notion of agency that is in no way exclusively human. The conception of the human that emerges is a being around whom lines cannot be definitively drawn and whose powers cannot be pre-emptively defined. As he insists on the inability of the mind to master its body, he declares that 'no one has yet determined what the body can do' (*E* III p2s). Mind–body identity entails that, likewise, no one knows what the mind can do. These limitless possibilities ascribed to mind and body include not only those we call human but also the ideal and corporeal powers of beasts, computers, and collectivities.[52]

And this means that we should not limit the conception of the production of a non-subjectivist and collective, militant and self-critical intellectuality only to political parties or other traditional political forms. Hardt and Negri have insisted on the creative, affective, and insurrectionary aspects inscribed in what they define as the biopolitics of the multitude, including how both current 'biopolitical' forms of capitalist production tend also to produce antagonistic subjectivities. Consequently, for Hardt and Negri, current movements also include a 'struggle over the control or autonomy of the production of subjectivity. The multitude makes itself by composing in the common the singular subjectivities that result from this process'.[53] This leads them to suggest a combination of insurrection and institution, thus entering into a very interesting dialogue with Gramsci:

> The making of the multitude and the composition and consolidation of its capacities for democratic decision making in revolutionary institutions is exactly the kind of production of subjectivity that Gramsci sees as necessary for an active rather than passive revolution. Such a return to the Leninist Gramsci on the biopolitical terrain allows us to bring together the seemingly divergent strands of his thought. We are not faced with an alternative – either insurrection or institutional struggle, either passive or active revolution. Instead revolution must simultaneously be both insurrection and institution, structural and superstructural transformation. This is the path of the 'becoming-Princ' of the multitude.[54]

These questions are not simply theoretical; they are also relevant to important questions in contemporary struggles. It is not only necessary to think this pro-

---

52   Sharp 2011. p. 23.
53   Hardt and Negri 2009, p. x.
54   Hardt and Negri 2009, p. 367.

cess of creating collective militant intellectualities in terms of the party form; it is also necessary in relation to various forms of collective action. I think that it is crucial not only to establish forms of democracy and openness within existing political formations – in contrast to the hierarchical character of the party in the Leninist tradition – but also to experiment with those collective practices that would turn movements and collectivities into sites producing militant intellectualities, both in the sense of critical and politically engaged theoretical production oriented toward projects for emancipation and in the sense of mass intellectuality and a change in common sense and mass ideological practices. Social movements, especially when they are politicised in a collective and non-hierarchical manner, are also knowledge processes. People engaging in them learn from the very collective experience of struggle. Consequently, we need to go beyond any relation of externality between the movement and critical theory and build new institutions of knowledge within the movement itself: new knowledge practices and new forms of militant research. This will help us to produce new readings of the conjuncture and also to discuss new projects and alternative social forms.[55]

Despite the limits and contradictions of Althusser's theorisation of political subjectivity, a simple return to an ethics of the subject would be a theoretical retreat. The alternative is not some mechanistic conception of simple structural determination, but rather a return to the possibility of theorising the *production* of political knowledge, political subjectivity, and mass critical intellectuality within forms of collective political militancy and intervention.

---

55   For a more expanded form of the argument suggested here, see Sotiris 2013.

CHAPTER 21

The Limits of Althusserian Politics

From the survey of Althusser's confrontation with questions of politics, political practice and organisation, I think one can realise, at the same time, the political character of Althusser's theoretical endeavour, the politics of his theoretical intervention, but also the limits of this effort.

Althusser's refusal, until a very late stage, when it was impossible for him to continue to be a public intellectual, to think of revolutionary politics outside the Party through new forms of social and political struggle, his self-limiting to a politics of theory, which is the common denominator of both the idealism and scientism of the initial attempt toward a theoretical correction of a political line and the later emphasis on the relation between class struggle and theory, his inability to think through and not simply acknowledge the crisis of the communist movement, his tendency (as part of the 'bending of the stick to the other side' strategy) to discard concepts and theorists that offered important insights (his rejection of Gramsci, and the unease towards Poulantzas's positions, to cite some examples), and above all the huge difficulty of thinking, in terms of a radically novel strategy for proletarian hegemony, all these can account for the impossibility of Althusserian politics. If we try to simply project or articulate Althusser's interventions, in their complex and uneven development, into a coherent strategy, we will soon realise that in this sense there can be no Althusserian politics. Althusser's own silences exemplify this.

However, there are also theoretical limits that we must take into consideration. Mainly these have to do with the very complexity of class politics. Althusser, in many cases, thinks in terms of a rather schematic conception of the working class as a revolutionary force. The contradictions of the actual 'social and political composition' of the working class, to borrow the terms of the workerists, in most cases are not dealt with. This leads to the simplistic opposition between powerful movements on the one hand and communist political parties in crisis on the other. By contrast, what is needed is also a conception of a crisis of both political organisations and the state. Because the crisis of the communist movement and the Left, especially in Europe, at the beginning of the neoliberal era cannot be described in terms of a contradiction between powerful movements and parties without strategy. A series of defeats of the labour movement, the beginning of a process of capitalist restructuring, the subsequent unleashing of the first wave of neoliberal reforms, some of them by social-democratic governments, along with processes of fragmentation and displacement of strongholds of labour militancy and radical politics, created the conditions for a double crisis of both the Left and the labour movement, eroding collective representations that were more favourable to left-wing politics, creating new fragmentations and posing the challenge of re-founding social alliances. And this can account for another contradiction of Althusser's interventions in the 1970s. Although he opposed what he saw as a right-wing deviation, he nevertheless did not distance himself from a dominant conception, shared by most Western European communist parties, namely that the situation was ripe for 'progressive' change under the influence of a strong Left and the initiative of the popular masses, but it did not entail the possibility of more radical or revolutionary change, nor did it confront the open questions regarding what might be described as the second defeat of the revolution in the West. Even his political and theoretical confrontation with the positions of 'left-wing euro-communists' such as Poulantzas tended to take more the form of a drawing of lines of demarcation than an actual articulation of an alternative strategy to Poulantzas's version of the 'democratic road to socialism'.

Moreover, Althusser has no concept of 'historical bloc', in the sense of a social or even worse electoral alliance, but of the potential complex dialectic of social alliance, political programme, organisation and revolutionary strategy.[1] This

---

[1] Traditionally the concept of the historical bloc has been read as referring simply to the articulation of base and superstructure or material practice and ideology. Some of Gramsci's own references suggest such a reading, such as the one referring to the historical bloc as 'the unity between nature and spirit (structure and superstructure)' (Q13, §10; *SPN*, p. 137). But I also think that it would be much better to define it as the description of the social, political, and ideological processes and conditions that can lead to a social class – or an alliance of social classes – becoming a historical force of transformation, through the dialectic of ideology, practice, and strategy. In this sense it is also a position about the complexity of the social whole as the terrain of political intervention. This is my reading of Gramsci's reference that '[s]tructures and superstructures form a "historical bloc". That is to say the complex contradictory and discordant ensemble of the superstructures is the reflection of the ensemble of the social relations of production' (Q8, §182; *SPN*, p. 366). This possible reading is reinforced in my opinion by Gramsci's insistence that in his conception of the historical bloc 'material forces are the content and ideologies are the form, though this distinction between form and content has purely didactic value, since the material forces would be inconceivable historically without form and the ideologies would be individual fancies without the material forces' (Q7, §21; *SPN*, p. 377). Moreover, the full force of Gramsci's conception of the historical bloc not simply as a reference to the relation between structures and superstructures, but – and mainly – to the processes, practices, and conditions (in terms of economics, politics, ideology, and mass intellectuality) that make possible hegemony and consequently social transformation, comes to the fore in extracts like the following. 'If the relationship between intellectuals and people-nation, between the leaders and the led [...] is provided by an organic cohesion

adds to the limits of Althusser's thinking of the political party. His insistence on the need for revolutionary parties to be open and democratic and in a relation to social movements that not only respects their autonomy but also acknowledges the importance of the dynamics and knowledge coming from them, are surely necessary starting points. But what is missing is a conception of the party as a laboratory of mass intellectualities in the sense suggested by Gramsci. Moreover, Althusser in most of his interventions thought about the process of restarting the communist project more in terms of a left-wing self-reform of communist parties through a combination of theoretical renovation and radicalism coming from the movements. What is missing is exactly the need for a complex and uneven process of a 'refoundation' of the communist movement through the political and organisational articulation and synthesis, in necessarily new political forms, of various anti-capitalist collective experiences, social, political, theoretical, with the aim of rethinking the possibility of communist politics and working-class hegemony. And if this was already becoming evident in the 1980s, with the full eruption of the crisis of Western European communism (along with the decline and collapse of Soviet 'socialism'), it subsequently became more urgent than ever.

But the fact that there can be no Althusserian politics does not mean that there is no use to be made of Althusser's work in any attempt to rethink radical and even revolutionary politics today.

First of all, revolutionary politics – and politics in general – is not the expression or manifestation of laws of history or some form of metaphysical grounding. Nor does it entail simply waiting for the unexpected. Politics means intervening in the conjuncture, its dynamics, working towards lasting encounters. It is the dialectic of attempting to influence or affect the conjuncture while at the same time being constantly conditioned by its aleatory (in)determinacy. In this sense, revolutionary politics is always dealing with the exception, the singular case, the specific conjuncture, the necessarily aleatory character of a historically specific balance of forces. Knowledge of structural (namely durable) tendencies and determinations is necessary, it provides an apprehension of the terrain of struggle, but at a certain moment revolutionary politics actually demands that we seize the moment and make choices without guarantees. This also means that a certain – and uneven – dialectic is at play here: revolutionary politics includes both the patient work of the *longue durée*

---

in which feeling-passion becomes understanding and thence knowledge (not mechanically but in a way that is alive), then and only then is the relation one of representation. Only then [...] can the shared life be realized, which alone is a social force – with the creation of the "historical bloc"' (Q11, § 67; *SPN*, p. 418).

of organisation building, education, alliance forming, creating ties and relations of representation (Gramsci's war of position), as well as the ability to act, even unprepared, in conditions that at the same time seem promising and unripe.

Secondly, revolutionary politics cannot be centred on the state, despite the importance of state power in the articulation of political power. If Marxism performs a certain theoretical short-circuit between economics and politics, going beyond their division in bourgeois politics, then communist politics aims simultaneously at and beyond the state; it is a new practice of politics, not simply a different content or a different political line. Aiming at political and governmental power must always be accompanied with the experimentation with forms of counter-power from below, autonomous spaces of the movements, forms of self-management, experimentation with new productive practices, in a relation of autonomy to the state even if they receive some form of institutional recognition: in short, what one might describe as a contemporary form of dual power. Certain forms of self-organisation and coordination practiced in today's movements along with networks of solidarity and various forms of community building can be considered embryonic forms of a potential dual power. It means at the same time a socialisation of politics (the intrusion of social movements at the level of decision making, extended forms of social and workers' control, extended forms of popular participation in areas such as the justice system, experimentation with forms of representation based on work or class determination instead of abstract citizenship), and an extended politicisation of the social (the political struggle for the transformation of productive practices, the extended powers of labour collectivities, new forms of self-management). At the same time, the revolutionary process cannot be reduced to the unstable co-existence of the state and forms of popular power or self-management. In the end, a process of deep revolutionary transformation of state apparatuses is more than necessary, which must include new forms of direct democracy, institutionalised forms of social and worker control, and a dismantling of the repressive apparatus: in short, a process that revolutionises the state and 'destroys' its class character in directions that go beyond the limits of the liberal constitutional tradition.

Thirdly, political parties and organisations cannot be considered as bearers of political truths. They are more like nodal points and political procedures that can help the elaboration of a political line. The force of the movement can also be a determinant factor in politics; it can even be the 'epistemological condition' of determining a correct line in a given conjuncture. Parties and organisations must be open to the dynamics and the contradictions coming from actual struggles, must find ways to incorporate them into their internal political process, and must avoid any simplistic conception of being the vanguard. And this gives another dimension to the question to intra-Party democracy. It is not simply a question of free discussion or of militants' rights; this would remain well within a 'juridical' or 'parliamentary' conception of politics. Party democracy is necessary in order for it to be an open and necessarily contradictory process of elaboration of social and political dynamics into political line and programme. Revisiting the question of the Party form remains an urgent task today, in a period when what is needed is not only resistance and struggle but, at least in some 'weak links of the chain', (counter-)hegemonic projects, programmes, concrete utopias and alternative narratives for the future of whole societies, along with a new and fresh conception of the party-form. Above all we must think of radical left parties, political fronts and organisations as knowledge practices and laboratories of new forms of mass critical intellectuality. In a period of economic and political crisis but also of new possibilities to challenge capitalist rule, questions of political organisation gain new relevance. Thinking of organisation simply in terms of practical or of communicative skills for mobilisation or of electoral fronts and tactics is not enough. We need forms of organisation that not only enable coordination and networking, democratic discussion and effective campaigning, but also bring together different experiences, combine critical theory with the knowledge coming from the different sites of struggle, and are also learning processes that produce both concrete analyses but also mass ideological practises and new forms of radical 'common sense'.

Fourthly, the ability of Marxism to be of actual use in revolutionary politics is itself determined by class struggle. Marxism is not the negation of proletarian ideology (in the sense of the complex ensemble of practical knowledge, representation, visions of emancipation arising from the economic, social, and political practices of the subaltern classes), nor is it a simple elaboration, projection, and theoretical articulation of proletarian ideology. It is the result of a transformation of the ideological representations of the subaltern classes, the gaps and contradictions in 'dominant ideology', the inherent contradictions of the theoretical and ideological elements that accompanied the rise of the bourgeoisie to hegemony and its traumatic encounter with proletarian resistance. Consequently, Marxism is never a complete theory; it is necessarily ridden with contradictions, open questions, and theoretical lacunae. We cannot think of its evolution outside of the history of the workers' movement, nor is it possible to imagine its development without the 'experimental processes' presented by actual struggles and collective experiences. We cannot deny the existence of open questions and whole areas that have not been dealt with theoretically. In this sense, Althusser's tormented realisation of the limits of Marxism as an unfinished theoretical project is more pertinent today than ever. Accepting this is a necessary condition of initiating a process of renovation of Marxist theory.

Fifthly, the possibility that things can go in the wrong direction is always greater. The elaboration of political lines and strategies on the part of movements and the political left is always a stake of the actual balance of forces. The long history of the crises of the communist movement exemplifies how easy it is to move to the logic or the terrain of the opponent, in most cases unconsciously. This is the logic of deviation; it describes a material tendency or potentiality, not a 'mistake' or a 'sin'. That is why criticism and self-criticism, both theoretical and political, is a necessary element of any potential revolutionary politics. If there are no 'Archimedean' points in a particular social and political conjuncture, it is necessary to act as if one is always in the possibility of error, and therefore in constant need to be open to criticism and self-criticism. It is the only way to come to terms with the recurring possibility of deviation or of wrong political choices. This is necessary not only in theory, in the sense of how to deal with the necessarily 'scissionist' character of Marxism, but also in politics and the elaboration of the political line, strategy, and tactics. And this process of criticism and self-criticism can never be limited to 'intra-party' debate and democracy, but should also include all the common space between the movement and political forms, in an attempt to actually be subject to the 'criticism of the masses' (and to learn from them).

These are starting points that one can find in the long trajectory of Althusser's theoretical and in the last instance political confrontation with questions of communist politics. And they are still valid and necessary. Even Althusser's own shortcomings are useful in this regard.

Although an Althusserian politics never actually existed, a confrontation with Althusser's theoretical trajectory remains indispensable for anyone wishing to rethink revolutionary politics today. Current developments and the worldwide return of mass protest and radical demands show that indeed history has more imagination than us.

Conclusion

The extent of the influence of Althusser in the Marxist – and not only Marxist – debates of the last 50 years provides ample reason for attempting to come to terms with his theoretical and political significance. This can also account for the recurring interest in his work by consecutive waves of Marxist scholars. The reason for this continuous confrontation with Althusser's work lies in the importance and urgency of the questions with which he engaged.

One might say that the main strength of Althusser's theoretical endeavour has less to do with the answers he sought to offer – most of them provisional and tentative, always subject to almost immediate correction and, in some cases, negation; rather, it has to do with the questions themselves. It was exactly this manner of stressing questions and of questioning answers that were taken as given that defined Althusser's intervention from the very outset. The special status of Marxist philosophy in relation to Marxist science; the scientificity of Marxism as a science of history; the status of philosophy as a theoretical and political operation; the particular status of social relations as structures and/or conjunctural encounters; the theory of ideology as a production of subjectivities and forms of subjection; the question of human essence and of theoretical humanism; the question of teleology and direction in history; all these represent crucial open questions and points of bifurcation or even scission and conflict, which, in one way or another, traverse both Marxism and much of contemporary critical social theory and philosophy. In this sense, even as a confrontation with a very harsh and difficult testing ground, such a theoretical trajectory retains its importance. It is a path that anyone wishing to confront the challenge of a materialist practice of philosophy must follow even they do not wish to follow the answers proffered by Althusser.

The first major contribution of Althusser lies in the rethinking of materialism or a *materialist position* in theory and politics. Althusser's materialism is in no sense an ontological and metaphysical materialism. Nor is it simply a theory of social activity or of praxis, at least not of praxis in the more or less phenomenological sense of intentional and more or less conscious activity. Rather, it is a relational materialism of singularities and singular encounters and of the apparatuses and rituals that make them lasting and reproduce them as 'structures' which remain, however, always open to change and transformation. Althusser's materialism is also the absence of any form of teleology of any form of historical direction. Idealism in Althusser is never simply about spiritualism or belief in the autonomous existence of ideas; rather it is about any form of metaphysical thinking, even in materialist guise, from empiricist 'realism' to historicist teleology. History in this sense is never a unified narrative, but an open terrain of struggles under constant transformation. Moreover, this conception also redefines a materialist position within the sciences. Althusser always rejected any empiricist conception of knowledge in the sense of any possibility of a direct contact with the reality of any presence of the real or the empirical within knowledge. In a certain Spinozist conception of knowledge, the knowledge process always begins within ideology and only through conceptual breaks, on the ground of the inherently contradictory and antagonistic terrain of ideology, breaks, and ruptures that are in many cases unintended, something that can account for the reproduction of various 'spontaneous philosophies of the sciences'. Consequently, knowledge is always a result, a possible outcome, in a certain sense the product of a 'process without a subject'. In this sense 'objectivity' is produced and is never taken as a given, the 'given' taken as always the expression of ideological miscognition. Its production is never simply the result of 'theoretical processes of production' – this is in a certain sense the 'theoreticism' of Althusser's early texts; it also has to do with all forms of practices, it is the result of how practices irrupt the closure of the ideological terrain producing knowledge as a result in a never-ending process. In this sense, class struggles and antagonism also have a knowledge effect insofar as it is exactly the materiality of struggle, confrontation, and antagonism that undermines the tendency of the ideological towards closure and suture.

However, it is in this thinking of the materiality of immanent singularity that we can see both the strength and the limitation of Althusser. However important it might be as a corrective to metaphysical thinking, at the same time it runs the risk of an atomisation of reality. It is here that one aspect of Althusser's inability to come to terms with Gramsci becomes plainly evident, namely the theoretical importance of Gramsci's conception of hegemony. If hegemony, in its broadest sense, deals with the ways in which the multitude of singular social practices, the 'molecular' aspect, always emphasised by Gramsci, is transformed into class projects providing a non-metaphysical way of transforming singular practices into historical tendencies.

In light of this conception of a materialist position we can also consider Althusser's attempt to rethink the dialectic. For Althusser the dialectic is never about simply a theory of the self-becoming of an essence, either historical or cosmological. His philosophical coming of age being mainly a confrontation with a variety of historicist, Hegelian Marxism, he always drew a line of demarcation with any move towards such a hypostatisation of the dialectic, which represented for him pure metaphysics. The dialectic for Althusser is an extension of materiality, in the sense defined above, that is, of how to confront social relationality as antagonism and encounter, as constant singular encounters and constitutive antagonisms. Althusser's later evolution, especially in the form of aleatory materialism, seems like an abandonment of any form of the dialectic, the chance encounter or the contingent aleatory sequence making impossible any 'labour of the negative'. However, this does not imply a substitution of the dialectic by a variation of the Pascalian wager. Rather, Althusser attempts to make sure that any conception of the dialectic, that is, the incorporation in theory of the efficacy of always overdetermined practices, struggles, and antagonisms, is devoid of any metaphysical directionality. In this sense, for Althusser a dialectical thinking is never an attempt to think of History in general; rather, it is what he defined in *Machiavelli and Us* as thinking *under* the conjuncture, that is, a thinking that not only confronts an open and overdetermined terrain of struggles and encounters, but is also itself traversed by the very contradictory tendencies and 'lines of flight' that are active within this terrain. That is why Althusser from the beginning introduces overdetermination, that is, the thinking of the conjuncture in its singularity, a dialectical aspect par excellence, in sharp contrast to any essentialist conception of the dialectic. In this sense, a dialectical thinking in Althusser is never a thinking about how conceptual transformations attempt to 'express' actual historical processes; rather it is a constant discursive intervention, in the form of a constant 'bending of the stick to the other side', to use one of Althusser's favourite metaphors of Lenin. A materialist practice of philosophy, attempting to draw lines of demarcation while at the same time intrinsically interwoven with the terrain in which it intervenes, is thus a dialectical practice. However, the dialectical practice *par excellence* is *political practice*, the constitutive political gesture that can enable the emergence of new social and political forms out of any conjuncture. The constant distancing of Althusser from any conception of the dialectic, towards the immanent dynamics of the contradictions of the conjuncture, towards a thinking of the constitutive political gesture that creates new forms out of the void of the conjuncture, is not simply a theoretical displacement. Rather it is a political realisation of the extent of the crisis of historical forms of the working-class movement, as a result of both capitalist counter-offensives and the crisis of the communist movement. That is why the dialectical or non-dialectical character of any conjuncture is not a question of theoretical choice; rather it is itself a political stake, a different balance of forces in the conjuncture.

All this can also account for another of Althusser's major preoccupations, namely his conception of Marxism itself as a terrain of struggle. In Althusser's entire trajectory, even at the height of the theoreticism of High Althusserianism, there is an acute apprehension of the struggles traversing Marxism. The very notion of the epistemological break is a philosophical conceptualisation of the politics of theory and the political stake inherent in the emergence of any potentially scientific theory. Althusser's topography of the constant interplay of class struggle, ideology, philosophy, and scientific theory is a highly original conception of the emergence of a scientific theory as an overdetermined conceptual and ideological 'war of positions'. In the case of Marxism, as a series of always unfinished breaks, this means the terrain of social and ideological struggle upon which Marxism enters and intervenes, is, in turn, internalised in Marxism itself, as the constant efficacy of antagonistic tendencies. Here lies the importance of Althusser's conception of Marxism – and psychoanalysis – as 'scissionist sciences', as sciences that intervene and intensify contradictions and antagonisms traversing the social body, inducing important political and ideological transformations and potentially revolutions, causing constant counterattacks and attempts towards both annihilation and incorporation, while at the same time internalising these contradictions, antagonisms, and counterattacks. One might also say that Althusser offers here a potential theory of 'revisionism', not in the theological sense of a flight from 'orthodoxy' but of the actuality – tragically documented in the history of the working-class movement – of such an internalisation of the counterattacks that it ends up as simply an apologia for repressive and exploitative social relations. In contrast to any attempt to find some political and ideological 'safety' in the supposed theoretical vigour of Marxism, Althusser suggest that we must go the opposite way. Not only face the unfinished, overdetermined, contradictory, and crisis-prone character of Marxism, but also embrace and accept it as an inescapable point of departure. In a strange resonance with Gramscian themes, the answer to the open questions and limits of theory can never be theoretical; only the actual *revolutionäre Praxis* of the working-class movement can offer tentative answers in its very attempt to materialise an alternative to capitalist exploitation.

Althusser never ceased to be a philosopher. In all the evolution of his conception of philosophy, from the Theory of theoretical practice, to philosophy as in the last instance class struggle in theory, to the poetics of aleatory materialism, he never ceased to stress the importance and necessity of philosophy as a distinct theoretical and political practice for any emancipatory political project. Althusser's project was never about simply 'deconstructing' idealist philosophy; it was about facing the inescapability of philosophy. Philosophy, for Althusser, is a necessity. It is an unavoidable terrain of theoretical, ideological, and in the last instance political struggle, since as he showed the contradictions traversing the encounter of science, ideology, and class struggle necessarily take the form of philosophical questions, both conscious and 'spontaneous'. At the same time, it is a necessary terrain, since only philosophy can serve as the laboratory of concepts and worldview, the testing ground and the experimental site not only of forms of dominant class hegemony, but also of forms, practices, discursive tropes, argumentation strategies, and theoretical interventions that can liberate the potential to actually think the practices, struggles, and counter-hegemonic projects arising out of the struggles of the subaltern classes. This practice of philosophy, this new materialist practice of philosophy, in tandem with a new practice of politics, is antagonistic to the tendency of traditional idealist philosophy to incorporate and annul these dynamics, and attempts to liberate dynamics, to liberate practices, to liberate discourses in an attempt to think the extreme, the not yet possible, the actual alternative. In this sense, a materialist practice of philosophy is the attempt to think communism *par excellence*; it can be by itself a communist political practice. This is both the challenge and the responsibility of anyone attempting to think what it means to be a communist in philosophy.

Louis Althusser lived, wrote, and died a communist philosopher. This was his work. This is his legacy. This is the challenge we still face today. Not just as intellectuals, but as part of a broader movement to rethink in practice the possibility of social transformation, the actuality of communism. History has more imagination than us; but we still need philosophy to think this. The more collective philosophy becomes as a practice, as collective thinking and ingenuity, the closer we come to actually grasping this potential for hope. Not as certainty, but as the least possible and yet more hopeful of outcomes of our neverending struggles. The future, indeed, lasts a long time ...

References

Abse, Tobias 1985, 'Judging the PCI', *New Left Review* 1/153: 5–40.
Agamben, Giorgio 1993, *The Coming Community*, translated by Michael Hardt, Minneapolis: University of Minnesota Press.
Agamben, Giorgio 2009, *The Signature of All Things: On Method*, translated by Luca D'Isanto with Kevin Attell, New York: Zone Books.
Althusser, Louis 1959, *Montesquieu: la politique et l'histoire*, Paris: Presses Universitaires de France.
Althusser, Louis [1964] 2011, 'Student Problems', *Radical Philosophy* 170: 11–15.
Althusser, Louis 1967, 'Sur le "contrat social"', *Cahiers pour l'analyse* 8: 5–42.
Althusser, Louis [1969] 2006, 'À propos de l'article de Michel Verret sur "Mai étudiant"', in Louis Althusser, *Les dossiers de* La Pensée, Paris: Les temps de cerises.
Althusser, Louis 1969, *For Marx*, London: Allen Lane.
Althusser, Louis 1971, *Lenin and Philosophy and Other Essays*, translated by Ben Brewster, New York: Monthly Review Books.
Althusser, Louis 1972a, *Politics and History: Montesquieu, Rousseau, Marx*, translated by Ben Brewster, London: New Left Books.
Althusser, Louis 1972b, *Lénine et la philosophie. Suivie de Marx & Lénine devant Hegel*, Paris: Maspero.
Althusser, Louis 1973, *Réponse à John Lewis*, Paris: Maspero.
Althusser, Louis 1974a, *Philosophie et philosophie spontanée des savants (1967)*, Paris: Maspero.
Althusser, Louis 1974b, *Éléments d'autocritique*, Paris: Hachette.
Althusser, Louis 1976a, *Essays in Self-Criticism*, translated by Grahame Locke, London: New Left Books.
Althusser, Louis 1976b, 'The Transformation of Philosophy', in Althusser 1990.
Althusser, Louis [1977] 1998, 'Enfin la crise du marxisme', in *La Solitude de Machiavel*, Paris: PUF.
Althusser, Louis [1977] 1999, 'Althusser's Solitude', in *Machiavelli and Us*, London: Verso.
Althusser, Louis 1977, 'On the Twenty-Second Congress of the French Communist Party', *New Left Review* 1/194: 3–32.
Althusser, Louis 1978a, 'The Crisis of Marxism', *Marxism Today* July.
Althusser, Louis 1978b, *Ce qui ne plus durer dans le parti communiste*, Paris: Maspero.
Althusser, Louis 1978c, 'What Must Change in the Party', *New Left Review* 1/109: 19–45.
Althusser, Louis 1978d, *Nuevos escritos (La crisis des movimiento comunist internacional frente a la teoría marxista)*, Barcelona: Editorial Laia.
Althusser, Louis 1986, 'Theses de Juin', mim.

Althusser, Louis 1988, *Filosofía y Marxismo. Entrevista por Fernanda Navarro*, Mexico: Siglo veintiuno editores.

Althusser, Louis 1990, *Philosophy and the Spontaneous Philosophy of the Scientists*, edited by Gregory Elliott, translated by B. Brewster, J. Kavanagh, T. Lewis, G. Lock, and W. Montag, London: Verso.

Althusser, Louis 1992, *Journal de Captivité. Stalag XA 1940–1945*, Paris: STOCK/IMEC.

Althusser, Louis 1993a, 'Sur la pensée marxiste', in *Future anterieur, Sur Althusser. Passages*, Paris: L'Harmattan, pp. 11–29.

Althusser, Louis 1993b, *The Future Lasts Forever*, New York: The New Press.

Althusser, Louis 1993c, *Écrits sur la psychanalyse. Freud et Lacan*, Paris: Stock/IMEC.

Althusser, Louis 1994a, *L'avenir dure longtemps. Suivi de Les Faits*, Paris: Stock/IMEC.

Althusser, Louis 1994b, *Sur la philosophie*, Paris: Gallimard.

Althusser, Louis 1995a, *Écrits philosophiques et politiques. Tome II*, Paris: Stock/IMEC.

Althusser, Louis 1995b, *Sur la reproduction*, edited by Jacques Bidet, Paris: Presses Universitaires de France.

Althusser, Louis 1997a, 'The Only Material Tradition. Part 1: Spinoza', in *The New Spinoza*, edited by Warren Montag and Ted Stolze, Minnesota: University of Minnesota Press.

Althusser, Louis 1997b, *Lettres à Franca (1961–1973)*, Paris: Stock/IMEC.

Althusser, Louis 1997c, *The Spectre of Hegel: Early Writings*, translated by G.M. Goshgarian, London: Verso.

Althusser, Louis 1998, *Solitude de Machiavel*, edited by Ives Sintomer, Paris: PUF.

Althusser, Louis 1999a, *Machiavelli and Us*, translated by Gregory Elliott, London: Verso.

Althusser, Louis 1999b, *Writings on Psychoanalysis: Freud and Lacan*, translated by Jeffrey Mehlham, New York: Columbia University Press.

Althusser, Louis 2003, *The Humanist Controversy*, translated by G.M. Goshgarian, London: Verso.

Althusser, Louis 2005, 'Du matérialisme aléatoire', *Multitudes* 21: 179–93.

Althusser, Louis 2006a, *Philosophy of the Encounter: Later Writings 1978–86*, translated by G.M. Goshgarian, London: Verso.

Althusser, Louis 2006b, *Politique et Histoire de Machiavel à Marx. Cours à l'École normale supérieure 1955–1972*, Paris: Seuil.

Althusser, Louis 2006c, *Les dossiers de pensée*, Paris: Le temps de cerises.

Althusser, Louis 2007, 'Letter to the Central Committee of the PCF, 18 March 1966', *Historical Materialism* 15, no. 2: 153–72.

Althusser, Louis 2009, *Machiavel et nous. Suivi de 'Des problèmes qu'il faudra appeler d'un autre nom et peut-être politique'. Althusser et instabilité de la politique et de 'La récurrence du vide chez Althusser' par François Matheron*, Paris: Texto.

Althusser, Louis 2011, *Lettres à Hélène*, Paris: Grasset/IMEC.

Althusser, Louis 2013a, *Cours sur Rousseau*, edited by Yves Vargas, Paris: Le temps de cerises.

REFERENCES

Althusser, Louis 2013b, 'Sur la genèse', *Décalages* 1, no. 2, http://scholar.oxy.edu/deca lages/vol1/iss2/9 (last accessed 30 July 2015).

Althusser, Louis 2014a, *Initiation à la philosophie pour les non-philosophes*, edited by G.M. Goshgarian, Paris: PUF.

Althusser, Louis 2014b, *On the Reproduction of Capitalism: Ideology and Ideological State Apparatuses*, translated by G.M. Goshgarian, London: Verso.

Althusser, Louis 2014c, 'Conférence sur la dictature de prolétariat à Barcelone. Un texte inédit de Louis Althusser', *Période*, http://revueperiode.net/un-texte-inedit-de-louis-althusser-conference-sur-la-dictature-du-proletariat-a-barcelone/ (last accessed 1 July 2019).

Althusser, Louis 2015a, *Être marxiste en philosophie*, edited by G.M. Goshgarian, Paris: PUF.

Althusser, Louis 2015b, 'Some Questions Concerning the Crisis of Marxist Theory and of the International Communist Movement', translated by David Broder, *Historical Materialism* 23:1: 152–78.

Althusser, Louis 2016, *Les Vaches noires. Interview imaginaire*, edited by G.M. Goshgarian, Paris: PUF.

Althusser, Louis 2017a, *Philosophy for Non-Philosophers*, translated by G.M. Goshgarian, London: Bloomsbury.

Althusser, Louis 2017b, *How to be a Marxist in Philosophy*, translated by G.M. Goshgarian, London: Bloomsbury.

Althusser, Louis 2018a, *Écrits sur l'histoire*, edited by G.M. Goshgarian, Paris: PUF.

Althusser, Louis 2018b, *Que faire*, edited by G.M. Goshgarian, Paris: PUF.

Althusser, Louis 2019, *Lessons on Rousseau*, translated by G.m. Goshgarian, London: Verso.

Althusser, Louis and Étienne Balibar 1970, *Reading Capital*, translated by Ben Brewster, London: New Left Books.

Althusser, Louis, Étienne Balibar, Jacques Ranciére, Roger Establet, and Pierre Macherey 1996, *Lire le Capital*, Paris: PUF.

Althusser, Louis, Étienne Balibar, Roger Establet, Pierre Macherey and Jacques Rancière 2016, *Reading Capital: The Complete Edition*, translated by Ben Brewster and David Fernbach, London: Verso.

Amariglio, Jack 1987, 'Marxism Against Economic Science: Althusser's Legacy', *Research in Political Economy*, 10: 159–94.

Anderson, Perry 1979, *Considerations on Western Marxism*, second edition, London: New Left Books.

Anderson, Perry 1980, *Arguments within English Marxism*, London: Verso.

Anon. [Althusser, Louis] 1966, *Sur la révolution culturelle*, *Cahiers Marxistes – Léninistes*, 14: 5–16.

Arthur, Charles J. 2002, *The New Dialectic and Marx's Capital*, Leiden: Brill.

Ashton, T.H. and C.H.E. Philpin (eds) 1987, *The Brenner Debate: Agrarian Class Structure and Economic Development in Pre-Industrial Europe*, Cambridge: Cambridge University Press.

Badiou, Alain 2001, *Ethics: An Essay on the Understanding of Evil*, London: Verso.

Badiou, Alain 2005a, *Metapolitics*, translated by Jason Barker, London: Verso.

Badiou, Alain 2005b, *Being and Event*, translated by Oliver Feltham, London: Continuum.

Badiou, Alain 2005c, 'The Triumphant Restoration', *Positions* 13, no. 3: 659–62.

Badiou, Alain 2005d, 'The Cultural Revolution: The Last Revolution?', *Positions* 13, no. 3: 481–514.

Badiou, Alain 2009a, *Logics of Worlds: Being and Event II*, translated by Alberto Toscano, London: Continuum.

Badiou, Alain 2009b, *Theory of the Subject*, translated by Bruno Bosteels, London: Continuum.

Balibar, Étienne 1973, 'Sur la dialectique historique. Quelques remarques critiques à propos de "Lire le Capital"', *La Pensée* 170: 27–47.

Balibar, Étienne 1974, *Cinque études du matérialisme historique*, Paris: Maspero.

Balibar, Étienne 1977a, 'An nouveau sur la contradiction. Dialectique de luttes de classes et lutte de classes dans la dialectique', in *Sur la dialectique*, Centre d'Études et de Recherches Marxistes, Paris: Éditions Sociales.

Balibar, Étienne 1977b, *On the Dictatorship of the Proletariat*, translated by Graham Locke, London: New Left Books.

Balibar, Étienne 1978, 'Marx, Engels et le Party revolutionaire', *La Pensée* 201: 120–35.

Balibar, Étienne 1979, 'Etat, Parti, Transition', *Dialectiques* 27: 81–92.

Balibar, Étienne 1990a, 'Les apories de la "transition" et les contradictions de Marx', *Sociologie et societés* 22, no. 1: 83–91.

Balibar, Étienne 1990b, 'Individualité, causalité, substance. Réflexions sur l'ontologie de Spinoza', in *Spinoza: Issues and Directions. The Proceedings of the Chicago Spinoza Conference*, edited by Edwin Curley and Pierre-François Moreau, Leiden: Brill.

Balibar, Étienne 1992, 'Foucault and Marx: The Question of Nominalism', in *Michel Foucault, Philosopher*, translated by Timothy Armstrong, Hempsted: Harvester Wheatsheaf.

Balibar, Étienne 1993a, 'L'objet d'Althusser', in *Politique et philosophie dans l'œuvre de Louis Althusser*, edited by Sylvain Lazarus, Paris: PUF.

Balibar, Étienne 1993b, *La philosophie de Marx*, Paris: La Découverte.

Balibar, Étienne 1993c, 'The Non-contemporaneity of Althusser', in *The Althusserian Legacy*, edited by E. Ann Kaplan and Michael Sprinker, London: Verso.

Balibar, Étienne 1994a, 'Althusser's Object', *Social Text* 39: 157–88.

Balibar, Étienne 1994b, *Masses, Classes, Ideas: Studies on Politics and Philosophy Before and After Marx*, translated by James Swenson, London: Routledge.

Balibar, Étienne 1995, *The Philosophy of Marx*, translated by Chris Turner, London: Verso.
Balibar, Étienne 1996, 'Avant-propos', in *Pour Marx*, Paris: La Découverte/Poche.
Balibar, Étienne 1997, *La crainte de masses. Politique et philosophie avant et après Marx*, Paris: Galilée.
Balibar, Étienne 1998, *Spinoza and Politics*, translated by Peter Snowdon, London: Verso.
Balibar, Étienne 2002, *Politics and the Other Scene*, London: Verso.
Balibar, Étienne 2003, 'Structuralism: A Destitution of the Subject?', *Differences* 14, no. 1: 1–21.
Balibar, Étienne 2009, 'Une rencontre en Romagne', in Althusser 2009, pp. 9–30.
Balibar, Étienne 2012, 'Préface', in *Althusser. L'adieu infini*, by Emilio de Ípola, Paris: PUF.
Balibar, Étienne and Yves Duroux 2012, 'A Philosophical Conjuncture: An Interview with Étienne Balibar and Yves Duroux', in *Concept and Form: Volume Two, Interviews and Texts from the Cahiers pour l'analyse*, edited by Peter Hallward and Knox Peden, London: Verso.
Balibar, Étienne, Christine Buci-Glucksmann, Mark Abeles, David Kaisergruber, Jacques Guilhaumou, and Georges Labica 1977, 'Table ronde: sur et autour de la dictature du prolétariat', *Dialectiques* 17: 3–34.
Baltas, Aristidis and Giorgos Fourtounis 1994, *Louis Althusser and the End of Classical Marxism* [in Greek], Athens: Politis.
Bensaïd, Daniel 1974, 'Les intellectuels du PCF, dos au stalinisme', in *Contre Althusser*, Paris: 10/18.
Bensaïd, Daniel 1978, 'Le P.C.F. à la croisée des chemins', *Dialectiques* 23: 47–61.
Bensaïd, Daniel 2004, 'Alain Badiou and the Miracle of the Event', in *Think Again: Alain Badiou and the Future of Philosophy*, edited by Peter Hallward, London: Continuum.
Benton, Ted 1984, *The Rise and Fall of Structural Marxism: Althusser and his Influence*, London: Macmillan.
Berlinguer, Enrico 1973, 'Riflessioni sull'Italia dopo i fatti del Cile', http://www.sitocomunista.it/pci/documenti/berlinguer/berlinguercile.htm (last accessed 30 July 2019).
Besse, Guy 1966, 'Communisme, culture et dialogue', *Cahiers du Commoynisme* 5–6: 179–91.
Bettelheim, Charles 1974, *Cultural Revolution and Industrial Organization in China: Changes in Management and the Division of Labour*, translated by Alfred Ehrenfeld, New York: Monthly Review Press.
Bettelheim, Charles 1975, *Economic Calculation and Forms of Property*, translated by John Taylor, New York: Monthly Review Press.
Bettelheim, Charles 1976–77, *Class Struggle in the USSR*, 2 vols., translated by Brian Pearce, New York: Monthly Review Press.
Bosteels, Bruno 2011, *Badiou and Politics*, Durham, NC: Duke University Press.

Bourdin, Jean Claude 2008, 'Matérialisme aléatoire et pensée de la conjoncture. Au-delà de Marx', in *Althusser: une lecture de Marx*, edited by Jean Claude Bourdin, Paris: PUF.

Brand, Urlich and Miriam Heigl, '"Inside" and "Outside": The State, Movements and "Radical Transformation" in the Work of Nicos Poulantzas', in *Reading Poulantzas*, edited by Alexander Gallas, Lars Bretthauer, John Kannankulam, and Ingo Stützle, London: Merlin.

Brenner, Robert 1987a, 'Agrarian Class Structure and Economic Development in Pre-Industrial Europe', in *The Brenner Debate: Agrarian Class Structure and Economic Development in Pre-Industrial Europe*, edited by T.H. Ashton and C.H.E. Philpin, Cambridge: Cambridge University Press.

Brenner, Robert 1987b, 'The Agrarian Roots of European Capitalism', in *The Brenner Debate: Agrarian Class Structure and Economic Development in Pre-Industrial Europe*, edited by T.H. Ashton and C.H.E. Philpin, Cambridge: Cambridge University Press.

Brown, Nathan 2011, 'Red Years: Althusser's Lesson, Rancière's Error and the Real Movement of History', *Radical Philosophy* 170: 16–24.

Buci-Glucksmann, Christine 1979, 'Pour un eurocommunisme de gauche', in *Changer le PC? Debats sur le gallocommunisme*, edited by Olivier Duhamel and Henri Weber, Paris: PUF.

Buci-Glucksmann, Christine 1980, *Gramsci and the State*, translated by David Fernbach, London: Lawrence and Wishart.

Burgio, Alberto 2014, *Gramsci. Il sistema in movimento*, Roma: Derive Approndi.

Butler, Judith 1997, *The Psychic Life of Power*, Stanford: Stanford University Press.

Callari, Antonio and David F. Ruccio 1996, 'Introduction', in *Postmodern Materialism and the Future of Marxist Theory*, edited by Antonio Callari and David F. Ruccio, Hanover and London: Wesleyan University Press.

Callinicos, Alex 1976, *Althusser's Marxism*, London: Pluto.

Castoriadis, Cornelius 1988a, *Political and Social Writings: Volume 1*, translated by David Ames Curtis, Minneapolis: University of Minnesota Press.

Castoriadis, Cornelius 1988b, *Political and Social Writings: Volume 2*, translated by David Ames Curtis, Minneapolis: University of Minnesota Press.

Cavaillés, Jean 1960, *Sur la logique et la théorie de la science*, 2nd edition, Paris: PUF.

Cavazzini, Andrea 2009a, *Crise du Marxisme et Critique de l'Etat. La dernière batail d'Althusser*, Paris: Le Clou dans le Fer.

Cavazzini, Andrea 2009b, 'Introduction à la Révolution Culturelle', http://f.hypotheses.org/wp-content/blogs.dir/1106/files/2013/01/GRM3.R.C.Cavazzini.pdf (last accessed 30 June 2019).

Cavazzini, Andrea 2011, 'La pratique d'Althusser: d'un marxisme à l'autre', in *Le moment philosophique des années 1960 en France*, edited by Patrice Maniglier, Paris: PUF.

CC du PCF 1966, 'Resolution sur les problèmes idéologiques et culturelles', *Cahiers du Communisme* 5–6: 264–80.

REFERENCES 541

Choi, Won 2013, 'Inception or Interpellation? The Slovenian School, Butler, and Althusser', *Rethinking Marxism* 25, no. 1: 23–37.

Claudin, Fernando 1975, *The Communist Movement: From Comintern to Cominform*, translated by Brian Pearce and Francis MacDonagh, London: Penguin.

Cohen, G.A. 2000, *Karl Marx's Theory of History: A Defense*, 2nd edition, Princeton: Princeton University Press.

Collective, *Contre Althusser*, Paris: 10/18.

Colletti, Lucio 1975, 'Marxism and the Dialectic', *New Left Review* I/93: 3–29.

Communist Party of China 1965, *The Polemic on the General Line of the International Communist Movement*, Peking: Foreign Languages Press.

Cotten, Jean-Pierre 1993, 'Althusser et Spinoza', in *Spinoza au XXe siècle*, edited by Olivier Bloch, Paris: PUF.

de Ípola, Emilio 2012, *Althusser. L'adieu infini*, Paris: PUF.

de Lara Philippe (ed.) 1978, 'Réponses à Louis Althusser', *Dialectiques* 24–25: 73–82.

Deleuze, Gilles 1988, *Spinoza: Practical Philosophy*, translated by Robert Hurley, San Francisco: City Lights Books.

Deleuze, Gilles 2004a, *The Logic of Sense*, edited by Constantine Boundas, translated by Mark Lester, London: Continuum.

Deleuze, Gilles 2004b, *Desert Islands and Other Texts 1953–1974*, edited by David Lapoujade, translated by Michael Taormina, New York: Semiotext(e).

Deleuze, Gilles 2004c, *Difference and Repetition*, translated by Paul Patton, London: Continuum.

Deleuze, Gilles and Félix Guattari 2004, *Anti-Oedipus: Capitalism and Schizophrenia*, translated by Robert J. Hurley, Mark Seem, and Helen R. Lane, London: Continuum.

Deleuze, Gilles and Claire Parnet 1987, *Dialogues*, translated by Hugh Tomlison and Barbara Habberjam, New York: Columbia University Press.

Derrida, Jacques 1972, *Positions*, Paris: Seuil.

Derrida, Jacques 1981, *Dissemination*, translated by Barbara Johnson, London: The Athlone Press.

Derrida, Jacques 1982, *Margins of Philosophy*, translated by Alan Bass, Sussex: The Harvester Press.

Derrida, Jacques 2001, *Writing and Difference*, translated by Alan Bass, London: Routledge.

Derrida, Jacques 2011, *Voice and Phenomenon: Introduction to the Problem of the Sign in Husserl's Phenomenology*, Evanston, IL: Northwestern University Press.

Di Maggio, Marco 2009, 'Le Parti communiste français à travers le débat interne et le rôle des intellectuels (1958–1978)', http://www.marxau21.fr/index.php?option=com_content&view=article&id=76:le-parti-communiste-francaise-a-travers-le-debat-interne-et-le-role-des-intellectuels-1958-1978&catid=60:marx-en-politiques&Itemid=83 (last accessed 30 June 2015).

Di Maggio, Marco 2013, *Les intellectuelles et la stratégie communiste. Une crise d'hégémonie*, Paris: Éditions Sociales.

Dimoulis, Dimitri and John Milios 2004, 'Commodity Fetishism vs. Capital Fetishism: Marxist Interpretations vis-à-vis Marx's Analyses in *Capital*', *Historical Materialism* 12:3: 3–42.

Dolar, Mladen 1998, 'Cogito as the Subject of the Unconscious', in *Cogito and the Unconscious*, edited by Slavoj Žižek, Durham, NC: Duke University Press.

Duhamel, Olivier and Henri Weber (eds) 1979, *Changer le PC? Debats sur le gallocommunisme*, Paris: PUF.

Elliott, Gregory 1993, 'Althusser's Solitude', in *The Althusserian Legacy*, edited by E. Ann Kaplan and Michael Sprinker, London: Verso.

Elliott, Gregory 2006, *Althusser: The Detour of Theory*, 2nd edition, Leiden: Brill.

Engels, Friedrich 1987, *Anti-Dühring*, Moscow: Editions du Progrés.

Engels, Friedrich 2003, *Socialism, Utopian and Scientific*, http://www.marxists.org/archive/marx/works/1880/soc-utop/index.htm (last accessed 30 July 2019).

Farris, Sara R. 2013, 'Althusser and Tronti: The Primacy of Politics versus the Autonomy of the Political', in *Encountering Althusser: Politics and Materialism in Contemporary Radical Thought*, edited by Katja Diefenbach, Sara R. Farris, Gal Kirn, and Peter D. Thomas, London: Bloomsbury.

Foucault, Michel 2002, *The Order of Things: An Archaeology of the Human Sciences*, London: Routledge.

Fourtounis, Giorgos, '"An Immense Aspiration to Being": The Causality and the Temporality of the Aleatory', in *Encountering Althusser: Politics and Materialism in Contemporary Radical Thought*, edited by Katja Diefenbach, Sara R. Farris, Gal Kirn, and Peter D. Thomas, London: Bloomsbury.

Franchi, Stefano 2011, 'Les jeux anaclastiques de Lévi-Strauss', in *Le moment philosophique des années 1960 en France*, edited by Patrice Maniglier, Paris: PUF.

Fromm, Erich (ed.) 1965, *Socialist Humanism: An International Symposium*, New York: Doubleday.

Frosini, Fabio 2003, *Gramsci e la filosofia. Saggio sui Quaderni del carcere*, Rome: Carocci.

Frosini, Fabio 2006, 'Lenin e Althusser. Rileggendo «Contraddizione e surdeterminazione»', *Critica marxista*, 6: 62–70.

Frosini, Fabio 2009, 'Immanenza', in *Dizionario Gramsciano 1926–37*, edited by Guido Liguori and Pasquale Voza, Roma: Carocci.

Futur Antérieur (ed.) 1993, *Sur Althusser. Passages*, Paris: L'Harmattan.

Gallas, Alexander, Lars Bretthauer, Jon Kannnkulam, and Ingo Stützle (eds) 2011, *Reading Poulantzas*, London: Merlin.

Garaudy, Roger 1966, 'Dogmatisme, pluralisme, problèmes de la religion', *Cahiers du Communisme* 5–6: 9–40.

Geerlandt, Robert 1978, *Garaudy et Althusser. Le débat sur l'humanisme dans le Parti communiste français et son enjeu*, Lille: PUF.

Geras, Norman 1977, 'Althusser's Marxism: An Assessment', in *Western Marxism: A Critical Reader*, edited by New Left Review, London: New Left Books.

Geras, Norman 1983, *Marx and Human Nature: Refutation of a Legend*, London: Verso.

Gillot, Pascale 2009, *Althusser et la psychanalyse*, Paris: PUF.

Girval-Palotta, Julien 2009, 'Révoltes étudiantes et Révolution culturelle chez Althusser (11)', http://f.hypotheses.org/wp-content/blogs.dir/1106/files/2013/01/GRM3.RC_.Pallotta.pdf (last accessed 30 June 2019).

Glucksmann, André 1972, 'A Ventriloquist Structuralism', *New Left Review* I/72: 68–92.

Goldmann, Lucien 1959, *Le Dieu caché. Étude sur la vision tragique dans les Pensées de Pascal et dans le théâtre de Racine*, Paris: Gallimard.

Goldmann, Lucien 2013 [1964], *The Hidden God: A Study of Tragic Vision in the Pensées of Pascal and the Tragedies of Racine*, translated by Philip Thody, London: Routledge.

Goshgarian, G.M. 2003, 'Introduction', in Althusser 2003.

Goshgarian, G.M. 2006, 'Introduction', in Althusser 2006.

Goshgarian, G.M. 2013, 'The Very Essence of the Object, the Soul of Marxism and Other Singular Things: Spinoza in Althusser 1959–67', in *Encountering Althusser: Politics and Materialism in Contemporary Radical Thought*, edited by Katja Diefenbach, Sara R. Farris, Gal Kirn, and Peter D. Thomas, London: Bloomsbury.

Goshgarian, G.M. 2015a, 'Preface', in Althusser 2015, pp. 9–41.

Goshgarian, G.M. 2015b, 'Philosophie et Révolution. Althusser sans le théoricisme. Entretien avec G.M. Goshgarian', *Période*, http://revueperiode.net/philosophie-et-revolution-althusser-sans-le-theoricisme-entretien-avec-g-m-goshgarian/ (last accessed 1 July 2019).

Goshgarian, G.M. 2016, 'Note d'édition', in Althusser 2016, pp. 9–31.

Gramsci, Antonio 1971, *Selection from Prison Writings*, edited and translated by Quintin Hoare and Geoffrey Nowell-Smith, London: Lawrence and Wishart.

Gramsci, Antonio 1975, *Quaderni del carcere*, 4 vols., edited by Valentino Gerratana, Rome: Einaudi.

Gramsci, Antonio 1978, *Cahiers de prison. Cahiers 10, 11, 12 et 13*, edited by Robert Paris, translated by P. Fulcignoni, G. Granel, and N. Negri, Paris: Gallimard.

Gramsci, Antonio 1996, *Further Selections from the Prison Notebooks*, edited and translated by Derek Boothman, London: Lawrence and Wishart.

Gramsci, Antonio 2007, *Prison Notebooks*, 3 vols., edited and translated by Joseph Buttigieg, New York: Columbia University Press.

Gueroult, Martial 1968, *Spinoza. Dieu. (Ethique, 1)*, Paris: Aubier-Montaigne.

Gueroult, Martial 1974, *Spinoza. L'âme (Ethique 2)*, Paris: Aubier-Montaigne.

Habermas, Jürgen 1985, 'A Philosophico-Political Profile', *New Left Review* I/151: 75–105.

Hallward, Peter and Knox Peden (eds.) 2012a, *Concept and Form: Volume One, Key Texts from the Cahiers pour l'analyse*, London: Verso.

Hallward, Peter and Knox Peden (eds.) 2012b, *Concept and Form: Volume Two, Interviews and Essays on the Cahiers pour l'analyse*, London: Verso.

Hardt, Michael and Antonio Negri 2009, *Commonwealth*, Cambridge, MA: Belknap Press.

Harman, Chris 1979, 'Crisis of the European Revolutionary Left', *International Socialism* 2, no. 4, http://www.marxists.org/archive/harman/1979/xx/eurevleft.html (last accessed 30 October 2013).

Hastings-King, Stephen 2014, *Socialisme ou Barbarie and the Problem of Worker Writing*, Leiden: Brill.

Hegel, Georg Wilhelm Friedrich 1873, *Hegel's Encyclopaedia of the Philosophical Sciences. Part One: The Shorter Logic*, translated by William Wallace, http://www.marxists.org/reference/archive/hegel/sl_index.htm (last accessed 30 October 2018).

Hegel, Georg Wilhelm Friedrich 1999, *Political Writings*, edited by Laurence Dickey and H.B. Nisbet, translated by H.B. Nisbet, Cambridge: Cambridge University Press.

Hegel, Georg Wilhelm Friedrich 2010, *The Science of Logic*, translated by George di Giovanni, Cambridge: Cambridge University Press.

Heidegger, Martin 1994, *Basic Writings*, London: Routledge.

Heinrich, Michael 1999, *Die Wissenschaft vom Wert. Die Marxische Kritik der politischen Ökonomie zwischen wissenschaftlicher Revolution und klassischer Tradition*, Münster: Verlag Westfälisches Dampfboot.

Honneth, Axel 1994, 'History and Interaction: On the Structuralist Interpretation of Historical Materialism', translated by James Gordon Finlayson, in *Althusser: A Critical Reader*, edited by Gregory Elliott, London: Blackwell, pp. 73–103.

Hume, David 1964, *A Treatise on Human Nature*, in *The Philosophical Works, Volumes 1 and 2*, Aalen: Scientia Verlag.

Ichida, Yoshihiko and François Matheron 2005, 'Un, deux, trois, quatre, dix milles Althusser?', *Multitudes* 21: 167–77.

Il Manifesto 1970, 'Progetto di tesi', *Il Manifesto* September.

Ingrao, Pietro 1977a, *Masse e Potere*, Rome: Editori Riuniti.

Ingrao, Pietro 1977b, 'Le P.C.I. aujourd'hui: stratégie politique et dialectique sociale', *Dialectiques* 18–19: 7–17.

Ingrao, Pietro 1978, 'Parlamento, Partiti e Societa Civile, Intervista di Pietro Ingrao a cura di Guliano Amato', in *Quale Riforma dello Stato?*, Quaderni di Mondo Operaio.

Jalley, Émile 2014, *Louis Althusser et quelques autres. Notes de cours 1958–1959. Hypollite, Badiou, Lacan, Hegel, Marx, Alain, Wallon*, Paris: L'Harmattan.

Jameson, Fredric 1997, 'Marx's Purloined Letter', in *Ghostly Demarcations: A Symposium on Jacques Derrida's Spectres of Marx*, London: Verso.

Jessop, Bob 1985, *Nikos Poulantzas: Marxist Theory and Political Strategy*, London: Macmillan.

REFERENCES

Jiang, Hongsheng 2014, *La Commune de Shanghai et la Commune de Paris*, translated by Eric Hazan, Paris: Fabrique.

Kant, Immanuel 2007, *Critique of Judgment*, translated by James Creed Meredith, edited by Nicholas Walker, Oxford: Oxford University Press.

Kaplan, E. Ann and Michael Sprinker (eds) 1993, *The Althusserian Legacy*, London: Verso.

Karsz, Saül 1974, *Théorie et politique: Louis Althusser*, Paris: Fayard.

Keck, Frédéric 2011, 'La Pensée sauvage aujourd'hui: d'August Comte à Claude Lévi-Strauss', in *Le moment philosophique des années 1960 en France*, edited by Patrice Maniglier, Paris: PUF.

Kołakowski, Leszek 1971, 'Althusser's Marx', *Socialist Register* 8: 111–28.

Kouvélakis, Eustache 2003, *Philosophie et Révolution. De Kant à Marx*, Paris: Actuel Marx/PUF.

Kouvélakis, Eustache and Vincent Charbonier (eds) 2005, *Sartre, Lukács, Althusser: Des marxistes en philosophie*, Paris: PUF.

Krailsheiner, A.J. 1966, 'Introduction', in Pascal 1966.

Krasucki, Henri 1966, 'La culture, les intellectuelles et la nation', *Cahiers du Communisme* 5–6: 158–78.

Labica, Georges 1979, 'Pour les pratiques nouvelles', in *Changer le PC? Debats sur le gallocommunisme*, edited by Olivier Duhamel and Henri Weber, Paris: PUF.

Labica, Georges 1980, *Marxism and the Status of Philosophy*, translated by Kate Soper and Martin Ryle, London: Harvester Press.

Labica, Georges 1987, *Karl Marx: Les Thèses sur Feuerbach*, Paris: PUF.

Lahtinen, Mikko 2009, *Politics and Philosophy: Niccoló Machiavelli and Louis Althusser's Aleatory Materialism*, Leiden: Brill.

Lazarus, Sylvain (ed.) 1993, *Politique et philosophie dans l'œuvre de Louis Althusser*, Paris: PUF.

Lecourt, Dominique 1975, *Marxism and Epistemology: Bachelard, Canguilhem and Foucault*, translated by Ben Brewster, London: New Left Books.

Lecourt, Dominique 1981, *L'ordre et les jeux. Le positivisme logique en question*, Paris: Grasset.

Lecourt, Dominique 1982, *La philosophie sans feinte*, Paris: J.-E. Hallier/Albin Michel.

Lefort, Claude 1986, *Le travail de l'oeuvre Machiavel*, 2nd edition, Paris: Gallimard.

Lenin, V.I. [1917] 1974, *State and Revolution*, in *Collected Works*, Volume 25, Moscow: Progress Publishers.

Lenin, V.I. 1920, 'KOMMUNISMUS, Journal of the Communist International', http://www.marxists.org/archive/lenin/works/1920/jun/12.htm (last accessed 30 July 2019).

Lévi-Strauss, Claude 1966, *The Savage Mind*, London: Weidenfeld and Nicholson.

Lewis, William S. 2005, *Louis Althusser and the Traditions of French Marxism*, London: Lexington Books.

Liguori, Guido 2006, *Sentieri Gramsciani*, Rome: Carocci.

Liguori, Guido and Pasquale Voza (eds), *Dizionario Gramsciano*, Roma: Carocci.

Lipietz, Alain 1993, 'From Althusserianism to "Regulation Theory"', in *The Althusserian Legacy*, edited by E. Ann Kaplan and Michael Sprinker, London: Verso.

Long, Anthony Arthur and David Sedley 1987, *The Hellenistic Philosophers, Volume 1*, Cambridge: Cambridge University Press.

Luxemburg, Rosa [1904], *Organizational Questions of the Russian Social Democracy [Leninism or Marxism?]*, http://www.marxists.org/archive/luxemburg/1904/questions-rsd/index.htm (last accessed 14 June 2010).

Macciocchi, Maria Antoinetta 1973, *Letters from the Inside of the Italian Communist Party to Louis Althusser*, London: New Left Books.

Macherey, Pierre 1964, 'La philosophie de la science de Georges Canguilhem. Epistémologie et histoire des sciences', *La Pensée* 113: 50–74.

Macherey, Pierre 1976, 'L'histoire de la philosophie comme lutte de tendances', *La Pensée* 185: 3–25.

Macherey, Pierre 1979, *Hegel ou Spinoza*, Paris: Maspero.

Macherey, Pierre 1992, *Avec Spinoza*, Paris: PUF.

Macherey, Pierre 1994–98, *Introduction à l'Ethique de Spinoza*, 5 vols., Paris: PUF.

Macherey, Pierre 1997, *Introduction à l'Éthique de Spinoza. La seconde partie. La realité mentale*, Paris: PUF.

Macherey, Pierre 1999, *Histoire de dinosaure. Faire de la philosophie, 1965–1997*, Paris: PUF.

Macherey, Pierre 2004, 'Out of Melancholia: Notes on Judith Butler's *The Psychic Life of Power: Theories in Subjection*', *Rethinking Marxism* 16, no. 1: 7–17.

Macherey, Pierre 2005a, 'Pascal et la machine', https://philolarge.hypotheses.org/files/2017/09/09-11-2005.pdf (last accessed 30 July 2019).

Macherey, Pierre 2005b, 'Between Pascal and Spinoza: The Vacuum', in *Current Continental Theory and Modern Philosophy*, edited by Stephen H. Daniel, Evanston, IL: Northwestern University Press.

Macherey, Pierre 2008, *Marx 1845. Le 'Thèses' sur Feuerbach*, Paris: Éditions Amsterdam.

Macherey, Pierre 2011a, *Hegel or Spinoza*, translated by Susan M. Ruddick, Minneapolis: University of Minnesota Press.

Macherey, Pierre 2011b, 'Spinoza: 1968: Guéroult et/ou Deleuze', in *Le moment philosophique des années 1960 en France*, edited by Patrice Maniglier, Paris: PUF.

Magri, Lucio 2011, *The Tailor of Ulm: Communism in the Twentieth Century*, London: Verso.

Maniglier, Patrice (ed.) 2011, *Le moment philosophique des années 1960 en France*, Paris: PUF.

Maniglier, Patrice 2012, 'Acting Out the Structure', in *Concept and Form: Volume Two*,

Interviews and Texts from the Cahiers pour l'analyse, edited by Peter Hallward and Knox Peden, London: Verso.

Mao, Tse-Tung 1967, *Selected Works of Mao Tse-Tung*, Peking: Foreign Language Press.

Martin, James 2008, 'Introduction', in *The Poulantzas Reader: Marxism, Law and the State*, edited by James Martin, London: Verso.

Marx, Karl 1841, *Difference between the Democritean and Epicurean Philosophy of Nature*, in Karl Marx and Friedrich Engels 1975–2005, *Collected Works, Volume 1*, London: Lawrence and Wishart.

Marx, Karl 1845, *Theses on Feuerbach*, http://www.marxists.org/archive/marx/works/1845/theses/index.htm (last accessed: 30 July 2019).

Marx, Karl 1875, *Critique of the Gotha Program*, http://www.marxists.org/archive/marx/works/1875/gotha/index.htm (last accessed 30 July 2019).

Marx, Karl 1893, *Das Kapital, Band II*, http://www.mlwerke.de/me/me24/me24_000.htm.

Marx, Karl 1894, *Capital, Volume 3*, http://www.marxists.org/archive/marx/works/1894-c3 (last accessed 30 July 2019).

Marx, Karl 1973, *Grundrisse*, translated by Martin Nicolaus, London: Pelican.

Marx, Karl 1974, *Capital, Volume 2*, Moscow: Progress Publishers.

Marx, Karl and Friedrich Engels 1845, *The German Ideology*, http://www.marxists.org/archive/marx/works/1845/german-ideology/index.htm (last accessed 30 July 2019).

Marx, Karl and Friedrich Engels 1970, *Manifesto of the Communist Party*, Peking: Foreign Language Press.

Marx, Karl and Friedrich Engels 1975–2005, *Collected Works*, London: Lawrence and Wishart.

Marx, Karl and Friedrich Engels 1982, *Selected Correspondence*, Moscow: Progress Publishers.

Matheron, Alexandre 1988, *Individu et communauté chez Spinoza*, 2nd edition, Paris: Les editions de Minuit.

Matheron, Alexandre 2011, *Études sur Spinoza et les philosophies de l'âge classique*, Lyon: ENS Éditions.

Matheron, François 1997a, 'Introduction', in *The Spectre of Hegel: Early Writings*, by Louis Althusser, London: Verso.

Matheron, François 1997b, 'La récurrence de vide chez Louis Althusser', in *Lire Althusser aujourd'hui*, by *Futur Antérieur*.

Matheron, François 2012, 'Louis Althusser et le "groupe Spinoza"', in *Lectures contemporaines de Spinoza*, edited by Pierre-François Moreau, Claude Cohen-Boulaki, and Mireille Delibraccio, Paris: PUF, pp. 77–93.

Matheron, François and Yoshihiko Ichida 2011, 'Althusser, un "typapart" une bibliothèque à part?', *Les Temps Modernes* 3, no. 664: 194–209.

Mavroudeas, Stavros 1999, 'Regulation Theory: The Road from Creative Marxism to Post-modern Disintegration', *Science and Society* 63, no. 3: 310–37.

Merleau-Ponty, Maurice 2002, *Phenomenology of Perception*, London: Routledge.
Milios, John, Dimitri Dimoulis and George Economakis 2002, *Karl Marx and the Classics: An Essay on Value, Crises, and the Capitalist Mode of Production*, Aldershot: Ashgate.
Miller, Jacques-Alain 2012 [1964], 'Action of the Structure', in *Concept and Form: Volume One, Key Texts from the Cahiers pour l'analyse*, edited by Peter Hallward and Knox Peden, London: Verso.
Molina, Gérard and Yves Vargas 1979, 'Des contradictions au sein du Parti', in *Changer le PC? Debats sur le gallocommunisme*, edited by Olivier Duhamel and Henri Weber, Paris: PUF.
Montag, Warren 1993, 'Spinoza and Althusser Against Hermeutics: Interpretation or Intervention', in *The Althusserian Legacy*, edited by E. Ann Kaplan and Michael Sprinker, London: Verso.
Montag, Warren 1998a, 'Althusser's Nominalism: Structure and Singularity (1962–5)', *Rethinking Marxism* 10, no. 3: 64–73.
Montag, Warren 1998b, 'Introduction', in *In a Materialist Way*, by Pierre Macherey, London: Verso.
Montag, Warren 1999, *Bodies, Masses, Power: Spinoza and his Contemporaries*, London: Verso.
Montag, Warren 2003, *Althusser*, Houndsmills: Palgrave Macmillan.
Montag, Warren 2005, 'La dialectique à la cantonade: Althusser devant l'art', in *Sartre, Lukács, Althusser: des marxistes en philosophie*, edited by Eustache Kouvélakis and Vincent Charbonier, Paris: Actuel Marx/PUF.
Montag, Warren 2013, *Althusser and his Contemporaries: Philosophy's Perpetual War*, Durham, NC: Duke University Press.
Montag, Warren 2015, 'Introduction to Louis Althusser, "Some Questions Concerning the Crisis of Marxist Theory and of the International Communist Movement"', *Historical Materialism* 23, no. 1: 141–51.
Moreau, Pierre-François 1975, *Spinoza*, Paris: Seuil.
Moreau, Pierre-François 1993, 'Althusser et Spinoza', in *Althusser philosophe*, edited by Pierre Reymond, Paris: PUF, pp. 75–86.
Moreau, Pierre-François 1994, *Spinoza: L'expérience et l'éternité*, Paris: PUF.
Morfino, Vittorio 2005, 'An Althusserian Lexicon', translated by Jason Smith, *Borderlands* 4, no. 2, http://www.borderlands.net.au/vol4no2_2005/morfino_lexicon.htm (last accessed 30 July 2019).
Morfino, Vittorio 2007, 'The Primacy of the Encounter over Form', http://www.theseis.com/synedrio/03_a_Morfino.pdf. (last accessed 30 July 2019)
Morfino, Vittorio 2010, *Le temps de la Multitude*, Paris: Amsterdam.
Morfino, Vittorio 2015a, 'Althusser lecteur de Gramsci', *Actuel Marx* 57: 62–81.
Morfino, Vittorio 2015b, *Plural Temporality: Transindividuality and the Aleatory. Between Spinoza and Althusser*, Leiden: Brill.

Morfino, Vittorio and Luca Pinzolo 2005 'Le primat de la rencontre sur la forme. Le dernier Althusser entre nature et histoire', *Multitudes* 21: 149–58.

Moulier Boutang, Yann 1997, 'L'interdit biographique et l'autorisation de l'œuvre', in *Futur Antérieur, Lire Althusser aujourd'hui*, Paris: L'Harmattan.

Moulier Boutang, Yann 2002, *Louis Althusser, une biographie. La formation du mythe. Vol. 1 1918–1945: La matrice. Vol. 2 1945–56: Ruptures et plis.*, 2nd edition, Paris: Livre de Poche.

Moulier Boutang, Yann 2005, 'Le matérialisme comme politique aléatoire', *Multitudes* 21: 159–66.

Negri, Antonio 1991, *The Savage Anomaly: The Power of Spinoza's Metaphysics and Politics*, Minnesota: University of Minnesota Press.

Negri, Antonio 1996, 'Notes on the Evolution of the Thought of the Later Althusser', in *Postmodern Marxism and the Future of Marxist Theory*, edited by David Callari and David F. Ruccio, London: Wesleyan University Press.

Negri, Antonio 1997, 'Machiavel selon Althusser', in *Lire Althusser aujourd'hui*, by *Futur Antérieur*, Paris: L'Harmattan, pp. 139–58.

New Left Review (ed.) 1977, *Western Marxism: A Critical Reader*, London: New Left Books.

Özselçuk, Ceren 2013, 'Louis Althusser and the Concept of Economy', In *Encountering Althusser: Politics and Materialism in Contemporary Radical Thought*, edited by Katja Diefenbach, Sara R. Farris, Gal Kirn, and Peter D. Thomas, London: Bloomsbury.

Pascal, Blaise 1966, *Pensées*, edited and translated by A.J. Kreilsheimer, London: Penguin.

Pascal, Blaise 2001, *Préface sur la traité du vide*, Paris: édition ebookFrance (English translation at http://www.bartleby.com/48/3/10.html).

Pêcheux, Michel 1982, *Language, Semantics and Ideology: Stating the Obvious*, translated by H. Nagpal, London: Macmillan.

Peden, Knox 2014, *Spinoza contra Phenomenology: French Rationalism from Cavaillés to Deleuze*, Stanford: Stanford University Press.

Portantiero, Juan C. 1981, *Los usos de Gramsci*, Mexico: Folios Ediciones.

Poulantzas, Nicos 1975, *Classes in Contemporary Capitalism*, translated by David Fernbach, London: New Left Books.

Poulantzas, Nicos 1980, *Repères*, Paris: Maspero.

Poulantzas, Nicos 2000, *State, Power, Socialism*, London: Verso.

Poulantzas, Nicos 2008, *The Poulantzas Reader: Marxism, Law and the State*, edited by James Martin, London: Verso.

Rancière, Jacques 2011, *Althusser's Lesson*, London: Continuum.

Raymond, Gino G. 2005, *The French Communist Party during the Fifth Republic: A Crisis of Leadership and Ideology*, London: Palgrave Macmillan.

Raymond, Pierre 1973, *Le passage au matérialisme*, Paris: Maspero.

Raymond, Pierre 1975, *De la combinatoire aux probabilités*, Paris: Maspero.

Raymond, Pierre 1976, '... et la theorie dans la lutte des classes', *Dialectiques* 15–16: 137–48.

Raymond, Pierre 1982, *La résistible fatalité de l'histoire*, Paris: J.-E. Hallier/Albin Michel.

Raymond, Pierre (ed.) 1997, *Althusser philosophe*, Paris: PUF.

Raymond, Pierre 2015, 'Althusser's Materialism', translated by Ted Stolze, *Historical Materialism* 23, no. 2: 176–88.

Ricœur, Paul 1986, *Lectures on Ideology and Utopia*, edited by George H. Taylor, New York: Columbia University Press.

Rizk, Hadi 1992, 'Ubiquité de la liberté: Groupe et action commune, entre Spinoza et Sartre', *Futur Antérieur*, 9, http://www.multitudes.net/Ubiquite-de-la-liberte-groupe-et/ (last accessed 10 June 2014).

Rossanda, Rossana 2010, *The Comrade from Milan*, translated by Romy Clark Giuliani, London: Verso.

Rousseau, Jean-Jacques 1997, *The Discourses and Other Early Political Writings*, translated by Victor Gourevitch, Cambridge: Cambridge University Press.

Rousseau, Jean-Jacques 1999, *The Social Contract*, translated by Christopher Betts, Oxford: Oxford University Press.

Rubin, Isaak Il'ich 1973, *Essays on Marx's Theory of Value*, translated by Miloš Samardžija and Fredy Perlman, Montreal: Black Rose Books.

Sébag, Lucien 1964, *Marxisme et structuralisme*, Paris: Payot.

Sève, Lucien 1966, 'Pour un développement créatif du marxisme', *Cahiers du communisme* 5–6: 89–108.

Sève, Lucien 1997, 'Althusser et la dialectique', in *Althusser philosophe*, edited by Pierre Raymond, Paris: PUF.

Sharp, Hasana 2011, *Spinoza and the Politics of Renaturalization*, Chicago: University of Chicago Press.

Sibertin-Blanc, Guillaume 2006, *Politique et Clinique. Recherche sur la philosophie pratique de Gilles Deleuze*, Thèse de Doctorat, Université Lille 3.

Sibertin-Blanc, Guillaume 2009, 'Révoltes étudiantes et Révolution culturelle chez Althusser: la théorie à l'épreuve de la conjoncture', http://f.hypotheses.org/wp-content/blogs.dir/1106/files/2013/01/GRM3.RC_.Sibertin-Blanc.pdf (last accessed 30 June 2015).

Sibertin-Blanc, Guillaume 2011, 'De la théorie du théâtre à la scène de la théorie: reflexions sur "Le 'Piccolo': Bertolazzi et Brecht" d'Althusser', in *Le moment philosophique des années 1960 en France*, edited by Patrice Maniglier, Paris: PUF.

Simon, Michel 1966, 'Pour un travail toujours plus fécond, sur des bases théoriques toujours mieux assurées', *Cahiers du Communisme* 5–6: 109–35.

Sotiris, Panagiotis 1999, *Louis Althusser's Attempt to Define the Special Terrain of Philosophy and the Redefinition of a Marxist Practice of Philosophy* [in Greek], PhD Dissertation, Athens, Panteion University.

Sotiris, Panagiotis 2008, 'Review of Louis Althusser's *Philosophy of the Encounter: Later Writings 1978–1987*', *Historical Materialism* 16, no. 3: 147–78.
Sotiris, Panagiotis 2009, 'Review of Warren Montag's *Althusser*, William Lewis' *Louis Althusser and the Traditions of French Theory* and Gregory Elliott's *Althusser: The Detour of Theory*', *Historical Materialism* 17, no. 4: 121–42.
Sotiris, Panagiotis 2011, 'Beyond Simple Fidelity to the Event: The Limits of Alain Badiou's Ontology', *Historical Materialism* 19, no. 2: 35–59.
Sotiris, Panagiotis 2013, 'Hegemony and Mass Critical Intellectuality', *International Socialism* 137, http://www.isj.org.uk/index.php4?id=871&issue=137.
Spinoza, Baruch 2002, *Complete Works*, translated by Samuel Shirley, Indianapolis: Hackett.
Stalin, Joseph 1976, *Problems of Leninism*, Peking: Foreign Languages Press.
Stolze, Ted 1998, 'Deleuze and Althusser: Flirting with Structuralism', *Rethinking Marxism* 10, no. 3: 51–3.
Stolze, Ted 2014, 'An Ethics for Marxism: Spinoza on Fortitude', *Rethinking Marxism* 26, no. 4: 561–80.
Suchting, Wal 2004, 'Althusser's Late Thinking about Materialism', *Historical Materialism* 12, no. 1: 3–70.
Terray, Emmanuel 1996, 'An Encounter: Althusser and Machiavelli', in *Postmodern Materialism and the Future of Marxist Theory*, edited by Antonio Callari and David F. Ruccio, Hanover: Wesleyan University Press.
Thomas, Peter D. 2002, 'Philosophical Strategies: Althusser and Spinoza', *Historical Materialism* 10, no. 3: 71–113.
Thomas, Peter D. 2009, *The Gramscian Moment: Philosophy, Hegemony and Marxism*, Leiden: Brill.
Thomas, Peter D. 2013, 'Althusser's Last Encounter: Gramsci', in *Encountering Althusser: Politics and Materialism in Contemporary Radical Thought*, edited by Katja Diefenbach, Sara R. Farris, Gal Kirn, and Peter D. Thomas, London: Bloomsbury.
Thompson, Edward P. 1981, *The Poverty of Theory and Other Essays*, London: Merlin.
Tosel, André 1994, *Du Matérialisme de Spinoza*, Paris: Kimé.
Tosel, André 2005, 'Les aléas du matérialisme aléatoire dans la dernière philosophie de Louis Althusser', in *Sartre, Lukács, Althusser. Des marxistes en philosophie*, edited by Stathis Kouvélakis and Vincent Charbonier, Paris: Actuel Marx/PUF.
Tosel, André 2008, *Spinoza ou l'autre (in)finitude*, Paris: L'Harmattan.
Tosel, André 2012, 'Matérialisme de la rencontre et pensée de l'événement-miracle', in *Autour d'Althusser. Penser un matérialisme aléatoire: problèmes et perspectives*, edited by Annie Ibrahim, Paris: Le temps de cerises, pp. 19–53.
Tosel, André 2013, 'The Hazards of Aleatory Materialism in the Late Philosophy of Louis Althusser', in *Encountering Althusser: Politics and Materialism in Contemporary Radical Thought*, edited by Katja Diefenbach, Sara R. Farris, Gal Kirn, and Peter D. Thomas, London: Bloomsbury.

Tronti, Mario 2006 [1971], *Operai e capitale*, Roma: Derive Approdi.
UJCML (Union de la Jeneusse Communiste Marxiste-Léniniste) 1966, *Faut-il réviser la théorie marxiste-léniniste? Le marxisme n'est pas un humanisme*, http://archivescommunistes.chez-alice.fr/ujcml/ujcml1.html (last accessed 30 July 2019).
Vargas, Yves 2008, 'L'horreur dialectique (description d'un itinéraire)', in *Althusser: une lecture de Marx*, edited by Jean Claude Bourdin, Paris: PUF.
Vargas, Yves (ed.) 2012, 'Introduction', in *Cours sur Rousseau*, Paris: Le temps de cerises.
Verret, Michel 1969, 'Mai étudiant ou les substitutions', *Le Pensée*, Février: 3–36.
Vilar, Pierre 1973, 'Marxist History, a History in the Making: Towards a Dialogue with Althusser', *New Left Review* I/80: 65–106.
Wald Lasowski, Aliocha 2016, *Althusser et nous. Vingt Conversations*, Paris: PUF.
Weber, Henri 1979, 'Les raisons de la colére', in *Changer le PC? Debats sur le gallocommunisme*, edited by Olivier Duhamel and Henri Weber, Paris: PUF.
Wood, Ellen Meiksins 1991, *The Pristine Nature of Capitalism: A Historical Essay on Old Regimes and Modern States*, London: Verso.
Wood, Ellen Meiksins 1995, *Democracy against Capitalism: Renewing Historical Materialism*, Cambridge: Cambridge University Press.
Wood, Ellen Meiksins 2002, *The Origin of Capitalism: A Longer View*, London: Verso.
Wood, Ellen Meiksins 2003, *Empire of Capital*, London: Verso.
Žižek, Slavoj (ed.) 1998, *Cogito and the Unconscious*, Durham, NC: Duke University Press.
Žižek, Slavoj 1999, *The Ticklish Subject: The Absent Centre of Political Ontology*, London: Verso.

Index

Abse, Tobias   397n, 441n
Agamben, Giorgio   305
Alienation   10, 28, 55, 76, 80, 101, 103, 106–107, 111–112, 114, 120, 167, 197n, 351, 353n, 355–356, 367–370, 428–429
Althusserianism   9, 11, 12, 15, 51, 69, 71, 125, 169, 463, 531
Amariglio, Jack   512
Anderson, Perry   19–20, 23, 169
Anti-empiricism   10, 66, 165, 175
Anti-humanism   12, 23, 25, 32, 57, 312, 331, 353–357, 360–377, 504
Aquinas, Thomas   233
Aristotle   192, 253, 257, 265, 283, 285, 331n, 361

Bachelard, Gaston   21–22, 151, 216, 220–221, 279, 301, 308, 369
Badiou, Alain   58n, 74, 247–248, 381, 395n, 441, 484–485, 505, 509, 511
Balibar, Étienne   21, 50–51, 57, 65, 73–74, 88, 89n, 145n, 157n, 166n, 169, 202, 204–207, 215, 230n, 282, 329n, 335n, 358–360, 388–390, 398–404, 405, 409, 426, 427n, 433, 443–450, 506, 499, 467, 512, 520
Baltas, Aristidis   422n
Barthes, Roland   69
Bensäid, Daniel   74n, 164n, 416n
Benton, Ted   14
Berlinguer, Enrico   396n
Besse, Guy   365n
Bettelheim, Charles   381n, 390, 415
Bosteels, Bruno   56n, 58n
Bourdin, Jean Claude   460n
Brand, Urlich   442n
Brewster, Ben   88n
Brown, Nathan   351n
Buci-Glucksmann, Christine   313n, 416, 459
Burgio, Alberto   313n
Butler, Judith   506–508

Callari, Antonio   85
Callinicos, Alex   17–18, 393n
Caputo, Renato   324n
Cassirer, Ernst   39

Castoriadis, Cornelius   344n
Cavaillés, Jean   179–180
Cavazzini, Andrea   52, 53n, 381n, 443
Chinese Cultural Revolution   20, 22, 243, 344, 380–382, 397, 415, 444–445
Choi, Won   509
Claudin, Fernando   342n
Clausewitz, Carl von   154, 156, 487
Clinamen   90n, 93, 115, 143, 158–160, 257, 304, 491
Cohen, G.A.   9
Colletti, Lucio   204n
Communism   12–13, 23, 80, 86, 155, 159, 197, 199, 255, 290, 292, 299–300, 304, 310, 319, 322, 323, 335, 341, 343–344, 345–346, 353, 355, 357, 394n, 397, 399, 402–404, 405–407, 409–412, 427–428, 435–440, 443–444, 452, 475, 498–502, 533
Contradiction   25, 33, 41, 43, 52, 53–56, 66, 73–75, 96, 108, 115,-116, 152–153, 164, 166–168, 198–199, 200–207, 210,-211, 233, 260, 286–287, 296, 300, 307, 319, 323, 340, 348, 375, 381, 410, 418, 427, 440, 444–446, 526, 531–532
Conjuncture   24, 25, 32, 36, 48, 50–58, 71, 74, 80–81, 86, 90, 94, 122–123, 140, 148, 158, 165, 168, 171, 181, 184–185, 195, 200–201, 204, 206–211, 215, 223, 225–228, 233, 236, 240, 242, 247, 251, 257, 272, 275, 304, 320, 327n, 328, 333, 340, 348–350, 353, 354n, 355, 366, 378–379, 381, 397, 404–405, 415, 419–420, 426, 448, 453, 456, 460, 466–470, 473–474, 476–479, 481–485, 491–497, 502, 511, 518, 522
Cotten, Jean-Pier   197–198n
Cournot, Antoine Augustin   90, 146, 155

Darwin, Charles   147n
Della Volpe, Galvano   19, 220
Deborin, Abram   197
De Lara, Phillipe   423n
Deleuze, Gilles   57–59, 72n, 89–90, 200, 201n, 496, 502
Democritus   143n, 191n, 273n

Derrida, Jacques   143–145, 191, 247, 255, 302, 354
Descartes, René   131, 192, 194, 201, 242, 265, 276, 287–288, 290
De Ípola, Emilio   499, 513
Di Maggio, Marco   342n, 343n, 354n, 363n, 364n, 365
Dialectic   11, 17, 19, 21, 25, 30, 33, 41, 48, 50–52, 61, 63n, 70, 84, 85, 100–101, 104, 116, 120, 149, 152, 158, 167, 169, 188, 204–209, 217, 227, 228n, 234, 245, 250–252, 258, 260, 262, 283, 313, 322, 325, 326, 330, 332, 368–371, 397, 417, 420n, 426, 438n, 467, 469, 472, 494, 499, 503, 507, 516, 524–525, 530–531
   Hegelian   26–30, 32, 35, 294, 339, 367
   Marxist   347
   Materialist   55, 86, 166, 171, 176, 180, 200, 204–209, 217, 348
   Of history   38
Dictatorship of the proletariat   255, 345, 355, 387–388, 397–404, 404–419, 431–432, 435, 437, 500
Diderot, Denis   264, 266, 367
Dimoulis, Dimitris   166n, 433n
Dolar, Mladen   506, 509
Duhamel, Olivier   416n
Duménil, Gerard   82
Duroux, Yves   230n

Economakis, George   166n, 433n
Eisenmann, Charles   42
Elliot, Gregory   20–23, 71n, 172, 220, 221, 354n, 390n, 393–394, 481n
Encounter   24, 47, 84–97, 98, 102, 104–105, 114–115, 117–124, 126, 130, 139–141, 142–146, 156–166, 167, 181, 185, 191–192, 198, 201, 203, 206, 208n, 253, 257, 258, 263, 265–266, 273, 281–283, 299, 302, 304, 309–311, 359, 372, 378, 383, 425, 446, 460, 466, 474, 477–480, 483, 489n, 490–496, 498–503, 505, 519, 525, 529–532
   Philosophy of   84–97, 146–151, 304
Engels, Friedrich   28, 31, 50, 75, 149, 150n, 167n, 175, 218, 222, 226, 240, 244, 260, 294, 305, 307, 327, 371, 388, 389n, 400, 425, 428, 433n, 434, 471, 487
Epicurus   90, 93–95, 122, 143, 145, 148, 160, 162, 191, 257, 258, 266, 273, 302, 304, 307, 479
Eurocommunism   23, 329, 405–407, 414–416, 446, 455, 525

Feuerbach, Ludwig   75–80, 203, 238, 355–356, 358, 366–370, 429
Fourtounis, George   422n
Franchi, Stephano   354n
Freud, Sigmund   13, 56n, 227, 239, 284–285, 506
Fromm, Erich   355
Frosini, Fabio   313n, 314n, 321, 327n
Foucault, Michel   137, 206, 247, 354, 364, 434

Garaudy, Roger   363–366
Geerlandt, Robert   354n, 363n, 365n
Gerratana, Valentino   459
Geras, Norman   12, 354n
Giap, Vo Nguyen   154
Gillot, Pascale   354n
Goldmann, Lucien   78n, 131–132, 140
Goshgarian, G.M.   44n, 46–47, 52, 63, 64n, 85–87, 90n, 125n, 165n, 181, 182n, 246, 329n, 350, 353, 364, 404n, 505
Glucksmann, André   12
Gramsci, Antonio   35, 144, 259, 260, 264–265, 289, 291–294, 296, 299, 310n, 311–335, 406, 423, 449, 450–459, 461, 464–466, 471, 472, 473, 477, 482, 495, 501, 502, 514–18, 521, 523, 524n, 525, 526, 530, 532
Guattari, Félix   89–90
Gueroult, Martial   160n, 174, 178

Habermas, Jürgen   9
Hardt, Michael   201, 521
Harman, Chris   397n
Hastings-King, Stephen   344
Hegel, Georg Wilhelm Friedrich   9, 19, 24, 25–49, 54, 61, 73, 75–76, 101, 152, 167n, 171, 175, 186, 187, 188–189, 194, 199, 204n, 217, 219–220, 228n, 251, 253, 258–259, 270, 273, 291, 293, 307n, 318, 339, 347, 360n, 367–372, 376, 427, 461, 464
Hegelianism   24, 30–32, 204, 327, 330, 364
Hegemony   150, 166, 235, 289, 291, 297, 299, 312, 313, 315–316, 318–320, 323–326, 328–329, 333, 364, 392, 397, 406–407,

420, 448–449, 451–459, 465, 495, 523, 524n, 525, 527, 530, 533
Heidegger, Martin 143, 146, 159, 191, 198, 247, 252, 254, 259, 302
Heigl, Miriam 442n
Heinrich, Michael 222n
Hobbes, Thomas 39, 101–102, 105, 107, 110, 145, 170, 191, 199, 248, 253, 302, 519
Humanism 12, 14, 16, 29, 143n, 222, 239, 345, 350, 360–377, 380, 391, 392
   Socialist 12, 346, 353–357, 390
   Theoretical 12, 75, 80, 190, 222, 512, 529
Hume, David 149, 151, 165
Hyppolite, Jean 32, 98

Ichida, Yoshihiko 85, 146n, 163n
Ideology 13, 15, 18, 29, 34, 54, 60, 62, 71, 72, 77–80, 90, 102, 108, 110, 133–138, 141, 155, 161, 171, 173, 186–187, 190, 192, 194, 196, 208n, 216, 217, 219–220, 222, 223, 224, 228n, 229, 232, 234, 236, 238–239, 241, 244–245, 252, 258, 260–262, 264, 271, 272, 275, 279–282, 288–292, 295–300, 306n, 307, 315–316, 318, 322, 326, 328n, 332–335, 339, 347, 352, 356–357, 362, 365, 368, 370, 373, 377, 381–382, 387–388, 391–392, 399, 400, 407, 410–412, 419–421, 422n, 423, 425–426, 427n, 428, 432–433, 439, 443, 446, 450n, 452, 456, 471, 476, 487–488, 498, 500, 504–522, 524n, 527, 529–530, 532
   Ideological Apparatuses of the State 71, 132, 241, 260, 281, 328, 384–386, 439, 445, 450
Ingrao, Pietro 441n

Jalley, Émile 101, 102n
Jameson, Fredric 298n
Jankélévitch, Vladimir 98
Jessop, Bob 396n
Jiang, Hongseng 381n, 393n

Kant, Immanuel 19, 26, 31, 138, 153, 194, 220, 231, 235, 242, 253–254, 258, 285, 290, 356, 367
Karsz, Saül 55
Kautsky, Karl 15
Keck, Fréderic 354

Kojéve, Alexandre 30–31
Kolakowski, Leszek 9
Korsch, Karl 330
Kouvelakis, Stathis 222
Krailsheiner, A.J. 134n

Labica, Georges 222, 358–359, 416n
Labriola, Antonio 293
Lacan, Jacques 62, 137, 284–285, 354n, 364n, 508–509
Lahtinen, Mikko 74, 86, 348n, 461n, 467, 468n, 469n, 483n
Lecourt, Dominique 221, 300–301, 308
Lefort, Claude 463
Leibniz, Wilhelm Gottfried 68, 151, 160, 183, 192, 201, 239, 253, 266
Lenin, Vladimir Ilich 13, 24, 36, 50, 55–56, 171, 182, 215, 226, 228, 230, 231, 233, 236–237, 240–242, 244, 251–253, 264, 292, 299, 303, 364n, 374, 375, 385, 392, 399, 406, 411, 415, 430, 432, 439, 444–445, 465, 467, 482, 514–515, 518, 531
Lévi-Strauss, Claude 67–69, 79, 182, 224, 239, 247, 309, 354, 509
Lewis, William 243, 343n, 345–346n, 393
Liguori, Guido 314n, 324n
Locke, John 102–103, 110
Lucretius 93, 140, 143n, 191, 257, 302
Lukács, Georg 19, 263, 292, 327, 330
Luxemburg, Rosa 420–421

Macciocchi, Maria-Antoinetta 91, 92n
Macherey, Pierre 68–70, 90n, 127n, 128n, 135, 150n, 153, 160n, 161n, 162n, 165n, 169, 182, 201–203, 235n, 287n, 298n, 359, 508
Machiavelli, Nicolo 35, 36, 48, 51, 80–81, 86, 92–93, 109, 121–122, 125, 138, 141, 144, 145n, 153, 162, 170, 185, 191, 253, 266, 281, 302, 326, 329, 380, 450, 453, 455–457, 460–503, 531
Madonia, Franca 68n, 183–184, 227, 326, 328n, 350, 379–380, 460n, 461n, 462
Magri, Lucio 344n, 397n
Il Manifesto 353, 422, 439
Maniglier, Patrice 509
Mao Zedong 17, 20, 22, 227, 244, 292, 343, 380, 385, 487, 518
Maoism 13, 16, 18, 243, 383, 397

Marchais, George   417
Martin, James   396n
Marx, Karl   9, 13, 15–16, 21, 25, 27–28, 31–32, 34–35, 36, 39, 40, 44, 46–47, 49, 56, 65, 66n, 75, 81–83, 89–91, 101, 124, 136, 143, 149, 150–151, 153, 157, 162n, 165n, 166, 167, 171, 176–178, 182, 186, 188, 189, 191, 195, 203, 211n, 217–218, 220–223, 224–225, 227, 228n, 236–237, 240, 242, 251, 253, 256, 259–260, 263, 282–283, 291–292, 294, 299, 302–303, 307, 327, 328n, 330, 331n, 333, 345, 349, 353n, 354n, 355–356, 358–360, 361–362, 364, 366–372, 376–377, 388, 389n, 399–400, 403, 405–408, 415, 425, 426n, 427–430, 433–435, 440, 443, 449, 471, 476, 492, 497, 512
Marxism   9–10, 14, 15, 17, 19–20, 23, 25–26, 50, 52, 56n, 77, 79, 85, 142, 149n, 156, 183, 198, 240–241, 245, 252–253, 266, 272, 275, 293–294, 304, 312, 314, 320, 328, 330, 334, 343n, 350, 354, 360, 364, 366, 379, 392, 395n, 401, 404, 424, 426, 428, 434, 446, 450, 455, 458, 494n, 499, 504, 506, 509, 512–514, 526–528, 529–532
  Marxism-Leninism   22–23, 345, 373
  Soviet Marxism   95, 253, 393
  Western   19
  Crisis of Marxism   84, 140, 142, 300, 329n, 397, 420–424, 439, 463, 501, 503
Materialism   10, 29, 130, 167, 169, 175, 176, 200, 240, 244, 247–248, 251, 259–260, 264, 266, 269, 275, 277–278, 298, 300, 305, 307–308, 319–321, 367, 378, 417, 457, 490, 529
  Historical   11, 13, 17, 20–23, 25, 31, 52, 64, 76, 84, 99, 102, 125, 155, 197, 210, 215, 222–223, 236, 242, 247, 260, 262, 280, 283, 303–304, 312–313, 317, 328, 330, 334, 347, 362–363, 378, 473, 475, 511, 514
  Aleatory / of the encounter   24, 84–97, 98, 118, 121–125, 126, 130, 140–141, 142–167, 169, 191–199, 210, 246, 255, 262, 281, 302, 478–479, 491–496, 499–502, 531–532
  Dialectical   20, 149, 223, 230, 236, 239, 245, 301
Matheron, Alexandre   167, 197, 201, 520

Matheron, François   81n, 85, 90, 146n, 161n, 162n, 163n, 169n, 170n, 184–185, 201
Mavroudeas, Stavros   166n
Merleau-Ponty, Maurice   26n, 77
Milios, John   166n, 222n, 433n
Miller, Jacques-Alain   60–62
Molina, Gerard   416n
Montag, Warren   29n, 32n, 47–48, 57–58, 61n, 62n, 63, 68, 69n, 78n, 79n, 164n, 180, 182, 199, 201, 354n, 405n, 520
Montaigne, Michel de   129
Montesquieu   36–49, 52, 85, 87–88, 98–99, 125, 133, 148, 170, 467
Moreau, Pierre-François   170n, 175, 177n, 191n, 519
Morfino, Vittorio   86–87, 146n, 147n, 157, 158n, 160, 175, 326, 329, 519
Moulier-Boutang, Yann   84, 85n, 126, 127n, 164n, 340, 341n

Navarro, Fernanda   137, 142, 150n, 255n, 306n, 307
Negri, Antonio   84, 124, 201 462n, 486, 496n, 503n, 521
New practice of politics   95, 246, 282, 292, 388–389, 404, 409, 415, 437, 443, 460, 490, 503, 526, 533

Overdetermination   21, 33, 40, 52, 54, 56n, 73–75, 171, 181, 183, 200, 202, 204, 207, 320, 340, 348, 490, 493, 500–501, 531
Özselçuk, Ceren   512

Pascal, Blaise   126–141, 151, 153, 159, 162, 199, 531
PCF (Parti Communiste Français)   22, 341–343, 350–351, 353n, 354, 363–366, 381–382, 383, 393, 396, 398, 404–405, 412–421, 434–435, 437–438, 448, 500
Pêcheux, Michel   511–512
Peden, Knox   169n, 171–172, 174, 180, 183
Philosophy   9, 15–16, 22, 24, 25, 26–28, 31, 34, 48, 49, 55, 76, 77, 79, 84, 90, 92, 93–94, 98, 102, 109–111, 122–123, 125, 126, 131–133, 139–141, 142–146, 150–152, 159, 161, 163–154, 174, 176, 178–185, 188–192, 194, 196, 198–199, 210–220, 222–224, 225–245, 246–301, 302–311, 312–335, 344, 349, 350, 353n, 354n, 367, 378, 382,

450n, 454–455, 463, 464n, 479, 493, 499, 503, 510, 517, 519, 532
Idealist   150, 178, 187, 235, 246, 250–251, 258, 272, 277, 306–307, 339, 367, 427
Marxist   17, 20–21, 25, 36, 81, 186, 211, 218, 226, 240, 243, 252, 262, 334, 375, 384, 529
Materialist   25, 34, 95, 150, 162, 232, 237, 246, 262, 266–267, 291, 330, 375, 379, 460n, 490
New practice of   86, 168, 221, 229, 238, 241, 263, 296–300, 302, 306, 311, 440, 503, 529, 531, 533
Pinzolo, Luca   86n, 147n, 157, 158n
Plato   39, 231, 306, 242, 253, 256, 265, 268, 253, 288, 349
Popper, Karl   149n, 247
Portantiero, Juan, Carlos   328n
Poulantzas, Nicos   66n, 208, 396, 416, 430–434, 441–443, 450, 523–524
Praxis   11–13, 53, 132, 180, 275–276, 283, 285, 293, 310n, 312, 333, 354n, 360, 370, 516, 519–520, 529, 532
    Philosophy of   241, 294, 312–333, 455
Psychoanalysis   64n, 149n, 183, 224, 227, 229, 247, 284–285, 354n, 532

Ranciére, Jacques   14–16, 62, 222, 346n, 349, 351
Raymond, Gino   342n
Raymond, Pierre   146n, 150n, 151–156, 245
Ricoeur, Paul   13
Rizk, Hadi   519
Rossanda, Rossana   300, 344n, 424, 440, 500
Rousseau, Jean-Jacques   36, 41, 48, 92, 98–125, 145, 148, 170, 191, 199, 253–254, 302–303, 305, 367
Rubin I.I.   222n
Ruccio, David F.   85
Rytman, Hélène   327n, 330n, 341

Sartre, Jean-Paul   19, 30, 273, 354, 372, 519
Sébag, Lucien   79
Sève, Lucien   364
Sharp, Hasana   520–521
Sibertin-Blanc, Guillaume   61, 381, 502
Smith, Adam   218
Spinoza, Baruch   19, 21, 35, 59n, 64, 68, 69n, 125, 136, 145, 148, 159, 160–162, 165, 167, 169–199, 201, 202, 203, 249, 250–251, 258–259, 267, 272, 302, 307, 376, 403n, 406, 464, 490, 502, 519–521
Stalin, Joseph   15, 18, 20, 292–294, 380, 385n, 391, 393n, 394, 405–406, 412
Stalinism   11–12, 14, 17–23, 329–330, 344–346, 350, 354n, 364, 385, 390–395, 396, 405, 414, 424, 515
State Monopoly Capitalism (theory of)   413, 419, 432, 453
State Theory   72, 313, 318, 329, 396–440, 441–450, 451–453, 455
Stolze, Ted   58, 198n
Structuralism   9–13, 24, 47–48, 51, 57–60, 66–70, 75, 79–80, 84, 140n, 181, 208, 224, 247–248, 250, 281, 506
Structure   12, 24, 25, 29, 40, 41, 47, 48, 50–83, 84, 87–88, 89–90, 96, 104, 131, 136, 147–149, 158, 162, 169, 177, 182, 185, 198, 200, 203–204, 206–208, 209, 211, 220, 224, 227–228, 239, 285, 331n, 348n, 350, 369, 371–372, 373, 378, 384, 401, 454, 499, 505, 506, 529
Suchting, Wal   86, 143n, 146n

Terray, Emmanuel   81n, 468n, 482, 490, 494n
Theoretical practice   17, 26, 53, 63, 178, 184, 215–217, 226, 242, 262, 317, 325, 332–333, 347, 469, 510
    Theory of   17, 55, 64, 185, 215, 223, 225–226, 298, 303, 312, 330, 349, 357, 378–379, 532
Thomas, Peter   145n, 169, 180, 186, 310n, 313n, 317n, 321, 328n, 330, 331n, 458n, 517
Togliatti, Palmiro   458
Topography   227–229, 275, 506, 532
Tosel, André   86n, 146n, 157n, 158–160, 162, 167n, 176, 190, 197–198, 519
Totality   26, 29–31, 33–34, 39–40, 51, 53–55, 70, 150, 158–159, 161, 171, 177, 180, 193, 197n, 201, 203, 209, 228n, 272, 331, 339–340, 347, 359
Thompson, Edward P.   9–14, 20, 21, 354

UJCML (*Union des jeunesses communistes marxistes-léninistes*) 380, 383
Underdetermination 73–75, 200, 202, 204, 348

Vargas, Yves 121n, 124n, 167, 416n
Verret, Michel 383

Vilar, Pierre 14, 209
Voza, Pasquale 324n

Weber, Henri 416, 449n
Wittgenstein, Ludwig 86, 145, 146n, 300

Žižek, Slavoj 167n